CW01497049

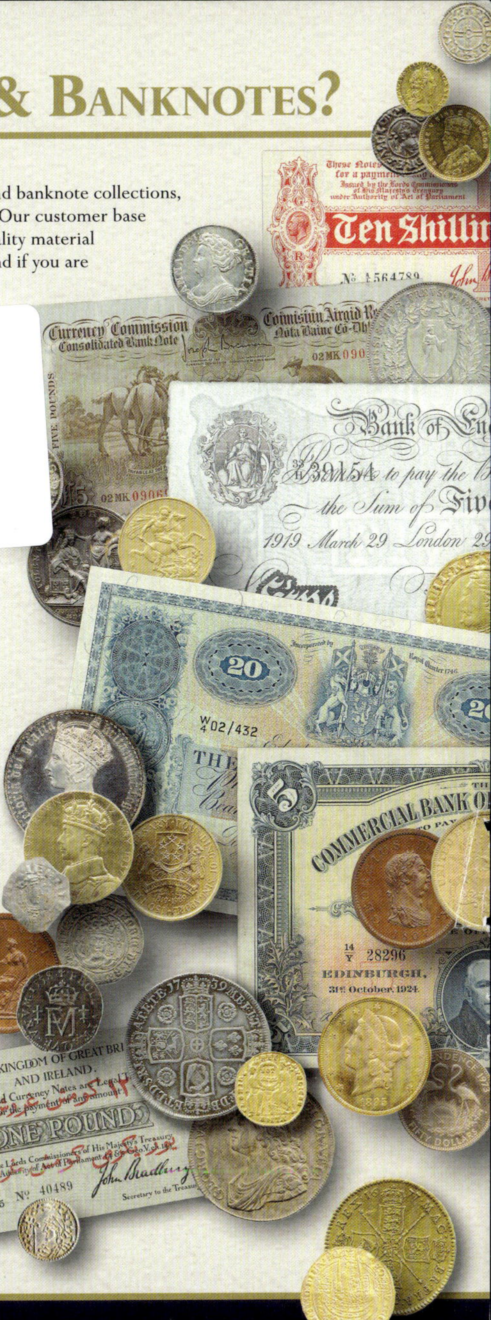
Ten Shillin
Currency Commission
Consolidated Bank Note
Bank of Eng
1919 March 29 London
COMMERCIAL BANK OF
EDINBURGH,
31st October, 1924
UNITED KINGDOM OF GREAT BRI
AND IRELAND.
ONE POUND

THE COIN Yearbook

2025

Edited by
Carol Hartman & Philip Mussell
and the Editorial Team of COIN NEWS

ISBN 978-1-908828-70-5

Published by
TOKEN PUBLISHING LIMITED
8 Oaktree Place, Manaton Close, Exeter, Devon EX2 8WA
Telephone: 01404 46972
email: info@tokenpublishing.com. Website: www.tokenpublishing.com

Printed in Great Britain by Stephens & George Ltd.

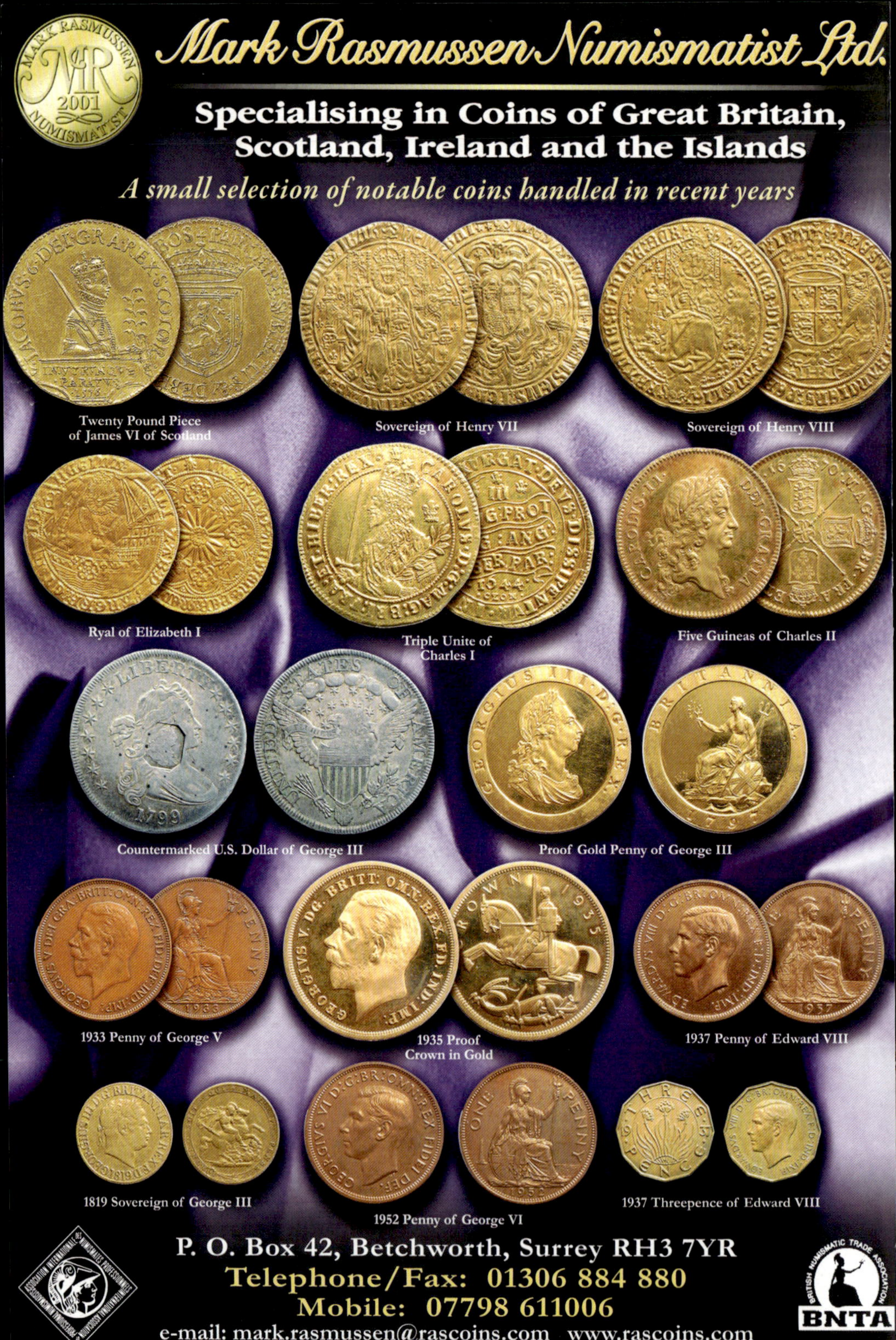
MARK RASMUSSEN MR 2001 NUMISMATIST
Mark Rasmussen Numismatist Ltd.
Specialising in Coins of Great Britain, Scotland, Ireland and the Islands
A small selection of notable coins handled in recent years
Twenty Pound Piece of James VI of Scotland
Sovereign of Henry VII
Sovereign of Henry VIII
Ryal of Elizabeth I
Triple Unite of Charles I
Five Guineas of Charles II
Countermarked U.S. Dollar of George III
Proof Gold Penny of George III
1933 Penny of George V
1935 Proof Crown in Gold
1937 Penny of Edward VIII
1819 Sovereign of George III
1952 Penny of George VI
1937 Threepence of Edward VIII
P. O. Box 42, Betchworth, Surrey RH3 7YR
Telephone/Fax: 01306 884 880
Mobile: 07798 611006
e-mail: mark.rasmussen@rascoins.com www.rascoins.com
BRITISH NUMISMATIC TRADE ASSOCIATION
BNTA

Contents

Foreword

WELCOME to the 2025 edition of the COIN YEARBOOK, the best value price guide to English, Scottish and Irish coins available! Regular readers will perhaps note that this year's book has gone up slightly and although it's still excellent value for money, we simply couldn't sustain the previous "under a tenner" price that we have had in place for nearly three decades! In fact the book used to be more expensive, in its first incarnation it was B5 size and £12.95, with far fewer pages. We brought the price down for the 1997 edition and maintained it for 27 years. Sadly, inflationary pressure means it isn't possible to sustain this, but we had a good run!

Of course, had the book kept up with coin prices it would be far higher than the £11.95 you've just paid, coin values continue to remain very strong with just about every element of our hobby seeing increases. The most obvious ones being where precious metals make a difference, gold in particular has gone up and up and up, silver is healthy too and consequently many coins not collected for their numismatic element have seen their prices increase dramatically. But it isn't only precious metal coins that have seen gains. Across the hobby record prices are being asked, and fetched; whether this is because of an investment angle or simply a renewed interest in coin collecting isn't obvious, and it doesn't really matter—what counts is that collecting coins seems to be becoming more and more popular, which can only be a good thing.

Regular readers will also note that the coins of the Channel Islands are, once again, not included this year. Unfortunately, there are simply too many issued for us to keep track of. As the islands all issue coins for the collector market they are often sent directly to specialist marketing companies and we never get to hear about them. It's only when they come up for sale on the secondary market that we are even aware they exist! This has, of course, been the same for some time now, but in recent years the numbers of coins being produced has increased at an incredible rate and to try to keep track of them all is impossible.

Collectors can't have failed to note that it isn't just the Channel Islands that have ramped up their production, the Royal Mint have released dozens of new coin designs in the past year. There are of course the new King Charles III definitives, the coins we will use every day, with their nature theme so reminiscent of the Irish Barnyard series taking over from the "jigsaw shield designs", but in addition to those we have the commemoratives and the bullion issues too!

Not that all of these coins are aimed at coin collectors though; whilst some do still try to buy everything the Royal Mint produces, it isn't so easy these days. But when the Mint produces a Harry Potter coin or a Star Wars piece, it isn't actually we numismatists it is aiming for but rather it is the fans of those film franchises who are the intended market. That said, what can and does happen, is some of those people who are Harry Potter fans and who buy the coins then start wondering what other coins are out there and before you know it, they are collecting other new issues; then maybe some older coins too. So whilst they may only have started on the coin route because of their obsession with bespectacled wizard, they carry on travelling on it because coins really are quite interesting in their own right.

Coin collecting is one of the oldest hobbies around. If you think about it for a moment, what other collecting interest stretches back well over 2,000 years? Of all the traditional collecting pastimes, stamps, postcards, cigarette cards, phone cards, model cars, trains et al are all relative newcomers, only coins have endured for so long. Of course, many of these hobbies have faded in popularity as the things themselves fell out of everyday use. Postcards aren't sent like they used to be, phone cards are obsolete, cigarette cards, later superseded by tea cards found in PG Tips have gone and stamps are so expensive these days that fewer and fewer people are sending letters, especially now texts and emails are so easy. So does this mean that as cash slowly disappears so too coin collecting will fade? Fortunately, that's unlikely to happen for a number of reasons—firstly cash isn't going anywhere any time soon, cash use is actually on the up as it helps people budget and secondly many people collect Roman coins, Greek coins, Anglo-Saxon coins, they haven't been used in centuries but are still highly collectable! It is perhaps inevitable that our smaller denomination coins will go in time, inflationary pressures make our small coins worth less and less every year; we lost the 1/2p back in 1984 and the farthing some 24 years before that. The fact that the farthing went is no surprise at all, it was a coin worth a quarter of a penny at a time when there were 240 pennies in the pound, so it was actually worth 1/960th of a pound! Can you imagine that today? But even when we do lose our penny and 2p coins they will still be collected, they're interesting, fun to collect and, if you're lucky, can be worth a bit too—which is where books like this one come in!

We reach the prices included here in a variety of ways, mainly by checking dealers' lists and auction results, however, we also have specialists in their field check things over for us to ensure there aren't any glaring errors and, to that end, we would like to extend our thanks to the following: Chris Rudd and Elizabeth Cottam for their work on the Celtic Section; John Philpotts of Silbury Coins for the Roman and Hammered sections and Roy Norbury of West Essex Coin Investments for helping with the Milled coinage. Nick Swabey has once again helped on the Maundy Section as has Dave Stuart (Scottish), Mike Southall (Isle of Man) and Charles Riley (Medals). The other sections have been checked and rechecked by the wonderful Token Team in-house, so we take full responsibility for those! We would, as ever, like to extend our thanks to the Royal Mint, and in Particular Dr Kevin Clancy of the Royal Mint Museum and to the various auctions houses who have permitted us to use their illustrations. These include, but aren't limited to: Baldwins, Morton & Eden, Noonans of Mayfair, Spink & Son, and St James's. We would also like to thank all those in the hobby, dealers, auction houses and collectors who continue to support us year in year out.

Monarchs of England

Here we list the Kings and Queens from Anglo-Saxon times to the present, with the dates of their rule. Before Eadgar became the King of all England the country had been divided up into small kingdoms, each with their own ruler.

ANGLO-SAXON KINGS

The Anglo-Saxon monarchs ruled over the various kingdoms which existed in England following the withdrawal of the Romans in the 5th century AD. The most prominent kingdoms in the land were Kent, Sussex, Wessex, Mercia and Northumbria. Each kingdom produced its own coinage but in 973 Eadgar introduced a new coinage that became the standard for the whole of the country.

Eadgar (959–975)
Edward the Martyr (975–978)
Aethelred II (978–1016)
Cnut (1016–1035)
Harold I (1035–1040)
Harthacanut (1035–1042)
Edward the Confessor (1042–1066)
Harold II (1066)

NORMAN KINGS

The Normans came to Britain from their native France following the establishment of a kingdom in Sicily and southern Italy. An expedition led by the powerful Duke William of Normandy culminated in the battle of Hastings in 1066 where he defeated Harold II and was proclaimed King of All England. Their influence spread from these new centres to the Crusader States in the Near East and to Scotland and Wales in Great Britain, and to Ireland. Today their influence can be seen in their typical Romanesque style of architecture.

William I (1066–1087)
William II (1087–1100)
Henry I (1100–1135)
Stephen (1135–1154)

PLANTAGENETS

The Plantagenet kings of England were descended from the first House of Anjou who were established as rulers of England through the Treaty of Wallingford, which passed over the claims of Eustace and William, Stephen of Blois's sons, in favour of Henry of Anjou, son of the Empress Matilda and Geoffrey V, Count of Anjou.

Henry II (1154–1189)
Richard I (1189–1199)
John (1199–1216)
Henry III (1216–1272)
Edward I (1272–1307)
Edward II (1307–1327)
Edward III (1327–1377)
Richard II (1377–1399)

HOUSE OF LANCASTER

The House of Lancaster, a branch of the English royal House of Plantagenet, was one of the opposing factions involved in the Wars of the Roses, the civil war which dominated England and Wales during the 15th century. Lancaster provided England with three Kings

Henry IV (1399–1413)
Henry V (1413–1422)
Henry VI (1422–1461 and again 1470)

HOUSE OF YORK

The House of York was the other branch of the House of Plantagenet involved in the disastrous Wars of the Roses. Edward IV was descended from Edmund of Langley, 1st Duke of York, the fourth surviving son of Edward III.

Edward IV (1461–1483 and again 1471–83)
Richard III (1483–1485)

TUDORS

The House of Tudor was an English royal dynasty that lasted 118 years, from 1485 to 1603. The family descended from the Welsh courtier Owen Tudor (Tewdwr). Following the defeat of Richard III at Bosworth, the battle that ended the Wars of the Roses, Henry Tudor, 2nd Earl of Richmond, took the throne as Henry VII.

Henry VII (1485–1509)
Henry VIII (1509–1547)
Edward VI (1547–1553)
Mary (1553–1558)
Philip & Mary (1554–1558)
Elizabeth I (1558–1603)

STUARTS

The House of Stuart ruled Scotland for 336 years, between 1371 and 1707. Elizabeth I of England's closest heir was James VI of Scotland via her grandfather Henry VII of England, who was founder of the Tudor dynasty. On Elizabeth's death, James Stuart ascended the thrones of England and Ireland and inherited the English claims to the French throne. The Stuarts styled themselves "Kings and Queens of Great Britain", although there was no parliamentary union until the reign of Queen Anne, the last monarch of the House of Stuart.

James I (1603–1625)
Charles I (1625–1649)
The Commonwealth (1653–1658)
Charles II (1660–1685)
James II (1685–1688)
William III & Mary (1688–1694)
William III (1694–1702)
Anne (1702–1714)

HOUSE OF HANOVER

The House of Hanover was a Germanic royal dynasty which ruled the Duchy of Brunswick-Lüneburg and the Kingdom of Hanover. George Ludwig ascended to the throne of the Kingdom of Great Britain and Ireland through the female line from Princess Elizabeth, sister of Charles I.

George I (1714–1727)
George II (1727–1760)
George III (1760–1820)
George IV (1820–1830)
William IV (1830–1837)
Victoria (1837–1901)

HOUSES OF SAXE-COBURG-GOTHA AND WINDSOR

The name Saxe-Coburg-Gotha was inherited by Edward VII from his father Prince Albert, the second son of the Duke of Saxe-Coburg-Gotha and husband of Victoria. During World War I the name was changed to Windsor to avoid the Germanic connotatiion.

Edward VII (1901–1910)
George V (1910–1936)
Edward VIII (1936)
George VI (1936–1952)
Elizabeth II (1952–2022)
Charles III (2022—)

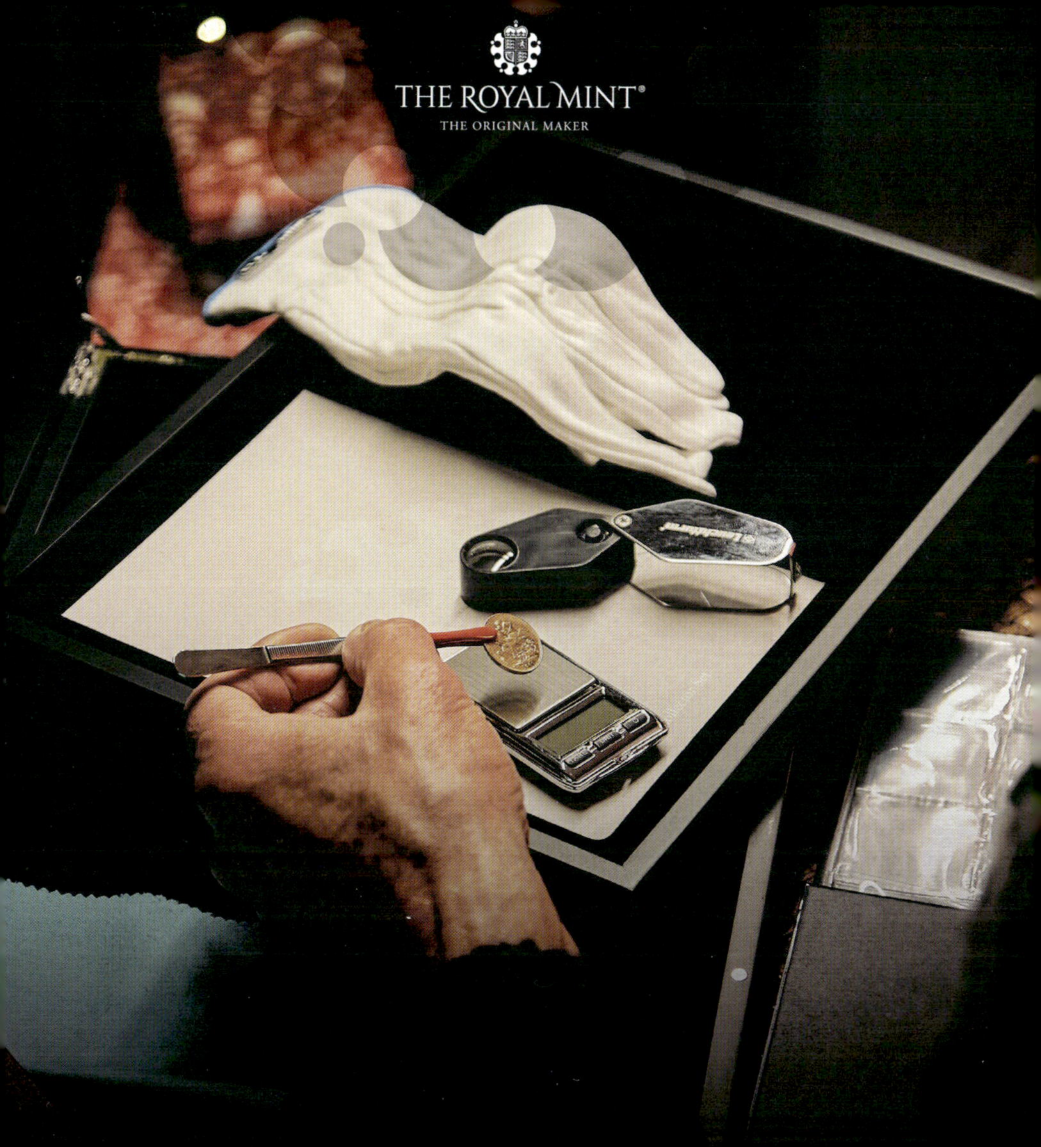
THE ROYAL MINT®
THE ORIGINAL MAKER

Realise
the True
Value
of your
Collection
Halls 1845
Inviting consignments
for our regular coin auctions.
Get in touch with our
specialist for a free valuation
of your collection.
01743 450 700
fineart@hallsgb.com
fineart.hallsgb.com

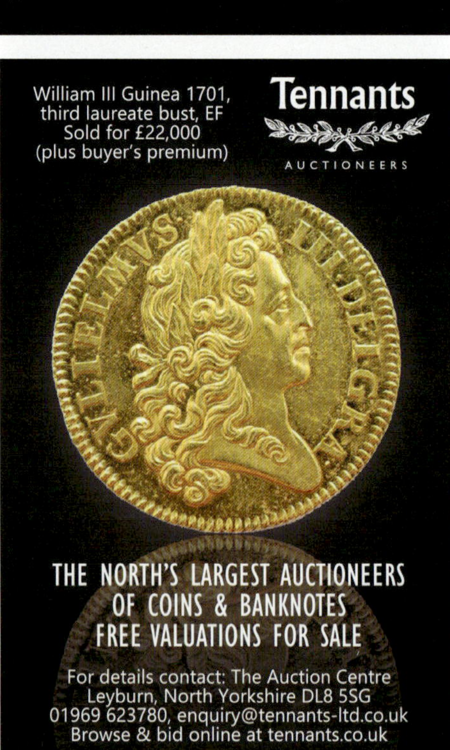
William III Guinea 1701,
third laureate bust, EF
Sold for £22,000
(plus buyer's premium)
Tennants
AUCTIONEERS
THE NORTH'S LARGEST AUCTIONEERS
OF COINS & BANKNOTES
FREE VALUATIONS FOR SALE
For details contact: The Auction Centre
Leyburn, North Yorkshire DL8 5SG
01969 623780, enquiry@tennants-ltd.co.uk
Browse & bid online at tennants.co.uk

Care
of coins

There is no point in going to a great deal of trouble and expense in selecting the best coins you can afford, only to let them deteriorate in value by neglect and mishandling. Unless you give some thought to the proper care of your coins, your collection is unlikely to make a profit for you if and when you come to sell it. Housing your coins is the biggest problem of all, so it is important to give a lot of attention to this.

Storage

The ideal, but admittedly the most expensive, method is the coin cabinet, constructed of air-dried mahogany, walnut or rosewood (*never* oak, cedar or any highly resinous timber likely to cause chemical tarnish). These cabinets have banks of shallow drawers containing trays made of the same wood, with half-drilled holes of various sizes to accommodate the different denominations of coins. Such cabinets are handsome pieces of furniture but, being largely handmade, tend to be rather expensive. Occasionally good specimens can be picked up in secondhand furniture shops, or at the dispersal of house contents by auction, but the best bet is still to purchase a new cabinet, tailored to your own requirements. These collectors cabinets are hand-made using certified solid mahogany, as specified by leading museums, as mahogany does not contain any chemicals or resins that could result in the discolouration of the collection inside the cabinet. The polish used on the outside of the cabinets is based on natural oils and hand applied then finished with bees wax. The trays are left as untreated mahogany so as not to introduce any harmful contaminants. The coin trays are available as single thickness or double thickness for holding thicker coins, capsules or artifacts.

For the coin connoisseur there are beautiful, hand-made cabinets such as this one from Rob Davis Cabinets.

Rob Davis Cabinets of Ticknall, Derbyshire (telephone: 01332 862755, www.robdaviscabinets), provides a first-class bespoke service with cabinets made to client's personal specifications. Made out of mahogany or English walnut, the storage options range from glassed-topped display cabinets suitable for a table top (with "secret" drawers) through to free-standing pieces as used by museums and institutions where security as well as safe-storage is a requirement. **Peter Nichols Cabinet Makers** (telephone 0115 9224149, www.coincabinets.com) was established in 1967 and is now run by Geoff Skinner and Shirley Watts. Based in Nottingham, the family-run business provides specialist display and storage systems to suit every need from standard cabinets for the average collector all the way up to the massive 40-tray specials supplied to the British Museum. All of these manufacturers use materials from sustainable sources and their products are exquisite examples of the cabinet maker's craft.

An excellent storage option is provided by a number of firms who manufacture coin trays in durable, felt-lined, man-made materials with shallow compartments to suit the various sizes of coins. Most of these trays interlock so that they build up into a cabinet of the desired size, and there are also versions designed as carrying cases, which are ideal for transporting coins.

The popular and extensive **Lighthouse** range is available from **Curtis Coin Care**. To view the current range of stock, go to www.curtiscoincare.com. This range includes a wide variety of cases and albums for the general collector in basic or deluxe styles as required, as well as printed albums for the specialist. Their cases, including the popular aluminium range, are manufactured to the highest standards, lined with blue plush which displays any coin to its best advantage. The red-lined single trays come in deep or standard size and make an ideal cabinet when stacked together or housed in their attractive aluminium case, which is available separately. The trays themselves come with a variety of compartments for every size of coin. Their complete range can be viewed on-line.

The extensive **Lindner** range is supplied in the UK by Prinz Publications UK Ltd of Unit 20A, Longrock Industrial Estate, Longrock, Cornwall TR20 8HX (telephone 01736 751910, www.prinz.co.uk). Well-known for their wide range of philatelic and numismatic accessories, but these include a full array of coin boxes, capsules, carrying cases and trays. The basic Lindner coin box is, in fact, a shallow tray available in a standard version or a smoked glass version. These trays have a crystal clear frame, red felt inserts and holes for various diameters of coins and medals. A novel feature of these trays is the rounded insert which facilitates the removal of coins from their spaces with the minimum of handling. These boxes are designed in such a manner that they interlock and can be built up into banks of trays, each fitted with a draw-handle and sliding in and out easily. Various types of chemically inert plastic capsules and envelopes have been designed for use in combination with plain shallow trays, without holes drilled. Lindner also manufacture a range of luxury cases lined in velvet and Atlas silk with padded covers and gold embossing on the spines, producing a most tasteful and elegant appearance.

Safe Albums of 16 Falcon Business Park, 38 Ivanhoe Road, Finchampstead, Berkshire RG40 4QQ (telephone 0118 932 8976, www.safealbums.co.uk) are the UK agents for the German Stapel-Element, a drawer-stacking system with clear plasticiser-free trays that fit into standard bookshelves. The sliding coin compartments, lined with blue velvet, can be angled for display to best advantage. Stackable drawers can be built up to any height desired. A wide range of drawer sizes is available, with compartments suitable for the smallest coins right up to four-compartment trays designed for very large artefacts such as card-cases or cigarette cases. The Mobel-Element cabinet is a superb specialised cabinet constructed of the finest timber with a steel frame and steel grip bars which can be securely locked.

There are also various other storage systems, such as the simple cardboard or plastic box which is made specifically to hold coins stored in see-through envelopes of chemically-inert plastic of various sizes, or white acid-free envelopes, usually 50mm square.

An alternative to these is the card coin holder which has a window made of inert cellophane-type see-through material. The card is folded over with the coin inside and is then stapled or stuck together with its own self-adhesive lining. The cards are a standard 50mm square with windows of various sizes from 15 to 39mm and fit neatly into the storage box or album page.

Coin Albums

When coin collecting became a popular hobby in the 1960s, several firms marketed ranges of coin albums. They had clear plastic sleeves divided into tiny compartments of various sizes and had the merit of being cheap and taking up little room on a bookshelf.

They had several drawbacks, however, not the least being the tendency of the pages to sag with the weight of the coins, or even, in extreme cases, to pull away from the pegs or rings holding them on to the spine.

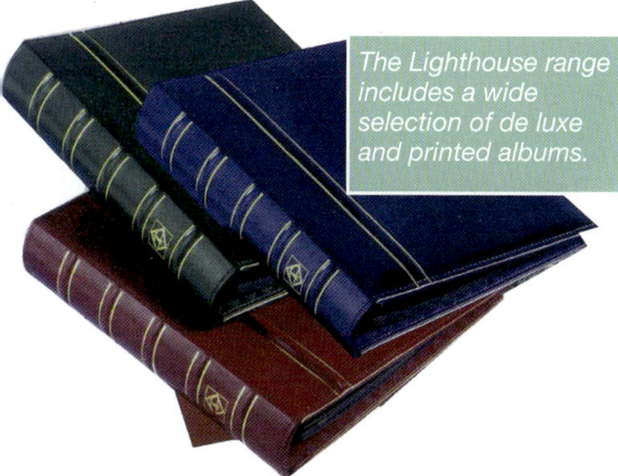
The Lighthouse range includes a wide selection of de luxe and printed albums.

They required very careful handling as the coins could easily fall out of the top row as the pages were turned. The more expensive albums had little flaps that folded over the top of the coin to overcome this problem.

Arguably the worst aspect of these albums was the use of polyvinyl chloride (PVC) in the construction of the sleeves. Collectors soon discovered to their horror that this reacted chemically with their coins, especially those made of silver and many fine collections were ruined as a result.

Fortunately the lesson has been learned and the coin albums now on the market are quite safe. Lighthouse and Lindner offer a wide range of albums designed to house coins, medals or banknotes. The old problem about sagging pages is overcome by the use of a multi-ring binding welded to a very stout spine, while the sleeves contain neither Styrol nor PVC and will not affect any metals at all. In addition to pages with pockets of uniform size, the Karat range of albums operates on a slide principle which enables the user to insert vertical strips of different sizes on the same page, so that the coins of one country or series, or perhaps a thematic display of coins from different countries, can be displayed side by side.

Safe Albums offer a wide range of albums in the Coinholder System and Coin-Combi ranges. These, too, offer the choice of fixed pages with uniform-sized pockets, or interchangeable sliding inserts for different sizes side by side.

The "slab"

In the United States in the past few decades one of the preferred methods for keeping coins in pristine condition is the use of "slabs"—these tough plastic rectangles cannot be easily broken into, meaning that the coin inside remains in exactly the same condition as when it was placed in there. This has led to the rise of professional grading and encapsulation companies who not only "slab" your coin but also grade it and guarantee that grade. This allows coins to be bought and sold with both vendor and purchaser knowing exactly what the grade is, thus taking out the subjectivity of dealer or collector—an issue that can mean a huge difference in the value of the coin. Slabbing in this way is essentially a tool to help a coin maintain a grade and thus more easily guarantee its value, however, many collectors prefer it as a method of protecting their coins as it allows them to be stored or transported easily with no fear of damage.

The biggest companies in the United States for the encapsulation of coins are **NGC** (Numismatic Gauaranty Corporation) and **PCGS** (Professional Coin Grading Service) . They have been in business for many, many years and in America the "slabbed" coin is a common sight. It is less common in the UK, with many collectors still unsure about the benefits of the "slab", but undoubtedly with the US companies opening offices and grading centres throughout the world more and more collectors are using the service and the "slab" is becoming accepted everywhere. However, anyone wishing to photograph a coin undoubtedly has a problem, as can be seen in many auction catalogues offering such items. The tell-tale grips that hold the coin obscure part of the edge of the coin.

Cleaning
coins

This is like matrimony—it should not be embarked on lightly. Indeed, the advice given by the magazine *Punch* in regard to marriage is equally sound in this case—don't do it! It is far better to have a dirty coin than an irretrievably damaged one. Every dealer has horror stories of handling coins that previous owners have cleaned, to their detriment. Probably the worst example was a display of coins found by a metal detectorist who "improved" his finds by abrading them in the kind of rotary drum used by lapidarists to polish gemstones. If you really must remove the dirt and grease from coins, it is advisable to practise on coins of little value.

Warm water containing a mild household detergent or washing-up liquid will work wonders in removing surface dirt and grease from most coins, but silver is best washed in a weak solution of ammonia and warm water—one part ammonia to ten parts water. Gold coins can be cleaned with diluted citric acid, such as lemon juice. Copper or bronze coins present more of a problem, but patches of verdigris can usually be removed by careful washing in a 20 per cent solution of sodium sesquicarbonate. Wartime coins made of tin, zinc, iron or steel can be cleaned in a 5 per cent solution of caustic soda containing some aluminium or zinc foil or filings, but they must be rinsed afterwards in clean water and carefully dried. Cotton buds are ideal for gently prising dirt out of coin legends and crevices in the designs. Soft brushes (with animal bristles—*never* nylon or other artificial bristles) designed for cleaning silver are most suitable for gently cleaning coins.

Coins recovered from the soil or the sea bed present special problems, due to chemical reaction between the metals and the salts in the earth or sea water. In such cases, the best advice is to take them to the nearest museum and let the professional experts decide on what can or should be done.

There are a number of proprietary coin-cleaning kits and materials on the market suitable for gold, silver, copper and other metals but all of these should be used with caution and always read the instructions that come with them. When using any type of chemical cleaner rubber gloves should be worn and care taken to avoid breathing fumes or getting splashes of liquid in your eyes or on your skin. Obviously, the whole business of cleaning is a matter that should not be entered into without the utmost care and forethought.

POLISHING: A WARNING

If cleaning should only be approached with the greatest trepidation, polishing is definitely OUT! Beginners sometimes fall into the appalling error of thinking that a smart rub with metal polish might improve the appearance of their coins. Short of actually punching a hole through it, there can hardly be a more destructive act. Polishing a coin may improve its superficial appearance for a few days, but such abrasive action will destroy the patina and reduce the fineness of the high points of the surface.

Even if a coin is only polished once, it will never be quite the same again, and an expert can tell this a mile off.

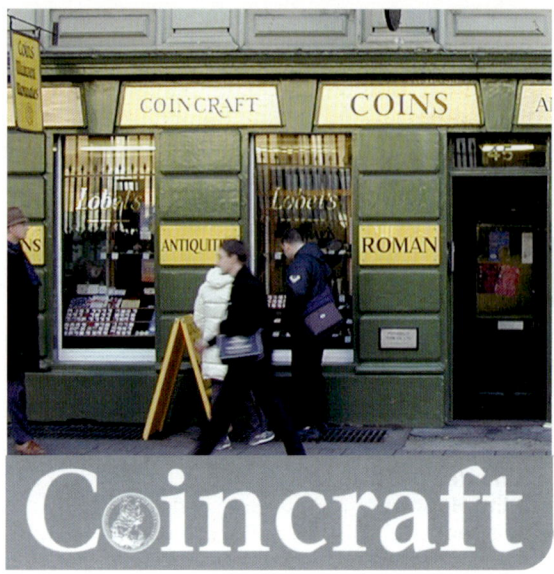

Celtic
coinage of Britain

Celtic coins were the first coins made in Britain, from c.120 BC to c.AD 50. They were minted by the rulers of thirteen tribal groups situated to the southeast of a line from the Humber to the Severn. Today's prices typically range from £50 to £5,000. Celtic specialist CHRIS RUDD introduces this increasingly popular series.

Britain was the last part of Celtic Europe to conform to the uniform bureaucracy of Roman colonisation and then only partially. Like Britons themselves, the essence of Ancient British coins is freedom. Tribal rulers were free to mint their own coins to their own designs, often influenced by their local Druids, in my view. The imagery of British Celtic coins is free—surrealistic, not realistic. For me this free spirit is symbolised by two great British freedom fighters and their coins: Cassivellaunos who fought Caesar in 54 BC and Caratacus who fought Claudius from AD 43 to 51.

Cassivellaunos with winged sceptre and winged helmet, as seen on silver unit, ABC 2472.

Whaddon Chase gold stater of Cassivellaunos, ABC 2436, with his winged sceptre.

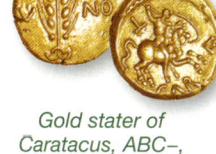

Gold stater of Caratacus, ABC–, sold by Chris Rudd for £88,000, world record price for a Celtic coin.

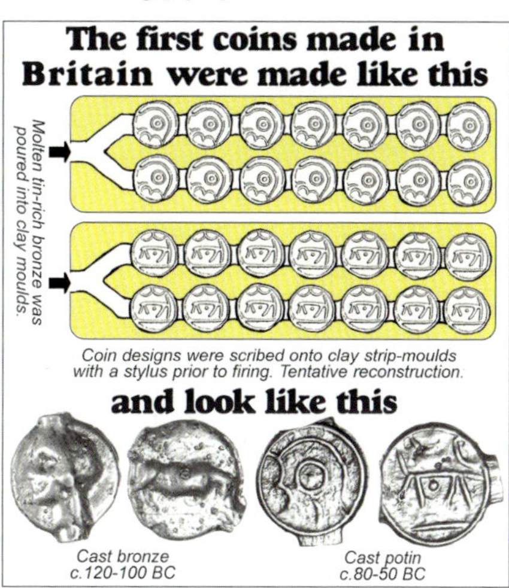

Marseilles inspired Britain's first homemade coinage: potin coins cast in clay strip-moulds, with Apollo on one side and a bull on the other, plus MA for Massalia (Marseilles). Made in Kent c. 120–100 BC, these cast potins circulated alongside gold coins imported from Gaul. During the Gallic Wars (58–51 BC) many other Gaulish coins—gold, silver and bronze—came to Britain, some brought by refugees, others by British mercenaries, others by trade.

Imported Coriosolites silver stater, ABC 70. Many were in the Jersey hoard, 2012, which contained 70,000 coins and was valued by Chris Rudd at £6 million.

The most famous Gallic migrant was Commios "friend", a former ally of Caesar, who became king of the Regini and Atrebates in the south of England c. 50–25 BC. Commios was the first British ruler to place his name on coins. His three sons—Tincomarus (great in peace), Eppillus (little horse) and Verica (the high one), made the Commian dynasty one of the wealthiest and most powerful in Britain. Most of their coins adopted Roman imagery and archaeology indicates that they imported Roman luxury goods, especially Italian wine. Many coins of Verica show grapes, vine leaves and wine cups.

The main rivals of the Regini and Atrebates were the Catuvellauni of Hertfordshire. Their first known ruler was probably Cassivellaunos "bronze commander", leader of the British coalition against Caesar in 54 BC. Many of Britain's earliest gold coins were probably struck to fund resistance to Caesar and then to pay tribute to him. Cassivellaunos may have organised this war money. Addedomaros "great in chariots" (c. 45–25 BC) was the first ruler north of the Thames to inscribe his coins, perhaps copying Commios.

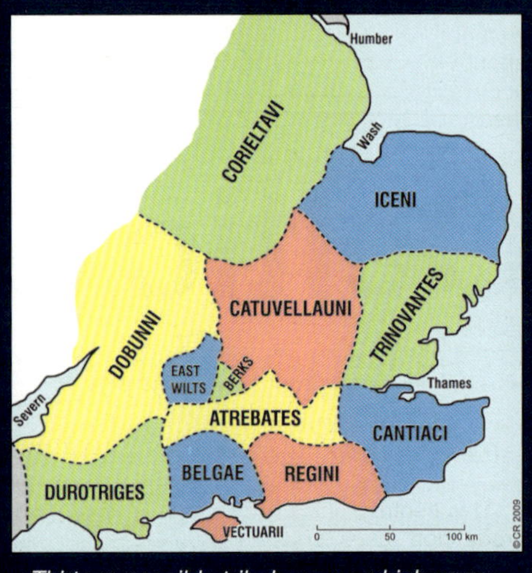

Thirteen possible tribal groups which were producing coins by c.50-40 BC (Cantiaci much earlier). By c.30 BC the Belgae, East Wiltshire and Berkshire group had apparently stopped minting independently.

Gold stater of Commios (ABC 1022) the first British king to place his name on coins. There are two hidden faces on the obverse.

Verica silver minim with wine cup (ABC 1331) and Verica gold stater with vine leaf (ABC 1193)—evidence of Britain's thirst for fine Italian wine and Roman silverware.

Catuvellaunian expansion continued under Tasciovanos "killer of badgers" whose coins became increasingly Roman in style. His son Cunobelinus "hound of Belenus"—Shakespeare's *Cymbeline*) was the most potent tribal king in Atlantic Europe. Suetonius called him "king of the Britons". During his thirty-year reign (c. AD 8–41) Cunobelinus may have minted well over a million gold staters, most of them displaying a corn ear and CAMV— short for *Camulodunon* (Colchester). When his brother Epaticcus "leader of horsemen" and his son Caratacus "the beloved"—both clad as Hercules on their silver coins—crossed the Thames and attacked the Atrebates, Verica fled to Claudius who invaded Britain in AD 43. The minting of tribal coins ceased shortly afterwards.

Other tribes that issued coins included the Cantiaci of Kent, the Belgae of Hampshire, the Durotriges of Dorset, the Dobunni of the West Midlands, the Trinovantes of Essex, the Iceni of East Anglia and the Corieltavi of Lincolnshire. However, only a minority of people in the British Isles used coins regularly—the moneyed minority in southeast England. Cornwall, Devon, Wales, northern England, Scotland and Ireland remained coinless. Which is why ancient British coins are relatively rare. For example, whereas Greek coins were minted for about 600 years, Roman for about 800 years and Gaulish for about 250 years, ancient British coins were produced for little more than 150 years, and often in much smaller runs.

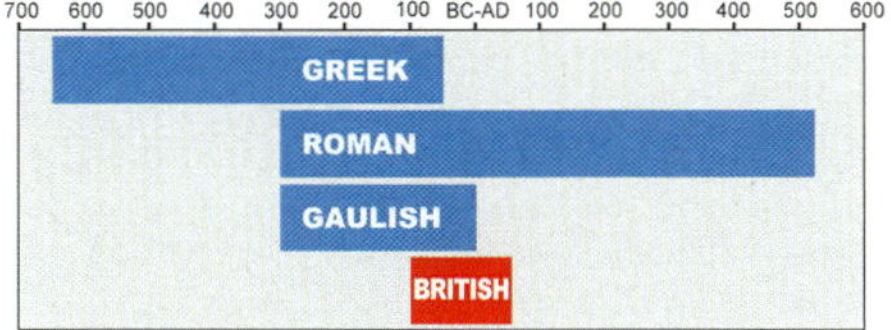

Ancient British coins weren't minted for as long as Greek, Roman or Gaulish coins were. That's one of the reasons they are so scarce.

This century and a half of Ancient British coin production generated a remarkable flowering of insular creativity and insular technology, unmatched by any other northern European nation of the period. Though initially influenced by Gallic minting techniques and Gallic iconography, Ancient British coinage rapidly developed its own denominational systems, its own gold standards and its own highly distinctive coin designs—often inspired by Roman prototypes, but invariably modified to suit local needs. Between c. 110 BC and c. AD 45 around a thousand different coin types were minted in Britain. Many if not most of these thousand types displayed what might loosely be described as "religious" imagery. Not surprising, really, when one recalls that Caesar says that Druidism originated in Britain. Moreover, Tasciovanos struck coins in no fewer than five different denominations, whereas most Gaulish rulers issued no more than two or three.

The history of late iron age Britain, particularly the century prior to the Claudian conquest, has largely been rewritten with the help of Ancient British coins. Most of the recent advances in our knowledge of this period have been due to amateur metal detecting. As a direct result of coin finds made by metal detectorists since the 1970s four new coin-issuing groups and maybe ten new rulers, previously unknown or unrecognised, have been identified. Not bad for barely forty years of unfunded, unofficial fieldwork.

Unlike Gaul, most of the British Isles was virtually coinless throughout the late iron age (and later). Coin production was confined to south-east Britain. That's why, overall, Ancient British coins are much rarer than Gaulish coins.

What is it about Ancient British coins that is making them increasingly popular with collectors all over the world? Having been involved with them for many years (I excavated my first in 1952) I'll tell you why they appeal to me.

I love the *primal antiquity* of Celtic coins. They were the first coins made in Britain over two thousand years ago. When you see the flamboyant freedom of their designs you realise that they are the most boisterously British coins ever minted, unlike the unsmiling Roman, Anglo-Saxon and Norman series that marched soberly in their dancing footsteps.

I love the *anarchic regality* of Celtic coins. Like the rumbustious tribal kings that issued them, their personality is wild, strong and highly irregular. These coins were made by the first British rulers known by name to us—unruly, quarrelsome, beer-swilling, tribal warlords such as Cassivellaunos who fought Julius Caesar in 54 BC and Caratacus, the British resistance leader who opposed Claudius in AD 43.

I love the *imaginative imagery* you find on Celtic coins: all the different gods and goddesses, armed warriors, chariot wheels, hidden faces, decapitated heads, suns, moons, stars, thunderbolts, floral motifs, magic signs and phallic symbols. Plus an amazing menagerie of wild animals, birds and mythical beasts.

I love the *myths, mystery and mysticism* behind Celtic coins. Look closely at this late iron age money of Albion and you'll catch glimpses

Ancient British denominations

There was no national currency in pre-Roman Britain and little consistency from region to region. Different tribes issued different mixtures of low, medium and high value coins. Here are the most common denominations used by the ancient Brits. The names are ours, not theirs. We've no idea what they called their coins, shown here actual size.

GOLD STATERS

Can also be silver, billon or bronze

Norfolk Wolf, ABC 1393

GOLD QUARTER STATERS

Can also be silver or billon

Irstead Smiler, ABC 1480

SILVER UNITS

Norfolk God, ABC 1567

SILVER HALF UNITS

Aunt Cost Half, ABC 1953

SILVER MINIMS

Verica Sphinx, ABC 1340

BRONZE UNITS

Cunobelinus Centaur, ABC 2957

BRONZE HALF UNITS

Tasciovanos Goat, ABC 2709

CAST POTIN UNITS

Nipples, ABC 174

of long-lost legends and ancient pagan rituals such as head-hunting, bull sacrificing and shape-shifting. You'll marvel at the plethora of occult signs and arcane symbols and you may even feel the secret power of the Druids.

I love the *palpitating unpredictability* of Celtic coins. Even after seventy years of heart-racing intimacy they are constantly and delightfully surprising me. Attributions, names and dates are always being revised. Not long ago the Coritani were renamed Corieltavi and Tincommios was rechristened Tincomarus. Almost every month exciting new types and new variants keep leaping out of the ground, thanks to metal detectorists.

Bronze units of Cunobelinus, son of Tasciovanos,showing a bull being sacrificed (ABC 2972) and a man—perhaps a Druid priest?—carrying a severed human head (ABC 2987).

For example, on September 4, 2010 the late Danny Baldock discovered the first recorded coin of Anarevitos, a Kentish ruler previously unknown to history.

I love the *uncommon scarcity* of Celtic coins. Ask any metdet how many Ancient British coins he or she has found and you'll immediately realise that they are rarer than Roman coins—at least a thousand times rarer on average—for the reasons stated above.

Finally I love the *galloping good value* of this horsey money (some Celtic horses have three tails, some breathe fire, others have a human

Silver unit of freedom-fighter Caratacus (ABC 1376) who defied the Roman invaders for eight years until he was betrayed by Cartimandua, queen of the Brigantes.

torso). Their greater rarity doesn't mean they are costlier than other Ancient coins. In fact, they are often cheaper because demand determines price and because there are far fewer collectors of Ancient British coins than there are, say, of Greek or Roman coins. For example, a very fine British gold stater typically costs less than half the price—sometimes even a third the price of a Roman aureus or English gold noble of comparable quality and rarity. But the disparity is gradually diminishing as more and more canny collectors are appreciating the untamed beauty and undervalued scarcity of British Celtic coins.

Coin Yearbook provides a great guide to current prices of commoner Celtic types, but because new types keep turning up and because big hoards are sometimes found (causing values to fluctuate temporarily) you'd be well advised to also keep an eye on dealers' catalogues and prices realised at auction. If you're buying in Britain, buy from people who are members of the BNTA (British Numismatic Trade Association). If you're buying overseas, check that your suppliers belong to the IAPN (International Association of Professional Numismatists). And, if you're a beginner, beware of dodgy traders on the internet, or you could end up with a fistful of fakes and no refund.

A unique gold stater of Anarevitos, a previously unknown ruler of the Cantiaci, probably a son of Eppillus, king of Calleva (Silchester). Sold by Elizabeth Cottam of Chris Rudd for £21,000. (Coin News, *December 2010).*

I'd also counsel you to spend a day at the British Museum. Its collection of almost 7,000 Ancient British coins is the most comprehensive, publicly accessible collection of its kind in the world. As former curator, Ian Leins, says: "They're public coins . . . your coins, and they're here for you to see. So come and see them. We'll be pleased to show them to you". Access to the collection is free for everyone. But you'll need to make an appointment before you go, and take some photo ID and proof of address. Email: coins@thebritishmuseum.ac.uk or telephone: 020 7323 8607.

Before you buy coins—any coins of any period—it always pays to read about them first. As an old adman I'm not shy about blowing my own trumpet. The best little introduction to Celtic coins is *Britain's First Coins* by Chris Rudd (2013) and the most comprehensive catalogue of the series is *Ancient British Coins* also by Chris Rudd (2010), known in the trade as ABC. If you have even half the fun I've had with Ancient British coins (and am still having)—I can promise you that you'll be a very happy person indeed. Never bored, and never with a complete collection.

Chris Rudd started studying Ancient British coins 70 years ago and has written over a hundred articles about them, many published by COIN NEWS.

Collecting
ancient coins

An Introduction to Roman Coinage by Hugh Smith, ancient coin specialist at Silbury Coins Ltd.

Although the systematic conquest of Britain by the Romans did not take place until AD 43 under the Emperor Claudius there had been increasing contact and trade between the two cultures since the expeditions carried out by Julius Caesar nearly 100 years earlier. This led to a certain Romanisation of local Celtic coinage prior to the invasion of AD 43.

The introduction of Britain into the Roman Empire initiated a complete change of the currency which endured for the next 350 years. The main denominations of coinage, which could be used throughout the Roman Empire, initially were:

The gold aureus = 25 denarius

Silver denarius = 4 Sestertius

Bronze sestertius = 2 dupondius

Copper dupondius = 4 as

Copper as

The typical wage for a Roman legionary soldier at this time was 1 denarius a day. The denarius also came to denote the silver penny which was later issued from the Anglo-Saxon period.

In addition to the official coinage local copies of the Roman coinage began to appear due to initial shortages of currency and increased trade. One of the most popular was the copper as of Claudius depicting Minerva on the reverse. Some of these copies were well executed whilst others were very crude.

Roman coins typically had a portrait of the emperor on the obverse. This was important, as it is today, to show who was in charge. On the reverse a remarkable array of images are shown and is where much of their historical interest will be found. Typical depictions include deities and personifications, there being many pagan gods both male and female. There were also frequent appearances by the emperor and his family. Other popular themes include types of military conquest and victories. Animal and architecture types are also common. Coins were also used for propaganda. For instance depictions include the reform or lowering of taxes, distribution of the corn supply or feeding of the poor.

As the decades past the empire expanded further into Britain and by the time of Hadrian in the early 2nd century his famous wall was constructed between the Solway and the Tyne. Further expeditions into Scotland were short lived and the wall became the official boundary between the Romans and the Picts for the next 250 years. The peace and security offered by the occupation brought a flood of Roman coinage into the country as trade flourished and considerable urban expansion also took place.

When the empire ceased to expand, an increase in taxes, as well as a run of poor emperors, led to unrest and inflation as well as deepening political and economic crisis. The currency became increasingly devalued and the silver content in the denarius was reduced. By the middle of the 3rd century silver coins were largely made of bronze. The denarius was increasingly replaced by the antoninianus, nominally worth 2 denarius, but this too was debased and reduced in size.

The 3rd century saw a succession of short-lived emperors and as anarchy and unrest spread there were various uprisings throughout the empire. In Britain, and North West Gaul one of the uprisings was led by Carausius. Carausius was one of the most famous usurpers and defied Rome for seven years before being assassinated and replaced by a rival, Allectus. Both men issued their own coinage from local mints which were set up in London and Colchester. There was also a large increase in the issue of local and unofficial coins at around this time. These coins were often modelled on the official Roman bronze coinage and are usually classified as Barbarous Radiates. Typically these radiates are smaller and more crudely made.

The Empire was eventually stabilised under Diocletian. In AD 296 Allectus was deposed, and Britain brought back under Roman rule. Diocletian brought in many reforms which included the division of the empire for administrative purposes. The currency was also stabilised and reformed. The new coins include:

Gold solidus

Silver siliqua

Billon follis later to become the centenionalis

Again, these coins typically depict the emperor on the obverse together with a diverse array of reverses. The conversion of the empire to Christianity under Constantine the Great meant that the depiction of pagan gods was replaced by Christian symbols typically the Chi Rho. During the 4th century the minting of coins was decentralised and for several decades coins were minted in provincial towns such as Trier, Lyon and London.

By the end of the 4th century AD the Roman Empire, which had been divided into the East and the West, was again in decline. There was increasing unrest, particularly on the borders, which led to incursions into the empire by neighbouring barbarian tribes. These culminated in the eventual sacking of Rome in AD 476 together with the fall of the western part of the empire. In the east however the empire, which was centred on Constantinople, continued under the Byzantines, for another 1,000 years.

The Romans started to withdraw from Britain towards the end of the 4th century AD and in AD 410 the Roman province was told that it could no longer rely on the protection of the Roman army. Many Romans had by then settled in Britain and some of these chose to remain. Although there was an increasing number of incursions into the province during the 5th century it would be several decades before the Anglo-Saxons became dominant and the influence of Rome disappeared. Indeed, some of the coins from the early Anglo-Saxon period retained a distinctly Romanic appearance.

Roman solidus

Anglo-Saxon thrymsa

A Roman coin provides a direct link to Roman culture. When a coin and its inscription has been identified an insight is provided not only on the emperor under whose reign the coin was struck but also often some of the important historical and cultural events of the time. Due to the large number of coins found through metal detecting, especially where hoards have been discovered, acquiring a collection of Roman coinage is relatively easy. Whilst museums often retain some of the rarer or more unusual finds. Roman coin hoards, particularly from the later Roman period, have produced a vast array of high-quality bronze and silver coinage available to the private collector. Coinage minted under Constantine the Great and his descendants for instance are usually available and are often relatively inexpensive (under £100). Some of these hoard coins were almost uncirculated when they were buried. Not only does this provide some insight as to when the coins were buried but the high quality of workmanship of many of these coins can now be enjoyed by their new owners.

As with coins from all periods there are many forgeries, both contemporary and modern, also available for sale. It is therefore important, particularly when inexperienced, to acquire coins from reputable sources. Most dealers now show what coins they have available for sale online. Searching their websites can provide a useful source of information and will often help the collector to decide what coins are of interest and where to begin their collection.

For further reading on the subject try David R. Sears' excellent titles *Roman Coins and their Values* (Volumes 1-5).

The Ropsley Hoard, found 2018.

Hammered coinage

The hammered currency of Medieval Britain is among some of the most interesting coinage in the world. The turbulent history of these islands is reflected in the fascinating changes in size, design, fineness and workmanship, culminating in the many strange examples that emanated from the strife of the Civil War.

The Norman Conquest of England in 1066 and succeeding years had far-reaching effects on all aspects of life. Surprisingly, however, it had little impact on the coinage. William the Conqueror was anxious to emphasise the continuity of his reign, so far as the ordinary people were concerned, and therefore he retained the fabric, size and general design pattern of the silver penny. Almost 70 mints were in operation during this reign, but by the middle of the 12th century the number was reduced to 55 and under Henry II (1154–89) it fell to 30 and latterly to only eleven. By the early 14th century the production of coins had been centralised on London and Canterbury, together with the ecclesiastical mints at York and Canterbury. The silver penny was the principal denomination throughout the Norman period, pieces cut along the lines of the cross on the reverse continuing to serve as halfpence and farthings.

Eight types of penny were struck under William I and five under his son William Rufus, both profiles (left and right) and facing portraits being used in both reigns allied to crosses of various types. Fifteen types were minted under Henry I (1100–35), portraiture having now degenerated to crude caricature, the lines engraved on the coinage dies being built up by means of various punches. Halfpence modelled on the same pattern were also struck, but very sparingly and are very rare.

On Henry's death the succession was contested by his daughter Matilda and his nephew Stephen of Blois. Civil war broke out in 1138 and continued till 1153. Stephen controlled London and its mint, but Matilda and her supporters occupied the West Country and struck their own coins at Bristol. Several of the powerful barons struck their own coins, and there were distinct regional variants of the regal coinage. Of particular interest are the coins

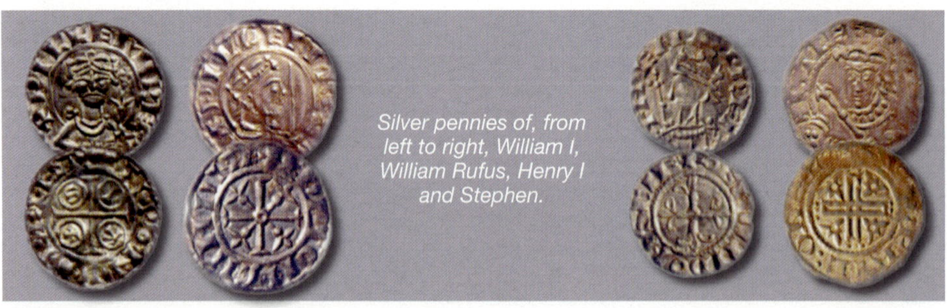

Silver pennies of, from left to right, William I, William Rufus, Henry I and Stephen.

struck from obverse dies with Stephen's portrait erased or defaced, believed to date from 1148 when the usurper was under papal interdict.

Peace was restored in 1153 when it was agreed that Matilda's son Henry should succeed Stephen. On the latter's death the following year, Henry II ascended the throne. Coins of Stephen's last type continued to be minted till 1158, but Henry then took the opportunity to overhaul the coinage which had become irregular and sub-standard during the civil war. The new "Cross Crosslet" coins, usually known as the Tealby coinage (from the hoard of over 5,000 pennies found at Tealby, Lincolnshire in 1807), were produced at 30 mints, but when the recoinage was completed this number was reduced to a dozen. The design of Henry's coins remained virtually the same throughout more than two decades, apart from minor variants. Then, in 1180, a new type, known as the Short Cross coinage, was introduced. This was a vast improvement over the poorly struck Cross Crosslet coins and continued without alteration, not only to the end of the reign of Henry II in 1189, but throughout the reigns of his sons Richard (1189–99) and John (1199–1216) and the first half of the reign of his grandson Henry III (1216–46). Throughout that 66 year period, however, there were minor variations in portraits and lettering which enable numismatists to attribute the HENRICUS coins to specific reigns and periods.

"Tealby" type penny (top), and "Short Cross" penny of Henry II.

The style and workmanship of the Short Cross coinage deteriorated in the reign of Henry III. By the 1220s coin production was confined to the regal mints at London and Canterbury, the sole exception being the ecclesiastical mint maintained by the Abbot of Bury St Edmunds. Halfpence and farthings were briefly struck in 1221–30, though halfpence are now extremely rare and so far only a solitary farthing has been discovered.

By the middle of this reign the coinage was in a deplorable state, being poorly struck, badly worn and often ruthlessly clipped. In 1247 Henry ordered a new coinage and in this the arms of the cross on the reverse were extended to the rim as a safeguard against clipping. This established a pattern of facing portrait and long cross on obverse and reverse respectively that was to continue till the beginning of the 16th century. Several provincial mints were re-activated to assist with the recoinage but they were all closed down again by 1250, only the regal mints at London and Canterbury and the ecclesiastical mints at Durham and Bury St Edmunds remaining active.

"Long Cross" pennies of Henry III (top), and Edward I.

In 1257 Henry tentatively introduced a gold penny (worth 20 silver pence and twice the weight of a silver penny). The coin was undervalued and soon disappeared from circulation.

The Long Cross coinage of Henry III continued under Edward I till 1279 when the king introduced a new coinage in his own name. The penny continued the style of its predecessors, though much better designed and executed; but new denominations were now added. Henceforward halfpence and farthings became a regular issue and, at the same time, a fourpenny coin known as the groat (from French *gros*) was briefly introduced (minting ceased in 1282 and was not revived till 1351). Due to the centralisation of coin production the name of the moneyer was now generally dropped, although it lingered on a few years at Bury St Edmunds. The provincial mints were again revived in 1299–1302 to recoin the lightweight foreign imitations of pennies which had flooded in from the Continent.

The coinage of Edward II (1307–27) differed only in minor respects from that of his father, and a similar pattern prevailed in the first years of Edward III. In 1335 halfpence and farthings below the sterling fineness were struck. More

Pre-Treaty Noble of Edward III which contained reference to France in the legend.

importantly, further attempts were made to introduce gold coins. In 1344 the florin or double leopard of six shillings was introduced, along with its half and quarter. This coinage was not successful and was soon replaced by a heavier series based on the noble of 80 pence (6*s.* 8*d.*), half a mark or one third of a pound. The noble originally weighed 138.5 grains but it was successively reduced to120 grains, at which weight it continued from 1351. During this reign the protracted conflict with France known as the Hundred Years' War erupted. Edward III, through his mother, claimed the French throne and inscribed this title on his coins. By the Treaty of Bretigny (1361) Edward temporarily gave up his claim and the reference to France was dropped from the coins, but when war was renewed in 1369 the title was resumed, and remained on many English coins until the end of the 18th century. The silver coinage followed the pattern of the previous reign, but in 1351 the groat was re-introduced and with it came the twopence or half-groat. Another innovation was the use of mintmarks at the beginning of the inscriptions. Seven types of cross and one crown were employed from 1334 onwards and their sequence enables numismatists to date coins fairly accurately.

Noble of Edward IV, issued before he was forced to abandon the throne of England.

The full range of gold (noble, half-noble and quarter-noble) and silver (groat, half-groat, penny, halfpenny and farthing) continued under Richard II (1377–99). Little attempt was made to alter the facing portrait on the silver coins,

Noble of Henry IV which was reduced in weight due to the shortage of gold.

by now little more than a stylised caricature anyway.

Under Henry IV (1399–1413) the pattern of previous reigns prevailed, but in 1412 the weights of the coinage were reduced due to a shortage of bullion. The noble was reduced to 108 grains and its sub-divisions lightened proportionately. The penny was reduced by 3 grains, and its multiples and sub-divisions correspondingly reduced. One interesting change was the reduction of the fleur de lis of France from four to three in the heraldic shield on the reverse of the noble; this change corresponded with the alteration in the arms used in France itself. The Calais mint, opened by Edward III in 1363, was closed in 1411. There was no change in the designs used for the coins of Henry V (1413–22) but greater use was now made of mintmarks to distinguish the various periods of production. Coins were by now produced mainly at London, although the episcopal mints at Durham and York were permitted to strike pennies.

The supply of gold dwindled early in the reign of Henry VI and few nobles were struck after 1426. The Calais mint was re-opened in 1424 and struck a large amount of gold before closing finally in 1440. A regal mint briefly operated at York in 1423–24. Mintmarks were now much more widely used and tended to correspond more closely to the annual trials of the Pyx. The series of civil upheavals known as the Wars of the Roses erupted in this period.

In 1461 Henry VI was deposed by the Yorkist Earl of March after he defeated the Lancastrians at Mortimer's Cross. The Yorkists advanced on London where the victor was crowned Edward IV. At first he continued the gold series of his predecessor, issuing nobles and quarter-nobles, but in 1464 the weight of the penny was reduced

Groat of Richard III (1483–85).

to 12 grains and the value of the noble was raised to 100 pence (8*s*. 4*d*.).The ryal or rose-noble of 120 grains, together with its half and quarter, was introduced in 1465 and tariffed at ten shillings or half a pound. The need for a coin worth a third of a pound, however, led to the issue of the angel of 80 grains, worth 6*s*. 8*d*., but this was initially unsucessful and very few examples are now extant. The angel derived its name from the figure of the Archangel Michael on the obverse; a cross surmounting a shield appeared on the reverse.

In 1470 Edward was forced to flee to Holland and Henry VI was briefly restored. During this brief period (to April 1471) the ryal was discontinued but a substantial issue of angels and half-angels was made both at London and Bristol. Silver coins were struck at York as well as London and Bristol, the issues of the provincial mints being identified by the initials B or E (Eboracum, Latin for York). Edward defeated the Lancastrians at Tewkesbury and deposed the luckless Henry once more. In his second reign Edward struck only angels and half-angels as well as silver from the groat to halfpenny. In addition to the three existing mints, silver coins were struck at Canterbury, Durham and the archiepiscopal mint at York. Mintmarks were now much more frequent and varied. Coins with a mark of a halved sun and rose are usually assigned to the reign of Edward IV, but they were probably also struck in the nominal reign of Edward V, the twelve-year-old prince held in the Tower of London under the protection of his uncle Richard, Duke of Gloucester. Coins with this mark on the reverse had an obverse mark of a boar's head, Richard's personal emblem. The brief reign of Richard III (1483–5) came to an end with his defeat at Bosworth and the relatively scarce coins of this period followed the pattern of the previous reigns, distinguished by the sequence of mint marks and the inscription RICAD or RICARD.

In the early years of Henry VII's reign the coinage likewise followed the previous patterns, but in 1489 the first of several radical changes was effected, with the introduction of the gold sovereign of 20 shillings showing a full-length portrait of the monarch seated on an elaborate throne. For reverse, this coin depicted a Tudor rose surmounted by a heraldic shield. A similar reverse appeared on the ryal of 10 shillings, but the angel and angelet retained previous motifs. The silver coins at first adhered to the medieval pattern, with the stylised facing portrait and long cross, but at the beginning of the 16th century a large silver coin, the testoon or shilling of 12 pence, was introduced and adopted a realistic profile of the king, allied to a reverse showing a cross surmounted by the royal arms. The same design was also used for the later issue of groat and half groat.

First coinage Angel of Henry VIII which retained the traditional 23.5 carat fineness.

This established a pattern which was to continue till the reign of Charles I. In the reign of Henry VIII, however, the coinage was subject to considerable debasement. This led to the eventual introduction of 22 carat (.916 fine) gold for the crown while the traditional 23 1/2 carat gold was retained for the angel and ryal. This dual system continued until the angel was discontinued at the outset of the Civil War in 1642; latterly it had been associated with the ceremony of touching for "King's Evil" or scrofula, a ritual used by the early Stuart monarchs to bolster their belief in the divine right of kings.

Under the Tudors and Stuarts the range and complexity of the gold coinage increased, but it was not until the reign of Edward VI that the silver series was expanded. In 1551 he introduced the silver crown of five shillings, the first English coin to bear a clear date on the obverse. Under Mary dates were extended to the shilling and sixpence.

The mixture of dated and undated coins continued under Elizabeth I, a reign remarkable for the range of denominations—nine gold and eight silver. The latter included the sixpence, threepence, threehalfpence and threefarthings, distinguished by the rose which appeared behind the Queen's head.

The magnificent second coinage Rose-Ryal of James I (1603–25).

Images courtesy of Spink.

The coinage of James I was even more complex, reflecting the king's attempts to unite his dominions. The first issue bore the legend ANG: SCO (England and Scotland), but from 1604 this was altered to MAG: BRIT (Great Britain). This period witnessed new denominations, such as the rose-ryal and spur-ryal, the unite, the Britain crown and the thistle crown, and finally the laurel of 20 shillings and its sub-divisions.

In the reign of Elizabeth experiments began with milled coinage under Eloi Mestrell. These continued sporadically in the 17th century, culminating in the beautiful coins struck by Nicholas Briot (1631–39). A branch mint was established at Aberystwyth in 1637 to refine and coin silver from the Welsh mines. Relations between King and Parliament deteriorated in the reign of Charles I and led to the Civil War (1642). Parliament controlled London but continued to strike coins in the King's name. The Royalists struck coins, both in pre-war and new types, at Shrewsbury, Oxford, Bristol, Worcester, Exeter, Chester, Hereford and other Royalist strongholds, while curious siege pieces were pressed into service at Newark, Pontefract and Scarborough.

After the execution of Charles I in 1649 the Commonwealth was proclaimed and gold and silver coins were now inscribed in English instead of Latin. Patterns portraying Cromwell and a crowned shield restored Latin in 1656. Plans for milled coinage were already being considered before the Restoration of the monarchy in 1660. Hammered coinage appeared initially, resuming the style of coins under Charles I, but in 1662 the hand-hammering of coins was abandoned in favour of coins struck on the mill and screw press. The hammered coins of 1660–62 were undated and bore a crown mintmark, the last vestiges of medievalism in British coinage.

Coin grading

Condition is the secret to the value of virtually anything, whether it be antiques, jewellery, horses or second-hand cars—and coins are certainly no exception. When collecting coins it is vital to understand the recognised standard British system of grading, i.e. accurately assessing a coin's condition or state of wear. Grading is an art which can only be learned by experience and so often it remains one person's opinion against another's, therefore it is important for the beginner or inexperienced collector to seek assistance from a reputable dealer or knowledgeable numismatist when making major purchases.

The standard grades as used in the Price Guide are as follows:	
UNC	**Uncirculated** A coin that has never been in circulation, although it may show signs of contact with other coins during the minting process.
EF	**Extremely Fine** A coin in this grade may appear uncirculated to the naked eye but on closer examination will show signs of minor friction on the highest surface.
VF	**Very Fine** A coin that has had very little use, but shows signs of wear on the high surfaces.
F	**Fine** A coin that has been in circulation and shows general signs of wear, but with all legends and date clearly visible.
Other grades used in the normal grading system are:	
BU	**Brilliant Uncirculated** As the name implies, a coin retaining its mint lustre.
Fair	A coin extensively worn but still quite recognisable and legends readable.
Poor	A coin very worn and only just recognisable.
Other abbreviations used in the Price Guide are:	
Obv	**Obverse**
Rev	**Reverse**
Other abbreviations, mintmarks, etc. can be identified under the appropriate section of this Yearbook.	

A SIMPLIFIED PRICE GUIDE TO

ANCIENT COINS USED IN BRITAIN

PART I Ancient British

The prices given in this section are those that you would expect to pay from a reputable dealer and not the prices at which you could expect to sell coins.

The list below, which has been generously provided by Celtic coin dealer Elizabeth Cottam of Chris Rudd, contains most of the commonly available types: a fully comprehensive guide is beyond the scope of this book. Prices are for coins with good surfaces which are not weakly struck or struck from worn dies. Examples which are struck from worn or damaged dies can be worth considerably less. Particularly attractive examples of bronze Celtic coins command a very high premium. Where a price is given for an issue of which there are many varieties, the price is for the most common type.The illustrations are representative examples only and are not shown actual size.

UNINSCRIBED COINAGE

GOLD STATERS	F	VF	EF
Broad Flan	£700	£1775	£5750
Gallic War Uniface	£300	£600	£1000
Remic types	£250	£400	£800
Wonersh types	£250	£450	£2200
Chute	£200	£300	£750
Cheriton	£250	£450	£975
Iceni (various types)	£300	£500	£1350
Norfolk "wolf" type			
fine gold	£250	£475	£1500
brassy gold	£175	£300	£695
very debased	£120	£200	£475
Corieltauvi (various types)	£200	£400	£1000
Dobunni	£250	£500	£1500
Whaddon Chase types	£275	£475	£1300

Cheriton Smiler gold stater

GOLD QUARTER STATERS	F	VF	EF
Gallic Imported Types	£300	£450	£850
Kent types	£200	£300	£550
Southern types	£125	£200	£500
Iceni	£150	£250	£500
Corieltauvi	£125	£200	£500
Dobunni	£175	£300	£700
East Wiltshire	£300	£500	£1000
Durotriges	£120	£225	£750
North Thames types	£220	£300	£550

SILVER COINAGE	F	VF	EF
Armorican billion staters	£125	£250	£500
Kent Types	£150	£300	£675
South Thames types	£120	£175	£375

Cranborne Chase silver stater

	F	VF	EF
Iceni ('crescent' types)...........................	£85	£125	£275
Iceni ('Norfolk God' types)....................	£100	£200	£400
Corieltavi...	£50	£110	£225
Dobunni	£85	£125	£295
Durotriges full stater			
fine silver..	£80	£175	£350
base silver..	£30	£55	£175
Durotriges quarter silver	£25	£35	£95
(Note—most examples are for base coins as better quality items are appreciably higher)			
North Thames types	£110	£195	£375

Hengistbury cast bronze

POTIN COINAGE

	F	VF	EF
Kent	£75	£100	£200

BRONZE COINAGE

	F	VF	EF
Durotriges debased stater....................	£30	£75	£125
Durotriges cast bronze	£65	£125	£350
North Thames types. Various issues from:	£45	£110	£450

INSCRIBED CELTIC COINAGE

Vosenos gold quarter stater

CANTIACI

	F	VF	EF
Dubnovellaunos			
stater..	£320	£600	£1500
silver unit...	£135	£220	£575
bronze unit	£65	£175	£395
Vosenos			
stater..	£1100	£2500	£6000
quarter stater	£350	£850	£1500
silver unit...	£200	£600	£850
Sam			
stater (unique)	—	—	—
silver unit...	£250	£650	£1000
bronze unit	£110	£275	£550
Eppillus			
stater..	£1100	£2000	£5000
quarter stater	£150	£265	£575
silver unit...	£75	£145	£395
bronze unit	£65	£125	£495
bronze minim......................................	£85	£175	£300
Anarevitos			
stater (unique)			—
Touto			
silver unit...	£200	£450	£875
Verica..			
silver unit...	£200	£350	£695
bronze unit	£165	£300	£635
Sego			
stater..	£525	£1000	£5000
quarter stater	£220	£500	£1275
silver unit...	£150	£350	£675
silver minim..	£80	£200	£425
bronze unit	£80	£165	£495
Amminus			
silver unit...	£175	£400	£600
silver minim..	£110	£215	£475
bronze unit	£85	£175	£535
Solidus			
silver unit...	£535	£1000	£1500
silver minim..	£300	£650	£1000

Verica gold stater

Sego Warrior gold stater

	F	VF	EF
REGINI & ATREBATES			
Commios			
stater	£450	£1250	£2000
silver unit	£120	£300	£425
silver minim	£65	£125	£295
Tincomarus			
stater	£465	£895	£2250
quarter stater	£150	£250	£475
silver unit	£75	£145	£300
silver minim	£65	£125	£200
Eppillus			
stater	£1000	£2500	£6000
quarter stater	£160	£245	£575
silver unit	£80	£165	£345
Verica			
stater	£500	£850	£1750
quarter stater	£200	£500	£750
silver unit	£100	£200	£375
silver minim	£85	£150	£275
Epaticcus			
stater	£1000	£2000	£4250
silver unit	£50	£100	£275
silver minim	£55	£120	£295
Caratacus			
stater (unique)			–
silver unit	£175	£320	£475
silver minim	£110	£220	£345
VECTUARII			
Crab			
silver unit	£165	£325	£695
silver minim	£120	£295	£435
ICENI			
Cani Duro			
silver unit	£115	£275	£575
Antedios			
stater	£425	£1000	£2500
silver unit	£40	£100	£275
silver half unit	£45	£100	£150
Ecen			
stater	£425	£1200	£2575
silver unit	£45	£100	£275
silver half unit	£50	£100	£175
Saenu			
silver unit	£65	£125	£325
Aesu			
silver unit	£65	£125	£325
Ale Scavo			
silver unit	£275	£500	£1000
Prasutagus			
silver unit	£425	£1000	£2000
CORIELTAUVI			
Cat			
silver unit	£400	£1100	£2200
silver half unit (unique)			–
VEPOCUNAVOS			
stater	£450	£1000	£1750
silver unit	£85	£150	£350
Esuprasu			
stater	£350	£675	£1375
silver unit	£85	£150	£350

Tincomarus gold stater

Norfolk Wolf gold stater

Ale Scavo silver unit

Vep CorF gold stater

	F	VF	EF
Aunt Cost			
stater	£500	£850	£1500
silver unit	£90	£195	£350
silver half unit	£90	£150	£250
Lat Ison			
stater	£1000	£2100	£4300
silver unit	£175	£425	£1175
silver half unit	£160	£300	£575
Dumnocoveros Tigirseno			
stater	£600	£1200	£2500
silver unit	£100	£195	£595
silver half unit	£100	£210	£625
Volisios Dumnocoveros			
stater	£350	£675	£1350
silver unit	£100	£185	£500
silver half unit	£100	£175	£275
Volisios Cartivellaunos			
stater	£1000	£2000	£4100
silver half unit	£300	£675	£1200
Volisios Dumnovellaunos			
stater	£500	£1000	£1750
silver half unit	£150	£300	£500
DOBUNNI			
Bodvoc			
stater	£1000	£2250	£3250
quarter stater (unique)			—
silver unit	£200	£500	£895
Corio			
stater	£275	£560	£1550
quarter stater	£200	£350	£675
Comux			
stater	£285	£560	£1550
Catti			
stater	£285	£565	£1600
Inamn			
plated stater (unique)			—
silver unit (unique)			—
Anted			
stater	£450	£750	£2000
silver unit	£85	£125	£325
Eisu			
stater	£450	£750	£2000
silver unit	£75	£125	£335
TRINOVANTES			
Dubnovellaunos			
stater	£300	£550	£1750
quarter stater	£175	£350	£750
silver unit	£75	£150	£375
silver half unit	£100	£200	£475
bronze unit	£65	£140	£295
CATUVELLAUNI			
Addedomaros			
stater	£300	£600	£1500
quarter stater	£175	£350	£750
silver unit	£100	£200	£420
silver half unit	£100	£200	£475
bronze unit	£35	£95	£295

Bodvoc Bold gold stater

Catti gold stater

Dumno Tigir Seno gold stater

Addedomaros gold stater

	F	VF	EF
Tasciovanos			
stater	£500	£850	£2500
quarter stater	£250	£450	£850
silver unit	£85	£175	£395
bronze unit	£60	£135	£275
bronze half unit	£60	£135	£295
Andoco			
stater	£600	£1000	£3000
quarter stater	£200	£420	£775
silver unit	£155	£400	£600
bronze unit	£85	£225	£300
Dias			
silver unit	£100	£200	£500
bronze unit	£50	£150	£425
Rues			
bronze unit	£50	£150	£425
Cat			
plated silver unit (unique)			–
CATUVELLAUNI & TRINOVANTES			
Cunobelinus			
stater	£400	£1000	£2000
quarter stater	£200	£400	£600
silver unit	£185	£400	£600
bronze unit	£60	£145	£395
bronze half	£60	£145	£285
Trocc			
bronze unit	£50	£150	£550
Agr			
quarter stater	£400	£850	£1200
silver unit	£300	£850	£1000
bronze unit (only two known)		(too rare to price)	
Dubn			
quarter stater (only three)	£1000	£3000	£7500

Tasciovanos gold stater

Cunobelinus gold stater

Illustrations by courtesy of Chris Rudd

SILBURY
COINS
IRON AGE GREEK ROMAN
SAXON NORMAN MEDIEVAL
View our stock online at
www.silburycoins.com
We are looking to buy high value single items
and collections of coins.
Email: info@silburycoins.com | Tel: 01242 898107
BNTA

A SIMPLIFIED PRICE GUIDE TO

ANCIENT COINS USED IN BRITAIN

PART II

Roman Britain

Throughout the centuries, Roman coinage has been subject to many changes, driven by the economic climate of the times giving rise to a range of denominations predominantly in gold, silver and bronze, together with alloys of these metals, typically as a result of debasement. Beginning with the Republican period, we see denominations like the denarius, quinarius and some cast-bronze coinage which was unsuccessful and quickly phased out. Imperatorial and Imperial coinage is a mix of the gold aureus, silver denarius and bronze sestertius, as and dupondius. In the 2nd century AD the silver antoninianus was introduced—a double denarius. The late 3rd century sees the appearance of the silver argenteus, quickly followed by silver siliqua and miliarense, circulated alongside the gold solidus until the Roman's left Britain in AD 410.

All of the coins listed here can be found in Britain and with the increasing popularity of the hobby of metal detecting, more coins are becoming available to budding collectors who in the past may not have seen such coins for sale. This guide offers an indicative price for Fine and Very Fine grade coins; Extremely Fine examples will be worth considerably more and popular types often sell at higher prices. Our grateful thanks go to John Philpotts of Silbury Coins Ltd (www.silburycoins.com) who has completely revised and updated this section.

REPUBLICAN COINAGE 290–41 BC

	F	VF
Republican		
Quadrigatus (or Didrachm) (Janus/Quadriga)	£250	£850
Victoriatus (Jupiter/Victory)	£40	£200
+Denarius (Roma/Biga)	£25	£100
+Denarius (other types)	£35	£150
Denarius (Gallic warrior—L.Hostilius Saserna)	£500	£2500
Quinarius	£35	£125
Cast Aes Grave, As	£250	£900
Struck As/Semis/Litra	£40	£200
Struck Triens/Quadrands	£25	£150

Republican

IMPERATORIAL COINAGE 71–27 BC

	F	VF
Pompey the Great		
Denarius (Hd. of Pompilius/Prow)	£250	£750
Scipio		
Denarius (Jupiter/Elephant	£100	£350
Cato Uticensis		
Quinarius (Bacchus/Victory)	£45	£150
Gnaeus Pompey Junior		
Denarius (Roma/Hispania)	£150	£500
Sextus Pompey		
Denarius (his bust)	£275	£900
Denarius (other types)	£150	£500
As	£160	£600

Gnaeus Pompey Junior

	F	VF
Julius Caesar		
Aureus	£2000	£6500
Denarius ("elephant" type)	£250	£700
Denarius (Caesar portrait)	£750	£3500
Denarius (heads of godesses)	£250	£650
Brutus		
Aureus	Extremely rare	
Denarius (his portrait/EID MAR)	£10,000	£75,000
Denarius (others)	£300	£850
Cassius		
Denarius	£200	£600
Ahenobarbus		
Denarius	£450	£1500
Mark Antony		
Denarius ("Galley" type)	£100	£400
Denarius (with portrait)	£200	£600
Denarius (other types)	£70	£300
Mark Antony & Lepidus		
AR quinarius	£75	£195
Mark Antony & Octavian		
AR denarius	£250	£850
Quninarius	£50	£175
Mark Antony & Lucius Antony		
AR denarius	£350	£950
Mark Antony & Octavia		
AR Cistophorus	£250	£800
Cleopatra VII & Mark Antony		
AR denarius	£2000	£5000
Fulvia		
AR quinarius	£125	£375
Octavian (later known as Augustus)		
Aureus	£1500	£5500
Denarius	£150	£500
Quinarius (ASIA RECEPTA)	£100	£250
Octavian & Divos Julius Caesar		
AE sestertius	£275	£1500

Julius Caesar

Brutus

Mark Antony

Mark Antony Legionary Series

IMPERIAL COINAGE—Julio-Claudian Dynasty 27 BC–AD 69

	F	VF
Augustus		
Aureus (Caius & Lucius Caesar)	£1500	£5000
AR Cistophorus	£250	£850
Denarius (Caius & Lucius Caesar)	£100	£450
Denarius (other types)	£125	£500
AR quinarius	£75	£250
Sestertius (large SC)	£150	£600
Dupondius or as (large SC)	£55	£250
Quadrans	£25	£100
Divus Augustus (struck under Tiberius)		
As	£70	£450
Augustus & Agrippa		
Dupondius (Crocodile rev)	£100	£350
Livia		
Sestertius or Dupondius	£200	£800
Gaius Caesar		
AR denarius	£250	£1000
Tiberius		
Aureus (Tribute penny)	£1200	£4500
Denarius (Tribute penny)	£100	£400
Sestertius	£200	£650
Dupondius	£125	£500
As	£125	£400
Drusus		
Sestertius	£275	£950
As (Large S C)	£125	£450

Augustus

Tiberius

Caligula

	F	VF
Caligula		
Denarius (rev. portrait)	£750	£3500
Sestertius (PIETAS & Temple)	£300	£2000
As (VESTA)	£100	£350
Agrippa (struck under Caligula)		
As	£75	£300
Germanicus (struck under Caligula or Claudius)		
As (Large S C)	£125	£500
Agrippina Senior (struck under Caligula)		
Sestertius (Carpentum)	£250	£1250
Nero & Drusus (struck under Caligula)		
Dupondius (On horseback, galloping)	£200	£750
Claudius		
Aureus ("DE BRITANN" type)	£2000	£5500
Denarius as above	£500	£2500
Didrachm as above	£375	£1250
Denarius other types	£400	£1250
Sestertius	£225	£750
Dupondius	£60	£350
As	£45	£250
Quadrans	£20	£75
Irregular British Sestertius	£50	£250
Irregular British As	£20	£150
Claudius & Agrippina Junior or Nero		
Denarius	£450	£2000
Nero Cludius Drusus (struck under Claudius)		
Sestertius	£200	£950
Antonia (struck under Claudius)		
Dupondius	£150	£650
Britannicus		
Sestertius	£2500	£17,500
Nero		
Aureus	£1000	£4500
Denarius	£100	£450
Sestertius	£150	£750
Sestertius (Port of Ostia)	£2500	£15000
Dupondius	£85	£350
As	£50	£275
Semis	£45	£150
Quadrans	£25	£85
Civil War		
Denarius	£200	£700
Galba		
Denarius	£125	£600
Sestertius	£170	£700
Dupondius	£180	£525
As	£110	£400
Otho		
Denarius	£200	£800
Vitellius		
Denarius	£100	£400
Sestertius	£750	£3000
Dupondius	£350	£1000
As	£195	£700

Agrippina Senior

Claudius

Claudius De Britann

Nero

Galba

IMPERIAL COINAGE—Flavian Dynasty AD 69–96

	F	VF
Vespasian		
Aureus	£1000	£4500
Denarius	£40	£200
Denarius (IVDAEA)	£85	£350
Sestertius	£195	£625
Dupondius	£70	£250
As	£55	£210

Vespasian

	F	VF
Titus		
Aureus	£1000	£4500
Denarius as Caesar	£40	£250
Denarius as Augustus	£45	£250
Sestertius	£200	£650
Dupondius	£75	£250
As	£50	£200
As (IVDAEA CAPTA)	£200	£650
Julia Titi		
Denarius	£200	£650
Domitian		
Aureus	£1500	£5000
Cistophorus	£200	£650
Denarius as Caesar	£35	£150
Denarius as Augustus	£35	£150
Sestertius	£100	£550
Dupondius	£50	£200
As	£35	£200
Ae Semis	£30	£120
Ae Quadrands	£25	£100
Domitia		
Cistophorus	£250	£750

Titus

Domitian

IMPERIAL COINAGE—Adoptive Emperors AD 96–138

	F	VF
Nerva		
Aureus	£2000	£7000
Denarius	£50	£300
Sestertius	£140	£750
Sestertius (Palm-tree)	£500	£2500
Dupondius	£70	£250
As	£65	£175
Trajan		
Aureus	£1200	£4000
Denarius	£25	£150
Denarius (Trajan's Column)	£40	£300
Sestertius	£100	£600
Sestertius (Dacian rev.)	£100	£700
Dupondius or as	£35	£250
Ae Quadrands	£25	£95
Plotina, Marciana or Matidia		
Denarius	£450	£1350
Hadrian		
Aureus	£1250	£4500
Cistophourus	£125	£550
Denarius (Provinces)	£45	£250
Denarius other types	£30	£150
Sestertius	£75	£500
Sestertius (RETITVTORI province types)	£150	£600
Sestertius (Britannia std)	£5000	£20,000
Dupondius or As	£35	£250
As (Britannia std)	£200	£1250
Ae Semiis or Quadrands	£30	£125
Egypt, Alexandrian Billon Tetradrachm	£30	£200
Sabina		
Denarius	£30	£250
Sestertius	£115	£475
As or Dupondius	£70	£225
Aelius Ceasar		
Denarius	£70	£250
Sestertius	£150	£550
As or Dupondius	£65	£200

Nerva

Trajan

Hadrian

Sabina

IMPERIAL COINAGE—The Antonines AD 138–193

	F	VF
Antoninus Pius		
Aureus	£1200	£3000
Denarius	£25	£150
Sestertius Britannia seated	£500	£3000
Sestertius other types	£40	£350
As - Britannia rev.	£50	£250
Dupondius or As other types	£50	£200
Antoninus Pius & Marcus Aurelius		
Denarius (bust each side)	£30	£250
Diva Faustina Senior		
Denarius	£25	£100
Sestertius	£45	£250
As or Dupondius	£25	£125
Marcus Aurelius		
Aureus	£1200	£4000
Denarius as Caesar	£25	£200
Denarius as Augustus	£25	£250
Sestertius	£45	£500
As or Dupondius	£25	£200
Faustina Junior		
Denarius	£25	£150
Sestertius	£40	£300
As or Dupondius	£30	£125
Lucius Verus		
Denarius	£25	£150
Sestertius	£45	£300
As or Dupondius	£30	£150
Lucilla		
Denarius	£25	£150
Sestertius	£65	£250
As or Dupondius	£30	£150
Commodus		
Aureus	£1500	£5000
Denarius as Caesar	£30	£150
Denarius as Augustus	£25	£150
Sestertius	£45	£300
Sestertius (VICT BRIT)	£150	£525
As or Dupondius	£25	£150
Crispina		
Denarius	£25	£150
Sestertius	£70	£250
As or Dupondius	£35	£150

Antoninus Pius

Marcus Aurelius

Faustina

Pertinax

IMPERIAL COINAGE—The Severan Dynasty AD 193–235

	F	VF
Pertinax		
Denarius	£225	£750
Sestertius	£500	£2000
Didius Julianus		
Denarius	£400	£1250
Sestertius or Dupondius	£325	£1500
Manlia Scantilla or Didia Clara		
Denarius	£300	£1500
Pescennius Niger		
Denarius	£275	£800
Clodius Albinus		
Denarius as Caesar	£45	£150
Denarius as Augustus	£85	£300
Sestertius	£250	£1000
As	£85	£265

Didius Julianus

Clodius Albinus

	F	VF
Septimius Severus		
Aureus	£1500	£5000
Aureus (VICT BRIT)	£1500	£6000
+Denarius (Mint of Rome)	£25	£100
+Denarius (Mints of Emesa & Laodicea)	£25	£75
Denarius (LEG XIIII)	£30	£175
Denarius (VICT BRIT)	£30	£150
Sestertius other types	£75	£350
Sestertius (VICT BRIT)	£300	£1250
Dupondius or as	£50	£225
Dupondius or As (VICT BRIT)	£125	£450
Julia Domna		
Denarius	£25	£75
Sestertius	£75	£250
As or Dupondius	£50	£175
Caracalla		
Aureus (VICT BRIT)	£1500	£5500
Denarius as Caesar	£25	£75
Denarius as Augustus	£25	£75
Denarius (VICT BRIT)	£30	£100
Antoninianus	£50	£150
Sestertius	£100	£350
Sestertius (VICT BRIT)	£300	£1500
Dupondius or As	£50	£175
Dupondius or As (VICT BRIT)	£100	£325
Plautilla		
Denarius	£25	£75
Geta		
Denarius as Caesar	£25	£75
Denarius as Augustus	£25	£75
Denarius (VICT BRIT)	£30	£125
Sestertius	£125	£375
Sestertius (VICT BRIT)	£250	£850
Dupondius or as	£75	£250
As (VICT BRIT)	£120	£500
Macrinus		
Antoninianus	£100	£350
Denarius	£45	£150
Sestertius	£125	£425
Diadumenian		
Denarius	£75	£350
Dupondius or As	£135	£450
Elagabalus		
Aureus	£1500	£5000
Antoninianus	£50	£150
Denarius	£30	£80
Sestertius	£100	£350
Dupondius or As	£60	£185
Julia Paula		
Denarius	£30	£120
Aquilla Severa		
Denarius	£55	£200
Julia Soaemias		
Denarius	£30	£80
Dupondius or As	£65	£250
Julia Maesa		
Denarius	£25	£65
Sestertius	£85	£300
Severus Alexander		
Aureus	£1500	£4500
Denarius as Caesar	£65	£200
Denarius as Augustus	£25	£50
Sestertius	£45	£150
Dupondius or As	£35	£120

Septimus Severus

Julia Domna

Caracalla

Geta

Macrinus

Diadumenian

Elagabalus

Julia Maesa

	F	VF
Orbiana		
Denarius	£65	£300
As	£100	£350
Julia Mamaea		
Denarius	£20	£65
Sestertius	£35	£150

Severus Alexander

IMPERIAL COINAGE—Military Anarchy AD 235–270

	F	VF
Maximinus I		
Denarius	£25	£80
Sestertius, Dupondius or As	£45	£150
Diva Paula		
Denarius	£150	£500
Maximus Caesar		
Denarius	£70	£275
Sestertius	£65	£250
Gordian I & II, Africanus		
Denarius	£550	£2000
Sestertius	£550	£2000
Balbinus & Pupienus		
Antoninanus	£90	£450
Denarius	£80	£425
Gordian III		
Antoninianus	£15	£50
Denarius	£25	£50
Sestertius or As	£25	£100
Tranquillina		
Common Colonial	£30	£115
Philip I		
Antoninianus "Animal":		
Lion, stag, antelope, wolf & twins	£25	£75
Other Antoninianus	£15	£50
Sestertius, Dupondius or As	£35	£100
Otacilla Severa		
Antoniniaus	£15	£50
Antoninianus "Hipo"	£25	£125
Sestertius	£25	£125
Philip II		
Antoninianus	£15	£55
Antoninianus "Goat"	£20	£75
Sestertius, Dupondius or As	£35	£100
Pacatian		
Antoninianus	1000	£4000
Trajan Decius		
Antoninianus	£15	£50
Antoninianus (DIVI series Augustus, Trajan etc)	£40	£150
Double Sestertius	£275	£1250
Sestertius, Dupondius or As	£25	£100
Herennius Etruscilla		
Antoniniaus	£15	£50
Sestertius, Dupondius or As	£30	£150
Herennius Etruscus		
Antoninianus	£20	£75
Sesterius, Dupondius or As	£55	£225
Hostilian		
Antoninianus as Caesar	£30	£150
Antoninianus as Augustus	£70	£250
Trebonianus Gallus		
Antoninianus	£15	£50
Sestertius or As	£30	£125
Volusian		
Antoninianus	£15	£55
Sestertius	£30	£150

Maximinus I

Balbinus

Gordian III

Philip I

Trajan Decius

Volusian

	F	VF
Aemilian		
Antoninianus	£45	£175
Valerian I		
Antoninianus	£15	£50
Sestertius & As	£50	£175
Diva Mariniana		
Antoninianus	£35	£150
Gallienus		
Silver Antoninianus	£12	£45
Ae Antoninianus	£5	£25
Ae Antoninianus (Military bust)	£10	£50
Ae Antoninianus (Legionary)	£50	£250
Ae Sestertius	£45	£200
Ae Denarius	£50	£150
Saloninus		
Ae Antoninianus	£5	£25
Valerian II		
Billon Antoninianus	£12	£45
Saloninus		
Antoninianus	£15	£45
Macrianus & Quietus		
Billon Antoninianus	£45	£150
Regalianus or Dryantilla		
Billon Antoninianus	£1500	£5000
Postumus		
Silver Antoninianus	£5	£40
Ae Antoninianus	£5	£25
Radiated sestertius	£50	£250
Laelianus		
Ae Antoninianus	£225	£875
Marius		
Ae Antoninianus	£45	£175
Victorinus		
Ae Antoninianus	£5	£30
Tetricus I & II		
Ae Antoninianus	£5	£30
Claudius II Gothicus		
Ae Antoninianus	£4	£30
Egypt, Alexandrian Billon tetradrachm	£8	£35
DIVO Ae Antoninianus	£8	£35
Quintillus		
Ae Antoninianus	£12	£45

Gallienus

Postumus

Laelianus

Aurelian

IMPERIAL COINAGE—The Illyrian Emperors—AD 270–285

	F	VF
Aurelian		
Ae Antoninianus	£8	£50
Ae Denarius	£20	£75
Vabalathus & Aurelian		
Ae Antoninianus (bust both sides)	£20	£75
Vabalathus		
Ae Antoninianus	£250	£1000
Severina		
Ae Antoninianus	£15	£50
Ae As	£35	£125
Zenobia		
Eygpt, Alexandrian Billon Tetradrachm	£750	£3000
Tacitus		
Ae Antoninianus	£15	£35
Florian		
Ae Antoninianus	£25	£150

Tacitus

Florian

	F	VF
Probus		
Gold Aureus	£1500	£5000
Ae Antoninianus	£10	£50
Antoninianus (military or imp. Busts RIC G or H)	£20	£100
Antoninianus (Other military or imp NOT BUSTS G or H)	£50	£250
Antoninianus (VICTOR GERM rev.)	£20	£100
Egypt, Alexandrian Billon tetradrachm	£15	£80
Carus		
Ae Antoninianus	£15	£50
Numerian		
Ae Antoninianus	£15	£50
Carinus		
Ae Antoninianus	£12	£50
Magna Urbica		
Ae Antoninianus	£50	£250
Julian of Pannonia		
Ae Antoninianus	£650	£3000

Probus

Numerian

IMPERIAL COINAGE—The Tetrarchy AD 285–307

	F	VF
Diocletian		
Gold Aureus	£1500	£5000
AR Argenteus	£100	£350
Ae Antoninianus & Radiates	£10	£50
Ae Follis (London Mint)	£15	£75
As above with LON mint mark	£100	£500
Ae Follis (other mints)	£10	£50
Ae Follis (Imperial bust)	£25	£150
Maximianus		
AR Argenteus	£100	£350
Ae Follis (London mint)	£15	£75
Ae Follis (other mints)	£10	£50
Ae Follis (MONETA rev.)	£10	£80
Carausius		
Aureus	Extremely rare	
Denarius	£600	£3000
Ae Antoninianus (PAX)	£25	£175
As above but full silvering	£35	£500
Legionary Antoninianus	£75	£600
Expectate Veni Antoninianus	£100	£500
In the name of Diocletian or Maximian	£35	£200
Allectus		
Aureus	Extremely rare	
Ae Antoninianus	£25	£300
As above but full silvering	£45	£500
Quinarius	£25	£150
Constantius I		
AR Argenteus	£20	£350
Ae Follis (London Mint)	£15	£75
Ae Follis (other mints)	£10	£50
Ae Follis (SALVS rev.)	£15	£55
Ae 4 (Lion or Eagle)	£10	£50
Galerius		
Ae Follis (London mint)	£15	£80
Ae Follis (other mints)	£10	£55
Galeria Valeria		
Ae Follis	£35	£100
Severus II		
Ae Follis (London mint)	£35	£200
Ae Follis (other mints)	£30	£125
Ae Radiate	£25	£75
Ae Denarius	£25	£200

Diocletian

Carausius

Allectus

Galerius

	F	VF
Maximinus II		
Ae Follis (London mint)	£15	£75
Ae Follis (other mints)	£10	£55
Ae Radiate	£5	£50
Maxentius		
Ae Follis	£10	£45
Romulus		
Ae Follis	£50	£250
Licinius I		
Billon Argenteus	£50	£175
Ae Follis (London mint)	£12	£50
Ae Follis (other mints)	£12	£40
AE3	£5	£30
Licinius II		
AE3	£10	£35
Alexander or Martinian		
AE	£1200	£4000

Maximinus II

Constantine I

IMPERIAL COINAGE—Family of Constantine AD 307–350

	F	VF
Constantine I		
Billon Argenteus	£50	£175
Ae Follis (London mint)	£12	£50
As above—helmeted bust	£15	£125
Ae Follis (other mints) as Caesar	£15	£50
Ae Follis (other mints) as Augustus	£5	£50
AE3	£5	£30
AE3 (London mint)	£10	£50
AE3 (SARMATIA rev)	£12	£50
Urbs Roma / Wolf & twins AE3/4	£5	£30
Constantinopolis AE3/4	£5	£25
Fausta & Helena		
AE3 (London mint)	£50	£175
AE3 (other mints)	£15	£75
Theodora		
AE4	£10	£35
Crispus		
AE3 (London mint)	£10	£45
AE3	£10	£30
Delmatius		
AE3/4	£15	£50
Hanniballianus Rex		
AE4	£75	£250
Constantine II		
AE3 (London mint)	£10	£40
AE3	£8	£30
AE3/4	£8	£25
Constans		
AE2 (centenionalis)	£10	£30
AE3 (half centenionalis)	£8	£25
AE4	£8	£25
Constantius II		
Gold Solidus	£300	£1000
Siliqua	£25	£100
AE2 (or centenionalis)	£10	£35
AE3 (or half centenionalis)	£8	£20
AE3 (London mint)	£15	£50
AE3	£8	£20

Fausta

Crispus

Constans

IMPERIAL COINAGE—Late period to the collapse of the Empire AD 350 to end

	F	VF
Magnentius		
Gold Solidus	£1000	£4000
Silver Siliqua	£300	£1250
Double centenionalis	£45	£250
Centenionalis	£15	£60

Magnentius

	F	VF
Decentius		
Double centenionalis	£75	£300
Centenionalis	£25	£75
Vetranio		
AE2 (centenionalis)	£40	£150
AE3 (half centenionalis)	£50	£175
Nepotian		
AE2 (centenionalis)	£1500	£6000
Constantius Gallus		
AE2 (centenionalis)	£15	£45
AE3 (half centenionalis)	£8	£30
Julian II		
Siliqua	£30	£100
AE1	£45	£150
AE3 (helmeted bust)	£12	£40
Anonymous, Serapis + Jupiter AE3	£200	£600
Jovian		
AE1	£65	£250
AE3	£15	£55
Valentinian I		
Gold Solidus	£250	£900
Silver Milliarense	£200	£800
Siliqua	£25	£100
AE3	£8	£25
Valens		
Gold Solidus	£250	£800
Silver Milliarense	£200	£700
Siliqua	£25	£100
AE3	£8	£25
Procopius		
AE3	£45	£150
Gratian		
Silver Milliarense	£200	£750
Siliqua	£25	£100
AE3	£8	£45
AE4	£8	£35
Valentinian II		
Solidus	£250	£1000
Siliqua	£25	£125
AE2	£12	£35
AE4	£5	£15
Theodosius I		
Solidus	£250	£1000
Siliqua	£30	£125
AE2	£12	£50
AE3	£10	£45
Aelia Flaccilla		
AE2	£30	£125
AE4	£15	£50
Magnus Maximus		
Solidus (AVGOB)	£7500	£25,000
Solidus	£1250	£3500
Siliqua	£45	£150
Siliqua (AVGPS)	£750	£2500
AE2	£25	£75
Flavius Victor		
Silver Sliqua	£150	£700
AE4	£30	£85
Eugenius		
Silver Siliqua	£100	£550

Julian II

Jovian

Valens

Magnus Maximus

Gratian

Eugenius

	F	VF
Arcadius		
Gold Solidus	£250	£1000
Silver Siliqua	£25	£150
Silver Half-siliqua	£150	£500
AE2	£12	£50
AE4	£5	£25
Eudoxia		
AE3	£25	£85
Honorius		
Gold Solidus	£250	£850
Silver Siliqua	£30	£150
AE4	£8	£25
Constantine III		
Silver Siliqua	£200	£650
Theodosius II		
Gold Solidus	£225	£700
Johannes		
AE4	£125	£500
Valentinian III		
Gold Soldius	£250	£850
AE4	£25	£75

Ae = bronze; AE 1, 2, 3, 4 = bronze coins in descending order of size.

Arcadius

Honorius

Valentinian III

Coin illustrations by courtesy of Silbury Coins.

A SIMPLIFIED PRICE GUIDE TO

ENGLISH HAMMERED COINS

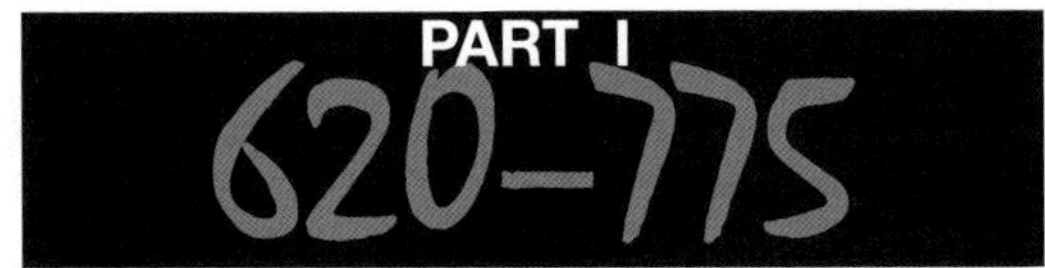

AN INTRODUCTION TO EARLY ANGLO-SAXON COINAGE

The withdrawal of Roman forces from Britain in the 5th Century AD led to a rapid demise in society including areas such as coinage. In fact, there was nearly 200 years where no coins at all were struck (we can say this with confidence as if coins had been made during this period they would have been lost and found as with all other periods). Imagine if such a thing happened nowadays, the demise of our monetary system and a return to bartering, one wonders what you could buy with a gram of gold at the local Sainsbury's . . . Sometime in the early 7th century the value of stamping design on said gram of gold became apparent once again and the first Thrymsa's started to appear. These are very rare and many of the early pieces known were found in one location in AD 1828, later to be known as the Crondall Hoard (worth a visit to the Ashmoleon Museum in Oxford just to see this). The first silver coins (referred to as a Sceat or Sceatta) made an appearance in the late 7th century and are thought to have been made in South East England. These were joined by the Continental series which includes the "Porcupine" sceat (series E) among a few other types. The 8th century brought what is known as the "Secondary Phase" which is by far the most diverse with some 20–30 main types, each with several variations. The art on the secondary series is mesmerising. Much of it has hidden meaning which the Saxons are famous for and we can only guess at, some is clearer than others, for example, the bird fighting with a serpent on the series Q coins is accepted to be depicting the fight between good and evil. The 7th century coins are generally made of good silver while the 8th century (secondary) coins are often base metal and porous. AD 685 sees the introduction of an organised monetary system in the Kingdom of Northumbria with Kings and Archbishops being named on silver sceats, also the introduction of a bronze coin called the Styca. AD 758 sees the transitional sceat/penny of Beonna, King of East Anglia and marks the end of a truly fascinating period. Collecting the coinage from this period is like diving into a good fictional novel, immersed in the world of fanciful beasts and horned gods, brought to life by these little masterpieces. Here we lay out the standard types in gold, silver and copper alloy. Pricing is very much dependant on condition and variation. For further reading we'd recommend: *Sceattas, An Illustrated Guide* by Tony Abramson or for a more indepth publication *Sceatta List*, also by Tony Abramson.

Values given for standard types, varionts can be worth more.

J. PHILPOTTS

GOLD COINAGE—THRYMSAS OR SHILLINGS

	F	VF
CRONDALL TYPES—circa AD 620–655		
Witmen Type		
Bust right with trident		
Blundered legend, central cross................	£1500	£5000
London types		
Head right or facing		
Blundered legend, central cross................	£4000	£12500
Eadbald of Kent—AD 616–640 (minted at London or Canterbury)		
Bust right		
Mint name around orb	£10000	£17500
Wuneetton type		
Bust right, cross before		
Blundered legend, central cross................	£3000	£7500
York type		
Stylised figure facing with crosses		
Blundered legend, central cross................	£3000	£10000
POST CRONDALL TYPES—circa AD 655–675		
Crispus type		
Helmeted bust right		
Crosses within runic inscription.................	£4000	£12500
Concordia type		
Radiate bust right		
Clasped hands..	£3000	£12000
Oath-taking type		
Bust r. or l. holding cross		
Lyre-shaped object..................................	£2500	£7500
Two emperors type		
Helmeted bust right		
Angel between two seated figures	£1500	£5000
Pada types (I, II & III)		
Helmeted bust right		
Runic PADA in centre or legend	£1000	£4000
Vanimundus type		
Helmeted bust r. holding sceptre		
Blundered legend, central cross................	£1000	£4000
Base examples of previous types		
Bust right		
Blundered legend, central cross..................	£500	£2500

SILVER COINAGE—SCEATTAS

	F	VF
PRIMARY PHASE—circa AD 680–710		
Series A		
Radiate bust right		
Standard, TOTII in centre	£100	£450
Series B		
Bust right or facing		
Bird on cross with annulets	£120	£400
Series C		
Bust right		
Standard, TOTII in centre	£80	£200
Aethelred of Mercia—AD 674–704		
Degenerate head right		
Runic Aethilraed in 2 lines	£500	£1000
Series F		
Bust right with helmet		
Cross on steps, annulets and letters	£100	£275
Series Z		
Facing bust with beard (Christ?)		
Hound running right	£500	£1500
Vernus types		
Degenerate head right		
Standard, various styles	£150	£450
Saroaldo type		
Stylised bust right		
SAROALDO around standard	£250	£750
Stepped Cross		
Degenerate 'porcupine' head		
Stepped cross, annulet at centre	£100	£250
SEDE type		
Quilled serpent around cross		
S E D E in centre of circle with saltires	£400	£1250
Series W		
Standing figure		
Cross crosslet on Saltire	£350	£1200
CONTINENTAL ISSUES—circa AD 695–740		
Series E		
Degenerate head or bird/porcupine		
Votive standard	£60	£160
Series D		
Bust right		
Plain cross, pellets in angles	£50	£140
Interlace Cross typo		
Crude head left		
Quatrefoil interlaced cross	£250	£750

	F	VF
Hexagon type Hexagram enclosing cross Radial arrangement, cross in centre..........	£200	£650
Series X Facing Wodan head Crested monster..	£250	£750
SECONDARY PHASE—circa AD 710–760		
Series G Diademed bust right Standard with saltires................................	£120	£375
Series H (Hamwic, Southampton mint) Pecking bird, Facing head or Whorl of wolves Celtic cross or Pecking bird	£200	£600
Series J (York) Diademed bust or busts Birds and or Serpents	£150	£450
Series K (Kent) Bust right Wolf, Hound or Standing figure in boat	£250	£750
Series L (London) Bust right Standing figure, Figures holding crosses ..	£200	£700
Series M Sinuous animal Spiral vine..	£250	£750
Series N Two standing figures Crested monster..	£150	£450
Series O Bust, standing figures or monster Bird, standing figure, monster or standard	£175	£500
Series Q Standing figures or Bust with crosses Quadruped animal or Bird, sometimes fighting serpant..	£250	£750
Series R Bust, mainly right Standard, Bird or Quadruped....................	£120	£300
Series S Female centaur left Whorl of wolf heads..................................	£200	£650
Series T Diademed bust right, legend before Degenerate 'porcupine' head....................	£250	£750

	F	VF
Series U		
Standing figure in boat holding crosses		
Pecking bird	£250	£800
Series V		
Wolf and twins		
Bird in wheat stalks	£400	£1250
Carip group		
Bust right. Blundered CARIP		
Pecking bird, wolf serpent or standing figure	£200	£600
Triquetras group		
Man, bust or pecking bird		
Interlaced cross with triquetra terminals	£250	£1000
Celtic Cross		
Bust, figure, wolfworm or bird		
Celtic cross	£250	£700
Monita Scorum		
Diademed bust right, inscription		
Degenerate porcupine	£500	£1500
Archer		
Kneeling archer right		
Swan like bird looking back	£750	£2500
Hen		
Hen		
Swan like bird looking back	£500	£1750
Victory		
Victory standing with wreath		
Standing figure holding crosses or bust	£350	£1500
Animal Mask		
Facing animal		
Standing figure with bird, cross or monster	£500	£1750
Fledgling		
Wolf head right		
Running fledgling with fish in mouth	£600	£2250
Annulet Cross		
Bust, Wodan face or serpent		
Annulet cross	£200	£600
Saltire Standard		
Two standing figures or bust left		
Saltire standard	£150	£500
Wodan head		
Facing Wodan head		
Two standing figures	£250	£800

	F	VF
KINGDOM OF NORTHUMBRIA—circa AD 685–855		
Aldfrith AD 685-705		
ALDFRIDVS around central boss		
Triple tailed lion	£400	£1250
Eadberht AD 737–758		
EADBERHTVS around small cross		
Stylized stag, various ornaments	£175	£450
Aethelwald Moll AD 759–765		
AD+ELAATDRE around central boss		
AEDILRED+R around cross.......................	£4500	£13500
Alchred AD 765–774		
ALCHRED around small cross		
Stylized stag...	£350	£1000
Aethelred I AD 774–780 (1st reign)		
EDILRED around small cross		
Stylized stag...	£500	£1500
Aelfwald I AD 779–788		
AELFWALDVS (partially runic) around small cross		
Stylized stag...	£500	£1600
Aethelred I AD 789–796 (2nd reign)		
EDILRED around central ornament		
Moneyers name around motif....................	£150	£400
Eardwulf AD 796–806		
EARDVVLFRX around small cross		
Moneyers name around motif....................	£2000	£6000
Aelfwald II AD 806–808		
AELFWALDVS (partially runic) around small cross		
CVDhEARD around cross on rear	£500	£1750
Eanred AD 810–841		
EANRED REX around motif		
Moneyers name around motif....................	£120	£300
Archbishop Eanbald II AD 796–835		
EANBALD around motif		
Moneyers name around motif....................	£200	£450
JOINT ISSUES		
Eadberht with Archbishop Ecgberht AD 737–758		
EADBERHTVS around small cross		
ECGBERHT AR, Figure holding two crosses	£250	£750
Aethelwald Moll with Archbishop Ecgberht AD 759–765		
AD+ELAATDRE around cross		
ECGBERHT AR around cross....................	£2500	£7500
Alchred with Archbishop Ecgberht AD 765–766		
ALCHRED around small cross		
ECGBERHT AR around cross....................	£300	£900

	F	VF
Aethelred I with Archbishop Eanbald I AD 779–780		
AEDILRED around central motif		
EANBALD around cross	£300	£900
BRONZE COINAGE—Stycas		
Eanred AD 810-841		
EANRED REX around motif		
Moneyers name around motif....................	£70	£225
Aethelred II AD 841-850		
EDILRED REX around motif		
Moneyers name around motif....................	£50	£175
Redwulf AD 843-844		
REDWVLF REX around motif		
Moneyers name around motif....................	£150	£350
Osberht AD 849-867		
OSBERHT REX around motif		
Moneyers name around motif....................	£150	£350
Archbishop Wigmund AD 837-850		
WIGMVND AREP around motif		
Moneyers name around motif....................	£125	£250
Archbishop Wulfhere AD 849-900		
VVLFHERE AR around motif		
VVLFRED around motif.............................	£200	£500
Irregular Issues AD 843-855		
Various types, legends blundered	£45	£125

A SIMPLIFIED PRICE GUIDE TO

ENGLISH HAMMERED COINS

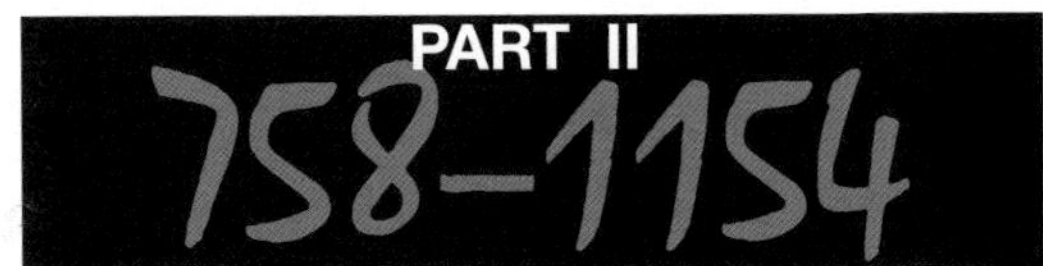

Middle Saxon Period AD 758–973

Starting with the first prototype penny in AD 758 struck by King Beonna in the Kingdom of East Anglia and spanning right through the kingdoms being united by the dynasty of Edward the Elder in the late 10th century AD. Many of these coins are extremely rare, even more so in good condition.

England was split in to seven Kingdoms during the first part of this period, five of which produced coins. These were Northumbria, Mercia, East Anglia, Kent and Wessex. Offa (King of Mercia) built a Dyke stretching from the Severn Estuary to the north coast to keep the Welsh out of his kingdom. The River Thames divided Mercia and Wessex with London being occupied by both tribes at some point—likely peacefully for a time as we see joint issues of these two tribes. The Vikings successfully occupied Northumbria and East Anglia, centred in York, which must have created much unrest; many battles were fought and bribes paid. Eventually Edward the Elder, the last King of Wessex, and his son, Aethelstan united the kingdoms and a new "unified" England was formed, which we still see in place today. Aethelstan created Burghs, each of which had a church and mint. The later part of this period saw kings proclaiming themselves as "king of all Britain(s)".

The British Isles during the mid-Saxon period.

ANGLO SAXON KINGDOMS

KENT

	F	VF
Heaberht (c. 765)	£15,000	£50,000
Ecgberht (c. 780)	£2,250	£7,500
Eadberht Praen (796–798)	£3,000	£8,500
Cuthred (798–807) (Portrait type)	£2,000	£5,500
Baldred (c. 823–825)	£2,500	£6,500

Cuthred (798–807)

Baldred (c. 823–825)

ARCHBISHOPS OF CANTERBURY

	F	VF
Jaenberht (765–792)	£2,000	£6,000
Aethelheard (792–805)	£1,500	£4,000
Wulfred (805–832)	£1,000	£4,000
Ceolnoth (833–870)	£1,000	£4,000
Aethelred (870–889)	£3,000	£10,000
Plegmund (890–914)	£1,250	£4,000

Wulfred (805–832)

Ceolnoth (833–870)

Plegmund (890–914)

MERCIA

	F	VF
Offa (757–796) (portrait)	£1,500	£4,000
— — (non portrait)	£750	£2,000
Cynethryth (wife of Offa)	£3,500	£9,000
Bishop Eadberht (died 789)	£1,500	£4,500
Coenwulf (796–821) (portrait)	£1,500	£4,500
Coenwulf (796–821) (non portrait)	£800	£2,000
Ceolwulf I (821–823)	£2,500	£6,500
Beornwulf (823–825)	£2,500	£6,500
Ludica (825–827)	£7,500	£30,000
Wiglaf (827–829)	£6,000	£17,500
Berhtwulf (840–852)	£2,500	£7,000
Burgred (852–874)	£750	£1,750
Ceolwulf II (874–880)	£5,000	£22,500

Offa (757–796)

Offa (757–796)

Coenwulf (796–821)

Ceolwulf I (821–823)

Burgred (852–874)

	F	VF
EAST ANGLIA		
Beonna (c. 758)	£1,500	£5,000
Alberht (749–?)	£5,750	£22,500
Aethelberht (d. 794)	£7,250	£27,500
Eadwald (c. 798)	£1,500	£5,500
Aethelstan I (c.825–840) (non portrait)	£750	£2,250
Aethelweard (c.840–855)	£1,500	£5,000
Eadmund (855–870)	£750	£2,250

Beonna (c. 758)

Aethelweard (c.840–855)

Eadmund (855–870)

	F	VF
ANGLO-VIKING COINAGE circa 885–954		
St Edmund (Danish East Anglia 855–915)	£250	£800
— — half penny	£1,000	£3,750
Southern Danelaw Imitations		
Cnut (Viking Kingdom of York c. 895–920)	£500	£1,500

St Edmund (Danish East Anglia 855–915)

Cnut (Viking Kingdom of York c. 895–920)

	F	VF
HIBERNO-NORSE VIKINGS AT YORK (c.919–954)		
Sihtric (921–927)	£4,000	£15,000
St Peter coinage	£2,500	£6,500
Anlaf Guthfrithsson (939–941)	£5,000	£15,000
Anlaf Sihtricsson (941–944 & 948–952)	£3,500	£13,500
Eric Blood-Axe (948–954)	£15,000	£60,000

St Peter coinage

Anlaf Guthfrithsson (939–941)

	F	VF
WESSEX		
Beorhtric (786–924)	£10,000	£40,000
Ecgberht (802–839)	£2,000	£6,000
Aethelwulf (839–858)	£1,500	£5,000
Aethelberht (858–865)	£1,500	£5,000

Ecgberht (802–839)

Aethelberht (858–865)

	F	VF
Aethelred I (865–871)	£1,500	£5,000
Alfred The Great (871–899) (portrait)	£1,500	£5,500
— — (non portrait)	£1,250	£2,750
Edward the Elder (899–924) (portrait)	£1,500	£5,000
— — (non portrait)	£450	£1,250
— — (Ornamental types)	£2,500	£11,000

Alfred The Great (871–899)

Edward the Elder (899–924)

Edward the Elder (899–924) (Ornamental types)

KINGS OF ALL ENGLAND

	F	VF
Aethelstan (924–939) (portrait)	£1,750	£5,500
— — (non portrait)	500	£1,500
— — (with mint name)	£1,000	£2,500
Eadmund (939–946) (portrait)	£1,500	£5,000
— — (non portrait)	£500	£1,250
Eadred (946–955) (portrait)	£1,500	£4,500
— — (non portrait)	£500	£1,250
Howel Dda (d. 949–950)	£17,500	£60,000
Eadwig (955–959) (portrait)	£12,000	£40,000
— — (non portrait)	£1,250	£4,000
Eadgar (959–975) (portrait)	£1,250	£4,500
— — (non portrait)	£450	£1,000

Aethelstan (924–939)

Eadmund (939–946)

Eadred (946–955)

Eadwig (955–959)

Eadgar (959–975)

Edward The Martyr (975–978)

Late Saxon Period AD 973–1066

In AD 973 Eadgar introduced a new coinage. A "royal portrait" now became a regular feature and various reverse designs all incorporate a legend identifying mint and moneyer. The silver used was of much higher quality than previously and closely regulated, with the moneyers names recorded on every coin. Debasement would be easily and quickly spotted, with the offending moneyer located and lucky if he only lost a hand or other body part!

With the diversity of mints now striking various coin types, this is an interesting and wide area to collect. Some collectors focus on coins minted in their locality or perhaps go for a coin of each modern county or mint. Some mints had a very high output; coins from the likes of London, Canterbury, Winchester and York, etc. are often seen where as coins from mints such as Cadbury, Winchcombe, Malmesbury and Newport, to name but a few, are rarely available to commerce. The period ends in AD 1066 with King Harold II and the Battle of Hastings.

	F	VF
LATE ANGLO-SAXON COINAGE		
Eadgar (reform coinage 973–975)	£1,000	£4,000
Edward The Martyr (975–978)	£2,500	£6,000
Aethelred II (978–1016)		
Hand type	£250	£700
Benediction Hand type	£1,500	£5,500
Crux type	£200	£600
Small Cross type (last)	£200	£500
Long Cross type	£200	£500
Helmet type	£250	£600
Agnus Dei type	£9,500	£30,000

Aethelred II (978–1016)
(Hand type)

Aethelred II (978–1016)
(Crux type)

Aethelred II (978–1016)
(Long Cross type)

	F	VF
Cnut (1016–1035)		
Quatrefoil type	£200	£600
Pointed Helmet type	£200	£550
Short Cross type	£175	£500
Posthumous Jewel Cross type	£850	£3,000

Cnut (1016–1035)
Quatrefoil type

Cnut (1016–1035)
Short Cross type

	F	VF
Harold I "Harefoot" (1035–1040)		
Short Cross type	£1,500	£5,250
Jewel Cross type	£450	£1,250
Fleur-de-Lis type	£450	£1,250
Harthacnut (1035–1042)		
Jewel Cross (Regency) bust left or right	£1,250	£3,500
Arm and Sceptre type (Sole Reign)	£1,000	£2,500
— — (name given as Cnut)	£750	£2,000
Danish types	£550	£1,500
Edward the Confessor (1042–1066)		
Arm and Sceptre type	£1,500	£5,250
Pacx type	£300	£900
Radiate/Small Cross type	£250	£650
Trefoil Quadrilateral type	£250	£650
Small Flan type	£175	£500
Expanding Cross type	£250	£700
— (heavy issue)	£300	£800
— (in gold)	£57,500	£200,000
Pointed Helmet type	£250	£750
Sovereign/Eagles type	£300	£800
Hammer Cross type	£250	£650
Facing bust/Small Cross type	£200	£600
Pyramids type	£250	£700
Transitional Pyramids type	£2,250	£7,500

Harold I "Harefoot" (1035–1040)
Jewel Cross type

Harthacnut (1035–1042)
(Jewel Cross—Regency)

Edward the Confessor (1042–1066)
(Pacx type)

Edward the Confessor (1042–1066)
(Expanding Cross type—heavy issue)

Edward the Confessor (1042–1066)
(Pointed Helmet type)

Edward the Confessor (1042–1066)
(Sovereign/Eagles type)

Edward the Confessor (1042–1066)
(Pyramids type)

	F	VF
Harold II (1066)		
Pax type	£1,500	£5,000
— (without sceptre)	£2,000	£6,000
— (bust right)	£3,750	£12,500

Harold II (1066)
(Pax type)

Norman Kings, AD 1066–1154

Starting with William the Conqueror (AD 1066–87) who was the first Norman king of England, prior to his accession he was Duke of Normandy and cousin to Edward the Confessor who's death sparked a battle for the throne which saw Harold II seize power for a short time before being dispatched by William at the Battle of Hastings (AD 1066). His son, William Rufus (AD 1087–1100) followed but his reign was short lived as he died in a hunting accident in the New Forest. William's third son, Henry I (AD 1100–35) then ruled. He actioned much administrative reform and military advancement, in an attempt to secure the kingdom for his daughter, Matilda. This was unsuccessful and Stephen (AD 1135–54) seized the English throne following the death of his uncle, Henry in AD 1135. Civil War followed and the country was torn apart as Matilda had much support from England's people. Coins of this period are hard to come across, especially so in good grade.

	F	VF
William I "the Conqueror"		
Profile Left type	£750	£2,000
Bonnet type	£500	£1,350
Canopy type	£650	£2,000
Two Sceptres type	£550	£1,850
Two Stars type	£450	£1,500
Sword type	£650	£2,000
Profile Right type	£800	£2,250
Paxs type	£350	£900

William I "the Conqueror" (Profile Left type)

William I "the Conqueror" (Two Sceptres type)

William I "the Conqueror" (Sword type)

William I "the Conqueror" (Paxs type)

	F	VF
William II (1087–1100)		
Profile type	£1,250	£3,250
Cross in Quatrefoil type	£1,000	£2,500
Voided Cross type	£1,000	£2,500
Cross Pattee and Fleury type	£1,000	£2,500
Cross Fleury and Piles type	£1,250	£3,000

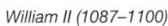

William II (1087–1100)

William II (1087–1100) (Cross in Quatrefoil type)

	F	VF
Henry I (1100–1135)		
Annulets type	£750	£2,000
Profile/Cross Fleury type	£450	£1,250
Paxs type	£450	£1,250
Annulets and Piles type	£350	£900
Voided Cross and Fleurs type	£1,000	£2,500

Henry I (1100–1135) (Voided Cross and Fleurs type)

	F	VF
Pointing Bust and Stars type	£1,250	£3,500
Facing bust /Quatrefoil with Piles type	£600	£1,500
Large Profile/Cross and Annulets type	£1,500	£5,000
Facing Bust/Cross in Quatrefoil type	£1,250	£3,000
Facing Bust/Cross Fleury type	£450	£1,000
Double Inscription type	£1,250	£2,750
Small Profile/Cross and Annulets type	£550	£1,500
Star in Lozenge Fleury type	£600	£1,750
Pellets in Quatrefoil type	£350	£900
Quadrilateral on Cross Fleury type	£250	£750
Halfpenny	£2,000	£6,000

Henry I (1100–1135)
(Star in Lozenge Fleury type)

Henry I (1100–1135)
(Pellets in Quatrefoil type)

Stephen 1135–1154AD

	F	VF
Cross Moline (Watford) type	£325	£1,000
Voided Cross and Stars type	£300	£1,000
Cross and Piles type	£350	£1,250
Cross Pommee (Awbridge) type	£275	£900
Many Provincial varients exist	varied	varied

Stephen 1135–1154AD
(Cross Moline "Watford" type)

Stephen 1135–1154AD
(Southern variant)

Angevin Party c. 1139–1183

	F	VF
Matilda (1139–1148)	£3,000	£10,000
Henry	£2,500	£7,000
Earls & Lords	varied	varied

Plantagenet Kings, AD 1154–1399

In the period following Henry I's death, England descended into what has become known as "The Anarchy" (See COIN NEWS, JULY 2023), a Civil War between the forces of Empress Maude (Matilda, Henry's daughter and wife of Geoffrey V, Count of Anjou) and Stephen of Blois (Henry's nephew). During the next 18 years the throne of England was claimed by both Matilda and Stephen with both reigning at different points. Stephen was crowned in 1135 but was then captured at the Battle of Lincoln in 1141 upon which Matilda declared herself Queen. She was never crowned but even after Stephen was released (exchanged for Matilda's half-brother Robert of Gloucester who himself had been captured in battle) she retained her claim. In 1148 she returned to Normandy, leaving the campaign against Stephen in the hands of her son Henry. Following a military campaign in 1153 Stephen agreed to recognise Henry as his heir in an attempt to bring about an end to the conflict that neither side looked like winning. In October the following year, Stephen died and by December Henry II was crowned in Westminster Abbey. The rule of the Plantagenets (named for the planta genista, the yellow broom flower, emblem of the Counts of Anjou) had begun—it was to last for over 300 years.

HENRY II (1154–89)

There were two distinct issues struck during this reign. The first, Cross and Crosslets or "Tealby" coinage (named after Tealby in Lincolnshire, where a large hoard was found), continued to be very poorly made and lasted 20 years. However, in 1180 the new and superior "Short Cross" issue commenced, being issued from only twelve major towns.

	F	VF	EF
Henry II, Penny, Tealby	£135	£450	–
Henry II, Penny, Short Cross	£90	£240	£495

RICHARD I (1189–99)

There were no major changes during this reign, in fact pennies continued to be struck with his father Henry's name throughout the reign. The coins struck under Richard tend to be rather crude in style.

	F	VF	EF
Richard I, Penny	£125	£275	–

JOHN
(1199–1216)

As with his brother before him, there were no major changes during the reign of King John, and pennies with his father's name were struck throughout the reign, although they tended to be somewhat neater in style than those struck during the reign of Richard I.

	F	VF
John, Penny	£90	£200

HENRY III
(1216–72)

The coinage during Henry III's reign continued as before with the short cross issue. However, in 1247 a new long cross design was introduced to prevent clipping. This design was to last in one form or another for many centuries. Late in the reign saw a brief appearance of the 1st English gold coin.

	F	VF	EF
Henry III, Penny, Short Cross	£50	£140	£360
Henry III, Penny, Long Cross	£50	£100	£275

EDWARD I
(1272–1307)

After a few years of issuing similar pieces to his father, and in his farther's name in 1279 Edward I ordered a major re-coinage. This consisted of well-made pennies, halfpennies and farthings in relatively large quantities, and for a brief period a groat (four pence) was produced. These were often mounted and gilded, the price is for an undamaged piece.The pennies are amongst the most common of all hammered coins.

	F	VF	EF
Edward I (and Edward II)			
Groat (often damaged) see above	£2750	£7500	–
Penny	£30	£80	–
Halfpenny	£30	£90	–
Farthing	£30	£90	–

Edward I penny

EDWARD II (1307–27)

	F	VF	EF
Edward II, long cross Pennies, Halfpennies and Farthings continued in very similar style to his father (Edward I)			
Pennies	£30	£90	–
Halfpennies	£70	£180	–
Farthings	£35	£125	–

EDWARD III (1327–77)

This was a long reign which saw major changes in the coinage, the most significant being the introduction of a gold coinage (based on the Noble, valued at 6s 8d, and its fractions) and a regular issue of a large silver groat (and half groat). The provincial mints were limited to a few episcopal cities but coins of English type were also struck in the newly-acquired Calais Mint.

	F	VF	EF
Gold			
Noble	£2500	£5000	–
Half Noble	£1000	£2500	–
Quarter Noble	£500	£1000	–
Silver			
Groat	£70	£190	£900
Half Groat	£50	£150	£600
Penny	£40	£120	£500
Half Penny	£25	£90	£300
Farthing	£50	£130	£400

Gold Noble

RICHARD II (1377–99)

The denominations continued during this reign much as before. However, coins are quite scarce mainly due to the lack of bullion gold and silver going into the mints, mainly because of an inbalance with European weights and fineness.

	F	VF	EF
Gold			
Noble	£2000	£5000	–
Half Noble	£1500	£4700	–
Quarter Noble	£600	£1400	–
Silver			
Groat	£600	£2000	–
Half Groat	£300	£900	–
Penny	£80	£350	–
Half Penny	£40	£150	–
Farthing	£150	£550	–

Gold Noble

HENRY IV
(1399–1413)

Because of the continuing problems with the scarcity of gold and silver the coinage was reduced by weight in 1412, towards the end of the reign. All coins of this reign are quite scarce.

	F	VF
Gold		
Noble, Light coinage	£2000	£6500
Half Noble, Light coinage	£2500	£8000
Quarter Noble, Light coinage	£900	£2500
Silver		
Groat, Light coinage	£1600	£5800
Half Groat, Heavy coinage	£800	£3500
Penny	£500	£1300
Half Penny	£300	£800
Farthing	£850	£2750

Noble

HENRY V
(1413–22)

Monetary reform introduced towards the end of his father's reign in 1412 improved the supply of bullion and hence coins of Henry V are far more common. All of the main denominations continued as before.

	F	VF	EF
Gold			
Noble	£1600	£5500	–
Half Noble	£1300	£3500	–
Quarter Noble	£600	£1300	–
Silver			
Groat, class "C"	£200	£750	–
Half Groat	£120	£375	–
Penny	£50	£200	–
Half Penny	£40	£150	–
Farthing	£450	£1500	–

Groat

HENRY VI
(1422–61 and again 1470–71)

Although there were no new denominations except for the Angel and Halfangel during the 2nd reign (see Edward IV opposite), Henry's first reign saw eleven different issues, each for a few years and distinguished by privy marks, i.e. annulets, pinecones, mascles, leaves etc.

HENRY VI *continued*

	F	VF	EF
Gold			
First reign—			
Noble, Annulet issue	£1300	£4500	–
Half Noble, Annulet issue	£1000	£3000	–
Quarter Noble, Annulet issue	£450	£1000	–
2nd reign—			
Angel	£2000	£6000	–
Half Angel	£4600	£13,000	–
Silver			
Groat, Annulet issue	£85	£250	£450
Half Groat, Annulet issue	£40	£150	£400
Penny	£40	£120	£375
Half Penny, Annulet issue	£35	£80	£200
Farthing, Annulet issue	£150	£475	–

Noble

EDWARD IV (1461–70 and again 1471–83)

The significant changes during these reigns were the replacement of the noble by the rose ryal (and revalued at 10 shillings) and the continuation of the angel at the old noble value. We also start to see mint-marks or initial marks appearing, usually at the top of the coin, they were used to denote the period of issue for dating purposes and often lasted for two to three years e.g. rose, lis, crown etc. Groats were issued at London, Bristol, Coventry, Norwich and York.

	F	VF	EF
Gold			
Noble and quarter noble (Heavy Coinage)			Very rare
Ryal	£1200	£3800	–
"Flemish" copy of Ryal	£1000	£2800	–
Half Ryal	£1100	£3000	–
Quarter Ryal	£600	£1500	–
Angel, 2nd reign	£2000	£4200	–
Half Angel, 2nd reign	£1000	£3000	–
Silver			
Groat	£80	£200	£550
Half Groat Canterbury	£60	£180	£475
Penny	£45	£180	£375
Half Penny	£40	£140	–
Farthing, Heavy coinage	£600	£1500	–

Angel

RICHARD III (1483–85)

The close of the Yorkist Plantagenet and Medieval period come together at this time. There are no new significant numismatic changes but most silver coins of Richard whilst not really rare, continue to be very popular and priced quite high. The smaller denominations are usually poor condition.

	F	VF	EF
Gold			
Angel	£5800	£19,000	–
Half Angel	£9750	£32,000	–
Silver			
Groat	£900	£2000	–
Half Groat	£1600	£6000	–
Penny	£450	£1400	–
Half Penny	£375	£1000	–
Farthing	£1700	£4750	–

Groat

PART III
1485–1663

Among the more significant features of the post-Renaissance period as it affected coinage is the introduction of realistic portraiture during the reign of Henry VII. We also have a much wider and varied number of new and revised denominations, for example, 11 different gold denominations of Henry VIII and the same number of silver for Elizabeth I. Here we only mention the introduction or changes in the main denominations, giving a value for all of them, once again listing the commonest type.

HENRY VII
(1485–1509)

The gold sovereign of 20 shillings makes its first appearance in 1489 as does the testoon (later shilling) in about 1500. The silver penny was re-designed to a rather crude likeness of the sovereign, enthroned.

	F	VF	EF
Gold			
Sovereign	£30000	£110,000	–
Ryal	£32500	£140,000	–
Angel	£925	£2750	–
Half Angel	£750	£2350	–
Silver			
Testoon 1/-	£17500	£42,500	–
Groat, facing bust	£85	£250	£1100
Half Groat	£45	£165	£550
Penny, sovereign type	£45	£140	£400
Half Penny	£30	£90	–
Farthing	£550	£1500	–

Profile Groat

HENRY VIII
(1509–47)

After a long initial period of very little change in the coinage, in 1526 there were many, with an attempt to bring the gold/silver ratio in line with the continental currencies. Some gold coins only lasted a short time and are very rare. The crown (in gold) makes its first appearance. Towards the end of the reign we see large issues of debased silver coins (with a high copper content) bearing the well-known facing portrait of the ageing King. These tend to turn up in poor condition and include the shilling in greater numbers. Similar posthumous issues were minted during the early reign of Edward VI.

	F	VF	EF
Gold			
Sovereign, 3rd coinage	£6750	£25,000	–
Half Sovereign	£1050	£3350	–
Angel	£1000	£3000	–
Half Angel	£800	£2500	–
Quarter Angel	£875	£2650	–
George Noble	£11,000	£40,000	–
Half George Noble	£9250	£37,500	–
Crown of the rose	£7000	£25,000	–
Crown of the double rose	£900	£3000	–
Half Crown of the double rose	£650	£1850	–
Silver			
Testoon 1/-	£1300	£4750	–
Groat, 2nd coinage	£165	£400	£1350
Half Groat, 2nd coinage	£70	£200	£700
Penny	£50	£150	£425
Half Penny	£35	£135	–
Farthing	£325	£850	–

Gold Sovereign

EDWARD VI
(1547–53)

Some of the coins struck in the first few years of this short reign could really be called Henry VIII posthumous issues as there is continuity in both name and style from his father's last issue. However, overlapping this period are portrait issues of the boy King, particularly shillings (usually poor quality coins). This period also sees the first dated English coin (shown in Roman numerals) MDXLIX (1549). In 1551 however, a new coinage was introduced with a restored silver quality from the Crown (dated 1551) down to the new sixpence and threepence.

	F	VF	EF
Gold			
Sovereign (30s)	£7250	£22,500	—
Half Sovereign (in own name)	£2100	£7250	—
Crown	£2000	£7250	—
Half Crown	£1600	£5250	—
Angel	£14,000	£40,000	—
Half Angel	—	£45,000	—
Sovereign (20s)	£7500	£22,000	—
Silver			
Crown	£1150	£3650	—
Half Crown	£750	£2200	—
Shilling (Fine coinage)	£165	£575	—
Sixpence (Fine coinage)	£170	£650	—
Groat	£800	£4650	—
Threepence	£275	£1350	—
Half Groat	£475	£1600	—
Penny	£75	£250	—
Half Penny	£400	£1450	—
Farthing	£1500	£5000	—

Crowned bust half sovereign

MARY
(1553–54)

The early coins of Mary's sole reign are limited and continue to use some of the same denominations as Edward, except that the gold ryal was reintroduced.

	F	VF
Gold		
Sovereign (30s)	£9000	£28,500
Ryal	£35,000	—
Angel	£2250	£6000
Half Angel	£6350	£17,000
Silver		
Groat	£225	£750
Half Groat	£725	£2650
Penny	£650	£2350

Groat

PHILIP & MARY (1554–58)

After a very short reign alone, Mary married Philip of Spain and they technically ruled jointly (although not for very long in practise) until her death. After her marriage we see both her and Philip on the shillings and sixpences with both full Spanish and then English titles alone.

	F	VF
Gold		
Angel	£6500	£21,500
Half Angel	£14,000	–
Silver		
Shilling	£500	£2150
Sixpence	£425	£1600
Groat	£225	£775
Half Groat	£550	£2150
Penny	£85	£250

Shilling

ELIZABETH I (1558–1603)

As might be expected with a long reign there are a number of significant changes in the coinage which include several new denominations—so many in silver that every value from the shilling downwards was marked and dated to distinguish them. Early on we have old base Edward VI shillings countermarked to a new reduced value (not priced here). Also due to a lack of small change and the expense of making a miniscule farthing we have a new threehalfpence and threefarthings. Finally we see the beginnings of a milled (machine produced) coinage for a brief period from 1561–71.

	F	VF	EF
Gold			
Sovereign (30s)	£8000	£25,000	–
Ryal (15s)	£22,500	£65,000	–
Angel	£1300	£4000	–
Half Angel	£1100	£3250	–
Quarter Angel	£1000	£3100	–
Pound (20s)	£4000	£13,500	–
Half Pound	£1900	£5650	–
Crown	£1300	£3850	–
Half Crown	£1250	£3750	–
Silver			
Crown (mm I)	£2000	£5350	–
Half Crown (mm I)	£1150	£3250	–
Shilling	£120	£550	£1850
Sixpence	£80	£260	£1500
Groat	£85	£325	£900
Threepence	£60	£225	£650
Half Groat	£40	£125	£325
Threehalfpence	£65	£235	£450
Penny	£40	£125	£300
Threefarthings	£85	£300	£425
Half Penny	£50	£125	£175

Shilling

JAMES I
(1603–25)

Although the size of the gold coinage remains much the same as Elizabeth's reign, the name and weight or value of the denominations have several changes, i.e. Pound = Sovereign = Unite = Laurel. A new four shilling gold coin (thistle crown) was introduced. A number of the silver coins now have their value in Roman numerals on the coin. Relatively few angels were made from this period onwards and they are usually found pierced.

	F	VF	EF
Gold			
Sovereign (20s)	£4000	£15000	–
Unite	£750	£2000	–
Double crown/half unite	£550	£1650	–
Crown	£350	£800	–
Thistle Crown	£350	£1000	–
Half Crown	£300	£625	–
Rose Ryal (30s)	£4000	£14,000	–
Spur Ryal (15s)	£10,000	£33,500	–
Angel (pierced)	£725	£2000	–
Half Angel (Unpierced)	£4000	£11,500	–
Laurel	£725	£2100	–
Half Laurel	£525	£1600	–
Quarter Laurel	£350	£800	–
Silver			
Crown	£900	£2150	–
Half Crown	£375	£950	–
Shilling	£100	£335	–
Sixpence	£70	£275	–
Half Groat	£25	£75	£175
Penny	£25	£70	£135
Half Penny	£20	£55	£135

Gold Unite, second bust

Silver Halfcrown

CHARLES I
(1625–49)

This reign is probably the most difficult to simplify as there are so many different issues and whole books have been produced on this period alone. From the beginning of the King's reign and throughout the Civil War, a number of mints operated for varying lengths of time, producing both regular and irregular issues. The Tower mint was taken over by Parliament in 1642 but before this a small quantity of milled coinage was produced alongside the regular hammered issues. The Court then moved to Oxford from where, for the next three years, large quantities of gold and silver were struck (including rare triple unites and large silver pounds). The most prolific of the provincial mints were those situated at Aberystwyth, York, Oxford, Shrewsbury, Bristol, Exeter, Truro, Chester and Worcester as well as some smaller mints mainly situated in the West Country. Among the more interesting coins of the period are the pieces struck on unusually-shaped flans at Newark and Pontefract whilst those towns were under siege. As many of the coins struck during the Civil War were crudely struck on hastily gathered bullion and plate, they provide a fascinating area of study. The prices indicated below are the minimum for the commonest examples of each denomination irrespective of town of origin.

	F	VF	EF
Gold			
Triple Unite (£3) (Oxford)	£14,000	£38,000	–
Unite	£850	£2400	–
Double crown/Half unite	£500	£1500	–
Crown	£340	£875	–
Angel (pierced)	£725	£2250	–
Angel (unpierced)	£2600	£9250	–
Silver			
Pound (20 shillings—Oxford)	£4250	£12,000	–
Half Pound (Shrewsbury)	£1500	£4000	–
Crown (Truro, Exeter)	£500	£1400	–
Half Crown	£100	£325	–
Shilling	£60	£200	£1000
Sixpence	£50	£190	£875
Groat (Aberystwyth)	£100	£240	£600
Threepence (Aberystwyth)	£90	£220	£550
Half Groat	£25	£90	£250
Penny	£25	£75	£225
Half Penny	£20	£60	£100

Triple unite

Oxford Halfcrown

Above: Newark siege shilling.

THE COMMONWEALTH
(1649–60)

After the execution of Charles I, Parliament changed the design of the coinage. They are simple non- portrait pieces with an English legend.

	F	VF	EF
Gold			
Unite	£2400	£6000	–
Double crown/Half unite	£1800	£5500	–
Crown	£1500	£4000	–
Silver			
Crown	£1500	£3250	£7500
Half Crown	£400	£1000	£3500
Shilling	£325	£700	£2750
Sixpence	£250	£625	£2250
Half Groat	£65	£170	£350
Penny	£60	£165	£335
Halfpenny	£50	£115	£200

Crown

CHARLES II
(1660–85)

Although milled coins had been produced for Oliver Cromwell in 1656–58, after the Restoration of the monarchy hammered coins continued to be produced until 1663, when the machinery was ready to manufacture large quantities of good milled pieces.

	F	VF	EF
Gold			
Unite (2nd issue)	£2300	£6400	–
Double crown/Half unite	£1700	£5000	–
Crown (1st issue)	£2000	£5750	–
Silver			
Half Crown (3rd issue)	£275	£850	–
Shilling (3rd issue)	£180	£675	–
Sixpence (3rd issue)	£150	£525	–
Fourpence (3rd issue)	£45	£150	£325
Threepence (3rd issue)	£45	£150	£325
Twopence (3rd issue)	£25	£75	£175
Penny (3rd issue)	£40	£115	£235

Halfcrown

A COMPREHENSIVE PRICE GUIDE
TO THE COINS OF

THE UNITED KINGDOM 1656–2024

including

When referring to this price guide one must bear a number of important points in mind. The points listed here have been taken into consideration during the preparation of this guide and we hope that the prices given will provide a true reflection of the market at the time of going to press. Nevertheless, the publishers can accept no liability for the accuracy of the prices quoted, which are the prices one could expect to pay for a coin.

1. "As struck" examples with flaws will be worth less than the indicated price.
2. Any coin which is particularly outstanding, with an attractive natural toning or in superb state will command a much *higher* price than that shown.
3. These prices refer strictly to the British market, and do not reflect outside opinions.
4. Some prices given for coins not seen in recent years are estimates based on a knowledge of the market.
5. In the case of coins of high rarity, prices are not generally given.
6. In the listing, "—" indicates, where applicable, one of the following:
    a. Metal or bullion value only
    b. Not usually found in this grade
    c. Not collected in this condition
7. Proof coins are listed in FDC under the UNC column.
8. All prices are quoted in £ sterling, exclusive of VAT (where applicable).

FIFTY SHILLINGS

OLIVER CROMWELL (1656–58)

	F	VF	EF
1656	£35,000	£110,000	£330,000

Opinions differ as to whether the portrait coinage of Oliver Cromwell was ever meant for circulation but for the sake of completeness it has been decided to include it in this Yearbook. The fifty shillings gold coin is unique as it was only struck during Cromwell's time using the same dies that were used for the broad or 20 shillings coin but with a weight of approximately 2.5 times that of the broad.

FIVE GUINEAS

CHARLES II (1660–85)

	F	VF	EF
1668 First bust	£8500	£22,000	£115,000
1668 — Elephant below bust	£8500	£22,000	£115,000
1669 —	£8500	£22,000	—
1669 — Elephant	£8500	£22,000	—
1670 —	£9000	£22,000	£110,000
1670 — Proof		Exceedingly Rare	
1671 —	£8500	£18,000	£110,000
1672 —	£8500	£18,000	£110,000
1673 —	£8500	£19,000	£110,000
1674 —	£8500	£18,000	£110,000
1675 —	£8000	£17,000	£110,000
1675 — Elephant	£10000	£25,000	—
1675 — Elephant & Castle below bust	£11000	£25,000	£130,000
1676 —	£8500	£21,000	£110,000
1676 — Elephant & Castle	£9000	£22,000	£110,000
1677 —	£8500	£21,000	£110,000
1677/5 — Elephant	£11000	£26,000	£130,000
1677 — Elephant & Castle	£10000	£21,000	£120,000
1678/7 — 8 over 7	£9000	£21,000	£110,000
1678/7 — Elephant & Castle	£9000	£22,000	£115,000
1678/7 Second Bust	£9000	£21,000	£115,000
1679 —	£9000	£22,000	£100,000
1680 —	£9000	£22,000	£100,000
1680 — Elephant & Castle	£9000	£22,000	£120,000
1681 —	£9000	£21,000	£110,000
1681 — Elephant & Castle	£10000	£24,000	£130,000
1682 —	£8000	£19,000	£110,000
1682 — Elephant & Castle	£9500	£22,000	£115,000
1683 —	£8000	£19,000	£100,000
1683 — Elephant & Castle	£9500	£24,000	£120,000
1684 —	£8000	£22,000	£95,000
1684 — Elephant & Castle	£9000	£23,000	£100,000

Charles II

JAMES II (1685–88)

	F	VF	EF
1686	£9000	£20,000	£110,000
1687	£9000	£20,000	£110,000
1687 Elephant & Castle	£10000	£20,000	£110,000
1688	£8500	£19,000	£95,000
1688 Elephant & Castle	£11000	£24,000	£115,000

WILLIAM AND MARY (1688–94)

	F	VF	EF
1691	£8000	£20,000	£120,000
1691 Elephant & Castle	£8000	£21,000	£120,000
1692	£8000	£20,000	£120,000
1692 Elephant & Castle	£9000	£22,000	£130,000
1693	£8000	£22,000	£120,000
1693 Elephant & Castle	£9000	£22,000	£130,000
1694	£8500	£21,000	£115,000
1694 Elephant & Castle	£9000	£22,000	£120,000

WILLIAM III (1694–1702)

	F	VF	EF
1699 First bust	£9500	£21,000	£110,000
1699 — Elephant & Castle	£10500	£22,000	£120,000
1700 —	£9000	£21,000	£110,000
1701 Second bust “fine work”	£8500	£22,000	£105,000

(1701 "fine work"—beware recent forgeries)

ANNE (1702–14)

	F	VF	EF
Pre-Union with Scotland			
1703 VIGO below bust	£65,000	£170,000	£650,000
1705	£15,000	£40,000	£160,000
1706	£13,000	£35,000	£160,000
Post-Union (different shields)			
1706	£9500	£22,000	£110,000
1709 Narrow shields	£9500	£22,000	£115,000
1711 Broader shields	£9000	£20,000	£110,000
1713 —	£11,000	£24,000	£110,000
1714 —	£10,000	£22,000	£110,000
1714/3	£10,000	£22,000	£110,000

William & Mary

GEORGE I (1714–27)

	F	VF	EF
1716	£10000	£24,000	£125,000
1717	£11000	£25,000	£130,000
1720	£11000	£25,000	£130,000
1726	£12000	£25,000	£125,000

GEORGE II (1727–60)

	F	VF	EF
1729 Young head	£10000	£21,000	£110,000
1729 — E.I.C. below head	£9000	£20,000	£110,000
1731 —	£10000	£24,000	£110,000
1735 —	£10000	£24,000	£115,000
1738 —	£9000	£20,000	£120,000
1741	£9000	£19,000	£100,000
1741/38 41 over 38	£9000	£21,000	£100,000
1746 Old head, LIMA	£8500	£20,000	£100,000
1748 —	£8500	£20,000	£95,000
1753 —	£8500	£21,000	£90,000

GEORGE III (1760–1820)

	F	VF	EF
1770 Patterns	–	–	£440,000
1773	–	–	£440,000
1777	–	–	£440,000

Anne

TWO GUINEAS

Charles II

CHARLES II (1660–85)

	F	VF	EF
1664 First bust	£2700	£7000	£27,000
1664 — Elephant	£2500	£6500	£25,000
1665 —		Extremely rare	
1669 —		Extremely rare	
1671 —	£3500	£9000	£37,500
1673 First bust		Extremely rare	
1675 Second bust	£3000	£7500	£32,000
1676 —	£3000	£7000	£35,000
1676 — Elephant & Castle	£3000	£7000	£35,000
1677 —	£3000	£7000	£30,000
1677 — Elephant & Castle		Extremely rare	
1678/7 —	£3000	£7000	£30,000
1678 — Elephant		Extremely rare	
1678 — Elephant & Castle	£3000	£7000	£32,000
1679 —	£3000	£7000	£32,000
1680 —	£3500	£8000	£34,000
1681 —	£3000	£7000	£32,000
1682 — Elephant & Castle	£3000	£7000	£32,000
1683 —	£3000	£6500	£35,000
1683 — Elephant & Castle	£3000	£7000	£36,000
1684 —	£3000	£7000	£35,000
1684 — Elephant & Castle	£3000	£7500	£42,000

James II

JAMES II (1685–88)

	F	VF	EF
1687	£4000	£12,000	£40,000
1688/7	£4500	£13,000	£45,000

WILLIAM AND MARY (1688–94)

	F	VF	EF
1691 Elephant & Castle		Exceedingly rare	
1693	£3500	£10000	£40,000
1693 Elephant & Castle	£3500	£10000	£40,000
1694 — 4 over 3	£3500	£9000	£32,000
1694/3 Elephant & Castle	£3750	£11000	£37,500

WILLIAM III (1694–1702)

	F	VF	EF
1701 "fine work"	£3500	£8500	£37,000

ANNE (1702–14)

	F	VF	EF
1709 Post Union	£2200	£7000	£25,000
1711	£2200	£7000	£25,000
1713	£2200	£7500	£27,000
1714/3	£2350	£8000	£30,000

GEORGE I (1714–27)

	F	VF	EF
1717	£2800	£7000	£35,000
1720	£2800	£7000	£35,000
1720/17	£3300	£7500	£35,000
1726	£2500	£7500	£35,000

Anne

GEORGE II (1727–60)

	F	VF	EF
1733 Proof only FDC		Extremely Rare	
1734 Young head 4 over 3	£3000	£8000	—
1735 —	£3000	£7000	£25,000
1738 —	£950	£3000	£8000
1739 —	£1000	£3000	£8000
1739 Intermediate head	£950	£3000	£8500
1740 —	£1000	£2750	£9000
1748 Old head	£1500	£4000	£1100
1753 —	£1700	£4000	£12000

George II

GEORGE III (1760–1820)

	F	VF	EF
1768 Patterns only	—	Extremely Rare	
1773 Patterns only	—	Extremely Rare	
1777 Patterns only	—	Extremely Rare	

GUINEAS

CHARLES II (1660–85)

	F	VF	EF
1663 First bust	£5000	£16,000	£62,500
1663 — Elephant below	£4000	£13,000	—
1663 Second bust	£3500	£12,000	£48,000
1664 Second bust	£3500	£11,000	—
1664 — Elephant	£4000	£12,000	£47,000
1664 Third bust	£1500	£4500	£18,000
1664 — Elephant	£2000	£6000	£20,000
1665 —	£1500	£4000	£16,000
1665 — Elephant	£2000	£6000	£22,000
1666 —	£1400	£4000	£16,000
1667 —	£1400	£4000	£16,000
1668 —	£1300	£4250	£16,000
1668 — Elephant		Extremely rare	
1669 —	£1500	£3500	£16,000
1670 —	£1500	£3500	£15,000
1671 —	£1500	£3500	£15,000
1672 —	£1500	£4000	£18,000
1672 Fourth bust	£1200	£3000	£12,000
1673 Third bust	£1200	£3200	£16,000
1673 Fourth bust	£1000	£3000	£13,000
1674 —	£1000	£3000	£13,000
1674 — Elephant & Castle		Extremely rare	
1675 —	£1100	£3000	£13,000
1675 — CRAOLVS Error		Extremely rare	
1675 — Elephant & Castle	£1500	£4500	£17,000
1676 —	£1000	£3000	£12,000
1676/4 — 6 over 4	£1000	£3000	£12,000
1676 — Elephant & Castle	£1000	£4500	£16,000
1677 —	£1000	£4000	£14,000
1677 — GRATIR Error		Extremely rare	
1677/5 — Elephant 7 over 5		Extremely rare	
1677 — Elephant & Castle	£1300	£4000	£16,000
1678 —	£1000	£3000	£14,000
1678 — Elephant		Extremely rare	
1678 — Elephant & Castle	£1400	£4000	£16,000

Charles II, third bust

Charles II, fourth bust, elephant & castle below

	F	VF	EF
1679 —	£1200	£3000	£12,000
1679 — Elephant & Castle	£1250	£3500	£15,000
1680 —	£1000	£3000	£12,000
1680 — Elephant & Castle	£1300	£4000	£15,000
1681 —	£1100	£3250	£13,000
1681 — Elephant & Castle	£1300	£4000	£17,000
1682 —	£1000	£3200	£12,000
1682 — Elephant & Castle	£1500	£4500	£20,000
1683 —	£1000	£2500	£12,000
1683 — Elephant & Castle	£1300	£5000	£17,000
1684 —	£1000	£3000	£14,000
1684 — Elephant & Castle	£1500	£4500	£19,000

James II, first bust, elephant & castle below

JAMES II (1685–88)

	F	VF	EF
1685 First bust	£1500	£3500	£13,000
1685 — Elephant & Castle	£1600	£4500	£16,000
1686 —	£1300	£3000	£14,000
1686 — Elephant & Castle		Extremely rare	
1686 Second bust	£1400	£3500	£13,000
1686 — Elephant & Castle	£1600	£4000	£17,000
1687 —	£1700	£5000	£15,000
1687 —Elephant & Castle	£1500	£4000	£17,500
1688 —	£1400	£3000	£14,000
1688 — Elephant & Castle	£1400	£4500	£15,000

James II, second bust

WILLIAM AND MARY (1688–94)

	F	VF	EF
1689	£1200	£3600	£12,000
1689 Elephant & Castle	£1300	£3500	£13,000
1690	£1200	£3600	£13,000
1690 GVLIFLMVS	£1200	£3600	£13,000
1690 Elephant & Castle	£1200	£3650	£16,000
1691	£1200	£3500	£14,000
1691 Elephant & Castle	£1200	£3500	£14,000
1692	£1100	£3400	£13,000
1692 Elephant	£1250	£4250	£13,000
1692 Elephant & Castle	£1200	£4250	£13,000
1693	£1200	£3250	£13,000
1693 Elephant	£1600	£4750	£19,000
1693 Elephant & Castle	£1500	£4750	£18,000
1694	£1300	£3500	£14,000
1694/3	£1200	£3500	£13,000
1694 Elephant & Castle	£1300	£3500	£13,000
1694/3 Elephant & Castle	£1300	£3500	£14,000

(Note: there are several overstamp errors of this reign. Prices are similar to standard issues)

WILLIAM III (1694–1702)

	F	VF	EF
1695 First bust	£1100	£3000	£11,000
1695 — Elephant & Castle	£1500	£6000	£16,500
1696 —	£1000	£3000	£12,000
1696 — Elephant & Castle		Extremely rare	
1697 —	£1200	£4000	£12,000
1697 Second bust	£1200	£3500	£12,000
1697 — Elephant & Castle	£2000	£7000	£20,000
1698 —	£1100	£3000	£11,000
1698 — Elephant & Castle	£1800	£5500	£15,000
1699 —	£1100	£3500	£12,000
1699 — Elephant & Castle		Extremely rare	
1700 —	£1100	£3000	£11,000
1700 — Elephant & Castle	£1600	£6000	—
1701 —	£950	£2750	£10,000
1701 — Elephant & Castle		Extremely rare	
1701 Third bust "fine work"	£2000	£6750	£20,000

William III, second bust

ANNE (1702–14)

	F	VF	EF
1702 (Pre-Union) First bust	£1500	£6000	£20,000
1703 — VIGO below	£25,000	£65,000	£150,000
1705 —	£1600	£6000	£20,000
1706 —	£1600	£6000	£20,000
1707 —	£1700	£6500	£21,000
1707 — (Post-Union)	£1100	£3500	£15,000
1707 — Elephant & Castle	£1800	£6000	£20,000
1707 Second bust	£1100	£3500	£14,000
1708 First bust	£1200	£3500	£15,000
1708 Second bust	£1100	£3000	£11,000
1708 — Elephant & Castle	£1700	£6000	£20,000
1709 —	£1500	£5000	£14,000
1709 — Elephant & Castle	£1500	£5000	£17,000
1710 Third bust	£850	£2000	£10,000
1711 —	£850	£2000	£10,000
1712 —	£850	£2200	£10,000
1713 —	£800	£2000	£11,000
1714 —	£800	£2000	£11,000
1714 GRΛTIΛ	£1000	£2200	£12,000

Anne, third bust

GEORGE I (1714–27)

	F	VF	EF
1714 First bust (Prince Elector)	£2200	£6000	£20,000
1715 Second bust	£900	£2200	£7000
1715 Third bust	£850	£2200	£6500
1716 —	£900	£2200	£8000
1716 Fourth bust	£900	£2000	£6500
1717 —	£950	£2200	£7000
1718/7 — 8 over 7		Extremely rare	
1718 —		Extremely rare	
1719 —	£900	£2000	£7000
1720 —	£900	£2000	£7000
1721 —	£950	£2200	£7500
1721 — Elephant & Castle		Extremely rare	
1722 —	£900	£2000	£7000
1722 — Elephant & Castle		Extremely rare	
1723 —	£900	£2000	£7000
1723 Fifth bust	£900	£2000	£7000
1724 —	£950	£2200	£7000
1725 —	£950	£2200	£7000
1726 —	£900	£2200	£7000
1726 — Elephant & Castle	£2500	£8000	£25,000
1727 —	£900	£2500	£8500

George I, fifth bust

GEORGE II (1727–60)

	F	VF	EF
1727 First young head, early large shield	£1700	£5500	£18,000
1727 — Larger lettering, early small shield	£1700	£5500	£18,000
1728 — —	£1650	£5500	£17,000
1729 2nd young head E.I.C. below	£1800	£5000	£18,000
1729 — Proof			Very Rare
1730 —	£950	£2250	£10,000
1731 —	£850	£2500	£10,000
1731 — E.I.C. below	£1600	£5000	£16,500
1732 —	£900	£2500	£9500
1732 — E.I.C. below	£1500	£4500	£17,000
1732 — Larger lettering obverse	£800	£2250	£8500
1732 — — E.I.C. below	£1650	£5000	£18,000
1733 — —	£700	£1800	£7500
1734 — —	£700	£1800	£7500
1735 — —	£700	£1800	£7500
1736 — —	£700	£1900	£7500
1737 — —	£700	£1900	£7500

George II, 1760, old head, large lettering

	F	VF	EF
1738 — —	£800	£2000	£8000
1739 Intermediate head	£900	£2000	£9500
1739 — E.I.C. below	£1600	£5500	£17,000
1740 —	£900	£2200	£10,000
1741/39 —	£1100	£3000	£11,000
1743 —	£1100	£3000	£12,000
1745 — Larger lettering obv. Older bust	£700	£1800	£8000
1745 — LIMA below	£2500	£7500	£32,500
1746 — (GEORGIVS) Larger lettering obv.	£800	£2000	£8000
1747 Old head, large lettering	£650	£1600	£6000
1748 —	£650	£1600	£6500
1749 —	£700	£1600	£6500
1750 —	£650	£1500	£6000
1751 — small lettering	£650	£1500	£6000
1753 —	£650	£1500	£6000
1755 —	£650	£1600	£5500
1756 —	£650	£1600	£5500
1758 —	£650	£1600	£5500
1759 —	£650	£1600	£5500
1760 —	£650	£1600	£5500

George III third head

GEORGE III (1760–1820)

	F	VF	EF
1761 First head	£2200	£6500	£15,000
1763 Second head	£1600	£4500	£12,000
1764 —	£1400	£4500	£13,000
1764 – No stop above bust	£2200	£5000	£13,000
1765 Third head	£500	£950	£2300
1766 —	£500	£950	£2300
1767 —	£600	£1200	£3250
1768 —	£500	£900	£2350
1769 —	£500	£900	£2350
1770 —	£1500	£3250	£8000
1771 —	£500	£750	£2000
1772 —	£500	£750	£2000
1773 —	£500	£750	£2100
1774 Fourth head	£500	£750	£1650
1775 —	£475	£750	£1500
1776 —	£475	£750	£1700
1777 —	£475	£750	£1700
1778 —	£850	£1400	£4000
1779 —	£500	£800	£1600
1781 —	£450	£725	£1550
1782 —	£450	£725	£1550
1783 —	£450	£700	£1550
1784 —	£450	£700	£1450
1785 —	£475	£700	£1450
1786 —	£500	£750	£1500
1787 Fifth head, "Spade" reverse	£425	£575	£1150
1788 —	£425	£575	£1150
1789 —	£425	£575	£1200
1790 —	£450	£650	£1350
1791 —	£400	£600	£1200
1792 —	£400	£600	£1200
1793 —	£400	£650	£1300
1794 —	£400	£650	£1200
1795 —	£400	£650	£1200
1796 —	£400	£650	£1200
1797 —	£400	£700	£1300
1798 —	£400	£675	£1300
1799 —	£500	£825	£2000
1813 Sixth head, "Military" reverse	£1400	£2750	£7500

(Beware of counterfeits of this series—many dangerous copies exist)

Fourth head

Fifth head, Spade reverse

Sixth "Military" head

HALF GUINEAS

CHARLES II (1660–85)

	F	VF	EF
1669 First bust	£800	£2200	£8000
1670 —	£750	£2000	£8000
1671 —	£850	£2200	£9000
1672 —	£850	£2500	£9000
1672 Second bust	£700	£1800	£7000
1673 —	£700	£1900	£7500
1674 —	£700	£2200	£7500
1675 —	£700	£2000	£7500
1676 —	£700	£2000	£7000
1676 — Elephant & Castle	£1000	£3250	—
1677 —	£750	£2000	£7500
1677 — Elephant & Castle	£900	£2500	£9000
1678 —	£800	£2000	£8000
1678/7 —	£850	£2000	£7500
1678/7 — Elephant & Castle	£900	£2500	£9500
1679 —	£700	£1850	£7000
1680 —	£700	£2200	£7000
1680 — Elephant & Castle	£1000	£3000	£10,500
1681 —	£725	£2000	£7500
1682 —	£700	£2000	£7000
1682 — Elephant & Castle	£900	£2750	£10,000
1683 —	£700	£1850	£7000
1683 — Elephant & Castle		Extremely rare	
1684 —	£700	£1800	£7500
1684 — Elephant & Castle	£900	£2750	£9500

Charles II, second bust

JAMES II (1685–88)

	F	VF	EF
1686	£700	£2000	£7500
1686 Elephant & Castle	£1100	£4000	£10,500
1687	£800	£2200	£7500
1688	£750	£2200	£7500

James II

WILLIAM AND MARY (1688–94)

	F	VF	EF
1689 First busts	£750	£2200	£7500
1690 Second busts	£750	£2200	£7500
1691 —	£750	£2200	£7500
1691 — Elephant & Castle	£800	£2400	£8000
1692 —	£750	£2300	£7500
1692 — Elephant		Extremely rare	
1692 — Elephant & Castle	£750	£2500	£7500
1693 —		Extremely rare	
1694 —	£750	£2250	£7500

William & Mary, second busts

WILLIAM III (1694–1702)

	F	VF	EF
1695	£600	£1500	£6000
1695 Elephant & Castle	£900	£2500	£8000
1696 —	£650	£1850	£6500
1697 Larger Harp rev.	£800	£2200	£7500
1698	£650	£1500	£5250
1698 Elephant & Castle	£750	£2200	£7000
1699		Extremely rare	
1700	£600	£1600	£6000
1701	£550	£1500	£5750

William III

	F	VF	EF

ANNE (1702–14)

	F	VF	EF
1702 (Pre-Union)	£1400	£3500	£14,000
1703 VIGO below bust	£12,000	£37,500	£90,000
1705	£1300	£3500	£12,500
1707 (Post-Union)	£500	£1200	£5000
1708	£550	£1300	£5500
1709	£525	£1200	£5000
1710	£500	£1100	£5000
1711	£500	£1100	£5000
1712	£550	£1250	£5250
1713	£500	£1100	£5000
1714	£500	£1100	£5000

Anne

GEORGE I (1714–27)

	F	VF	EF
1715 First bust	£750	£1800	£8000
1717 —	£500	£1100	£5000
1718 —	£500	£1100	£5000
1718/7 —	£500	£1100	£5000
1719 —	£500	£1000	£4750
1720 —	£475	£1150	£5000
1721 —			Extremely rare
1721 — Elephant & Castle			Extremely rare
1722 —	£500	£1100	£5000
1723 —	£550	£1100	£5000
1724 —	£600	£1200	£6000
1725 Second bust	£450	£1000	£4500
1726 —	£450	£1000	£4600
1727 —	£450	£1000	£4750

George I, second bust

GEORGE II (1727–60)

	F	VF	EF
1728 Young head	£700	£1600	£7000
1728 — Proof			Extremely rare
1729 —	£700	£1750	£6500
1729 — E.I.C.	£750	£1800	£7000
1730 —	£600	£1300	£6000
1730 — E.I.C.	£950	£2250	—
1731 —	£500	£1100	£5000
1731 — E.I.C.			Extremely rare
1732 —	£500	£1200	£5250
1732 — E.I.C.			Extremely rare
1733 —			Unknown
1734 —	£500	£1100	£4500
1735 —			Unknown
1736 —	£500	£1100	£5000
1737 —	£500	£1100	£5250
1738 —	£500	£1100	£5000
1739 —	£500	£1100	£5000
1739 — E.I.C.			Extremely rare
1740 Intermediate head	£500	£1100	£5000
1743 —			Extremely rare
1745 —	£600	£1300	£5250
1745 — LIMA	£1300	£4000	£13,000
1746 —	£400	£900	£3750
1747 Old head	£550	£950	£4250
1748 —	£450	£900	£4000
1749 —	£600	£1500	£6000
1750 —	£550	£1200	£5000
1751 —	£450	£950	£3500
1752 —	£450	£950	£3500
1753 —	£400	£950	£3500
1755 —	£400	£900	£3500
1756 —	£400	£750	£3000
1758 —	£350	£750	£3000
1759 —	£350	£750	£2750
1759/8	£350	£750	£3000
1760 —	£350	£750	£3000

George II, young head

George II, old head

GEORGE III (1760–1820)

	F	VF	EF
1762 First head	£725	£2000	£5500
1763 —	£850	£2700	£6500
1764 Second head	£400	£700	£1800
1765 —	£600	£1600	£4250
1766 —	£375	£700	£2000
1768 —	£375	£700	£2000
1769 —	£400	£800	£2100
1772 —		Extremely rare	
1773 —	£400	£800	£2250
1774 —	£450	£900	£2500
1774 Third head		Extremely rare	
1775 —	£1500	£4000	£11,000
1775 Fourth head	£300	£500	£1300
1775 — Proof		Extremely rare	
1776 —	£350	£625	£1700
1777 —	£300	£600	£1300
1778 —	£300	£600	£1300
1779 —	£300	£600	£1400
1781 —	£300	£600	£1350
1783 —	£500	£1800	—
1784 —	£300	£550	£1250
1785 —	£250	£500	£1200
1786 —	£250	£500	£1200
1787 Fifth head, "Spade" rev.	£250	£500	£1200
1788 —	£250	£500	£1200
1789 —	£250	£500	£1200
1790 —	£250	£500	£1000
1791 —	£250	£500	£1000
1792 —	£1500	£4000	—
1793 —	£250	£475	£1000
1794 —	£250	£475	£1000
1795 —	£250	£525	£1100
1796 —	£250	£475	£1000
1797 —	£250	£475	£1000
1798 —	£250	£475	£1000
1800 —	£400	£1000	£2750
1801 Sixth head, Shield in Garter rev.	£240	£375	£900
1802 —	£240	£375	£900
1803 —	£240	£375	£900
1804 Seventh head	£240	£375	£900
1805		Extremely rare	
1806 —	£250	£425	£900
1808 —	£250	£425	£900
1899 —	£250	£425	£900
1810 —	£250	£425	£900
1811 —	£400	£600	£1600
1813 —	£375	£600	£1250
1813 — Proof			Very rare

George III, first head

George III, second head

George III, third head

George III, fourth head

George III, fifth head

George III, sixth head

George III, seventh head

THIRD GUINEAS

DATE	F	VF	EF
GEORGE III (1760–1820)			
1797 First head, date in legend	£150	£275	£750
1798 — —	£150	£275	£750
1799 — —	£475	£1100	£2000
1800 — —	£160	£325	£800
1801 Date under crown	£170	£350	£850
1802 —	£170	£400	£850
1803 —	£170	£350	£800
1804 Second head	£150	£275	£700
1806 —	£150	£300	£700
1808 —	£150	£350	£750
1809 —	£150	£350	£750
1810 —	£150	£350	£750
1811 —	£600	£1300	£3000
1813 —	£300	£650	£1350

George III, date in legend

George III, date under crown

QUARTER GUINEAS

DATE	F	VF	EF
GEORGE I (1714–27)			
1718	£250	£450	£1200
GEORGE III (1760–1820)			
1762	£250	£525	£900

George I

FIVE POUNDS

DATE	Mintage	F	VF	EF	UNC
GEORGE III (1760–1820)					
1820 (pattern only)	—				Extremely rare
GEORGE IV (1820–30)					
1826 proof only	—	—	—		£200,000 (FDC)
VICTORIA (1837–1901)					
1839 Una & The Lion. Proof.					*

** In recent months the prices paid for Una & the Lion coins has risen astronomically. In August 2021 Hertiage Auctions sold an example for over $1 million.*

DATE	Mintage	F	VF	EF	UNC
1887	53,844	£2000	£2800	£4000	£5500
1887 Proof	797	—	—	—	£25,000 (FDC)
1887 S on ground on rev. (Sydney Mint)					Excessively rare
1893	20,405	£2200	£2800	£5000	£8250
1893 Proof	773	—	—	—	£30,000
EDWARD VII (1902–10)					
1902	34,910	£2000	£2350	£2950	£4000
1902 Matt proof	8,066	—	—	—	£4500

DATE	MINTAGE	F	VF	EF	UNC

GEORGE V (1911–36)

1911 Proof only	2,812	–	–	–	£15,000

GEORGE VI (1937–52)

1937 Proof only	5,501	–	–	–	£8000

Later issues are listed in the Decimal section.

TWO POUNDS

GEORGE III (1760–1820)

1820 (pattern only)	–	–	–	Extremely rare	

GEORGE IV (1820–30)

1823 St George reverse	–	£900	£1300	£3000	£4500
1826 Proof only, shield reverse	–	–	–	Extremely rare	

WILLIAM IV (1830–37)

1831 Proof only	225	–	–	–	£22,500

VICTORIA (1837–1901)

1887	91,345	£1000	£1400	£1800	£2500
1887 Proof	797	–	–	–	£6000
1887 S on ground of rev. (Sydney Mint)				Excessively rare	
1893	52,212	£1000	£1400	£2500	£4500
1893 Proof	773	–	–	–	£9000

EDWARD VII (1902–10)

1902	45,807	£750	£950	£1300	£2200
1902 Matt proof	8,066	–	–	–	£2500

GEORGE V (1911–36)

1911 Proof only	2,812	–	–	–	£4500

GEORGE VI (1937–52)

1937 Proof only	5,501	–	–	–	£4500

Later issues are listed in the Decimal section.

CROMWELL GOLD

OLIVER CROMWELL (1656–58)

	F	VF	EF
1656 Fifty Shillings	£35,000	£110,000	£325,000
1656 Twenty Shillings	£9,000	£22,000	£55,000

SOVEREIGNS

George III

GEORGE III (1760–1820)

DATE	MINTAGE	F	VF	EF	UNC
1817	3,235,239	£800	£1100	£2500	£5500
1818	2,347,230	£800	£1400	£5000	£8500
1819	3,574		Exceedingly rare		
1820	931,994	£800	£1000	£2250	£5500

George IV, shield reverse

GEORGE IV (1820–30)

DATE	MINTAGE	F	VF	EF	UNC
1821 First bust, St George reverse	9,405,114	£500	£800	£2000	£4500
1821 — Proof	incl. above	—	—	—	£15,000
1822 —	5,356,787	£450	£800	£2000	£4500
1823 —	616,770	£1100	£3000	£8500	£11,000
1824 —	3,767,904	£550	£1000	£2250	£4500
1825 —	4,200,343	£800	£2400	£8000	£10,000
1825 Second bust, shield reverse	incl. above	£550	£800	£2000	£5000
1826 —	5,724,046	£550	£800	£1800	£4000
1826 — Proof	—	—	—	—	£12,000
1827 —	2,266,629	£550	£800	£1850	£4000
1828 —	386,182	£6000	£15,000	£30,000	£40,000
1829 —	2,444,652	£550	£900	£2500	£4500
1830 —	2,387,881	£575	£825	£2500	£4500

William IV

WILLIAM IV (1830–37)

DATE	MINTAGE	F	VF	EF	UNC
1831	598,547	£600	£1000	£3250	£6000
1831 Proof, plain edge	—	—	—	—	£15,000
1832	3,737,065	£550	£1000	£2700	£5000
1833	1,225,269	£550	£1000	£2700	£4500
1835	723,441	£550	£1000	£2700	£7000
1836	1,714,349	£550	£1000	£2500	£6000
1836 N. of Anno struck on shield	—	£6000	£11,000	—	£22,000
1837	1,172,984	£550	£1100	£2750	£3500

Note—from the Victoria reign onwards, the prices of coins in lower grade are usually subject to the bullion price of gold.

VICTORIA (1837–1901)

Many of the gold coins struck at the colonial mints found their way into circulation in Britain, for the sake of completeness these coins are listed here. These can easily be identified by a tiny initial letter for the appropriate mint which can be found below the base of the reverse shield or, in the case of the St George reverse, below the bust on the obverse of the Young Head issues, or on the "ground" below the horse's hoof on the later issues.

YOUNG HEAD ISSUES

Shield reverse

(Note—Shield back sovereigns in Fine/VF condition, common dates, are normally traded as bullion + a percentage—subject to market movement changes)

DATE	MINTAGE	F	VF	EF	UNC
1838	2,718,694	£900	£1500	£4000	£7500
1839	503,695	£1300	£3000	£4500	£8500
1839 Proof, plain edge	—	—	—	—	£27,000
1841	124,054	£5000	£10,000	£23,500	£35,000
1842	4,865,375	£400	£500	£1000	£2500
1843	5,981,968	£400	£500	£1000	£2000
1843 "Narrow shield" variety	incl. above	£5250	£10,000	—	£35,000
1843 Roman I in date	—	£750	£1750	—	—
1844	3,000,445	£400	£450	£1000	£2000
1845	3,800,845	£400	£450	£1000	£2500
1846	3,802,947	£400	£450	£1000	£2250
1847	4,667,126	£400	£450	£1000	£2250

Victoria Young Head

DATE	MINTAGE	F	VF	EF	UNC
1848	2,246,701	£400	£460	£1000	£2500
1849	1,755,399	£400	£460	£1000	£2500
1850	1,402,039	£400	£460	£1000	£2000
1851	4,013,624	£400	£460	£750	£2000
1852	8,053,435	£400	£460	£850	£2000
1853	10,597,993	£400	£460	£750	£1750
1853 Proof	—	—	—	—	£30,000
1854 Incuse WW	3,589,611	£400	£460	£750	£2000
1854 Surface raised WW	3,589,611	£400	£460	£750	£2250
1855	4,806,160	£400	£460	£750	£2000
1856	8,448,482	£400	£460	£750	£2000
1857	4,495,748	£400	£460	£750	£2000
1858	803,234	£400	£460	£750	£2000
1859	1,547,603	£400	£460	£750	£2000
1859 "Ansell" (additional line on lower part of hair ribbon)	—	£750	£1800	£10,000	—
1860	2,555,958	£400	£450	£650	£2000
1861	7,624,736	£400	£450	£600	£1000
1862	7,836,413	£400	£450	£650	£1350
1863	5,921,669	£400	£450	£600	£1350
1863 Die No 827 on Truncation...				Extremely rare	
1863 with Die number below shield	incl. above	£400	£450	£600	£1100
1864 —	8,656,352	£400	£450	£650	£1350
1865 —	1,450,238	£400	£450	£650	£1350
1866 —	4,047,288	£400	£450	£600	£1350
1868 —	1,653,384	£400	£450	£550	£1200
1869 —	6,441,322	£400	£450	£550	£1200
1870 —	2,189,960	£400	£450	£550	£1200
1871 —	8,767,250	£400	£450	£500	£1000
1872 —	13,486,708	£400	£450	£500	£1000
1872 no Die number	incl. above	£400	£450	£500	£1000
1873 with Die number	2,368,215	£400	£450	£600	£1300
1874 —	520,713	£2000	£4200	£11,000	£15,000
M below reverse shield (Melbourne Mint)					
1872	748,180	£400	£450	£500	£1000
1874	1,373,298	£400	£450	£500	£900
1880	3,053,454	£700	£1700	£3000	£8000
1881	2,325,303	£400	£450	£480	£1750
1882	2,465,781	£400	£450	£480	£1000
1883	2,050,450	£400	£450	£600	£1300
1884	2,942,630	£400	£450	£480	£1000
1885	2,967,143	£400	£450	£480	£1000
1886	2,902,131	£1800	£4000	£6500	£20,000
1887	1,916,424	£600	£1350	£3500	£10,000
S below reverse shield (Sydney Mint)					
1871	2,814,000	£400	£450	£480	£800
1872	1,815,000	£400	£450	£480	£900
1873	1,478,000	£400	£450	£480	£900
1875	2,122,000	£400	£450	£480	£900
1877	1,590,000	£400	£450	£480	£900
1878	1,259,000	£400	£450	£480	£950
1879	1,366,000	£400	£450	£480	£900
1880	1,459,000	£400	£450	£480	£900
1881	1,360,000	£400	£450	£480	£1500
1882	1,298,000	£400	£450	£480	£900
1883	1,108,000	£400	£450	£480	£900
1884	1,595,000	£400	£450	£480	£900
1885	1,486,000	£400	£450	£480	£850
1886	1,667,000	£400	£450	£480	£850
1887	1,000,000	£400	£450	£480	£900

The die number appears between the wreath and the bottom rose, below the shield

The mint initial appears between the wreath and the bottom rose, below the shield, i.e. "S" indicates that this coin was struck at the Sydney Mint

IMPORTANT NOTE: The prices quoted in this guide are set at August 2024 with the price of gold at £1,950 per ounce and silver £21.70 per ounce—market fluctuations can have a marked effect on the values of modern precious metal coins.

DATE	MINTAGE	F	VF	EF	UNC
St George & Dragon reverse					
1871	incl. above	£400	£440	£450	£850
1872	incl. above	£400	£440	£450	£1000
1873	incl. above	£400	£440	£450	£1000
1874	incl. above	£400	£440	£450	£900
1876	3,318,866	£400	£440	£450	£1000
1878	1,091,275	£400	£440	£450	£1050
1879	20,013	£600	£1500	£5000	£20,000
1880	3,650,080	£400	£440	£450	£900
1884	1,769,635	£400	£440	£450	£900
1885	717,723	£400	£440	£450	£900
M below bust on obverse (Melbourne Mint)					
1872	incl. above	£400	£500	£600	£900
1873	752,199	£400	£450	£490	£900
1874	incl. above	£400	£450	£490	£900
1875	incl. above	£400	£450	£490	£800
1876	2,124,445	£400	£450	£490	£900
1877	1,487,316	£400	£450	£490	£800
1878	2,171,457	£400	£450	£490	£800
1879	2,740,594	£400	£450	£490	£800
1880	incl. above	£400	£450	£490	£800
1881	incl. above	£400	£450	£490	£800
1882	incl. above	£400	£450	£490	£800
1883	incl. above	£400	£450	£490	£800
1884	incl. above	£400	£450	£490	£800
1885	incl. above	£400	£450	£490	£800
1886	incl. above	£400	£450	£490	£850
1887	incl. above	£400	£450	£490	£850
S below bust on obverse (Sydney Mint)					
1871	2,814,000	£400	£450	£490	£900
1872	incl. above	£400	£450	£490	£850
1873	incl. above	£400	£450	£490	£850
1874	1,899,000	£400	£450	£490	£850
1875	inc above	£400	£450	£490	£850
1876	1,613,000	£400	£450	£490	£900
1877	—				Unknown
1879	incl. above	£400	£450	£490	£900
1880	incl. above	£400	£450	£490	£900
1881	incl. above	£400	£450	£490	£900
1882	incl. above	£400	£450	£490	£850
1883	incl. above	£400	£450	£490	£850
1884	incl. above	£400	£450	£490	£850
1885	incl. above	£400	£450	£490	£850
1886	incl. above	£400	£450	£490	£850
1887	incl. above	£400	£450	£490	£850
JUBILEE HEAD ISSUES					
1887	1,111,280	£400	£450	£480	£2700
1887 Proof	797	—	—	—	£7000
1888	2,717,424	£400	£450	£480	£2500
1889	7,257,455	£400	£450	£480	£550
1890	6,529.887	£400	£450	£480	£900
1891	6,329,476	£400	£450	£480	£2000
1892	7,104,720	£400	£450	£480	£850
M on ground on reverse (Melbourne Mint)					
1887	940,000	£400	£450	£480	£1100
1888	2,830,612	£400	£450	£480	£550
1889	2,732,590	£400	£450	£480	£850
1890	2,473,537	£400	£450	£480	£850
1891	2,749,592	£400	£450	£480	£2,500
1892	3,488,750	£400	£450	£480	£850
1893	1,649,352	£400	£450	£480	£850

M below bust indicates Melbourne Mint

S below bust indicates Sydney Mint

Jubilee head type

"M" below the horse's hoof above the date indicates that the coin was struck at the Melbourne Mint

DATE	MINTAGE	F	VF	EF	UNC
S on ground on reverse (Sydney Mint)					
1887	1,002,000	£400	£450	£1600	£2900
1888	2,187,000	£400	£450	£480	£550
1889	3,262,000	£400	£450	£480	£550
1890	2,808,000	£400	£450	£480	£550
1891	2,596,000	£400	£450	£480	£550
1892	2,837,000	£400	£450	£480	£550
1893	1,498,000	£400	£450	£480	£550
OLD HEAD ISSUES					
1893	6,898,260	£400	£450	£480	£550
1893 Proof	773	—	—	—	£7000
1894	3,782,611	£400	£450	£480	£550
1895	2,285,317	£400	£450	£480	£550
1896	3,334,065	£400	£450	£480	£550
1898	4,361,347	£400	£450	£480	£550
1899	7,515,978	£400	£450	£480	£550
1900	10,846,741	£400	£450	£480	£550
1901	1,578,948	£400	£450	£480	£550
M on ground on reverse (Melbourne Mint)					
1893	1,914,000	£400	£450	£480	£550
1894	4,166,874	£400	£450	£480	£550
1895	4,165,869	£400	£450	£480	£550
1896	4,456,932	£400	£450	£480	£550
1897	5,130,565	£400	£450	£480	£550
1898	5,509,138	£400	£450	£480	£550
1899	5,579,157	£400	£450	£480	£550
1900	4,305,904	£400	£450	£480	£550
1901	3,987,701	£400	£450	£480	£550
P on ground on reverse (Perth Mint)					
1899	690,992	£400	£450	£525	£800
1900	1,886,089	£400	£450	£480	£525
1901	2,889,333	£400	£450	£480	£525
S on ground on reverse (Sydney Mint)					
1893	1,346,000	£400	£450	£480	£550
1894	3,067,000	£400	£450	£480	£550
1895	2,758,000	£400	£450	£480	£550
1896	2,544,000	£400	£450	£480	£600
1897	2,532,000	£400	£450	£480	£525
1898	2,548,000	£400	£450	£480	£525
1899	3,259,000	£400	£450	£480	£525
1900	3,586,000	£400	£450	£480	£525
1901	3,012,000	£400	£450	£480	£525

Old head type

EDWARD VII (1902–10)

DATE	MINTAGE	F	VF	EF	UNC
1902	4,737,796	£400	£450	£480	£500
1902 Matt proof	15,123	—	—	—	£1150
1903	8,888,627	£400	£450	£480	£500
1904	10,041,369	£400	£450	£480	£500
1905	5,910,403	£400	£450	£480	£500
1906	10,466,981	£400	£450	£480	£500
1907	18,458,663	£400	£450	£480	£500
1908	11,729,006	£400	£450	£480	£500
1909	12,157,099	£400	£450	£480	£500
1910	22,379,624	£400	£450	£480	£500
C on ground on reverse (Ottawa Mint)					
1908 Satin finish Proof only	633			Extremely rare	
1909	16,300	£400	£450	£500	£750
1910	28,020	£400	£450	£500	£700

DATE	MINTAGE	F	VF	EF	UNC
M on ground on reverse (Melbourne Mint)					
1902	4,267,157	£400	£450	£480	£525
1903	3,521,780	£400	£450	£480	£525
1904	3,743,897	£400	£450	£480	£525
1905	3,633,838	£400	£450	£480	£525
1906	3,657,853	£400	£450	£480	£525
1907	3,332,691	£400	£450	£480	£525
1908	3,080,148	£400	£450	£480	£525
1909	3,029,538	£400	£450	£480	£525
1910	3,054,547	£400	£450	£480	£525
P on ground on reverse (Perth Mint)					
1902	3,289,122	£400	£450	£480	£525
1903	4,674,783	£400	£450	£480	£525
1904	4,506,756	£400	£450	£480	£525
1905	4,876,193	£400	£450	£480	£525
1906	4,829,817	£400	£450	£480	£525
1907	4,972,289	£400	£450	£480	£525
1908	4,875,617	£400	£450	£480	£525
1909	4,524,241	£400	£450	£480	£525
1910	4,690,625	£400	£450	£480	£525
S on ground on reverse (Sydney Mint)					
1902	2,813,000	£400	£450	£480	£525
1902 Proof	incl. above			Extremely rare	
1903	2,806,000	£400	£450	£480	£525
1904	2,986,000	£400	£450	£480	£525
1905	2,778,000	£400	£450	£480	£525
1906	2,792,000	£400	£450	£480	£525
1907	2,539,000	£400	£450	£480	£525
1908	2,017,000	£400	£450	£480	£525
1909	2,057,000	£400	£450	£480	£525
1910	2,135,000	£400	£450	£480	£525

IMPORTANT NOTE: The prices quoted in this guide are set at August 2024 with the price of gold at £1,950 per ounce and silver £21.70 per ounce—market fluctuations can have a marked effect on the values of modern precious metal coins.

GEORGE V (1911–36)

(Extra care should be exercised when purchasing as good quality forgeries exist of virtually all dates and mintmarks)

DATE	MINTAGE	F	VF	EF	UNC
1911	30,044,105	£400	£450	£480	£475
1911 Proof	3,764	—	—	—	£3200
1912	30,317,921	£400	£450	£480	£475
1913	24,539,672	£400	£450	£480	£475
1914	11,501,117	£400	£450	£480	£475
1915	20,295,280	£400	£450	£480	£475
1916	1,554,120	£400	£450	£500	£650
1917	1,014,714	£1500	£5500	£20,000	£22,000
1925	4,406,431	£400	£450	£480	£475
C on ground on reverse (Ottawa Mint)					
1911	256,946	£400	£450	£500	£650
1913	3,715	£400	£500	£1750	£4000
1914	14,891	£400	£450	£1500	2000
1916	6,111			Extremely rare	
1917	58,845	£400	£450	£600	£645
1918	106,516	£400	£450	£500	£600
1919	135,889	£400	£450	£500	£600
I on ground on reverse (Bombay Mint)					
1918	1,295,372	£400	£450	£480	£525
M on ground on reverse (Melbourne Mint)					
1911	2,851,451	£400	£450	£480	£525
1912	2,469,257	£400	£450	£480	£525
1913	2,323,180	£400	£450	£480	£525
1914	2,012,029	£400	£450	£480	£525
1915	1,637,839	£400	£450	£480	£525
1916	1,273,643	£400	£450	£480	£525
1917	934,469	£400	£450	£500	£650
1918	4,969,493	£400	£450	£480	£525
1919	514,257	£400	£450	£480	£525

"I" on reverse ground for the Bombay Mint

DATE	MINTAGE	F	VF	EF	UNC
1920	530,266	£1350	£2000	£3000	£4000
1921	240,121	£4000	£7000	£8000	£24,000
1922	608,306	£4000	£7000	£8000	£25,000
1923	510,870	£400	£450	£500	£675
1924	278,140	£400	£450	£500	£675
1925	3,311,622	£400	£450	£480	£525
1926	211,107	£400	£450	£480	£525
1928	413,208	£400	£900	£1800	£3000
1929	436,719	£900	£1000	£1800	£3000
1930	77,547	£400	£450	£500	£650
1931	57,779	£400	£450	£650	£1000
P on ground on reverse (Perth Mint)					
1911	4,373,165	£400	£450	£480	£525
1912	4,278,144	£400	£450	£480	£525
1913	4,635,287	£400	£450	£480	£525
1914	4,815,996	£400	£450	£480	£525
1915	4,373,596	£400	£450	£480	£525
1916	4,096,771	£400	£450	£480	£525
1917	4,110,286	£400	£450	£480	£525
1918	3,812,884	£400	£450	£480	£525
1919	2,995,216	£400	£450	£480	£525
1920	2,421,196	£400	£450	£480	£525
1921	2,134,360	£400	£450	£480	£525
1922	2,298,884	£400	£450	£480	£525
1923	2,124,154	£400	£450	£480	£525
1924	1,464,416	£400	£450	£480	£525
1925	1,837,901	£400	£450	£500	£650
1926	1,313,578	£500	£850	£1500	£3000
1927	1,383,544	£400	£450	£500	£650
1928	1,333,417	£400	£450	£480	£600
1929	1,606,625	£400	£450	£480	£525
1930	1,915,352	£400	£450	£500	£650
1931	1,173,568	£400	£450	£480	£525
S on ground on reverse (Sydney Mint)					
1911	2,519,000	£400	£450	£480	£525
1912	2,227,000	£400	£450	£480	£525
1913	2,249,000	£400	£450	£480	£525
1914	1,774,000	£400	£450	£480	£525
1915	1,346,000	£400	£450	£480	£525
1916	1,242,000	£400	£450	£480	£525
1917	1,666,000	£400	£450	£480	£525
1918	3,716,000	£400	£450	£480	£525
1919	1,835,000	£400	£450	£480	£525
1920	—		Excessively rare		
1921	839,000	£600	£900	£1750	£3000

Melbourne Mint (M on ground)

Perth Mint (P on ground)

DATE	MINTAGE	F	VF	EF	UNC
1922	578,000			Extremely rare	
1923	416,000			Extremely rare	
1924	394,000	£600	£1100	£1500	£3250
1925	5,632,000	£400	£450	£480	£525
1926	1,031,050			Extremely rare	
1928		£425	£800	£1200	£2200
SA on ground on reverse (Pretoria Mint)					
1923	719	—	£15,000	—	—
1923 Proof	655			Extremely rare	
1924	3,184	—	£3000	£6000	£9000
1925	6,086,264	£400	£470	£495	£525
1926	11,107,611	£400	£470	£495	£525
1927	16,379,704	£400	£470	£495	£525
1928	18,235,057	£400	£470	£495	£525
1929	12,024,107	£400	£470	£495	£525
1930	10,027,756	£400	£470	£495	£525
1931	8,511,792	£400	£470	£495	£525
1932	1,066,680	£400	£470	£495	£525

Pretoria Mint (SA on ground)

GEORGE VI (1937–52)

DATE	MINTAGE	F	VF	EF	UNC
1937 Proof only	5,501	—	—	£3750	£5000

ELIZABETH II (1952–2022)

Pre Decimal Issues

DATE	MINTAGE	F	VF	EF	UNC
1957	2,072,000	£400	£420	£440	£525
1958	8,700,140	£400	£420	£440	£530
1959	1,358,228	£400	£420	£440	£525
1962	3,000,000	£400	£420	£440	£530
1963	7,400,000	£400	£420	£440	£530
1964	3,000,000	£400	£420	£440	£530
1965	3,800,000	£400	£420	£440	£530
1966	7,050,000	£400	£420	£440	£530
1967	5,000,000	£400	£420	£440	£530
1968	4,203,000	£400	£420	£440	£530

Later issues are included in the Decimal section.

HALF SOVEREIGNS

GEORGE III (1760–1820)

DATE	MINTAGE	F	VF	EF	UNC
1817	2,080,197	£250	£400	£1000	£2000
1818	1,030,286	£250	£475	£1000	£1800
1820	35,043	£250	£475	£1000	£1500

GEORGE IV (1820–30)

DATE	MINTAGE	F	VF	EF	UNC
1821 First bust, ornate shield reverse	231,288	£650	£1600	£3750	£5000
1821 — Proof	unrecorded	—	—	—	£9000
1823 First bust, Plain shield rev.	224,280	£250	£400	£1000	£2500
1824 —	591,538	£250	£400	£850	£2000
1825 —	761,150	£250	£400	£800	£2000
1826 Bare head, shield with full legend reverse	344,830	£250	£375	£1000	£2500
1826 — Proof	unrecorded	—	—	—	£8000
1827 —	492,014	£250	£375	£1000	£2500
1828 —	1,224,754	£250	£375	£900	£2000

DATE	MINTAGE	F	VF	EF	UNC

WILLIAM IV (1830–37)

DATE	MINTAGE	F	VF	EF	UNC
1831 Proof only	unrecorded	—	—	—	£7000
1834	133,899	£350	£800	£1500	£3000
1835	772,554	£350	£800	£1200	£2500
1836	146,865	£350	£700	£1400	£3000
1836 obverse from 6d die	incl. above	£2500	£5000	£10,000	£17,000
1837	160,207	£350	£650	£1800	£3000

VICTORIA (1837–1901)

YOUNG HEAD ISSUES

Shield reverse

DATE	MINTAGE	F	VF	EF	UNC
1838	273,341	£220	£300	£1100	£2000
1839 Proof only	1,230	—	—	—	£8000
1841	508,835	£250	£325	£1400	£2200
1842	2,223,352	£220	£325	£1000	£2000
1843	1,251,762	£220	£325	£1000	£2000
1844	1,127,007	£220	£275	£850	£1700
1845	887,526	£350	£800	£3000	£5000
1846	1,063,928	£200	£275	£850	£1700
1847	982,636	£200	£275	£750	£1600
1848	410,595	£200	£275	£850	£1700
1849	845,112	£200	£275	£750	£1600
1850	179,595	£240	£700	£3000	—
1851	773,573	£200	£275	£700	£1600
1852	1,377,671	£200	£275	£750	£1600
1853	2,708,796	£200	£275	£700	£1600
1853 Proof	unrecorded	—	—	—	£15,000
1855	1,120,362	£200	£275	£700	£1600
1856	2,391,909	£200	£275	£700	£1600
1857	728,223	£200	£275	£700	£1600
1858	855,578	£200	£275	£700	£1600
1859	2,203,813	£200	£275	£700	£1600
1860	1,131,500	£200	£275	£700	£1600
1861	1,130,867	£200	£275	£700	£1600
1862	unrecorded	£800	£2500	£10,000	£12,000
1863	1,571,574	£200	£250	£700	£1600
1863 with Die number	incl. above	£200	£250	£800	£1700
1864 —	1,758,490	£200	£250	£650	£1500
1865 —	1,834,750	£200	£250	£650	£1500
1866 —	2,058,776	£200	£250	£650	£1500
1867 —	992,795	£200	£250	£650	£1500
1869 —	1,861,764	£200	£250	£650	£1500
1870 —	1,159,544	£200	£250	£650	£1500
1871 —	2,062,970	£200	£250	£650	£1500
1872 —	3,248,627	£200	£250	£650	£1500
1873 —	1,927,050	£200	£250	£650	£1500
1874 —	1,884,432	£200	£250	£650	£1500
1875 —	516,240	£200	£250	£650	£1500
1876 —	2,785,187	£200	£250	£650	£1500
1877 —	2,197,482	£200	£250	£650	£1500
1878 —	2,081,941	£200	£250	£650	£1500
1879 —	35,201	£200	£250	£650	£1500
1880 —	1,009,049	£200	£250	£650	£1500
1880 no Die number	incl. above	£200	£250	£900	£1600
1883 —	2,870,457	£200	£250	£600	£1350
1884 —	1,113,756	£200	£250	£650	£1500
1885 —	4,468,871	£200	£250	£600	£1350

London Mint die number on reverse

M below shield (Melbourne Mint)

DATE	MINTAGE	F	VF	EF	UNC
1873	165,034	£200	£400	£5000	—
1877	80,016	£200	£400	£5000	—
1881	42,009	£200	£500	£7000	—
1882	107,522	£200	£500	£1600	—
1884	48,009	£200	£250	£1750	—
1885	11,003	£200	£600	£4000	—
1886	38,008	£200	£600	£7000	—
1887	64,013	£200	£750	£12,000	£20,000

Melbourne Mint (M below shield)

Date	Mintage	F	VF	EF	UNC
S below shield (Sydney Mint)					
1871	180,000 (?)	£200	£250	£750	£900
1872	356,000	£200	£250	£750	£900
1875	unrecorded	£200	£250	£750	£975
1879	94,000	£200	£250	£650	£775
1880	80,000	£200	£250	£850	–
1881	62,000	£200	£400	£1250	–
1882	52,000			Extremely rare	
1883	220,000	£200	£250	£900	–
1886	82,000	£200	£250	£600	–
1887	134,000	£200	£250	£800	£4500

JUBILEE HEAD ISSUES

Date	Mintage	F	VF	EF	UNC
1887	871,770	£200	£250	£500	£550
1887 Proof	797	£200	£250	–	£1900
1890	2.266,023	£200	£250	£500	£600
1891	1,079,286	£200	£250	£300	£500
1892	13,680,486	£200	£250	£300	£600
1893	4,426,625	£200	£250	£300	£400
M below shield (Melbourne Mint)					
1887	incl. above	£200	£250	£400	£500
1893	110,024	£200	£250	£450	£850
S below shield (Sydney Mint)					
1887	incl. above	£200	£250	£300	£400
1889	64,000	£200	£280	£1500	–
1891	154,000	£200	£250	£1000	–

OLD HEAD ISSUES

Date	Mintage	F	VF	EF	UNC
1893	incl. above	£200	£250	£300	£350
1893 Proof	773	–	–	–	£3000
1894	3,794,591	£200	£250	£300	£350
1895	2,869,183	£200	£250	£300	£350
1896	2,946,605	£200	£250	£300	£350
1897	3,568,156	£200	£250	£300	£350
1898	2,868,527	£200	£250	£300	£350
1899	3,361,881	£200	£250	£300	£350
1900	4,307,372	£200	£250	£300	£350
1901	2,037,664	£200	£250	£300	£350
M on ground on reverse (Melbourne Mint)					
1893	unrecorded			Extremely rare	
1896	218,946	£200	£250	£450	£500
1899	97,221	£200	£250	£550	£600
1900	112,920	£200	£250	£600	£650
P on ground on reverse (Perth Mint)					
1900	119,376	£200	£350	£600	£3000
S on ground on reverse (Sydney Mint)					
1893	250,000	£200	£250	£800	–
1897	unrecorded	£200	£250	£700	–
1900	260,00	£200	£250	£650	–

EDWARD VII (1902–10)

Date	Mintage	F	VF	EF	UNC
1902	4,244,457	£200	£250	£300	£320
1902 Matt proof	15,123		–	–	£750
1903	2,522,057	£200	£250	£300	£320
1904	1,717,440	£200	£250	£300	£320
1905	3,023,993	£200	£250	£300	£320
1906	4,245,437	£200	£250	£300	£320
1907	4,233,421	£200	£250	£350	£375
1908	3,996,992	£200	£250	£350	£400
1909	4,010,715	£200	£250	£350	£500
1910	5,023,881	£200	£250	£300	£350
M on ground on reverse (Melbourne Mint)					
1906	82,042	£200	£250	£750	£1000
1907	405,034	£200	£250	£300	£375
1908	incl. above	£200	£250	£300	£1750
1909	186,094	£200	£250	£600	£850

DATE		F	VF	EF	UNC
P on ground on reverse (Perth Mint)					
1904	60,030				Very Rare
1908	24,668	£200	£250	£950	£1250
1909	44,022	£200	£250	£500	£750
S on ground on reverse (Sydney Mint)					
1902	84,000	£200	£250	£300	£320
1902 Proof					Extremely rare
1903	231,000	£200	£250	£300	£400
1906	308,000	£200	£250	£300	£400
1908	538,000	£200	£250	£300	£320
1910	474,000	£200	£250	£300	£320

GEORGE V (1911–36)

DATE		F	VF	EF	UNC
1911	6,104,106	£200	£250	£300	£375
1911 Proof	3,764	—	—	—	£1750
1912	6,224,316	£200	£250	£300	£375
1913	6,094,290	£200	£250	£300	£375
1914	7,251,124	£200	£250	£300	£375
1915	2,042,747	£200	£250	£300	£375
M on ground on reverse (Melbourne Mint)					
1915	125,664	£200	£250	£300	£375
P on ground on reverse (Perth Mint)					
1911	130,373	£200	£250	£300	£400
1915	136,219	£200	£250	£300	£400
1918	unrecorded	£220	£600	£2000	£5000
1919	56,786				Rare
1920	53,208				Rare
S on ground on reverse (Sydney Mint)					
1911	252,000	£200	£250	£300	£375
1912	278,000	£200	£250	£300	£375
1914	322,000	£200	£250	£300	£375
1915	892,000	£200	£250	£300	£375
1916	448,000	£200	£250	£300	£375
SA on ground on reverse (Pretoria Mint)					
1923 Proof only	655	—	—	—	£2000
1925	946,615	£200	£250	£300	£375
1926	806,540	£200	£250	£300	£375

GEORGE VI (1937–52)

DATE		F	VF	EF	UNC
1937 Proof only	5,501	—	—	—	£1750

Later issues are included in the Decimal section.

BRITISH NUMISMATIC TRADE ASSOCIATION
BNTA

ANA
1891
MEMBER

CROWNS

DATE	F	VF	EF	UNC
OLIVER CROMWELL				
1658 8 over 7 (always)	£2200	£4700	£11,000	–
1658 Dutch Copy			Extremely rare	
1658 Patterns. In Various Metals			Extremely rare	
CHARLES II (1660–85)				
1662 First bust, rose (2 varieties)	£250	£1000	£9000	–
1662 — no rose (2 varieties)	£250	£1000	£9000	–
1663 —	£250	£1000	£9000	–
1664 Second bust	£220	£1000	£9500	–
1665 —	£2000	£5500	—	–
1666 —	£300	£1200	£10,000	–
1666 — error RE.X for REX			Extremely rare	
1666 — Elephant below bust	£1250	£4500	£20,000	–
1667 —	£200	£750	£7500	–
1668/7 — 8 over 7	£220	£750	—	–
1668 —	£220	£750	£7500	–
1669/8 — 9 over 8	£350	£800	—	–
1669 —	£350	£1300	£9000	–
1670/69 — 70 over 69	£250	£1500	—	–
1670 —	£220	£750	£8000	–
1671	£220	£900	£7000	–
1671 Third bust	£220	£850	£7000	–
1672 —	£220	£700	£7000	–
1673 —	£220	£700	£7000	–
1674 —			Extremely rare	
1675 —	£800	£3250	—	–
1675/3 —	£700	£3000	—	–
1676 —	£200	£750	£8000	–
1677 —	£200	£750	£7500	–
1677/6 — 7 over 6	£200	£1000	—	–
1678/7 —	£200	£900	—	–
1678/7 — 8 over 7	£275	£1000	—	–
1679 —	£200	£800	£7500	–
1679 Fourth bust	£200	£800	£6500	–
1680 Third bust	£200	£1000	£7500	–
1680/79 — 80 over 79	£250	£850	—	–
1680 Fourth bust	£220	£900	£7000	–
1680/79 — 80 over 79	£250	£1100	—	–
1681 —	£220	£900	£8000	–
1681 — Elephant & Castle below bust	£5500	£15000	—	–
1682/1 —	£260	£950	£8000	–
1682 — edge error QVRRTO for QVARTO	£300	—	—	–
1683 —	£400	£1200	£8000	–
1684 —	£400	£1300	—	–
JAMES II (1685–88)				
1686 First bust	£325	£1300	£8500	–
1686 — No stops on obv	£425	£1800	—	–
1687 Second bust	£300	£800	£7000	–
1688/7 — 8 over 7	£350	£950	—	–
1688 —	£280	£900	£7000	–
WILLIAM AND MARY (1688–94)				
1691	£850	£2200	£9000	–
1692	£850	£2400	£9000	–
1692 2 over upside down 2	£850	£2400	£9000	–

WILLIAM III (1694–1702)

DATE	F	VF	EF	UNC
1695 First bust	£110	£425	£3250	–
1696 —	£110	£340	£2800	–
1696 — no stops on obv.	£225	£500	–	–
1996 — no stops obv./rev.	£250	£550	–	–
1696 — GEI for DEI	£750	£1800	–	–
1696 — Last 6 over 5	£200	£550	–	–
1696 Second bust			Unique	
1696 Third bust	£120	£400	£3500	–
1697 —	£2800	£10,000	£45,000	–
1700 Third bust variety edge year DUODECIMO	£150	£550	£3500	–
1700 — edge year DUODECIMO TERTIO..	£150	£550	£3500	–

ANNE (1702–14)

DATE	F	VF	EF	UNC
1703 First bust, VIGO	£600	£1700	£12,000	–
1705 — Plumes in angles on rev.	£850	£2500	£14,000	–
1706 — Roses & Plumes in angles on rev...	£325	£900	£5000	–
1707 — —	£300	£800	£4500	–
1707 Second bust, E below	£250	£700	£4500	–
1707 — Plain	£250	£700	£5000	–
1708 — E below	£250	£700	£4500	–
1708/7 — 8 over 7	£250	£800	–	–
1708 — Plain	£250	£750	£4500	–
1708 — — error BR for BRI			Extremely rare	
1708 — Plumes in angles on rev.	£250	£800	£5000	–
1713 Third bust, Roses & Plumes in angles on rev.	£280	£800	£5500	–

GEORGE I (1714–27)

DATE	F	VF	EF	UNC
1716	£750	£1800	£7250	–
1718 8 over 6	£750	£1800	£7500	–
1720 20 over 18	£750	£1800	£7250	–
1723 SSC in angles on rev. (South Sea Co.)	£750	£1800	£7000	–
1726	£750	£2000	£8000	–

GEORGE II (1727–60)

DATE	F	VF	EF	UNC
1732 Young head, Plain, Proof	–	–	£27,500	
1732 — Roses & Plumes in angles on rev ..	£450	£1200	£5500	–
1734 — —	£450	£1200	£5500	–
1735 — —	£450	£1200	£5500	–
1736 — —	£425	£1200	£5500	–
1739 — Roses in angles on rev.	£400	£1000	£4700	–
1741 — —	£400	£1000	£4700	–
1743 Old head, Roses in angles on rev.	£400	£1000	£4000	–
1746 — — LIMA below bust	£400	£1100	£4250	–
1746 — Plain, Proof	–	–	£18,000	–
1750 — —	£550	£1400	£5500	–
1751 — —	£600	£1700	£6500	–

GEORGE III (1760–1820)

DATE	F	VF	EF	UNC
Dollar with oval counterstamp	£175	£650	£1000	–
Dollar with octagonal counterstamp	£225	£700	£1000	–
1804 Bank of England Dollar, Britannia rev.	£120	£275	£1000	–
1818 LVIII	£50	£130	£700	£2000
1818 LIX	£50	£130	£700	£2000
1819 LIX	£50	£130	£700	£2000
1819 LIX 9 over 8	£56	£175	£800	–
1819 LIX no stops on edge	£65	£170	£700	£2000
1819 LX	£55	£160	£700	£1900
1820 LX	£45	£150	£700	£1800
1820 LX 20 over 19	£55	£240	£750	–

DATE	MINTAGE	F	VF	EF	UNC
GEORGE IV (1820–30)					
1821 First bust, St George rev. SECUNDO on edge	437,976	£55	£210	£750	£2250
1821 — — Proof		—	—	—	£7000
1821 — — Proof TERTIO (error edge)		—	—	—	£10000
1822 — — SECUNDO	124,929	£60	£220	£900	£2350
1822 — — TERTIO	Incl above	£60	£220	£900	£2350
1823 — — Proof only				Extremely rare	
1826 Second bust, shield rev, SEPTIMO Proof only		—	—	—	£20,000
WILLIAM IV (1830–37)					UNC
1831 Proof only W.W. on truncation		—	—	—	£35,000
1831 Proof only W. WYON on truncation		—	—	—	£40,000
1834 Proof only		—	—	—	£60,000
VICTORIA (1837–1901)					
YOUNG HEAD ISSUES					
1839 Proof only	—	—	—	—	£30,000
1844 Star stops on edge	94,248	£80	£350	£1500	£4500
1844 Cinquefoil stops on edge	incl. above	£90	£350	£1600	£4250
1845 Star stops on edge	159,192	£80	£400	£1700	£4250
1845 Cinquefoil stops on edge	ncl. above	£80	£400	£1800	£4250
1847	140,976	£120	£425	£2000	£6500
GOTHIC HEAD ISSUES (Proof only)					
1847 mdcccxlvii UNDECIMO on edge	8,000	£1200	£2500	£5000	£15,000
1847 — Plain edge	—	—	—	—	£20,000
1853 mdcccliii SEPTIMO on edge	460	—	—	—	£32,000
1853 — Plain edge	—	—	—	—	Very rare
JUBILEE HEAD ISSUES					
1887	173,581	£30	£45	£90	£300
1887 Proof	1,084	—	—	—	£3250
1888 Narrow date	131,899	£28	£45	£110	£375
1888 Wide date	incl above	£40	£100	£450	—
1889	1,807,224	£25	£45	£100	£240
1890	997,862	£25	£45	£110	£400
1891	556,394	£25	£45	£110	£425
1892	451,334	£28	£50	£120	£450
OLD HEAD ISSUES (Regnal date on edge in Roman numerals)					
1893 LVI	497,845	£28	£60	£175	£500
1893 LVII	incl. above	£28	£60	£250	£600
1893 Proof	1,312	—	—	—	£3500
1894 LVII	144,906	£28	£60	£275	£650
1894 LVIII	incl. above	£28	£60	£275	£650
1895 LVIII	252,862	£28	£60	£250	£625
1895 LIX	incl. above	£28	£60	£250	£625
1896 LIX	317,599	£28	£60	£250	£625
1896 LX	incl. above	£28	£60	£250	£625
1897 LX	262,118	£28	£60	£250	£625
1897 LXI	incl. above	£28	£60	£250	£625
1898 LXI	166,150	£28	£60	£220	£850
1898 LXII	incl. above	£28	£60	£220	£625
1899 LXII	166,300	£28	£60	£220	£625
1899 LXIII	incl. above	£28	£60	£220	£625
1900 LXIII	353,356	£28	£60	£220	£625
1900 LXIV	incl. above	£28	£60	£220	£625

Victoria, Jubilee head

EDWARD VII (1901–10)

DATE	MINTAGE	F	VF	EF	UNC
1902	256,020	£90	£150	£260	£375
1902 "Matt Proof"	15,123	—	—	—	£400

GEORGE V (1910–36)

DATE	MINTAGE	F	VF	EF	UNC
1927 Proof only	15,030	—	£120	£225	£350
1928	9,034	£120	£200	£325	£550
1929	4,994	£120	£210	£350	£550
1930	4,847	£120	£200	£350	£575
1931	4,056	£120	£200	£350	£600
1932	2,395	£220	£500	£800	£1500
1933	7,132	£120	£200	£350	£600
1934	932	£800	£1600	£3500	£5500
1935 Jubilee issue. Incuse edge inscription	714,769	£15	£20	£30	£45
1935 — — error edge inscription	incl. above	—	—	—	£1500
1935 — Specimen in box	incl. above	—	—	—	£60
1935 — Proof. Raised edge inscription	2,500	—	—	—	£800
1935 — — fine lettering	incl. above	—	—	—	£1000
1935 — — error edge inscription	incl. above	—	—	—	Rare
1935 — Gold proof	30	—	—	Extremely rare	
1936	2,473	£250	£425	£725	£1100

GEORGE VI (1936–52)

DATE	MINTAGE	F	VF	EF	UNC
1937 Coronation	418,699	£18	£24	£35	£55
1937 Proof	26,402	—	—	—	£70
1951 Festival of Britain, Proof-like	1,983,540	—	£3	£6	£8

ELIZABETH II (1952–2022)

Pre-Decimal issues (Five Shillings)

DATE	MINTAGE	F	VF	EF	UNC
1953	5,962,621	—	—	£3	£6
1953 Proof	40,000	—	—	—	£25
1960	1,024,038	—	—	£3	£6
1960 Polished dies	70,000	—	—	—	£9
1965 Churchill	19,640,000	—	—	—	£1

Later issues are listed in the Decimal section.

DOUBLE FLORINS

VICTORIA (1837–1901)

DATE	MINTAGE	F	VF	EF	UNC
1887 Roman I	483,347	£20	£35	£60	£170
1887 Roman I Proof	incl. above	—	—	—	£1250
1887 Arabic 1	incl. above	£20	£35	£60	£170
1887 Arabic 1 Proof	incl. above	—	—	—	£1250
1888	243,340	£20	£50	£100	£250
1888 Second I in VICTORIA an inverted 1	incl. above	£30	£60	£110	£400
1889	1,185,111	£20	£35	£75	£190
1889 inverted 1	incl. above	£30	£60	£110	£450
1890	782,146	£20	£45	£80	£210

Patterns were also produced in 1911, 1914 and 1950 and are all extremely rare.

HALFCROWNS

OLIVER CROMWELL

DATE	MINTAGE	F	VF	EF	UNC
1656				Extremely rare	
1658		£2200	£3000	£6500	—
1658 Proof in Gold				Extremely rare	

CHARLES II (1660–85)

DATE	MINTAGE	F	VF	EF	UNC
1663 First bust		£200	£800	£6000	—
1663 — no stops on obv.		£220	£900	—	—
1664 Second bust		£300	£1200	£6500	—
1666 Third bust		£1000	—	—	—
1666 — Elephant		£950	£3750	—	—
1667/4 — 7 over 4				Extremely rare	
1668/4 — 8 over 4		£350	£1500	—	—
1669 —		£400	£1600	—	—
1669/4 — 9 over 4		£275	£1100	—	—
1670 —		£170	£600	£4000	—
1670 — MRG for MAG		£300	£1000	—	—
1671 —		£170	£700	£3600	—
1671/0 — 1 over 0		£170	£700	£4500	—
1672 — Third bust				Extremely rare	
1672 Fourth bust		£170	£600	£4000	—
1673 —		£170	£600	£4000	—
1673 — Plumes both sides				Extremely rare	
1673 — Plume below bust		£9000	£25,000	—	—
1674 —		£170	£750	—	—
1675 —		£170	£600	£4000	—
1676 —		£160	£650	£3800	—
1676 — inverted 1 in date		£160	£650	£4000	—
1677 —		£160	£600	£3500	—
1678 —		£270	£1100	—	—
1679 — GRATTA error				Extremely rare	
1679 —		£180	£600	£3500	—
1680 —		£200	£900	—	—
1681/0 — 1 over 0		£300	—	—	—
1681 —		£220	£850	£4500	—
1681 — Elephant & Castle		£3750	£13000	—	—
1682 —		£180	£600	£4500	—
1683 —		£180	£600	£4500	—
1683 — Plume below bust				Extremely rare	
1684/3 — 4 over 3		£400	£1350	£8000	—

JAMES II (1685–88)

DATE	MINTAGE	F	VF	EF	UNC
1685 First bust		£250	£700	£6000	—
1686 —		£250	£700	£5000	—
1686/5 — 6 over 5		£275	£850	—	—
1686 — V over S		£270	£850	—	—
1687 —		£250	£700	£5000	—
1687/6 — 7 over 6		£325	£850	—	—
1687 Second bust		£250	£650	£4500	—
1688 —		£250	£650	£4250	—

WILLIAM AND MARY (1688–94)

DATE	MINTAGE	F	VF	EF	UNC
1689 First busts; first shield		£140	£400	£2750	—
1689 — — no pearls in crown		£140	£400	£2750	—
1689 — — FRA for FR		£170	£600	£2800	—
1689 — — No stop on obv.		£140	£600	£2600	—
1689 — Second shield		£140	£550	£2400	—
1689 — — no pearls in crown		£150	£550	£2500	—
1690 — —		£180	£700	£3250	—
1690 — — error GRETIA for GRATIA		£600	£1600	£6000	—
1691 Second busts		£200	£650	£3000	—
1692 —		£200	£650	£3000	—

DATE	MINTAGE	F	VF	EF	UNC
1693 —		£180	£550	£3000	—
1693 — 3 over inverted 3		£220	£800	£3750	—

WILLIAM III (1694–1702)

DATE	MINTAGE	F	VF	EF	UNC
1696 First bust, large shields, early harp		£90	£300	£1700	—
1696 — — — B (Bristol) below bust		£90	£325	£1800	—
1696 — — — C (Chester)		£100	£450	£2000	—
1696 — — — E (Exeter)		£170	£600	£2400	—
1696 — — — N (Norwich)		£140	£600	£2400	—
1696 — — — y (York)		£110	£425	£2750	—
1696 — — — — Scottish arms at date				Extremely rare	
1696 — — ordinary harp		£110	£400	£2500	—
1696 — — — C		£125	£600	£2500	
1696 — — — E		£130	£600	£2500	—
1696 — — — N		£200	£750	£3500	—
1696 — Small shields, ordinary harp		£90	£300	£1800	—
1696 — — — B		£110	£400	£2000	—
1696 — — — C		£110	£400	£2200	—
1696 — — — E		£140	£800	£3000	—
1696 — — — N		£130	£700	£2650	—
1696 — — — y		£110	£700	£2500	—
1696 Second bust				Only one known	
1697 First bust, large shields, ordinary harp		£90	£325	£1700	—
1697 — — — GRR for GRA				Extremely rare	
1697 — — — B		£140	£450	£2200	—
1697 — — — C		£140	£450	£2400	
1697 — — — E		£140	£450	£2400	—
1697 — — — N		£125	£450	£2500	—
1697 — — — y		£110	£425	£2400	—
1698 — —		£110	£400	£2000	—
1698/7 — — 8 over 7				Extremely rare	
1699 — —		£170	£600	£4000	—
1699 — — Scottish arms at date				Extremely rare	
1700 — —		£180	£500	£2750	—
1701 — —		£180	£600	£3000	—
1701 — — No stops on rev		£180	£700	—	—
1701 — — Elephant & Castle below		Fair £3250			
1701 — — Plumes in angles on rev.		£325	£1100	£5500	—

ANNE (1702–14)

DATE	MINTAGE	F	VF	EF	UNC
1703 Plain (pre-Union)		£750	£2500	—	—
1703 VIGO below bust		£160	£550	£3000	—
1704 Plumes in angles on rev.		£220	£800	£3250	—
1705 —		£220	£900	£3250	—
1706 Roses & Plumes in angles on rev.		£160	£600	£2400	—
1707 —		£120	£350	£1900	—
1707 Plain (post-Union)		£120	£325	£1700	—
1707 E below bust		£120	£325	£1700	—
1707 — SEPTIMO edge				Extremely rare	
1708 Plain		£130	£350	£1800	—
1708 E below bust		£135	£350	£1950	—
1708 Plumes in angles on rev.		£160	£450	£2300	—
1709 Plain		£120	£400	£1600	—
1709 E below bust		£300	£1250	—	—
1710 Roses & Plumes in angles on rev.		£120	£400	£2000	—
1712 —		£120	£400	£1900	—
1713 Plain		£120	£400	£2000	—
1713 Roses & Plumes in angles on rev.		£120	£400	£1850	—
1714 —		£120	£400	£1850	—
1714/3 4 over 3		£150	£500	—	—

GEORGE I (1714–27)

DATE	MINTAGE	F	VF	EF	UNC
1715 Roses & Plumes in angles on rev.		£500	£1000	£4500	—
1715 Plain edge				Extremely rare	
1717 —		£500	£1300	£4500	—
1720 —		£500	£1200	£4500	—
1720/17 20 over 17		£475	£1200	£4200	—
1723 SSC in angles on rev.		£475	£1200	£4250	—
1726 Small Roses & Plumes in angles on rev.		£5000	£15,000	—	—

GEORGE II (1727–60)

DATE	MINTAGE	F	VF	EF	UNC
1731 Young head, Plain, proof only		—	—	£15000	—
1731 — Roses & Plumes in angles on rev.		£180	£500	£2750	—
1732 — —		£180	£500	£2750	—
1734 — —		£180	£500	£2750	—
1735 — —		£180	£500	£2750	—
1736 — —		£180	£500	£2750	—
1739 — Roses in angles on rev.		£170	£500	£2400	—
1741/39 — — 41 over 30		£170	£600	—	—
1741 — —		£170	£500	£2250	—
1743 Old head, Roses in angles on rev.		£150	£300	£1600	—
1745 — —		£125	£350	£1600	—
1745 — LIMA below bust		£90	£275	£900	—
1746 — —		£90	£275	£900	—
1746/5 — — 6 over 5		£100	£350	£1000	—
1746 — Plain, Proof		—	—	£6500	—
1750 — —		£225	£600	£3200	—
1751 — —		£250	£750	£3500	—

GEORGE III (1760–1820)

DATE	MINTAGE	F	VF	EF	UNC
1816 "Bull head"	—	£30	£90	£350	£700
1817 —	8,092,656	£30	£90	£350	£700
1817 "Small head"	incl. above	£30	£90	£350	£700
1818 * —	2,905,056	£30	£90	£350	£700
1819/8 — 9 over 8	incl. above			Extremely rare	
1819 —	4,790,016	£30	£90	£300	£650
1820 —	2,396,592	£60	£160	£550	£1100

** Beware of recent copies.*

GEORGE IV (1820–30)

DATE	MINTAGE	F	VF	EF	UNC
1820 First bust, first reverse	incl. above	£30	£85	£400	£850
1821 — —	1,435,104	£30	£85	£400	£850
1821 — — Proof	incl. above	—	—	—	£4500
1823 — —	2,003,760	£1300	£4500	—	—
1823 — Second reverse	incl. above	£30	£90	£375	£900
1824 — —	465,696	£40	£100	£350	£950
1824 Second bust, third reverse	incl. above			Extremely rare	
1825 — —	2,258,784	£30	£90	£300	£800
1826 — —	2,189,088	£30	£90	£300	£800
1826 — — Proof	incl. above	—	—	—	£2500
1828 — —	49,890	£110	£300	£1100	£3000
1829 — —	508,464	£80	£180	£650	£1200

WILLIAM IV (1830–37)

DATE	MINTAGE	F	VF	EF	UNC
1831 Plain edge	—			Extremely rare	
1831 Proof (W.W. in script & block)	—	—	—	—	£4000
1834 W.W. in block	993,168	£35	£90	£425	£1500
1834 W.W. in script	incl. above	£35	£85	£400	£1500
1835	281,952	£45	£110	£450	£1250
1836	1,588,752	£35	£80	£375	£1200
1836/5 6 over 5	incl. above	£60	£125	£650	—
1837	150,526	£55	£200	£800	£1850

VICTORIA (1837–1901)

YOUNG HEAD ISSUES

DATE	MINTAGE	F	VF	EF	UNC
1839 (two varieties)	—	£1300	£4250	£11000	—
1839 Proof	—	—	—	—	£7500
1840	386,496	£60	£220	£1100	£3000
1841	42,768	£1000	£2000	£5000	£10000
1842	486,288	£60	£170	£800	£2000
1843	454,608	£170	£500	£2000	£4500
1844	1,900,000	£60	£175	£600	£2000
1845	2,231,856	£60	£175	£600	£2000
1846	1,539,668	£70	£180	£600	£2200
1848 Plain 8	367,488	£200	£600	£1800	£6000
1848/6	incl. above	£175	£600	£1500	£4500
1849	261,360	£80	£200	£750	£2800

DATE	MINTAGE	F	VF	EF	UNC
1849 Small date	incl. above	£100	£300	£1200	£3500
1850	484,613	£75	£300	£1000	£3000
1853 Proof only	—	—	—	—	£8000
1874	2,188,599	£25	£70	£350	£800
1875	1,113,483	£25	£70	£350	£750
1876	633,221	£40	£100	£400	£1000
1876/5 6 over 5	incl. above	£35	£80	£280	£900
1876/6 6 over 6	incl. above	£75	£150	£450	—
1877	447,059	£25	£70	£300	£800
1878	1,466,323	£25	£70	£300	£800
1879	901,356	£40	£100	£350	£1000
1880	1,346,350	£25	£70	£250	£700
1881	2,301,495	£25	£70	£250	£675
1882	808,227	£30	£80	£300	£800
1883	2,982,779	£25	£70	£250	£600
1884	1,569,175	£25	£70	£250	£600
1885	1,628,438	£25	£70	£250	£600
1886	891,767	£25	£70	£250	£600
1887	1,438,046	£25	£70	£275	£650
JUBILEE HEAD ISSUES					
1887	incl. above	£12	£18	£35	£90
1887 Proof	1,084	—	—	—	£750
1888	1,428,787	£15	£30	£70	£300
1889	4,811,954	£12	£25	£60	£200
1890	3,228,111	£14	£30	£90	£280
1891	2,284,632	£14	£30	£90	£300
1892	1,710,946	£14	£30	£90	£325
OLD HEAD ISSUES					
1893	1,792,600	£12	£25	£70	£175
1893 Proof	1,312	—	—	—	£1300
1894	1,524,960	£20	£45	£125	£350
1895	1,772,662	£15	£40	£100	£325
1896	2,148,505	£12	£30	£90	£300
1897	1,678,643	£12	£30	£90	£300
1898	1,870,055	£12	£30	£90	£300
1899	2,865,872	£12	£30	£90	£300
1900	4,479,128	£12	£30	£90	£300
1901	1,516,570	£12	£30	£90	£300

Victoria, Young head type

DATE	MINTAGE	F	VF	EF	UNC
EDWARD VII (1901–10)					
1902	1,316,008	£14	£32	£90	£200
1902 "Matt Proof"	15,123	—	—	—	£300
1903	274,840	£175	£550	£2200	£5000
1904	709,652	£60	£225	£500	£1500
1905	166,008	£550	£1500	£5000	£10000
1906	2,886,206	£14	£50	£225	£900
1907	3,693,930	£14	£50	£225	£900
1908	1,758,889	£22	£90	£450	£1500
1909	3,051,592	£14	£60	£350	£900
1910	2,557,685	£14	£45	£150	£500
GEORGE V (1910–36)					
First issue					
1911	2,914,573	£15	£35	£90	£300
1911 Proof	6,007	—	—	—	£425
1912	4,700,789	£12	£25	£60	£250
1913	4,090,169	£12	£28	£80	£275
1914	18,333,003	£8	£14	£40	£75
1915	32,433,066	£8	£14	£40	£75
1916	29,530,020	£8	£14	£40	£75
1917	11,172,052	£10	£16	£50	£120
1918	29,079,592	£8	£14	£40	£70
1919	10,266,737	£8	£15	£50	£110
Second issue—debased silver					
1920	17,982,077	£5	£9	£25	£80
1921	23,677,889	£5	£9	£30	£65
1922	16,396,724	£5	£10	£25	£70
1923	26,308,526	£6	£9	£20	£50
1924	5,866,294	£15	£35	£100	£275
1925	1,413,461	£30	£75	£300	£1000
1926	4,473,516	£12	£30	£70	£240
Third issue —Modified effigy					
1926	incl. above	£6	£14	£40	£125
1927	6,837,872	£6	£12	£35	£85
Fourth issue—New shield reverse					
1927 Proof	15,000	—	—	—	£100
1928	18,762,727	£5	£8	£22	£40
1929	17,632,636	£5	£8	£22	£40
1930	809,051	£18	£60	£325	£900
1931	11,264,468	£5	£8	£20	£40
1932	4,793,643	£6	£12	£30	£95
1933	10,311,494	£5	£8	£20	£45
1934	2,422,399	£10	£20	£75	£250
1935	7,022,216	£5	£8	£18	£30
1936	7,039,423	£5	£8	£18	£25
GEORGE VI (1936–52)					
1937	9,106,440	—	£6	£9	£15
1937 Proof	26,402	—	—	—	£25
1938	6,426,478	£5	£6	£15	£30
1939	15,478,635	£5	£6	£9	£12
1940	17,948,439	£5	£6	£9	£12
1941	15,773,984	£5	£6	£9	£12
1942	31,220,090	£5	£6	£9	£10
1943	15,462,875	£5	£6	£9	£10
1944	15,255,165	£5	£6	£9	£10
1945	19,849,242	£5	£6	£9	£10
1946	22,724,873	£5	£6	£9	£10
Cupro-nickel					
1947	21,911,484	—	£1	£2	£4
1948	71,164,703	—	£1	£2	£4
1949	28,272,512	—	£1	£2	£6
1950	28,335,500	—	£1	£2	£6
1950 Proof	17,513	—	—	—	£35
1951	9,003,520	—	£1	£2	£6
1951 Proof	20,000	—	—	—	£10
1952	Unknown		Only one known		

George V, fourth issue, new shield reverse

DATE	MINTAGE	F	VF	EF	UNC

ELIZABETH II (1952–2022)

DATE	MINTAGE	F	VF	EF	UNC
1953	4,333,214	—	—	£1	£3
1953 Proof	40,000	—	—	—	£10
1954	11,614,953	—	£1	£8	£45
1955	23,628,726	—	—	£1	£6
1956	33,934,909	—	—	£1	£6
1957	34,200,563	—	—	£1	£6
1958	15,745,668	—	£1	£6	£40
1959	9,028,844	—	£1	£9	£35
1960	19,929,191	—	—	£1	£3
1961	25,887,897	—	—	—	£2
1961 Polished dies	incl. above	—	—	£1	£2
1962	24,013,312	—	—	—	£1
1963	17,625,200	—	—	—	£1
1964	5,973,600	—	—	—	£2
1965	9,778,440	—	—	—	£1
1966	13,375,200	—	—	—	£1
1967	33,058,400	—	—	—	£1
1970 Proof	—	—	—	—	£8

FLORINS

VICTORIA (1837–1901)

YOUNG (CROWNED) HEAD ISSUES

"Godless" type (without D.G.—"Dei Gratia")

DATE	MINTAGE	F	VF	EF	UNC
1848 "Godless" Pattern only plain edge	—			Very rare	
1848 "Godless" Pattern only milled edge	—			Extremely rare	
1849	413,820	£33	£80	£300	£600

(Beware of recent forgeries)

"Gothic" type, i.e. date in Roman numerals in obverse legend

"brit." in legend. No die no.

DATE	MINTAGE	F	VF	EF	UNC
1851 mdcccli Proof	1,540			Extremely rare	
1852 mdccclii	1,014,552	£35	£75	£300	£750
1853 mdcccliii	3,919,950	£35	£75	£320	£775
1853 — Proof	incl. above	—	—	—	£7000
1854 mdcccliv	550,413	£1200	£4000	—	—
1855 mdccclv	831,017	£35	£80	£350	£850
1856 mdccclvi	2,201,760	£35	£80	£350	£850
1857 mdccclvii	1,671,120	£35	£80	£350	£900
1858 mdccclviii	2,239,380	£35	£80	£350	£875
1859 mdccclix	2,568,060	£35	£80	£350	£800
1860 mdccclx	1,475,100	£40	£100	£350	£1000
1862 mdccclxii	594,000	£300	£800	£2000	£5500
1862 plain edge Proof				Very rare	
1863 mdccclxiii	938,520	£1300	£3000	£7500	£17500
1863 plain edge Proof				Very rare	

"brit" in legend. Die no. below bust

DATE	MINTAGE	F	VF	EF	UNC
1864 mdccclxiv	1,861,200	£35	£75	£350	£850
1864 Gothic Piedfort flan	incl. above			Extremely rare	
1865 mdccclxv	1,580,044	£45	£110	£500	£850
1866 mdccclxvi	914,760	£40	£100	£400	£750
1867 mdccclxvii	423,720	£55	£170	£550	£1350
1867—only 42 arcs in border	incl. above			Extremely rare	

"britt" in legend. Die no. below bust

DATE	MINTAGE	F	VF	EF	UNC
1868 mdccclxviii	896,940	£35	£90	£400	£900
1869 mdccclxix	297,000	£45	£110	£500	£1100
1870 mdccclxx	1,080,648	£35	£90	£350	£800
1871 mdccclxxi	3,425,605	£35	£90	£350	£800
1872 mdccclxxii	7,199,690	£35	£80	£300	£700
1873 mdccclxxiii	5,921,839	£35	£80	£300	£675
1874 mdccclxxiv	1,642,630	£35	£80	£300	£700
1874 — iv over iii in date	incl. above	£40	£90	£400	£850
1875 mdccclxxv	1,117,030	£40	£90	£300	£800
1876 mdccclxxvi	580,034	£60	£140	£600	£1300
1877 mdccclxxvii	682,292	£35	£80	£325	£700
1877 — 48 arcs in border no W.W.	incl. above	£35	£80	£325	£700

"Godless" florin

"Gothic" florin

DATE	MINTAGE	F	VF	EF	UNC
1877 — 42 arcs	incl. above	£35	£85	£325	£750
1877 — — no die number	incl. above			Extremely rare	
1878 mdccclxxviii with die number	1,786,680	£35	£85	£325	£750
1879 mdccixxix no die no	1,512,247			Extremely rare	
1879 — 48 arcs in border	incl. above	£35	£70	£325	£800
1879 — no die number	incl. above			Extremely rare	
1879 — 38 arcs, no W.W..	incl. above	£35	£70	£325	£800
1880 mdccclxxx Younger portrait	—			Extremely rare	
1880 — 34 arcs, Older portrait	2,167,170	£35	£70	£325	£700
1881 mdccclxxxi — —	2,570,337	£30	£70	£325	£700
1881 — xxΓi broken puncheon	incl. above	£35	£80	£300	£750
1883 mdccclxxxiii — —	3,555,667	£30	£75	£300	£675
1884 mdccclxxxiv — —	1,447,379	£30	£75	£300	£700
1885 mdccclxxxv — —	1,758,210	£30	£75	£300	£700
1886 mdccclxxxvi — —	591,773	£30	£75	£300	£700
1887 mdccclxxxvii — —	1,776,903	£50	£130	£350	£850
1887 — 46 arcs	incl. above	£50	£130	£375	£1000

JUBILEE HEAD ISSUES

DATE	MINTAGE	F	VF	EF	UNC
1887	incl. above	£8	£16	£35	£80
1887 Proof	1,084	—	—	—	£600
1888	1,547,540	£8	£20	£50	£160
1889	2,973,561	£9	£20	£50	£180
1890	1,684,737	£12	£32	£150	£400
1891	836,438	£25	£80	£350	£650
1892	283,401	£40	£150	£450	£1000

VICTORIA—OLD HEAD ISSUES

DATE	MINTAGE	F	VF	EF	UNC
1893	1,666,103	£10	£20	£60	£150
1893 Proof	1,312	—	—	—	£800
1894	1,952,842	£15	£30	£110	£320
1895	2,182,968	£12	£35	£100	£320
1896	2,944,416	£10	£30	£90	£250
1897	1,699,921	£10	£30	£90	£240
1898	3,061,343	£10	£30	£90	£250
1899	3,966,953	£10	£30	£90	£250
1900	5,528,630	£10	£30	£80	£220
1901	2,648,870	£10	£30	£80	£220

EDWARD VII (1901–10)

DATE	MINTAGE	F	VF	EF	UNC
1902	2,189,575	£10	£30	£75	£150
1902 "Matt Proof"	15,123	—	—	—	£250
1903	1,995,298	£12	£35	£170	£600
1904	2,769,932	£15	£45	£180	£550
1905	1,187,596	£65	£250	£750	£2000
1906	6,910,128	£14	£40	£150	£600
1907	5,947,895	£14	£40	£150	£600
1908	3,280,010	£20	£60	£350	£900
1909	3,482,829	£15	£50	£270	£700
1910	5,650,713	£15	£40	£150	£375

GEORGE V (1910–36)

First issue

DATE	MINTAGE	F	VF	EF	UNC
1911	5,951,284	£7	£12	£50	£140
1911 Proof	6,007	—	—	—	£275
1912	8,571,731	£8	£18	£50	£180
1913	4,545,278	£12	£30	£70	£225
1914	21,252,701	£7	£18	£30	£90
1915	12,367,939	£7	£18	£30	£90
1916	21,064,337	£7	£18	£30	£90
1917	11,181,617	£7	£22	£40	£110
1918	29,211,792	£7	£18	£30	£100
1919	9,469,292	£10	£22	£50	£150

***Second issue** —debased silver*

DATE	MINTAGE	F	VF	EF	UNC
1920	15,387,833	£4	£12	£40	£95
1921	34,863,895	£4	£12	£40	£75
1922	23,861,044	£4	£12	£40	£75
1923	21,546,533	£4	£10	£30	£70
1924	4,582,372	£12	£35	£100	£300
1925	1,404,136	£30	£75	£300	£1000
1926	5,125,410	£12	£30	£70	£225

George V first type

DATE	MINTAGE	F	VF	EF	UNC
***Fourth issue**—new reverse*					
1927 Proof only	101,497	—	—	—	£150
1928	11,087,186	£4	£8	£20	£50
1929	16,397,279	£4	£8	£20	£45
1930	5,753,568	£4	£8	£25	£65
1931	6,556,331	£4	£8	£25	£45
1932	717,041	£15	£50	£350	£900
1933	8,685,303	£4	£8	£20	£45
1935	7,540,546	£4	£8	£15	£40
1936	9,897,448	£4	£8	£15	£40

George V new reverse

GEORGE VI (1936–52)

DATE	MINTAGE	F	VF	EF	UNC
1937	13,006,781	£4	£5	£8	£16
1937 Proof	26,402	—	—	—	£35
1938	7,909,388	£6	£8	£18	£45
1939	20,850,607	£4	£5	£10	£15
1940	18,700,338	£4	£5	£8	£18
1941	24,451,079	£4	£5	£8	£15
1942	39,895,243	£4	£5	£8	£15
1943	26,711,987	£4	£5	£8	£15
1944	27,560,005	£4	£5	£8	£15
1945	25,858,049	£4	£5	£8	£15
1946	22,300,254	£4	£5	£8	£15
Cupro-nickel					
1947	22,910,085	—	—	£1	£3
1948	67,553,636	—	—	£1	£3
1949	28,614,939	—	—	£1	£5
1950	24,357,490	—	—	£2	£7
1950 Proof	17,513	—	—	£1	£9
1951	27,411,747	—	—	£2	£8
1951 Proof	20,000	—	—	—	£9

ELIZABETH II (1952–2022)

DATE	MINTAGE	F	VF	EF	UNC
1953	11,958,710	—	—	—	£3
1953 Proof	40,000	—	—	—	£10
1954	13,085,422	—	—	£8	£50
1955	25,887,253	—	—	£1	£5
1956	47,824,500	—	—	£1	£5
1957	33,071,282	—	—	£4	£30
1958	9,564,580	—	—	£4	£50
1959	14,080,319	—	—	£4	£40
1960	13,831,782	—	—	£1	£5
1961	37,735,315	—	—	£1	£2
1962	35,147,903	—	—	£1	£2
1963	26,471,000	—	—	£1	£2
1964	16,539,000	—	—	£1	£2
1965	48,163,000	—	—	—	£2
1966	83,999,000	—	—	—	£2
1967	39,718,000	—	—	—	£2
1970 Proof	—	—	—	—	£8

SHILLINGS

OLIVER CROMWELL

DATE	F	VF	EF	UNC
1658	£1100	£2250	£5500	—
1658 Dutch Copy			Extremely rare	

CHARLES II (1660–85)

DATE	F	VF	EF	UNC
1663 First bust	£140	£600	£1800	—
1663 — GARTIA error			Extremely rare	
1663 — Irish & Scottish shields transposed	£300	£800	—	—
1666 — Elephant below bust	£900	£3500	£8500	—
1666 "Guinea" head, elephant	£3000	£9000	—	—
1666 First bust variety	£700	£2750	—	—
1666 Second bust			Extremely rare	
1668 —	£140	£450	£2500	—
1668/7 — 8 over 7	£175	£650	—	—

Charles II

DATE	F	VF	EF	UNC
1669/6 First bust variety			Extremely rare	
1669			Extremely rare	
1669 Second bust			Extremely rare	
1670 —	£175	£650	£2750	—
1671 —	£200	£700	£3000	—
1671 — Plume below, plume in centre rev.	£800	£2500	£6500	—
1672 —	£200	£750	£3000	—
1673 —	£200	£750	£3000	—
1673 — Plume below, plume in centre rev.	£900	£3000	£7500	—
1673/2 — 3 over 2	£200	£800	—	—
1674/3 — 4 over 3	£250	£800	—	—
1674 —	£260	£800	£3200	—
1674 — Plume below bust, plume in centre rev.	£800	£2750	£7000	—
1674 — Plume rev. only	£2000	£6000	£12000	—
1674 Third bust	£900	£3250	—	—
1675 Second bust	£250	£900	—	—
1675/4 — 5 over 4	£240	£850	—	—
1675 — Plume below bust, plume in centre rev.	£900	£3000	£8000	—
1675 Third bust	£500	£2250	—	—
1676 Second bust	£180	£750	£2750	—
1676/5 — 6 over 5	£200	£750	—	—
1676 — Plume below bust, plume in centre rev.	£900	£3000	£8000	—
1677 —	£180	£650	£2750	—
1677 — Plume below bust	£2500	£7500	£18,000	—
1678 —	£200	£750	£3250	—
1678/7 — 8 over 7	£225	£850	—	—
1679 —	£175	£750	£3200	—
1679 — Plume below bust, plume in centre rev.	£850	£3000	£8500	—
1679 — Plume below bust	£2000	£6000	£10000	—
1679 — 9 over 7	£220	£800	—	—
1680 —			Extremely rare	
1680/79 — Plume below bust, plume in centre rev.	£1500	£5500	£10500	—
1681 —	£500	£1600	£6000	—
1681 — 1 over 0	£550	£1500	£4000	—
1681/0 Elephant & Castle below bust	£6000	£16000	—	—
1682/1 — 2 over 1	£1200	£3750	—	—
1683 —			Extremely rare	
1683 Fourth (Larger) bust	£275	£1000	£4000	—
1684 —	£275	£1000	£4000	—

James II

JAMES II (1685–88)

DATE	F	VF	EF	UNC
1685	£225	£650	£3250	—
1685 Plume in centre rev. rev			Extremely rare	
1685 No stops on rev.	£280	£800	—	—
1686	£250	£700	£3250	—
1686/5 6 over 5	£275	£750	£3500	—
1687	£275	£750	£3800	—
1687/6 7 over 6	£270	£700	£3250	—
1688	£280	£750	£3400	—
1688/7 last 8 over 7	£275	£750	£3500	—

William & Mary

WILLIAM & MARY (1688–94)

DATE	F	VF	EF	UNC
1692	£225	£650	£3200	—
1692 inverted 1	£225	£675	£3250	—
1693	£225	£700	£3250	—
1690 9 over 0	£275	£700	£3000	—

WILLIAM III (1694–1702)

Provincially produced shillings carry privy marks or initials below the bust: B: Bristol. C: Chester. E: Exeter. N: Norwich. Y or y: York.

DATE	F	VF	EF	UNC
1695 First bust	£45	£120	£750	—
1696 —	£45	£120	£650	—
1696 — no stops on rev.	£70	£160	£900	—
1696 — MAB for MAG			Extremely rare	
1696 — 1669 error			Extremely rare	
1696 — 1669 various GVLELMVS errors			Extremely rare	
1696 — B below bust	£75	£225	£1200	—
1696 — C	£90	£225	£1200	—
1696 — E	£95	£240	£1300	—

DATE	F	VF	EF	UNC
1696 — N	£100	£300	£1350	—
1696 — y	£90	£250	£1300	—
1696 — Y	£80	£250	£1300	—
1696 Second bust			Only one known	
1696 Third bust C below	£175	£550	£1900	—
1696 — Y			Extremely rare	
1697 First bust	£55	£140	£600	—
1697 — GRI for GRA error			Extremely rare	
1697 — Scottish & Irish shields transposed			Extremely rare	
1697 — Irish arms at date			Extremely rare	
1697 — no stops on rev	£80	£240	£1100	—
1697 — GVLELMVS error			Extremely rare	
1697 — B	£90	£220	£1200	—
1697 — C	£80	£220	£1200	—
1697 — E	£100	£250	£1350	—
1697 — N	£85	£250	£1350	—
1697 — — no stops on obv.			Extremely rare	
1697 — y	£80	£225	£1200	—
1697 — — arms of France & Ireland transposed			Extremely rare	
1697 — Y	£90	£225	£1100	—
1697 Third bust	£50	£130	£700	—
1697 — B	£100	£225	£1200	—
1697 — C	£110	£220	£1200	—
1697 — — Fr.a error	£150	£500	—	—
1697 — — no stops on obv.	£100	£350	—	—
1697 — — arms of Scotland at date			Extremely rare	
1697 — E	£110	£275	£1300	—
1697 — N	£100	£250	£1350	—
1697 — y	£100	£300	£1400	—
1697 Third bust variety	£70	£170	£750	—
1697 — B	£100	£300	£1500	—
1697 — C	£150	£900	—	—
1698 —	£110	£325	£1500	—
1698 — Plumes in angles of rev.	£275	£750	£3000	—
1698 Fourth bust "Flaming hair"	£225	£750	£3000	—
1698 Plain Edge Proof			Extremely rare	
1699 —	£200	£625	£2700	—
1699 Fifth bust	£130	£400	£1600	—
1699 — Plumes in angles on rev.	£275	£900	£2750	—
1699 — Roses in angles on rev.	£250	£900	£2800	—
1700 —	£70	£150	£700	—
1700 — Small round oo in date	£70	£150	£700	—
1700 — no stop after DEI	£60	£160	£700	—
1700 — Plume below bust	£4000	£12500	—	—
1701 — Plumes in angles on rev.	£200	£750	£2500	—

William III First bust

William III Fifth bust

ANNE (1702–14)

DATE	F	VF	EF	UNC
1702 First bust (pre-Union with Scotland)	£125	£350	£1600	—
1702 — Plumes in angles on rev.	£125	£400	£1800	—
1702 — VIGO below bust	£120	£350	£1650	—
1702 — — colon before ANNA			Extremely rare	
1703 Second bust, VIGO below	£110	£350	£1400	—
1704 — Plain	£600	£2000	—	—
1704 — Plumes in angles on rev.	£150	£500	£2000	—
1705 — Plain	£230	£750	£2500	—
1705 — Plumes in angles on rev.	£120	£500	£1600	—
1705 — Roses & Plumes in angles on rev.	£120	£400	£1600	—
1707 — —	£130	£400	£1800	—
1707 Second bust (post-Union) E below bust	£100	£400	£1450	—
1707 — E* below bust	£100	£400	£1450	—
1707 Third bust, Plain	£45	£130	£800	—
1707 — Plumes in angles on rev.	£60	£200	£1000	—
1707 — E below bust	£50	£125	£750	—
1707 2nd "E" bust Plain Edge Proof			Extremely rare	
1708 Second bust, E below	£110	£300	£1200	—
1708 — E* below bust	£130	£400	£13 00	—
1708/7 — — 8 over 7			Extremely rare	

Anne, first bust, VIGO below

DATE	MINTAGE	F	VF	EF	UNC
1708 — Roses & Plumes in angles on rev.		£100	£450	£1000	–
1708 Third bust, Plain		£55	£175	£600	–
1708 — Plumes in angles on rev.		£100	£300	£1000	–
1708 Third bust, E below bust		£100	£275	£950	–
1708/7 — — 8 over 7		£200	£450	–	–
1708 — Roses & Plumes in angles on rev.		£100	£250	£900	–
1708 "Edinburgh" bust, E* below		£100	£250	£850	–
1709 Third bust, Plain		£60	£180	£650	–
1709 "Edinburgh" bust, E* below		£60	£190	£850	–
1710 Third bust, Roses & Plumes in angles		£75	£200	£900	–
1710 Fourth bust, Roses & Plumes in angles		£90	£240	£1000	–
1711 Third bust, Plain		£70	£160	£600	–
1711 Fourth bust, Plain		£35	£80	£275	–
1712 — Roses & Plumes in angles on rev.		£80	£200	£850	–
1713 — —		£70	£180	£700	–
1713/2 — 3 over 2		£100	£275	–	–
1714 — —		£80	£200	£600	–
1714/3 —		£120	£300	£1000	–

Anne, Fourth bust, roses and plumes reverse type

GEORGE I (1714–27)

DATE	MINTAGE	F	VF	EF	UNC
1715 First bust, Roses & Plumes in angles on rev.		£80	£270	£1000	–
1716 — —		£150	£500	£2000	–
1717 — —		£130	£400	£1700	–
1718 — —		£85	£250	£950	–
1719 — —		£140	£600	£1600	–
1720 — —		£110	£350	£1200	–
1720/18 — —		£150	£500	£1500	–
1720 — Plain		£50	£160	£750	–
1721 — Roses & Plumes in angles on rev.		£130	£400	£2000	–
1721/0 — — 1 over 0		£110	£400	£1300	–
1721 — Plain		£200	£650	£2000	–
1721/19 — — 21 over 19		£125	£400	–	–
1721/18 21 over 18 error, Plumes & Roses		£500	£1800	–	–
1722 — Roses & Plumes in angles on rev.		£110	£350	£1500	–
1723 — —		£120	£350	£1500	–
1723 — SSC rev., Arms of France at date		£100	£325	£1100	–
1723 — SSC in angles on rev		£35	£110	£450	–
1723 Second bust, SSC in angles on rev.		£50	£170	£600	–
1723 — Roses & Plumes in angles		£110	£400	£1400	–
1723 — WCC (Welsh Copper Co) below bust		£1100	£3000	£10000	–
1724 — Roses & Plumes in angles on rev.		£120	£350	£1400	–
1724 — WCC below bust		£1100	£3000	£10000	–
1725 — Roses & Plumes in angles on rev.		£110	£300	£1400	–
1725 — — no stops on obv.		£120	£300	£1400	–
1725 — WCC below bust		£1150	£3000	£10000	–
1726 — — Roses & Plumes		£700	£2500	£7500	–
1726 — WCC below bust		£1200	£3000	£10500	–
1727 — —				Extremely rare	
1727 — — no stops on obv.				Extremely rare	

George I First bust with SSC in angles on reverse

George I Second bust, roses and plumes reverse type

GEORGE II (1727–60)

DATE	MINTAGE	F	VF	EF	UNC
1727 Young head, Plumes in angles on rev.		£150	£525	£2500	–
1727 — Roses & Plumes in angles on rev.		£120	£350	£1200	–
1728 — —		£130	£400	£1500	–
1728 — Plain		£120	£350	£1500	–
1729 — Roses & Plumes in angles on rev.		£120	£350	£1600	–
1731 — —		£125	£350	£1600	–
1731 — Plumes in angles on rev.		£150	£600	£1800	–
1732 — Roses & Plumes in angles on rev.		£125	£350	£1600	–
1734 — —		£70	£250	£950	–
1735 — —		£70	£250	£950	–
1736 — —		£70	£250	£900	–
1736/5 — — 6 over 5		£70	£250	£950	–
1737 — —		£65	£225	£850	–
1739 — Roses in angles on rev.		£60	£220	£800	–
1739/7 — — 9 over 7					Rare
1741 — —		£50	£200	£700	–
1741/39 — — 41 over 39					Rare
1743 Old head, Roses in angles on rev.		£35	£130	£550	–
1745 — —		£35	£130	£550	–
1745 — — LIMA below bust		£35	£120	£600	–

George II Young head, roses and plumes reverse type

DATE	MINTAGE	F	VF	EF	UNC
1745/3 — — — 5 over 3		£60	£180	£700	–
1746 — — —		£60	£220	£800	–
1746/5 — — — 6 over 5		£100	£300	–	–
1746 — Plain, Proof		–	–	£4000	–
1747 — Roses in angles on rev.		£50	£150	£800	–
1750 — Plain		£60	£200	£800	–
1750/46 — — 50 over 46		£75	£200	£800	–
1751 — —		£140	£600	£1750	–
1758 — —		£25	£60	£200	–

GEORGE III (1760–1820)

DATE	MINTAGE	F	VF	EF	UNC
1763 "Northumberland" bust (Beware of counterfeits)		£450	£800	£1600	–
First type,					
1787 rev. no semée of hearts in 4th shield		£25	£50	£140	–
1787 — No stop over head		£30	£50	£160	–
1787 — No stop at date		£50	£90	£190	–
1787 — No stops on obv		£400	£800	£2500	–
1787 rev. with semée of hearts in shield		£35	£65	£160	–
1798 "Dorrien Magens" bust		–	–	£30,000+	
NEW COINAGE—shield in garter reverse					
1816	–	£12	£25	£75	£200
1817	3,031,360	£12	£35	£85	£220
1817 GEOE for GEOR	incl. above	£120	£250	£700	–
1818	1,342,440	£25	£50	£150	£500
1819	7,595,280	£15	£35	£100	£260
1819/8 9 over 8	incl. above	£20	£50	£160	–
1820	7,975,440	£15	£30	£100	£275

GEORGE IV (1820–30)

DATE	MINTAGE	F	VF	EF	UNC
1821 First bust, first reverse	2,463,120	£20	£55	£240	£650
1821 — — Proof	incl. above	–	–	–	£2000
1823 — Second reverse	693,000	£55	£95	£300	£800
1824 — —	4,158,000	£18	£55	£225	£550
1825 — —	2,459,160	£25	£60	£225	£700
1825/3 — — 5 over 3	incl. above			Extremely rare	
1825 Second bust, third reverse	incl. above	£10	£35	£100	£400
1825 — — Roman I	incl. above			Extremely rare	
1826 — —	6,351,840	£10	£30	£80	£250
1826 6 over 2				Does this exist?	
1826 — — Proof	incl. above	–	–	–	£1500
1827 — —	574,200	£45	£110	£400	£950
1829 — —	879,120	£30	£70	£250	£700

WILLIAM IV (1830–37)

DATE	MINTAGE	F	VF	EF	UNC
1831Proof only, Plain Edge	–	–	–	–	£1800
1834	3,223,440	£18	£45	£250	£600
1835	1,449,360	£20	£60	£250	£650
1836	3,567,960	£18	£45	£220	£600
1837	478,160	£25	£80	£350	£800

VICTORIA (1837–1901)

DATE	MINTAGE	F	VF	EF	UNC
YOUNG HEAD ISSUES					
First head					
1838 WW on truncation	1,956,240	£20	£50	£220	£500
1839 —	5,666,760	£35	£80	£280	£750
Second head					
1839 — Proof only, Plain Edge	incl. above	–	–	–	£3500
1839 no WW	incl. above	£20	£50	£180	£500
(Rare Proofs exist)					
1840	1,639,440	£20	£60	£240	£550
1841	875,160	£25	£65	£300	£600
1842	2,094,840	£20	£50	£250	£575
1843	1,465,200	£25	£65	£275	£650
1844	4,466,880	£18	£50	£200	£500
1845	4,082,760	£22	£55	£200	£500
1846	4,031,280	£20	£50	£200	£500
1848 last 8 of date over 6	1,041,480	£90	£225	£850	£1800

George II Old head, plain reverse

George III First type

George III New coinage Shield reverse type

George IV second bust second reverse type

Victoria Second head type

DATE	MINTAGE	F	VF	EF	UNC
1849	845,480	£30	£75	£250	£700
1850	685,080	£800	£2200	£6500	£9000
1850/49	incl. above	£850	£2000	£6000	–
1851	470,071	£50	£120	£550	£1500
1852	1,306,574	£15	£35	£180	£450
1853	4,256,188	£15	£35	£180	£450
1853 Proof	incl. above	–	–	–	£3000
1854	552,414	£250	£650	£2500	£5250
1854/1 4 over 1	incl. above	£300	£900	–	–
1855	1,368,400	£15	£30	£175	£425
1856	3,168,000	£15	£30	£175	£425
1857	2,562,120	£15	£30	£175	£425
1857 error F:G with inverted G	incl. above	£250	£600	–	–
1858	3,108,600	£15	£35	£170	£425
1859	4,561,920	£15	£35	£170	£425
1860	1,671,120	£15	£35	£225	£525
1861	1,382,040	£15	£40	£225	£600
1862	954,360	£70	£180	£500	£1600
1863	859,320	£140	£400	£1000	£2500
1863/1 3 over 1				Extremely rare	
Die no. added above date up to 1879					
1864	4,518,360	£12	£30	£150	£400
1865	5,619,240	£12	£30	£150	£400
1866	4,984,600	£12	£30	£150	£400
1866 error BBITANNIAR	incl. above	£80	£300	£1100	–
1867	2,166,120	£15	£35	£150	£425
Third head—with die no					
1867	incl. above	£175	£500	–	–
1868	3,330,360	£12	£40	£150	£400
1869	736,560	£20	£60	£200	£500
1870	1,467,471	£15	£40	£170	£400
1871	4,910,010	£12	£40	£140	£400
1872	8,897,781	£12	£40	£150	£400
1873	6,489,598	£12	£40	£150	£400
1874	5,503,747	£15	£40	£150	£425
1875	4,353,983	£12	£40	£140	£400
1876	1,057,487	£20	£65	£200	£650
1877	2,989,703	£12	£40	£140	£400
1878	3,127,131	£12	£40	£140	£400
1879				Extremely rare	
Fourth head—no die no					
1879 no Die no.	incl. above	£10	£30	£140	£300
1880	4,842,786	£10	£30	£140	£300
1881	5,255,332	£10	£30	£140	£300
1882	1,611,786	£25	£80	£200	£600
1883	7,281,450	£10	£30	£110	£250
1884	3,923,993	£10	£30	£110	£250
1885	3,336,526	£10	£30	£110	£250
1886	2,086,819	£10	£30	£110	£250
1887	4,034,133	£10	£30	£110	£250
JUBILEE HEAD ISSUES					
1887	incl. above	£5	£10	£18	£45
1887 Proof	1,084	–	–	–	£500
1888	4,526,856	£6	£12	£40	£100
1889	7,039,628	£50	£150	£450	–
1889 Large bust (until 1892)	incl. above	£6	£15	£60	£130
1890	8,704,042	£6	£15	£60	£130
1891	5,665,348	£6	£15	£60	£140
1892	4,591,622	£6	£15	£60	£150
OLD HEAD ISSUES					
1893	7,039,074	£8	£15	£50	£110
1893 small lettering	incl. above	£8	£15	£50	£110
1893 Proof	1,312	–	–	–	£450
1894	5,953,152	£10	£30	£75	£200
1895	8,880,651	£9	£30	£65	£190
1896	9,264,551	£8	£15	£50	£125
1897	6,270,364	£8	£15	£50	£125
1898	9,768,703	£8	£15	£50	£125
1899	10,965,382	£8	£15	£50	£125
1900	10,937,590	£8	£15	£50	£125
1901	3,426,294	£8	£15	£50	£125

Victoria Third head, with die no.

Victoria Fourth head, no die no.

Victoria Jubilee head

Victoria Old or Veiled head

EDWARD VII (1901–10)

DATE	MINTAGE	F	VF	EF	UNC
1902	7,809,481	£6	£15	£50	£110
1902 Proof matt	13,123	—	—	—	£175
1903	2,061,823	£10	£35	£170	£550
1904	2,040,161	£8	£35	£170	£525
1905	488,390	£110	£325	£1500	£4000
1906	10,791,025	£6	£14	£60	£160
1907	14,083,418	£6	£14	£60	£170
1908	3,806,969	£12	£30	£180	£625
1909	5,664,982	£9	£25	£125	£450
1910	26,547,236	£6	£12	£45	£110

GEORGE V (1910–36)

DATE	MINTAGE	F	VF	EF	UNC
First issue					
1911	20,065,901	£6	£10	£25	£80
1911 Proof	6,007	—	—	—	£160
1912	15,594,009	£6	£14	£35	£110
1913	9,011,509	£7	£20	£60	£180
1914	23,415,843	£5	£8	£30	£70
1915	39,279,024	£5	£8	£30	£70
1916	35,862,015	£5	£8	£30	£70
1917	22,202,608	£5	£8	£30	£80
1918	34,915,934	£5	£8	£30	£70
1919	10,823,824	£6	£8	£35	£80
Second issue—debased silver					
1920	22,825,142	£2	£5	£25	£60
1921	22,648,763	£2	£5	£25	£60
1922	27,215,738	£2	£5	£25	£70
1923	14,575,243	£2	£5	£25	£60
1924	9,250,095	£7	£20	£65	£180
1925	5,418,764	£6	£12	£50	£150
1926	22,516,453	£3	£8	£30	£120
(Trial Proofs of 1923 and 1924 were struck in cupro nickel—both Rare)					
Third issue—Modified bust					
1926	incl. above	£3	£6	£30	£65
1927 —	9,247,344	£3	£6	£30	£65
Fourth issue— new reverse: large lion and crown on rev., date in legend					
1927	incl. above	£3	£6	£20	£55
1927 Proof	15,000	—	—	—	£70
1928	18,136,778	£3	£6	£15	£45
1929	19,343,006	£3	£6	£15	£45
1930	3,172,092	£3	£6	£20	£55
1931	6,993,926	£3	£6	£15	£45
1932	12,168,101	£3	£6	£15	£50
1933	11,511,624	£3	£6	£15	£40
1934	6,138,463	£3	£6	£18	£50
1935	9,183,462	£3	£6	£12	£30
1936	11,910,613	£3	£6	£12	£30

George V First reverse

George V Fourth issue, Second reverse

GEORGE VI (1936–52)

E = England rev. (lion standing on large crown). S = Scotland rev. (lion seated on small crown holding sword and mace)

DATE	MINTAGE	F	VF	EF	UNC
1937 E	8,359,122	—	£2	£4	£6
1937 E Proof	26,402	—	—	—	£25
1937 S	6,748,875	—	£2	£4	£6
1937 S Proof	26,402	—	—	—	£25
1938 E	4,833,436	—	£3	£10	£20
1938 S	4,797,852	—	£3	£10	£20
1939 E	11,052,677	—	£2	£4	£6
1939 S	10,263,892	—	£2	£4	£6
1940 E	11,099,126	—	—	£4	£7
1940 S	9,913,089	—	—	£4	£7
1941 E	11,391,883	—	—	£4	£6
1941 S	8,086,030	—	—	£4	£5
1942 E	17,453,643	—	—	£4	£5

DATE	MINTAGE	F	VF	EF	UNC
1942 S	13,676,759	–	–	£4	£5
1943 E	11,404,213	–	–	£5	£7
1943 S	9,824,214	–	–	£5	£6
1944 E	11,586,751	–	–	£5	£6
1944 S	10,990,167	–	–	£5	£6
1945 E	15,143,404	–	–	£5	£7
1945 S	15,106,270	–	–	£5	£6
1946 E	16,663,797	–	–	£5	£6
1946 S	16,381,501	–	–	£5	£6
Cupro-nickel					
1947 E	12,120,611	–	–	–	£2
1947 S	12,283,223	–	–	–	£2
1948 E	45,576,923	–	–	–	£2
1948 S	45,351,937	–	–	–	£2
1949 E	19,328,405	–	–	–	£5
1949 S	21,243,074	–	–	–	£5
1950 E	19,243,872	–	–	–	£5
1950 E Proof	17,513	–	–	–	£20
1950 S	14,299,601	–	–	–	£5
1950 S Proof	17,513	–	–	–	£20
1951 E	9,956,930	–	–	–	£5
1951 E Proof	20,000	–	–	–	£20
1951 S	10,961,174	–	–	–	£6
1951 S Proof	20,000	–	–	–	£20

English reverse

Scottish reverse

ELIZABETH II (1952–2022)

E = England rev. (shield with three lions). S = Scotland rev. (shield with one lion).

DATE	MINTAGE	F	VF	EF	UNC
1953 E	41,942,894	–	–	–	£1
1953 E Proof	40,000	–	–	–	£4
1953 S	20,663,528	–	–	–	£1
1953 S Proof	40,000	–	–	–	£4
1954 E	30,262,032	–	–	–	£2
1954 S	26,771,735	–	–	–	£2
1955 E	45,259,908	–	–	–	£2
1955 S	27,950,906	–	–	–	£2
1956 E	44,907,008	–	–	–	£10
1956 S	42,853,639	–	–	–	£10
1957 E	42,774,217	–	–	–	£1
1957 S	17,959,988	–	–	–	£10
1958 E	14,392,305	–	–	–	£10
1958 S	40,822,557	–	–	–	£1
1959 E	19,442,778	–	–	–	£1
1959 S	1,012,988	£1	£3	£10	£70
1960 E	27,027,914	–	–	–	£1
1960 S	14,376,932	–	–	–	£1
1961 E	39,816,907	–	–	–	£1
1961 S	2,762,558	–	–	–	£3
1962 E	36,704,379	–	–	–	£1
1962 S	17,475,310	–	–	–	£1
1963 E	49,433,607	–	–	–	£1
1963 S	32,300,000	–	–	–	£1
1964 E	8,590,900	–	–	–	£1
1964 S	5,239,100	–	–	–	£1
1965 E	9,216,000	–	–	–	£1
1965 S	2,774,000	–	–	–	£2
1966 E	15,002,000	–	–	–	£1
1966 S	15,604,000	–	–	–	£1
1970 E Proof	–				£10
1970 S Proof	–				£10

English reverse

Scottish reverse

SIXPENCES

DATE	F	VF	EF	UNC

OLIVER CROMWELL

DATE	F	VF	EF	UNC
1658 Patterns by Thos. Simon & Tanner Four varieties			Extremely rare	

CHARLES II (1660–85)

Charles II

DATE	F	VF	EF	UNC
1674	£75	£300	£1000	–
1675	£80	£300	£1100	–
1675/4 5 over 4	£85	£300	£1100	–
1676	£85	£300	£1000	–
1676/5 6 over 5	£90	£300	£1100	–
1677	£80	£300	£1000	–
1678/7	£80	£300	£1100	–
1679	£80	£300	£1000	–
1680	£110	£500	£1300	–
1681	£85	£300	£1100	–
1682/1	£85	£300	£1100	–
1682	£120	£400	£1400	–
1683	£85	£300	£1000	–
1684	£90	£300	£1000	–

JAMES II (1685–88)

James II

DATE	F	VF	EF	UNC
1686 Early shields	£150	£450	£1400	–
1687 Ealy Shields	£175	£500	£1600	–
1687/6 — 7 over 6	£175	£500	£1450	–
1687 Late shields	£170	£500	£1600	–
1687/6 — 7 over 6	£180	£550	£1600	–
1688 —	£170	£500	£1550	–

WILLIAM & MARY (1688–94)

William and Mary

DATE	F	VF	EF	UNC
1693	£150	£450	£1400	–
1693 error inverted 3	£250	£550	£1750	–
1694	£160	£525	£1500	–

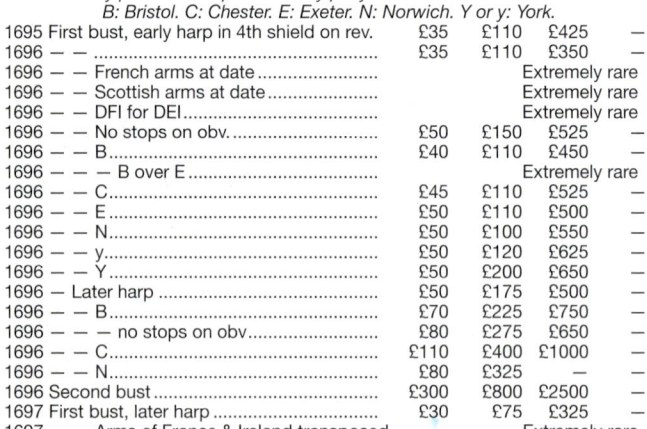

WILLIAM III (1694–1702)

Provincially produced sixpences carry privy marks or initials below the bust: B: Bristol. C: Chester. E: Exeter. N: Norwich. Y or y: York.

William III first bust

DATE	F	VF	EF	UNC
1695 First bust, early harp in 4th shield on rev.	£35	£110	£425	–
1696 — —	£35	£110	£350	–
1696 — — French arms at date			Extremely rare	
1696 — — Scottish arms at date			Extremely rare	
1696 — — DFI for DEI			Extremely rare	
1696 — — No stops on obv.	£50	£150	£525	–
1696 — — B	£40	£110	£450	–
1696 — — — B over E			Extremely rare	
1696 — — C	£45	£110	£525	–
1696 — — E	£50	£110	£500	–
1696 — — N	£50	£100	£550	–
1696 — — y	£50	£120	£625	–
1696 — — Y	£50	£200	£650	–
1696 — Later harp	£50	£175	£500	–
1696 — — B	£70	£225	£750	–
1696 — — — no stops on obv	£80	£275	£650	–
1696 — — C	£110	£400	£1000	–
1696 — — N	£80	£325	–	–
1696 Second bust	£300	£800	£2500	–
1697 First bust, later harp	£30	£75	£325	–
1697 — — Arms of France & Ireland transposed			Extremely rare	

DATE	MINTAGE	F	VF	EF	UNC
1697 — — B		£60	£140	£550	—
1697 — — C		£80	£225	£600	—
1697 — — — Irish shield at date			Extremely rare		
1697 — — E		£70	£200	£550	—
1697 — — — error GVLIEMVS			Extremely rare		
1697 — — y		£65	£150	£550	—
1697 — — — Irish shield at date			Extremely rare		
1697 Second bust		£220	£600	£2000	—
1697 Third bust		£35	£75	£350	—
1697 — error GVLIEIMVS			Extremely rare		
1697 — B		£60	£150	£550	—
1697 — — IRA for FRA			Extremely rare		
1697 — C		£90	£270	£650	—
1697 — E		£80	£250	£650	—
1697 — Y		£60	£220	£600	—
1698 —		£80	£300	£750	—
1698 — Plumes in angles on rev.		£100	£300	£900	—
1699 —		£110	£300	£950	—
1699 — Plumes in angles on rev.		£90	£300	£1000	—
1699 — Roses in angles on rev.		£100	£325	£1000	—
1699 — — error G∀LIELMVS			Extremely rare		
1700 —		£45	£110	£425	—
1700 — Plume below bust		£2500	—	—	—
1701 —		£75	£200	£600	—

William III third bust

ANNE (1702–14)

DATE	MINTAGE	F	VF	EF	UNC
1703 VIGO below bust Before Union with Scotland		£40	£150	£600	—
1705 Plain		£60	£170	£625	—
1705 Plumes in angles on rev.		£70	£200	£700	—
1705 Roses & Plumes in angles on rev.		£70	£180	£650	—
1707 Roses & Plumes in angles on rev.		£50	£180	£650	—
1707 (Post-Union), Plain		£40	£100	£450	—
1707 E (Edinburgh) below bust		£45	£110	£500	—
1707 Plumes in angles on rev.		£50	£150	£500	—
1708 Plain		£45	£125	£525	—
1708 E below bust		£50	£130	£475	—
1708 E* below bust		£70	£150	£500	—
1708 "Edinburgh" bust E* below		£50	£150	£475	—
1708 Plumes in angles on rev.		£60	£175	£650	—
1710 Roses & Plumes in angles on rev.		£60	£175	£625	—
1711 Plain		£35	£90	£375	—

Queen Anne

GEORGE I (1714–27)

DATE	MINTAGE	F	VF	EF	UNC
1717 Roses & Plumes in angles on rev.		£120	£350	£1000	—
1717 Plain edge			Extremely rare		
1720 —		£120	£350	£1000	—
1723 SSC in angles on rev.		£30	£80	£300	—
1723 Larger lettering		£30	£80	£300	—
1726 Small Roses & Plumes in angles on rev.		£90	£275	£825	—

George I

GEORGE II (1727–60)

DATE	MINTAGE	F	VF	EF	UNC
1728 Young head, Plain		£70	£200	£600	—
1728 — Proof		—	—	£4000	—
1728 — Plumes in angles on rev.		£45	£150	£500	—
1728 — Roses & Plumes in angles on rev.		£40	£150	£475	—
1731 — —		£45	£150	£500	—
1732 — —		£45	£150	£500	—
1734 — —		£45	£150	£500	—
1735 — —		£45	£150	£500	—
1735/4 5 over 4		£50	£160	£525	—
1736 — —		£45	£150	£500	—
1739 — Roses in angles on rev.		£40	£125	£425	—
1741 —		£40	£125	£400	—
1743 Old head, Roses in angles on rev.		£25	£75	£340	—
1745 — —		£25	£75	£340	—
1745 — — 5 over 3		£30	£90	£350	—

George II, young head

DATE	MINTAGE	F	VF	EF	UNC
1745 — Plain, LIMA below bust		£35	£110	£350	—
1746 — — —		£35	£100	£375	—
1746 — — Proof		—	—	£1800	—
1750 — —		£35	£140	£350	—
1751 — —		£40	£150	£425	—
1757 — —		£20	£40	£140	—
1758 — —		£20	£40	£140	—

George II, old head

GEORGE III (1760–1820)

DATE	MINTAGE	F	VF	EF	UNC
1787 rev. no semée of hearts on 4th shield		£15	£35	£90	£130
1787 rev. with semée of hearts		£15	£35	£90	£130

NEW COINAGE

DATE	MINTAGE	F	VF	EF	UNC
1816	—	£7	£18	£60	£175
1817	10,921,680	£8	£18	£60	£175
1818	4,284,720	£14	£35	£110	£220
1819	4,712,400	£8	£18	£60	£150
1819 very small 8 in date	incl. above	£12	£25	£70	£160
1820	1,488,960	£10	£20	£80	£200

George III new coinage

GEORGE IV (1820–30)

DATE	MINTAGE	F	VF	EF	UNC
1821 First bust, first reverse	863,280	£15	£40	£150	£425
1821 error BBRITANNIAR		£100	£325	£950	—
1821 — — Proof	incl. above	—	—	—	£1800
1824 — Second (garter) reverse	633,600	£15	£35	£150	£425
1825 —	483,120	£18	£40	£150	£420
1826 — —	689,040	£40	£100	£300	£700
1826 Second bust, third (lion on crown) reverse	incl. above	£15	£35	£100	£375
1826 — — Proof	incl. above	—	—	—	£1400
1827 — —	166,320	£40	£130	£350	£800
1828 — —	15,840	£20	£60	£200	£425
1829 — —	403,290	£20	£60	£200	£425

George IV second reverse

WILLIAM IV (1830–37)

DATE	MINTAGE	F	VF	EF	UNC
1831	1,340,195	£15	£40	£140	£375
1831 Proof, milled edge	incl. above	—	—	—	£1500
1834	5,892,480	£15	£40	£150	£425
1835	1,552,320	£15	£40	£150	£425
1836	1,987,920	£15	£45	£180	£450
1837	506,880	£25	£65	£300	£700

William IV

VICTORIA (1837–1901)

YOUNG HEAD ISSUES

First head

DATE	MINTAGE	F	VF	EF	UNC
1838	1,607,760	£15	£40	£130	£375
1839	3,310,560	£15	£40	£130	£375
1839 Proof (plain edge)	incl. above	—	—	—	£1600
1840	2,098,800	£15	£40	£130	£400
1841	1,386,000	£20	£60	£175	£500
1842	601,920	£15	£40	£150	£400
1843	3,160,080	£15	£40	£150	£400
1844	3,975,840	£15	£40	£160	£425
1844 Large 44 in date	incl. above	£18	£45	£150	£475
1845	3,714,480	£15	£35	£120	£450
1846	4,226,880	£15	£35	£120	£450
1847		Extremely rare			
1848	586,080	£100	£300	£1000	£2750
1848/6 final 8 over 6	incl. above	£100	£300	£1000	£2750
1850	498,960	£15	£40	£120	£450
1850/3 0 over 3	incl. above	£18	£40	£130	£425
1851	2,288,107	£12	£30	£110	£425
1852	904,586	£12	£30	£150	£425
1853	3,837,930	£12	£30	£150	£425
1853 Proof	incl above	—	—	—	£2000

DATE	MINTAGE	F	VF	EF	UNC
1854	840,116	£300	£650	£1600	3500
1855	1,129,684	£12	£30	£120	£350
1855/3 last 5 over 3	incl. above	£15	£45	£150	£400
1856	2,779,920	£12	£40	£120	£375
1857	2,233,440	£12	£40	£120	£375
1858	1,932,480	£10	£40	£120	£375
1859	4,688,640	£10	£40	£120	£375
1859/8 9 over 8	incl. above	£12	£40	£120	£500
1860	1,100,880	£10	£35	£120	£400
1862	990,000	£110	£300	£800	£2200
1863	491,040	£80	£200	£550	£1500
Die no. added above date from 1864 to 1879					
1864	4,253,040	£10	£25	£125	£375
1865	1,631,520	£10	£25	£125	£375
1866	4,140,080	£10	£25	£125	£375
1866 no Die no.	incl. above			Extremely Rare	

Second head

DATE	MINTAGE	F	VF	EF	UNC
1867	1,362,240	£12	£30	£130	£325
1868	1,069,200	£12	£30	£120	£325
1869	388,080	£12	£30	£120	£375
1870	479,613	£12	£30	£120	£350
1871	3,662,684	£10	£30	£100	£350
1871 no Die no.	incl. above	£10	£30	£100	£325
1872	3,382,048	£10	£30	£100	£325
1873	4,594,733	£10	£30	£100	£325
1874	4,225,726	£10	£30	£110	£300
1875	3,256,545	£10	£30	£100	£300
1876	841,435	£10	£30	£100	£350
1877	4,066,486	£10	£30	£100	£300
1877 no Die no	incl. above	£10	£30	£100	£300
1878	2,624,525	£10	£30	£100	£325
1878/7 8 struck over 7 Error	incl. above	£45	£200	£750	—
1878 Dritanniar Error	incl. above	£160	£400	£1200	—
1879	3,326,313	£10	£25	£100	£325
1879 no Die no	incl. above	£10	£25	£100	£325
1880 no Die no	3,892,501	£10	£25	£100	£325

Third head

DATE	MINTAGE	F	VF	EF	UNC
1880	incl above	£10	£24	£90	£240
1881	6,239,447	£10	£24	£90	£240
1882	759,809	£15	£50	£150	£500
1883	4,986,558	£10	£25	£80	£220
1884	3,422,565	£10	£25	£80	£220
1885	4,652,771	£10	£25	£80	£220
1886	2,728,249	£10	£25	£80	£220
1887	3,675,607	£10	£25	£80	£220

JUBILEE HEAD ISSUES

DATE	MINTAGE	F	VF	EF	UNC
1887 Shield reverse	incl. above	£6	£10	£20	£30
1887 — Proof	incl. above	—	—	—	£500
1887 — Proof (wreath) milled edge	incl. above	—	—	—	£1500
1887 Six Pence in wreath reverse	incl. above	£6	£10	£20	£40
1888 —	4,197,698	£8	£12	£35	£70
1889 —	8,738,928	£8	£12	£35	£80
1890 —	9,386,955	£8	£12	£35	£80
1891 —	7,022,734	£8	£12	£35	£100
1892 —	6,245,746	£8	£12	£40	£110
1893 —	7,350,619	£800	£1500	£4000	—

OLD HEAD ISSUES

DATE	MINTAGE	F	VF	EF	UNC
1893	incl. above	£7	£12	£25	£50
1893 Proof	1,312	—	—	—	£500
1894	3,467,704	£8	£18	£60	£160
1895	7,024,631	£8	£18	£60	£140
1896	6,651,699	£7	£15	£50	£95
1897	5,031,498	£7	£15	£50	£95
1898	5,914,100	£7	£15	£50	£95
1899	7,996,80	£7	£15	£50	£90
1900	8,984,354	£7	£15	£50	£90
1901	5,108,757	£7	£15	£50	£90

Victoria first young head

Victoria Jubilee head, shield reverse

Jubilee head, wreath reverse

Victoria Old Head

DATE	MINTAGE	F	VF	EF	UNC
EDWARD VII (1901–10)					
1902	6,367,378	£5	£14	£40	£75
1902 "Matt Proof"	15,123	—	—	—	£150
1903	5,410,096	£7	£20	£50	£170
1904	4,487,098	£15	£50	£175	£500
1905	4,235,556	£8	£20	£70	£220
1906	7,641,146	£7	£12	£40	£120
1907	8,733,673	£7	£12	£45	£130
1908	6,739,491	£10	£30	£110	£350
1909	6,584,017	£8	£20	£55	£180
1910	12,490,724	£5	£8	£35	£75
GEORGE V (1910–36)					
First issue					
1911	9,155,310	£4	£8	£18	£45
1911 Proof	6,007	—	—	—	£150
1912	10,984,129	£4	£8	£25	£70
1913	7,499,833	£4	£10	£24	£90
1914	22,714,602	£4	£8	£15	£40
1915	15,694,597	£4	£8	£15	£50
1916	22,207,178	£4	£8	£15	£35
1917	7,725,475	£8	£25	£70	£150
1918	27,553,743	£4	£8	£14	£30
1919	13,375,447	£4	£8	£14	£40
1920	14,136,287	£4	£8	£10	£35
Second issue—debased silver					
1920	incl. above	£1	£3	£10	£40
1921	30,339,741	£1	£3	£10	£40
1922	16,878,890	£1	£3	£10	£35
1923	6,382,793	£4	£10	£45	£110
1924	17,444,218	£1	£5	£10	£35
1925	12,720,558	£1	£3	£10	£35
1925 Broad rim	incl. above	£1	£3	£10	£35
1926 —	21,809,621	£1	£3	£10	£35
Third issue—Modified bust					
1926	incl. above	£1	£2	£10	£40
1927	8,924,873	—	£2	£10	£40
Fourth issue—New design (oakleaves)					
1927 Proof only	15,000	—	—	—	£75
1928	23,123,384	£2	£4	£10	£35
1929	28,319,326	£2	£4	£10	£35
1930	16,990,289	£2	£4	£10	£40
1931	16,873,268	£2	£4	£10	£35
1932	9,406,117	£2	£4	£10	£40
1933	22,185,083	£2	£4	£10	£40
1934	9,304,009	£2	£4	£14	£45
1935	13,995,621	£2	£4	£8	£22
1936	24,380,171	£2	£4	£8	£22
GEORGE VI (1936–52)					
First type					
1937	22,302,524	—	—	£2	£6
1937 Proof	26,402	—	—	—	£15
1938	13,402,701	—	£2	£6	£20
1939	28,670,304	—	—	£2	£6
1940	20,875,196	—	—	£2	£6
1941	23,086,616	—	—	£2	£6
1942	44,942,785	—	—	£2	£6
1943	46,927,111	—	—	£2	£6
1944	36,952,600	—	—	£2	£6
1945	39,939,259	—	—	£2	£4
1946	43,466,407	—	—	£2	£4
Cupro-nickel					
1947	29,993,263	—	—	£1	£3
1948	88,323,540	—	—	£1	£3
Second type—new cypher on rev.					
1949	41,335,515	—	—	£1	£3
1950	32,741,955	—	—	£1	£3
1950 Proof	17,513	—	—	—	£8
1951	40,399,491	—	—	£1	£3

Edward VII

George V first reverse

George V second reverse (fourth issue)

George VI first reverse

George VI second reverse

DATE	MINTAGE	F	VF	EF	UNC
1951 Proof	20,000	–	–	–	£10
1952	1,013,477	£15	£35	£70	£200

ELIZABETH II (1952–2022)

DATE	MINTAGE	F	VF	EF	UNC
1953	70,323,876	–	–	–	£2
1953 Proof	40,000	–	–	–	£4
1954	105,241,150	–	–	–	£3
1955	109,929,554	–	–	–	£1
1956	109,841,555	–	–	–	£1
1957	105,654,290	–	–	–	£1
1958	123,518,527	–	–	–	£3
1959	93,089,441	–	–	–	£1
1960	103,283,346	–	–	–	£3
1961	115,052,017	–	–	–	£3
1962	166,483,637	–	–	–	25p
1963	120,056,000	–	–	–	25p
1964	152,336,000	–	–	–	25p
1965	129,644,000	–	–	–	25p
1966	175,676,000	–	–	–	25p
1967	240,788,000	–	–	–	25p
1970 Proof	–				£8

GROATS OR FOURPENCES

The earlier fourpences are included in the Maundy oddments section as they are generally considered to have been issued for the Maundy ceremony.

WILLIAM IV (1831–37)

DATE	MINTAGE	F	VF	EF	UNC
1836	–	£8	£20	£45	£95
1837	962,280	£8	£20	£45	£100

VICTORIA (1838–1901)

DATE	MINTAGE	F	VF	EF	UNC
1837	Extremely Rare Proofs or Patterns only				
1838	2,150,280	£7	£15	£50	£120
1838 over last 8 on its side		£10	£20	£65	£150
1839	1,461,240	£7	£16	£60	£140
1839 Proof	incl. above				Rare
1840	1,496,880	£7	£15	£55	£140
1840 Small 0 in date	incl. above	£7	£15	£55	£140
1841	344,520	£7	£15	£55	£140
1842/1 2 over 1	incl. above	£7	£15	£55	£140
1842	724,680	£7	£15	£50	£140
1843	1,817640	£8	£18	£55	£170
1843 4 over 5	incl. above	£7	£15	£55	£160
1844	855,360	£7	£15	£55	£140
1845	914,760	£7	£15	£55	£140
1846	1,366,200	£7	£15	£55	£135
1847 7 over 6	225,720	£15	£35	£140	–
1848	712,800	£7	£15	£55	£125
1848/6 8 over 6	incl. above	£30	£110	–	–
1848/7 8 over 7	incl. above	£8	£20	£70	£140
1849	380,160	£8	£18	£70	£140
1849/8 9 over 8	incl. above	£8	£20	£80	£160
1851	594,000	£40	£90	£300	£500
1852	31,300	£55	£130	£450	–
1853	11,880	£80	£170	£650	–
1853 Proof Milled Rim	incl. above	–	–	–	£1300
1853 Plain edge Proof				Extremely rare	
1854	1,096,613	£7	£15	£50	£130
1855	646,041	£7	£15	£50	£130
1855/3 Last 5 over 3	–	£12	£25	£85	£225
1857 Proofs only				Extremely rare	
1862 Proofs only				Extremely rare	
1888 Jubilee Head	–	£15	£30	£60	£140

THREEPENCES

The earlier threepences are included in the Maundy oddments section.

WILLIAM IV (1830–37)

Wiliam IV

DATE	MINTAGE	F	VF	EF	UNC
(issued for use in the West Indies)					
1834		£12	£25	£100	£250
1835		£10	£20	£80	£240
1836		£10	£20	£90	£250
1837		£15	£35	£130	£320

VICTORIA (1837–1901)

Victoria Young head type

DATE	MINTAGE	F	VF	EF	UNC
1838 BRITANNIAB error				Extremely rare	
1838	—	£15	£30	£80	£250
1839	—	£15	£30	£90	£275
1840	—	£15	£30	£90	£275
1841	—	£18	£32	£100	£300
1842	—	£15	£30	£100	£300
1843	—	£15	£30	£75	£220
1843/34 43 over 34	—	£15	£30	£90	£250
1844	—	£16	£30	£90	£250
1845	1,319,208	£16	£30	£80	£250
1846	52,008	£30	£75	£275	£550
1847	4,488			Extremely rare	
1848	incl. above			Extremely rare	
1849	131,208	£12	£30	£100	£250
1850	954,888	£12	£30	£80	£240
1851	479,065	£12	£30	£80	£230
1851 reads 1551				Very rare	
1851 5 over 8	incl. above	£25	£50	£220	—
1852	4,488	£90	£240	£700	£1100
1853	36,168	£60	£140	£300	£700
1854	1,467,246	£8	£30	£75	£220
1855	383,350	£12	£30	£90	£275
1856	1,013,760	£10	£25	£90	£225
1857	1,758,240	£10	£25	£80	£250
1858	1,441,440	£10	£28	£90	£240
1858 BRITANNIAB error	incl. above			Extremely rare	
1858/6 final 8 over 6	incl. above	£15	£30	£200	—
1858/5 final 8 over 5	incl. above	£10	£30	£150	—
1859	3,579,840	£10	£25	£80	£220
1860	3,405,600	£12	£30	£85	£275
1861	3,294,720	£10	£25	£70	£200
1862	1,156,320	£10	£30	£75	£200
1863	950,400	£30	£70	£125	£350
1864	1,330,560	£7	£22	£60	£180
1865	1,742,400	£7	£22	£70	£200
1866	1,900,800	£7	£22	£60	£180
1867	712,800	£7	£22	£60	£180
1868	1,457,280	£7	£22	£60	£190
1868 RRITANNIAR error	incl. above			Extremely rare	
1869	—	£25	£175	£300	£650
1870	1,283,218	£6	£20	£70	£160
1871	999,633	£6	£20	£70	£150
1872	1,293,271	£5	£16	£60	£140
1873	4,055,550	£5	£16	£60	£140
1874	4,427,031	£5	£16	£60	£150
1875	3,306,500	£5	£16	£60	£140
1876	1,834,389	£5	£16	£60	£140
1877	2,622,393	£5	£16	£60	£140
1878	2,419,975	£6	£18	£60	£175
1879	3,140,265	£5	£16	£40	£120

DATE	MINTAGE	F	VF	EF	UNC
1880	1,610,069	£5	£16	£40	£110
1881	3,248,265	£5	£16	£40	£100
1882	472,965	£8	£30	£75	£200
1883	4,369,971	£5	£10	£40	£85
1884	3,322,424	£5	£12	£40	£90
1885	5,183,653	£5	£12	£40	£100
1886	6,152,669	£5	£12	£35	£75
1887	2,780,761	£5	£12	£35	£70

Dates of 1838, 1839, 1840, 1841, 1842, 1843, 1844, 1847, 1848 and 1853 were issued for colonial use.

JUBILEE HEAD ISSUES

DATE	MINTAGE	F	VF	EF	UNC
1887	incl. above	£3	£5	£15	£30
1887 Proof	incl. above	—	—	—	£250
1888	518,199	£3	£6	£20	£45
1889	4,587,010	£3	£6	£20	£50
1890	4,465,834	£3	£6	£20	£50
1891	6,323,027	£3	£6	£20	£50
1892	2,578,226	£3	£6	£20	£60
1893	3,067,243	£20	£60	£180	£450

Victoria Jubilee head

OLD HEAD ISSUES

DATE	MINTAGE	F	VF	EF	UNC
1893	incl. above	£2	£5	£16	£40
1893 Proof	incl. above	—	—	—	£275
1894	1,608,603	£4	£7	£25	£80
1895	4,788,609	£2	£5	£22	£60
1896	4,598,442	£2	£5	£18	£45
1897	4,541,294	£2	£5	£18	£45
1898	4,567,177	£2	£5	£18	£45
1899	6,246,281	£2	£5	£18	£45
1900	10,644,480	£2	£5	£18	£45
1901	6,098,400	£2	£5	£15	£35

Victoria Old or Veiled head

EDWARD VII (1901–10)

DATE	MINTAGE	F	VF	EF	UNC
1902	8,268,480	£2	£3	£10	£20
1902 "Matt Proof"	incl. above	—	—	—	£60
1903	5,227,200	£2	£5	£20	£55
1904	3,627,360	£4	£12	£50	£120
1905	3,548,160	£2	£5	£25	£65
1906	3,152,160	£3	£9	£40	£90
1907	4,831,200	£2	£4	£20	£60
1908	8,157,600	£2	£3	£20	£55
1909	4,055,040	£2	£4	£20	£60
1910	4,563,380	£2	£4	£18	£45

Edward VII

GEORGE V (1910–36)

First issue

DATE	MINTAGE	F	VF	EF	UNC
1911	5,841,084	—	—	£3	£12
1911 Proof	incl. above	—	—	—	£70
1912	8,932,825	—	—	£3	£15
1913	7,143,242	—	—	£3	£15
1914	6,733,584	—	—	£3	£14
1915	5,450,617	—	—	£3	£16
1916	18,555,201	—	—	£3	£12
1917	21,662,490	—	—	£3	£12
1918	20,630,909	—	—	£3	£10
1919	16,845,687	—	—	£3	£10
1920	16,703,597	—	—	£3	£10

Second issue—debased silver

DATE	MINTAGE	F	VF	EF	UNC
1920	incl. above	—	—	£3	£14
1921	8,749,301	—	—	£3	£14
1922	7,979,998			£5	£40
1925	3,731,859	—	—	£4	£28
1926	4,107,910	—	—	£4	£35

George V second issue

Third issue—Modified bust

DATE	MINTAGE	F	VF	EF	UNC
1926	incl. above	—	—	£8	£25

DATE	MINTAGE	F	VF	EF	UNC
Fourth issue—new design (oakleaves)					
1927 Proof only	15,022	—	—	—	£140
1928	1,302,106	£4	£10	£30	£65
1930	1,319,412	£2	£4	£10	£40
1931	6,251,936	—	—	£2	£7
1932	5,887,325	—	—	£2	£7
1933	5,578,541	—	—	£2	£7
1934	7,405,954	—	—	£2	£7
1935	7,027,654	—	—	£2	£7
1936	3,328,670	—	—	£2	£7

George V, fourth issue oak leaves design reverse

GEORGE VI (1936–52)

DATE	MINTAGE	F	VF	EF	UNC
Silver					
1937	8,148,156	—	—	£1	£5
1937 Proof	26,402	—	—	—	£20
1938	6,402,473	—	—	£1	£5
1939	1,355,860	—	—	£4	£15
1940	7,914,401	—	—	£1	£4
1941	7,979,411	—	—	£1	£4
1942	4,144,051	£2	£5	£12	£35
1943	1,397,220	£3	£8	£15	£40
1944	2,005,553	£10	£25	£50	£100
1945			Only one known		
1942, 1943, 1944, 1945 were for colonial issue only.					
Nickel brass					
1937	45,707,957	—	—	£1	£4
1937 Proof	26,402	—	—	—	£20
1938	14,532,332	—	—	£1	£25
1939	5,603,021	—	—	£5	£50
1940	12,636,018	—	—	£4	£35
1941	60,239,489	—	—	£1	£10
1942	103,214,400	—	—	£1	£10
1943	101,702,400	—	—	£1	£10
1944	69,760,000	—	—	£1	£12
1945	33,942,466	—	—	£5	£25
1946	620,734	£6	£25	£240	£950
1948	4,230,400	—	—	£7	£60
1949	464,000	£6	£28	£250	£1000
1950	1,600,000	—	£2	£20	£140
1950 Proof	17,513	—	—	—	£25
1951	1,184,000	—	£4	£35	£170
1951 Proof	20,000	—	—	—	£25
1952	25,494,400	—	—	—	£12

George VI small silver 3d

George VI "Thrift" design of the nickel brass 3d

ELIZABETH II (1952–2022)

DATE	MINTAGE	F	VF	EF	UNC
1953	30,618,000	—	—	—	£1
1953 Proof	40,000	—	—	—	£12
1954	41,720,000	—	—	—	£5
1955	41,075,200	—	—	—	£5
1956	36,801,600	—	—	—	£6
1957	24,294,500	—	—	—	£6
1958	20,504,000	—	—	—	£9
1959	28,499,200	—	—	—	£6
1960	83,078,400	—	—	—	£2
1961	41,102,400	—	—	—	£1
1962	51,545,600	—	—	—	£1
1963	39,482,866	—	—	—	£1
1964	44,867,200	—	—	—	—
1965	27,160,000	—	—	—	—
1966	53,160,000	—	—	—	—
1967	151,780,800	—	—	—	—
1970 Proof	—				£6

TWO PENCES

DATE		F	VF	EF	UNC

GEORGE III (1760–1820)

1797 "Cartwheel"	722,972	£35	£90	£450	£1200
1797 — Copper Proofs		Many types from £1000+			

VICTORIA (1837–1901)

For use in the Colonies

Small silver

	F	VF	EF	UNC
1838	£4	£10	£20	£45
1848	£4	£12	£20	£50

Earlier issues of the small silver two pences are listed in the Maundy section.

THREE-HALFPENCES

WILLIAM IV (1830–37)

For use in the Colonies

	F	VF	EF	UNC
1834	£6	£18	£40	£100
1835	£10	£25	£75	£225
1835 over 4	£7	£18	£40	£120
1836	£8	£20	£50	£125
1837	£15	£40	£120	£350

VICTORIA (1837–1901)

For use in the Colonies

	F	VF	EF	UNC
1838	£6	£15	£35	£100
1839	£6	£15	£35	£100
1840	£8	£20	£60	£160
1841	£6	£15	£40	£90
1842	£6	£18	£50	£130
1843	£6	£15	£40	£90
1860	£15	£35	£110	£250
1862	£20	£40	£110	£300

PENNIES

The earlier small silver pennies are included in the Maundy oddments section.

GEORGE III (1760–1820)

Note: Mintage figures are from an on-line thesis by Sue Tungate, Birmingham University, October 2011 (information supplied by Dennis Onions).

Soho Mint

		F	VF	EF	UNC
1797 "Cartwheel" type, 10 laurel leaves	43,969,204	£25	£60	£320	£1000
Numerous proofs in different metals are known for this issue—all are rare.					
1797 — 11 laurel leaves	incl. above	£25	£60	£320	£1000
1806 (34mm)	19,355,480	£7	£22	£90	£300
1807	11,290,168	£7	£22	£90	£300
1808	—				Unique

George III "Cartwheel" penny reverse. The obverse is as the two pence above.

GEORGE IV (1820–30)

		F	VF	EF	UNC
1825	1,075,200	£18	£45	£275	£750
1826 (varieties)	5,913,600	£18	£45	£275	£750
1826 Proof	—	—	—	—	£1200
1827	1,451,520	£300	£1000	£5000	—

DATE	MINTAGE	F	VF	EF	UNC

WILLIAM IV (1830–37)

DATE	MINTAGE	F	VF	EF	UNC
1831 (varieties)	806,400	£30	£75	£425	£1300
1831 Proof	—	—	—	—	£1600
1834	322,560	£32	£75	£425	£1400
1837	174,720	£70	£210	£850	£3000

VICTORIA (1837–1901)

YOUNG HEAD ISSUES

Copper

Victoria copper penny

DATE	MINTAGE	F	VF	EF	UNC
1839 Proof	unrecorded	—	—	—	£3500
1841	913,920	£10	£50	£300	£875
1841 No colon after REG	incl. above	£8	£20	£175	£550
1843	483,840	£100	£375	£2000	£5000
1844	215,040	£12	£30	£200	£650
1844 Proofs exist	—			Extremely rare	
1845	322,560	£15	£35	£300	£850
1846	483,840	£15	£25	£275	£800
1846 FID: DEF colon spaced	incl. above	£15	£25	£275	£800
1846 FID:DEF colon close	incl. above	£16	£30	£280	£800
1847	430,080	£12	£25	£200	£600
1848	161,280	£12	£25	£200	£600
1848/7 final 8 over 7	incl. above	£9	£22	£160	£500
1848/6 final 8 over 6	incl. above	£20	£120	£525	—
1849	268,800	£250	£600	£2500	—
1851	432,224	£15	£45	£240	£825
1853	1,021,440	£7	£15	£100	£225
1853 Proof	—	—	—	—	£3500
1854	6,720,000	£8	£22	£120	£300
1854/3 4 over 3	incl. above	£15	£50	£200	—
1855	5,273,856	£8	£20	£120	£350
1856 Plain trident close colon DEF:	1,212,288	£110	£250	£1100	£3000
1856 Orn trident far colon DEF: ..	—	£120	£270	£1100	£3200
1856 Proofs exists	—			Extremely rare	
1857 Plain trident	752,640	£7	£20	£110	£350
1857 Ornamental trident	incl. above	£7	£20	£100	£370
1858/7 final 8 over 7	incl. above	£7	£20	£100	£370
1858/6 final 8 over 6	—	£40	£120	£550	—
1858/3 final 8 over 3	incl. above	£25	£90	£400	—
1858	1,599,040	£7	£16	£100	£400
1859	1,075,200	£10	£28	£180	£525
1860/59	32,256	£900	£2200	£4000	£7000

Note all are 60/59. All have a prominent die flan under Victoria's chin.

Bronze

Prices of bronze Victoria Young "bun" head pennies are for the common types. There are many known varieties which are listed in detail in other more specialised publications. Prices for coins in mint with full lustre will be considerably higher.

Victoria Young or "Bun" head bronze penny

DATE	MINTAGE	F	VF	EF	UNC
1860 Beaded border	5,053,440	£40	£100	£250	£1000
1860 Toothed border	incl. above	£10	£30	£80	£400
1860 — Piedfort flan	—		Extremely rare		
1861	36,449,280	£8	£15	£55	£400
1862	50,534,400	£8	£15	£55	£375
1862 8 over 6	incl. above		Extremely rare		
1863	28,062,720	£8	£15	£60	£340
1863 Die no below date	incl. above		Extremely rare		
1864 Plain 4	3,440,640	£30	£175	£700	£3500
1864 Crosslet 4	incl. above	£35	£185	£800	£4000
1865	8,601,600	£8	£20	£60	£400
1865/3 5 over 3	incl. above	£50	£160	£600	—
1866	9,999,360	£8	£25	£110	£500
1867	5,483,520	£8	£25	£150	£900
1868	1,182,720	£20	£80	£300	£2500
1869	2,580,480	£150	£500	£2000	£6000
1870	5,695,022	£18	£50	£200	£800
1871	1,290,318	£45	£150	£600	£2750
1872	8,494,572	£8	£25	£80	£325

DATE	MINTAGE	F	VF	EF	UNC
1873	8,494,200	£8	£25	£90	£350
1874	5,621,865	£8	£25	£90	£350
1874 H	6,666,240	£8	£25	£80	£400
1874 Later (older) bust	incl. above	£18	£50	£130	£600
1875	10,691,040	£8	£25	£75	£350
1875 H	752,640	£35	£125	£1000	£2750
1876 H	11,074,560	£8	£15	£65	£400
1877	9,624,747	£8	£15	£65	£400
1878	2,764,470	£8	£15	£65	£400
1879	7,666,476	£6	£20	£65	£400
1880	3,000,831	£6	£18	£60	£380
1881	2,302,362	£8	£18	£60	£350
1881 H	3,763,200	£12	£20	£65	£350
1882 H	7,526,400	£8	£18	£60	£325
1882 no H	—		Extremely Rare		
1883	6,237,438	£8	£18	£70	£320
1884	11,702,802	£8	£20	£70	£320
1885	7,145,862	£8	£18	£65	£320
1886	6,087,759	£8	£18	£65	£320
1887	5,315,085	£8	£18	£65	£320
1888	5,125,020	£8	£18	£70	£350
1889	12,559,737	£8	£18	£60	£425
1890	15,330,840	£8	£18	£60	£300
1891	17,885,961	£8	£15	£60	£300
1892	10,501,671	£10	£20	£100	£320
1893	8,161,737	£8	£15	£55	£275
1893 3 over 2	—	£90	£250	£375	£600
1894	3,883,452	£15	£45	£160	£400
OLD HEAD ISSUES					
1895 Trident 2mm from P(ENNY)	5,395,830	£20	£90	£300	£850
1895 Trident 1mm from P	incl. above	—	£2	£18	£75
1896	24,147,156	—	£2	£18	£65
1897	20,756,620	—	£2	£15	£60
1897 Raised dot after O of ONE (O·NE)		£150	£275	£900	—
1898	14,296,836	—	£3	£18	£65
1899	26,441,069	—	£3	£16	£60
1900	31,778,109	—	£3	£16	£45
1901	22,205,568	—	£3	£10	£30

Victoria Old head

EDWARD VII (1901–10)

DATE	MINTAGE	F	VF	EF	UNC
1902	26,976,768	—	£1	£8	£30
1902 "Low tide" to sea line	incl. above	£4	£15	£75	£250
1903	21,415,296	—	£3	£15	£90
1904	12,913,152	—	£4	£25	£200
1905	17,783,808	—	£3	£15	£85
1906	37,989,504	—	£3	£15	£75
1907	47,322,240	—	£3	£15	£75
1908	31,506,048	—	£3	£18	£140
1909	19,617,024	—	£3	£22	£200
1910	29,549,184	—	£3	£15	£65

Edward VII

GEORGE V (1910–36)

DATE	MINTAGE	F	VF	EF	UNC
1911	23,079,168	—	£3	£12	£65
1912	48,306,048	—	£3	£12	£65
1912 H next to date	16,800,000	—	£4	£40	£250
1913	65,497,812	—	£3	£15	£80
1914	50,820,997	—	£3	£18	£85
1915	47,310,807	—	£3	£20	£90
1916	86,411,165	—	£3	£15	£65
1917	107,905,436	—	£3	£15	£60
1918	84,227,372	—	£3	£12	£55
1918 H	3,660,800	£1	£15	£150	£700
1918 KN	incl. above	£8	£80	£600	£2500
1919	113,761,090	—	£2	£15	£55
1919 H	5,209,600	£1	£20	£275	£1100
1919 KN	incl. above	£15	£120	£800	£3200
1920	124,693,485	—	£2	£12	£30
1921	129,717,693	—	£2	£12	£40
1922	16,346,711	—	£3	£28	£160
1922 with reverse of 1927	Unknown				Very rare

George V

DATE	MINTAGE	F	VF	EF	UNC
1926	4,498,519	—	£6	£25	£150
1926 Modified effigy	incl above	£25	£150	£800	£3000
1927	60,989,561	—	£2	£10	£45
1928	50,178,00	—	£2	£10	£40
1929	49,132,800	—	£2	£10	£45
1930	29,097,600	—	£2	£20	£80
1931	19,843,200	—	£2	£10	£55
1932	8,277,600	—	£2	£15	£110
1933	Very limited numbers, certainly under 15				
1934	13,965,600	—	£2	£25	£110
1935	56,070,000	—	—	£2	£15
1936	154,296,000	—	—	£2	£12

George VI

GEORGE VI (1936–52)

DATE	MINTAGE	F	VF	EF	UNC
1937	88,896,000	—	—	—	£4
1937 Proof	26,402	—	—	—	£15
1938	121,560,000	—	—	—	£6
1939	55,560,000	—	—	—	£15
1940	42,284,400	—	—	£8	£25
1944 Mint Dark	42,600,000	—	—	—	£8
1945 Mint Dark	79,531,200	—	—	—	£8
1946 Mint Dark	66,855,600	—	—	—	£8
1947	52,220,400	—	—	—	£5
1948	63,961,200	—	—	—	£5
1949	14,324,400	—	—	—	£8
1950	240,000	£8	£16	£30	£50
1950 Proof	17,513	—	—	—	£25
1951	120,000	£20	£28	£50	£75
1951 Proof	20,000	—	—	—	£40

Elizabeth II

ELIZABETH II (1952–2022)

DATE	MINTAGE	F	VF	EF	UNC
1953	1,308,400	—	—	£2	£5
1953 Proof	40,000	—	—	—	£10
1954				Only one known	
1961	48,313,400	—	—	—	£2
1962	143,308,600	—	—	—	50p
1963	125,235,600	—	—	—	50p
1964	153,294,000	—	—	—	50p
1965	121,310,400	—	—	—	50p
1966	165,739,200	—	—	—	50p
1967	654,564,000	—	—	—	—
1970 Proof	—				£8

Later issues are included in the Decimal section.

HALFPENNIES

CHARLES II (1660–85)

DATE	F	VF	EF	UNC
1672	£70	£375	£1500	—
1672 CRAOLVS error		Extremely rare		
1673	£70	£325	£1450	—
1673 CRAOLVS error		Extremely rare		
1673 No rev. stop	£100	£600	—	—
1673 No stops on obv.		Extremely rare		
1675	£65	£500	£1500	—
1675 No stops on obv.	£80	£550	—	—
1675/3 5 over 3	£175	£650	—	—

JAMES II (1685–88)

Tin (with copper plug)

DATE	F	VF	EF	UNC
1685	£250	£800	£4250	—
1686	£300	£800	£4400	—
1687	£325	£850	£4250	—

Charles II

DATE	F	VF	EF	UNC

WILLIAM & MARY (1688–94)

	F	VF	EF	UNC
Tin (with copper plug)				
1689 Small draped busts, edge dated			Extremely rare	
1690 Large cuirassed busts, edge dated	£200	£750	£3500	–
1691 — date on edge and in exergue	£180	£700	£3400	–
1692 — —	£200	£750	£3500	–
Copper				
1694 Large cuirassed busts, date in exergue	£80	£300	£1300	–
1694 — — GVLIEMVS error		Extremely rare		
1694 — — MΛRIΛ error		Extremely rare		
1694 — — No stops on rev.		Extremely rare		

Copper halfpenny of William & Mary

WILLIAM III (1694–1702)

	F	VF	EF	UNC
1695 *First issue* (date in exergue)	£50	£220	£1200	–
1695 — No stop after BRITANNIA on rev.		Extremely rare		
1696 —	£40	£180	£1000	–
1696 — TERTVS error		Extremely rare		
1697 —	£50	£200	£1000	–
1697 — No stop after TERTIVS on obv.	£55	£325	–	–
1698 —	£50	£240	£1200	–
1698 *Second issue* (date in legend)	£55	£200	–	–
1698 — No stop after date	£50	£200	–	–
1699 —	£55	£220	£1200	–
1699 — No stop after date	£250	–	–	–
1699 *Third issue* (date in exergue) (Britannia with right hand on knee)	£40	£200	£900	–
1699 — No stop after date		Extremely rare		
1699 — BRITΛNNIΛ error	£225	–	–	–
1699 — TERTVS error		Extremely rare		
1699 — No stop on rev.		Extremely rare		
1699 — No stops on obv.	£90	£400	–	–
1700 —	£50	£200	£1000	–
1700 — No stops on obv.	£100	£375	–	–
1700 — No stops after GVLIELMUS	£100	£375	–	–
1700 — BRITVANNIA error		Extremely rare		
1700 — GVIELMS error	£100	£350	–	–
1700 — GVLIEEMVS error	£100	£350	–	–
1701 —	£50	£200	£1000	–
1701 — BRITΛNNIΛ error	£80	£300	–	–
1701 — No stops on obv.		Extremely rare		
1701 — inverted As for Vs	£90	£350	–	–

William III first issue

GEORGE I (1714–27)

	F	VF	EF	UNC
1717 *"Dump" issue*	£50	£270	£900	–
1718 —	£40	£250	£850	–
1719 — Patterns				Rare
1719 *Second issue*	£40	£200	£900	–
1720 —	£35	£175	£800	–
1721 —	£35	£160	£800	–
1721 — Stop after date	£45	£175	–	–
1722 —	£35	£150	£700	–
1722 —inverted A for V on obv.		Extremely rare		
1723 —	£35	£160	£650	–
1723 —No stop on rev.	£110	£500	–	–
1724 —	£40	£160	£700	–

George I "Dump" type

GEORGE II (1727–60)

	F	VF	EF	UNC
1729 *Young head*	£30	£100	£500	–
1729 — No stop on rev.	£30	£100	£500	–
1730 —	£25	£100	£500	–
1730 — GEOGIVS error	£90	£300	£900	–
1730 — Stop after date	£30	£130	£500	–
1730 — No stop after REX on obv.	£35	£160	£525	–
1731 —	£25	£120	£475	–

DATE	MINTAGE	F	VF	EF	UNC
1731 — No rev. stop		£28	£125	£450	—
1732 —		£25	£110	£450	—
1732 — No rev. stop		£28	£140	£500	—
1733 —		£25	£100	£500	—
1734/3 — 4 over 3		£35	£220	—	—
1734 — No stop on obv.		£35	£220	—	—
1735 —		£25	£90	£475	—
1736 —		£25	£90	£475	—
1737 —		£25	£95	£500	—
1738 —		£25	£90	£425	—
1739 —		£20	£80	£375	—
1740 *Old head*		£20	£75	£350	—
1742 —		£20	£75	£350	—
1742/0 — 2 over 0		£25	£150	£500	—
1743 —		£18	£75	£400	—
1744 —		£18	£75	£400	—
1745 —		£18	£75	£400	—
1746 —		£18	£75	£350	—
1747 —		£18	£75	£350	—
1748 —		£18	£75	£350	—
1749 —		£18	£75	£350	—
1750 —		£18	£75	£350	—
1751 —		£18	£75	£350	—
1752 —		£18	£75	£350	—
1753 —		£18	£75	£350	—
1754 —		£18	£75	£350	—

George II "Old" head

GEORGE III (1760–1820)

DATE	MINTAGE	F	VF	EF	UNC
First type—Royal Mint					
1770		£18	£60	£300	—
1770 No stop on rev.		£25	£70	£350	—
1771		£12	£50	£300	—
1771 No stop on rev.		£20	£70	£325	—
1772 Error GEORIVS		£80	£250	£850	
1772		£12	£50	£250	—
1772 No stop on rev		£20	£65	£300	—
1773		£10	£45	£280	—
1773 No stop after REX		£35	£110	£450	—
1773 No stop on rev.		£20	£70	£300	—
1774		£12	£40	£240	—
1775		£12	£40	£240	—
Second type—Soho Mint					
1799	42,481,116	£5	£12	£55	£120
Third type					
1806	87,993,526	£5	£12	£60	£110
1807	41,394,384	£5	£12	£60	£110

George III second "Soho" type

GEORGE IV (1820–30)

DATE	MINTAGE	F	VF	EF	UNC
1825	215,040	£12	£45	£190	£425
1826 (varieties)	9,031,630	£12	£45	£190	£425
1826 Proof	—	—	—	—	£900
1827	5,376,000	£12	£45	£170	£400

WILLIAM IV (1830–37)

DATE	MINTAGE	F	VF	EF	UNC
1831	806,400	£12	£30	£130	£340
1831 Proof	—	—	—	—	£900
1834	537,600	£12	£30	£130	£325
1837	349,440	£12	£30	£130	£325

William IV

VICTORIA (1837–1901)

DATE	MINTAGE	F	VF	EF	UNC
Copper					
1838	456,960	£8	£20	£80	£320

DATE	MINTAGE	F	VF	EF	UNC
1839 Proof	268,800	—	—	—	£1200
1841	1,075,200	£6	£18	£75	£300
1843	967,680	£50	£100	£300	£1100
1844	1,075,200	£12	£40	£180	£425
1845	1,075,200	£275	£600	£2300	—
1846	860,160	£12	£25	£85	£300
1847	725,640	£12	£22	£85	£300
1848	322,560	£12	£25	£80	£300
1848/7 final 8 OVER 7	incl. above	£15	£35	£110	£325
1851	215,040	£7	£18	£80	£325
1852	637,056	£10	£22	£90	£325
1853	1,559,040	£5	£10	£40	£135
1853/2 3 over 2	incl. above	£15	£30	£60	£275
1853 Proof	—	—	—	—	£1300
1854	12,354,048	£5	£9	£40	£170
1855	1,455,837	£5	£9	£40	£170
1856	1,942,080	£12	£30	£100	£380
1857	1,820,720	£6	£18	£60	£180
1858	2,472,960	£5	£12	£50	£160
1858/7 final 8 over 7	incl. above	£5	£12	£50	£160
1858/6 final 8 over 6	incl. above	£5	£12	£50	£175
1859	1,290,240	£8	£25	£80	£300
1859/8 9 over 8	incl. above	£8	£25	£70	£325
1860	unrecorded	£2000	£3750	£7000	£13000
Bronze					
1860 Beaded border	6,630,400	£3	£10	£50	£200
1860 Toothed border		£4	£12	£70	£300
1861	54,118,400	£4	£10	£60	£200
1862 Die letter A, B or C to left of lighthouse				Extremely rare	
1862	61,107,200	£3	£9	£55	£180
1863	15,948,800	£3	£9	£75	£175
1864	537,600	£3	£12	£80	£270
1865	8,064,000	£4	£18	£90	£350
1865/3 5 over 3	incl. above	£50	£120	£450	—
1866	2,508,800	£5	£15	£80	£325
1867	2,508,800	£5	£15	£75	£300
1868	3,046,400	£5	£15	£80	£340
1869	3,225,600	£30	£100	£400	£1200
1870	4,350,739	£5	£15	£60	£275
1871	1,075,280	£60	£100	£500	£1600
1872	4,659,410	£4	£10	£50	£220
1873	3,404,880	£4	£10	£50	£220
1874	1,347,655	£6	£25	£110	£350
1874 H	5,017,600	£3	£10	£60	£270
1875	5,430,815	£3	£8	£60	£220
1875 H	1,254,400	£5	£12	£60	£250
1876 H	5,809,600	£5	£12	£75	£300
1877	5,209,505	£3	£10	£60	£225
1878	1,425,535	£6	£20	£100	£400
1878 Wide date		£100	£200	£550	—
1879	3,582,545	£3	£10	£40	£200
1880	2,423,465	£4	£12	£60	£210
1881	2,007,515	£4	£12	£50	£200
1881 H	1,792,000	£3	£10	£50	£240
1882 H	4,480,000	£3	£10	£50	£250
1883	3,000,725	£3	£12	£60	£275
1884	6,989,580	£3	£10	£45	£200
1885	8,600,574	£3	£10	£45	£200
1886	8,586,155	£3	£10	£45	£200
1887	10,701,305	£3	£10	£45	£200
1888	6,814,670	£3	£10	£45	£200
1889	7,748,234	£3	£10	£45	£200

Victoria copper halfpenny

Victoria bronze halfpenny

DATE	MINTAGE	F	VF	EF	UNC
1889/8 9 over 8	incl. above	£30	£60	£250	—
1890	11,254,235	£3	£10	£45	£150
1891	13,192,260	£3	£10	£40	£150
1892	2,478,335	£3	£10	£50	£175
1893	7,229,344	£3	£10	£40	£160
1894	1,767,635	£6	£15	£85	£220
OLD HEAD ISSUES					
1895	3,032,154	£2	£8	£25	£95
1896	9,142,500	£1	£4	£10	£60
1897	8,690,315	£1	£4	£10	£60
1898	8,595,180	£1	£5	£12	£75
1899	12,108,001	£1	£4	£10	£60
1900	13,805,190	£1	£4	£10	£45
1901	11,127,360	£1	£3	£8	£40

Victoria bronze Old head halfpenny

EDWARD VII (1901–10)

DATE	MINTAGE	F	VF	EF	UNC
1902	13,672,960	£2	£4	£8	£35
1902 "Low tide"	incl. above	£22	£90	£180	£450
1903	11,450,880	£2	£5	£20	£90
1904	8,131,200	£2	£6	£25	£115
1905	10,124,800	£2	£5	£20	£90
1906	16,849,280	£2	£5	£25	£100
1907	16,849,280	£2	£5	£20	£100
1908	16,620,800	£2	£5	£20	£100
1909	8,279,040	£2	£5	£20	£110
1910	10,769,920	£2	£5	£20	£100

Edward VII

GEORGE V (1910–36)

DATE	MINTAGE	F	VF	EF	UNC
1911	12,570,880	£1	£4	£15	£40
1912	21,185,920	£1	£3	£15	£40
1913	17,476,480	£1	£3	£15	£45
1914	20,289,111	£1	£3	£15	£45
1915	21,563,040	£2	£3	£20	£55
1916	39,386,143	£1	£2	£15	£45
1917	38,245,436	£1	£2	£15	£35
1918	22,321,072	£1	£2	£15	£35
1919	28,104,001	£1	£2	£15	£35
1920	35,146,793	£1	£2	£15	£40
1921	28,027,293	£1	£2	£15	£40
1922	10,734,964	£1	£4	£25	£45
1923	12,266,282	£1	£2	£15	£35
1924	13,971,038	£1	£2	£15	£30
1925	12,216,123	—	£2	£15	£30
1925 Modified effigy	incl. above	£4	£10	£50	£90
1926	6,172,306	—	£2	£10	£40
1927	15,589,622	—	£2	£10	£40
1928	20,935,200	—	£2	£8	£35
1929	25,680,000	—	£2	£8	£35
1930	12,532,800	—	£2	£8	£35
1931	16,137,600	—	£2	£8	£35
1932	14,448,000	—	£2	£8	£35
1933	10,560,000	—	£2	£8	£35
1934	7,704,000	—	£2	£12	£50
1935	12,180,000	—	£1	£6	£20
1936	23,008,800	—	£1	£5	£15

George V

GEORGE VI (1936–52)

DATE	MINTAGE	F	VF	EF	UNC
1937	24,504,000	—	—	£1	£5
1937 Proof	26,402	—	—	—	£25
1938	40,320,000	—	—	£1	£6
1939	28,924,800	—	—	£1	£5
1940	32,162,400	—	—	£4	£15

DATE	MINTAGE	F	VF	EF	UNC
1941	45,120,000	—	—	£1	£8
1942	71,908,800	—	—	£1	£5
1943	76,200,000	—	—	£1	£5
1944	81,840,000	—	—	£1	£5
1945	57,000,000	—	—	£1	£5
1946	22,725,600	—	—	£1	£6
1947	21,266,400	—	—	£1	£6
1948	26,947,200	—	—	£1	£4
1949	24,744,000	—	—	£1	£4
1950	24,153,600	—	—	£1	£5
1950 Proof	17,513	—	—	—	£18
1951	14,868,000	—	—	£1	£6
1951 Proof	20,000	—	—	—	£18
1952	33,784,000	—	—	£1	£4

George VI

ELIZABETH II (1952–2022)

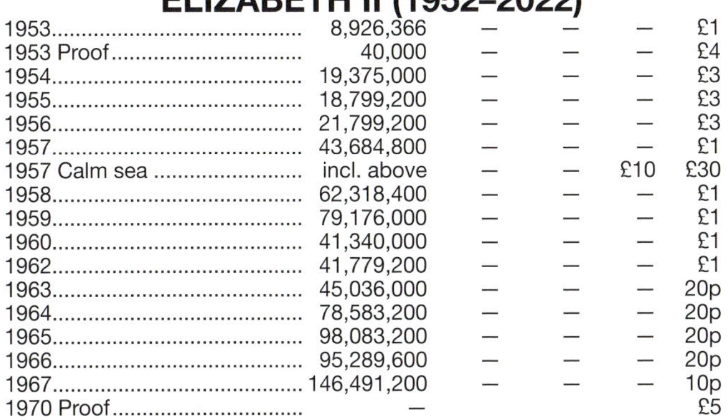

DATE	MINTAGE	F	VF	EF	UNC
1953	8,926,366	—	—	—	£1
1953 Proof	40,000	—	—	—	£4
1954	19,375,000	—	—	—	£3
1955	18,799,200	—	—	—	£3
1956	21,799,200	—	—	—	£3
1957	43,684,800	—	—	—	£1
1957 Calm sea	incl. above	—	—	£10	£30
1958	62,318,400	—	—	—	£1
1959	79,176,000	—	—	—	£1
1960	41,340,000	—	—	—	£1
1962	41,779,200	—	—	—	£1
1963	45,036,000	—	—	—	20p
1964	78,583,200	—	—	—	20p
1965	98,083,200	—	—	—	20p
1966	95,289,600	—	—	—	20p
1967	146,491,200	—	—	—	10p
1970 Proof	—				£5

Elizabeth II

Later issues are included in the Decimal section.

FARTHINGS

OLIVER CROMWELL

DATE	F	VF	EF	UNC
Undated (copper) Draped bust, shield rev. Variations			Extremely rare	

CHARLES II (1660–85)

DATE	F	VF	EF	UNC
Copper				
1672	£45	£250	£800	—
1672 No stops on obv.	£70	£300	£950	
1673	£50	£275	£950	—
1673 CAROLA for CAROLO error	£150	£550	—	—
1673 No stops on obv.			Extremely rare	
1673 No stop on rev.			Extremely rare	
1674	£55	£300	£900	—
1675	£50	£250	£875	—
1675 No stop after CAROLVS			Extremely rare	
1679	£60	£300	£1000	—
1679 No stop on rev.	£70	£350	—	—
Tin (with copper plug)				
1684 with date on edge	£250	£900	—	—
1685 —			Extremely rare	

Charles II copper issue

DATE	F	VF	EF	UNC
JAMES II (1685–88)				
Tin (with copper plug)				
1684 Cuirassed bust			Extremely rare	
1685 —	£200	£700	£3000	—
1686 —	£220	£700	£3100	—
1687 —			Extremely rare	
1687 Draped bust	£250	£1000	—	—
WILLIAM & MARY (1688–94)				
Tin (with copper plug)				
1689 Small draped busts	£300	£700	—	—
1689) — with edge date 1690			Extremely rare	
1690 Large cuirassed busts	£180	£700	£3000	—
1690 — with edge date 1689			Extremely rare	
1691 —	£200	£700	—	—
1692 —	£200	£700	£3000	—
Copper				
1694 —	£70	£300	£1000	—
1694 — No stop after MARIΛ			Extremely rare	
1694 — No stop on obv.			Extremely rare	
1694 — No stop on rev.			Extremely rare	
1694 — Unbarred As in BRITANNIA			Extremely rare	
WILLIAM III (1694–1702)				
1695 *First issue* (date in exergue)	£50	£250	£900	—
1695 — GVLIELMV error			Extremely rare	
1696 —	£50	£240	£900	—
1697 —	£50	£240	£900	—
1697 — GVLIELMS error			Extremely rare	
1698 —	£220	£800	—	—
1698 *Second issue* (date in legend)	£50	£275	£950	—
1699 *First issue*	£40	£250	£900	—
1699 *Second issue*	£40	£250	£900	—
1699 — No stop after date	£50	£350	—	—
1700 *First issue*	£35	£160	£800	—
1700 — error RRITANNIA			Extremely rare	
ANNE (1702–14)				
1714 pattern	£425	£700	£1500	—
GEORGE I (1714–27)				
1717 First small "Dump" issue	£200	£650	£1250	—
1718 1 Known				—
1719 Second issue	£40	£175	£650	—
1719 — No stop on rev.	£70	£375	—	—
1719 — No stops on obv.	£70	£325	—	—
1720 —	£30	£180	£650	—
1721 —	£25	£180	£650	—
1721/0 — Last 1 over 0	£40	£200	—	—
1722 —	£35	£170	£625	—
1723 —	£35	£170	£650	—
1723 — R over sideways R in REX			Extremely rare	
1724 —	£35	£170	£650	—
GEORGE II (1727–60)				
1730 Young head	£15	£65	£370	—
1731 —	£15	£65	£370	—
1732 —	£15	£85	£420	—
1733 —	£15	£90	£425	—
1734 —	£15	£75	£420	—
1734 — No stop on obv.	£30	£120	£475	—

James II tin issue with central copper plug

William III

Queen Anne

George I, first "Dump" type

George I second type

DATE	MINTAGE	F	VF	EF	UNC
1735 —		£15	£75	£400	—
1735 — 3 over 5		£25	£120	£450	—
1736 —		£15	£60	£425	—
1737 —		£15	£60	£400	—
1739 —		£15	£60	£400	—
1741 Old Head		£15	£55	£375	—
1744 —		£15	£55	£375	—
1746 —		£15	£55	£350	—
1746 — V over LL in GEORGIVS				Extremely rare	
1749 —		£18	£70	£360	—
1750 —		£15	£55	£320	—
1754 —		£10	£35	£220	—
1754 — 4 over 0		£30	£130	£375	—

George II Young head

GEORGE III (1760–1820)

DATE	MINTAGE	F	VF	EF	UNC
1771 *First* (London) issue		£20	£65	£300	—
1773 —		£12	£40	£240	—
1773 — No stop on rev.		£20	£60	£260	—
1773 — No stop after REX		£25	£80	£340	—
1774 —		£12	£40	£240	—
1775 —		£12	£40	£240	—
1797 *Second* (Soho Mint) issue				Patterns only	
1799 *Third* (Soho Mint) issue	4,225,428	£2	£8	£40	£100
1806 *Fourth* (Soho Mint) issue	4,833,768	£2	£8	£40	£100
1807 —	1,075,200	£2	£8	£40	£100

George III, third (Soho Mint) issue

GEORGE IV (1820–30)

DATE	MINTAGE	F	VF	EF	UNC
1821 *First bust* (laureate, draped), first reverse (date in exergue)	2,688,000	£4	£12	£60	£150
1822 —	5,924,350	£4	£12	£60	£150
1823 —	2,365,440	£4	£12	£60	£150
1823 I for 1 in date	incl. above	£25	£75	£300	£600
1825 —	4,300.800	£4	£12	£60	£160
1826 —	6,666,240	£4	£12	£60	£150
1826 *Second bust* (couped, date below), second reverse (ornament in exergue)	incl. above	£4	£12	£60	£150
1826 — Proof	—	—	—	—	£750
1827 —	2,365,440	£4	£12	£60	£170
1828 —	2,365,440	£4	£12	£60	£170
1829 —	1,505,280	£4	£12	£60	£170
1830 —	2,365,440	£4	£12	£60	£170

George III, fourth (Soho Mint) issue

WILLIAM IV (1830–37)

DATE	MINTAGE	F	VF	EF	UNC
1831	2,688,000	£5	£12	£50	£150
1831 Proof	—	—	—	—	£800
1834	1,935,360	£5	£12	£50	£160
1835	1.720,320	£5	£15	£60	£180
1836	1,290.240	£5	£12	£55	£160
1837	3.010,560	£5	£12	£55	£200

William IV

VICTORIA (1837–1901)

FIRST YOUNG HEAD (COPPER) ISSUES

DATE	MINTAGE	F	VF	EF	UNC
1838	591,360	£5	£15	£60	£200
1839	4,300,800	£5	£15	£60	£200
1839 Proof	—	—	—	—	£900
1840	3,010,560	£4	£15	£50	£180
1841	1,720,320	£4	£15	£50	£190
1841 Proof				Extremely rare	
1842	1,290,240	£12	£40	£140	£400
1843	4,085,760	£5	£14	£40	£190

George IV

DATE	MINTAGE	F	VF	EF	UNC
1843 I for 1 in date		£90	£425	£900	–
1844	430,080	£80	£250	£800	£2200
1845	3,225,600	£6	£10	£60	£180
1846	2,580,480	£7	£20	£55	£220
1847	3,879,720	£5	£12	£50	£175
1848	1,290,240	£5	£12	£50	£175
1849	645,120	£50	£100	£375	£900
1850	430,080	£5	£10	£45	£180
1851	1,935,360	£8	£20	£80	£250
1851 D over sideways D in DEI	incl. above	£80	£110	£450	–
1852	822,528	£10	£20	£80	£300
1853	1,028,628	£4	£7	£30	£70
1853 Proof	–	–	–	–	£1400
1854	6,504,960	£4	£10	£45	£110
1855	3,440,640	£4	£10	£45	£120
1856	1,771,392	£10	£25	£80	£300
1856 R over E in VICTORIA	incl. above	£20	£50	£300	–
1857	1,075,200	£4	£10	£40	£110
1858	1,720,320	£4	£10	£40	£110
1859	1,290,240	£12	£25	£90	£350
1860	unrecorded	£1600	£3750	£7000	–

Victoria Young Head first (copper) issue

SECOND YOUNG OR "BUN" HEAD (BRONZE) ISSUES

DATE	MINTAGE	F	VF	EF	UNC
1860 Toothed border	2,867,200	£2	£5	£40	£120
1860 Beaded border	incl. above	£3	£7	£40	£130
1860 Toothed/Beaded border mule	incl. above			Extremely rare	
1861	8,601,600	£2	£5	£35	£120
1862	14,336,000	£1	£5	£35	£120
1862 Large 8 in date	incl. above			Extremely rare	
1863	1,433,600	£45	£90	£300	£725
1864	2,508,800	£1	£5	£30	£110
1865	4,659,200	£1	£5	£30	£110
1865 5 over 2	incl. above	£10	£20	£70	–
1866	3,584,000	£1	£5	£25	£120
1867	5,017,600	£1	£5	£25	£120
1868	4,851,210	£1	£5	£25	£135
1869	3,225,600	£3	£10	£55	£200
1872	2,150,400	£1	£5	£25	£110
1873	3,225,620	£1	£5	£25	£110
1874 H	3,584,000	£1	£5	£25	£130
1874 H both Gs over sideways G	incl. above	£150	£350	£1000	–
1875	712,760	£4	£12	£40	£160
1875 H	6,092,800	£1	£5	£20	£85
1876 H	1,175,200	£5	£18	£70	£250
1878	4,008,540	£1	£4	£22	£90
1879	3,977,180	£1	£4	£22	£90
1880	1,842,710	£1	£4	£22	£90
1881	3,494,670	£1	£4	£22	£90
1881 H	1,792,000	£1	£4	£22	£90
1882 H	1,792,000	£1	£5	£25	£110
1883	1,128,680	£5	£20	£70	£170
1884	5,782,000	£1	£4	£20	£65
1885	5,442,308	£1	£4	£20	£65
1886	7.707,790	£1	£4	£20	£65
1887	1,340,800	£1	£4	£20	£65
1888	1,887,250	£1	£4	£20	£65
1890	2,133,070	£1	£4	£20	£65
1891	4,959,690	£1	£4	£20	£65
1892	887,240	£4	£15	£60	£170
1893	3,904,320	£1	£4	£20	£60
1894	2,396,770	£1	£4	£25	£75
1895	2,852,852	£10	£30	£90	£300

Victoria Young Head second (bronze) issue

DATE	MINTAGE	F	VF	EF	UNC
OLD HEAD ISSUES					
1895 Bright finish	incl. above	£1	£2	£16	£40
1896 —	3,668,610	£1	£2	£16	£30
1897 —	4,579,800	£1	£2	£16	£30
1897 Dark finish	incl. above	£1	£2	£16	£30
1898 —	4,010,080	£1	£2	£16	£30
1899 —	3,864,616	£1	£2	£16	£30
1900 —	5,969,317	£1	£2	£16	£30
1901 —	8,016,460	£1	£2	£10	£28

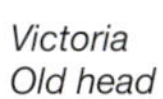

Victoria Old head

EDWARD VII (1901–10)

DATE	MINTAGE	F	VF	EF	UNC
1902	5,125,120	50p	£1	£10	£16
1903	5,331,200	50p	£1	£12	£20
1904	3,628,800	£2	£5	£20	£45
1905	4,076,800	£1	£2	£12	£40
1906	5,340,160	50p	£1	£12	£30
1907	4,399,360	50p	£1	£10	£25
1908	4,264,960	50p	£1	£10	£25
1909	8,852,480	50p	£1	£10	£25
1910	2,298,400	£5	£10	£30	£80

Edward VII

GEORGE V (1910–36)

DATE	MINTAGE	F	VF	EF	UNC
1911	5,196,800	50p	£1	£6	£14
1912	7,669,760	50p	£1	£8	£14
1913	4,184,320	50p	£1	£6	£14
1914	6,126,988	50p	£1	£5	£14
1915	7,129,255	50p	£1	£5	£16
1916	10,993,325	50p	£1	£5	£14
1917	21,434,844	25p	50p	£4	£10
1918	19,362,818	25p	50p	£4	£10
1919	15,089,425	25p	50p	£4	£10
1920	11,480,536	25p	50p	£4	£8
1921	9,469,097	25p	50p	£4	£8
1922	9,956,983	25p	50p	£4	£8
1923	8,034,457	25p	50p	£4	£8
1924	8,733,414	25p	50p	£4	£8
1925	12,634,697	25p	50p	£4	£8
1926 Modified effigy	9,792,397	25p	50p	£4	£8
1927	7,868,355	25p	50p	£4	£8
1928	11,625,600	25p	50p	£4	£8
1929	8,419,200	25p	50p	£4	£8
1930	4,195,200	25p	50p	£4	£8
1931	6,595,200	25p	50p	£4	£8
1932	9,292,800	25p	50p	£4	£8
1933	4,560,000	25p	50p	£4	£8
1934	3,052,800	25p	50p	£4	£8
1935	2,227,200	£1	£3	£15	£30
1936	9,734,400	25p	50p	£3	£6

George V

GEORGE VI (1936–52)

DATE	MINTAGE	F	VF	EF	UNC
1937	8,131,200	—	—	50p	£1
1937 Proof	26,402	—	—	—	£8
1938	7,449,600	—	—	£1	£6
1939	31,440,000			50p	£1
1940	18,360,000	—	—	50p	£1
1941	27,312,000	—	—	50p	£1
1942	28,857,600	—	—	50p	£1
1943	33,345,600	—	—	50p	£1
1944	25,137,600	—	—	50p	£1

George VI

DATE	MINTAGE	F	VF	EF	UNC
1945	23,736,000	–	–	50p	£1
1946	24,364,800	–	–	50p	£1
1947	14,745,600	–	–	50p	£1
1948	16,622,400	–	–	50p	£1
1949	8,424,000	–	–	50p	£1
1950	10,324,800	–	–	50p	£1
1950 Proof	17,513	–	–	50p	£8
1951	14,016,000	–	–	50p	£1
1951 Proof	20,000	–	–	50p	£8
1952	5,251,200	–	–	50p	£1

Elizabeth II

ELIZABETH II (1952–2022)

DATE	MINTAGE	F	VF	EF	UNC
1953	6,131,037	–	–	–	£1
1953 Proof	40,000	–	–	–	£8
1954	6,566,400	–	–	–	£2
1955	5,779,200	–	–	–	£2
1956	1,996,800	–	£1	£2	£6

HALF FARTHINGS

William IV

GEORGE IV (1820–30)

DATE	MINTAGE	F	VF	EF	UNC
1828 (two different obverses) (issued for Ceylon)	7,680,000	£10	£22	£60	£225
1830 (large or small date) (issued for Ceylon)	8,766,320	£10	£22	£60	£225

WILLIAM IV (1830–37)

DATE	MINTAGE	F	VF	EF	UNC
1837 (issued for Ceylon)	1,935,360	£25	£75	£200	£400

VICTORIA (1837–1901)

DATE	MINTAGE	F	VF	EF	UNC
1839	2,042,880	£5	£10	£35	£100
1842	unrecorded	£4	£8	£30	£100
1843	3,440,640	£3	£6	£25	£70
1844	6,451,200	£3	£6	£15	£55
1844 E over N in REGINA	incl. above	£10	£45	£100	–
1847	3,010,560	£6	£12	£40	£130
1851	unrecorded	£6	£12	£40	£150
1851 5 over 0	unrecorded	£8	£20	£60	£180
1852	989,184	£6	£12	£45	£160
1853	955,224	£6	£15	£50	£200
1853 Proof	incl. above	–	–	–	£850
1854	677,376	£9	£30	£80	£220
1856	913,920	£9	£30	£80	£220
1868 Proof	unrecorded			Very Rare	

Victoria

THIRD FARTHINGS

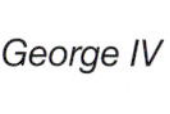

George IV

DATE	MINTAGE	F	VF	EF	UNC
GEORGE IV (1820–30)					
1827 (issued for Malta)	unrecorded	£8	£20	£50	£125
WILLIAM IV (1830–37)					
1835 (issued for Malta)	unrecorded	£8	£25	£60	£170
VICTORIA (1837–1901)					
1844 (issued for Malta)	1,301,040	£15	£35	£110	£250
1844 RE for REG	incl. above	£30	£70	£275	—
1866	576,000	£6	£15	£35	£75
1868	144,000	£6	£15	£35	£70
1876	162,000	£6	£15	£35	£90
1878	288,000	£6	£15	£35	£80
1881	144,000	£6	£15	£35	£80
1884	144,000	£6	£15	£35	£80
1885	288,000	£6	£15	£35	£80
EDWARD VII (1902–10)					
1902 (issued for Malta)	288,000	£5	£10	£25	£45
GEORGE V (1911–36)					
1913 (issued for Malta)	288,000	£5	£10	£25	£45

Victoria

QUARTER FARTHINGS

DATE	MINTAGE	F	VF	EF	UNC
VICTORIA (1837–1901)					
1839 (issued for Ceylon)	3,840,000	£50	£80	£150	£300
1851 (issued for Ceylon)	2,215,680	£50	£80	£150	£300
1852 (issued for Ceylon)	unknown	£50	£80	£150	£300
1853 (issued for Ceylon)	unknown	£50	£80	£150	£325
1853 Proof	unknown	—	—	—	£1500

EMERGENCY ISSUES

GEORGE III (1760–1820)

To alleviate the shortage of circulating coinage during the Napoleonic Wars the Bank of England firstly authorised the countermarking of other countries' coins, enabling them to pass as English currency. The coins, countermarked with punches depicting the head of George III, were mostly Spanish American 8 reales of Charles III. Although this had limited success it was later decided to completely overstrike the coins with a new English design on both sides—specimens that still show traces of the original host coin's date are avidly sought after by collectors. This overstriking continued for a number of years although all the known coins are dated 1804. Finally, in 1811 the Bank of England issued silver tokens which continued up to 1816 when a completely new regal coinage was introduced.

DATE	F	VF	EF	UNC
DOLLAR				
Oval countermark of George III				
On "Pillar" type 8 reales	£200	£850	£1500	—
*On "Portrait" type............	£200	£400	£1250	—
Octagonal countermark of George III				
On "Portrait" type.............	£200	£750	£1400	—
HALF DOLLAR				
Oval countermark of George III				
On "Portrait" type 4 reales	£200	£500	£1400	—
FIVE SHILLINGS OR ONE DOLLAR				
These coins were overstruck on Spanish-American coins				
1804.................................	£150	£350	£750	—
— With details of original coin still visible add from 10%.				

BANK OF ENGLAND TOKENS

DATE	F	VF	EF	UNC
THREE SHILLINGS				
1811 Draped bust.............	£35	£75	£275	—
1812 —	£35	£75	£300	—
1812 Laureate bust	£35	£65	£250	—
1813 —	£35	£65	£250	—
1814 —	£35	£65	£250	—
1815 —	£35	£65	£250	—
1816 —	£250	£600	£1850	—
ONE SHILLING AND SIXPENCE				
1811 Draped bust.............	£20	£50	£110	£260
1812 —	£20	£50	£110	£260
1812 Laureate bust	£20	£50	£110	£260
1812 Proof in platinum				Unique
1813 —	£20	£45	£90	£260
1813 Proof in platinum				Unique
1814 —	£20	£55	£90	£260
1815 —	£20	£55	£90	£260
1816 —	£20	£55	£90	£260
NINEPENCE				
1812 Pattern (three types)				from £3000

MAUNDY SETS

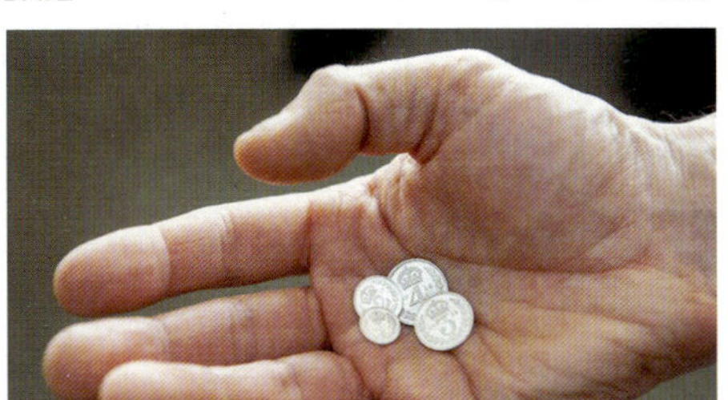

CHARLES II (1660–85)

DATE	F	VF	EF	UNC
Undated	£255	£375	£825	–
1670	£260	£370	£825	–
1671	£280	£450	£875	–
1672	£250	£380	£775	–
1673	£240	£350	£720	–
1674	£240	£340	£735	–
1675	£220	£325	£715	–
1676	£245	£375	£770	–
1677	£210	£310	£690	–
1678	£305	£460	£850	–
1679	£235	£360	£775	–
1680	£225	£345	£745	–
1681	£270	£380	£800	–
1682	£235	£360	£750	–
1683	£235	£360	£750	–
1684	£255	£365	£780	–

JAMES II (1685–88)

DATE	F	VF	EF	UNC
1686	£250	£375	£770	–
1687	£245	£370	£765	–
1688	£265	£410	£790	–

WILLIAM & MARY (1688–94)

DATE	F	VF	EF	UNC
1689	£875	£1250	£1900	–
1691	£650	£900	£1550	–
1692	£725	£925	£1650	–
1693	£675	£900	£1750	–
1694	£470	£735	£1300	–

WILLIAM III (1694–1702)

DATE	F	VF	EF	UNC
1698	£250	£480	£870	–
1699	£505	£700	£1575	–
1700	£280	£490	£925	–
1701	£260	£450	£900	–

ANNE (1702–14)

DATE	F	VF	EF	UNC
1703	£250	£440	£775	–
1705	£255	£450	£800	–
1706	£205	£375	£680	–
1708	£650	£1000	£1900	–
1709	£260	£475	£850	–
1710	£280	£500	£850	–
1713	£275	£435	£775	–

Sets in contemporary dated boxes are usually worth a higher premium. For example approximately £30 can be added to sets from Victoria to George VI in contemporary undated boxes and above £40 for dated boxes.

GEORGE I (1714–27)

DATE	F	VF	EF	UNC
1723	£285	£460	£825	–
1727	£275	£4505	£800	–

GEORGE II (1727–60)

DATE	F	VF	EF	UNC
1729	£225	£350	£675	–
1731	£225	£350	£675	–
1732	£210	£320	£660	–
1735	£210	£340	£660	–
1737	£205	£325	£640	–
1739	£190	£320	£625	–
1740	£175	£300	£600	–
1743	£350	£445	£900	–
1746	£175	£300	£575	–
1760	£190	£325	£615	–

GEORGE III (1760–1820)

DATE	F	VF	EF	UNC
1763	£170	£290	£475	–
1763 Proof	–			£22000
1766	£225	£350	£550	–
1772	£190	£300	£525	–
1780	£250	£350	£675	–
1784	£195	£320	£500	–
1786	£195	£310	£515	–
1792 Wire	£300	£450	£675	£900
1795	£120	£200	£325	£405
1800	£120	£200	£300	£375
New Coinage				
1817	£155	£260	£305	£500
1818	£155	£245	£290	£480
1820	£150	£255	£300	£475

GEORGE IV (1820–30)

DATE	F	VF	EF	UNC
1822	–	£180	£250	£450
1823	–	£160	£255	£450
1824	–	£175	£260	£450
1825	–	£150	£255	£400
1826	–	£145	£245	£400
1827	–	£150	£255	£405
1828	–	£160	£250	£425
1828 Proof	–	–	–	£4500
1829	–	£150	£250	£395
1830	–	£150	£240	£400

WILLIAM IV (1830–37)

DATE	F	VF	EF	UNC
1831	–	£175	£280	£460
1831 Proof	–	–	–	£1900
1831 Proof Gold	–	–		£41000
1832	–	£225	£315	£485
1833	–	£180	£275	£425
1834	–	£185	£280	£450
1835	–	£170	£265	£415
1836	–	£185	£285	£440
1837	–	£220	£350	£490

VICTORIA (1837–1901)

YOUNG HEAD ISSUES

DATE	MINTAGE	EF	UNC
1838	4,158	£270	£450
1838 Proof	unrecorded		£3400
1838 Proof Gold			£42000
1839	4,125	£325	£575
1839 Proof	unrecorded	£700	£1900
1840	4,125	£300	£445
1841	2,574	£405	£690
1842	4,125	£450	£635
1843	4,158	£260	£425
1844	4,158	£355	£585
1845	4,158	£225	£415
1846	4,158	£505	£790
1847	4,158	£625	£1125
1848	4,158	£600	£1125
1849	4,158	£375	£550
1850	4,158	£250	£425
1851	4,158	£305	£475
1852	4,158	£615	£1175
1853	4,158	£635	£1125
1853 Proof	unrecorded		£2300
1854	4,158	£275	£400
1855	4,158	£315	£525
1856	4,158	£235	£375
1857	4,158	£275	£425
1858	4,158	£240	£375
1859	4,158	£215	£315
1860	4,158	£250	£385
1861	4,158	£205	£385
1862	4,158	£250	£425
1863	4,158	£275	£450
1864	4,158	£240	£345
1865	4,158	£240	£355
1866	4,158	£225	£340
1867	4,158	£250	£350
1867 Proof	unrecorded	–	£3300
1868	4,158	£200	£325
1868 Proof	unrecorded		£3200
1869	4,158	£275	£395
1870	4,458	£190	£290
1871	4,488	£185	£280
1871 Proof	unrecorded	–	£3000
1872	4,328	£180	£280
1873	4,162	£180	£275
1874	4,488	£185	£275
1875	4,154	£180	£270
1876	4,488	£190	£275
1877	4,488	£180	£265
1878	4,488	£185	£265
1878 Proof	unrecorded	–	£2750
1879	4,488	£190	£250
1879 Proof	unrecorded	–	£2850
1880	4,488	£190	£260
1881	4,488	£180	£260
1881 Proof	unrecorded	–	£2500
1882	4,146	£215	£285
1882 Proof	unrecorded	–	£2700
1883	4,488	£160	£240
1884	4,488	£160	£240
1885	4,488	£160	£240
1886	4,488	£165	£240
1887	4,488	£180	£285

JUBILEE HEAD ISSUES

DATE	MINTAGE	EF	UNC
1888	4,488	£160	£235
1888 Proof	unrecorded	–	£2400
1889	4,488	£170	£255
1890	4,488	£160	£240
1891	4,488	£160	£240
1892	4,488	£180	£260

OLD HEAD ISSUES

DATE	MINTAGE	EF	UNC
1893	8,976	£115	£190
1894	8,976	£135	£225
1895	8,976	£120	£195
1896	8,976	£120	£195
1897	8,976	£120	£195
1898	8,976	£125	£200
1899	8,976	£130	£200
1900	8,976	£110	£185
1901	8,976	£110	£175

EDWARD VII (1902–10)

DATE	MINTAGE	EF	UNC
1902	8,976	£95	£170
1902 Matt proof	15,123	–	£225
1903	8,976	£100	£170
1904	8,976	£110	£180
1905	8,976	£110	£180
1906	8,800	£100	£170
1907	8,760	£100	£175
1908	8,769	£100	£170
1909	1,983	£175	£290
1910	1,440	£195	£300

GEORGE V (1911–36)

DATE	MINTAGE	EF	UNC
1911	1,786	£150	£260
1911 Proof	6,007	–	£460
1912	1,246	£160	£260
1913	1,228	£155	£260
1914	982	£205	£305
1915	1,293	£165	£270
1916	1,128	£160	£260
1917	1,237	£160	£260
1918	1,375	£165	£265
1919	1,258	£160	£265
1920	1,399	£160	£255
1921	1,386	£160	£255
1922	1,373	£165	£260
1923	1,430	£165	£275
1924	1,515	£165	£275
1925	1,438	£150	£245
1926	1,504	£150	£245
1927	1,647	£155	£255
1928	1,642	£165	£270
1929	1,761	£170	£270
1930	1,724	£150	£240
1931	1,759	£150	£240
1932	1,835	£145	£250
1933	1,872	£140	£240
1934	1,887	£140	£240
1935	1,928	£170	£260
1936	1,323	£250	£315

GEORGE VI (1936–52)

DATE	MINTAGE	EF	UNC
1937	1,325	£140	£175
1937 Proof	20,900	£140	£210
1938	1,275	£175	£255

DATE	MINTAGE	EF	UNC
1939	1,234	£180	£265
1940	1,277	£175	£255
1941	1,253	£180	£265
1942	1,231	£175	£255
1943	1,239	£175	£260
1944	1,259	£175	£260
1945	1,355	£180	£255
1946	1,365	£175	£255
1947	1,375	£185	£275
1948	1,385	£185	£280
1949	1,395	£190	£280
1950	1,405	£195	£285
1951	1,468	£195	£290
1952	1,012	£215	£305
1952 Proof (copper)			£19,000

ELIZABETH II (1952–2022)

DATE AND PLACE OF ISSUE	MINTAGE	UNC
1953 St. Paul's Cathedral	1,025	£1200
1953 Proof in gold	unrecorded	Ex. rare
1953 Proof Matt		Very rare
1954 Westminster Abbey	1,020	£210
1955 Southwark Cathedral	1,036	£210
1955 Proof Matt		£3500
1956 Westminster Abbey	1,088	£205
1957 St. Albans Cathedral	1,094	£205
1958 Westminster Abbey	1,100	£205
1959 St. George's Chapel, Windsor	1,106	£205
1960 Westminster Abbey	1,112	£205
1961 Rochester Cathedral	1,118	£205
1962 Westminster Abbey	1,125	£200
1963 Chelmsford Cathedral	1,131	£200
1964 Westminster Abbey	1,137	£200
1965 Canterbury Cathedral	1,143	£200
1966 Westminster Abbey	1,206	£205
1967 Durham Cathedral	986	£235
1968 Westminster Abbey	964	£245
1969 Selby Cathedral	1,002	£220
1970 Westminster Abbey	980	£240
1971 Tewkesbury Abbey	1,018	£215
1972 York Minster	1,026	£220
1973 Westminster Abbey	1,004	£215
1974 Salisbury Cathedral	1,042	£215
1975 Peterborough Cathedral	1,050	£215
1976 Hereford Cathedral	1,158	£220
1977 Westminster Abbey	1,138	£240
1978 Carlisle Cathedral	1,178	£215
1979 Winchester Cathedral	1,188	£215
1980 Worcester Cathedral	1,198	£215
1981 Westminster Abbey	1,178	£215
1982 St David's Cathedral	1,218	£220
1983 Exeter Cathedral	1,228	£215
1984 Southwell Minster	1,238	£215
1985 Ripon Cathedral	1,248	£215
1986 Chichester Cathedral	1,378	£225
1987 Ely Cathedral	1,390	£225
1988 Lichfield Cathedral	1,402	£220
1989 Birmingham Cathedral	1,353	£220
1990 Newcastle Cathedral	1,523	£220
1991 Westminster Abbey	1,384	£220
1992 Chester Cathedral	1,424	£225
1993 Wells Cathedral	1,440	£225
1994 Truro Cathedral	1,433	£225
1995 Coventry Cathedral	1,466	£225
1996 Norwich Cathedral	1,629	£230
1997 Birmingham Cathedral	1,786	£230
1998 Portsmouth Cathedral	1,654	£230
1999 Bristol Cathedral	1,676	£235
2000 Lincoln Cathedral	1,686	£225
2000 Silver Proof	13,180	£200
2001 Westminster Abbey	1,132	£250
2002 Canterbury Cathedral	1,681	£225
2002 Gold Proof	2,002	£2500
2003 Gloucester Cathedral	1,608	£235
2004 Liverpool Cathedral	1,613	£240
2005 Wakefield Cathedral	1,685	£240
2006 Guildford Cathedral	1,937	£240
2006 Silver Proof	6,394	£195
2007 Manchester Cathedral	1,822	£295
2008 St Patrick's Cathedral (Armagh)	1,833	£710
2009 St. Edmundsbury Cathedral	1,602	£600
2010 Derby Cathedral	1,617	£550
2011 Westminster Abbey	1,734	£550
2012 York Minster	1,633	£625
2013 Christ Church Cathedral Oxford	1,627	£650
2014 Blackburn Cathedral	1,693	£750
2015 Sheffield Cathedral	1,721	£650
2016 St. George's Chapel, Windsor	1,940	£625
2017 Leicester Cathedral	1,919	£700
2018 St. George's Chapel, Windsor	1,993	£725
2019 St. George's Chapel, Windsor	1,997	£750
2020 Service cancelled due to the Pandemic. Recipients received the coins in the post	2,010	£815
2021 Service cancelled. Recipients received the coins in the post	1,995	£800
2022 St. George's Chapel, Windsor	1,920	£850

CHARLES III (2022–)

DATE AND PLACE OF ISSUE	MINTAGE	UNC
2023 York Minster		£900
2024 Worcester Cathedral		£900

Despite the decimalisation of the coinage in 1971, in keeping with ancient tradition the Royal Maundy sets are still made up of four silver coins (4p, 3p, 2p and 1p). The designs for the reverse of the coins are a crowned numeral in a wreath of oak leaves—basically the same design that has been used for Maundy coins since George IV.

MAUNDY ODDMENTS SINGLE COINS

FOUR PENCE

CHARLES II (1660–85)

DATE	F	VF	EF
Undated	£80	£140	£200
1670	£80	£150	£235
1671	£100	£200	£290
1672/1	£80	£125	£185
1673	£75	£120	£180
1674	£70	£115	£175
1674 7 over 6	£75	£130	£205
1675	£65	£115	£165
1675/4	£75	£115	£190
1676	£75	£110	£195
1676 7 over 6	£80	£125	£205
1677	£55	£95	£160
1678	£55	£95	£160
1678 8 over 6	£60	£100	£165
1678 8 over 7	£65	£115	£175
1679	£55	£95	£155
1680	£55	£100	£160
1681	£60	£115	£170
1681 B over R in HIB	£70	£135	£200
1682	£65	£95	£180
1682/1	£70	£100	£195
1683	£65	£95	£180
1684	£70	£120	£200
1684 4 over 3	£85	£130	£215

JAMES II (1685–88)

DATE	F	VF	EF
1686	£80	£120	£205
1686 Date over crown	£85	£135	£225
1687	£75	£115	£185
1687 7 over 6	£80	£115	£190
1687 8 over 7	£75	£115	£200
1688	£85	£125	£220
1688 1 over 8	£110	£150	£230
1688/7	£85	£130	£225

WILLIAM & MARY (1688–94)

DATE	F	VF	EF
1689	£85	£145	£215
1689 GV below bust	£85	£155	£220
1689 GVLEELMVS	£150	£260	£335
1690	£80	£140	£235
1690 No stop after "G" in D.G	£110	£175	£275
1690 6 over 5	£100	£145	£240
1691	£100	£155	£245
1691 1 over 0	£90	£160	£245
1692	£150	£210	£285
1692 MAR•IA	£220	£315	£400
1692 2 over 1	£130	£170	£270
1693	£145	£250	£370
1693 3 over 2	£155	£265	£385
1694	£95	£150	£225
1694 small lettering	£100	£160	£230

WILLIAM III (1694–1702)

DATE	F	VF	EF
1697—Reported	—	—	—
1698	£90	£160	£235
1699	£75	£130	£215
1700	£100	£165	£250
1701	£95	£155	£235
1702	£95	£150	£235

It is nowadays considered that the early small denomination silver coins 4d–1d were originally struck for the Maundy ceremony although undoubtedly many subsequently circulated as small change—therefore they are listed here under "Maundy silver single coins".

Charles II

William & Mary

Queen Anne

George I

ANNE (1702–14)

DATE	F	VF	EF	UNC
1703	£95	£140	£225	–
1704	£80	£125	£185	–
1705	£150	£220	£300	–
1706	£80	£130	£185	–
1708	£85	£140	£220	–
1709	£80	£130	£205	–
1710	£60	£115	£165	–
1713	£80	£135	£200	–

GEORGE I (1714–27)

DATE	F	VF	EF	UNC
1717	£85	£135	£190	–
1721	£85	£135	£185	–
1723	£95	£150	£230	–
1727	£95	£145	£235	–

George II

GEORGE II (1727–60)

DATE	F	VF	EF	UNC
1729	£75	£120	£180	–
1731	£70	£120	£170	–
1732	£70	£110	£170	–
1735	£70	£100	£165	–
1737	£70	£115	£170	–
1739	£65	£105	£160	–
1740	£55	£95	£145	–
1743	£145	£205	£310	–
1743 3 over 0	£155	£235	£330	
1746	£55	£90	£140	–
1760	£65	£115	£160	–

George III

GEORGE III (1760–1820)

DATE	F	VF	EF	UNC
1763 Young head	£60	£95	£145	–
1763 Proof	–	–	Extremely rare	
1765	£500	£900	£1200	–
1766	£70	£115	£160	–
1770	£175	£270	£390	–
1772	£80	£130	£200	–
1776	£70	£130	£180	–
1780	£55	£100	£140	–
1784	£50	£95	£130	–
1786	£70	£120	£170	–
1792 Older head, Thin 4	£110	£185	£250	£325
1795	–	£60	£100	£140
1800	–	£55	£95	£130
1817 New coinage	–	£65	£100	£150
1818	–	£65	£95	£145
1820	–	£60	£95	£150

George IV

GEORGE IV (1820–30)

DATE	F	VF	EF	UNC
1822	–	–	£100	£160
1823	–	–	£95	£150
1824	–	–	£90	£150
1826	–	–	£85	£140
1827	–	–	£85	£145
1828	–	–	£90	£140
1829	–	–	£85	£135
1830	–	–	£90	£140

WILLIAM IV (1830–37)

DATE	F	VF	EF	UNC
1831–37	–	–	£85	£160
1831 Proof	–	–	£350	£515

Victoria

VICTORIA (1837–1901)

DATE	F	VF	EF	UNC
1838 Proof	–	–	–	£1100
1839 Proof	–	–	–	£550
1853 Proof	–	–	–	£725
1838–87 (Young Head)	–	–	£40	£60
1841	–	–	£50	£75
1888–92 (Jubilee Head)	–	–	£35	£55
1893–1901 (Old Head)	–	–	£30	£50

DATE	F	VF	EF	UNC
EDWARD VII (1901–10)				
1902–08	–	–	£30	£45
1902 Proof	–	–	£40	£60
1909 & 1910	–	–	£60	£110
GEORGE V (1910–36)				
1911–36	–	–	£45	£65
1911 Proof	–	–	£60	£85
GEORGE VI (1936–52)				
1937–52	–	–	£50	£70
1937 Proof	–	–	£40	£60
ELIZABETH II (1952–2022)				
1953	–	–	£210	£275
1954–85	–	–	£45	£75
1986–2007	–	–	£65	£85
2002 in Gold Proof	–	–	£550	£825
2008	–	–	–	£190
2009	–	–	–	£180
2010	–	–	–	£160
2011	–	–	–	£150
2012	–	–	–	£160
2013	–	–	–	£165
2014	–	–	–	£210
2015	–	–	–	£165
2016	–	–	–	£170
2017	–	–	–	£200
2018	–	–	–	£210
2019	–	–	–	£210
2020	–	–	–	£220
2021	–	–	–	£225
2022	–	–	–	£250
CHARLES III (2022–)				
2023	–	–	–	£300
2024	–	–	–	£300

Elizabeth II

Charles III

THREEPENCE

DATE	F	VF	EF	UNC
CHARLES II (1660–85)				
Undated	£75	£130	£200	–
1670	£75	£125	£185	–
1671	£75	£130	£185	–
1671 GRVTIA	£85	£160	£245	–
1672	£80	£130	£195	–
1673	£70	£110	£175	–
1674	£70	£110	£175	–
1675	£70	£110	£180	–
1676	£75	£125	£220	–
1676 6 over 5	£90	£140	£240	–
1676 ERA for FRA	£115	£170	£250	–
1677	£65	£90	£165	–
1678	£55	£85	£140	–
1679	£50	£80	£140	–
1679 O/A in CAROLVS	£125	£180	£275	–
1680	£65	£100	£175	–
1681	£70	£110	£190	–
1682/1	£65	£110	£175	–
1682	£65	£115	£175	–
1683	£65	£110	£170	–
1684	£70	£115	£175	–
1684/3	£75	£115	£180	–
JAMES II (1685–88)				
1685	£85	£125	£200	–
1685 Struck on fourpence flan	£160	£235	£350	–
1686	£80	£120	£175	–
1687	£80	£120	£170	–

James II

William & Mary

DATE	F	VF	EF	UNC
1687 7 over 6	£85	£115	£175	–
1688	£85	£130	£215	–
1688 8 over 7	£95	£140	£225	–

WILLIAM & MARY (1688–94)

DATE	F	VF	EF	UNC
1689	£85	£130	£195	–
1689 No stop on reverse	£90	£135	£200	–
1689 LMV over MVS (obverse)	£120	£160	£240	–
1690	£100	£150	£210	–
1690 9 over 6	£105	£155	£225	–
1690 6 over 5	£100	£150	£220	–
1691 First bust	£370	£570	£850	–
1691 Second bust	£245	£365	£525	–
1692	£120	£180	£275	–
1692 G below bust	£125	£185	£275	–
1692 GV below bust	£125	£180	£270	–
1692 GVL below bust	£125	£180	£275	–
1693	£150	£220	£300	–
1693 3 over 2	£155	£245	£310	–
1694	£95	£120	£200	–
1694 MARIΛ	£140	£180	£265	–
1694 GV below bust	£105	£135	£210	–
1694 GVL below bust	£105	£140	£220	–

William III

WILLIAM III (1694–1702)

DATE	F	VF	EF	UNC
1698	£80	£145	£225	–
1699	£75	£135	£200	–
1700	£85	£150	£220	–
1701 Small lettering	£80	£140	£215	–
1701 GBA instead of GRA	£100	£170	£240	–
1701 Large lettering	£90	£145	£215	–

Queen Anne

ANNE (1702–14)

DATE	F	VF	EF	UNC
1703	£80	£125	£205	–
1703 7 of date above crown	£90	£150	£230	–
1704	£75	£105	£180	–
1705	£90	£140	£225	–
1706	£70	£105	£175	–
1707	£65	£105	£155	–
1708	£75	£125	£185	–
1708 8 over 7	£75	£130	£195	–
1709	£70	£145	£195	–
1710	£55	£105	£150	–
1713	£75	£135	£190	–

George I

GEORGE I (1714–27)

DATE	F	VF	EF	UNC
1717	£80	£125	£180	–
1721	£80	£125	£180	–
1723	£90	£145	£210	–
1727	£85	£140	£205	–

George II

GEORGE II (1727–60)

DATE	F	VF	EF	UNC
1729	£60	£110	£155	–
1731	£60	£110	£160	–
1731 Small lettering	£75	£120	£180	–
1732	£60	£105	£160	–
1732 Stop over head	£75	£120	£175	–
1735	£70	£110	£175	–
1737	£65	£100	£170	–
1739	£65	£100	£175	–
1740	£55	£95	£145	–
1743 Small and large lettering	£65	£95	£160	–
1743 Stop over head	£70	£100	£170	–
1746	£50	£80	£140	–
1746 6 over 3	£60	£90	£155	–
1760	£65	£95	£160	–

DATE	F	VF	EF	UNC
GEORGE III (1760–1820)				
1762	£30	£50	£70	–
1763	£30	£50	£75	–
1763 Proof	–	–	Extremely rare	
1765	£425	£650	£975	–
1766	£70	£110	£185	–
1770	£95	£135	£215	–
1772	£60	£90	£120	–
1780	£65	£95	£125	–
1784	£80	£115	£195	–
1786	£80	£110	£190	–
1792	£120	£175	£250	£340
1795	–	£45	£80	£120
1800	–	£50	£85	£130
1817	–	£55	£95	£170
1818	–	£55	£95	£170
1820	–	£55	£95	£170
 **GEORGE IV (1820–30)**				
1822	–	–	£90	£180
1823	–	–	£80	£160
1824	–	–	£80	£170
1825–30	–	–	£80	£165
WILLIAM IV (1830–37)				
1831 Proof	–	–	£425	£700
1831	–	–	£110	£175
1832	–	–	£130	£220
1833–1836	–	–	£90	£160
1837	–	–	£115	£205
VICTORIA (1837–1901)				
1838	–	–	£120	£225
1838 Proof	–	–	–	£1750
1839	–	–	£235	£400
1839 Proof	–	–	–	£650
1840	–	–	£160	£290
1841	–	–	£325	£550
1842	–	–	£305	£455
1843	–	–	£130	£235
1844	–	–	£225	£365
1845	–	–	£85	£165
1846	–	–	£415	£725
1847	–	–	£495	£900
1848	–	–	£475	£875
1849	–	–	£230	£375
1850	–	–	£115	£225
1851	–	–	£185	£350
1852	–	–	£500	£925
1853	–	–	£485	£895
1853 Proof	–	–	–	£1250
1854	–	–	£160	£300
1855	–	–	£195	£370
1856	–	–	£100	£220
1857	–	–	£160	£290
1858	–	–	£120	£235
1859	–	–	£100	£195
1860	–	–	£145	£255
1861	–	–	£145	£245
1862	–	–	£165	£290
1863	–	–	£195	£315
1864	–	–	£145	£250
1865	–	–	£140	£260
1866	–	–	£130	£255
1867	–	–	£135	£245
1868	–	–	£115	£215
1869	–	–	£175	£295

George III

George IV

William IV

Victoria

DATE	F	VF	EF	UNC
1870	—	—	£110	£195
1871	—	—	£105	£190
1872	—	—	£95	£185
1873	—	—	£90	£175
1874	—	—	£90	£185
1875	—	—	£85	£180
1876	—	—	£85	£175
1877	—	—	£80	£170
1878	—	—	£90	£175
1879	—	—	£85	£170
1880	—	—	£80	£165
1881	—	—	£80	£160
1882	—	—	£145	£240
1883	—	—	£75	£155
1884	—	—	£75	£155
1885	—	—	£70	£140
1886	—	—	£70	£135
1887	—	—	£85	£175
1888–1892 (Jubilee Head)	—	—	£55	£110
1893–1901 (Old Head)	—	—	£40	£65

Edward VII

EDWARD VII (1901–10)

DATE	F	VF	EF	UNC
1902	—	—	£30	£50
1902 Proof	—	—	—	£65
1903	—	—	£40	£80
1904	—	—	£55	£100
1905	—	—	£55	£90
1906	—	—	£45	£85
1907	—	—	£45	£85
1908	—	—	£40	£75
1909	—	—	£80	£135
1910	—	—	£90	£150

George V

GEORGE V (1910–36)

DATE	F	VF	EF	UNC
1911–34	—	—	£60	£85
1911 Proof	—	—	—	£135
1935	—	—	£65	£110
1936	—	—	£85	£140

GEORGE VI (1936–52)

DATE	F	VF	EF	UNC
1937–52	—	—	£50	£80
1937 Proof	—	—	—	£70

Elizabeth

ELIZABETH II (1952–2022)

DATE	F	VF	EF	UNC
1953	—	—	£225	£325
1954–85	—	—	£45	£75
1986–2007	—	—	£55	£80
2002 In gold (proof)	—	—	—	£650
2008	—	—	—	£155
2009	—	—	—	£145
2010	—	—	—	£150
2011	—	—	—	£130
2012	—	—	—	£140
2013	—	—	—	£140
2014	—		—	£170
2015	—	—	—	£155
2016	—	—	—	£150
2017	—	—	—	£170
2018	—	—	—	£180
2019	—	—	—	£190
2020	—	—	—	£200
2021	—	—	—	£210
2022	—	—	—	£215

Charles III

CHARLES III (2022–)

DATE	F	VF	EF	UNC
2023	—	—	—	£275
2024	—	—	—	£275

TWOPENCE

CHARLES II (1660–85)

DATE	F	VF	EF	UNC
Undated	£65	£110	£165	–
1668	£70	£110	£175	–
1670	£55	£80	£155	–
1671	£55	£90	£155	–
1672	£55	£90	£150	–
1672/1	£65	£110	£165	–
1673	£55	£85	£155	–
1674	£60	£95	£150	–
1675	£50	£90	£140	–
1676	£60	£100	£155	–
1677	£45	£85	£135	–
1678	£40	£80	£130	–
1679	£45	£75	£125	–
1679 HIB over FRA	£50	£100	£150	–
1680	£50	£85	£135	–
1680 over 79	£45	£80	£145	–
1681	£55	£80	£135	–
1682	£65	£90	£165	–
1682/1 ERA for FRA	£80	£125	£225	–
1683	£60	£100	£165	–
1683 over 2	£60	£110	£185	–
1684	£60	£100	£160	–

JAMES II (1685–88)

DATE	F	VF	EF	UNC
1686	£65	£110	£165	–
1686 reads IACOBVS	£90	£140	£240	–
1687	£70	£100	£165	–
1687 ERA for FRA	£80	£135	£235	–
1688	£55	£90	£155	–
1688/7	£65	£95	£170	–

WILLIAM & MARY (1688–94)

DATE	F	VF	EF	UNC
1689	£75	£115	£185	–
1691	£70	£115	£170	–
1692	£80	£140	£210	–
1693	£75	£125	£205	–
1693 GV below bust	£85	£125	£200	–
1693/2	£70	£110	£190	–
1694	£55	£95	£150	–
1694 MARLA error	£90	£160	£260	–
1694 GVLI under bust	£70	£110	£195	–
1694 GVL under bust	£65	£110	£190	–
1694/3	£65	£115	£200	–

WILLIAM III (1694–1702)

DATE	F	VF	EF	UNC
1698	£70	£130	£190	–
1699	£55	£100	£155	–
1700	£75	£130	£195	–
1701	£70	£120	£175	–

ANNE (1702–14)

DATE	F	VF	EF	UNC
1703	£70	£120	£195	–
1704	£50	£80	£135	–
1704 No stops on obverse	£60	£100	£170	–
1705	£65	£110	£170	–
1706	£85	£140	£200	–
1707	£55	£90	£150	–
1708	£75	£115	£185	–
1709	£90	£150	£230	–
1710	£50	£80	£115	–
1713	£75	£125	£205	–

James II

William & Mary

William III

Queen Anne

George II

DATE	F	VF	EF	UNC
GEORGE I (1714–27)				
1717	£50	£85	£135	–
1721	£50	£90	£130	–
1723	£70	£110	£170	–
1726	£60	£90	£135	–
1727	£65	£105	£155	–
GEORGE II (1727–60)				
1729	£55	£90	£130	–
1731	£55	£90	£130	–
1732	£55	£90	£125	–
1735	£55	£85	£125	–
1737	£50	£85	£125	–
1739	£50	£80	£125	–
1740	£45	£75	£120	–
1743	£45	£70	£115	–
1743/0	£50	£80	£125	–
1746	£40	£70	£95	–
1756	£35	£65	£95	–
1759	£35	£70	£95	–
1760	£50	£75	£110	–
GEORGE III (1760–1820)				
1763	£45	£70	£95	–
1763 Proof			Extremely rare	
1765	£425	£650	£875	–
1766	£50	£75	£95	–
1772	£45	£70	£95	–
1772 second 7 over 6	£45	£80	£105	–
1780	£40	£70	£95	–
1784	£40	£70	£90	–
1786	£55	£85	£100	–
1792	–	£95	£150	£210
1795	–	£35	£60	£85
1800	–	£35	£70	£85
1817	–	£40	£75	£90
1818	–	£40	£70	£90
1820	–	£45	£80	£100
GEORGE IV (1820–30)				
1822–30	–	–	£45	£70
1825 TRITANNIAR	–	–	£65	£125
1826 TRITANNIAR	–	–	£65	£125
WILLIAM IV (1830–37)				
1831–37	–	–	£45	£80
1831 Proof	–	–	£150	£260
VICTORIA (1837–1901)				
1838–87 (Young Head)	–	–	£35	£50
1859 BEITANNIAR	–	–	£80	£135
1861 6 over 1	–	–	£40	£85
1888–92 (Jubilee Head)	–	–	£35	£55
1893–1901 (Old Head	–	–	£30	£45
1838 Proof	–	–	–	£475
1839 Proof	–	–	–	£350
1853 Proof	–	–	–	£370
EDWARD VII (1901–10)				
1902–08	–	–	£25	£35
1902 Proof	–	–	£30	£60
1909	–	–	£45	£85
1910	–	–	£50	£90

George III

George IV

William IV

Victoria

DATE	F	VF	EF	UNC
GEORGE V (1910–36)				
1911–34	–	–	£35	£60
1911 Proof	–	–	£45	£80
1935	–	–	£40	£65
1936	–	–	£50	£80
GEORGE VI (1936–52)				
1937–47	–	–	£40	£65
1937 Proof	–	–	£35	£60
1948–52	–	–	£45	£75
ELIZABETH II (1952–2022)				
1953	–	–	£160	£225
1954–85	–	–	£40	£55
1986–2007	–	–	£40	£70
2002 Gold Proof	–	–	–	£425
2008	–	–	–	£125
2009	–	–	–	£115
2010	–	–	–	£110
2011	–	–	–	£90
2012	–	–	–	£115
2013	–	–	–	£120
2014	–	–	–	£140
2015	–	–	–	£115
2016	–	–	–	£135
2017	–	–	–	£170
2018	–	–	–	£170
2019	–	–	–	£175
2020	–	–	–	£185
2021	–	–	–	£175
2022	–	–	–	£180
CHARLES III (2022–)				
2023	–	–	–	£250
2024	–	–	–	£225

Elizabeth II

Charles III

PENNY

DATE	F	VF	EF	UNC
CHARLES II (1660–85)				
Undated	£80	£130	£200	–
1670	£75	£120	£180	–
1671	£75	£120	£175	–
1672/1	£70	£120	£175	–
1673	£70	£120	£170	–
1674	£70	£120	£175	–
1674 Ↄratia (error)	£110	£170	£250	–
1675	£70	£120	£170	–
1675 Ↄratia (error)	£110	£175	£260	–
1676	£85	£125	£190	–
1676 Ↄratia (error)	£120	£180	£275	–
1677	£60	£110	£165	–
1677 Ↄratia (error)	£95	£150	£235	–
1678	£150	£255	£365	–
1678 Ↄratia (error)	£180	£290	£380	–
1679	£85	£125	£210	–
1680	£85	£120	£200	–
1680 on 2d flan	£130	£250	£300	
1681	£110	£155	£230	–
1682	£75	£125	£195	–
1682 ERA for FRA	£90	£155	£245	–
1683	£85	£120	£195	–
1683/1	£85	£150	£225	–
1684	£125	£210	£260	–
1684/3	£130	£215	£270	–
JAMES II (1685–88)				
1685	£75	£130	£185	–
1686	£80	£130	£180	–

James II

William & Mary

DATE	F	VF	EF	UNC
1687	£80	£135	£190	–
1687 7 over 6	£90	£140	£195	–
1687/8	£85	£135	£195	–
1688	£65	£120	£180	–
1688/7	£75	£120	£190	–

WILLIAM & MARY (1688–94)

DATE	F	VF	EF	UNC
1689	£465	£700	£1000	–
1689 MΛRIΛ	£480	£700	£975	–
1689 GVIELMVS (Error)	£465	£715	£1000	–
1690	£90	£160	£240	–
1691	£90	£160	£230	–
1691/0	£90	£170	£255	–
1692	£230	£350	£500	–
1692/1	£240	£355	£530	–
1693	£115	£190	£275	–
1694	£85	£150	£230	–
1694 HI for HIB	£125	£180	£275	–
1694 No stops on obverse	£105	£165	£245	–

WILLIAM III (1694–1702)

DATE	F	VF	EF	UNC
1698	£90	£150	£200	–
1698 HI. BREX (Error)	£115	£175	£270	–
1698 IRA for FRA	£105	£170	£215	–
1699	£250	£395	£550	–
1700	£95	£165	£225	–
1701	£90	£140	£210	–

ANNE (1702–14)

DATE	F	VF	EF	UNC
1703	£85	£130	£195	–
1705	£75	£115	£180	–
1706	£70	£95	£165	–
1708	£415	£535	£775	–
1709	£60	£95	£150	–
1710	£145	£200	£305	–
1713/0	£85	£140	£190	–

GEORGE I (1714–27)

DATE	F	VF	EF	UNC
1716	£55	£90	£115	–
1718	£55	£90	£115	–
1720	£60	£95	£125	–
1720 HIPEX (Error)	£75	£125	£205	–
1723	£80	£125	£180	–
1725	£50	£85	£130	–
1726	£50	£85	£125	–
1727	£75	£120	£170	–

GEORGE II (1727–60)

DATE	F	VF	EF	UNC
1729	£45	£80	£125	–
1731	£50	£80	£125	–
1732	£50	£80	£120	–
1735	£45	£70	£100	–
1737	£40	£70	£105	–
1739	£40	£70	£100	–
1740	£45	£70	£100	–
1743	£40	£65	£95	–
1746	£45	£80	£115	–
1746/3	£50	£80	£120	–
1760	£35	£60	£85	–
1752	£35	£60	£85	–
1752/0	£40	£65	£90	–
1753	£35	£60	£85	–
1754	£35	£60	£85	–
1755	£35	£60	£85	–
1756	£35	£60	£80	–

William III

Anne

George I

George III

DATE	F	VF	EF	UNC
1757	£35	£60	£80	–
1757 No colon after Gratia	£45	£75	£90	–
1758	£35	£60	£85	–
1759	£35	£60	£80	–
1760	£40	£75	£95	–

GEORGE III (1760–1820)

DATE	F	VF	EF	UNC
1763	£55	£75	£115	–
1763 Proof	–	–	Extremely rare	
1766	£40	£70	£90	–
1770	£60	£95	£120	–
1772	£40	£70	£85	–
1780	£120	£165	£220	–
1781	£35	£60	£85	–
1784	£45	£65	£90	–
1786	£40	£60	£90	–
1792	£40	£70	£105	£140
1795	–	£25	£50	£70
1800	–	£25	£45	£70
1817	–	£30	£45	£70
1818	–	£30	£45	£70
1820	–	£35	£50	£75

GEORGE IV (1820–30)

DATE	F	VF	EF	UNC
1822–30	–	–	£40	£60

WILLIAM IV (1830–37)

DATE	F	VF	EF	UNC
1831–37	–	–	£45	£65
1831 Proof	–	–	£185	£250

VICTORIA (1837–1901)

DATE	F	VF	EF	UNC
1838–87 (Young Head)	–	–	£30	£45
1888–92 (Jubilee Head)	–	–	£30	£40
1893–1901 (Old Head)	–	–	£25	£30
1838 Proof	–	–	–	£295
1839 Proof	–	–	–	£190
1853 Proof	–	–	–	£225

EDWARD VII (1901–10)

DATE	F	VF	EF	UNC
1902–08	–	–	£20	£30
1902 Proof	–	–	£30	£40
1909	–	–	£50	£80
1910	–	–	£55	£90

GEORGE V (1910–36)

DATE	F	VF	EF	UNC
1911–14	–	–	£45	£75
1911 Proof	–	–	£50	£100
1915	–	–	£50	£85
1916–19	–	–	£45	£80
1920	–	–	£45	£80
1921–28	–	–	£45	£75
1929	–	–	£45	£80
1930–34	–	–	£40	£75
1935	–	–	£45	£80
1936	–	–	£55	£85

GEORGE VI (1936–52)

DATE	F	VF	EF	UNC
1937–40	–	–	£50	£75
1937 Proof	–	–	£45	£80
1941	–	–	£55	£85
1942–47	–	–	£50	£85
1948–52	–	–	£60	£90

ELIZABETH II (1952–2022)

DATE	F	VF	EF	UNC
1953	–	–	£315	£465
1965–85	–	–	£45	£75
1986–2007	–	–	£50	£80
2002 Proof in gold	–	–	–	£425

George IV

William IV

Victoria

Edward VII

George V

Elizabeth II

DATE	F	VF	EF	UNC
2008	–	–	–	£145
2009	–	–	–	£140
2010	–	–	–	£120
2011	–	–	–	£110
2012	–	–	–	£130
2013	–	–	–	£125
2014	–	–	–	£150
2015	–	–	–	£120
2016	–	–	–	£135
2017	–	–	–	£150
2018	–	–	–	£155
2019	–	–	–	£160
2020	–	–	–	£170
2021	–	–	–	£185
2022	–	–	–	£190

Charles III

CHARLES III (2022–)

DATE	F	VF	EF	UNC
2023	–	–	–	£225
2024	–	–	–	£225

Maundy 2024—1p, 2p, 3p and 4p reverses (shown enlarged).

The 2024 Maundy Service was held at the graceful Worcester Cathedral (right). For the first time this year, due to the ill health of King Charles III, a Consort, Queen Camilla, distributed the Royal Maundy (image courtesy Worcester Cathedral).

	Coin Size	Coin Weight
Decimal		
Half Penny	17.10mm	1.78g
Penny	20.30mm	3.56g
Two Pence	25.90mm	7.12g
Old Five Pence	23.60mm	5.56g
New Five Pence	18.00mm	3.25g
Old Ten Pence	28.50mm	11.31g
New Ten Pence	24.3mm	6.5g
Twenty Pence	21.40mm	5g
Twenty Five Pence	38.61mm	28.28g
Old Fifty Pence	30.00mm	13.5g
Fifty Pence	27.30mm	8g
One Pound	22.50mm	9.5g
One Pound (2017)	23.43mm	8.75g
Two Pound	28.40mm	12.49g
Five Pound (Crown)	38.61mm	28.28g
Quarter Sovereign	13.50mm	2g
Half Sovereign	19.30mm	3.994g
Sovereign	22.05mm	7.988g
Two Sovereigns (Double)	28.40mm	15.98g
Five Sovereigns	36.00mm	39.94g
Two Sovereigns	28.40mm	15.98g
Five Sovereigns	36.00mm	39.94g

	Coin Size	Coin Weight
Pre Decimal (Milled)		
Farthing 1860–1956	20.19mm	2.83g
Farthing 1821–1860	22.00mm	4.72g
Farthing 1799	23.50mm	6.3g
Farthing 1806/7	21.50mm	4.72g
Half Penny	25.48mm	5.67g
Half Penny 1799	30.50mm	12.6g
Half Penny 1806/7	29.00mm	9.41g
Half Penny 1825–1860	28.00mm	9.49g
Penny 1825–1860	34.00mm	18.8g
Penny 1806–1807	35.00mm	18.9g
Penny 1860–1967	30.86mm	9.45g
Silver Threepence up to 1817 after 1817 Brass Threepence	 17.00mm 16.00mm 21.00mm	 1.2g 1.2g 6.8g
Groat	16.00mm	1.9g
Sixpence	19.41mm	2.83g
Shilling	23.60mm	5.65g
Florin	28.50mm	11.3g
Double Florin	36.00mm	22.6g
Half Crown	32.31mm	14014g
Crown	38.61mm	28.28g
Half Sovereign	19.30mm	3.994g
Sovereign	22.05mm	7.988g
Two Sovereigns	28.40mm	15.98g
Five Sovereigns	36.00mm	39.94g

EARLY PROOF SETS

These very important G.B. proof sets have been moved from the decimal coin sections (as seen in previous editions of the COIN YEARBOOK) to the main milled section. Putting a price on these sets in no easy task, hence they have been divided into three sections.

DATE FDC

SECTION 1: The three first sets (1826, 1831 and 1839)

These three sets were available to order on a bespoke basis, via application to the Royal Mint Chief Engraver, William Wyon. They were available to order for some years after the first date of issue.

GEORGE IV

1826 £5–farthing (11 coins) .... £150,000 to £200.000

WILLIAM IV

1831 Coronation £2–farthing (14 coins) .... £75,000 to £100,000

VICTORIA

1839 "Una and the Lion" £5–farthing (15 coins) .... Upwards of £100,000

SECTION 2: 1853 Proof Set

In 1851 the Mint went through a major re-organisation under the new Mint Master, John Herschel the Astronomer, which phased out the handling of orders by the Chief Engraver which meant customers had to apply for sets of coins through the Royal Mint's agent, Hunt & Roskell (the court jewellers). Again, such sets would have been sold for some years after 1853.

VICTORIA

1853 Sovereign–quarter farthing, including "Gothic" crown (16 coins) .... £100,000 to £150,000

SECTION 3: 1887 and onwards

In 1887, the Royal Mint finally commercialised their sale of sets by bringing the application and order process in-house. The public could now order sets from the Mint itself, and if you wanted a case, you would have to pay extra for it. Of course, major coin dealers like Spink & Son and jewellery firms would have also bought stock from the Mint to supply to their own clientele, which is why we see bespoke coin cases with the names of such firms on, or inside, the lids. All of these early proof sets will command high prices being housed in bespoke cases.

There are many other factors in pricing these sets, most importantly, the quality. We have indicated a price for the sets based on recent private and auction sales. We have also introduced a spread pricing system. For example, 1937 silver sets range from £250 to £500, subject to quality.

The two sets of 1950 and 1951 were issued in low-quality cardboard boxes, very possibly due to financial constraints as the country got back on its feet after World War II. Sets of these two years will command very good prices if the cardboard boxes they are housed in are still in good condition.

VICTORIA

1887 Golden Jubilee £5–3d (11 coins) .... £35,000 to £57,500
1887 Golden Jubilee Crown–3d (7 coins) .... £6000 to £9000
1893 £5–3d (10 coins) .... £40,000 to £62,500
1893 Crown–3d (6 coins) .... £7000 to £9000

This 1839 Una and the Lion 5 Sovereign sold in Sincona's Auction 83 on May 15–17, 2023. It was graded NGC PF60 Ultra Cameo and sold for 180,000 CHF (£160.000).

DATE	FDC
EDWARD VII	
1902 Coronation £5–Maundy penny, matt proofs (13 coins)	£6000 to £8000
1902 Coronation Sovereign–Maundy penny, matt proofs (11 coins)	£2000 to £2500
GEORGE V	
1911 Coronation £5–Maundy penny (12 coins)	£20000 to £35,000
1911 Sovereign–Maundy penny (10 coins)	£3000 to £4000
1911 Coronation Halfcrown–Maundy penny (8 coins)	£900 to £1250
1927 New types Crown–3d (6 coins)	£500 to £750
GEORGE VI	
1937 Coronation £5–half sovereign (4 coins)	£9500 to 16,500
1937 Coronation Crown–farthing including Maundy money (15 coins)	£250 to £500
1950 Mid-century Halfcrown–farthing (9 coins)	£80 to £160
1951 Festival of Britain, Crown–farthing (10 coins)	£100 to £225
ELIZABETH II	
1953 Proof Coronation Crown–farthing (10 coins)*	£70 to £125
1970 Proof Last £sd coins (issued from 1972) Halfcrown–halfpenny (8 coins)	£10 to £20

*An uncirculated 1953 Coronation set also exists, these retail at £25–35.

1953 Proof Coronation Set (Picture courtesy of the Royal Mint).

I would like to pay special thanks to Steve Hill of Sovereign Rarities, Keith Bayford of K. B. Coins and Steve Locket of London Coin Auctions, for their invaluable assistance to me in preparing this update.

Royston Norbury, West Essex Coin Investments

DECIMAL COINAGE

Since the introduction of the Decimal system in the UK, many coins have been issued for circulation purposes in vast quantities. In addition, from 1982 sets of coins to non-proof standard, and including examples of each denomination found in circulation, have been issued each year. For 1982 and 1983 they were to "circulation" standard and described as "Uncirculated". Individual coins from these sets are annotated "Unc" on the lists that follow. From 1984 to the present day they were described as "Brilliant Uncirculated" (BU on the lists), and from around 1986 these coins are generally distinguishable from coins intended for circulation. They were from then produced by the Proof Coin Division of the Royal Mint (rather than by the Coin Production Room which produces circulation-standard coins). For completeness however, we have included the annotations Unc and BU back to 1982, the start year for these sets.

It is emphasised that the abbreviations Unc and BU in the left-hand columns adjacent to the date refer to an advertising description or to an engineering production standard, not the preservation condition or grade of the coin concerned. Where no such annotation appears adjacent to the date, the coin is circulation-standard for issue as such.

We have included the "mintage" figures for circulation coins down to Half Penny where known. The figure given for the 1997 Two Pounds, is considerably less than the actual quantity struck, because many were scrapped before issue due to failing an electrical conductivity test. Where a coin is available in uncirculated grade at, or just above, face value no price has been quoted. NOTE: *For many of the later issues, especially the latest issue precious metal coins, the price quoted is the issue price.*

Base metal Proof issues of circulation coinage (£2 or £1 to one or half penny) of the decimal series were only issued, as with Unc or BU, as part of Year Sets, but many of these sets have been broken down into individual coins, hence the appearance of the latter on the market.

The lists do not attempt to give details of die varieties, except where there was an obvious intention to change the appearance of a coin, e.g. 1992 20p.

2008 saw new reverses and modified obverses for all circulation denominations from the One Pound to the One Penny. All seven denominations were put into circulation dated 2008, all with both the old and the new reverses.

The circulation standard mintage figures have mainly been kindly supplied by courtesy of the Head of Historical Services and the Department of UK Circulation Coin Sales, both at the Royal Mint.

KILO COINS
(gold and silver)

The UK's first-ever Kilo coins were struck to commemorate the 2012 Olympic Games in 0.999 fine gold and 0.999 fine silver. These and subsequent issues are listed in detail below, and all were struck to proof standard and to similar metallic standards. They are also listed under their relevant "series" where appropriate. In addition some issues were struck in 2, 5 or 10 kilos but these are not specifically listed here.

DATE	FACE VALUE	AUTHORISED ISSUE QTY.	NO. ISSUED	ISSUE PRICE
2012 Olympic Gold; obverse: 1998 Ian Rank-Broadley's Royal Portrait reverse: Sir Anthony Caro's "Individual Endeavour"	£1,000	60	20	£100,000
2012 Olympic Silver; obverse: 1998 Rank-Broadley Royal Portrait reverse: Tom Phillip's "Team Endeavour"	£500	2,912	910	£3,000
2012 Diamond Jubilee Gold; obverse: Queen in Garter Robes (Rank-Broadley) reverse: Royal Arms (Buckingham Palace Gates)	£1,000	21	21	£60,000
2012 Diamond Jubilee Silver; obverse: Queen in Garter Robes (Rank-Broadley) reverse: Royal Arms (Buckingham Palace Gates)	£500	1,250	206	£2,600
2013 Coronation Anniversary Gold; obverse: 1998 Rank-Broadley Royal Portrait reverse: John Bergdahl's Coronation Regalia	£1,000	27	13	£50,000
2013 Coronation Anniversary Silver; obverse: 1998 Rank-Broadley Royal Portrait reverse: John Bergdahl's Coronation Regalia	£500	400	301	£2,600
2013 Royal Christening Gold; obverse: 1998 Rank-Broadley Royal Portrait reverse: John Bergdahl's Lily Font	£1,000	22	19	£48,000
2013 Royal Christening Silver; obverse: 1998 Rank-Broadley Royal Portrait reverse: John Bergdahl's Lily Font	£500	500	194	£2,600
2014 First World War Outbreak Gold; obverse: 1998 Rank-Broadley Royal Portrait reverse: Sandle's Hostile Environment	£1,000	25	10	£45,000
2014 First World War Outbreak Silver; obverse: 1998 Rank-Broadley Royal Portrait reverse: Sandle's Hostile Environment	£500	430	165	£2,000
2015 50th Anniversary of Death of Sir Winston Churchill Gold; obverse: 1998 Rank-Broadley Royal Portrait reverse: Millner's image of Churchill	£1,000	15	9	£45,000
2015 50th Anniversary of Death of Sir Winston Churchill Silver; obverse: 1998 Rank-Broadley Royal Portrait reverse: Milner's image of Churchill	£500	170	117	£2,000
2015 The Longest Reign Gold; obverse: Butler Royal Portrait reverse: Stephen Taylor Queen's Portraits	£1,000	15	15	£42,500
2016 The Longest Reign Silver; obverse: Butler Royal Portrait reverse: Stephen Taylor Queen's Portraits	£500	320	278	£2,000
2016 Year of the Monkey Gold; obverse: Clark Royal Portrait reverse: Wuon-Gean Ho's Rhesus monkey	£1,000	8	–	£42,500
2016 Year of the Monkey Silver; obverse: Butler Royal Portrait everse: Wuon-Gean Ho's Rhesus monkey	£500	88	–	£2,000
2016 Queen's 90th Birthday Gold; obverse: Clark Royal Portrait reverse: Christopher Hobbs Floral design	£1,000	25	15	–
2016 Queen's 90th Birthday Silver; obverse: Clark Royal Portrait reverse: Christopher Hobbs Floral design	£500	450	447	£2,000

DATE	FACE VALUE	AUTHORISED ISSUE QTY.	NO. ISSUED	ISSUE PRICE
2017 The Queen's Sapphire Accession Jubilee Silver; obverse: Clark Royal Portrait reverse: Gregory Cameron's design of Crowned Coat of Arms	£500	300	225	£2,050
2017 Lunar Year of the Rooster Gold; obverse: Clark Royal Portrait reverse: Wuon-Gean Ho's Rooster	£1,000	8	8	£42,500
2017 Lunar Year of the Rooster Silver; obverse: Clark Royal Portrait reverse: Wuon-Gean Ho's Rooster	£500	68	–	£2,050
2017 Platinum Wedding Gold; obverse: Etienne Millner Double Royal Portrait reverse: Heraldic shields by John Bergdahl	£1,000	31	15	£49,950
2017 Platinum Wedding Silver; obverse: Etienne Millner Double Royal Portrait reverse: Heraldic shields by John Bergdahl	£500	550	–	£2,025
2018 Anniversary of the Armistice Gold; obverse: Clark Royal Portrait reverse: Kneeling soldier by Paul Day	£1,000	10	–	£49,995
2018 Anniversary of the Armistice Silver; obverse: Clark Royal Portrait reverse: Kneeling soldier by Paul Day	£500	100	–	£2,025
2018 Lunar Year of the Dog Gold; obverse: Clark Royal Portrait reverse: Wuon-Gean Ho's Dog	£1,000	8	–	£42,500
2018 Lunar Year of the Dog Silver; obverse: Clark Royal Portrait reverse: Wuon-Gean Ho's Dog	£500	108	–	£2,025
2018 Britannia Silver; obverse: Clark Royal Portrait reverse: David Lawrence Stylised bust of Britannia	£500	250	–	£2,025
2018 Sapphire Coronation Jubilee Gold; obverse: Jody Clark Royal Portrait reverse: Dominique Evans The Queen in the Royal Coach	£1,000	15	–	£49,950
2018 Sapphire Coronation Jubilee Silver; obverse: Jody Clark Royal Portrait reverse: Dominique Evans The Queen in the Royal Coach	£500	250	–	£2,025

2015 50th Anniversary of Death of Sir Winston Churchill Silver

2021 Lunar— Year of the Ox

2017 Platinum Wedding Gold

2021 White Greyhound of Richmond

Illustrations on this page are not shown to scale.

DATE	FACE VALUE	AUTHORISED ISSUE QTY.	NO. ISSUED	ISSUE. PRICE
2019 Britannia Silver; obverse: Clark Royal Portrait reverse: David Lawrence's portrait of Britannia beside a lion	£500	115	–	£2,025
2019 Queen Victoria Silver; obverse: Clark Royal Portrait reverse: William Wyon portrait of Queen Victoria and Prince Albert	£500	125	–	£2,025
2019 Lunar Year of the Pig Gold; obverse: Clark Royal Portrait reverse: Harry Brockway's Pig	£1000	8	–	–
2019 Lunar Year of the Pig Silver; obverse: Clark Royal Portrait reverse: Harry Brockway's Pig	£500	38	–	£2,025
2019 The Falcon of the Plantagenets Gold; obverse: Clark Royal Portrait reverse: by Jody Clark	£1000	10	–	£59,995
2019 The Falcon of the Plantagenets Silver; obverse: Clark Royal Portrait reverse: by Jody Clark	£500	125	–	£2,050
2019 The Yale of Beaufort Gold; obverse: Clark Royal Portrait reverse: by Jody Clark	£1000	13	–	–
2019 The Yale of Beaufort Silver; obverse: Clark Royal Portrait reverse: by Jody Clark	£500	120	–	£2,025
2019 Great Engraver Series: Una & the Lion Silver (also in 2 and 5 kilos); obverse: Clark Royal Portrait reverse: William Wyon's Una	£5000	12	–	£59,995
2020 White Lion of Mortimer Gold; obverse: Clark Royal Portrait reverse: by Jody Clark	£1000	10	–	£59,995
2020 White Lion of Mortimer Silver; obverse: Clark Royal Portrait reverse: by Jody Clark	£500	90	–	£2,025
2020 White Horse of Hanover Gold; obverse: Clark Royal Portrait reverse: by Jody Clark	£1000	13	–	£57,750
2020 White Horse of Hanover Silver; obverse: Clark Royal Portrait reverse: by Jody Clark	£500	115	–	£2,050
2020 Lunar Year of the Rat Gold; obverse: Clark Royal Portrait reverse: P. J. Lynch's Rat	£1000	8	–	£59,995
2020 Lunar Year of the Rat Silver; obverse: Clark Royal Portrait reverse: P. J. Lynch's Rat	£500	28	–	£2,050
2021 Lunar Year of the Ox Gold, obverse: Clark Royal Portrait reverse: Harry Brockway	£1000	10	–	£63,865
2021 Lunar Year of the Ox Silver, obverse: Clark Royal Portrait reverse: Harry Brockway	£500	38	–	£2,050
2021 White Greyhound of Richmond Gold, obverse: Clark Royal Portrait reverse: Jody Clark	£1000	10	–	£63,865
2021 White Greyhound of Richmond Silver; obverse: Clark Royal Portrait reverse: Jody Clark	£500	80	–	£2,050

As the issuing of one kilo coins as part of a collection or series of coins has become a more regular occurrence for the Royal Mint, it has been decided to ONLY list later issues under their themes. Therefore for other 1 kilo coins see Precious Metal Bullion and Collector Coins (Series) for these and a more in-depth listing of the latest bullion coin releases.

FIVE-OUNCE COINS
(gold and silver)

Appearing for the first time in 2012 were Five-Ounce coins, minted in the same metals and standards as the Kilo Coins.The Five-Ounce Britannia coins, both gold (50mm) and silver (65mm) proofs, which appeared first in 2013 are listed in the Britannia section.

DATE	FACE VALUE	AUTHORISED ISSUE QTY.	NO ISSUED	ISSUE PRICE
2012 Olympic Gold; obverse: 1998 Rank-Broadley Royal Portrait reverse: Pegasus (C. Le Brun)	£10	500	193	£11,500
2012 Olympic Silver; obverse: 1998 Rank-Broadley Royal Portrait reverse: Pegasus (C. Le Brun)	£10	7,500	5,056	£525
2012 Diamond Jubilee Gold; obverse: Queen in Garter Robes (Rank-Broadley) reverse: Queen seated (facing)	£10	250	140	£9,500
2012 Diamond Jubilee Silver; obverse: Queen in Garter Robes (Rank-Broadley) reverse: Queen seated (facing)	£10	1,952	1,933	£450
2013 Coronation Anniversary Gold; obverse: 1998 Rank-Broadley Royal Portrait reverse: Regalia in Westminster Abbey (J. Olliffe)	£10	129	74	£9,500
2013 Coronation Anniversary Silver; obverse: 1998 Rank-Broadley Royal Portrait reverse: Regalia in Westminster Abbey (J. Olliffe)	£10	1,953	1,604	£450
2013 Royal Christening Gold; obverse: 1998 Rank-Broadley Royal Portrait reverse: Bergdahl's Lily Font	£10	150	48	£8,200
2013 Royal Christening Silver; obverse: 1998 Rank-Broadley Royal Portrait reverse: Bergdahl's Lily Font	£10	1,660	912	£450
2014 First World War Outbreak Gold; obverse: 1998 Rank-Broadley Royal Portrait reverse: Bergdahl's Britannia	£10	110	36	£7,500
2014 First World War Outbreak Silver; obverse: 1998 Rank-Broadley Royal Portrait reverse: Bergdahl's Britannia	£10	1,300	606	£395

DATE	FACE VALUE	AUTHORISED ISSUE QTY.	NO. ISSUED	ISSUE PRICE
2014 Lunar Year of the Horse Gold; obverse: 1998 Rank-Broadley Royal Portrait reverse: Wuon-Gean Ho's Horse	£500	–	–	£7,500
2014 Lunar Year of the Horse Silver; obverse: 1998 Rank-Broadley Royal Portrait reverse: Wuon-Gean Ho's Horse	£10	799	799	£395
2015 Year of the Sheep Gold; obverse: 1998 Rank-Broadley Royal Portrait reverse: Wuon-Gean Ho's Swaledale Sheep	£500	38	26	£7,500
2015 Year of the Sheep Silver; obverse: 1998 Rank-Broadley Royal Portrait reverse: Wuon-Gean Ho's Swaledale Sheep	£10	1,088	331	£395
2015 50th Anniversary of Death of Sir Winston Churchill Gold; obverse: Clark Royal Portrait reverse: Millner's image of Churchill	£10	60	58	£7,500
2015 50th Anniversary of Death of Sir Winston Churchill Silver; obverse: Clark Royal Portrait reverse: Millner's image of Churchill	£10	500	855 (?)	£450
2015 First World War Gold; obverse: Clark Royal Portrait reverse: James Butler Devastation of War	£500	50	17	£6,950
2015 First World War Silver; obverse: Clark Royal Portrait reverse: James Butler Devastation of War	£10	500	355	£395
2015 The Longest Reign Gold; obverse: Butler Royal Portrait reverse: Stephen Taylor Queen's Portraits	£500	180	180	£6,950
2015 The Longest Reign Silver; obverse: Butler Royal Portrait reverse: Stephen Taylor Queen's Portraits	£10	1,500	1499	£395
2015 Christening of Princess Charlotte; obverse: Clark Royal Portrait reverse: John Bergdahl Baroque design	£10	500	500	£400
2016 Year of the Monkey Gold; obverse: Clark Royal Portrait reverse: Wuon-Gean Ho's Rhesus monkey	£500	38	–	£7,500
2016 Year of the Monkey Silver; obverse: Butler Royal Portrait reverse: Wuon-Gean Ho's Rhesus monkey	£10	588	–	£395
2016 Queen's 90th Birthday Gold; obverse: Clark Royal Portrait reverse: Christopher Hobbs Floral design	£500	170	170	£7,500
2016 Queen's 90th Birthday Silver; obverse: Clark Royal Portrait reverse: Christopher Hobbs Floral design	£10	1,750	1727	£395
2016 First World War Gold; obverse: Clark Royal Portrait reverse: David Lawrence Four Soldiers walking	£500	30	–	£7,500
2016 First World War Silver; obverse: Clark Royal Portrait reverse: David Lawrence Four Soldiers walking	£10	500	–	£395
2016 2016 Shakespeare Gold; obverse: Clark Royal Portrait; reverse: Tom Phillips Shakespeare Portrait	£500	–	50	–
2016 Shakespeare Silver; obverse: Clark Royal Portrait; reverse: Tom Phillips Shakespeare Portrait	£10	750	343	£395
2017 Lunar Year of the Rooster Gold; obverse: Clark Royal Portrait reverse: Wuon-Gean Ho's Rooster	£500	38	35	£8,250
2017 Lunar Year of the Rooster Gold; obverse: Clark Royal Portrait reverse: Wuon-Gean Ho's Rooster	£10	388	369	£415
2017 The Queen's Sapphire Jubilee Gold; obverse: Clark Royal Portrait reverse: Gregory Cameron's Crowned Coat of Arms	£500	110	110	£8,250

DATE	FACE VALUE	AUTHORISED ISSUE QTY.	NO. ISSUED	ISSUE PRICE
2017 The Queen's Sapphire Jubilee Silver; obverse: Clark Royal Portrait reverse: Gregory Cameron's Crowned Coat of Arms	£10	1,500	1,445	£415
2017 First World War Gold; obverse: Clark Royal Portrait reverse: Philip Jackson Soldier	£500	50	–	£8,250
2017 First World War Silver; obverse: Clark Royal Portrait reverse: Philip Jackson Soldier	£10	450	–	£415
2017 Royal Platinum Wedding Gold; obverse: Royal Portraits by Etienne Millner reverse: John Bergdahl Heraldic design	£500	450	86	£415
2018 Lunar Year of the Dog Gold; obverse: Clark Royal Portrait reverse: Wuon-Gean Ho's Dog	£500	58	–	£8,565
2018 Lunar Year of the Dog Silver; obverse: Clark Royal Portrait reverse: Wuon-Gean Ho's Dog	£10	388	–	£420
2018 Four Generations of Royalty Gold; obverse: Clark Royal Portrait reverse: Timothy Noad Initials of the Royal succession	£500	100	–	£8,565
2018 Four Generations of Royalty Silver; obverse: Clark Royal Portrait reverse: Timothy Noad Initials of the Royal succession	£10	1,000	–	£420
2018 Sapphire Coronation Gold; obverse: Clark Royal Portrait reverse: Dominique Evans Queen in Coronation Coach	£500	85	–	£8,565
2018 Sapphire Coronation Silver; obverse: Clark Royal Portrait reverse: Dominique Evans Queen in Coronation Coach	£10	1,050	–	£420
2018 Anniversary of the Armistice Gold; obverse: Clark Royal Portrait reverse: Paul Day Lone Soldier	£500	50	–	£8,565
2018 Anniversary of the Armistice Silver; obverse: Clark Royal Portrait reverse: Paul Day Lone Soldier	£10	525	–	£420
2019 Queen Victoria Gold; obverse: Clark Royal Portrait reverse: W. Wyon's portrait of Queen Victoria and Prince Albert	£500	70	–	£8,645
2019 Queen Victoria Silver; obverse: Clark Royal Portrait reverse: W. Wyon's portrait of Queen Victoria and Prince Albert	£10	800	–	£420
2019 The Tower of London Gold; obverse: Clark Royal Portrait reverse: Glyn Davis Yeoman Warder	£500	45	–	£8,645
2019 The Tower of London Silver; obverse: Clark Royal Portrait reverse: Glyn Davis Yeoman Warder	£10	585	–	£420
2019 The Tower of London Gold; obverse: Clark Royal Portrait reverse: Glyn Davis Ceremony of the Keys	£500	45	–	£8,645
2019 The Tower of London Silver; obverse: Clark Royal Portrait reverse: Glyn Davis Ceremony of the Keys	£10	585	–	£420
2019 The Falcon of the Plantagenets Gold; obverse: Clark Royal Portrait reverse: Clark's Falcon	£500	85	–	£8,645
2019 The Falcon of the Plantagenets Silver; obverse: Clark Royal Portrait reverse: Clark's Falcon	£10	550	–	£420
2019 The Tower of London Gold; obverse: Clark Royal Portrait reverse: Glyn Davis Crown Jewels	£500	45	–	£8,645
2019 The Tower of London Silver; obverse: Clark Royal Portrait reverse: Glyn Davis Crown Jewels	£10	585	–	£420

DATE	FACE VALUE	AUTHORISED ISSUE QTY.	NO. ISSUED	ISSUE PRICE
2019 Lunar Year of the Pig Gold; obverse: Clark Royal Portrait reverse: Harry Brockway's Pig	£500	38	–	£8,645
2019 Lunar Year of the Pig Silver; obverse: Clark Royal Portrait reverse: Harry Brockway's Pig	£10	288	–	£420
2019 The Tower of London Gold; obverse: Clark Royal Portrait reverse: Glyn Davies Legend of the Ravens	£500	45	–	£8,645
2019 The Tower of London Silver; obverse: Clark Royal Portrait reverse: Glyn Davies Legend of the Ravens	£10	585	–	£420
2019 The Yale of Beaufort Gold; obverse: Clark Royal Portrait reverse: by Jody Clark	£500	70	–	£8,645
2019 The Yale of Beaufort Silver; obverse: Clark Royal Portrait reverse: by Jody Clark	£10	335	–	£420
2019 Great Engraver Series: Una & the Lion Gold; obverse: Clark Royal Portrait reverse: William Wyon	£500	65	–	£9,995
2020 White Lion of Mortimer Gold; obverse: Clark Royal Portrait reverse: by Jody Clark	£500	55	–	£9,995
2020 White Lion of Mortimer Silver; obverse: Clark Royal Portrait reverse: by Jody Clark	£10	250	–	£420
2020 White Horse of Hanover Gold; obverse: Clark Royal Portrait reverse: by Jody Clark	£500	69	–	£9,595
2020 White Horse of Hanover Silver; obverse: Clark Royal Portrait reverse: by Jody Clark	£10	315	–	£420
2020 Lunar Year of the Rat Gold; obverse: Clark Royal Portrait reverse: P. J. Lynch	£500	28	–	£9,995
2020 Lunar Year of the Rat Silver; obverse: Clark Royal Portrait reverse: P. J. Lynch	£10	188	–	£420
2021 Lunar Year of the Ox Gold; obverse: Clark Royal Portrait reverse: Harry Brockway	£500	38	–	£10,605
2021 Lunar Year of the Ox Silver; obverse: Clark Royal Portrait reverse: Harry Brockway	£10	198	–	£420

As the range of these larger, bullion pieces has expanded, later issues are now included in the Precious Metal Bullion Collector Coins (Series).

FIVE POUNDS (Sovereign series)

This series is all minted in gold, and, except where stated, have the Pistrucci St George and Dragon reverse. BU coins up to 2001 bear a U in a circle. From 2009 the initials B.P. in the exergue are replaced by PISTRUCCI in small letters on the left. From 2014 the denomination is called the "Five-Sovereign" piece by the Royal Mint in their marketing publications.

DATE	Mintage	UNC
1980 Proof	10,000	£2800
1981 Proof	5,400	£2800
1982 Proof	2,500	£6000
1984 BU	15,104	£2800
1984 Proof	8,000	£4500
1985 New portrait BU	13,626	£2800
1985 — Proof	6,130	£4000
1986 BU	7,723	£2800
1987 Uncouped portrait BU	5,694	£2800
1988 BU	3,315	£2800
1989 500th Anniversary of the Sovereign. Enthroned portrayal obverse and Crowned shield reverse BU	2,937	£4500
1989 — Proof	5,000	£6500
1990 Reverts to couped portrait BU	1,226	£2800
1990 Proof	1,721	£3250
1991 BU	976	£2800
1991 Proof	1,336	£3500
1992 BU	797	£2800
1992 Proof	1,165	£3500
1993 BU	906	£2800
1993 Proof	1,078	£3000
1994 BU	1,000	£2800
1994 Proof	918	£3000
1995 BU	1,000	£2800
1995 Proof	1,250	£3000
1996 BU	901	£2800
1996 Proof	742	£3000
1997 BU	802	£2800
1997 Proof	860	£3000
1998 New portrait BU	825	£2800
1998 Proof	789	£3000
1999 BU	970	£2800
1999 Proof	1,000	£3000
2000 ("Bullion")	10,000	£2800
2000 BU	994	£2800
2000 Proof	3,000	£3000
2001 BU	1,000	£2800
2001 Proof	3,500	£3000
2002 Shield rev. ("Bullion")	—	£3000
2002 BU	—	£3000
2002 Proof	3,000	£4000
2003 BU	812	£2800
2003 Proof	—	£3500
2004 BU	1,000	£2800
2004 Proof	—	£3000
2005 Noad's heraldic St George and Dragon BU	936	£3000
2005 — Proof	—	£3500
2006 BU	731	£2800
2006 Proof	—	£3000
2007 BU	768	£2800
2007 Proof		£3000
2008 BU	750	£2800
2008 Proof	—	£3500
2009 BU	1,000	£2800
2009 Proof	—	£3500
2010 BU	1,000	£2800
2010 Proof	—	£3500
2011 BU	657	£3500
2011 Proof	—	£3500
2012 Day's St George and Dragon BU	496	£4000
2012 — Proof	—	£4000
2013 BU	262	£3500

IMPORTANT NOTE: The prices quoted in this guide are set at August 2024 with the price of gold at £1,950 per ounce and silver £21.70 per ounce—market fluctuations can have a marked effect on the values of modern precious metal coins.

Pistrucci's famous rendering of St George and the Dragon which appears on all except special commemorative five pound coins.

The obverse of the 1989 500th Anniversary of the original Sovereign coin portrays HM the Queen enthroned.

DATE	Mintage	UNC
2013 Proof	—	£4000
2014 BU	645	£3000
2014 Proof	—	£4000
2015 Proof	—	£3500
2015 Jody Clark Portrait BU	609	£3000
2015 — Proof	—	£3000
2016 BU	498	£3500
2016 James Butler Portrait Proof	575	£5500
2017 200th Anniversary of the Sovereign (Clark portrait) BU	992	£4000
2017 — Proof	750	£5500
2018 BU	1,500	£3000
2018 Proof	850	£3500
2019 BU Matt finish	550	£2500
2020 200th Anniversary of death of George III With GR cypher privy mark	—	£2500
2021 BU	350	£2500
2022 Platinum Jubilee—Timothy Noad coat of arms BU	750	£2635
2022 Memorial of HM QEII Proof	1,113	£4000
2022 — BU Matt finish	661	£3000
2023 Standard reverse, crowned head obverse Proof	1,785	£4000
2023 — Matt Proof (sets only)	23	£4500
2023 — BU Matt finish	450	£3000
2024 Standard reverse, uncrowned head obverse Proof	9,260	£4000
2024 — BU Matt finish	—	£3000

2017 200th Anniversary reverse design as the original issue.

FIVE POUNDS (Crown series)

This series commenced in 1990 when the "Crown" was declared legal tender at £5, instead of 25p as all previous issues continued to be. Mintage is in cupro-nickel unless otherwise stated. BU includes those in individual presentation folders, and those in sets sold with stamp covers and/or banknotes.

DATE	Mintage	UNC
1990 Queen Mother's 90th Birthday.	2,761,431	£6
1990 — BU	48,477	£10
1990 — Silver Proof	56,800	£35
1990 — Gold Proof	2,500	£2300
1993 Coronation 40th Anniversary	1,834,655	£6
1993 — BU	—	£10
1993 — Proof	—	£15
1993 — Silver Proof	58,877	£35
1993 — Gold Proof	2,500	£2300
1996 HM the Queen's 70th Birthday	2,396,100	£6
1996 — BU	—	£10
1996 — Proof	—	£15
1996 — Silver Proof	39,336	£35
1996 — Gold Proof	2,127	£2300
1997 Royal Golden Wedding	1,733,000	£8
1997 — BU	—	£10
1997 — — with £5 note	5,000	£60
1997 — Proof	—	£15
1997 — Silver Proof	33,689	£35
1997 — Gold Proof	2,750	£2300
1998 Prince of Wales 50th Birthday	1,407,300	£9
1998 — BU	—	£10
1998 — Proof	—	£20
1998 — Silver Proof	13,379	£45
1998 — Gold Proof	—	£2500
1999 Princess of Wales Memorial.	1,600,000	£10
1999 — BU	—	£14
1999 — Proof	—	£20
1999 — Silver Proof	49,545	£60
1999 — Gold Proof	7,500	£3000
1999 Millennium	3,796,300	£8
1999 — BU	—	£12
1999 — Proof	—	£15
1999 — Silver Proof	49,057	£35
1999 — Gold Proof	2,500	£2300

DATE	Mintage	UNC
2000 –	3,147,092*	£10
2000 – BU	–	£18
2000 – – with special Millennium Dome mintmark	–	£25
2000 – Proof	–	£20
2000 – Silver Proof with gold highlight	14,255	£50
2000 – Gold Proof	2,500	£2300
2000 Queen Mother's 100th Birthday	–	£8
2000 – BU	–	£12
2000 – Silver Proof	31,316	£40
2000 – – – Piedfort	14,850	£65
2000 – Gold Proof	3,000	£2300
2001 Victorian Era	851,491	£10
2001 – BU	–	£12
2001 – Proof	–	£20
2001 – Silver Proof	19,216	£45
2001 – – with frosted relief	596	£150
2001 – Gold Proof	3,000	£2300
2001 – – with frosted relief	733	£2750
2002 Golden Jubilee	3,469,243*	£8
2002 – BU	–	£12
2002 – Proof	–	£15
2002 – Silver Proof	54,012	£45
2002 – Gold Proof	5,502	£2300
2002 Queen Mother Memorial	*incl. above**	£9
2002 – BU	–	£12
2002 – Silver Proof	16,117	£40
2002 – Gold Proof	3,000	£2300
2003 Coronation Jubilee	1,307,147	£10
2003 – BU	100,481	£13
2003 – Proof	–	£20
2003 – Silver Proof	28,758	£45
2003 – Gold Proof	1,896	£2300
2004 Entente Cordiale Centenary	1,205,594	£10
2004 – Proof Reverse Frosting	6,065	£15
2004 – Silver Proof	11,295	£50
2004 – – – Piedfort	2,500	£90
2004 – Gold Proof	926	£2300
2004 – Platinum Proof Piedfort	501	£4250
2005 Trafalgar Bicentenary	1,075 516*	£12
2005 – BU	–	£15
2005 – Proof	–	£20
2005 – Silver Proof	21,448	£45
2005 – – – Piedfort	2,818	£65
2005 – Gold Proof	1,805	£2300
2005 Bicentenary of the Death of Nelson	*incl. above**	£12
2005 – BU	–	£15
2005 – Proof	–	£20
2005 – Silver Proof	12,852	£45
2005 – – – Piedfort	2,818	£65
2005 – Gold Proof	1,760	£2300
2005 – Platinum Proof Piedfort	200	£4000
2006 Queen's 80th Birthday	52,267	£10
2006 – BU	–	£12
2006 – Proof	–	£15
2006 – Silver Proof	20,790	£45
2006 – – – Piedfort, selective gold plating on reverse	5,000	£60
2006 – Gold Proof	2,750	£2300
2006 – Platinum Proof Piedfort	250	£4000
2007 Queen's Diamond Wedding	30,561	£10
2007 – BU	–	£12
2007 – Proof	–	£15
2007 – Silver Proof	15,186	£45
2007 – – – Piedfort	2,000	£65
2007 – Gold Proof	2,380	£2300
2007 – Platinum Proof Piedfort	250	£4000
2008 Prince of Wales 60th Birthday	14,088	£12
2008 – BU	54,746	£15
2008 – Proof	–	£20
2008 – Silver Proof	6,264	£55

DATE	Mintage	UNC
2008 — — — Piedfort	1,088	£75
2008 — Gold Proof	867	£2300
2008 Elizabeth I 450th Anniversary of Accession	20,047	£12
2008 — BU	26,700	£15
2008 — Proof	—	£20
2008 — Silver Proof	9,216	£50
2008 — — — Piedfort	1,602	£75
2008 — Gold Proof	1,500	£2300
2008 — Platinum Proof Piedfort	125	£4000
2009 500th Anniversary of Henry VIII Accession	30,000	£12
2009 — BU	69,119	£15
2009 — Proof	—	£25
2009 — Silver Proof	10,419	£50
2009 — — — Piedfort	3,580	£75
2009 — Gold Proof	1,130	£2300
2009 — Platinum Proof Piedfort	100	£4250
2009 Olympic Countdown (3 years) BU	184,921	£12
2009 — Silver Proof	26,645	£55
2009 — — — Piedfort	4,874	£75
2009 — Gold Proof	1,860	£2300
2009 Olympic Celebration of Britain "The Mind" series (incl. green logo):		
Stonehenge Silver Proof	—	£60
Palace of Westminster/Big Ben Silver Proof	—	£60
— Cu Ni Proof	—	£20
Angel of the North Silver Proof	—	£60
Flying Scotsman Silver Proof	—	£60
Globe Theatre Silver Proof	—	£60
Sir Isaac Newton Silver Proof	—	£60
2010 350th Anniversary of the Restoration of the Monarchy	15,000	£15
2010 — BU	30,247	£20
2010 — Proof	—	£25
2010 — Silver Proof	6,518	£50
2010 — — — Piedfort	4,435	£90
2010 — Gold Proof	1,182	£2300
2010 — Platinum Proof Piedfort	—	£4000
2010 Olympic Countdown (2 years) BU	153,080	£12
2010 — Silver Proof	20,159	£55
2010 — — — Piedfort	2,197	£120
2010 — Gold Proof	1,562	£2300
2010 Olympic Celebration of Britain, "The Body" series (incl. red logo):		
Coastline of Britain (Rhossili Bay) Silver Proof	—	£65
Giants Causeway Silver Proof	—	£65
River Thames Silver Proof	—	£65
British Fauna (Barn Owl) Silver Proof	—	£65
British Flora (Oak Leaves and Acorn) Silver Proof	—	£65
Weather Vane Silver Proof	—	£65
2010 Olympic Celebration of Britain "The Spirit" series (incl. blue logo):		
Churchill Silver Proof	—	£75
— CuNi Proof	—	£20
Spirit of London (Kind Hearts etc.) Silver Proof	—	£75
— CuNi Proof	—	£20
Humour Silver Proof	—	£75
Unity (Floral emblems of Britain) Silver Proof	—	£75
Music Silver Proof	—	£75
Anti-slavery Silver Proof	—	£75
2011 90th Birthday of the Duke of Edinburgh BU	18,730	£35
2011 — Proof	—	£35
2011 — Silver Proof	4,599	£75
2011 — — — Piedfort	2,659	£90
2011 — Gold Proof	636	£2300
2011 — Platinum Proof Piedfort	—	£7500
2011 Royal Wedding of William and Catherine BU	250,000	£15
2011 — Silver Proof	26,069	£60
2011 — Gold-plated Silver Proof	7,451	£80
2011 — Silver Proof Piedfort	2,991	£100
2011 — Gold Proof	2,066	£2300
2011 — Platinum Proof Piedfort	—	£5500
2011 Olympic Countdown (1 year) BU	163,235	£12

DATE	Mintage	UNC
2011 — Silver Proof	25,877	£55
2011 — — — Piedfort	4,000	£75
2011 — Gold Proof	1,300	£2300
2012 Diamond Jubilee BU	484,775	£15
2012 — Proof	—	£20
2012 — Silver Proof	16,370	£50
2012 — — — Piedfort	3,187	£90
2012 — Gold-plated silver proof	12,112	£60
2012 — Gold proof	1,025	£2300
2012 — Platinum Piedfort Proof	20	£5500
2012 Olympic Countdown (Games Time) BU	52,261	£13
2012 — Silver Proof	12,670	£65
2012 — — — Piedfort	2,324	£85
2012 — Gold proof	1,007	£2300
2012 Official Olympic BU	315,983	£15
2012 — Silver Proof	20,810	£55
2012 — — — Piedfort	5,946	£85
2012 — Gold-plated silver proof	12,112	£60
2012 — Gold proof	1,045	£2300
2012 Official Paralympic BU	—	£15
2012 — Silver Proof	—	£55
2012 — — — Piedfort	—	£85
2012 — Gold proof	—	£2300
2013 60th Anniversary of the Queen's Coronation BU	57,262	£12
2013 — Proof	—	£35
2013 — Silver Proof	4,050	£80
2013 — — — Piedfort	2,626	£95
2013 — Gold-plated silver proof	2,547	£80
2013 — Gold proof	418	£2300
2013 — Platinum Piedfort Proof	106	£7500
2013 Queen's Portraits, 4 coins each with one of the four portraits, paired with James Butler's Royal Arms. Issued only as sets of 4 in precious metals (see under Proof and Specimen Set section)	—	—
2013 Royal Birth of Prince George (St George & Dragon), Silver Proof	7,460	£150
2013 Christening of Prince George BU	56,014	£20
2013 — Silver Proof	7,264	£80
2013 — — — Piedfort	2,251	£160
2013 — Gold Proof	486	£2300
2013 — Platinum Proof Piedfort	38	£7500
2014 300th Anniversary of the death of Queen Anne BU	12,181	£60
2014 — Proof	—	£60
2014 — Silver Proof	2,212	£80
2014 — — — Piedfort	636	£160
2014 — Gold-plated Silver Proof	627	£100
2014 — Gold Proof	253	£2300
2014 First Birthday of Prince George Silver Proof	7,451	£85
2014 100th Anniversary of the First World War Outbreak, issued only as set of 6 coins (see under Proof and Specimen Sets)	—	—
2014 Portrait of Britain, issued only as set of 4 coins, with trichromatic colour-printing (see under Proof and Specimen Sets section)	—	—
2015 50th Anniversary of death of Sir Winston Churchill BU	—	£15
2015 — Silver Proof	4,238	£60
2015— — — Piedfort	1,800	£100
2015 — Gold Proof	325	£2300
2015 — Platinum Proof Piedfort	90	£5000
2015 200th Anniversary of the Battle of Waterloo, BU	24,554	£15
2015 — Silver Proof	2,523	£80
2015 — — — Piedfort	896	£140
2015 — Gold Proof	273	£2300
2015 First World War 100th Anniversary, continued, issued only as set of 6 coins	807	—
New Portrait		
2015 2nd Birthday of Prince George, Silver Proof	4,009	£85
2015 Birth of Princess Charlotte, BU	—	£20

DATE	Mintage	UNC
2015 — Silver Proof	—	£80
2015 — Gold Proof	500	£2300
2015 Christening of Princess Charlotte, Silver Proof	4,842	£800
2015 — Gold Proof	350	£2300
2015 The Longest Reign, BU	48,848	£18
2015 — Silver Proof	10,249	£60
2015 — — — Piedfort	3,171	£95
2015 — Gold Proof	899	£2300
2015 — Platinum Proof Piedfort	88	£5000
2016 Queen's 90th Birthday, BU	74,195	£15
2016 — Proof	—	£25
2016 — Silver Proof	8,947	£60
2016 — — — Piedfort	3,099	£95
2016 — Gold Proof	906	£2300
2016 — Platinum Proof Piedfort	81	£4500
2016 Portraits of Britain, issued only as set of 4 coins, with trichromatic colour-printing (see under Proof and Specimen Sets section)	1,098	—
2016 First World War Centenary, continued, issued only as a set of 6 Silver Proof coins	1,916	—
2016 Battle of the Somme, Silver Proof	3,678	£75
2017 Portraits of Britain, issued only as set of 4 coins, with trichromatic colour-printing (see under Proof and Specimen Sets section)	1,500	—
2017 1000th Anniversary of Coronation of King Canute, BU	26,567	£15
2017 — Proof	—	£30
2017 — Silver Proof	2,925	£60
2017 — — Piedfort	1,069	£100
2017 — Gold Proof	150	£2300
2017 Prince Philip, Celebrating a Life of Service, BU	29,097	£20
2017 — Silver Proof	2,574	£85
2017 — — Piedfort	1,250	£155
2017 — Gold Proof	299	£2300
2017 Remembrance Day Poppy	—	£15
2017 — Silver Proof	5,000	£100
2017 — — Piedfort	1,500	£200
2017 First World War Centenary, continued, issued only as set of 6 Silver Proof coins	1,917	—
2017 House of Windsor Centenary, BU	—	£15
2017 — — in pack for Engagement of Prince Harry	5,000	£20
2017 — Proof	—	£30
2017 — Silver Proof	13,000	£85
2017 — — Piedfort	5,500	£185
2017 — Gold Proof	884	£2300
2017 Christmas Tree BU	—	£13
2018 Her Majesty's Sapphire Jubilee, BU	—	£15
2018 — Proof	—	£30
2018 — Silver Proof	8,260	£85
2018 — — Piedfort	2,471	£155
2018 — Gold Proof	648	£2300
2018 70th Birthday of the Prince of Wales BU	—	£15
2018 — Silver Proof	3,500	£85
2018 — — Piedfort	1,000	£155
2018 — Gold Proof	50	£2,500
2018 — Platinum Proof	525	£650
2018 — Platinum Proof Piedfort	70	£5,500
2018 Prince George's 5th Birthday	—	£15
2018 — Proof	—	£18
2018 — Silver Proof	—	£85
2018 — — Piedfort	—	£165
2018 — Gold Proof	650	£2300
2018 Four generations of the Royal Family	—	£15
2018 — Proof	—	£20
2018 — Silver Proof	5,000	£100
2018 — — Piedfort	2,000	£175

2017 Portrait of Britain, issued only as set of 4 coins, with trichromatic colour-printing.

DATE	Mintage	UNC
2018 — Gold Proof	500	£2300
2018 250 years of the Royal Academy	—	£15
2018 — Silver Proof	2,750	£100
2018 Royal Wedding of Prince Harry	12,000	£20
2018 — Proof	—	£25
2018 — Silver Proof	15,000	£100
2018 — — Piedfort	2,220	£175
2018 — Gold Proof	500	£2300
2018 Portraits of Britain, issued only as set of 4 coins, with trichromatic colour-printing (see under Proof and Specimen Sets section)	2,016	—
2018 Stories of War set of six coins (see under Proof and Specimen Sets section)	—	—
2019 The Ceremony of the Keys BU	—	£15
2019 — Silver Proof	4,000	£85
2019 — — Piedfort	1,160	£175
2019 — Gold	385	£2300
2019 The Tower of London 4 coin set BU	—	£85
2019 — Silver Proof	4,000	£350
2019 — — Piedfort	1,160	£650
2019 — Gold	385	£9200
2019 200th Anniversary of the Birth of Queen Victoria BU	—	£15
2019 —Silver Proof	7,500	£85
2019 — — Piedfort	2,750	£175
2019 — Gold Proof	725	£2300
2019 Pride of England BU	—	£13
2019 Centenary of Remembrance BU	—	£17
2019 — Silver Proof	3,240	£100
2019 — — Piedfort	775	£185
2019 — Gold	240	£2500
2020 The Tower of London series—The White Tower BU	—	£13
2020 —Silver Proof	2,500	£85
2020 — — Piedfort	450	£175
2020 — Gold Proof	125	£2500
2020 Reign of George III BU	—	£15
2020 — Silver Proof	2,500	£85
2020 — — Piedfort	550	£175
2020 — Gold Proof	250	£2500
2020 250th Anniversary of William Wordsworth BU	—	£15
2020 — Silver Proof	3,000	£85
2020 — Gold Proof	300	£2500
2020 Tower of London Collection—the Royal Menagerie BU	—	£15
2020 — Silver Proof	1,510	£85
2020 — — Piedfort	410	£175
2020 — Gold Proof	135	£2500
2020 Remembrance Day BU	—	£15
2020 — Silver Proof	1920	£85
2020 — — Piedfort	700	£185
2020 75th Anniversary of the end of World War II BU	—	£15
2020 — Silver Proof	2575	£85
2020 — — Piedfort	565	£175
2020 — Gold Proof	225	£2500
2020 150th Anniversary of the British Red Cross BU	—	£18
2020 — Silver Proof	4000	£850
2020 — — Piedfort	1150	£175
2020 — Gold Proof	250	£2500
2021 Alfred the Great BU	—	£13
2021 — Silver Proof	2,250	£90
2021 — — Piedfort	900	£167
2021 — Gold Proof	160	£2590

DATE	Mintage	UNC
2021 Remembrance Day 2021 BU	–	£17
2021 –Silver Proof	2021	£100
2021 – – Piedfort	600	£187
2021 95th Birthday of Her Majesty the Queen BU	–	£12
2021 –Silver Proof	2021	£100
2021 – – Piedfort	600	£187
2021 – Gold Proof	800	£2725
2021 150th Anniversary of the Royal Albert Hall BU	–	£15
– Silver Proof	1650	£100
– Gold Proof	170	£2900
2022 The Platinum Jubilee of Her Majesty the Queen BU	–	£10
2022 – Premium Exclusive	10,010	£18
2022 – Silver Proof	6,905	£92
2022 – – Piedfort	2,162	£172
2022 – Gold Proof	550	£2725
2022 – Platinum Piedfort	82	£5495
2022 The 40th Birthday of HRH The Duke of Cambridge BU	–	£13
2022 – Silver Proof	3,500	£92
2022 – – Piedfort	1,500	£172
2022 –Gold Proof	300	£2725
2022 The Queen's Reign with Signature–Honours and Investitures BU	–	£13
2022 – Silver Proof	4,000	£92
2022 – – Piedfort	1500	£172
2022 – Gold Proof	250	£2725
2022 Tutankamun BU	–	£14
2022 – Silver Proof	2,682	£95
2022 – – Piedfort	810	£180
2022 – Gold Proof	260	£2,975
2023 Coronation of His Majesty King Charles III BU	–	£14
2023 – Silver Proof	12,500	£95
2023 – – Piedfort	3,250	£180
2023 Gold Proof	500	£2,995
2023 Pride of England BU	–	£14
2023 – Silver Proof	–	£95
2023 Mary Seacole BU	–	£14.50
2023 – Silver Proof	1,500	£97.50
2023 – – Piedfort	750	£182.50
2023 – Gold Proof	125	£2,995
2023 75th Birthday of His Majesty King Charles III		
2023 – Silver Proof	3,000	£97.50
2023 – – Piedfort	1,000	£182.50
2023 Gold Proof	200	£2,995
2024 Buckingham Palace		
2024 – Silver Proof	3,760	£98.50
2024 – – Piedfort	1,060	£185
2024 – –	210	£2,995

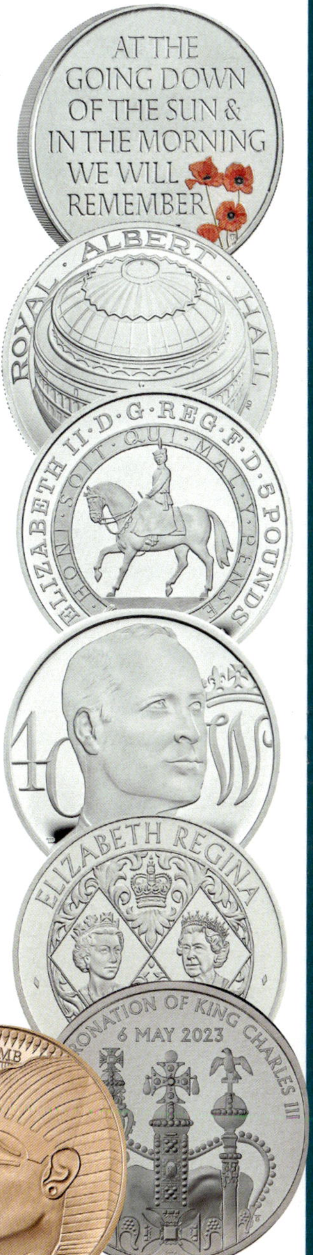

The Royal Mint also issue other coins of a specific theme in various denominations. To help the collector identify these special issues it has been decided to list them with their appropriate headings under "Precious Metal Bullion and Collector Coins" (series). For example, "The Queen's Beasts", "Music Legends" and other series as appropriate.

DOUBLE SOVEREIGN

As with the Sovereign series Five Pound coins, those listed under this heading bear the Pistrucci St George and Dragon reverse, except where otherwise stated, and are minted in gold. They are, and always have been, legal tender at £2, and have a diameter indentical to that of the base metal Two Pound coins listed further below under a different heading. The denomination does not appear on Double Sovereigns. Most were originally issued as part of Royal Mint sets.

DATE	Mintage	UNC
1980 Proof	10,000	£1250
1982 Proof	2,500	£1250
1983 Proof	12,500	£1250
1985 New Portrait Proof	5,849	£1250
1987 Proof	14,301	£1250
1988 Proof	12,743	£1250
1989 500th Anniversary of the Sovereign. Enthroned portrayal obverse and Crowned shield reverse Proof	2,000	£2500
1990 Proof	4,374	£1250
1991 Proof	3,108	£1250
1992 Proof	2,608	£1250
1993 Proof	2,155	£1250
1996 Proof	3,167	£1250
1998 New Portrait Proof	4,500	£1250
2000 Proof	2,250	£1500
2002 Shield reverse Proof	8,000	£1750
2003 Proof	2,250	£1250
2004 Proof	2,500	£1250
2005 Noad's heraldic St George and Dragon reverse Proof	–	£1750
2006 Proof	–	£1250
2007 Proof	–	£1250
2008 Proof	–	£1250
2009 Proof	–	£1250
2010 Proof	2,750	£1250
2011 Proof	2,950	£1250
2012 Day's stylised St George and Dragon reverse, BU	60	£1700
2012 – Proof	1,945	£2000
2013 BU	–	£1200
2013 Proof	1,895	£1250
2014 BU	1,300	£1700
2014 Proof	–	£1750
2015 Proof	1,100	£1250
2015 New Portrait by Jody Clark Proof	1,100	£1250
2016 Butler Portrait Proof	925	£1750
2017 200th Anniv. of the Sovereign design as 1817 issue	1,200	£1750
2018 Proof	1,600	£1750
2019 BU	–	£1500
2020 BU	–	£1250
2020 200th Anniversary of death of George III With GR cypher privy mark Proof	1,100	£1850
2021 BU	–	£1250
2022 Platinum Jubilee. Noad's reverse coat of arms BU	–	£1250
2022 – Proof		£1850
2022 – Piedfort Proof	–	£3500
King Charles III		
2022 Memorial edition Proof	1,787	£2000
2022 – – BU	–	£1250
2023 Coronation issue Proof	1,785	£2000
2023 – Matt Proof (in set)	23	£2250
2023 – – BU	–	£1250
2024 Proof	800	£2000
2024 – BU	–	£1250

Standard reverse

Reverse by Timothy Noad

Reverse by Paul Day

TWO POUNDS

This series commenced in 1986 with nickel-brass commemorative coins, with their associated base metal and precious metal BU and proof coins. From 1997 (actually issued in 1998) a thinner bi-metal version commenced with a reverse theme of the advance of technology, and from this date the coin was specifically intended to circulate. This is true also for the parallel issues of anniversary and commemorative Two Pound issues in 1999 and onwards. All have their BU and proof versions, as listed below.

In the case of Gold Proofs, a few have Certificates of Authenticity and/or green boxes of issue describing the coin as a Double Sovereign. All Gold Proofs since 1997 are of bi-metallic gold except for 2001 (red gold with the inner circle coated in yellow gold) and 2002 (Technology issue, uncoated red gold). After 2008 all RM boxes were black for all denominations.

A new definitive design was introduced during 2015 incorporating the Jody Clark portrait and Britannia by Antony Dufort but to date the mintage each year has been relatively low.

NOTE: The counterfeiting of circulation £2 coins has been around for several years but 2015 saw several proof-like base metal designs. Five types are known at present: 2011 (Mary Rose) and 2015 (all four designs).

DATE	Mintage	UNC
1986 Commonwealth Games	8,212,184	£5
1986 — BU	—	£8
1986 — Proof	59,779	£15
1986 — Silver BU	—	£35
1986 — — Proof	—	£45
1986 — Gold Proof	—	£1000
1989 Tercentenary of Bill of Rights.	4,392,825	£10
1989 — BU (issued in folder with Claim of Right)	—	£25
1989 — BU folder	—	£8
1989 — Proof	—	£15
1989 — Silver Proof	—	£35
1989 — — — Piedfort	—	£60
1989 Tercentenary of Claim of Right (issued in Scotland)	381,400	£30
1989 — BU (see above)	—	£35
1989 — Proof	—	£35
1989 — Silver Proof	—	£45
1989 — — — Piedfort	—	£65
1994 Tercentenary of the Bank of England	1,443,116	£10
1994 — BU	—	£12
1994 — Proof	—	£30
1994 — Silver Proof	27,957	£35
1994 — — — Piedfort	9,569	£65
1994 — Gold Proof	—	£1000
1994 — — — with Double Sovereign obverse (no denomination)	—	£1200
1995 50th Anniversary of End of WWII.	4,394,566	£10
1995 — BU	—	£12
1995 — Proof	—	£15
1995 — Silver Proof	35,751	£35
1995 — — — Piedfort	—	£65
1995 — Gold Proof	—	£1000
1995 50th Anniversary of The United Nations	1,668,575	£10
1995 — BU	—	£12
1995 — Proof	—	£15
1995 — Silver Proof	—	£40
1995 — — — Piedfort	—	£65
1995 — Gold Proof	—	£1000
1996 European Football Championships.	5,195,350	£10
1996 — BU	—	£12
1996 — Proof	—	£15
1996 — Silver Proof	25,163	£40
1996 — — — Piedfort	7,634	£65
1996 — Gold Proof	—	£1000
1997 Technology Standard rev. **First Bi-metallic issue**	13,734,625	£5
1997 — BU	—	£8
1997 — Proof	—	£12
1997 — Silver Proof	29,910	£35
1997 — — — Piedfort	16,000	£65
1997 — Gold Proof (red (outer) and yellow (inner) 22ct)	—	£1000

First bi-metal standard reverse

DATE	Mintage	UNC
1998 ***New Portrait by Ian Rank-Broadley***	91,110,375	£4
1998 BU	—	£8
1998 Proof	—	£12
1998 Silver Proof	19,978	£35
1998 — — Piedfort	7,646	£60
1999 Technology Standard rev.	33,719,000	£4
1999 Rugby World Cup	4,933,000	£6
1999 — BU	—	£10
1999 — Silver Proof (gold plated ring)	9,665	£45
1999 — — — Piedfort (Hologram)	10,000	£85
1999 — Gold Proof	—	£1000
2000 Technology Standard rev.	25,770,000	£4
2000 — BU	—	£6
2000 — Proof	—	£10
2000 — Silver Proof	—	£40
2001 Technology Standard rev.	34,984,750	£4
2001 — BU	—	£5
2001 — Proof	—	£10
2001 Marconi	4,558,000	£5
2001 — BU	—	£8
2001 — Proof	—	£10
2001 — Silver Proof (gold plated ring)	11,488	£40
2001 — — — Reverse Frosting (issued in set with Canada $5)	—	£65
2001 — — — Piedfort	6,759	£65
2001 — Gold Proof	—	£1000
2002 Technology Standard rev.	13,024,750	£4
2002 — BU	—	£6
2002 — Proof	—	£10
2002 — Gold Proof (red 22ct)	—	£1000
2002 Commonwealth Games, Scotland	771,750	£15
2002 — Wales	558,500	£15
2002 — Northern Ireland	485,500	£30
2002 — England	650,500	£15
2002 — BU (issued in set of 4)	—	£60
2002 — Proof (issued in set of 4)	—	£75
2002 — Silver Proof (issued in set of 4)	—	£250
2002 — — — Piedfort (painted) (issued in set of 4)	—	£350
2002 — Gold Proof (issued in set of 4)	—	£3500
2003 Technology Standard rev.	17,531,250	£4
2003 — BU	—	£8
2003 — Proof	—	£12
2003 DNA Double Helix	4,299,000	£5
2003 — BU	41,568	£8
2003 — Proof	—	£10
2003 — Silver Proof (Gold-plated ring)	11,204	£40
2003 — — — Piedfort	8,728	£65
2003 — Gold Proof	3,237	£1000
2004 Technology Standard rev.	11,981,500	£4
2004 — BU	—	£6
2004 — Proof	—	£12
2004 Trevithick Steam Locomotive	5,004,500	£5
2004 — BU	56,871	£8
2004 — Proof	—	£10
2004 — Silver BU	1,923	£25
2004 — — Proof (Gold-plated ring)	10,233	£45
2004 — — — Piedfort	5,303	£65
2004 — Gold Proof	1,500	£1000
2005 Technology Standard rev.	3,837,250	£4
2005 — BU	—	£6
2005 — Proof	—	£8
2005 Gunpowder Plot	5,140,500	£5
2005 — BU	—	£8
2005 — Proof	—	£10
2005 — Silver Proof	4,394	£40
2005 — — — Piedfort	4,585	£65
2005 — Gold Proof	914	£750

DATE	Mintage	UNC
2005 End of World War II	10,191,000	£5
2005 — BU	—	£8
2005 — Silver Proof	21,734	£40
2005 — — — Piedfort	4,798	£65
2005 — Gold Proof	2,924	£1000
2006 Technology Standard rev.	16,715,000	£4
2006 — Proof	—	£6
2006 Brunel, The Man (Portrait)	7,928,250	£5
2006 — BU	—	£6
2006 — Proof	—	£10
2006 — Silver Proof	7,251	£40
2006 — — — Piedfort	3,199	£65
2006 —Gold Proof	1,071	£1000
2006 Brunel, His Achievements (Paddington Station)	7,452,250	£5
2006 — BU	—	£6
2006 — Proof	—	£10
2006 — Silver Proof	5,375	£40
2006 — — — Piedfort	3,018	£65
2006 —Gold Proof	746	£1000
2007 Technology Standard rev.	10,270,000	£4
2007 — Proof	—	£8
2007 Tercentenary of the Act of Union	7,545,000	£5
2007 BU	—	£6
2007 — Proof	—	£8
2007 — Silver Proof	8,310	£40
2007 — — — Piedfort	4,000	£65
2007 — Gold Proof	750	£1000
2007 Bicentenary of the Abolition of the Slave Trade	8,445,000	£8
2007 — BU	—	£10
2007 — Proof	—	£12
2007 — Silver Proof	7,095	£40
2007 — — — Piedfort	3,990	£65
2007 — Gold Proof	1,000	£1000
2008 Technology Standard rev.	15,346,000	£4
2008 — BU	—	£6
2008 — Proof	—	£12
2008 Centenary of 4th Olympiad, London	910,000	£12
2008 — BU	—	£15
2008 — Proof	—	£20
2008 — Silver Proof	6,841	£40
2008 — — — Piedfort	1,619	£70
2008 — Gold Proof	1,908	£1000
2008 Olympic Games Handover Ceremony	853,000	£14
2008 — BU	47,765	£18
2008 — Silver Proof	30,000	£45
2008 — — — Piedfort	3,000	£75
2008 — Gold Proof	3,250	£1000
2009 Technology Standard rev.	8,775,000	£4
2009 — BU	—	£5
2009 — Proof	—	£10
2009 — Silver Proof	—	£40
2009 250th Anniversary of birth of Robert Burns	3,253,000	£5
2009 — BU	120,223	£12
2009 — Proof	—	£15
2009 — Silver Proof	9,188	£40
2009 — — — Piedfort	3,500	£70
2009 — Gold Proof	1,000	£1000
2009 200th Anniversary of birth of Charles Darwin	3,903,000	£5
2009 — BU	119,713	£12
2009 — Proof	—	£15
2009 — Silver Proof	9,357	£40
2009 — — — Piedfort	3,282	£70
2009 — Gold Proof	1,000	£1000
2010 Technology Standard rev.	6,890,000	£4
2010 — BU	—	£8
2010 — Proof	—	£12

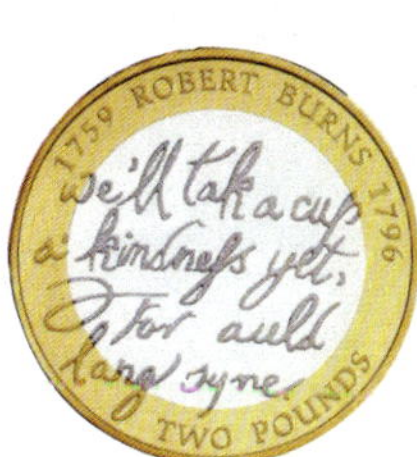

DATE	Mintage	UNC
2010 – Silver Proof	–	£40
2010 Florence Nightingale 150 Years of Nursing	6,175,000	£4
2010 – BU	73,160	£10
2010 – Proof	–	£12
2010 – Silver Proof	5,117	£40
2010 – – – Piedfort	2,770	£75
2010 – Gold Proof	472	£1000
2011 Technology Standard rev.	24,375,000	£4
2011 – BU	–	£5
2011 – Proof	–	£12
2011 – Silver Proof	–	£35
2011 500th Anniversary of the Mary Rose	1,040,000	£10
2011 – BU	53,013	£15
2011 – Proof	–	£20
2011 – Silver Proof	6,618	£40
2011 – – – Piedfort	2,680	£75
2011 – Gold Proof	692	£1000
2011 400th Anniversary of the King James Bible	975,000	£10
2011 – BU	56,268	£15
2011 – Proof	–	£20
2011 – Silver Proof	4,494	£40
2011 – – – Piedfort	2,394	£75
2011 – Gold Proof	355	£1000
2012 Technology Standard rev.	3,900,000	£3
2012 – BU	–	£8
2012 – Proof	–	£12
2012 – Silver Proof	–	£40
2012 – Gold Proof	–	£1000
2012 200th Anniversary of birth of Charles Dickens	8,190,000	£4
2012 – BU	15,035	£14
2012 – Proof	–	£17
2012 – Silver Proof	2,631	£40
2012 – – – Piedfort	1,279	£75
2012 – Gold Proof	202	£1000
2012 Olympic Handover to Rio	845,000	£14
2012 – BU	28,356	£20
2012 Proof	–	£25
2012 – Silver Proof	3,781	£40
2012 – – – Piedfort	2,000	£120
2012 – Gold Proof	771	£1000
2013 Technology Standard rev.	15,860,250	£4
2013 – BU	–	£10
2013 – Proof	–	£15
2013 – Silver Proof	–	£65
2013 – Gold Proof	–	£1000
2013 150th Anniversary of the London Underground, Roundel design	1,560,000	£6
2013 – BU	11,647	£15
2013 – Proof	–	£25
2013 – Silver Proof	3,389	£40
2013 – – – Piedfort	162	£100
2013 – Gold Proof	132	£1000
2013 150th Anniversary of the London Underground, Train design	1,690,000	£6
2013 – BU	11,647	£15
2013 – Proof	–	£25
2013 – Silver Proof	4,246	£40
2013 – – – Piedfort	186	£100
2013 – Gold Proof	140	£1000
2013 350th Anniversary of the Guinea	2,990,000	£5
2013 – BU	10,340	£12
2013 – Proof	–	£18
2013 – Silver Proof	1,640	£40
2013 – – – Piedfort	969	£100
2013 – Gold Proof	284	£1000

DATE	Mintage	UNC
2014 Technology Standard rev.	18,200,000	£4
2014 — BU	—	£10
2014 — Proof	—	£25
2014 — Silver Proof	—	£40
2014 100th Anniversary of First World War Outbreak	5,720,000	£4
2014 — BU	40,557	£15
2014 — Proof	—	£20
2014 — Silver Proof	4,983	£40
2014 — — — Piedfort	2,496	£100
2014 — Gold Proof	—	£1000
2014 500th Anniversary of Trinity House	3,705,000	£4
2014 — BU	10,521	£15
2014 — Proof	—	£20
2014 — Silver Proof	1,285	£40
2014 — — — Piedfort	652	£100
2014 — Gold Proof	204	£1000
2015 Technology Standard rev.	35,360,058	£4
2015 — BU	39,009	£10
2015 — Proof	3,930	£20
2015 — Silver Proof	1,512	£40
2015 — Gold Proof	406	£1000

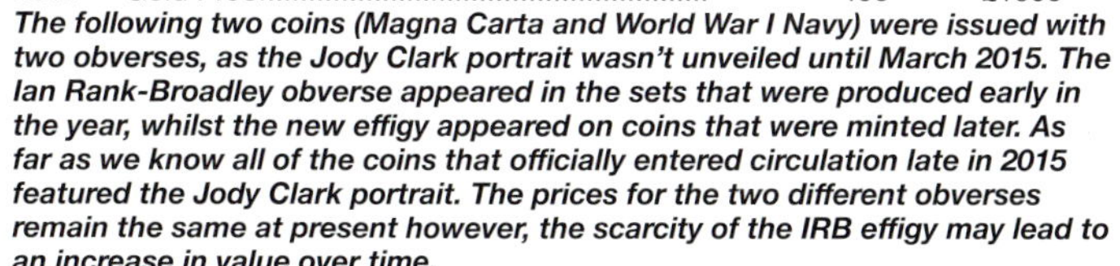
The following two coins (Magna Carta and World War I Navy) were issued with two obverses, as the Jody Clark portrait wasn't unveiled until March 2015. The Ian Rank-Broadley obverse appeared in the sets that were produced early in the year, whilst the new effigy appeared on coins that were minted later. As far as we know all of the coins that officially entered circulation late in 2015 featured the Jody Clark portrait. The prices for the two different obverses remain the same at present however, the scarcity of the IRB effigy may lead to an increase in value over time.

Britannia standard reverse

DATE	Mintage	UNC
2015 Anniversary of First World War—Royal Navy	650,000	£10
2015 — BU	39,009	£15
2015 — Proof	—	£20
2015 — Silver Proof	3,030	£40
2015 — — — Piedfort	1,512	£100
2015 — Gold Proof	406	£1000
2015 800th Anniversary of Magna Carta	1,495,000	£15
2015 — BU	32,818	£20
2015 — Proof	—	£25
2015 — Silver Proof	2,995	£40
2015 — — — Piedfort	1,988	£100
2015 — Gold Proof	399	£1000
2015 Britannia—**the new standard reverse design**	650,000	£8
2015 — BU	—	£10
2015 — Proof	—	£20
2015 — Silver Proof	—	£40
2015 — Gold Proof	—	£1000
2015 — Platinum Proof	—	£900
2016 Britannia Standard rev.	2,925,000	£5
2016 — BU	—	£12
2016 — Proof	—	£20
2016 — Silver Proof	—	£40
2016 400th Anniversary Shakespeare's death, Comedies	4,355,000	£4
2016 — — BU	—	£10
2016 — — Proof	—	£20
2016 — — Silver Proof	951	£40
2016 — — — — Piedfort	533	£125
2016 — — Gold Proof	152	£1000
2016 — Tragedies	5,695,000	£4
2016 — — BU	—	£10
2016 — — Proof	—	£20
2016 — — Silver Proof	1,004	£40
2016 — — — — Piedfort	679	£125
2016 — — Gold Proof	209	£1000

DATE	Mintage	UNC
2016 — Histories	4,615,000	£4
2016 — — BU	—	£10
2016 — — Proof	—	£20
2016 — — Silver Proof	965	£40
2016 — — — — Piedfort	624	£125
2016 — — Gold Proof	156	£1000
2016 350th Anniversary of Great Fire of London	5,135,000	£4
2016 — BU	23,215	£10
2016 — Proof	—	£20
2016 — Silver Proof	1,649	£50
2016 — — — Piedfort	1,356	£125
2016 — Gold Proof	259	£1000
2016 Anniversary of First World War—Army	9,550,000	£4
2016 — BU	19,066	£10
2016 — Proof	—	£20
2016 — Silver Proof	1,703	£50
2016 — — — Piedfort	931	£125
2016 — Gold Proof	279	£1000
2017 Britannia Standard rev. BU	—	£20
2017 — Proof	—	£30
2017 — Silver Proof	—	£50
2017 — Gold Proof	—	£1000
2017 Anniversary of First World War—Aviation BU	55,840	£15
2017 — Proof	—	£25
2017 — Silver Proof	7,000	£75
2017 — — — Piedfort	1,528	£125
2017 — Gold Proof	634	£1000
2017 Jane Austen BU	54,729	£15
2017 — Proof	—	£25
2017 — Silver Proof	7,498	£75
2017 — — — Piedfort	2,125	£125
2017 — Gold Proof	884	£1000
2018 Britannia Standard rev.	—	£3
2018 —BU	—	£20
2018 — Proof	—	£30
2018 — Silver Proof	—	£40
2018 — Gold Proof	—	£1000
2018 Bicentenary of Mary Shelley's "Frankenstein" BU	—	£17
2018 — Proof	—	£30
2018 — Silver Proof	—	£70
2018 — Gold Proof	—	£1000
2018 Journey to Armistice BU	—	£15
2018 — Proof	—	£30
2018 — Silver Proof	5,000	£50
2018 — — — Piedfort	2,500	£125
2018 — Gold Proof	750	£1000
2018 Centenary of the RAF BU	—	£15
2018 — Proof	—	£30
2018 — Silver Proof	7,500	£50
2018 — — — Piedfort	3,000	£125
2018 — Gold Proof	1,000	£1000
2018 250th Anniversary of Captain Cook's "Voyage of Discovery"—I BU	—	£20
2018 — Proof	—	£30
2018 — Silver Proof	4,795	£70
2018 —Gold Proof	340	£1000
2019 Britannia Standard rev. BU	—	£15
2019 — Proof	—	£25
2019 — Silver Proof	—	£50
2019 D-Day: 75th Anniversary BU	—	£10
2019 — Proof	—	£25
2019 — Silver Proof	8,750	£75
2019 — — Piedfort	3,010	£125
2019 — Gold Proof	750	£1000

DATE	Mintage	UNC
2019 Captain Cook II BU	—	£15
2019 — Proof	—	£25
2019 — Silver Proof	5,000	£85
2019 — Gold Proof	350	£1100
2019 Samuel Pepys BU	—	£15
2019 — Proof	—	£25
2019 — Silver Proof	3,500	£85
2019 — — Piedfort	2,019	£125
2019 — Gold Proof	350	£1100
2019 260th Anniversary of Wedgwood BU	—	£12
2019 — Proof	—	£25
2019 — Silver Proof	4,500	£100
2019 — — Piedfort	2,250	£125
2019 — Gold Proof	350	£1100
2020 Britannia Standard rev. BU	—	£10
2020 — Proof	—	£20
2020 — Silver Proof	—	£85
2020 Captain Cook III BU	—	£15
2020 — Proof	—	£25
2020 — Silver Proof	4,795	£85
2020 — Gold Proof	340	£1000
2020 VE Day Anniversary BU	—	£12
2020 — Proof	—	£25
2020 — Silver Proof	—	£85
2020 — — — Piedfort	—	£150
2020 — Gold Proof	—	£1100
2020 100 years of Agatha Christie BU	—	£15
2020 — Proof	—	£25
2020 — Silver Proof	—	£85
2020 — — — Piedfort	—	£150
2020 — Gold Proof	—	£1100
2020 Anniversary of the sailing of the "Mayflower" BU.	—	£12
2020 — Proof	—	£25
2020 — Silver Proof	—	£85
2020 — — — Piedfort	—	£150
2020 — Gold Proof	—	£1155
2021 Britannia Standard rev. BU	—	£10
2021 — Proof	—	£20
2021 — Silver Proof	—	£85
2021 Celebrating the life and work of H. G. Wells BU	—	£10
2021 — Proof	—	£25
2021 — Silver Proof	3135	£72.50
2021 — — Piedfort	985	£117.50
2021 — Gold Proof	330	£1095
2021 250th Anniversary of the birth of Sir. Walter Scott BU	—	£10
2021 — Proof	—	£25
2021 — Silver Proof	1771	£72.50
2021 — — Piedfort	771	£117.50
2021— Gold Proof	175	£1095
2022 Britannia Standard rev. BU	—	£10
2022 — Proof	—	£20
2022 — Silver Proof	—	£85
2022 Standard rev. BU with 26/22 privy mark	—	£20
2022 BU	—	£2
2022 Silver Proof	2,525	£78.50
2022 — Piedfort	1,425	£128.50
2022 Gold	275	£1250
2022 150 Years of the FA Cup BU	—	£12
2022 — Silver Proof	5,660	£72.50
2022 — — Piedfort	1,160	£117.50
2022 — Gold Proof	360	£1125
2022 Alexander Graham Bell BU	—	£10
2022 — Silver Proof	2,500	£72.50
2022 — — Piedfort	1,000	£117.50
2022 — Gold Proof	125	£1180

DATE	Mintage	UNC
2022 25 Years of the bi-metallic coin BU	—	£12
2022 Silver Proof	2,525	£75
2022 — — Piedfort	1,425	£125
2022 Gold Proof	275	£1,225
2023 Vaccination Pioneer—Edward Jenner BU	—	£12
2023 Silver Proof	2,510	£75
2023 — — Piedfort	1,260	£125
2023 Gold Proof	160	£1,225
2023 Centenary of the Flying Scotsman BU	—	£12
2023 BU (coloured coin)	15,000	£21
2023 Silver Proof (coloured coin)	4,475	£85
2023 — — Piedfort (coloured coin)	1,923	£135
2023 Gold Proof	300	£1,225
2023 The Enchantress of Numbers BU	—	£12
2023 Silver Proof	1,760	£77.50
2023 — — Piedfort	760	£127.50
2023 Gold Proof	85	£1,250
2023 Celebrating the Life and Work of J. R. R. Tolkien BU	—	£12
2023 — Silver Proof	4,500	£77.50
2023 — — Piedfort	2,000	£127.50
2023 Gold Proof	225	£1,250
2023 New definitive design Emblems of the UK (released in sets only), with commemorative Tudor crown privy mark, first year only		
2023 — BU		£34
2023 — Silver	—	£101.50
2023 — Gold		£7,225
2024 The National Gallery BU	—	£13.00
2024 — Silver Proof	2,760	£78.50
2024 — — Piedfort	1,210	£128.50
2024 — Gold Proof	185	£1,250

Note: The silver editions are silver centres with silver outers plated with gold. The gold issues are 22ct yellow gold centres with 22ct red gold outers.

SOVEREIGN

All are minted in gold, bear the Pistrucci St George and Dragon reverse except where stated, and are legal tender at one pound. From 2009 there is no streamer behind St George's Helmet in the Pistrucci design.

DATE	Mintage	UNC
1974	5,002,566	£530
1976	4,150,000	£530
1976 Brilliant Proof	—	£40,000
1978	6,550,000	£530
1979	9,100,000	£530
1979 Proof	50,000	£530
1980	5,100,000	£530
1980 Proof	91,200	£650
1981	5,000,000	£530
1981 Proof	32,960	£650
1982	2,950,000	£530
1982 Proof	22,500	£600
1983 Proof	21,250	£800
1984 Proof	19,975	£800
1985 **New portrait** Proof	17,242	£800
1986 Proof	17,579	£750
1987 Proof	22,479	£800
1988 Proof	18,862	£750
1989 500th Anniversary of the Sovereign—details as Five Pounds (Sov. Series). Proof	23,471	£2000
1990 Proof	8,425	£800
1991 Proof	7,201	£800
1992 Proof	6,854	£1100
1993 Proof	6,090	£900
1994 Proof	7,165	£900
1995 Proof	9,500	£950
1996 Proof	9,110	£900
1997 Proof	9,177	£900
1998 **New Portrait** Proof	11,349	£850
1999 Proof	11,903	£850
2000 (first Unc issue since 1982)	129,069	£550
2000 Proof	12,159	£850
2001	49,462	£525
2001 Proof	10,000	£900
2002 Golden Jubilee Shield Rev. ("bullion")	74,263	£550
2002 Proof	20,500	£900
2003 ("bullion")	43,208	£530
2003 Proof	12,433	£600
2004 ("bullion")	30,688	£300
2004 Proof	10,175	£550
2005 Timothy Noad's heraldic St George and Dragon	75,542	£650
2005 — Proof	12,500	£900
2006 ("bullion")	—	£550
2006 Proof	9,195	£650
2007 ("bullion")	75,000	£530
2007 Proof	8,199	£650
2008 ("bullion")	35,000	£530
2008 Proof	12,500	£700
2009 ("bullion")	75,000	£530
2009 Proof	9,770	£700
2010 ("bullion")	243,986	£530
2010 Proof	8,828	£700
2011 ("bullion")	250,000	£530
2011 Proof	15,000	£700

Standard reverse

500th Anniversary reverse

Golden Jubilee Shield reverse

Noad modern reverse

DATE	Mintage	UNC
2012 Paul Day's St George and Dragon BU "bullion".	250,000	£600
2012 — Proof	5,501	£1500
2013 BU ("bullion")	2,695	£530
2013 Proof	8,243	£650
2013 With "I" mintmark, minted by MMTC-PAMP, Haryana, India, under Licence from, and supervision of, the Royal Mint	—	£525
2014 BU ("bullion")	15,000	£530
2014 Proof	9,725	£900
2014 BU ("bullion") with "I" mintmark	—	£600
2015 BU ("bullion")	10,000	£530
2015 Proof	4,456	£700
2015 **New Portrait** by Jody Clark BU	10,000	£530
2015— Proof	7,494	£750
2016 BU ("bullion")	1,251	£530
2016 Queen's 90th Birthday, Butler portrait. Proof	7,995	£1300
2017 200th Anniversary of the Sovereign. Original 1817 "Garter" design. Proof-like	13,500	£1000
2017 — Piedfort	3,750	£2500
2017 BU with 200 Privy mark	—	£750
2017 Royal Platinum Wedding Strike on the day (no privy mark)	1,793	—
2018 BU ("bullion")	—	£550
2018 Proof	10,500	£700
2018 — Piedfort	2,675	£1500
2019 BU Matt finish	20,500	£600
2019 BU ("bullion")	—	£550
2019 Proof	9,500	£700
2019 — Piedfort	—	£1500
2020 BU ("bullion")	—	£550
2020 200th Anniversary of Death of George III With GR cypher privy mark	9,845	£750
2020 Matt finish, plain edge	—	£950
2021 BU ("bullion")	—	£550
2021 Proof Queen's 95th Birthday (95 millings on edge). Unique privy mark (Royal crown with the number 95 entwined)	9,850	£800
2022 Proof Platinum Jubilee, Royal Coat of Arms reverse	10,500	£700
2022 Memorial of Her Late Majesty Queen Elizabeth II passing—New portrait of King Charles III by Martin Jennings (obverse). Special Coat of Arms by Jody Clark (reverse)	17,500	£750
2022 — Piedfort Proof	2,022	£1500
2023 The Coronation of His Majesty King Charles III..		
Bullion	—	£550
Proof	17,875	£750
Piedfort	—	£1,400
Matt Proof	—	£750
BU Matt finish, plain edge (set only)	23	£1200
2023 BU Pistrucci reverse design, bare-headed obverse struck for 75th Birthday King Charles III	860	£550
2024 Pistrucci reverse design, bare-headed obverse		
Bullion	—	£550
Proof	8,950	£750

For coins struck on the day of a special event, see the table opposite.

Note: that coins struck on the actual day of the event are always accompanied by a certificate of authenticity from the Royal Mint. With many of these "Strike on the Day" coins this is the only means of identification as they do not all carry special privy marks. Only those with these privy marks are listed here.

Day's stylised reverse

200th Anniversary reverse

2020 Withdrawal from the EU

2021 Proof Queen's 95th Birthday

2022 Proof Platinum Jubilee, Royal Coat of Arms

2023 Coronation

SOVEREIGNS STRUCK ON THE DAY

To commemorate certain special occasions the Royal Mint strike a limited number of sovereigns on the day of the event. Listed below are the events so marked and the quantities issued. Some are only identified by a special certificate issued with the coin, but the later issues are marked with a special privy mark appropriate to the occasion. The first strike on the day was to mark the Diamond Jubilee of Her Majesty the Queen on June 2, 2012, followed by the 60th anniversary of the Coronation the following year. Since then various occasions have been celebrated and this has generated a great deal of interest among collectors, with the generally low quantities struck reflected in their values if kept in their original box accompanied by the certificate.

Date	Occasion struck	Quantity	Type	Privy mark
June 2, 2012	Diamond Jubilee of Her Majesty the Queen	1,990	BU	–
June 2, 2013	60th anniversary of the Coronation	900	BU	–
July 22, 2013	Birth of Prince George	2,013	BU	–
July 22, 2014	First birthday of Prince George	398	BU	–
May 2, 2015	Birth of Princess Charlotte	743	BU	–
July 22, 2015	Second birthday of Prince George	301	BU (Jody Clark obv.)	–
June 11, 2016	90th birthday of Her Majesty the Queen	499	BU	–
June 2, 2017	65th anniversary of the accession of Her Majesty the Queen	739	BU	–
July 1, 2017	200th anniversary of the issue of the 1817 sovereign	1,793	BU, plain edge	–
November 20, 2017	Platinum Wedding of Her Majesty the Queen and Prince Philip	745	BU	–
June 2, 2018	65th anniversary of the Coronation	323	BU, plain edge	65
July 22, 2018	5th birthday of Prince George	457	BU, plain edge	–
May 24, 2019	200th anniversary of birth of Queen Victoria	Limit 650	Matt, plain edge	VR
August 26, 2019	200th anniversary of birth of Prince Albert	Limit 650	Matt, plain edge	VA
January 31, 2020	"Brexit" Day	Limit 1,500	Matt, plain edge	Crowned portcullis
May 8, 2020	75th anniversary of VE Day	Limit 750	Matt, plain edge	VE75
August 15, 2020 Matt, plain edge	75th anniversary of the End of WWII VJ75	Limit 750		
April 21, 2021*	The 95th birthday of Her Majesty the Queen	Limit 1,295	Matt, plain edge	95 in Crown
February 6, 2022	Platinum Jubilee of Her Majesty the Queen (Royal Arms reverse design by the heraldic artist Timothy Noad)	Limit 1,200	BU	–
May 6, 2023	King's Coronation Day	Limit 1,250	Matt, plain edge	
November 14. 2023	King's 75th Birthday	Limit 860	Matt, plain edge	
June 6, 2024	80th Anniversary of D-Day	Limit 1,000,	Matt plain edge	Helmet above "80" in upper left of exergue

* Owing to the death of HRH Prince Philip this occasion was postponed until June 12, Her Majesty's official birthday.

In addition to the above, the Royal Mint have also adopted the policy of striking other denominations on appropriate dates and these are offered as "Strike on the Day" coins. It has been decided that these are outside of the scope of this publication and are therefore not recorded. For more information visit the Royal Mint website at www.royalmint.com

HALF SOVEREIGN

Legal Tender at 50 pence, otherwise the notes for the Sovereign apply. From 2009 the exergue in the Pistrucci design is larger in area, and the initials B.P. are absent. From 2011, however, the initials were restored.

DATE	Mintage	UNC
1980 Proof only	86,700	£400
1982	2,500,000	£320
1982 Proof	21,590	£400
1983 Proof	19,710	£375
1984 Proof	19,505	£375
1985 New portrait Proof	15,800	£375
1986 Proof	17,075	£375
1987 Proof	20,687	£375
1988 Proof	18,266	£375
1989 500th Anniversary of the Sovereign—details as Five Pounds (Sov. Series) Proof	21,824	£750
1990 Proof	7,889	£400
1991 Proof	6,076	£400
1992 Proof	5,915	£400
1993 Proof	4,651	£400
1994 Proof	7,167	£400
1995 Proof	7,500	£400
1996 New Portrait Proof	7,340	£400
1997 Proof	9,177	£400
1998 Proof	7,496	£400
1999 Proof	9,403	£400
2000	146,822	£250
2000 Proof	9,708	£400
2001	98,763	£250
2001 Proof	7,500	£400
2002 Golden Jubilee Shield reverse ("bullion")	61,347	£275
2002 — Proof	—	£500
2003 ("bullion")	47,805	£250
2003 Proof	—	£450
2004 ("bullion")	32,479	£250
2004 Proof	—	£450
2005 Timothy Noad's heraldic St George and Dragon	—	£450
2005 — Proof	—	£500
2006 ("bullion")	—	£250
2006 Proof	—	£400
2007 ("bullion")	—	£250
2007 Proof	—	£400
2008 ("bullion")	—	£250
2008 Proof	—	£425
2009 ("bullion")	—	£250
2009 Proof	—	£450
2010 ("bullion")	16,485	£250
2010 Proof	—	£500
2011 ("bullion")	—	£250
2011 Proof	—	£400
2012 Paul Day's stylised reverse. Diamond Jubilee BU	—	£350
2012 — Proof	—	£600
2013 BU "bullion"	—	£250
2013 Proof	—	£650
2014 BU "bullion"	—	£250
2014 Proof	—	£650
2014 BU "bullion" with "I" mintmark	—	£300
2015 BU "bullion"	500	£250
2015 Proof	1,704	£500
2015 New Jody Clark portrait. Proof		£550
2016 BU "bullion"	472	£250
2016 Queen's 90th Birthday, Butler portrait. Proof	1,995	£500
2017 200th Anniversary of the Sovereign. Original 1817 "Garter" design. Proof-like	1,817	£750
2017 With 200 Privy mark	—	£400

Standard reverse

500th Anniversary reverse

Golden Jubilee Shield reverse

Timothy Noad's Heraldic reverse

Paul Day's Diamond Jubilee reverse

DATE	Mintage	UNC
2018 BU "bullion"	—	£250
2018 Proof with 65 privy mark	2,500	£500
2019 BU Matt finish	4,620	£225
2019 Proof	—	£260
2020 Bullion	—	£250
2020 200th Anniversary of Death of George III With GR cypher privy mark	3,910	£500
2021 Proof with 95 privy mark	3,260	£550
2021 ("bullion")	—	£250
2022 Platinum Jubilee, Royal Coat of Arms reverse	2,000	£315
2022 Bullion	—	£250
2022 Proof	4,200	£500
2022 — Piedfort	70	£950
2022 Memorial of HM Queen Elizabeth II ("bullion")	—	£250
2022 — Proof	5,993	£500
2023 The Coronation of His Majesty King Charles III.. Bullion	—	£250
2023 — Proof	5,375	£500
2023 — Matt	In set 23	£850
2023 Pistrucci reverse design, bare-head obverse Bullion	—	£250
2023 — Proof	2,700	£500
2024 Pistrucci reverse design, bare-headed obverse Bullion	—	£250
2024 — Proof	2,710	£500

200th Anniversary reverse

QUARTER SOVEREIGN

Minted in 22ct gold, this denomination was introduced in 2009 in the same style as the rest of the sovereign series.

DATE	Mintage	UNC
2009 ("bullion")	50,000	£150
2009 Proof	13,495	£200
2010 ("bullion")	250,000	£150
2010 Proof	6,007	£200
2011 ("bullion")	50,000	£150
2011 Proof	7,764	£200
2012 Paul Day's stylised reverse Diamond Jubilee	137	£225
2012 — Proof	7,579	£275
2013 ("bullion")	—	£150
2013 Proof	1,729	£200
2014 ("bullion")	—	£150
2014 Proof	1,696	£200
2015 ("bullion")	—	£150
2015 Proof	1,808	£200
2015 Jody Clark portrait Proof	550	£175
2016 Butler portrait Proof	1,727	£225
2017 200th Anniversary Proof	5,100	£275
2018 Proof with 65 privy mark	—	£200
2019 BU Matt finish	1,750	£165
2019 Proof	—	£200
2020 200th Anniversary of Death of George III With GR cypher privy mark, proof	—	£225
2021 Proof with 95 privy mark	1,700	£220
2022 Platinum Jubilee, Royal Coat of Arms reverse	2,000	£315
2022 Bullion	—	£150
2022 Proof	2,200	£220
2022 Piedfort	70	£375
2022 Memorial of HM Queen Elizabeth II Bullion	—	£150
2022 — Proof	5,828	£200
2023 The Coronation of His Majesty King Charles III Bullion	—	£150
2023 — Proof	4,625	£200
2023 — Matt	In set 23	£500
2023 Pistrucci reverse design, bare-head obverse Bullion	—	£150
2023 — Proof	In set 1,450	£200
2024 Pistrucci reverse design, bare-headed obverse Bullion	—	£150
2024 — Proof	2,710	£200

ONE POUND

Introduced into circulation in 1983 to replace the £1 note, the original, £1 coins are minted in nickel-brass unless otherwise stated. The reverse changed yearly until 2008, and until 2008 the Royal Arms was the "definitive" version. 2008 also saw the introduction of the Matthew Dent Uncrowned Shield of the Royal Arms, a new "definitive", and this reverse appeared in 2008 and every year until 2017. A Capital Cities Series of two coins each year for two years commenced in 2010. From 2013 a further 4-coin series over two years was issued, portraying two floral emblems associated with each of the four countries making up the United Kingdom. Collectors and others should be aware of the many different counterfeit £1 coin versions that circulated up until 2017, a high proportion of which do not have matching obverses and reverses although many do. These original £1 coins have now been withdrawn from circulation. A 12-sided bi-metallic coin replaced the round £1 coin in 2017 which incorporates several security features to help defeat the counterfeiters.

DATE	Mintage	UNC
1983 Royal Arms	443,053,510	£3
1983 — BU	1,134,000	£8
1983 — Proof	107,800	£8
1983 — Silver Proof	50,000	£25
1983 — — — Piedfort	10,000	£85
1984 Scottish Thistle	146,256,501	£3
1984 — BU	199,430	£6
1984 — Proof	106,520	£8
1984 — Silver Proof	44,855	£25
1984 — — — Piedfort	15,000	£35
1985 ***New portrait.*** Welsh Leek	228,430,749	£3
1985 — BU	213,679	£5
1985 — Proof	102,015	£6
1985 — Silver Proof	50,000	£25
1985 — — — Piedfort	15,000	£35
1986 Northern Ireland Flax	10,409,501	£3
1986 — BU	—	£6
1986 — Proof	—	£7
1986 — Silver Proof	37,958	£25
1986 — — — Piedfort	15,000	£35
1987 English Oak	39,298,502	£3
1987 — BU	—	£5
1987 — Proof	—	£8
1987 — Silver Proof	50,000	£25
1987 — — — Piedfort	15,000	£35
1988 Crowned Shield Of The Royal Arms	7,118,825	£5
1988 — BU	—	£7
1988 — Proof	—	£8
1988 — Silver Proof	50,000	£25
1988 — — — Piedfort	10,000	£35
1989 Scottish Thistle	70,580,501	£4
1989 — BU	—	£6
1989 — Proof	—	£9
1989 — Silver Proof	22,275	£25
1989 — — — Piedfort	10,000	£35
1990 Welsh Leek	—	£4
1990 — BU	97,269,302	£6
1990 — Proof	—	£7
1990 — Silver Proof	23,277	£25
1991 Northern Ireland Flax	38,443,575	£3
1991 — BU	—	£6
1991 — Proof	—	£9
1991 — Silver Proof	22,922	£25

1983, 1993, 1998, 2003
EDGE: ***DECUS ET TUTAMEN***

1984, 1989
NEMO ME IMPUNE LACESSIT

1985, 1990
PLEIDIOL WYF I'M GWLAD

1986, 1991
DECUS ET TUTAMEN

1987, 1992
DECUS ET TUTAMEN

DATE	Mintage	UNC
1992 English Oak	36,320,487	£3
1992 — BU	—	£6
1992 — Proof	—	£7
1992 — Silver Proof	13,065	£25
1993 Royal Arms	114,744,500	£3
1993 — BU	—	£6
1993 — Proof	—	£7
1993 — Silver Proof	16,526	£25
1993 — — — Piedfort	12,500	£30
1994 Scottish Lion	29,752,525	£4
1994 — BU	—	£6
1994 — Proof	—	£8
1994 — Silver Proof	25,000	£25
1994 — — — Piedfort	11,722	£30
1995 Welsh Dragon	34,503,501	£3
1995 — BU	—	£6
1995 — — (Welsh)	—	£7
1995 — Proof	—	£10
1995 — Silver Proof	27,445	£25
1995 — — — Piedfort	8,458	£30
1996 Northern Ireland Celtic Cross	89,886,000	£4
1996 — BU	—	£6
1996 — Proof	—	£7
1996 — Silver Proof	25,000	£25
1996 — — — Piedfort	10,000	£30
1997 English Lions	57,117,450	£4
1997 — BU	—	£6
1997 — Proof	—	£7
1997 — Silver Proof	20,137	£30
1997 — — — Piedfort	10,000	£35
1998 ***New portrait.*** Royal Arms. BU	—	£15
1998 — Proof	—	£20
1998 — Silver Proof	13,863	£35
1998 — — — Piedfort	7,894	£40
1999 Scottish Lion. BU	—	£15
1999 — Proof	—	£20
1999 — Silver Proof	16,328	£30
1999 — — — Reverse Frosting	—	£45
1999 — — — Piedfort	9,975	£35
2000 Welsh Dragon	109,496,500	£3
2000 — BU	—	£6
2000 — Proof	—	£8
2000 — Silver Proof	15,913	£25
2000 — — — Reverse Frosting	—	£45
2000 — — — Piedfort	9,994	£35
2001 Northern Ireland Celtic Cross.	63,968,065	£3
2001 — BU	58,093,731	£6
2001 — Proof	—	£8
2001 — Silver Proof	11,697	£25
2001 — — — Reverse Frosting	—	£45
2001 — — — Piedfort	8,464	£35
2002 English Lions	77,818,000	£3
2002 — BU	—	£5
2002 — Proof	—	£8
2002 — Silver Proof	17,693	£35
2002 — — — Reverse Frosting	—	£45
2002 — — — Piedfort	6,599	£50
2002 — Gold Proof	—	£1100
2003 Royal Arms	61,596,500	£4
2003 — BU	23,760	£6
2003 — Proof	—	£8
2003 — Silver Proof	15,830	£30
2003 — — — Piedfort	9,871	£35

1988
DECUS ET TUTAMEN

1994, 1999
NEMO ME IMPUNE LACESSIT

1995, 2000
PLEIDIOL WYF I'M GWLAD

1996, 2001
DECUS ET TUTAMEN

1997, 2002
DECUS ET TUTAMEN

2004
PATTERNED EDGE

DATE	Mintage	UNC
2004 Forth Railway Bridge	39,162,000	£4
2004 — BU	24,014	£6
2004 — Proof	—	£10
2004 — Silver Proof	11,470	£30
2004 — — — Piedfort	7,013	£40
2004 — Gold Proof	—	£1100
2005 Menai Bridge	99,429,500	£4
2005 — BU	—	£6
2005 — Proof	—	£10
2005 — Silver Proof	8,371	£35
2005 — — — Piedfort	6,007	£40
2005 — Gold Proof	—	£1100
2006 Egyptian Arch	38,938,000	£4
2006 — BU	—	£6
2006 — Proof	—	£10
2006 — Silver Proof	14,765	£30
2006 — — — Piedfort	5,129	£40
2006 — Gold Proof	—	£1100
2007 Gateshead Millennium Bridge	26,180,160	£4
2007 — BU	—	£6
2007 — Proof	—	£10
2007 — Silver Proof	10,110	£35
2007 — — — Piedfort	5,739	£40
2007 — Gold Proof	—	£1100
2008 Royal Arms	3,910,000	£3
2008 — BU	18,336	£6
2008 — Proof	—	£8
2008 — Silver Proof	8,441	£30
2008 — Gold Proof	674	£1100
2008 — Platinum Proof	—	£600
2008 A series of 14 different reverses, the 25th Anniversary of the modern £1 coin, Silver Proof with selected gold highlighting on the reverses. the latter being all those used since 1983, the coins being with appropriate edge lettering	—	£450
2008 The same as above, Gold Proof (the 2008 Royal Arms being already listed above)	150	£6250
2008 ***New Rev.,*** Shield of the Royal Arms, no border beads on Obv.	29,518,000	£3
2008 BU	—	£5
2008 Proof	—	£6
2008 Silver Proof	5,000	£30
2008 Silver Proof Piedfort	2,456	£50
2008 Gold Proof	860	£1100
2008 Platinum Proof	—	£600
2009	7,820,000	£2
2009 BU	130,644	£5
2009 Proof	—	£6
2009 Silver Proof	8,508	£30
2009 Gold Proof	540	£1100
2010	38,505,000	£2
2010 BU	—	£8
2010 Proof	—	£6
2010 Silver BU	—	£30
2010 — Proof	—	£45
2010 City Series (London)	2,635,000	£3
2010 — BU	66,313	£10
2010 — Proof	—	£15
2010 — Silver Proof	7,693	£45
2010 — — — Piedfort	3,682	£65
2010 — Gold Proof	950	£1100
2010 City Series (Belfast)	6,205,000	£3
2010 — BU	64,461	£10

2005
PATTERNED EDGE

2006
PATTERNED EDGE

2007
PATTERNED EDGE

2008 (proof sets—silver and gold)
DECUS ET TUTAMEN

2008, 2009, 2010, 2011
DECUS ET TUTAMEN

2011
Y DDRAIG GOCH
DDYRY CYCHWYN

DATE	Mintage	UNC
2010 — Proof	—	£15
2010 — Silver Proof	5,805	£45
2010 — — — Piedfort	3,503	£65
2010 — Gold Proof	585	£1100
2011	25,415,000	£3
2011 BU	—	£10
2011 Proof	—	£15
2011 Silver BU (in 21st and 18th Birthday cards)	—	£30
2011 — Proof	—	£35
2011 City Series (Cardiff)	1,615,000	£5
2011 — BU	47,933	£10
2011 — Proof	—	£15
2011 — Silver Proof	5,553	£50
2011 — — — Piedfort	1,615	£70
2011 — Gold Proof	524	£1100
2011 City Series (Edinburgh)	935,000	£6
2011 — BU	47,896	£15
2011 — Proof	—	£20
2011 — Silver Proof	4,973	£60
2011 — — — Piedfort	2,696	£90
2011 — Gold Proof	499	£1100
2012	35,700,030	£3
2012 BU	—	£5
2012 Proof	—	£10
2012 Silver BU (in Silver Baby Gift)	—	£75
2012 Silver Proof	—	£45
2012 — with selective gold plating	—	£55
2012 Gold Proof	—	£1100
2013	13,090,500	£3
2013 BU	—	£10
2013 Proof	—	£15
2013 Silver BU	—	£60
2013 Silver Proof	—	£45
2013 Gold Proof	—	£1100
2013 Floral Series (England)	5,270,000	£2
2013 — BU	6112	£10
2013 — Proof	—	£15
2013 — Silver Proof	3,334	£60
2013 — — — Piedfort	1,071	£80
2013 — Gold Proof	284	£1100
2013 Floral Series (Wales)	5,270,000	£2
2013 — BU	6112	£15
2013 — Proof	—	£15
2013 — Silver Proof	3,094	£60
2013 — — — Piedfort	860	£80
2013 — Gold Proof	274	£1100
2013 Royal Coat of Arms (Sewell), Gold Proof	—	£1100
2013 Crowned Royal Arms (Gorringe), Gold Proof	—	£1100
(The above two coins are part of a set of three, along with the 2013 gold proof, with definitive reverse with Uncrowned Royal Arms (Dent)).		
2014	79,305,200	£3
2014 BU	—	£6
2014 Proof	—	£10
2014 Silver BU	—	£40
2014 Silver Proof	—	£45
2014 Floral Series (Scotland)	5,185,000	£2
2014 — BU	3,832	£6
2014 — Proof	—	£10
2014 — Silver Proof	1,540	£60
2014 — — — Piedfort	—	£80
2014 — Gold Proof	154	£1100

2011
NISI DOMINUS FRUSTRA

2013 Wales £1 Floral gold proof.

Most £1 coins are also available in precious metals.

2014 Scotland £1 Floral gold proof.

2015

DATE	Mintage	UNC
2014 Floral Series (Northern Ireland)	5,780,000	£2
2014 — BU	—	£10
2014 — Proof	—	£12
2014 — Silver Proof	1,502	£60
2014 — — — Piedfort	788	£80
2014 — Gold Proof	166	£1100
2015	29,580,000	£3
2015 BU	—	£8
2015 Proof	—	£12
2015 Silver Proof	—	£45
2015 Gold Proof	—	£1100
2015 Platinum Proof	—	—
2015 ***New Portrait*** BU	62,495,640	£3
2015 Proof	—	£10
2015 Silver Proof	7,500	£50
2015 Gold Proof	500	£550
2015 Heraldic Royal Arms	—	£3
2015 — BU	—	£6
2015 — Silver Proof	3,500	£50
2015 — — — Piedfort	2,000	£100
2015 — Gold Proof	500	£1100
2016 BU	—	£20
2016 Proof	—	£25
2016 Silver Proof	—	£50
2016 The Last Round Pound		
2016 — BU	96,089	£15
2016 — Proof	—	£20
2016 — Silver Proof	7,491	£45
2016 — — — Piedfort	2,943	£125
2016 — Gold Proof	499	£1100

2016 The last round pound

12-sided coin Nations of the Crown design

DATE	Mintage	UNC
2016	648,936,536	£3
2016 BU	—	£15
2016 BU cross crosslet mm in folder with Last Round £1	10,000	£75
2017	749,616,200	£3
2017 BU	—	£10
2017 Proof	—	£12
2017 Silver Proof	26,000	£50
2017 Silver Proof Piedfort	4,500	£250
2017 Gold Proof	2,008	£975
2017 Platinum Proof	232	£750
2018 BU	—	£10
2018 Proof	—	£12
2018 Silver Proof	—	£50
2019 BU	—	£12
2019 Proof	—	£15
2019 Silver Proof	—	£50
2020 BU	—	£12
2020 Proof	—	£15
2020 Silver Proof	—	£50
2021 BU	—	£12
2021 Proof	—	£15
2021 Silver Proof	—	£50
2022 BU	—	£12
2022 Proof	—	£15
2022 Silver Proof	—	£50
2022 Standard rev. BU with 26/22 privy mark —	—	£18
— BU —	—	£2
Silver —	—	£75
Gold	—	£1320
2023 New definitive design Honey bees (released in sets only) with commemorative Tudor crown privy mark, first year only		
2024 New definitive design Honey bees BU issued into circulation		
— BU	—	£2
Silver	—	£75
Gold		£1320

12-sided issue with Jody Clark portrait obverse and the reverse designed by 15-year-old David Pearce

FIFTY PENCE

Introduced as legal tender for 10 shillings to replace the banknote of that value prior to decimalisation, coins of the original size are no longer legal tender. Unless otherwise stated, i.e. for commemoratives, the reverse design is of Britannia. The reverse legend of NEW PENCE became FIFTY PENCE from 1982.

The description of "Unc" has been used against some 50 pence pieces dated 2009 and 2011 (for Olympic and Paralympic sports) to distinguish them from coins minted to circulation standard and BU standard, being a standard between the latter two. The uncirculated standard coins have a more even rim than the circulation standard examples, particularly observable on the obverse.

Since the surge of interest in collecting 50p coins prices have increased. The following values are for uncirculated coins. Any found in change will of course have been circulated and will not command such a high premium but the rarer ones will still be worth more than face value.

DATE	Mintage	UNC
1969	188,400,000	£2
1970	19,461,500	£5
1971 Proof	—	£10
1972 Proof	—	£12
1973 Accession to EEC	89,775,000	£3
1973 — Proof	—	£8
1973 — Silver Proof Piedfort	About 24	£3250
1974 Proof	—	£15
1975 Proof	—	£15
1976	43,746,500	£2
1976 Proof	—	£7
1977	49,536,000	£2
1977 Proof	—	£6
1978	72,005,000	£2
1978 Proof	—	£6
1979	58,680,000	£2
1979 Proof	—	£6
1980	89,086,000	£2
1980 Proof	—	£6
1981	74,002,000	£2
1981 Proof	—	£8
1982	51,312,000	£3
1982 Unc	—	£6
1982 Proof	—	£8
1983	62,824,000	£2
1983 Unc	—	£6
1983 Proof	—	£8
1984 BU (only issued in Year Sets)	158,820	£7
1984 Proof	—	£10
1985 ***New portrait***	682,103	£2
1985 BU (only issued in Year Sets)	—	£7
1985 Proof	—	£8
1986 BU (only issued in Year Sets)	—	£7
1986 Proof	—	£12
1987 BU (only issued in Year Sets)	—	£7
1987 Proof	—	£12
1988 BU (only issued in Year Sets)	—	£7
1988 Proof	—	£12
1989 BU (only issued in Year Sets)	—	£7
1989 Proof	—	£12
1990 BU (only issued in Year Sets)	—	£7
1990 Proof	—	£12
1991 BU (only issued in Year Sets)	—	£7
1991 Proof	—	£12
1992 BU (only issued in Year Sets)	—	£10

Accession to the EEC 1973.

Presidency of the EC Council 1992.

1994

DATE	Mintage	UNC
1992 Proof	—	£12
1992 Presidency of EC Council and EC accession 20th anniversary (includes 1993 date)	109,000	£45
1992 — BU	—	£50
1992 — Proof	—	£55
1992 — Silver Proof	26,890	£70
1992 — — — Piedfort	10,993	£90
1992 — Gold Proof	—	£1500
1993 BU (only issued in Year Sets)	—	£10
1993 Proof	—	£12
1994 50th Anniversary of the Normandy Landings	6,705,520	£3
1994 — BU (also in presentation folder)	—	£8
1994 — Proof	—	£10
1994 — Silver Proof	40,000	£30
1994 — — — Piedfort	10,000	£50
1994 — Gold Proof	—	£1500
1995 BU (only issued in Year Sets)	—	£9
1995 Proof	—	£12
1996 BU (only issued in Year Sets)	—	£9
1996 Proof	—	£12
1996 Silver Proof	—	£25
1997 BU	—	£8
1997 Proof	—	£10
1997 Silver Proof	—	£25
1997 ***New reduced size***	456,364,100	£2
1997 BU	—	£5
1997 Proof	—	£6
1997 Silver Proof	—	£20
1997 — — Piedfort	—	£35
1998 ***New portrait***	64,306,500	£2
1998 BU	—	£5
1998 Proof	—	£8
1998 Presidency and 25th anniversary of EU entry	5,043,000	£3
1998 — BU	—	£5
1998 — Proof	—	£8
1998 — Silver Proof	8,859	£30
1998 — — — Piedfort	8,440	£40
1998 — Gold Proof	—	£850
1998 50th Anniversary of the National Health Service	5,001,000	£3
1998 — BU	—	£5
1998 — Silver Proof	9,032	£30
1998 — — — Piedfort	5,117	£40
1998 — Gold Proof	—	£850
1999	24,905,000	£2
1999 BU	—	£5
1999 Proof	—	£10
2000	27,915,500	£2
2000 BU	—	£5
2000 Proof	—	£7
2000 150th Anniversary of Public Libraries	11,263,000	£2
2000 — BU	—	£6
2000 — Proof	—	£9
2000 — Silver Proof	7,634	£30
2000 — — — Piedfort	5,721	£40
2000 — Gold proof	—	£850
2001	84,998,500	£2
2001 BU	—	£5
2001 Proof	—	£7
2002	23,907,500	£2
2002 BU	—	£5
2002 Proof	—	£7
2002 Gold Proof	—	£850
2003	23,583,000	£2
2003 BU		£5
2003 Proof	—	£6
2003 Suffragette	3,124,030	£6
2003 — BU	9582	£9
2003 — Proof	—	£15
2003 — Silver Proof	6,267	£35

1998 EU Presidency

1998 NHS

2000 Public Libraries

2003 Suffragettes

DATE	Mintage	UNC
2003 — — — Piedfort	6,795	£45
2003 — Gold Proof	942	£850
2004	35,315,500	£2
2004 BU	—	£5
2004 Proof	—	£8
2004 Roger Bannister	9,032,500	£3
2004 — BU	10,371	£8
2004 — Proof	—	£10
2004 — Silver Proof	4,924	£35
2004 — — — Piedfort	4,054	£45
2004 — Gold Proof	644	£850
2005	25,363,500	£2
2005 BU	—	£6
2005 Proof	—	£8
2005 Samuel Johnson	17,649,000	£3
2005 — BU	—	£8
2005 — Proof	—	£10
2005 — Silver Proof	4,029	£35
2005 — — — Piedfort	3,808	£45
2005 — Gold Proof	—	£850
2006	24,567,000	£2
2006 Proof	—	£8
2006 Silver Proof	—	£25
2006 Victoria Cross, The Award	12,087,000	£3
2006 — BU	—	£6
2006 — Proof	—	£8
2006 — Silver Proof	6,310	£30
2006 — — — — Piedfort	3,532	£50
2006 — Gold Proof	866	£850
2006 Victoria Cross, Heroic Acts	10,000,500	£3
2006 — BU	—	£6
2006 — Proof	—	£8
2006 — Silver Proof	6,872	£30
2006 — — — — Piedfort	3,415	£50
2006 — Gold Proof	804	£850
2007	11,200,000	£2
2007 Proof	—	£8
2007 Centenary of Scout Movement	7,710,750	£3
2007 — BU	—	£8
2007 — Proof	—	£12
2007 — Silver Proof	10,895	£35
2007 — — — Piedfort	1,555	£65
2007 — Gold Proof	1,250	£850
2008	3,500,000	£2
2008 — BU	—	£8
2008 — Proof	—	£10
2008 — Silver Proof	—	£25
2008 — Gold Proof	—	£850
2008 — Platinum Proof	—	£1550
2008 ***New Shield Rev.*** Obv. rotated by approx. 26^0	22,747,000	£5
2008 BU	—	£8
2008 Proof	—	£10
2008 Silver Proof	—	£25
2008 Silver Proof Piedfort	—	£45
2008 Gold Proof	—	£850
2008 Platinum Proof	—	£1550

2004 Roger Bannister

2005 Samuel Johnson

2006 Victoria Cross—the Award

2006 Victoria Cross—Heroic Acts

2008 Shield design

The "Shield" design which replaced Britannia on the reverse of the circulating 50 pence coin was introduced in 2008 and continues in use as the standard reverse each year in addition to the many commemorative issues available.

2007 Centenary of Scouting

DATE	Mintage	UNC
2009 BU	–	£30
2009 Proof	–	£35
2009 Silver Proof	–	£35
2009 250th Anniversary of Kew Gardens	210,000	£150
2009 — BU	128,364	£175
2009 — Proof	–	£200
2009 — Silver Proof	7,575	£250
2009 — — — Piedfort	2,967	£350
2009 — Gold Proof	629	£3500
2009 Olympic and Paralympic Sports (Track & Field Athletics) Unc (Blue Peter Pack)	19,751	£125
2009 16 different reverses from the past marking the 40th Anniversary of the 50p coin. Proof	1,039	£500
2009 — Silver Proof	1,163	£800
2009 — Gold Proof	70	£15,000
2009 — — — Piedfort	40	£30,000
2010 BU	–	£25
2010 Proof	–	£30
2010 Silver Proof	–	£35
2010 100 years of Girl Guiding UK	7,410,090	£3
2010 — BU	99,075	£7
2010 — Proof	–	£12
2010 — Silver Proof	5,271	£30
2010 — — — Piedfort	2,879	£35
2010 — Gold Proof	355	£850
2011 BU	–	£30
2011 Proof	–	£40
2011 Silver Proof	–	£50
2011 50th Anniversary of the WWF	3,400,000	£4
2011 — BU	67,299	£10
2011 — Proof	–	£25
2011 — Silver Proof	24,870	£45
2011 — — — Piedfort	2,244	£80
2011 — Gold Proof	243	£850
2011 Olympic & Paralympic Sports Issues:		
Aquatics Unc, head clear of lines	2,179,000	£4
— Head with lines BU (as illustrated below)	–	£1100
— Head clear of lines. BU	–	£5
— Silver BU	30,000	£25
Archery Unc	3,345,000	£3
— BU	–	£4
— Silver BU	30,000	£25
Athletics Unc	2,224,000	£3
— BU	–	£4
— Silver BU	30,000	£25
Badminton Unc	2,133,000	£3
— BU	–	£4
— Silver BU	30,000	£25
Basketball Unc	1,748,000	£3
— BU	–	£5
— Silver BU	30,000	£25
Boccia Unc	2,166,000	£3
— BU	–	£4
— Silver BU	30,000	£25
Boxing Unc	2,148,000	£3
— BU	–	£4
— Silver BU	30,000	£25

2009 Kew Gardens

2010 100 years of Guiding

2011 WWF Anniversary

Archery
by Piotr Powaga

Aquatics—the rare error coin
by Jonathan Olliffe

Badminton
by Emma Kelly

Basketball
by Sarah Payne

Athletics
by Florence Jackson

Boccia
by Justin Chung

Boxing
by Shane Abery

Canoeing
by Timothy Lees

Cycling
by Theo Crutchley-Mack

Equestrian
by Thomas Babbage

Fencing
by Ruth Summerfield

Football
by Neil Wolfson

Goalball
by Jonathan Wren

Gymnastics
by Jonathan Olliffe

Handball
by Natasha Ratcliffe

Hockey
by Robert Evans

Judo
by David Cornell

Modern Pentathlon
by Daniel Brittain

Rowing
by Davey Podmore

Sailing
by Bruce Rushin

Shooting
by Pravin Dewdhory

Table Tennis
by Alan Linsdell

Taekwando
by David Gibbons

Tennis
by Tracy Baines

Triathlon
by Sarah Harvey

DATE	Mintage	UNC
Canoeing Unc	2,166,000	£3
— BU	—	£4
— Silver BU	30,000	£25
Cycling Unc	2,090,000	£3
— BU	—	£4
— Silver BU	30,000	£25
Equestrian Unc	2,142,000	£3
— BU	—	£4
— Silver BU	30,000	£25
Fencing Unc	2,115,000	£3
— BU	—	£4
— Silver BU	30,000	£25
Football Unc	1,125,000	£10
— BU	—	£15
— Silver BU	30,000	£35
Goalball Unc	1,615,000	£4
— BU	—	£7
— Silver BU	30,000	£25
Gymnastics Unc	1,720,000	£3
— BU	—	£4
— Silver BU	30,000	£25
Handball Unc	1,676,000	£4
— BU	—	£7
— Silver BU	30,000	£30
Hockey Unc	1,773,000	£3
— BU	—	£4
— Silver BU	30,000	£25
Judo Unc	1,161,000	£10
— BU	—	£15
— Silver BU	30,000	£35
Modern Pentathlon Unc	1,689,000	£3
— BU	—	£5
— Silver BU	30,000	£25
Rowing Unc	1,717,000	£3
— BU	—	£4
— Silver BU	30,000	£25
Sailing Unc	1,749,000	£3
— BU	—	£4
— Silver BU	30,000	£25
Shooting Unc	1,656,000	£3
— BU	—	£4
— Silver BU	30,000	£25
Table Tennis Unc	1,737,000	£3
— BU	—	£4
— Silver BU	30,000	£25
Taekwondo Unc	1,664,000	£3
— BU	—	£4
— Silver BU	30,000	£25
Tennis Unc	1,454,000	£4
— BU	—	£7
— Silver BU	30,000	£25
Triathlon Unc	1,163,000	£10
— BU	—	£15
— Silver BU	30,000	£30
Volleyball Unc	2,133,000	£3
— BU	—	£4
— Silver BU	30,000	£25
Weightlifting Unc	1,879,000	£3
— BU	—	£4
— Silver BU	30,000	£25
Wheelchair Rugby Unc	1,765,000	£3
— BU	—	£4
— Silver BU	30,000	£25
Wrestling Unc	1,129,000	£10
— BU	—	£15
— Silver BU	30,000	£35

Volleyball
by Daniela Boothman

Weight Lifting
by Rob Shakespeare

Wheelchair Rugby
by Natasha Ratcliffe

Wrestling
by Roderick Enriquez

Note—Each of the artists of the 29 Olympic sports above was presented with a gold proof coin with their own design. The Track & Field Athletics design coin was dated 2009, the Cycling was dated 2010, and the remaining issues 2011.

DATE	Mintage	UNC
2012	32,300,030	£2
2012 BU	—	£8
2012 Proof	—	£10
2012 Silver Proof with selective gold plating	—	£50
2012 Gold Proof	—	£850
2012 Olympic Gold Proof Piedfort. *The 11 Olympic sports in which the United Kingdom Team GB achieved a Gold Medal was celebrated with an issue limit of only 27 Piedfort coins for each sport, some in sets, some as individual coins (see under Proof and Specimen sets)*	27	—
2013	10,301,000	£2
2013 BU	—	£10
2013 Proof	—	£15
2013 Silver Proof	2,013	£55
2013 Gold Proof	198	£850
2013 100th anniversary of Birth of Christopher Ironside	7,000,000	£8
2013 — BU	4,403	£15
2013 — Proof	—	£20
2013 — Silver Proof	1,823	£45
2013 — — — Piedfort	816	£100
2013 — Gold Proof	198	£850
2013 Centenary of the Birth of Benjamin Britten	5,300,000	£8
2013 — BU	—	£25
2013 — Silver Proof	717	£200
2013 — — — Piedfort	515	£250
2013 — Gold Proof	70	£850
2014	49,001,000	£2
2014 BU	—	£10
2014 Proof	—	£15
2014 Silver Proof	—	£55
2014 XX Commonwealth Games	6,502,918	£8
2014 — BU	14,581	£10
2014 — Proof	—	£15
2014 — Silver Proof	2,610	£45
2014 — — — Piedfort	792	£100
2014 — Gold Proof	—	£850
2015	20,101,000	£2
2015 BU	—	£8
2015 Proof	—	£10
2015 Silver Proof	—	£30
2015 Gold Proof	—	£850
2015 Platinum Proof	—	—
2015 Battle of Britain 75th Anniversary BU (no denomination)	35,199	£5
2015 — Proof	—	£15
2015 — Silver Proof	2,839	£30
2015 — — — Piedfort	1,422	£80
2015 — Gold Proof	389	£850
New Portrait by Jody Clark		
2015 Battle of Britain 75th Anniversary (with denomination) UNC	5,900,000	£3
2015 Standard Shield rev.	—	£2
2015 BU	—	£8
2015 Proof	—	£12
2015 Silver Proof	—	£30
2015 Gold Proof	—	£850
2015 Platinum Proof	—	—
2016 BU	—	£20
2016 Proof	—	£25
2016 Silver Proof	—	£35
2016 Battle of Hastings 950th Anniversary	6,700,000	£3
2016 — BU	21,718	£7
2016 — Proof	—	£15
2016 — Silver Proof	2,338	£35
2016 — — — Piedfort	1,469	£155
2016 — Gold Proof	237	£450
2016 Beatrix Potter 150th Anniversary	6,900,000	£4
2016 — BU	61,658	£7
2016 — Silver Proof	7,471	£150
2016 — — — Piedfort	2,486	£200
2016 — Gold Proof	732	£850

2013 Christopher Ironside

2013 Benjamin Britten

2015 Battle of Britain

2016 Beatrix Potter

DATE	Mintage	UNC
2016 Beatrix Potter: Peter Rabbit	9,600,000	£4
2016 — BU	93,851	£7
2016 — Silver Proof with coloured highlights	15,245	£350
2016 Beatrix Potter: Jemima Puddle-Duck	2,100,000	£16
2016 — BU	54,929	£14
2016 — Silver Proof with coloured highlights	15,171	£85
2016 Beatrix Potter: Mrs. Tiggy-Winkle	8,800,000	£4
2016 — BU	47,597	£9
2016 — Silver Proof with coloured highlights	15,243	£50
2016 Beatrix Potter: Squirrel Nutkin	5,000,000	£4
2016 — BU	45,884	£7
2016 — Silver Proof with coloured highlights	15,143	£50
2016 Team GB for Olympics	6,400,000	£3
2016 — BU	34,162	£10
2016 — Silver Proof	4,456	£35
2016 — — — Piedfort	1,246	£95
2016 — Gold Proof	302	£850
2017 BU	—	£5
2017 Proof	—	£12
2017 Silver Proof	—	£30
2017 375th anniversary of Sir Isaac Newton's birth	1,801,500	£5
2017 — BU	54,057	£10
2017 — Proof	—	£15
2017 — Silver Proof	3,875	£50
2017 — — — Piedfort	1,935	£95
2017 — Gold Proof	282	£850
2017 Beatrix Potter: Peter Rabbit	19,900,000	£4
2017 — BU	221,866	£12
2017 — — Silver Proof with coloured highlights	40,000	£55
2017 — — Gold Proof	425	£850
2017 Beatrix Potter: Mr. Jeremy Fisher	9,900,000	£4
2017 — BU	165,618	£8
2017 — Silver Proof with coloured highlights	40,000	£50
2017 Beatrix Potter: Tom Kitten	9,500,000	£4
2017 — BU	159,302	£8
2017 — Silver Proof with coloured highlights	34,140	£50
2017 Beatrix Potter: Benjamin Bunny	25,000,000	£4
2017 — BU	—	£8
2017 — Silver Proof with coloured highlights	35,821	£50
2018 BU (sets only)	—	£10
2018 Proof	—	£12
2018 Silver Proof	—	£30
2018 375th anniversary of Sir Isaac Newton's birth (see above: 2018 only available from the Royal Mint Experience)		£75
2018 Anniversary of the Representation of the People Act	9,000,000	£3
2018 Beatrix Potter: Peter Rabbit	1,400,000	£10
2018 — BU	—	£5
2018 — Silver Proof with coloured highlights	—	£55
2018 — Gold Proof	450	£850
2018 Beatrix Potter: Flopsy Bunny	1,400,000	£4
2018 —BU	—	£5
2018 —Silver Proof with coloured highlights	—	£55

2016 Peter Rabbit

2016 Team GB

2017 Isaac Newton

2018 Peter Rabbit

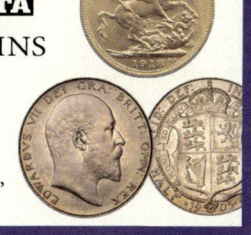

DATE	Mintage	UNC
2018 Beatrix Potter: The Tailor of Gloucester	3,900,000	£5
2018 — BU	—	£6
2018 —Silver Proof with coloured highlights	—	£55
2018 Beatrix Potter: Mrs Tittlemouse	1,700,000	£5
2018 — BU	—	£6
2018 —Silver Proof with coloured highlights	—	£55
2018 Paddington Bear at Paddington Station	5,001,000	£5
2018 — BU	—	£10
2018 — Silver Proof with coloured highlights 75,000	£40	
2018 — Gold Proof	1,250	£850
2018 Paddington Bear at Buckingham Palace	5,901,000	£5
2018 — BU	—	£10
2018 — Silver Proof with coloured highlights	75,000	£40
2018 — Gold Proof	1,250	£850
2018 The Snowman BU	—	£10
2018 — Silver Proof	15,000	£60
2018 — Gold Proof	400	£850
2019	122,000,000	£2
2019 BU	—	£5
2019 Proof	—	£12
2019 Silver Proof	—	£30
2019 Stephen Hawking BU	—	£10
2019 — Silver Proof	7,000	£55
2019 — — Piedfort	2,500	£95
2019 — Gold Proof	400	£850
2019 Sherlock Holmes BU	—	£10
2019 — Silver Proof	7,500	£55
2019 — — Piedfort	3,500	£95
2019 — Gold Proof	600	£850
2019 The Gruffalo BU	—	£10
2019 — Silver Proof	30,000	£40
2019 — Gold Proof	600	£850
2019 Peter Rabbit BU	—	£10
2019 — Silver Proof	30,000	£40
2019 — Gold Proof	500	£850
2019 Paddington Bear at the Tower of London	—	£3
2019 — BU	—	£10
2019 — Silver Proof with coloured highlights	25,000	£40
2019 — Gold Proof	600	£850
2019 Paddington Bear at St. Paul's	—	£3
2019 — BU	—	£10
2019 — Silver Proof with coloured highlights	25,000	£40
2019 — Gold Proof	600	£850
2019 50 years of the 50p BU	—	£10
2019 — Silver Proof Piedfort	1,969	£95
2019 — Silver Proof	3,500	£55
2019 — Gold Proof	300	£850
2019 20th Anniversary of the Gruffalo BU	—	£12
2019 — Silver Proof	25,000	£40
2019 — Gold (Red) Proof	600	£850
2019 The Snowman II BU	—	£10
2019 — Silver Proof	25,000	£65
2019 — Gold (Red) Proof	600	£850
2019 Wallace & Gromit BU	—	£18
2019 — Silver Proof	25,000	£65
2019 — Gold (Red) Proof	630	£850
2020	46,540,375	£2
2020 BU	—	£5
2020 Proof	—	£12
2020 Silver Proof	—	£30
2020 Withdrawal from the EU (Brexit)	10,001,000	£2
2020 Withdrawal from the EU (Brexit) BU	—	£10
2020 — BU (EEC 1973 + EU Withdrawal, 2-coin set)	5,000	£30
2020 — Silver Proof	47,000	£60
2020 — Gold (Red) Proof	1,500	£850
2020 Team GB BU	—	£10
2020 — Proof	—	£12
2020 — Silver Proof	—	£55
2020 Rosalind Franklin BU	—	£8
2020 — Proof	—	£15
2020 — Silver Proof	—	£55
2020 — Silver Proof Piedfort	—	£99

2018
Flopsy Bunny

Paddington at the Tower of London

2018 The Snowman

2019 Stephen Hawking

2019 Sherlock Holmes

Note: the prices given for recently-issued gold coins are the Royal Mint issue prices.

DATE	Mintage	UNC
2020 — Gold (Red) Proof	250	£850
2020 Dinosauria (Megalosaurus) BU	—	£10
2020 — BU (coloured coin)	50,000	£20
2020 — Silver Proof	3,000	£40
2020 — — Proof (coloured coin)	7,000	£45
2020 — Gold Proof	350	£850
2020 Dinosauria (Iguanodon) BU	—	£10
2020 — BU (coloured coin)	50,000	£20
2020 — Silver Proof	14,500	£35
2020 — — Proof (coloured coin)	7,000	£40
2020 — Gold Proof	500	£850
2020 Dinosauria (Hylaeosaurus) BU	—	£10
2020 — BU (coloured coin)	50,000	£20
2020 — Silver Proof	14,500	£35
2020 — — Proof (coloured coin)	7,000	£40
2020 — Gold Proof	500	£850
2020 Winnie the Pooh—Christopher Robin BU	—	£9
2020 — BU (coloured coin)	45,000	£20
2020 — Silver Proof	18,000	£50
2020 — Gold Proof	525	£850
2020 — Winnie the Pooh and friends BU	—	£10
2020 — BU (coloured coin)	45,000	£20
2020 — Silver Proof (coloured coin)	18,000	£50
2020 — Gold Proof	525	£850
2020 — Piglet BU	—	£9
2020 — BU (coloured coin)	45,000	£20
2020 — Silver Proof	18,000	£50
2020 — Gold Proof	525	£850
2020 The Snowman BU	—	£10
2020 — BU (coloured coin)	15,000	£20
2020 — Silver Proof	7,000	£60
2020 — Gold Proof	275	£850
2020 Diversity Built Britain	10,300,000	£2
2020 — BU	—	£6
2020 — Silver Proof	25,000	£57.50
2020 — — Piedfort	2,500	£100
2020 — Gold Proof	950	£850
2020 — — Piedfort	200	£2,225
2020 Peter Rabbit BU	—	£20
2020 — Silver Proof	15,000	£60
2020 — Gold Proof	500	£850
2021 50th Anniversay of Decimal Day BU	—	£10
2021 — Silver Proof	6,000	£57.50
2021 — — Piedfort	2,500	£100.00
2021— Gold Proof (coin struck on the day)	700	£1,250
2021 — —	450	£1,100
2021 — — Piedfort	200	£2,175
2021 Mary Anning Collection—Temnodantesaurus BU	—	£10
2021 — BU (coloured coin)	50,000	£20
2021 — Silver Proof	3,000	£62.50
2021 — — (coloured coin)	7,000	£67.50
2021 — Gold Proof	250	£850
2021 Mary Anning Collection—Plesiosaurus BU	—	£10
2021 — BU (coloured coin)	50,000	£20
2021 — Silver Proof	3,000	£62.50
2021 — — (coloured coin)	7,000	£67.50
2021 — Gold Proof	250	£850
2021 Mary Anning Collection—Dimporphodon BU	—	£10
2021 — BU (coloured coin)	50,000	£20
2021 — Silver Proof	3,000	£62.50
2021 — — (coloured coin)	7,000	£67.50
2021 — Gold Proof	250	£850
2021 John Logie Baird BU	—	£10
2021 — Silver Proof	5,010	£57.50
2021 — — Piedfort	2,200	£100
2021 — Gold Proof	405	£850

2020
Dinosauria—Iguanodon

DATE	Mintage	UNC
2021 Olympic Games Team 2020 (GB) BU	—	£10
2021 — BU (coloured coin)	12,021	£20
2021 — Silver Proof (coloured coin)	5,510	£67.50
2021.— — Piedfort	1,510	£105
2021 — Gold Proof	260	£850
2021 Winnie the Pooh & Friends BU	—	£10
2021 — (coloured coin)	45,000	£20
2021 — Silver Proof (coloured coin)	19,095	£67.50
2021 — Gold Proof	630	£850
2021 Winnie the Pooh—Owl BU	—	£9
2021 — (coloured coin)	45,000	£20
2021 — Silver Proof	18,000	£67.50
2021 — Gold Proof	535	£850
2021 Winnie the Pooh—Tigger BU	—	£9
2021 — (coloured coin)	45,000	£20
2021 — Silver Proof	18,000	£67.50
2021 — Gold Proof	535	£850
2021 Charles Babbage BU	—	£8
2021 — Silver Proof	4,000	£57.50
2021 — Silver Proof Piedfort	1,510	£102.50
2021 — Gold Proof	260	£850
2021 100 Years of Insulin BU	—	£12
2021 — Silver Proof	3,710	£57.50
2021 — Silver Proof Piedfort	1,510	£102.50
2021 — Gold Proof	260	£850
2021 The Snowman BU	—	£10
2021 — BU (coloured coin)	10,000	£20
2021 — Silver Proof (coloured coin)	7,000	£67.50
2021 — Gold Proof	300	£850
2022 Winnie the Pooh—Eeyore BU	—	£8
2022 — (coloured coin)	12,500	£20
2022 — Silver Proof (coloured coin)	6,010	£67.50
2022 — Gold Proof	160	£850
2022 Her Majesty the Queen's Platinum Jubilee 50p (John Bergdhal obverse Queen on horseback) BU	—	£7
2022 — Silver Proof	7,605	£57.50
2022 — — Piedfort	2,510	£102.50
2022 — Gold Proof	580	£850
2022 — — Piedfort	80	£2185
2022 — Platinum Proof	150	£1,395
2022 Her Majesty the Queen's Platinum Jubilee 50p for circulation at 50p (Jody Clark Obverse)	—	£2
2022 50 Years of Pride BU	—	£10
2022 — (coloured coin)	10,000	£18
2022 — Silver Proof (coloured coin)	4,000	£67.50
2022 — — Piedfort (coloured coin)	1,500	£112.50
2022 — Gold Proof	200	£850
2022 — — Piedfort	50	£2,185
2022 Birmingham 2022 Commonwealth Games BU	—	£10
2022 — (coloured coin) Team England	7,510	£18
2022 — (coloured coin) Team Wales	5,010	£18
2022 — (coloured coin) Team N Ireland	5,010	£18
2022 — (coloured coin) Scotland	5,010	£18
2022 — Silver Proof (coloured coin)	4,760	£67.50
2022 — — Piedfort (coloured coin)	1,260	£112.50
2022 — Gold Proof	410	£850
2022 Kanga and Roo BU	—	£10
2022 — (coloured coin)	12,500	£20
2022 — Silver Proof (coloured coin)	6,010	£67.50
2022 — Gold Proof	160	£850
2022 Winnie the Pooh and Friends BU	—	£10
2022 — (coloured coin)	12,500	£20
2022 — Silver Proof (coloured coin)	6,510	£67.50
2022 — Gold Proof	210	£1,150

DATE	Mintage	UNC
2022 100 Years of our BBC BU	—	£11
— Silver Proof	3,510	£59.50
— Silver Proof Piedfort	1,110	£110
— Gold Proof	360	£850
2022 Harry Potter BU	—	£11
2022 — (coloured coin)	—	£20
2022 — Silver Proof (coloured coin)	15,000	£69.50
2022 — Gold Proof	300	£900
2022 The Snowman and the Snowdog BU	—	£11
2022 — (coloured coin)	8,500	£20
2022 Silver Proof (coloured coin)	5,000	£69.50
2022 Gold Proof	125	£900
2022 The Hogwarts Express BU	—	£11
2022 — (coloured coin)	—	£20
2022 — Silver Proof (coloured coin)	15,000	£69.50
2022 — Gold Proof	300	£900
2022 Her Majesty Queen Elizabeth II Memorial Coin 50p for circulation at 50p (Martin Jennings Obverse)	—	£2
2022 — BU	—	£18
2022 — Silver Proof	—	£60
2022 — — Piedfort	—	£100
2022 — Gold Proof	—	£1,250
2022 — Platinum Proof	—	£1,450
2022 Standard rev. BU with 26/22 privy mark	—	£16
— BU	—	£1.50
Silver	—	£110
Gold	—	£1,464
2023 Professor Albus Dumbledore BU	—	£11
2023 — (coloured coin)	—	£20
2023 Silver Proof (coloured coin)	15,000	£69.50
2023 Gold Proof	300	£900
2023 Hogwarts School of Witchcraft and Wizardry BU	—	£11
2023 — (coloured coin)	—	£20
2023 Silver Proof (coloured coin)	15,000	£69.50
2023 Gold Proof	300	£900
2023 Coronation of His Majesty King Charles III BU	—	£11
2023 — Silver Proof	12,500	£59.50
2023 — — Piedfort	3,250	£110
2023 – Gold Proof	500	£950
2023 75th Anniversary of the NHS BU	—	£11
2023 Silver Proof	3,500	£59.50
2023 Gold Proof	250	£900
2023 75 Years of the Windrush Generation BU	—	£11
2023 — (coloured coin)	10,000	£20
2023 — Silver Proof (coloured coin)	1,948	£69.50
2023 — — Piedfort (coloured coin)	1,250	£120
2023 — Gold Proof	75	£900
2023 The Chronicles of Narnia—The Lion, the Witch and the Wardrobe BU	—	£11
2023 — (coloured coin)	10,000	£20
2023 Silver Proof (coloured coin)	5,000	£70.00
2023 Gold Proof	100	£1,220
2023 The Snowman BU	—	£11
2023 — (coloured coin)	10,000	£20
2023 — Silver Proof (coloured coin)	5,000	£70
2023 — Gold Proof	100	£1,220
2023 R2-D2 and C-3PO BU	—	£11
2023 — (coloured coin)	20,010	£20
2023 — Silver Proof (coloured coin)	12,510	£70
2023 — Gold Proof	200	£1,220
2023 Darth Vader and Emperor Palpatine BU	—	£11
2023 — BU (coloured coin)	20,010	£20
2023 — Silver Proof (coloured coin)	12,510	£70
2023 Luke Skywalker and Princess Leia BU	—	£11
2023 — BU (coloured coin)	20,010	£20
2023 — Silver Proof (coloured coin)	12,510	£70

DATE	Mintage	UNC
2023 New definitive design Salmon (released in sets only) with commemorative Tudor crown privy mark, first year only		
2023 New definitive design Salmon, BU	— —	£2
2023 — Proof	12,023	£5
2023 — Silver Proof	3,000	£110
2023 — Gold Proof	125	£1464
2024 Hans Solo and Chewbacca BU	—	£12
2024 — (coloured)	20,000	£21
2024 — Silver Proof (coloured)	12,500	£75
2024 — Gold Proof	200	£1,355
2024 Millenium Falcon BU	—	£12
2024 — BU (coloured coin)	20,010	£21.00
2024 — Silver Proof (coloured coin)	7,150	£71.00
2024 TIE fighter BU	—	£12.00
2024 — BU (coloured coin)	20,010	£21.00
2024 — Silver Proof (coloured coin)	7,150	£71.00
2024 Death Star BU	—	£12
2024 — (coloured)	20,000	£21
2024 — Silver Proof	7,500	£75
2024 — Gold Proof	100	£1,355
2024 X-Wing BU	—	£12
2024 — (coloured)	20,000	£21
2024 — Silver Proof	7,500	£75
2024 — Gold Proof	100	£1,355
2024 80th Anniversary of the D-Day Landings BU	—	£12
2024 — Silver Proof	5,000	£61
2024 — — Piedfort	1,944	£113.50
2024 — Gold Proof	350	£1,220
2024 Tyrosaurus BU	—	£11
2024 — (coloured coin)	15,000	£20
2024 — Silver Proof	500	£60
2024 — — (coloured coin)	5,000	£70
2024 — Gold Proof	100	£1,220
2024 Stegosaurus BU	—	£12
2024 — (coloured coin)	15,000	£21
2024 Silver Proof	500	£61
2024 — — (coloured coin)	5,000	£71
2024 — Gold Proof	100	£1,220
2024 Diplodocus BU	—	£12
2024 — (coloured coin)	15,000	£21
2024 — Silver Proof	500	£61
2024 — — (coloured coin)	5,000	£71
2024 — Gold Proof	100	£1,220
2024 200 Years of the RNLI BU	—	£12
2024 — BU (coloured coin)	—	£21
2024 — Silver Proof	4,510	£71
2024 — — Piedfort (coloured coin)	2,084	£123.50
2024 Team GB and Paralympics GB BU	—	£12
2024 — (coloured coin)	13,250	£21
2024 — Silver Proof (coloured coin)	5,010	£75
2024 — — Piedfort (coloured coin)	2,034	£128
2024 — Gold Proof	185	£1,355
2024 The Gruffalo's Child BU	—	£12
2024 — (coloured coin)	25,000	£21
2024 — Silver Proof (coloured coin)	7,500	£75

TWENTY-FIVE PENCE (CROWN)

This series is a continuation of the pre-decimal series, there having been four crowns to the pound. The coins below have a legal tender face value of 25p to this day, and are minted in cupro-nickel except where stated otherwise.

DATE	Mintage	UNC
1972 Royal Silver Wedding	7,452,100	£2
1972 — Proof	150,000	£8
1972 — Silver Proof	100,000	£36
1977 Silver Jubilee	37,061,160	£2
1977 — in Presentation folder	Incl. above	£3
1977 — Proof	193,000	£8
1977 — Silver Proof	377,000	£36
1980 Queen Mother 80th Birthday	9,306,000	£2
1980 — in Presentation folder	Incl. above	£3
1980 — Silver Proof	83,670	£36
1981 Royal Wedding	26,773,600	£2
1981 — in Presentation folder	Incl. above	£3
1981 — Silver Proof	218,140	£36

TWENTY PENCE

The series commenced in 1982, some 11 years after the introduction of decimal coinage. Its presence from introduction date meant that there was no requirement for ten pence circulation-standard coins until the latter's size was reduced in 1992. Its alloy is uniquely 84% copper and 16% nickel, unlike the 75/25 of the fifty pence.

ELIZABETH II (1952–2022)

DATE	Mintage	UNC
1982	740,815,000	£2
1982 Proof	—	£7
1982 Silver Proof Piedfort	25,000	£40
1983	158,463,000	£3
1983 Proof	—	£6
1984	65,350,000	£1
1984 BU	—	£3
1984 Proof	—	£7
New portrait		
1985	74,273,699	£2
1985 BU	—	£4
1985 Proof	—	£6
1986 BU	—	£7
1986 Proof	—	£10
1987	137,450,000	£1
1987 BU	—	£3
1987 Proof	—	£6
1988	38,038,344	£1
1988 BU	—	£3
1988 Proof	—	£5
1989	132,013,890	£1
1989 BU	—	£3
1989 Proof	—	£6
1990	88,097,500	£1
1990 BU	—	£3
1990 Proof	—	£6
1991	35,901,250	£1
1991 BU	—	£4
1991 Proof	—	£8
1992	Est. approx. 1,500,000	£4
1992 BU	—	£5
Enhanced effigy		
1992	Est. approx. 29,705,000	£4
1992 — BU	—	£5
1992 — Proof	—	£8
1993	123,123,750	£1
1993 BU	—	£3
1993 Proof	—	£6
1994	67,131,250	£1
1994 BU	—	£3
1994 Proof	—	£5
1995	102,005,000	£1
1995 BU	—	£3
1995 Proof	—	£5
1996	83,163,750	£2
1996 BU	—	£3
1996 Proof	—	£5
1996 Silver Proof	—	£20
1997	89,518,750	£2
1997 BU	—	£3
1997 Proof	—	£5

DATE	Mintage	UNC
New portrait		
1998	76,965,000	£2
1998 BU	—	£4
1998 Proof	—	£5
1999	73,478,750	£2
1999 BU	—	£3
1999 Proof	—	£5
2000	136,428,750	£2
2000 BU	—	£3
2000 Proof	—	£5
2000 Silver Proof	—	£35
2001	148,122,500	£2
2001 BU	—	£3
2001 Proof	—	£5
2002	93,360,000	£2
2002 BU	—	£3
2002 Proof	—	£5
2002 Gold Proof	—	£900
2003	153,383,750	£2
2003 BU	—	£4
2003 Proof	—	£6
2004	120,212,500	£2
2004 BU	—	£4
2004 Proof	—	£6
2005	124,488,750	£2
2005 BU	—	£4
2005 Proof	—	£6
2006	114,800,000	£2
2006 BU	—	£4
2006 Proof	—	£6
2006 Silver Proof	—	£35
2007	117,075,000	£2
2007 BU	—	£4
2007 Proof	—	£6
2008	11,900,000	£2
2008 BU	—	£4
2008 Proof	—	£7
2008 Silver Proof	—	£35
2008 Gold Proof	—	£900
2008 Platinum Proof	—	£800
New Reverse, date on Obverse		
2008	115,022,000	£2
2008 Mule—paired with old Obv. (thus no date)	Est. approx. 120,000 (?)	£75
2008 BU	—	£3
2008 Proof	—	£6
2008 Silver Proof	—	£35
2008 — — Piedfort	—	£50
2008 Gold Proof	—	£900
2008 Platinum Proof	—	£750
2009	121,625,300	£2
2009 BU	—	£5
2009 Proof	—	£7
2009 Silver Proof	—	£35
2010	112,875,500	£2
2010 BU	—	£5
2010 Proof	—	£7
2010 Silver Proof	—	£35
2011	191,625,000	£2
2011 BU	—	£5
2011 Proof	—	£8
2011 Silver Proof	—	£35
2012	69,650,030	£2
2012 BU	—	£5
2012 Proof	—	£8
2012 Silver Proof (issued in set with Victorian 4 Shilling piece)	—	£35
2012 — — with selective gold plating	—	£45
2012 Gold Proof	—	£900
2013	66,325,000	£2
2013 BU	—	£5
2013 Proof	—	£10
2013 Silver Proof	—	£35
2013 Gold Proof	—	£375
2014	173,775,000	£2
2014 BU	—	£5
2014 Proof	—	£10
2014 Silver Proof	—	£35
2015	63,175,000	£3
2015 BU	—	£5
2015 Proof	—	£10
2015 Silver Proof	—	£35
2015 Gold Proof	—	£900
2015 Platinum Proof	—	£800
New Portrait		
2015	131,250,000	£3
2015 BU	—	£5
2015 Proof	—	£5
2015 Silver Proof	—	£35
2015 Gold Proof	—	£900
2015 Platinum Proof	—	—
2016	212,625,000	£3
2016 BU	—	£5
2016 Proof	—	£10
2016 Silver Proof	—	£35
2017 BU	—	£10
2017 Proof	—	£10
2017 Silver Proof	—	£35
2018 BU	—	£10
2018 Proof	—	£10
2018 Silver Proof	—	£35
2019 BU	—	£5
2019 Proof	—	£10
2019 Silver Proof	—	£35
2020 BU	—	£5
2020 Proof	—	£10
2020 Silver Proof	—	£35
2021 BU	—	£5
2021 Proof	—	£10
2021 Silver Proof	—	£35
2022 BU	—	£5
2022 Proof	—	£10
2022 Silver Proof	—	£35
2022 Platinum Proof	—	£800
2022 Standard rev. BU with 26/22 privy mark—		£12
— BU—	—	£1
Silver—	—	£53
Gold	—	£1080

CHARLES III (2022–)

DATE	Mintage	UNC
2023 New definitive Reverse BU	—	£5
2023 — Proof	—	£10
2023 New definitive design Puffin (released in sets only) with commemorative Tudor crown privy mark, first year only		
2023 New definitive design Puffin, BU	—	£2
2023 — Proof	12,023	£5
2023 — Silver Proof	3,000	£53
2023 Gold Proof	125	£1080

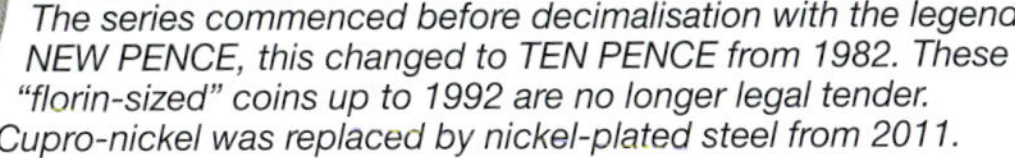

TEN PENCE

The series commenced before decimalisation with the legend NEW PENCE, this changed to TEN PENCE from 1982. These "florin-sized" coins up to 1992 are no longer legal tender. Cupro-nickel was replaced by nickel-plated steel from 2011.

DATE	Mintage	UNC
1968	336,143,250	£3
1969	314,008,000	£4
1970	133,571,000	£4
1971	63,205,000	£3
1971 Proof	–	£4
1972 Proof only	–	£7
1973	152,174,000	£3
1973 Proof	–	£4
1974	92,741,000	£3
1974 Proof	–	£4
1975	181,559,000	£3
1975 Proof	–	£4
1976	228,220,000	£3
1976 Proof	–	£4
1977	59,323,000	£6
1977 Proof	–	£8
1978 Proof	–	£10
1979	115,457,000	£2
1979 Proof	–	£4
1980	88,650,000	£3
1980 Proof	–	£4
1981	3,487,000	£10
1981 Proof	–	£15
1982 BU	–	£4
1982 Proof	–	£6
1983 BU	–	£3
1983 Proof	–	£4
1984 BU	–	£4
1984 Proof	–	£6
New portrait		
1985 BU	–	£5
1985 Proof	–	£7
1986 BU	–	£4
1986 Proof	–	£6
1987 BU	–	£4
1987 Proof	–	£7
1988 BU	–	£5
1988 Proof	–	£7
1989 BU	–	£6
1989 Proof	–	£9
1990 BU	–	£6
1990 Proof	–	£9
1991 BU	–	£6
1991 Proof	–	£9
1992 BU	–	£5
1992 Proof	–	£7
1992 Silver Proof	–	£30
Size reduced (24.5mm)		
1992	1,413,455,170	£3
1992 BU	–	£4
1992 Proof	–	£5
1992 Silver Proof	–	£30
1992 — — Piedfort	14,167	£35
1993 BU	–	£2
1993 Proof	–	£7
1994 BU	–	£2
1994 Proof	–	£7
1995	43,259,000	£1
1995 BU	–	£5
1995 Proof	–	£7
1996	118,738,000	£2
1996 BU	–	£4
1996 Proof	–	£7
1996 Silver Proof	–	£30
1997	99,196,000	£2
1997 BU	–	£4
1997 Proof	–	£4
New portrait		
1998 BU	–	£8
1998 Proof	–	£10
1999 BU	–	£4
1999 Proof	–	£11
2000	134,733,000	£1
2000 BU	–	£4
2000 Proof	–	£7
2000 Silver Proof	–	£30
2001	129,281,000	£1
2001 BU	–	£3
2001 Proof	–	£4
2002	80,934,000	£2
2002 BU	–	£3
2002 Proof	–	£5
2002 Gold Proof	–	£850
2003	88,118,000	£2
2003 BU	–	£3
2003 Proof	–	£5
2004	99,602,000	£1
2004 BU	–	£3
2004 Proof	–	£5
2005	69,604,000	£1
2005 BU	–	£2
2005 Proof	–	£4
2006	118,803,000	£1
2006 BU	–	£3
2006 Proof	–	£7
2006 Silver Proof	–	£30
2007	72,720,000	£1
2007 BU	–	£4
2007 Proof	–	£7
2008	9,720,000	£2
2008 BU	–	£5
2008 Proof	–	£8
2008 Silver Proof	–	£30
2008 Gold Proof	–	£850
2008 Platinum Proof	–	£600
New Reverse, no border beads on Obverse		
2008	71,447,000	£1
2008 BU	–	£4
2008 Proof	–	£5
2008 Silver Proof	–	£30
2008 — — Piedfort	–	£35
2008 Gold Proof	–	£850

Angel of the North

James Bond

Cricket

Double-decker bus

English breakfast

Fish and chips

Greenwich Mean Time

Houses of Parliament

Ice cream

Jubilee

King Arthur

Loch Ness

Mackintosh

NHS

Oak tree

Pillar box

Queueing

Robin

Stonehenge

Tea

Union Flag

Village

World Wide Web

X marks the spot

Yeoman warder

Zebra crossing

In 2018 and 2019 a special series was introduced for the 10p denomination. There are 26 coins, each depicting a letter of the alphabet as shown above.

DATE	Mintage	UNC
2008 Platinum Proof	—	£600
2009	84,360,000	£1
2009 BU	—	£3
2009 Proof	—	£5
2009 Silver Proof	—	£30
2010	96,600,500	£1
2010 BU	—	£5
2010 Proof	—	£7
2010 Silver Proof	—	£30
Nickel-plated steel		
2011	59,603,850	£1
2011 — BU	—	£5
2011 — Proof	—	£10
2011 Silver Proof	—	£30
2012	11,600,030	£1
2012 BU	—	£5
2012 Proof	—	£10
2012 Silver proof with selective gold plating	—	£35
2012 Gold Proof	—	£850
2013	320,200,750	£1
2013 BU	—	£5
2013 Proof	—	£10
2013 Silver Proof	—	£30
2013 Gold Proof	—	£850
2014	490,202,020	£1
2014 BU	—	£5
2014 Proof	—	£12
2014 Silver Proof	—	£30
2015	119,000,000	£1
2015 BU	—	£4
2015 Proof	—	£5
2015 Silver Proof	—	£30
2015 Gold Proof	—	£850
2015 Platinum Proof	—	£600
New portrait		
2015	91,900,000	£1
2015 BU	—	£5
2015 Proof	—	£6
2015 Silver Proof	—	£30
2015 Gold Proof	—	£850

DATE	Mintage	UNC
2016	135,380,000	£1
2016 BU	—	£8
2016 Proof	—	£10
2016 Silver Proof	—	£30
2017	32,300,000	£1
2017 BU	—	£4
2017 Proof	—	£10
2017 Silver Proof	—	£30
2018 BU	—	£1
2018 Proof	—	£4
2018 Silver Proof	—	£30
2018 Alphabet series (26 different letters)	220,000 of each coin	£2 each
2018 — Silver Proof	—	£30 each
2019 BU	—	£1
2019 Proof	—	£6
2019 Silver Proof	—	£30
2019 Alphabet series (26 different letters)	—	£2 each
2019 — Silver Proof	—	£30 each
2020 BU	—	£1
2020 Proof	—	£6
2020 Silver Proof	—	£30
2021 BU	—	£1
2021 Proof	—	£6
2021 Silver Proof	—	£30
2022 BU	—	£1
2022 Proof	—	£6
2022 Silver Proof	—	£30
2022 Standard rev. BU with 26/22 privy mark	—	£10
2022 BU	—	£1
2022 Silver	—	£80
2022 Gold	—	£1065
2023 New definitive design Capercaillie (released in sets only) with commemorative Tudor crown privy mark, first year only		
2023 New definitive design Capercaillie BU	—	£2
2023 — Proof	12,023	£20
2023 — Silver Proof	3,000	£80
—2023— Gold Proof	125	£1065

SIX PENCE

This "new" denomination has been struck, as part of the Royal Mint's gift range (originally priced at £30). They are of sterling silver to BU standard and 19.41mm in diameter. Being similar in size to the pre-decimal 6d they have also been marketed as part of coin sets along with old sixpences. Along with the highly popular "Christmas" sixpence for inclusion in Christmas puddings up and down the land, this diminutive denomination also makes an appearance as a lucky charm for any blushing bride. A silver sixpence is a traditional gift for the bride to place in her shoe on her wedding day as a token of good fortune. The attractive 2024 reverse image is based on Quentin Peacock's 1920 sixpence design. And if you are really fond of the happy couple, the Wedding sixpence is also available in 22 carat gold!

(Image shown enlarged.)

FIVE PENCE

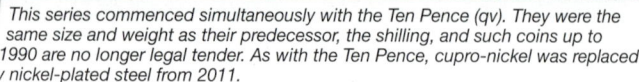

This series commenced simultaneously with the Ten Pence (qv). They were the same size and weight as their predecessor, the shilling, and such coins up to 1990 are no longer legal tender. As with the Ten Pence, cupro-nickel was replaced by nickel-plated steel from 2011.

DATE	Mintage	UNC
1968	98,868,250	£3
1969	120,270,000	£3
1970	225,948,525	£3
1971	81,783,475	£3
1971 Proof	–	£3
1972 Proof	–	£7
1973 Proof	–	£5
1974 Proof	–	£5
1975	141,539,000	£3
1975 Proof	–	£4
1976 Proof	–	£8
1977	24,308,000	£8
1977 Proof	–	£7
1978	61,094,000	£4
1978 Proof	–	£4
1979	155,456,000	£4
1979 Proof	–	£4
1980	220,566,000	£3
1980 Proof	–	£4
1981 Proof	–	£7
1982 BU Legend changed to FIVE PENCE	–	£7
1982 Proof	–	£8
1983 BU	–	£5
1983 Proof	–	£6
1984 BU	–	£4
1984 Proof	–	£5
***New Portrait*.**		
1985 BU	–	£2
1985 Proof	–	£7
1986 BU	–	£2
1986 Proof	–	£7
1987	48,220,000	£1
1987 BU	–	£3
1987 Proof	–	£5
1988	120,744,610	£1
1988 BU	–	£3
1988 Proof		£5
1989	101,406,000	£1
1989 BU	–	£4
1989 Proof	–	£5
1990 BU	–	£2
1990 Proof	–	£5
1990 Silver Proof	–	£20
Size reduced (18mm)		
1990	1,634,976,005	£2
1990 BU	–	£3
1990 Proof	–	£4
1990 Silver Proof	–	£20
1990 — — Piedfort	–	£25
1991	724,979000	£1
1991 BU	–	£3
1991 Proof	–	£5
1992	453,173,500	£1
1992 BU	–	£3
1992 Proof	–	£7
1993 BU	–	£5
1993 Proof	–	£9
1994	93,602,000	£1
1994 BU	–	£5

DATE	Mintage	UNC
1994 Proof	–	£7
1995	183,384,000	£1
1995 BU	–	£5
1995 Proof	–	£7
1996	302,902,000	£1
1996 BU	–	£4
1996 Proof	–	£7
1996 Silver proof	–	£20
1997	236,596,000	£1
1997 BU	–	£4
1997 Proof	–	£7
New portrait		
1998	217,376,000	£1
1998 BU	–	£4
1998 Proof	–	£7
1999	195,490,000	£1
1999 BU	–	£4
1999 Proof	–	£7
2000	388,512,000	£1
2000 BU	–	£4
2000 Proof	–	£7
2000 Silver Proof	–	£20
2001	337,930,000	£1
2001 BU	–	£3
2001 Proof	–	£5
2002	219,258,000	£1
2002 BU	–	£3
2002 Proof	–	£5
2002 Gold Proof	–	£500
2003	333,230,000	£1
2003 BU	–	£3
2003 Proof	–	£5
2004	271,810,000	£1
2004 BU	–	£3
2004 Proof	–	£5
2005	236,212,000	£1
2005 BU	–	£3
2005 Proof	–	£5
2006	317,697,000	£1
2006 BU	–	£3
2006 Proof	–	£7
2006 Silver Proof	–	£20
2007	246,720,000	£1
2007 BU	–	£5
2007 Proof	–	£7
2008	92,880,000	£1
2008 BU	–	£3
2008 Proof	–	£5
2008 Silver Proof	–	£20
2008 Gold Proof	–	£500
2008 Platinum Proof	–	£350
***New Reverse*, no border beads on Obverse**		
2008	155,172,000	£1
2008 BU	–	£4
2008 Proof	–	£5
2008 Silver Proof	–	£20
2008 — — Piedfort	–	£25
2008 Gold Proof	–	£500
2008 Platinum Proof	–	£350

DATE	Mintage	UNC
2009	132,960,300	£1
2009 BU	–	£6
2009 Proof	–	£7
2009 Silver Proof	–	£20
2010	296,245,500	£1
2010 BU	–	£4
2010 Proof	–	£5
2010 Silver Proof	–	£20
2011 Nickel-plated steel	50,400,000	£1
2011 — BU	–	£4
2011 — Proof	–	£6
2011 Silver Proof	–	£20
2012	339,802,350	£1
2012 BU	–	£5
2012 Proof	–	£8
2012 Silver Proof with selective gold plating	–	£25
2012 Gold Proof	–	£500
2013	318,800,750	£1
2013 BU	–	£5
2013 Proof	–	£8
2013 Silver Proof	–	£20
2013 Gold Proof	–	£500
2014	885,004,520	£1
2014 BU	–	£5
2014 Proof	–	£8
2014 Silver Proof	–	£20
New Portrait		
2015	536,600,000	£2
2015 BU	–	£4
2015 Proof	–	£6
2015 Silver Proof	–	£20
2015 Gold Proof	–	£500
2016	308,200,000	£2
2016 BU	–	£4
2016 Proof	–	£8
2016 Silver Proof	–	£20
2017	220,515,000	–
2017 BU	–	£4
2017 Proof	–	£6
2017 Silver Proof	–	£20
2017 Gold Proof	–	£500
2018 BU	–	£5
2018 Proof	–	£6
2018 Silver Proof	–	£20
2019 BU	–	£4
2019 Proof	–	£6
2019 Silver Proof	–	£20
2020 BU	–	£4
2020 Proof	–	£6
2020 Silver Proof	–	£20
2021 BU	–	£4
2021 Proof	–	£6
2021 Silver Proof	–	£20
2022 BU	–	£4
2022 Proof	–	£6
2022 Silver Proof	–	£20
2022 Standard rev. BU, 26/22 privy mark	–	£8
2022 BU	–	£1
2022 Silver	–	£30
2022 Gold	–	£625
2023 New definitive design Oak tree leaf (released in sets only) with commemorative Tudor crown privy mark, first year only		
2023 New definitive design Capercaillie BU	–	£2
2023 — Proof	12,023	£10
2023 — Silver Proof	3,000	£30
2023 — Gold Proof	125	£625

TWO PENCE

Dated from 1971, and legal tender from Decimal Day that year, early examples are found in the blue Specimen decimal set wallets of 1968. They were minted in bronze up to 1991, and mainly in copper-plated steel from 1992. However details of where this rule does not totally apply (1992, 1996, 1998–2000 and 2002, 2006, 2008 and 2009) are given below. As with other denominations, "NEW" was replaced by "TWO" from 1982. Note that some years the 2p is only issued in the Year Sets

DATE	Mintage	UNC
1971	1,454,856,250	£3
1971 Proof	–	£5
1972 Proof	–	£8
1973 Proof	–	£10
1974 Proof	–	£8
1975	Est. approx. 273,145,000	£3
1975 Proof	–	£5
1976	Est. approx. 53,779,000	£3
1976 Proof	–	£5
1977	109,281,000	£3
1977 Proof	–	£5
1978	189,658,000	£3
1978 Proof	–	£5
1979	260,200,000	£2
1979 Proof	–	£5
1980	408,527,000	£2
1980 Proof	–	£4
1981	353,191,000	£4
1981 Proof	–	£5
Legend changed to TWO PENCE		
1982	205,000	£4
1982 Proof	–	£6
1983	631,000	£2
1983 Error NEW instead of TWO	–	£1250
1983 Proof	–	£5
1984	158,820	£2
1984 Proof		£4
New portrait		
1985	107,113,000	£3
1985 BU	–	£2
1985 Proof	–	£4
1986	168,967,500	£2
1986 BU	–	£3
1986 Proof	–	£5
1987	218,100,750	£2
1987 BU	–	£3
1987 Proof	–	£5
1988	419,889,000	£2
1988 BU	–	£3
1988 Proof	–	£5
1989	359,226,000	£2
1989 BU	–	£3
1989 Proof	–	£5
1990	204,499,700	£2

DATE	Mintage	UNC
1990 BU	—	£3
1990 Proof	—	£5
1991	86,625,250	£2
1991 BU	—	£3
1991 Proof	—	£5
1992 Copper plated steel	102,247,000	£2
1992 Bronze BU	—	£3
1992 — Proof	—	£5
1993	235,674,000	£2
1993 BU	—	£3
1993 Proof	—	£4
1994	531,628,000	£2
1994 BU	—	£3
1994 Proof	—	£5
1995	124,482,000	£2
1995 BU	—	£3
1995 Proof	—	£5
1996	296,278,000	£2
1996 BU	—	£3
1996 Proof	—	£5
1996 Silver Proof	—	£25
1997	496,116,000	£2
1997 BU	—	£3
1997 Proof	—	£5
New Portrait		
1998	Est. approx. 120,243,000	£2
1998 BU	—	£3
1998 Proof	—	£5
1998 Bronze	Est. approx. 93,587,000	£2
1999	353,816,000	£2
1999 Bronze BU	—	£3
1999 — Proof	—	£5
2000	536,659,000	£2
2000 BU	—	£3
2000 Proof	—	£5
2000 Silver Proof	—	£25
2001	551,880,000	£2
2001 BU	—	£3
2001 Proof	—	£5
2002	168,556,000	£2
2002 BU	—	£3
2002 Proof	—	£5
2002 Gold Proof	—	£900
2003	260,225,000	£2
2003 BU	—	£3
2003 Proof	—	£5
2004	356,396,000	£2
2004 BU	—	£3
2004 Proof	—	£5
2005	280,396,000	£2
2005 BU	—	£3
2005 Proof	—	£5
2006	170,637,000	£2
2006 BU	—	£3
2006 Proof	—	£5
2006 Silver Proof	—	£25
2007	254,500,000	£2
2007 BU	—	£3
2007 Proof	—	£5
2008	10,600,000	£2
2008 BU	—	£3
2008 Proof	—	£5
2008 Silver Proof	—	£25
2008 Gold Proof	—	£900
2008 Platinum Proof	—	£750
New Rev., no border beads on Obv.		
2008	241,679,000	£2
2008 — BU	—	£3
2008 — Proof	—	£5
2008 — Silver Proof	—	£15
2008 — Silver Proof Piedfort	—	£65
2008 — Gold Proof	—	£900
2008 — Platinum Proof	—	£750
2009	150,500,500	£2
2009 BU	—	£3
2009 Proof	—	£5
2009 Silver Proof	—	£25
2010	99,600,000	£2
2010 BU	—	£3
2010 Proof	—	£6
2010 Silver Proof	—	£25
2011	144,300,000	£2
2011 BU	—	£3
2011 Proof	—	£6
2011 Silver Proof	—	£25
2012	67,800,000	£2
2012 BU	—	£3
2012 Proof	—	£8
2012 Silver Proof with selective gold plating	—	£50
2012 Gold Proof	—	£900
2013	40,600,000	£2
2013 BU	—	£5
2013 Proof	—	£8
2013 Silver Proof	—	£35
2013 Gold Proof	—	£900
2014	247,600,020	£2
2014 BU	—	£3
2014 Proof	—	£8
2014 Silver Proof	—	£45
New Portrait		
2015	139,200,000	£2
2015 BU	—	£3
2015 Proof	—	£5
2015 Silver Proof	—	£35
2015 Gold Proof	—	£900
2015 Platinum Proof	—	£750
2016	185,200,000	£2
2016 BU	—	£5
2016 Proof	—	£8
2016 Silver Proof	—	£35
2017	16,600,000	£2
2017 BU	—	£3
2017 Proof	—	£5
2017 Silver Proof	—	£35
2018 BU (available in sets only)	—	£5
2018 Proof	—	£8
2018 Silver Proof	—	£35
2019 BU (available in sets only)	—	£5
2019 Proof	—	£8
2019 Silver Proof	—	£35
2020 BU (available in sets only)	—	£5
2020 Proof	—	£8
2020 Silver Proof	—	£35
2021	117,700,000	£2
2021 BU	—	£5
2021 Proof	—	£8
2021 Silver Proof	—	£35
2022 BU (available in sets only)	—	£5
2022 Proof	—	£8
2022 Silver Proof	—	£35
2022 Gold Proof	—	£900
2022 Platinum Proof	—	£750
2022 Standard rev. BU with 26/22 privy mark	—	£6
2022 BU— —		£2
2022 Silver	—	£53
2022 Gold	—	£1125
2023 New definitive design Red Squirrel (released in sets only) with commemorative Tudor crown privy mark, first year only		
2023 New definitive design Red Squirrel BU	—	£2
2023 — Proof	12,023	£6
2023 — Silver Proof	3,000	£53
2023— Gold Proof	125	£1125

ONE PENNY

The history of this coin is very similar to that of the Two Pence coin (qv) except that all 1998 examples were of copper-plated steel.

DATE	Mintage	UNC
1971	1,521,666,250	£1
1971 Proof	—	£2
1972 Proof	—	£10
1973	280,196,000	£2
1973 Proof	—	£4
1974	330,892,000	£2
1974 Proof	—	£3
1975	221,604,000	£2
1975 Proof	—	£4
1976	300,160,000	£2
1976 Proof	—	£3
1977	285,430,000	£2
1977 Proof	—	£3
1978	292,770,000	£3
1978 Proof	—	£3
1979	459,000,000	£3
1979 Proof	—	£3
1980	416,304,000	£2
1980 Proof	—	£3
1981	301,800,000	£2
1981 Proof	—	£3
Legend changed to ONE PENNY		
1982	100,292,000	£2
1982 Unc	—	£3
1982 Proof	—	£5
1983	243,002,000	£1
1983 Unc	—	£2
1983 Proof	—	£4
1984	154,759,625	£1
1984 BU	—	£2
1984 Proof	—	£3
New portrait		
1985	200,605,245	£1
1985 BU	—	£2
1985 Proof	—	£3
1986	369,989,130	£1
1986 BU	—	£2
1986 Proof	—	£3
1987	4999,946,000	£1
1987 BU	—	£2
1987 Proof	—	£3
1988	793,492,000	£1
1988 BU	—	£2
1988 Proof	—	£3
1989	658,142,000	£1
1989 BU	—	£2
1989 Proof	—	£3
1990	529,047,500	£2
1990 BU	—	£3
1990 Proof	—	£4
1991	206,457,000	£1
1991 BU	—	£2
1991 Proof	—	£4
1992 Copper-plated steel	253,867,000	£3
1992 Bronze BU	—	£6
1992 — Proof	—	£4
1993	602,590,000	£1
1993 BU	—	£2
1993 Proof	—	£5
1994	843,834,000	£1

DATE	Mintage	UNC
1994 BU	—	£2
1994 Proof	—	£5
1995	303,314,000	£1
1995 BU	—	£3
1995 Proof	—	£5
1996	723,840,060	£1
1996 BU	—	£2
1996 Proof	—	£5
1996 Silver Proof	—	£30
1997	396,874,000	£1
1997 BU	—	£2
1997 Proof	—	£4
New portrait		
1998	739,770,000	£1
1998 — BU	—	£3
1998 Proof	—	£4
1999	891,392,000	£2
1999 Bronze BU	—	£4
1999 Bronze Proof	—	£8
2000	1,060,420,000	£1
2000 BU	—	£2
2000 Proof	—	£4
2000 Silver Proof	—	£25
2001	928,698,000	£1
2001 BU	—	£2
2001 Proof	—	£4
2002	601,446,000	£1
2002 BU	—	£2
2002 Proof	—	£4
2002 Gold Proof	—	£500
2003	539,436,000	£1
2003 BU	—	£2
2003 Proof	—	£3
2004	739,764,000	£1
2004 BU	—	£2
2004 Proof	—	£4
2005	536,318,000	£1
2005 BU	—	£2
2005 Proof	—	£3
2006	524,605,000	£1
2006 BU	—	£2
2006 Proof	—	£4
2006 Silver Proof	—	£25
2007	548,002,000	£1
2007 BU	—	£4
2007 Proof	—	£7
2008	180,600,000	£1
2008 BU	—	£3
2008 Proof	—	£5
2008 Silver Proof	—	£25
2008 Gold Proof	—	£500
2008 Platinum Proof	—	£400
New Rev, no border beads		
2008	507,952,000	£1
2008 — BU	—	£2
2008 — Proof	—	£3
2008 — Silver Proof	—	£25
2008 Silver Proof Piedfort	—	£35
2008 Gold Proof	—	£500
2008 Platinum Proof		£400

DATE	Mintage	UNC
2009	556,412,800	£1
2009 BU	—	£3
2009 Proof	—	£4
2009 Silver BU, in "Lucky Baby Gift Pack"	—	£25
2009 — Proof	—	£35
2010	609,603,000	£1
2010 BU	—	£3
2010 Proof	—	£4
2010 Silver BU, in "Lucky Baby Gift Card"	9,701	£25
2010 — Proof	—	£35
2011	431,004,000	£1
2011 BU	—	£2
2011 Proof	—	£3
2011Silver BU in "Lucky Baby Pack"	—	£25
2011 – Proof	—	£35
2012	227,201,000	£1
2012 BU	—	£2
2012 Proof	—	£4
2012 Silver BU (three different packagings)	—	£25
2012 Silver Proof with selective gold plating	—	£35
2012 Gold Proof	—	£500
2013	260,900,000	£1
2013 BU	—	£4
2013 Proof	—	£5
2013 Silver BU	—	£25
2013 — Proof	—	£30
2013 Gold Proof	—	£500
2014	464,801,520	£1
2014 BU	—	£2
2014 Proof	—	£5
2014 Silver BU	—	£25
2014 Silver Proof	—	£35
2015	154,600,000	£1
2015 BU	—	£2
2015 Proof	—	£5
2015 Silver BU	—	£25
2015 — Proof	—	£35
2015 Gold Proof	—	£500
2015 Platinum Proof	—	£400
New Portrait		
2015	418,201,016	£2
2015 BU	—	£3
2015 Proof	—	£6
2015 Silver Proof	—	£25
2015 Gold Proof	—	£500
2015 Platinum Proof	—	£400
2016	371,002,000	£1
2016 BU	—	£4
2016 Proof	—	£7
2016 Silver BU	2,842	£20
2016 Silver Proof	—	£25
2017	240,999,600	£1
2017 BU	—	£2
2017 Proof	—	£5
2017 Silver BU	—	£20
2017 Silver Proof	—	£25
2018 BU	—	£4
2018 Proof	—	£7
2018 Silver BU Portcullis birth of Prince Louis	—	£20
2018 Silver Proof	—	£25
2019 BU (only issued in year sets)	—	£5
2019 Proof	—	£8
2019 Silver BU Portcullis design date on reverse	—	£20
2019 Silver Proof	—	£30
2020	88,071,910	£1
2020 BU	—	£4
2020 Proof	—	£8
2020 Silver BU Portcullis design date on reverse	—	£20
2020 Silver Proof	—	£35
2021	56.000,000	£1
2021 BU	—	£4
2021 Proof	—	£8
2021 Silver BU Portcullis design but date on reverse	—	£20
2021 Silver Proof	—	£35
2022	30,000,000	£1
2022 BU	—	£2
2022 Silver Proof	—	£35
2022 Gold Proof	—	£500
2022 Platinum Proof	—	£400
2022 Standard rev. BU with 26/22 privy mark	—	£5
2022 BU	—	£2
2022 Silver	—	£53
2022 Gold	—	£625
2023 New definitive design Hazel Dormouse (released in sets only) with commemorative Tudor crown privy mark, first year only		
2023 New definitive design Hazel Dormouse BU	—	£2
2023 — Proof	12,023	£3
2023 Silver Proof	3,000	£53
2023 Gold Proof	125	£625

HALF PENNY

No longer legal tender, its history tracks that of the Two Pence and One Penny.

DATE	Mintage	UNC
1971	1,394,188,250	£2
1971 Proof	—	£3
1972 Proof	—	£15
1973	365,680,000	£2
1973 Proof	—	£3
1974	365,448,000	£2
1974 Proof	—	£3
1975	197,600,000	£2
1975 Proof	—	£3
1976	412,172,000	£2
1976 Proof	—	£3
1977	66,368,000	£1
1977 Proof	—	£3
1978	59,532,000	£1
1978 Proof	—	£4
1979	219,1322,000	£2
1979 Proof	—	£4
1980	202,788,000	£2
1980 Proof	—	£3
1981	46,748,000	£2
1981 Proof	—	£4
Legend changed to HALF PENNY		
1982	190,752,000	£1
1982 Unc	—	£2
1982 Proof	—	£3
1983	7,600,000	£1
1983 Unc	—	£1
1983 Proof	—	£6
1984	40,000	£4
1984 BU	—	£6
1984 Proof	—	£8

THE BRITANNIA SERIES

In addition to the large Britannia coin issues already listed, the series has grown to include many denominations and strikes in silver, gold and platinum. The coins are essentially bullion pieces and their values are usually related to the current price of precious metals, although the increasing popularity of the series in recent years has seen examples changing hands for figures well in excess of their bullion values, this is so especially with proof and other special strikes or the occasional mule or error. To ascertain the value of a piece it is usually only necessary to check with the prevailing price of precious metals. Hopefully this guide will give an indication of the recent market prices

SILVER

The silver Britannia series commenced in 1997, and, as with the Gold Britannia series, sets of the coins are listed in the "Proof and Specimen Sets" section. Coins contain one Troy ounce of fine silver (£2) alloyed to Britannia standard, i.e. 95.8 per cent fine silver, or fractions of one ounce as follows: half ounce (£1), quarter ounce (50 pence) and one tenth of an ounce (20 pence). Reverses change annually, all four coins of any particular date being of the same design. The reverses by Philip Nathan appear as follows:

1997 Chariot, 1998 Standing Britannia, 1999 Chariot, 2000 Standing Britannia, 2001 Una and the Lion, 2002 Standing Britannia, 2003 Britannia's Helmeted Head, 2004 Standing Britannia, 2005 Britannia Seated, 2006 Standing Britannia, 2009 Chariot.

The 2007 design is by Christopher Le Brun, and features a seated Britannia with Lion at her feet. The 2008 is by John Bergdahl, and features a standing Britannia facing left.

Two pounds Britannia coins to BU or "bullion" standard have been issued as individual coins for each year from 1998 onwards. 2010 features Suzie Zamit's Britannia with a portrait with a Corinthian style helmet.

The 2011 coins feature a seated Britannia and Union Flag, as described in the Britannia gold series below.

2012 saw the 15th anniversary of the Silver Series, but the reverse chosen was that of the Standing Britannia by Philip Nathan, which also marked the 25th Gold series. In addition, there is a 9-coin proof set of Half-Ounce silver coins dated 2012 featuring each of the Reverses used in the past, a 25th Anniversary collection. The story of the 2013 silver Britannia coins closely parallels that of the gold coins. The silver one-twentieth of an ounce has the logical face value of 10 pence.

The 2014 Silver Britannias closely follow the pattern of the three designs of 2014 Gold. This included the introduction of the silver one-fortieth of an ounce, with a face value of 5 pence. The Nathan Britannia has crenellated borders on both the obverse and the reverse, while the Year of the Horse has plain borders on both. Examples exist, however, of both One ounce silver bullion coins having the Other's obverse, thus producing two error coins, or "mules". 2014 also saw the SS *Gairsoppa* Quarter-ounce silver Britannia bullion coin with the edge inscription SS GAIRSOPPA. These coins have the Nathan Britannia reverse, and are struck from metal recovered from the vessel which was sunk by enemy action in 1941.

Both 2013 and 2014 one-ounce BU bullion Nathan Britannia coins exist with snakes or horses (respectively) on a plain edge. These were the result of a contract between the Royal Mint and the bullion dealers A-mark of Santa Monica,

California, and commemorate Chinese Lunar years. In 2015 Designer Jody Clark scored a first when his portrayal of Britannia was used on the £50 coin which also carried his new portrait of the Queen.

GOLD

In 1987 the gold Britannia £100 coin was introduced. It contained one Troy ounce of fine gold, alloyed to 22 carat, and this has continued to the present day. At the same time, and also continuing, gold coins of face value £50, £25 and £10 appeared, containing a half ounce, quarter ounce and one tenth of an ounce of fine gold respectively. From 1987 to 1989 the alloy was of copper (Red Gold), whereas from 1990 to the present day the alloy has been of silver and copper (yellow gold).

Proof sets of these coins are listed in the "Proof and Specimen Sets" section. In addition, non-proof coins have been minted, it is believed for each of the four coins for every year. The one ounce £100 Britannia is primarily issued as a bullion coin in the non-proof standard, originally in competition with the South African Krugerrand. Its price is quoted daily on the financial pages of some newspapers.

There were five reverse designs by Philip Nathan: 1987–96 Standing Britannia, 1997 Chariot, 1998–2000 Standing Britannia, 2001 Una and the Lion, 2002 Standing Britannia, 2003 Britannia's Helmeted Head, 2004 Standing Britannia, 2005 Britannia seated, 2006 Standing Britannia. For 2007 the design is a Seated Britannia with lion at her feet, by Christopher Le Brun. The 2008 design is of Britannia standing and facing left, by John Bergdahl. The 2009 reverse is similar to that of 1997, Britannia on a chariot, while 2010 has Suzie Zamit's Britannia potrait with a Corinthian style helmet. The 2011 design is by David Mach, and portrays a seated Britannia with trident and shield, replicating the design on a 1937 penny, superimposed on a Union Flag. The rotation of the coin from left to right, or vice-versa, creates an illusion of Britannia moving with the ripple of the flag.

In general the proof coins have reverse features frosted. The proofs with Standing Britannia and Una and the Lion reverses include P NATHAN on the reverse, whereas the equivalent bullion coins have NATHAN. The other three reverses have PN on both proofs and bullion coins.

2012 was the 25th anniversary of the Gold Britannia coin series, and the reverse design chosen was that of the 1987 coins, standing Britannia, by Philip Nathan. This was repeated in 2013, but only for Brilliant Uncirculated "Bullion" coins. A separate new series was introduced for Proof coins, a seated Britannia with an owl was featured, the artist being Robert Hunt. The range of Britannia Proofs was increased from 4 to 6, with the addition of a Five-ounce coin (qv) and a one-twentieth of an ounce, curiously denominated at One Pound and with a diameter of 12mm, just larger than a Maundy One Penny. All 2013 Gold Britannias are minted in 0.999 Au alloy.

2014 and 2015 each saw three Reverse designs. The Nathan outstretched arm of Britannia continued as the bullion coin. The series by new artists were of a standing Britannia facing left with lion (2014) by Jody Clark, and a "head and shoulders" Britannia holding the trident on her right shoulder, by Antony Dufont, the latter coin included the Clark portrayal of the Queen on the obverse.

The 2016 series Reverse was designed by Suzie Zamit and depicts Britannia as the Warrior Queen. The 2017 series celebrating the 30th anniversary of the gold Britannia used a design by Louis Tamlin which depicts a helmeted outline of Britain .

A further new denomination appeared in 2014, the gold one-fortieth of an ounce, diameter 8mm and face value 50 pence.

In 2018 David Lawrence chose to portray a beautiful head and shoulders of Britannia wearing a Corinthian helmet, returning to her classical roots. However, for 2019 David once again had her standing in a warlike pose with a lion at her feet and pointing her trident towards the sun. As David Lawrence himself explained: “My initial thoughts were influenced by the great engravers of the past. Their work has classical grace and gravitas I was keen to recreate . . . The end result is an Anglicised version of ancient Rome.”

In 2020 James Tottle echoed the Nathan reverse with a warlike Britannia again standing by crashing waves, trident in hand. Now though her shield bears the head of a lion and the previous shield design, the Union Flag, can be seen in the background. 2021 saw not one but two different designs by P.J. Lynch issued as proof coins alongside those bearing the Nathan reverse. The first showed a seated Britannia with a lion by her side, the second depicted a profile head with Roman style helmet. This latter design came to the attention of the press as it featured a Britannia whose facial features seemed more African than European and it was dubbed by some as the first “black Britannia”. Following the success of the “double designs” the previous year, 2022 saw another two coins issued in addition to the Nathan reverse. Created by Italian designer and sculptor Sandra Deina, the first depicts a warrior queen, wearing a helmet more Greek than Roman, with trident in hand and her shield once again bearing the lion’s head, the Union Flag appears again in the background. The second design, entitled “A celebration of Womanhood” shows not one but three female figures, a bear headed older woman, a be-helmeted Britannia and a young girl with a crown of laurel leaves. The Britannia range continues to expand and it seem likely that numerous dsigns inaddition to the standard one for bullion coins will feature heavily in the future.

On the following pages we have collated all the known information on the Britannia series and give the current market price you should expect to pay. However, for the later issues, many of which are still available from the Royal Mint, we have given the original issue price.

The Britannia was initially introduced as a bullion coin and changed hands at the prevailing rate, but today they are also collected for their numismatic interest and as such many of them can reach a value much higher than their intrinsic worth, so it is well worth checking before buying or selling coins of the series.

"Set only" indicates that the coin so listed was originally only available as part of a set and the prices are not given individually. BV indicates that the coin currently changes hands at the prevailing price of bullion gold or silver.

Note: whilst all British legal tender gold coins are VAT free, silver bullion coinage attracts VAT at the prevailing rate.

STANDING BRITANNIA
***Obverse* by Raphael Maklouf**
***Reverse* by Philip Nathan**

Date	Metal	Face value	Weight	No. struck	Value
1987	Gold Proof	£10.00	1/10oz	3,500	£320
1987	Gold Bullion	£10.00	1/10oz	Unlimited	BV
1987	Gold Proof	£25.00	1/4oz	3,500	£620
1987	Gold Bullion	£25.00	1/4oz	Unlimited	BV
1987	Gold Proof	£50.00	1/2oz	2,486	£1150
1987	Gold Bullion	£50.00	1/2oz	Unlimited	BV
1987	Gold Proof	£100.00	1oz	2,485	£2500
1987	Gold Bullion	£100.00	1oz	Unlimited	BV
1987	Gold Proof Set	£25 and £10		11,100	£820
1987	Gold Proof Set	£100, £50, £25 and £10		10,000	£4300
1988	Gold Proof	£10.00	1/10oz	2,694	£320
1988	Gold Bullion	£10.00	1/10oz	Unlimited	BV
1988	Gold Proof	£25.00	1/4oz	Set only	—
1988	Gold Bullion	£25.00	1/4oz	Unlimited	BV
1988	Gold Proof	£50.00	1/2oz	Set only	—
1988	Gold Bullion	£50.00	1/2oz	Unlimited	BV
1988	Gold Proof	£100.00	1oz	Set only	—
1988	Gold Bullion	£100.00	1oz	Unlimited	BV
1988	Gold Proof Set	£25 and £10		894	£820
1988	Gold Proof Set	£100, £50, £25 and £10		3,505	£4300
1989	Gold Proof	£10.00	1/10oz	1,609	£320
1989	Gold Bullion	£10.00	1/10oz	Unlimited	BV
1989	Gold Proof	£25.00	1/4oz	Set only	—
1989	Gold Bullion	£25.00	1/4oz	Unlimited	BV
1989	Gold Proof	£50.00	1/2oz	Set only	—
1989	Gold Bullion	£50.00	1/2oz	Unlimited	BV
1989	Gold Proof	£100.00	1oz	Set only	—
1989	Gold Bullion	£100.00	1oz	Unlimited	BV
1989	Gold Proof Set	£25 and £10		451	£820
1989	Gold Proof Set	£100, £50, £25 and £10		2,268	£4300
1990	Gold Proof	£10.00	1/10oz	1,571	£320
1990	Gold Bullion	£10.00	1/10oz	Unlimited	BV
1990	Gold Proof	£25.00	1/4oz	Set only	—
1990	Gold Bullion	£25.00	1/4oz	Unlimited	BV
1990	Gold Proof	£50.00	1/2oz	Set only	—
1990	Gold Bullion	£50.00	1/2oz	Unlimited	BV
1990	Gold Proof	£100.00	1oz	Set only	—
1990	Gold Bullion	£100.00	1oz	Unlimited	BV
1990	Gold Proof Set	£100, £50, £25 and £10		527	£4300
1991	Gold Proof	£10.00	1/10oz	(954)	£320
1991	Gold Bullion	£10.00	1/10oz	Unlimited	BV

1987 Gold Proof 1 ounce

Date	Metal	Face value	Weight	No. struck	Value
1991	Gold Proof	£25.00	1/4oz	Set only	—
1991	Gold Bullion	£25.00	1/4oz	Unlimited	BV
1991	Gold Proof	£50.00	1/2oz	Set only	—
1991	Gold Bullion	£50.00	1/2oz	Unlimited	BV
1991	Gold Proof	£100.00	1oz	Set only	—
1991	Gold Bullion	£100.00	1oz	Unlimited	BV
1991	Gold Proof Set	£100, £50, £25 and £10		509	£3750
1992	Gold Proof	£10.00	1/10oz	1,000	£320
1992	Gold Bullion	£10.00	1/10oz	Unlimited	BV
1992	Gold Proof	£25.00	1/4oz	Set only	—
1992	Gold Bullion	£25.00	1/4oz	Unlimited	BV
1992	Gold Proof	£50.00	1/2oz	Set only	—
1992	Gold Bullion	£50.00	1/2oz	Unlimited	BV
1992	Gold Proof	£100.00	1oz	Set only	—
1992	Gold Bullion	£100.00	1oz	Unlimited	BV
1992	Gold Proof Set	£100, £50, £25 and £10		500	£4300
1993	Gold Proof	£10.00	1/10oz	997	£320
1993	Gold Bullion	£10.00	1/10oz	Unlimited	BV
1993	Gold Proof	£25.00	1/4oz	Set only	—
1993	Gold Bullion	£25.00	1/4oz	Unlimited	BV
1993	Gold Proof	£50.00	1/2oz	Set only	—
1993	Gold Bullion	£50.00	1/2oz	Unlimited	BV
1993	Gold Proof	£100.00	1oz	Set only	—
1993	Gold Bullion	£100.00	1oz	Unlimited	BV
1993	Gold Proof Set	£100, £50, £25 and £10		462	£4300
1994	Gold Proof	£10.00	1/10oz	994	£320
1994	Gold Bullion	£10.00	1/10oz	Unlimited	BV
1994	Gold Proof	£25.00	1/4oz	Set only	—
1994	Gold Bullion	£25.00	1/4oz	Unlimited	BV
1994	Gold Proof	£50.00	1/2oz	Set only	—
1994	Gold Bullion	£50.00	1/2oz	Unlimited	BV
1994	Gold Proof	£100.00	1oz	Set only	—
1994	Gold Bullion	£100.00	1oz	Unlimited	BV
1994	Gold Proof Set	£100, £50, £25 and £10		435	£4300
1995	Gold Proof	£10.00	1/10oz	1,500	£320
1995	Gold Bullion	£10.00	1/10oz	Unlimited	BV
1995	Gold Proof	£25.00	1/4oz	Set only	—
1995	Gold Bullion	£25.00	1/4oz	Unlimited	BV
1995	Gold Proof	£50.00	1/2oz	Set only	—
1995	Gold Bullion	£50.00	1/2oz	Unlimited	BV
1995	Gold Proof	£100.00	1oz	Set only	—
1995	Gold Bullion	£100.00	1oz	Unlimited	BV
1995	Gold Proof Set	£100, £50, £25 and £10		500	£4300
1996	Gold Proof	£10.00	1/10oz	2,379	£320
1996	Gold Bullion	£10.00	1/10oz	Unlimited	BV
1996	Gold Proof	£25.00	1/4oz	Set only	—
1996	Gold Bullion	£25.00	1/4oz	Unlimited	BV
1996	Gold Proof	£50.00	1/2oz	Set only	—
1996	Gold Bullion	£50.00	1/2oz	Unlimited	BV
1996	Gold Proof	£100.00	1oz	Set only	—
1996	Gold Bullion	£100.00	1oz	Unlimited	BV
1996	Gold Proof Set	£100, £50, £25 and £10		483	£4300

BRITANNIA IN CHARIOT
***Obverse* by Raphael Maklouf**
***Reverse* by Philip Nathan**

Date	Metal	Face value	Weight	No. struck	Value
1997	Silver Proof	20 pence	1/10oz	8,686	£20
1997	Silver Proof	50 pence	1/4oz	Set only	—

Date	Metal	Face value	Weight	No. struck	Value
1997	Silver Proof	£1.00	1/2oz	Set only	–
1997	Silver Proof	£2.00	1oz	4,173	£175
1997	Silver Proof Set	£2, £1, 50p and 20p		11,832	£250
1997	Gold Proof	£10.00	1/10oz	1,821	£320
1997	Gold Bullion	£10.00	1/10oz	Unlimited	BV
1997	Gold Proof	£25.00	1/4oz	923	£620
1997	Gold Bullion	£25.00	1/4oz	Unlimited	BV
1997	Gold Proof	£50.00	1/2oz	Set only	–
1997	Gold Bullion	£50.00	1/2oz	Unlimited	BV
1997	Gold Proof	£100.00	1oz	164	£2500
1997	Gold Bullion	£100.00	1oz	Unlimited	BV
1997	Gold Proof Set	£100, £50, £25 and £10		892	£4300

STANDING BRITANNIA
***Obverse* by Ian Rank-Broadley**
***Reverse* by Philip Nathan**

Date	Metal	Face value	Weight	No. struck	Value
1998	Silver Proof	20 pence	1/10oz	2,724	£20
1998	Silver Proof	50 pence	1/4oz	Set only	–
1998	Silver Proof	£1.00	1/2oz	Set only	–
1998	Silver Proof	£2.00	1oz	Set only	–
1998	Silver Bullion	£2.00	1oz	88,909	£50
1998	Silver Proof Set	£2, £1, 50p and 20p		2,500	£200
1998	Gold Proof	£10.00	1/10oz	392	£320
1998	Gold Bullion	£10.00	1/10oz	Unlimited	BV
1998	Gold Proof	£25.00	1/4oz	560	£620
1998	Gold Bullion	£25.00	1/4oz	Unlimited	BV
1998	Gold Proof	£50.00	1/2oz	Set only	–
1998	Gold Bullion	£50.00	1/2oz	Unlimited	BV
1998	Gold Proof	£100.00	1oz	Set only	–
1998	Gold Bullion	£100.00	1oz	Unlimited	BV
1998	Gold Proof Set	£100, £50, £25 and £10		750	£4300

BRITANNIA IN CHARIOT (SILVER) / STANDING (GOLD)
***Obverse* by Ian Rank-Broadley**
***Reverse* by Philip Nathan**

Date	Metal	Face value	Weight	No. struck	Value
1999	Silver Bullion	£2.00	1oz	69,394	£50
1999	Gold Proof	£10.00	1/10oz	1,058	£320
1999	Gold Bullion	£10.00	1/10oz	Unlimited	BV
1999	Gold Proof	£25.00	1/4oz	1,000	£620
1999	Gold Bullion	£25.00	1/4oz	Unlimited	BV
1999	Gold Proof	£50.00	1/2oz	Set only	–
1999	Gold Bullion	£50.00	1/2oz	Unlimited	BV
1999	Gold Proof	£100.00	1oz	Set only	–
1999	Gold Bullion	£100.00	1oz	Unlimited	BV
1999	Gold Proof Set	£100, £50, £25 and £10		740	£4300

STANDING BRITANNIA
***Obverse* by Ian Rank-Broadley**
Reverse by Philip Nathan

Date	Metal	Face value	Weight	No. struck	Value
2000	Silver Bullion	£2.00	1oz	81,301	£50
2000	Gold Proof	£10.00	1/10oz	3,250	£320
2000	Gold Bullion	£10.00	1/10oz	Unlimited	BV
2000	Gold Proof	£25.00	1/4oz	1,250	£620
2000	Gold Bullion	£25.00	1/4oz	Unlimited	BV
2000	Gold Proof	£50.00	1/2oz	Set only	–
2000	Gold Bullion	£50.00	1/2oz	Unlimited	BV
2000	Gold Proof	£100.00	1oz	Set only	–
2000	Gold Bullion	£100.00	1oz	Unlimited	BV
2000	Gold Proof Set	£100, £50, £25 and £10		750	£4300

Date	Metal	Face value	Weight	No. struck	Value

UNA AND THE LION
***Obverse* by Ian Rank-Broadley**
***Reverse* by Philip Nathan**

Date	Metal	Face value	Weight	No. struck	Value
2001	Silver Proof	20 pence	1/10oz	10,000	£10
2001	Silver Proof	50 pence	1/4oz	Set only	—
2001	Silver Proof	£1.00	1/2oz	Set only	—
2001	Silver Proof	£2.00	1oz	10,000	£85
2001	Silver Bullion	£2.00	1oz	44,816	£50
2001	Silver Proof Set	"£2, £1, 50p and 20p"		Unknown	£225
2001	Gold Proof	£10.00	1/10oz	1,100	£300
2001	Gold Bullion	£10.00	1/10oz	Unlimited	BV
2001	Gold Proof	£25.00	1/4oz	500	£620
2001	Gold Bullion	£25.00	1/4oz	Unlimited	BV
2001	Gold Proof	£50.00	1/2oz	Set only	—
2001	Gold Bullion	£50.00	1/2oz	Unlimited	BV
2001	Gold Proof	£100.00	1oz	Set only	—
2001	Gold Bullion	£100.00	1oz	Unlimited	BV
2001	Gold Proof Set	£100, £50, £25 and £10		1,000	£4300

STANDING BRITANNIA
***Obverse* by Ian Rank-Broadley**
***Reverse* by Philip Nathan**

Date	Metal	Face value	Weight	No. struck	Value
2002	Silver Bullion	£2.00	1oz	36,543	£39
2002	Gold Proof	£10.00	1/10oz	2,500"	£300
2002	Gold Bullion	£10.00	1/10oz	Unlimited	BV
2002	Gold Proof	£25.00	1/4oz	1,750	£620
2002	Gold Bullion	£25.00	1/4oz	Unlimited	BV
2002	Gold Proof	£50.00	1/2oz	Set only	—
2002	Gold Bullion	£50.00	1/2oz	Unlimited	BV
2002	Gold Proof	£100.00	1oz	Set only	—
2002	Gold Bullion	£100.00	1oz	Unlimited	BV
2002	Gold Proof Set	£100, £50, £25 and £10		945	£4300

BRITANNIA'S HELMETED HEAD
***Obverse* by Ian Rank-Broadley**
***Reverse* by Philip Nathan**

Date	Metal	Face value	Weight	No. struck	Value
2003	Silver Proof	20 pence	1/10oz	1,179	£20
2003	Silver Proof	50 pence	1/4oz	Set only	—
2003	Silver Proof	£1.00	1/2oz	Set only	—
2003	Silver Proof	£2.00	1oz	2,016	£90
2003	Silver Bullion	£2.00	1oz	73,271	£50
2003	Silver Proof Set	£2, £1, 50p and 20p		3,669	£170
2003	Gold Proof	£10.00	1/10oz	1,382	£320
2003	Gold Bullion	£10.00	1/10oz	Unlimited	BV
2003	Gold Proof	£25.00	1/4oz	609	£620
2003	Gold Bullion	£25.00	1/4oz	Unlimited	BV
2003	Gold Proof	£50.00	1/2oz	Set only	—
2003	Gold Bullion	£50.00	1/2oz	Unlimited	BV
2003	Gold Proof	£100.00	1oz	Set only	—
2003	Gold Bullion	£100.00	1oz	Unlimited	BV
2003	Gold Proof Set	£50, £25 and £10		825	£2200
2003	Gold Proof Set	£100, £50, £25 and £10		1,250	£4300

STANDING BRITANNIA
***Obverse* by Ian Rank-Broadley**
***Reverse* by Philip Nathan**

Date	Metal	Face value	Weight	No. struck	Value
2004	Silver Proof	£2.00	1oz	2,174	£185
2004	Silver Bullion	£2.00	1oz	57,000	£40
2004	Gold Proof	£10.00	1/10oz	929	£300
2004	Gold Bullion	£10.00	1/10oz	Unlimited	BV
2004	Gold Proof	£25.00	1/4oz	750	£620
2004	Gold Bullion	£25.00	1/4oz	Unlimited	BV

Date	Metal	Face value	Weight	No. struck	Value
2004	Gold Proof	£50.00	1/2oz	Set only	—
2004	Gold Bullion	£50.00	1/2oz	Unlimited	BV
2004	Gold Proof	£100.00	1oz	Set only	—
2004	Gold Bullion	£100.00	1oz	Unlimited	BV
2004	Gold Proof Set	£50, £25 and £10		223	£2200
2004	Gold Proof Set	£100, £50, £25 and £10		973	£4300

BRTANNIA SEATED
***Obverse* by Ian Rank-Broadley**
***Reverse* by Philip Nathan**

Date	Metal	Face value	Weight	No. struck	Value
2005	Silver Proof	20 pence	1/10oz	913	£20
2005	Silver Proof	50 pence	1/4oz	Set only	—
2005	Silver Proof	£1.00	1/2oz	Set only	—
2005	Silver Proof	£2.00	1oz	1,539	£185
2005	Silver Bullion	£2.00	1oz	57,000	£55
2005	Silver Proof Set	£2, £1, 50p and 20p		2,360	£200
2005	Gold Proof	£10.00	1/10oz	1,225	£300
2005	Gold Bullion	£10.00	1/10oz	Unlimited	BV
2005	Gold Proof	£25.00	1/4oz	750	£620
2005	Gold Bullion	£25.00	1/4oz	Unlimited	BV
2005	Gold Proof	£50.00	1/2oz	Set only	—
2005	Gold Bullion	£50.00	1/2oz	Unlimited	BV
2005	Gold Proof	£100.00	1oz	Set only	—
2005	Gold Bullion	£100.00	1oz	Unlimited	BV
2005	Gold Proof Set	£50, £25 and £10		417	£2200
2005	Gold Proof Set	£100, £50, £25 and £10		1,439	£4300

STANDING BRITANNIA
***Obverse* by Ian Rank-Broadley**
***Reverse* by Philip Nathan**

Date	Metal	Face value	Weight	No. struck	Value
2006	Silver Proof	20 pence	1/10oz	Set only	—
2006	Silver Proof	50 pence	1/4oz	Set only	—
2006	Silver Proof	£1.00	1/2oz	Set only	—
2006	Silver Proof	£2.00	1oz	2,529	£185
2006	Silver Bullion	£2.00	1oz	50,300	£55
2006	Silver Proof "Silhouette" Set of five designs				
		5 x £2	1oz	3,000	£275
2006	Silver Proof Set	£2, £1, 50p and 20p		2,500	£200
2006	Gold Proof	£10.00	1/10oz	700	£300
2006	Gold Bullion	£10.00	1/10oz	Unlimited	BV
2006	Gold Proof	£25.00	1/4oz	728	£620
2006	Gold Bullion	£25.00	1/4oz	Unlimited	BV
2006	Gold Proof	£50.00	1/2oz	Set only	—
2006	Gold Bullion	£50.00	1/2oz	Unlimited	BV
2006	Gold Proof	£100.00	1oz	Set only	—
2006	Gold Bullion	£100.00	1oz	Unlimited	BV
2006	Gold Proof Set	£100, £50, £25 and £10		1,163	£4300
2006	Gold Proof Set of Five Designs				
		5 x £25	1/4oz	250	£3300

BRITANNIA SEATED LION AT FEET
***Obverse* by Ian Rank-Broadley**
***Reverse* by Christopher le Brun**

Date	Metal	Face value	Weight	No. struck	Value
2007	Silver Proof	20 pence	1/10oz	901	£20
2007	Silver Proof	50 pence	1/4oz	Set only	—
2007	Silver Proof	£1.00	1/2oz	Set only	—
2007	Silver Proof	£2.00	1oz	2,500	£175
2007	Silver Bullion	£2.00	1oz	94,000	£45
2007	Silver Proof Set (20th Anniversary) 6 Satin Finish Reverses				
		6 x £1	1/2oz	2,000	£200
2007	Silver Proof Set	£2, £1, 50p and 20p		2,500	£175
2007	Gold Proof	£10.00	1/10oz	893	£300

Date	Metal	Face value	Weight	No. struck	Value
2007	Gold Bullion	£10.00	1/10oz	Unlimited	BV
2007	Gold Proof	£25.00	1/4oz	1,000	£620
2007	Gold Bullion	£25.00	1/4oz	Unlimited	BV
2007	Gold Proof	£50.00	1/2oz	Set only	—
2007	Gold Bullion	£50.00	1/2oz	Unlimited	BV
2007	Gold Proof	£100.00	1oz	Set only	—
2007	Gold Bullion	£100.00	1oz	Unlimited	BV
2007	Gold Proof Set	£100, £50, £25 and £10		250	£4300
2007	Platinum Proof	£10	1/10oz	691	£190
2007	Platinum Proof	£25	1/4oz	210	£390
2007	Platinum Proof	£50	1/2oz	Set only	—
2007	Platinum Proof	£100	1oz	Set only	—
2007	Platinum Proof Set	£100, £50, £25 and £10		250	£2750

STANDING BRITANNIA ON WAVES
***Obverse* by Ian Rank-Broadley**
***Reverse* by John Bergdahl**

Date	Metal	Face value	Weight	No. struck	Value
2008	Silver Proof*	20 pence	1/10oz	2,500	£20
2008	Silver Proof*	50 pence	1/4oz	Set only	—
2008	Silver Proof*	£1.00	1/2oz	Set only	—
2008	Silver Proof*	£2.00	1oz	2,500	£125
2008	Silver Bullion	£2.00	1oz	100,000	£35
2008	Silver Proof Set	£2, £1, 50p and 20p		2,500	£130
2008	Gold Proof	£10.00	1/10oz	748	£300
2008	Gold Bullion	£10.00	1/10oz	Unlimited	BV
2008	Gold Proof	£25.00	1/4oz	1,000	£620
2008	Gold Bullion	£25.00	1/4oz	Unlimited	BV
2008	Gold Proof	£50.00	1/2oz	Set only	—
2008	Gold Bullion	£50.00	1/2oz	Unlimited	BV
2008	Gold Proof	£100.00	1oz	Set only	—
2008	Gold Bullion	£100.00	1oz	Unlimited	BV
2008	Gold Proof Set	£100, £50, £25 and £10		1,250	£4300
2008	Platinum Proof	£10	1/10oz	268	£190
2008	Platinum Proof	£25	1/4oz	100	£390
2008	Platinum Proof	£50	1/2oz	Set only	—
2008	Platinum Proof	£100	1oz	Set only	—
2008	Platinum Proof Set	£100, £50, £25 and £10		150	£2750

*Satin finish

BRITANNIA IN CHARIOT
***Obverse* by Ian Rank-Broadley**
***Reverse* by Philip Nathan**

Date	Metal	Face value	Weight	No. struck	Value
2009	Silver Proof	20 pence	1/10oz	2,500	£20
2009	Silver Proof	50 pence	1/4oz	2,500	£30
2009	Silver Proof	£1.00	1/2oz	2,500	£40
2009	Silver Proof	£2.00	1oz	6,784	£90
2009	Silver Bullion	£2.00	1oz	100,000	£40
2009	Silver Proof Set	£2, £1, 50p and 20p		2,500	£150
2009	Gold Proof	£10.00	1/10oz	1,546	£300
2009	Gold Bullion	£10.00	1/10oz	Unlimited	BV
2009	Gold Proof	£25.00	1/4oz	1,567	£620
2009	Gold Bullion	£25.00	1/4oz	Unlimited	BV
2009	Gold Proof	£50.00	1/2oz	797	£1150
2009	Gold Bullion	£50.00	1/2oz	Unlimited	BV
2009	Gold Proof	£100.00	1oz	797	£2200
2009	Gold Bullion	£100.00	1oz	Unlimited	BV
2009	Gold Proof Set	£100, £50, £25 and £10		797	£4300

BRITANNIA WEARING A CORINTHIAN HELMET
***Obverse* by Ian Rank-Broadley**
***Reverse* by Suzie Zamit**

Date	Metal	Face value	Weight	No. struck	Value
2010	Silver Proof	20 pence	1/10oz	4,486	£15
2010	Silver Proof	50 pence	1/4oz	3,497	£25
2010	Silver Proof	£1.00	1/2oz	3,497	£40
2010	Silver Proof	£2.00	1oz	6,539	£80
2010	Silver Bullion	£2.00	1oz	126,367	£40
2010	Silver Proof Set	£2, £1, 50p and 20p		3,500	£130
2010	Gold Proof	£10.00	1/10oz	2,102	£300
2010	Gold Bullion	£10.00	1/10oz	3,530	BV
2010	Gold Proof	£25.00	1/4oz	1,670	£620
2010	Gold Bullion	£25.00	1/4oz	1,501	BV
2010	Gold Proof	£50.00	1/2oz	1,053	£1200
2010	Gold Bullion	£50.00	1/2oz	1,301	BV
2010	Gold Proof	£100.00	1oz	867	£2200
2010	Gold Bullion	£100.00	1oz	13,860	BV
2010	Gold Proof Set First Strike	£100, £50, £25 and £10		500	£5000
2010	Gold Proof Set	£100, £50, £25 and £10		1,250	£4300

"PENNY" BRITANNIA SUPERIMPOSED ON A UNION FLAG
***Obverse* by Ian Rank-Broadley**
***Reverse* by David Mach**

Date	Metal	Face value	Weight	No. struck	Value
2011	Silver Proof	20 pence	1/10oz	2,483	£15
2011	Silver Proof	50 pence	1/4oz	2,483	£25
2011	Silver Proof	£1.00	1/2oz	2,483	£40
2011	Silver Proof	£2.00	1oz	4,973	£80
2011	Silver Bullion	£2.00	1oz	269,282	£40
2011	Silver Proof Set	£2, £1, 50p, 20p		3,500	£150
2011	Gold Proof	£10.00	1/10oz	3,511	£300
2011	Gold Proof	£25.00	1/4oz	698	£620
2011	Gold Bullion	£25.00	1/4oz	Unlimited	BV
2011	Gold Proof	£50.00	1/2oz	847	£1200
2011	Gold Bullion	£50.00	1/2oz	Unlimited	BV
2011	Gold Proof	£100.00	1oz	5,735	£2200
2011	Gold Bullion	£100.00	1oz	Unlimited	BV
2011	Gold Proof Set	£50, £25 and £10		250	£2300
2011	Gold Proof Set	£100, £50, £25 and £10		1,000	£4300

STANDING BRITANNIA
***Obverse* by Ian Rank-Broadley**
***Reverse* by Philip Nathan**

Date	Metal	Face value	Weight	No. struck	Value
2012	Silver Proof	20 pence	1/10oz	Set only	—
2012	Silver Proof	50 pence	1/4oz	Set only	—
2012	Silver Proof	£1.00	1/2oz	Set only	—
2012	Silver Proof	£2.00	1oz	5,550	£85
2012	Silver Bullion	£2.00	1oz	351,372	£35
2012	Silver BU	£2.00	1oz	Unknown	£40
2012	Silver Proof Set	£2, £1, 50p and 20p		2,595	£150
2012	Silver Proof Set 9 Reverse Portraits	9 x £1.00		1,656	£550
2012	Gold Proof	£10.00	1/10oz	1,249	£300
2012	Gold Proof	£25.00	1/4oz	316	£640
2012	Gold Bullion	£25.00	1/4oz	Unlimited	BV
2012	Gold Proof	£50.00	1/2oz	Set only	—
2012	Gold Bullion	£50.00	1/2oz	Unlimited	BV
2012	Gold Proof	£100.00	1oz	Set only	—
2012	Gold Bullion	£100.00	1oz	Unlimited	BV
2012	Gold Proof Set	£50, £25 and £10		99	£2200
2012	Gold Proof Set First Strike	£100, £50, £25 and £10		200	£5000
2012	Gold Proof Set	£100, £50, £25 and £10		352	£4300
2012	Gold Proof Set 9 Reverse Portraits	9 x £50		25	£11,000

Date	Metal	Face value	Weight	No. struck	Value

BRITANNIA SEATED WITH OWL
***Obverse* by Ian Rank-Broadley**
***Reverse* by Robert Hunt**

Date	Metal	Face value	Weight	No. struck	Value
2013	Silver Proof	10 pence	1/20oz	Set only	–
2013	Silver Proof	20 pence	1/10oz	Set only	–
2013	Silver Proof	50 pence	1/4oz	Set only	–
2013	Silver BU (SS *Gairsoppa)* Nathan Reverse				
		50 pence	1/4oz	584,946	£50
2013	Silver Proof	£1.00	1/2oz	Set only	–
2013	Silver Proof	£2.00	1oz	3,468	£125
2013	Silver Bullion (Nathan Reverse)				
		£2.00	1oz	Unlimited	£35
2013	Silver Bullion (Year of the Snake Privy Mark)				
		£2.00	1oz	Unlimited	£40
2013	Silver BU	£2.00	1oz	2,387	£35
2013	Silver Proof	£10.00	5oz	4,054	£450
2013	Silver Proof Set	£2, £1, 50p , 20p and 10 pence		3,087	£250
2013	Gold Proof	£1.00	1/20oz	2,496	£150
2013	Gold Proof	£10.00	1/10oz	1,150	£300
2013	Gold Proof	£25.00	1/4oz	Set only	–
2013	Gold Bullion (Nathan Reverse)				
		£25.00	1/4oz	Unlimited	BV
2013	Gold Proof	£50.00	1/2oz	Set only	–
2013	Gold Bullion (Nathan Reverse)				
		£50.00	1/2oz	Unlimited	BV
2013	Gold Proof	£100.00	1oz	Set only	–
2013	Gold Bullion (Nathan Reverse)				
		£100.00	1oz	Unlimited	BV
2013	Gold Proof	£500.00	5oz	61	£10,100
2013	Gold Proof Set	£50, £25 and £10		136	£2200
2013	Gold Proof Set (Premium)	£50, £25 and £10		90	£2500
2013	Gold Proof Set	£100, £50, £25 and £10		261	£4300

STANDING BRITANNIA WITH GLOBE
***Obverse* by Ian Rank-Broadley**
***Reverse* by Jody Clark**

Date	Metal	Face value	Weight	No. struck	Value
2014	Silver Proof	5 pence	1/40oz	Set only	–
2014	Silver Proof	10 pence	1/20oz	Set only	–
2014	Silver Proof	20 pence	1/10oz	Set only	–
2014	Silver Proof	50 pence	1/4oz	Set only	–
2014	Silver Bullion (SS *Gairsoppa*) Nathan Reverse				
		50 pence	1/4oz	19,214	£30
2014	Silver Proof	£1.00	1/2oz	Set only	–
2014	Silver Proof	£2.00	1oz	2,981	£350
2014	Silver Proof Gilded Britannia 24k Gold				
		£2.00	1oz	5,000	£120
2014	Silver Bullion (Nathan Reverse)				
		£2.00	1oz	623,741	£25
2014	Silver Bullion (Year of the Horse Privy Mark)				
		£2.00	1oz	Unlimited	£50
2014	Silver Bullion Year of the Horse Obverse Mule				
		£2.00	1oz	Unknown	–
2014	Silver BU	£2.00	1oz	1,493	£35
2014	Silver Proof	£10.00	5oz	1,348	£500
2014	Silver Proof Set	20p, 10p and 5 pence		998	£75
2014	Silver Proof Set	£2, £1, 50p , 20p and 10 pence		550	£500
2014	Silver Proof Set	£2, £1, 50p , 20p, 10p and 5 pence		1,735	£540
2014	Gold Proof	50 pence	1/40oz	5,521	£150
2014	Gold Proof	£1.00	1/20oz	993	£300
2014	Gold Proof	£10.00	1/10oz	Set only	–
2014	Gold Bullion (Nathan Reverse)				
		£10.00	1/10oz	Unlimited	BV

Date	Metal	Face value	Weight	No. struck	Value
2014	Gold Proof	£25.00	1/4oz	Set only	—
2014	Gold Bullion (Nathan Reverse)				
		£25.00	1/4oz	Unlimited	BV
2014	Gold Proof	£50.00	1/2oz	Set only	—
2014	Gold Bullion (Nathan Reverse)				
		£50.00	1/2oz	Unlimited	BV
2014	Gold Proof	£100.00	1oz	Set only	—
2014	Gold Bullion (Nathan Reverse)				
		£100.00	1oz	Unlimited	BV
2014	Gold Proof	£500.00	5oz	75	£13,000
2014	Gold Proof Set	£50, £25 and £10		140	£2500
2014	Gold Proof Set (Premium)	£50, £25 and £10		98	£3000
2014	Gold Proof Set	£100, £50, £25, £10 and £1		150	£5000
2014	Gold Proof Set (Premium)				
		£100, £50, £25, £10, £1 and 50 pence		225	£5500

BRITANNIA WITH TRIDENT
***Obverse* by Ian Rank-Broadley**
***Reverse* by Antony Dufort**

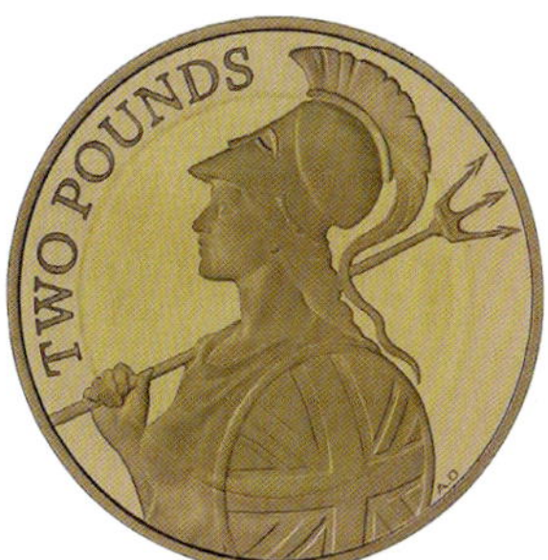

Date	Metal	Face value	Weight	No. struck	Value
2015	Silver Proof	5 pence	1/40oz	8,000	£15
2015	Silver Proof	10 pence	1/20oz	Set only	—
2015	Silver Proof	20 pence	1/10oz	Set only	—
2015	Silver Proof	50 pence	1/4oz	Set only	—
2015	Silver Proof	£1.00	1/2oz	Set only	—
2015	Silver Proof	£2.00	1oz	2,990	£70
2015	Silver Proof First Release				
		£2.00	1oz	1,250	£100
2015	Silver Proof Gilded Britannia 24k Gold				
		£2.00	1oz	5,000	£90
2015	Silver Bullion (Nathan Reverse)				
		£2.00	1oz	2,780,529	BV
2015	Silver Bullion (Year of the Sheep Privy Mark)				
		£2.00	1oz	1,000	£50
2015	Silver BU	£2.00	1oz	2,870	£30
2015	Silver Proof	£10.00	5oz	495	£500
2015	Silver Proof First Release				
		£10.00	5oz	500	£550
2015	Silver Proof	£50.00	31g	78,644	£65
2015	Silver Proof Set	£2, £1, 50p , 20p, 10p and 5 pence		1,009	£300
2015	Silver Proof Set First Release				
		£2, £1, 50p , 20p and 10 pence		550	£350
2015	Gold Proof	50 pence	1/40oz	3,075	£50
2015	Gold Proof	£1.00	1/20oz	Set only	—
2015	Gold Proof	£10.00	1/10oz	Set only	—
2015	Gold Bullion (Nathan Reverse)				
		£10.00	1/10oz	Unlimited	BV
2015	Gold Proof	£25.00	1/4oz	Set only	—
2015	Gold Bullion (Nathan Reverse)				
		£25.00	1/4oz	Unlimited	BV
2015	Gold Proof	£50.00	1/2oz	Set only	—
2015	Gold Bullion (Nathan Reverse)				
		£50.00	1/2oz	Unlimited	BV
2015	Gold Proof	£100.00	1oz	Set only	—
2014	Gold Bullion (Nathan Reverse)				
		£100.00	1oz	Unlimited	BV
2015	Gold Proof	£500.00	5oz	50	£10100
2015	Gold Proof First Release				
		£500.00	5oz	10	£12000
2015	Gold Proof Set	£50, £25 and £10		176	£2300
2015	Gold Proof Set (Premium)	£50, £25 and £10		99	£2500
2015	Gold Proof Set	£100, £50, £25, £10 and £1		96	£4750
2015	Gold Proof Set	£100, £50, £25, £10, £1 and 50 pence		138	£5200

Date	Metal	Face value	Weight	No. struck	Value

BRITANNIA AS WARRIOR QUEEN
***Obverse* by Jody Clark**
***Reverse* by Suzie Zamit**

Date	Metal	Face value	Weight	No. struck	Value
2016	Silver Proof	5 pence	1/40oz	Set only	–
2016	Silver Proof	10 pence	1/20oz	Set only	–
2016	Silver Proof	20 pence	1/10oz	Set only	–
2016	Silver Proof	50 pence	1/4oz	Set only	–
2016	Silver Proof	£1.00	1/2oz	Set only	–
2016	Silver Proof	£2.00	1oz	4,137	£100
2016	Silver Proof First Release				
		£2.00	1oz	416	£120
2016	Silver Bullion (Nathan Reverse)				
		£2.00	1oz	Unlimited	BV
2016	Silver Bullion (Year of the Monkey Privy Mark)				
		£2.00	1oz	1,000	£40
2016	Silver BU	£2.00	1oz	2,901	£40
2016	Silver BU	£2.00	1oz in Capsule	1,000	£40
2016	Silver Proof	£10.00	5oz	533	£450
2016	Silver Proof First Release				
		£10.00	5oz	25	£500
2016	Silver Proof 1oz Suzie Zamit and 1oz Nathan Reverse			500	£90
2016	Silver Proof Set £2, £1, 50p , 20p, 10p and 5 pence			1,050	£300
2016	Silver Proof Set Ultra Cameo Slabbed				
		£2, £1, 50p , 20p and 10 pence		250	£325
2016	Gold Proof	50 pence	1/40oz	1,447	£70
2016	Gold Proof	£1.00	1/20oz	Set only	–
2016	Gold Proof	£10.00	1/10oz	Set only	–
2016	Gold Proof	£25.00	1/4oz	620	£700
2016	Gold Proof First Release				
		£25.00	1/4oz	100	£800
2016	Gold Proof	£50.00	1/2oz	Set only	–
2016	Gold Proof	£100.00	1oz	Set only	–
2016	Gold Bullion (Nathan Reverse)				
		£100.00	1oz	Unlimited	BV
2016	Gold Proof	£500.00	5oz	54	£12,000
2016	Gold Proof First Release				
		£500.00	5oz	10	£13,000
2016	Gold Proof Set	£50, £25 and £10		69	
2016	Gold Proof Set	£100, £50, £25, £10, £1 and 50 pence		174	£8000

HELMETED OUTLINE OF BRITAIN
***Obverse* by Jody Clark**
***Reverse* by Louis Tamlyn**

Date	Metal	Face value	Weight	No. struck	Value
2017	Silver Proof	5 pence	1/40oz	Set only	–
2017	Silver Proof	10 pence	1/20oz	Set only	–
2017	Silver Proof	20 pence	1/10oz	Set only	–
2017	Silver Proof	50 pence	1/4oz	Set only	–
2017	Silver Proof	£1.00	1/2oz	Set only	–
2017	Silver BU	£2.00	1oz	3,977	£30
2017	Silver Proof	£2.00	1oz	5,225	£90
2017	Silver Bullion (Nathan Reverse)				
		£2.00	1oz	Unlimited	BV
2017	Silver Bullion (30th Anniversary Trident Privy Mark)				
		£2.00	1oz	120,000	£34
2017	Silver Bullion (Year of the Rooster Privy Mark)				
		£2.00	1oz	Unlimited	BV
2017	Silver Proof	£10.00	5oz	656	£500
2017	Silver Proof	£250.00	20oz	103	£2250
2017	Silver Proof Set £2, £1, 50p , 20p, 10p and 5 pence			1,347	£200
2017	Gold Proof	50 pence	1/40oz	871	£80
2017	Gold Proof	£1.00	1/20oz	Set only	–
2017	Gold Proof	£10.00	1/10oz	Set only	–

Date	Metal	Face value	Weight	No. struck	Value
2017	Gold bullion (Nathan Reverse)				
		£10.00	1/10oz	Set only	—
2017	Gold Proof	£25.00	1/4oz	687	£620
2017	Gold Bullion (Nathan Reverse)				
		£25.00	1/4oz	Set only	—
2017	Gold Proof	£50.00	1/2oz	Set only	—
2017	Gold Bullion (Nathan Reverse)				
		£50.00	1/2oz	Unlimited	BV
2017	Gold Proof	£100.00	1oz	Set only	—
2017	Gold Bullion (Nathan Reverse)				
		£100.00	1oz	Unlimited	BV
2017	Gold Bullion (30th Anniversary Trident Privy Mark)				
		£100.00	1oz	7,030	BV
2017	Gold Proof	£500.00	5oz	98	£10,100
2017	Gold Proof (30th Anniversary Trident Privy Mark)				
		£500.00	30oz	6	—
2017	Gold Proof Set	£50, £25 and £10		143	£2300
017	Gold Proof Set	£100, £50, £25, £10 and £1		62	£4750
2017	Gold Proof Set	£100, £50, £25, £10, £1 and 50 pence		176	£5200
2017	Platinum Bullion (Nathan Reverse)				
		£10	1/10oz	Unlimited	BV
2017	Platinum Proof	£25.00	1/4oz	538	£640
2017	Platinum Bullion (Nathan Reverse)				
		£25.00	1/4oz	Unlimited	BV
2017	Platinum Bullion (Nathan Reverse)				
		£100.00	1oz	Unlimited	BV

BRITANNIA FACING RIGHT WEARING A CORINTHIAN HELMET
***Obverse* by Jody Clark**
***Reverse* by David Lawrence**

Date	Metal	Face value	Weight	No. struck	Value
2018	Silver Proof	5 pence	1/40oz	Set only	—
2018	Silver Proof	10 pence	1/20oz	Set only	—
2018	Silver Proof	20 pence	1/10oz	Set only	—
2018	Silver Proof	50 pence	1/4oz	Set only	—
2018	Silver Proof	£1.00	1/2oz	Set only	—
2018	Silver Proof	£2.00	1oz	5,100	£85
2018	Silver Bullion (Nathan Reverse)				
		£2.00	1oz	Unlimited	BV
2018	Silver Bullion (Year of the Dog Privy Mark)				
		£2	1oz	Unlimited	£26
2018	Silver Bullion “Oriental Border” (Nathan Reverse)				
		£2.00	1oz	100,000	BV
2018	BU	£2.00	1oz	7,000	BV
2018	Silver Proof	£10.00	5oz	650	£420
2018	Silver Proof	£500.00	1kg	150	£2050
2018	Silver Proof Set	£2, £1, 50p , 20p, 10p and 5 pence		1,350	£210
2018	Gold Proof	50 pence	1/40oz	Set only	—
2018	Gold Proof	£1.00	1/20oz	Set only	—
2018	Gold Proof	£10.00	1/10oz	Set only	—
2018	Gold bullion (Nathan Reverse)				
		£10.00	1/10oz	Unlimited	BV
2018	Gold Proof	£25.00	1/4oz	1,080	£630
2018	Gold Bullion (Nathan Reverse)				
		£25.00	1/4oz	Unlimited	BV
2018	Gold Proof	£50.00	1/2oz	Set only	—
2018	Gold Bullion (Nathan Reverse)				
		£50.00	1/2oz	Set only	—
2018	Gold Bullion (Nathan Reverse)				
		£100.00	1oz	Unlimited	BV
2018	Gold bullion “Oriental Border” (Nathan Reverse)				
		£100.00	1oz	5,000	BV
2018	Gold Proof	£500.00	5oz	90	£10,100

Date	Metal	Face value	Weight	No. struck	Value
2018	Gold Proof Set	£100, £50, £25, £10, £1 and 50 pence		220	£4400
2018	Gold Proof Set	£50, £25 and £10		170	£1945
2018	Platinum Bullion (Nathan Reverse)				
		£100.00	1oz	5,000	BV
2018	Platinum Proof	£25.00	1/4oz	630	£650
2018	Platinum Bullion (Nathan Reverse)				
		£25.00	1/4oz	Unlimited	BV
2018	Platinum Bullion (Nathan Reverse)				
		£10	1/10oz	Unlimited	BV

STANDING BRITANNIA IN WARLIKE POSE
***Obverse* by Jody Clark**
***Reverse* by David Lawrence**

Date	Metal	Face value	Weight	No. struck	Value
2019	Silver Proof	5 pence	1/40oz	Set only	–
2019	Silver Proof	10 pence	1/20oz	Set only	–
2019	Silver Proof	20 pence	1/10oz	Set only	–
2019	Silver Proof	50 pence	1/4oz	Set only	–
2019	Silver Proof	£1.00	1/2oz	Set only	–
2019	Silver Proof	£2.00	1oz	5,200	£90
2019	Silver Proof Coin and Print Set				
		£2.00	1oz	200 each frame colour	£300
2019	Silver Bullion 'Oriental Border' (Nathan Reverse)				
		£2.00	1oz	Unlimited	BV
2019	Silver Bullion (Nathan Reverse)				
		£2.00	1oz	Unlimited	BV
2019	Silver Bullion (Year of the Pig Privy Mark)				
		£2.00	1oz	Unknown	£34
2019	BU (Year of the Pig Privy Mark)				
		£2.00	1oz	Unknown	
2019	Silver BU	£2.00	1oz	10,000	£60
2019	Silver BU	£10.00	5oz	250	£500
2019	Silver Proof	£500.00	1kg	85	£2050
2019	Silver Proof Set	£2, £1, 50p , 20p, 10p and 5 pence		950	£300
2019	Gold Proof	50 pence	1/40oz	Set only	–
2019	Gold Proof	£1.00	1/20oz	Set only	–
2019	Gold Proof	£10.00	1/10oz	Set only	–
2019	Gold bullion (Nathan Reverse)				
		£10.00	1/10oz	Unlimited	BV
2019	Gold Proof	£25.00	1/4oz	630	£555
2019	Gold Bullion (Nathan Reverse)				
		£25.00	1/4oz	Unlimited	BV
2019	Gold Proof	£50.00	1/2oz	Set only	–
2019	Gold Bullion (Nathan Reverse)				
		£50.00	1/2oz	Unlimited	BV
2019	Gold Bullion (Nathan Reverse)				
		£100.00	1oz	Unlimited	BV
2019	Gold bullion "Oriental Border" (Nathan Reverse)				
		£100.00	1oz	Unlimited	BV
2019	Gold Proof	£200.00	2oz	100	£4600
2019	Gold Proof	£500.00	5oz	57	£10,100
2019	Gold Proof Set	£100, £50, £25, £10, £1 and 50 pence		150	£4300
2019	Gold Proof Set	£50, £25 and £10		130	£2300
2019	Platinum Bullion (Nathan Reverse)				
		£10	1/10oz	Unlimited	BV
2019	Platinum Proof	£25.00	1/4oz	240	£650
2019	Platinum Bullion (Nathan Reverse)				
		£100.00	1oz	Unlimited	BV

STANDING BRITANNIA WITH UNION FLAG BACKGROUND
***Obverse* by Jody Clark**
***Reverse* by James Tottle**

Date	Metal	Face value	Weight	No. struck	Value
2020	Silver Proof	5 pence	1/40oz	Set only	–
2020	Silver Proof	10 pence	1/20oz	Set only	–
2020	Silver Proof	20 pence	1/10oz	Set only	–
2020	Silver Proof	50 pence	1/4oz	Set only	–
2020	Silver Proof	£1.00	1/2oz	Set only	–
2020	Silver Proof	£2.00	1oz	3,000	£85
2020	Silver Proof Coin and Print Set	£2.00	1oz	100	£245
2020	Silver Bullion (Nathan Reverse)	£2.00	1oz	Unlimited	BV
2020	Silver Bullion (Year of the Rat Privy Mark)	£2.00	1oz	Unlimited	£26
2020	Silver Proof Set: 1 x frosted reverse, 1 x standard	2 x £2	1oz	700	£170
2020	BU	£2.00	1oz	3,000	BV
2020	Silver Proof	£10.00	5oz	250	£420
2020	Silver Proof	£500.00	1kg	30	£2050
2020	Silver Proof Set	£2, £1, 50p , 20p, 10p and 5 pence		1,000	£210
2020	Gold Proof	50 pence	1/40oz	Set only	–
2020	Gold Proof	£1.00	1/20oz	Set only	–
2020	Gold Proof	£10.00	1/10oz	Set only	–
2020	Gold bullion (Nathan Reverse)	£10.00	1/10oz	Unlimited	BV
2020	Gold Proof	£25.00	1/4oz	700	£650
2020	Gold Bullion (Nathan Reverse)	£25.00	1/4oz	Unlimited	BV
2020	Gold Proof	£50.00	1/2oz	Set only	–
2020	Gold Bullion (Nathan Reverse)	£50.00	1/2oz	Set only	–
2020	Gold Proof	£100.00	1oz	Coin and print set 25	£2750
2020	Gold Bullion (Nathan Reverse)	£100.00	1oz	Unlimited	BV
2020	Gold bullion "Oriental Border" (Nathan Reverse)	£100.00	1oz	Unlimited	BV
2020	Gold Proof	£200.00	2oz	150	£4500
2020	Gold Proof Set	£100, £50, £25, £10, £1 and 50 pence		150	£4300
2020	Gold Proof Set	£50, £25 and £10		130	£2000
2020	Gold Proof Coin and Print Set	£100	1oz	25	£2750
2020	Gold Proof	£500	5oz	50	£11,000
2020	Platinum Bullion (Nathan Reverse)	£10	1/10oz	Unlimited	BV
2020	Platinum Proof	£25.00	1/4oz	160	£650
2020	Platinum Bullion (Nathan Reverse)	£25.00	1/4oz	Unlimited	BV
2020	Platinum Bullion (Nathan Reverse)	£100.00	1oz	Unlimited	BV

Most of the later prices given above are the original Royal Mint issue prices as very few of the coins have come onto the market.

BRITANNIA SEATED WITH LION AND BRITANNIA IN PROFILE FOR PREMIUM EXCLUSIVE COINS

***Obverse* by Jody Clark**
***Reverse* by P.J. Lynch**

Date	Metal	Face value	Weight	No. struck	Value
2021	Silver Proof	5 pence	1/40oz	Set only	—
2021	Silver Proof	10 pence	1/20oz	Set only	—
2021	Silver Proof	20 pence	1/10oz	Set only	—
2021	Silver Proof	50 pence	1/4oz	Set only	—
2021	Silver Proof	£1.00	1/2oz	Set only	—
2021	Silver Proof Britannia Seated with Lion				
		£2.00	1oz	2,900	£95
2021	Silver Bullion (Nathan Reverse)				
		£2.00	1oz	Unlimited	BV
2021	Silver Proof set Britannia Seated with Lion - 1 x frosted reverse, 1 x standard				
		2 x £2	1oz	500	£185
2021	Premium Exclusive (Britannia in Profile) BU				
		£2.00	1oz	7,500 (7,510 struck)	£60
	Silver Proof (Britannia seated with Lion)				
		£2.00	1oz	4860	£100
2021	Silver Proof Premium Exclusive (Britannia in Profile)				
		£5.00	2oz	550 (560 struck)	£200
2021	Silver Proof (Britannia seated with Lion)				
		£10.00	5oz	285	£475
2021	Premium Exclusive' Britannia in Profile Silver Proof				
		£500.00	1kg	40 (50 Struck)	£2500
2021	Silver Proof (Britannia seated with Lion)				
		£1000.00	2kg	110	£4890
2021	Silver Proof Set (Britannia seated with Lion)				
		£2, £1, 50p , 20p, 10p and 5 pence		1,100	£250
2021	Gold Proof	50 pence	1/40oz	Set only	—
2021	Gold Proof	£1.00	1/20oz	Set only	—
2021	Gold Proof	£10.00	1/10oz	Set only	—
2021	Gold bullion (Nathan Reverse)				
		£10.00	1/10oz	Unlimited	BV
2021	Gold Proof Set (Britannia seated with Lion)				
		£25.00	1/4oz	775 (1060 minted)	£700
2021	Gold Bullion (Nathan Reverse)				
		£25.00	1/4oz	Unlimited	BV
2021	Gold Proof	£50.00	1/2oz	Set only	
2021	Gold Bullion (Nathan Reverse)				
		£50.00	1/2oz	Set only	BV
2021	Gold Bullion (Nathan Reverse)				
		£100.00	1oz	Unlimited	BV
2021	Gold Proof (Britannia seated with Lion)				
		£200.00	2oz	103	£8200
			Sold price at LondonCoin Auctions		
2021	Gold Proof Premium Exclusive (Britannia in Profile)				
		£200.00	2oz	220 (230 struck)	£4750
2021	Gold Proof (Britannia seated with Lion)				
		£500.00	5oz	83	£12,000
2021	Gold Proof Premium (Britannia in Profile)				
		£1000.00	1kg	5 (6 struck)	£85,000
2021	Gold Proof Premium Exclusive (Britannia in Profile)				
	£100, £50, £25, £10, £1 and 50 pence			150	£5500
2021	Gold Proof Set (Briannia seated with Lion)				
		£50, £25 and £10		115	£2300
2021	Platinum Bullion (Nathan Reverse)				
		£10	1/10oz	Unlimited	BV
2021	Platinum Proof (Britannia seated with Lion)				
		£25.00	1/4oz	150	£650
2021	Platinum Bullion (Nathan Reverse)				
		£100.00	1oz	Unlimited	BV

Date	Metal	Face value	Weight	No. struck	Value

BRITANNIA WITH LION SHIELD ON PROOF COIN REVERSE. THREE AGES OF BRITANNIA IN PROFILE FOR EXCLUSIVE EDITION
Mintage (Brackets indicate maximum struck). Values—Royal Mint issue price
***Obverse* by Jody Clark**
***Reverse* by Dan Thorne (unless stated otherwise).**

Date	Metal	Face value	Weight	No. struck	Value
2022	Silver Proof	5 pence	1/40oz	Set only	—
2022	Silver Proof	10 pence	1/20oz	Set only	—
2022	Silver Proof	20 pence	1/10oz	Set only	—
2022	Silver Proof	50 pence	1/4oz	Set only	—
2022	Silver Proof	£1.00	1/2oz	Set only	—
2022	Silver Proof	£2.00	1oz	3,500 (3,610)	£95
2022	Silver Bullion (Nathan Reverse)	£2.00	1oz	Unlimited	BV
2022	Silver BU Exclusive Edition Sandra Deiana Three Women Reverse		1oz	5,000 (5,010)	£63
2022	Silver Proof Set 1 x frosted reverse, 1 x standard	2 x £2	1oz	1,110	£170
2022	Silver Proof Exclusive Edition Sandra Deiana Three Women Reverse	£5.00	2oz	550 (556)	£200
2022	Silver Proof	£10.00	5oz	350 (386)	£500
2022	Silver Proof Exclusive Edition Sandra Deiana Three Women Reverse	£500.00	1kg	40 (43)	£2500
2022	Silver Proof	£1000.00	2kg	75 (78)	£5000
2022	Silver Proof Set £2, £1, 50p , 20p, 10p and 5 pence			1,300 (1,310)	£250
2022	Gold Proof	50 pence	1/40oz	Set only	—
2022	Gold Proof	£1.00	1/20oz	Set only	—
2022	Gold Proof	£10.00	1/10oz	Set only	—
2022	Gold bullion (Nathan Reverse)	£10.00	1/10oz	Unlimited	BV
2022	Gold Proof	£25.00	1/4oz	775	£725
2022	Gold Bullion (Nathan Reverse)	£25.00	1/4oz	Unlimited	BV
2022	Gold Proof	£50.00	1/2oz	Set only	
2022	Gold Bullion (Nathan Reverse)	£50.00	1/2oz	Unlimited	BV
2022	Gold Bullion (Nathan Reverse)	£100.00	1oz	Unlimited	BV
2022	Gold Proof	£200.00	2oz	100 (106)	£5800
2022	Gold Proof Exclusive Edition Sandra Deiana Three Women Reverse	£200.00	2oz	100 (106)	£5500
2022	Gold Proof	£500.00	5oz	100 (106)	£14,000
2022	Gold Proof Exclusive Edition Sandra Deiana Three Women Reverse	£1000.00	1kg	5 (6)	£80,000
2022	Gold Proof 6 Coin Set	£100, £50, £25, £10, £1 and 50 pence		150	£5500
2022	Gold Proof 3 Coin Set	£50, £25 and £10		150	£2400
2022	Platinum Bullion (Nathan Reverse)	£10	1/10oz	Unlimited	BV
2022	Platinum Proof	£25.00	1/4oz	150 (160)	£650
2022	Platinum Bullion (Nathan Reverse)	£100.00	1oz	Unlimited	BV

BRITANNIA STANDING ON BULLION ISSUES
***Obverse* by Jody Clark—Queen Elizabeth II or Martin Jennings—King Charles III**
***Reverse* by Philip Nathan**

BRITANNIA WITH SEA CHARIOT AND HORSES ON PROOF ISSUES
Mintage (Brackets indicate maximum struck). Values—Royal Mint issue price
***Obverse* by Martin Jennings—King Charles III**
***Reverse* by Jonathan Olliffe**

Date	Metal	Face value	Weight	No. struck	Value
2023	Silver Proof	5 pence	1/40oz	Set only	—
2023	Silver Proof	10 pence	1/20oz	Set only	—
2023	Silver Proof	20 pence	1/10oz	Set only	—
2023	Silver Proof	50 pence	1/4oz	Set only	—
2023	Silver Proof	£1	1/2oz	Set only	—
2023	Silver Proof	£2	1oz	3,450 (5,210)	£99
2023	Silver Bullion (Nathan Reverse)				
	QEII	£2	1oz	Unlimited	BV
2023	Silver Bullion (Nathan Reverse)				
	KCIII	£2	1oz	Unlimited	BV
2023	Silver Proof set (Frosted reverse)				
		2 x £2	1oz	520	£170
2023	Silver Proof	£5	2oz	1,000 (1,010)	£170
2023	Silver Proof	£10	5oz	420	£490
2023	Silver Bullion (Nathan Reverse)				
	QEII	£500	1kg	Unlimited	BV
2023	Silver Bullion (Nathan Reverse)				
	KCIII	£500	1kg	Unlimited	BV
2023	Silver Proof Frosted Reverse Set 5p, 10p, 50p & £2			350	£175
2023	Silver Proof Set £2, £1, 50p , 20p, 10p and 5 pence			950	£250
2023	Gold Proof	50 pence	1/40oz	Set only	—
2023	Gold Proof	£1	1/20oz	Set only	—
2023	Gold Proof	£10	1/10oz	Set only	—
2023	Gold Bullion (Nathan Reverse)				
	QEII	£10	1/10oz	Unlimited	BV
2023	Gold Bullion (Nathan Reverse)				
	KCIII	£10	1/10oz	Unlimited	BV
2023	Gold Proof	£25	1/4oz	970 (1,345)	£725
2023	Gold Bullion (Nathan Reverse)				
	QEII	£25	1/4oz	Unlimited	BV
2023	Gold Bullion (Nathan Reverse)				
	KCIII	£25	1/4oz	Unlimited	BV
2023	Gold Proof	£50	1/2oz	Set only	—
2023	Gold Bullion (Nathan Reverse)				
	QEII	£50	1/2oz	Unlimited	BV
2023	Gold Bullion (Nathan Reverse)				
	KCIII	£50	1/2oz	Unlimited	BV
2023	Gold Proof	£100	1oz	Set Only	—
2023	Gold Bullion (Nathan Reverse)				
	QEII	£100	1oz	Unlimited	BV
2023	Gold Bullion (Nathan Reverse)				
	KCIII	£100	1oz	Unlimited	BV
2023	Gold Proof	£200	2oz	125	£5000
2023	Gold Proof	£500	5oz	65	£14,000
2023	Gold Proof Set £100, £50, £25, £10, £1 and 50 pence			175	£5500
2023	Gold Proof Set £50, £25 and £10			150	£2700
2023	Gold Proof Frosted Reverse Set				
	50p, £1, £25 and £100			50	£3750
2023	Platinum Proof	£25	1/4oz	200	£650
2023	Platinum Bullion (Nathan Reverse) 1oz/£100			—	BV
2023	Platinum Bullion (Nathan Reverse) QEII 2kg			—	BV

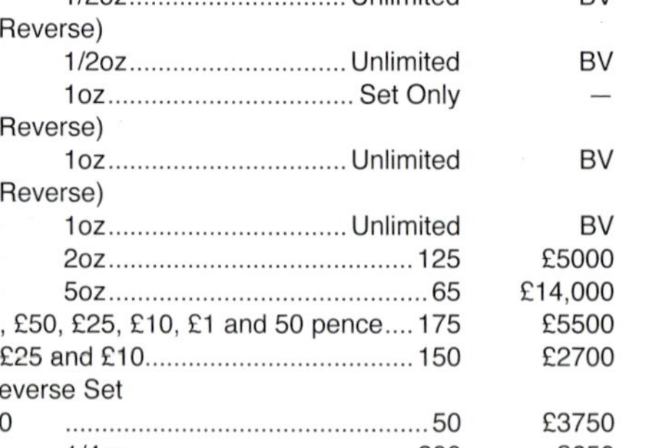

Date	Metal	Face value	Weight	No. struck	Value

BRITANNIA AND LIBERTY
Mintage (Brackets indicate maximum struck). Values—Royal Mint issue price
***Obverse* by Martin Jennings**
Reverse by Gordon Summers/Joseph Menna

Date	Metal	Face value	Weight	No. struck	Value
2024	Silver Proof	£2	1oz	12,300 (12,560)	£99.50
2024	Silver Bullion	£2	1oz	260,000 max	BV
2024	Silver Proof	£5	2oz	1500 (1510)	£190
2024	Silver Proof	£10	5oz	500 (506)	£480
2024	Silver Proof	£500	1kg	75 (77)	£2,390
2024	Gold Proof	50p	1/40oz	1776 (1,786)	£85
2024	Gold Proof	£25	1/4oz	700 (760)	£750
2024	Gold Bullion	£25	1/4oz	Unlimited	BV
2024	Gold Proof	£100	1oz	800 (810)	£2,770
2024	Gold Bullion	£100	1oz	Unlimited	BV
2024	Gold Proof	£1,000	1kg	8 (10)	£77,565

BRITANNIA WITH WAVE AND CRESCENT MOON ON PROOF ISSUES
Mintage (Brackets indicate maximum struck). Values—Royal Mint issue price
***Obverse* by Martin Jennings—King Charles III**
***Reverse* by Jonathan Olliffe**

Date	Metal	Face value	Weight	No. struck	Value
2024	Silver Proof	5 pence	1/40oz	Set only	—
2024	Silver Proof	10 pence	1/20oz	Set only	—
2024	Silver Proof	20 pence	1/10oz	Set only	—
2024	Silver Bullion (Nathan Reverse)	20 pence	1/10oz	Unlimited	BV
2024	Silver Proof	50 pence	1/4oz	Set only	—
2024	Silver Proof	£1	1/2oz	Set only	—
2024	Silver Proof	£2	1oz	3500 (5610)	£103.50
2024	Silver Bullion (Nathan Reverse)	£2	1oz	Unlimited	BV
2024	Silver Proof set (Frosted reverse)	2 x £2	1oz	850	£199
2024	Silver Proof	£5	2oz	1250 (1256)	£195
2024	Silver Proof	£10	5oz	550 (556)	£490
2024	Silver Bullion (Nathan Reverse)	£500	1kg	Unlimited	BV
2024	Silver Proof Frosted Reverse Set 5p, 10p, 50p & £2			1000	£170
2024	Silver Proof Set £2, £1, 50p , 20p, 10p and 5 pence			1250	£250
2024	Gold Proof	50 pence	1/40oz	2024 (2284)	£99.50
2024	Gold Proof	£1	1/20oz	Set only	—
2024	Gold Proof	£10	1/10oz	Set only	—
2024	Gold Bullion (Nathan Reverse)	£10	1/10oz	Unlimited	BV
2024	Gold Proof	£25	1/4oz	1000 (1760)	£750
2024	Gold Bullion (Nathan Reverse)	£25	1/4oz	Unlimited	BV
2024	Gold Proof	£50	1/2oz	Set only	—
2024	Gold Bullion (Nathan Reverse)	£50	1/2oz	Unlimited	BV
2024	Gold Proof	£100	1oz	Set Only	—
2024	Gold Bullion (Nathan Reverse)	£100	1oz	Unlimited	BV
2024	Premium Proof Set £100, £50, £25, £10, £1 & 50 pence			250	£5125
2024	Gold Proof Set £50, £25 and £10			500	£1125
2024	Platinum Bullion (Nathan Reverse)	£10	1/10oz	Unlimited	BV
2024	Platinum Bullion (Nathan Reverse)	£100	1oz	Unlimited	BV

PRECIOUS METAL BULLION AND COLLECTOR COINS (SERIES)

The Shengxiào Lunar Collection

The Shengxiào Collection of Lunar Coins by designer Wuon-Gean Ho was begun for the Year of the Horse in 2014 bringing the Royal Mint in line with most other major mints of the world. The Shengxiào series ended in 2018 but the Lunar series continues to be issued each year. We list them separately here, however, the larger denominatiions have also been listed under their respective headings.

Date	Weight Face value/	Auth. issue qty	No. Issued	Issue price
2014 YEAR OF THE HORSE				
Silver bullion	1 ounce /£2	—	—	BV
Silver Proof	1 ounce/£2	8,888	—	£85
Silver Proof	5 ounces/£10	1,488	—	£450
Gold BU	One-tenth ounce/£10	2,888	1,779	£225
Gold bullion	1 ounce/£100	—	—	BV
Gold Proof	1 ounce/£100	888	811	£1950
2015 YEAR OF THE SHEEP				
Silver bullion	1 ounce /£2	—	—	BV
Silver Proof	1 ounce/£2	9,888	4,463	£85
Silver Proof with gold plating	1 ounce/£2	4,888	1,358	£120
Silver Proof	5 ounces/£10	1,088	—	£395
Gold BU	One-tenth ounce/£10	2,888	922	£225
Gold bullion	1 ounce/£100	—	—	BV
Gold Proof	1 ounce/£100	888	548	£1950
Gold Proof	5 ounces/£500	38	—	£7500
2016 YEAR OF THE MONKEY				
Silver bullion	1 ounce /£2	—	—	BV
Silver Proof	1 ounce/£2	8,888	—	£85
Silver Proof	5 ounces/£10	588	—	£395
Silver Proof	1 kilo/£500	88	—	£2000
Gold BU	One-tenth ounce/£10	1,888	—	£175
Gold bullion	1 ounce/£100	—	—	BV
Gold Proof	1 ounce/£100	888	—	£1495
Gold Proof	5 ounces/£500	38	—	£7500
Gold Proof	1 kilo/£1,000	8	—	£42,500
2017 YEAR OF THE ROOSTER				
Silver bullion	1 ounce /£2	—	—	BV
Silver Proof	1 ounce/£2	3,888	3,846	£85
Silver Proof	5 ounces/£10	388	369	£415
Silver Proof	1 kilo/£500	88	—	£2050
Gold BU	One-tenth ounce/£10	2,088	980	£205
Gold bullion	1 ounce/£100	—	—	BV
Gold Proof	1 ounce/£100	688	—	£1780
Gold Proof	5 ounces/£500	38	35	£8250
Gold Proof	1 kilo/£1,000	8	8	£49,995
2018 YEAR OF THE DOG				
Silver bullion	1 ounce /£2	—	—	BV
Silver Proof	1 ounce/£2	5,088	—	£85
Silver Proof	5 ounces/£10	388	—	£415
Silver Proof	1 kilo/£500	108	—	£2050
Gold BU	One-tenth ounce/£10	1,088	—	£175
Gold bullion	1 ounce/£100	—	—	BV
Gold Proof	1 ounce/£100	888	—	£1795

The Lunar series, *continued*

From 2019 the Royal Mint has invited various artists to create the reverses for the Lunar serties as noted in each section below.

Date	Weight/ Face value	Auth. issue qty	No. Issued	Issue price
2019 LUNAR YEAR OF THE PIG				
Obverse: Jody Clark Royal portrait Reverse: by Harry Brockway				
Silver bullion	1 ounce /£2	—	—	BV
Silver Proof	1 ounce/£2	3,888	—	£85
Silver Proof	5 ounces/£10	288	—	£420
Silver Proof	1 kilo/£500	38	—	£2025
Gold BU	One-tenth ounce/£10	1,088	—	£210
Gold bullion	1 ounce/£100	—	—	BV
Gold Proof	1 ounce/£100	888	—	£1880
Gold Proof	5 ounces/£500	38	—	£8645
Gold Proof	1 kilo/£1,000	8	—	—
2020 LUNAR YEAR OF THE RAT;				
Obverse: Jody Clark Royal portrait Reverse: by P. J. Lynch				
Silver bullion	1 ounce /£2	—	—	BV
Silver Proof	1 ounce/£2	2,588	—	£85
Silver Proof	5 ounces/£10	188	—	£420
Silver Proof	1 kilo/£500	28	—	£2050
Gold BU	One-tenth ounce/£10	1,088	—	£210
Gold Proof	Quarter ounce/£25	388	—	£530
Gold bullion	1 ounce/£100	—	—	BV
Gold Proof	1 ounce/£100	888	—	£2100
Gold Proof	5 ounces/£500	28	—	£9995
Gold Proof	1 kilo/£1,000	8	—	£59,995
2021 LUNAR YEAR OF THE OX;				
Obverse: Jody Clark Reverse: Harry Brockway				
Silver bullion	1 ounce /£2	—	—	BV
Silver Proof	1 ounce/£2	3,998	—	£85
Silver Proof	5 ounces/£10	198	—	£420
Silver Proof	1 kilo/£500	38	—	£2050
Gold Proof	Quarter ounce/£25	398	—	£585
Gold Proof	1 ounce/£100	898	—	£2,320
Gold Proof	5 ounces/£500	38	—	£10,605
Gold Proof	1 kilo/£1,000	10	—	£63,865
2022 LUNAR YEAR OF THE TIGER				
Obverse: Jody Clark Reverse: David Lawrence				
Gold Proof	1 kilo/£1000	10	—	£67,500
Gold Proof	Five ounces/£500	128	—	£11,125
Gold Proof	One ounce/£100	898	—	£2,440
Gold Proof	Quarter ounce/£25	398	—	£650
Silver Proof	1 kilo/£500	38	—	£2,330
Silver Proof	Five ounces/£10	228	—	£465
Silver Proof	One ounce/£2	3,998	—	£95
Cu-Ni BU	£5	—	—	£13
2023 LUNAR YEAR OF THE RABBIT				
Obverse: Jody Clark Reverse: Louie Maryon				
Gold Proof	1 kilo/£1000	10	—	£73,205
Gold Proof	Five ounces/£500	138	—	£12,015
Gold Proof	One ounce/£100	898	—	£2,625
Gold Proof	Quarter ounce/£25	398	—	£700
Silver Proof	1 kilo/£500	52	—	£2,330
Silver Proof	Five ounces/£10	238	—	£465
Silver Proof	One ounce/£2	3,998	—	£95
Cu-Ni BU	£5	—	—	£13

Date Face value/	Weight issue qty	Auth.No. Issued	Issue price
2024 LUNAR YEAR OF THE DRAGON			
Obverse: Martin Jennings Reverse: William Webb			
Gold Proof	Kilo/£1000	10	£77,565
Gold Proof	Five ounces/£500	138	£12,725
Gold Proof	One ounce/£100	898	£2,770
Gold Proof	Quarter Ounce/£25	398	£750
Silver Proof	Kilo/£500	52	£2,422.50
Silver Proof	Five ounces/£10	298	£485
Silver Proof	One Ounce/£2	5008	£102.50
Cu-Ni BU	£5	–	£14.50

The Queen's Beasts

In 2016 a new series of coins was introduced by the Royal Mint entitled "The Queen's Beasts". These are intended as a homage to Her Majesty becoming Britain's longest reigning monarch and each coin in the series represents one of the heraldic animals sculpted by James Woodford, RA, for the Coronation ceremony held in Westminster Abbey in 1953. The 6-foot tall sculptures each symbolised the various strands of royal ancestry and were inspired by the King's Beasts of Henry VIII that still line the bridge at Hampton Court. In total 20 different designs have been struck, 10 for bullion coins and 10 for collector coins in proof. The bullion coins all have a patterned background whilst the proof coins have a polished field. We have included only the proof collector coins here as the bullion coins, struck in 2oz and 10oz silver and 1oz platinum and gold, will be priced according to the prevailing precious metal values. The coins all carry the effigy of Her Majesty the Queen by Jody Clark on the obverse with the heraldic beasts, by the same designer, appearing on the reverse. ***PLEASE NOTE: The prices listed in this section, are the issue price. Certain series have proved more popular than others hence, a number of these precious metal Collector Series issues, such as*** **The Queen's Beasts** ***and*** **The Great Engravers*****, are now securing high prices on the secondary market. However, not ALL of these new issues are as collectable and trends can change.***

Date	Weight Face value/	Auth. issue qty	No. Issued	Issue price
THE LION OF ENGLAND				
2016 Silver bullion	2 ounces/£5	–	–	BV
2016 Gold bullion	1 ounce/£100	–	–	BV
2017 Cu-Ni BU	£5	–	31,838	£13
2017 Silver Proof	1 ounce/£2	8,500	8,376	£85
2017 Silver Proof	5 ounces/£10	2,500	674	£415
2017 Silver Proof	1 kilo/£500	350	117	£2050
2017 Gold Proof	Quarter ounce/£25	2,500	2,492	£475
2017 Gold Proof	1 ounce/£100	1,000	591	£1780
2017 Gold Proof	5 ounces/£500	125	100	£8250
2017 Gold proof	1 kilo/£1,000	–	13	£49,995
THE UNICORN OF SCOTLAND				
2017 Cu-Ni BU	£5	–	31,978	£13
2017 Silver Proof	1 ounce/£2	6,250	5,952	£85
2017 Silver Proof	5 ounces/£10	750	458	£415
2017 Silver Proof	10 ounces/£10	850	–	£795
2017 Silver Proof	1 kilo/£500	225	–	£2050
2017 Gold Proof	Quarter ounce/£25	1,500	1,499	£475
2017 Gold Proof	1 ounce/£100	500	418	£475
2017 Gold Proof	5 ounces/£500	–	75	£475
2017 Gold Proof	1 kilo/£1,000	–	8	£475
THE RED DRAGON OF WALES				
2018 Cu-Ni BU	£5	–	–	£13
2018 Silver Proof	1 ounce/£2	6,000	–	£85
2018 Silver Proof	5 ounces/£10	700	–	£420
2018 Silver Proof	10 ounces/£10	600	–	£795
2018 Silver Proof	1 kilo/£500	150	–	£2025
2018 Gold Proof	Quarter ounce/£25	1,500	–	£475
2018 Gold Proof	1 ounce/£100	500	–	£1850
2018 Gold Proof	5 ounces/£500	85	–	£8565
2018 Gold Proof	1 kilo/£1000	–	–	£49,995
THE BLACK BULL OF CLARENCE				
2018 Cu-Ni BU	£5	–	–	£13
2018 Silver Proof	1 ounce/£2	6,000	–	£85
2018 Silver Proof	5 ounces/£10	700	–	£420
2018 Silver Proof	10 ounces/£10	600	–	£795
2018 Silver Proof	1 kilo/£500	150	–	£2025
2018 Gold Proof	Quarter ounce/£25	1,500	1,499	£475
2018 Gold Proof	1 ounce/£100	500	–	£1850
2018 Gold Proof	5 ounces/£500	85	–	£8565
2018 Gold Proof	1 kilo/£1000	–	–	£49,995

Date	Weight Face value/	Auth. issue qty	No. Issued	Issue price
THE YALE OF BEAUFORT				
2019 Cu-Ni BU	£5	–	–	£13
2019 Silver Proof	1 ounce/£2	5,500	–	£85
2019 Silver Proof	5 ounces/£10	400	–	£420
2019 Silver Proof	10 ounces/£10	240	–	£795
2019 Silver Proof	1 kilo/£500	120	–	£2025
2019 Gold Proof	1/4 ounce/£25	1,250	–	£475
2019 Gold Proof	1 ounce/£100	400	–	£1850
2019 Gold Proof	5 ounces/£500	70	–	£8645
2019 Gold Proof	1 kilo/£1000	13	–	£59,995
FALCON OF THE PLANTAGENETS				
2019 Cu-Ni BU	£5	–	–	£13
2019 Silver Proof	1 ounce/£2	5,510	–	£85
2019 – Proof	5 ounces/£10	400	–	£420
2019 – Proof	10 ounces/£10	350	–	£795
2019 – Proof	1 kilo/£500	100	–	£2050
2019 Gold Proof	1/4 ounce/£25	1250	–	£475
2019 – Proof	1 ounce/£100	400	–	£1900
2019 – Proof	5 ounces/£500	75	–	£9995
2019 – Proof	1 kilo/£1000	10	–	£59,995
WHITE LION OF MORTIMER				
2020 Cu-Ni BU	£5	–	–	£13
2020 Silver Proof	1 ounce/£2	4,250	–	£85
2020 – Proof	5 ounces/£10	250	–	£420
2020 – Proof	10 ounces/£10	200	–	£795
2020 – Proof	1 kilo/£500	90	–	£2025
2020 Gold Proof	1/4 ounce/£25	1,000	–	£500
2020 – Proof	1 ounce/£100	390	–	£1900
2020 – Proof	5 ounces/£500	55	–	£9995
2020 – Proof	1 kilo/£1000	10	–	–
WHITE HORSE OF HANOVER				
2020 Cu-Ni BU	£5	–	–	£13
2020 Silver Proof	1 ounce/£2	4,310	–	£85
2020 – Proof	5 ounces/£10	315	–	£420
2020 – Proof	10 ounces/£10	235	–	£795
2020 – Proof	1 kilo/£500	115	–	£2050
2020 Gold Proof	1/4 ounce/£25	1,000	–	£510
2020 – Proof	1 ounce/£100	435	–	£2020
2020 – Proof	5 ounces/£500	69	–	£9595
2020 – Proof	1 kilo/£1000	13	–	£57,750
WHITE GREYHOUND OF RICHMOND				
2021 Cu-Ni BU	£5	–	–	£13
2021 Silver Proof	1 ounce/£2	3,960	–	£85
2021 – Proof	5 ounces/£10	370	–	£420
2021 – Proof	10 ounces/£10	195	–	£795
2021– Proof	1 kilo/£500	80	–	£2025
2021 Gold Proof	1/4 ounce/£25	1,010	–	£585
2021 – Proof	1 ounce/£100	425	–	£2320
2021 – Proof	5 ounces/£500	69	–	£10,605
2021 – Proof	1 kilo/£1000	10	–	£63,865
GRIFFIN OF EDWARD III				
2021 Cu Ni BU	£5	–	–	£13
2021 Silver Proof	1 ounce/£2	4,400	–	£92.50
2021 – Proof	5 ounces/£10	290	–	£455
2021 – Proof	10 ounces/£10	140	–	£865
2021– Proof	1 kilo/£500	70	–	£2270
2021 Gold Proof	1/4 ounce/£25	1,240	–	£605
2021 – Proof	1 ounce/£100	500	–	£2370
2021 – Proof	5 ounces/£500	115	–	£10,820

Date	Weight Face value/	Auth. issue qty	No. Issued	Issue price
2021 — Proof	1 kilo/£1000	10	—	£65,275
THE QUEEN'S BEASTS 2021—COMPLETER COIN				
2021 Cu-Ni BU	£5	—	—	£13
2021 Silver Proof	1 ounce/£2	7,460	—	£85
2021 Silver Proof	1kilo/£500	—	—	—
2021 Gold Proof	1 ounce/£100	—	—	—
2021 Gold Proof	1 kilo/£1000	16	—	—

The above coins were issued in 2021/2 depicting all 10 designs from the Queen's Beasts series, called the "completer coin" it rounds up this popular collection.

The Valiant

The Valiant series of silver bullion-related coins portraying St George slaying the Dragon by artist Etienne Millner was introduced in 2018 with an attractive 10 ounce silver piece with the weight shown in the field. In 2019 the design was modified to give the weight in the legend around the circumference of the reverse. The obverse carries the effigy of Her Majesty the Queen by Jody Clark.

Date	Weight Face value/	Auth. issue qty	Issue price
2018 silver	10 ounces	—	£191.58
2019 silver	1 ounce	100,000	£19.76
2019 silver	10 ounces	—	£198.60
2020 silver	1 ounce	100,000	£25.19
2020 silver	10 ounces	—	£250.76
2021 silver	10 ounces	—	£256.00
2021 silver	1 ounce	100,000	£25.49

The information contained in this section is as supplied and is correct at the time of going to press (August 2024) but the quantities struck and the issue prices can be subject to change by the Royal Mint. To keep up to date on the new releases visit www.royalmint.com and www.royalmintbullion.com or check in COIN NEWS magazine every month.

The Royal Arms

Another bullion coin aimed at the investor, The Royal Arms series in gold and silver was introduced in 2019. The coins carry the Royal Arms as depicted by Eric Sewell in 1983 but reinterpreted in this design by Timothy Noad. The common obverse carries the effigy of Her Majesty the Queen by Jody Clark.

These coins are available in one ounce gold, one ounce platinum, 10 ounce silver and one ounce silver. As they are intended as bullion investment coins rather than for the collector market the prices asked for them will vary according to the prevailing metal markets.

In addition to their various investor coins, the Royal Mint regularly introduces other series of interest in various metals and weights. All can be found on the Mint's website which gives full details and issue prices

Great Engravers series

This new series commemorates the work of the great designers of the past. The first issue released in November 2019 celebrates the skill of William Wyon, his original Una and the Lion design has been skilfully remastered using modern technology by Royal Mint engraver Gordon Summers. In addition to those listed below, just one example was struck as a 5 kilo coin. ***PLEASE NOTE: The prices listed in this section, are the issue price. Certain series have proved more popular than others hence, a number of these precious metal Collector Series issues, such as*** **The Queen's Beasts** ***and*** **The Great Engravers*****, are now securing high prices on the secondary market. However, not ALL of these new issues are as collectable and trends do change.***

Date	Weight Face value/	Auth. issue qty	Issue price
UNA & THE LION—WILLIAM WYON			
2019 Silver Proof	2 ounces/£5	2980	£180
2019 Gold Proof	2 ounces/£200	205	£3995
2019 — Proof	5 ounces/£500	65	£9995
2019 — Proof	1 kilo/£1000	7	£59,995
2019 — Proof	2 kilos/£2000	4	£119,950
THE THREE GRACES—WILLIAM WYON			
2020 Silver Proof	2 ounces/£5	3500	£185
2020 Gold Proof	2 ounces/£200	325	£4995
2020 — Proof	5 ounces/£500	150	£11,995
2020 — Proof	1 kilo/£1000	20	£74,000
THE GOTHIC CROWN—Wyon REVERSE (issued 2022, dated 2021)			
2021 Silver Proof	2 ounce/£5	4,006	£
2021 — —	5 ounces/£10	506	£
2021 — —	10 ounces/£10	231	£
2021— —	1 kilo/£500	128	£
2021— —	2 kilos/£1000	53	£
2021 Gold Proof	2 ounce/£200	411	£4,775
2021 — —	5 ounces/£500	181	£11,430
2021 — —	10 ounces/£500	56	£22,855
2021— —	1 kilo/£1000	22	£69,445
2021— —	2 kilos/£2000	9	£151,135
2021— —	5 kilos/£5000	2	£385,200
2021— —	10 kilos/£10,000	1	£385,200

Date	Weight Face value/	Auth. issue qty	Issue price
THE GOTHIC CROWN—Wyon OBVERSE (issued 2022, dated 2021)			
2021 Silver Proof	2 ounce/£5	4,006	—
2021 — —	5 ounces/£10	506	—
2021 — —	10 ounces/£10	231	—
2021— —	1 kilo/£500	128	—
2021— —	2 kilo/£1000	53	—
2021 Gold Proof	2 ounce/£200	411	£4,775
2021 — —	5 ounces/£500	181	£11,430
2021 — —	10 ounces/£500	56	£22,855
2021— —	1 kilo/£1000	22	£69,445
2021— —	2 kilo/£2000	9	£151,135
2021— —	5 kilo/£5000	2	£385,200
2021— —	10 kilo/£10,000	1	£385,200
THE PETITION CROWN—THOMAS SIMON (two coin sets, obverse & reverse design)			
2023 Silver Proof	2 ounce/£5	3250	£560
2023 — —	5 ounces/£10	500	£1190
2023 — —	10 ounces/£10	150	£2375
2023 Gold Proof	1 kilo/£1000	6	£172,865
2023— —	5 kilo/£5000	1	POA
2023 Gold Proof	2 ounce/£200	300	£11,610
2023 — —	5 ounces/£500	125	£27,935

Date	Weight Face value/	Auth. issue qty	Issue price
ST GEORGE & THE DRAGON—BENEDETTO PISTRUCCI			
2024 Silver Proof	2 ounce/£5	3060	£275
2024 — —	5 ounce/£10	460	£577
2024 — —	10 ounce/£10	100	£1,065
2024 Gold Proof	2 ounce/£200	221	£5,545
2024 — —	1kg/£1,000	7	£84,380
2024 — —	2kg/£2,000	2	£176,850
2024 — —	5kg/£5,000	1	£437,130

The James Bond Collection

Released to coincide with the 25th James Bond movie "No Time to Die" in 2020, the commemorative coin collection offered three coins in several editions from BU to precious metal including just one 7 kilo coin, a first for the Royal Mint. Precious metal gold and silver bars were also available. Designers of the reverse images were Matt Dent, Christian Davies and Laura Clancy. The common obverse carries the effigy of Her Majesty the Queen by Jody Clark.

Date	Weight Face value/	Auth. issue qty	Issue price
CORE RANGE—ASTON MARTIN			
2020 BU	£5	—	£13
2020 Silver Proof	1/2 ounce/£1	15,017	£65
2020 — Proof	1 ounce/£2	8,517	£87.50
2020 Gold Proof	1/4 ounce/£25	1,067	£517
2020 — Proof	1 ounce/£100	360	£2,070
INSPIRED INNOVATION RANGE—SUBMARINE CAR			
2020 Silver Proof	2 ounce/£5	2017	£235
2020 Gold Proof	2 ounce/£200	260	£3,985
SPECIAL ISSUE RANGE—JAMES BOND'S JACKET AND TIE			
2020 Silver Proof	5 ounce/£10	700	£485
2020 Gold Proof	5 ounce/£500	64	£9,895
2020 — Proof	1 kilo coin/£1,000	20	£59,750
2020 — Proof	2 kilo coin/£2,000	10	£129,990
2020 — Proof	7 kilo coin/£7,000	1	POA

Six Decades of 007

Following the success of the James Bond Collection issued in 2020, the Royal Mint returned to the theme of the iconic British spy with a new seven coin series in 2023–24. The new coins feature the most memorable images from the films made in the 1960s. The first release in the collection depicted the autogyro from You Only Live Twice.

Date	Weight Face value/	Auth. issue qty	Issue price
BOND FILMS OF THE 1960s—*You Only Live Twice*			
2023 BU	£5	—	£15.50
2023 Silver Proof	1ounce/£2	4,007	£110
2023 — —	2 ounce/£5	760	£213
2023 — —	5 ounce/£10	510	£520
2023 Gold Proof	1/4 ounce/£25	660	£700
2023 — —	1 ounce/£100	260	£2,995
2023 — —	2 ounce/£200	110	£5,890

BOND FILMS OF THE 1970s—*The Spy Who Loved Me*

2023 Silver Proof	1ounce/£2	4,007	£102.50
2023 — —	2 ounce/£5	760	£192.50
2023 — —	5 ounce/£10	360	£485
2023 Gold Proof	1/4 ounce/£25	660	£750
2023 — —	1 ounce/£100	260	£2,770
2023 — —	2 ounce/£200	85	£5,305

BOND FILMS OF THE 1980s—*Octopussy*

2024 Silver Proof	1ounce/£2	4,007	£103.50
2024 — —	2 ounce/£5	760	£195
2024 — —	5 ounce/£10	360	£487.50
2024 Gold Proof	1/4 ounce/£25	660	£750
2024 — —	1 ounce/£100	260	£2,770
2024 — —	2 ounce/£200	110	£5,305

BOND FILMS OF THE 1990s—*The World is Not Enough*

2024 Silver Proof	1ounce/£2	4,007	£103.50
2024 — —	2 ounce/£5	760	£195
2024 — —	5 ounce/£10	260	£487.50
2024 Gold Proof	1/4 ounce/£25	660	£750
2024 — —	1 ounce/£100	260	£2,770
2024 — —	2 ounce/£200	110	£5,305

BOND FILMS OF THE 2000s—D*ie Another Day*

2024 Silver Proof	1ounce/£2	4,007	£103.50
2024 — —	2 ounce/£5	756	£195
2024 — —	5 ounce/£10	356	£487.50
2024 Gold Proof	1/4 ounce/£25	660	£750
2024 — —	1 ounce/£100	260	£2,770
2024 — —	2 ounce/£200	81	£5,305

BOND FILMS OF THE 2010s—*Spectre*

2024 Silver Proof	1ounce/£2	—	£110.00
2024 — —	2 ounce/£5	750	£213
2024 — —	5 ounce/£10	350	£520
2024 Gold Proof	1/4 ounce/£25	650	£799
2024 — —	1 ounce/£100	250	£2,995
2024 — —	2 ounce/£200	75	£5,890

The 50th anniversary of the Mr Men Collection

This delightful series of coins marked the 50th anniversary of the creation of these much-loved characters commencing with Mr Tickle who was created by Roger Hargreaves in 1971. The Mr Men, and later Little Miss, characters were featured in over 90 books, translated into 17 different languages. In 1988, the role of illustrating Mr Men and Little Miss characters was taken over by Adam Hargreaves, Roger's son. Adam provided the reverse designs for the Royal Mint 50th anniversary series. The common obverse carries the effigy of Her Majesty the Queen by Jody Clark.

50TH ANNIVERSARY OF MR MEN—LITTLE MISS SUNSHINE

2021 BU	£5	—	£13
2021 — (coloured coin)	£5	15,000	£22.50
2021 Silver Proof	1/2 ounce/£1	9,000	£65
2021 — Proof	1 ounce/£2	6,500	£97.50
2021 Gold Proof	1/4 ounce/£25	750	£595
2021 — Proof	1 ounce/£100	275	£2315

50TH ANNIVERSARY OF MR MEN—MR HAPPY

2021 BU	£5	—	£13
2021 — (coloured coin)	£5	15,000	£22.50
2021 Silver Proof	1/2 ounce/£1	9,000	£65
2021 — Proof	1 ounce/£2	6,500	£97.50
2021 Gold Proof	1/4 ounce/£25	750	£650
2021 — Proof	1 ounce/£100	275	£2440

Date	Weight Face value/	Auth. issue qty	Issue price
50TH ANNIVERSARY OF MR MEN—MR STRONG AND LITTLE MISS GIGGLES			
2021 BU	£5	–	£13
2021 — (coloured coin)	£5	15,000	£22.50
2021 Silver Proof	1/2 ounce/£1	9,000	£65
2021 — Proof	1 ounce/£2	6,500	£97.50
2021 Gold Proof	1/4 ounce/£25	750	£650
2021 — Proof	1 ounce/£100	275	£2440

The Alice Collection

Two-coin set to mark 160 years since the publication by Lewis Carroll of *Alice's Adventures in Wonderland* and the later *Through the Looking Glass*. Issued as part of the Treasury of Tales and in partnership with the Victoria & Albert Museum, the designs depict the exquisite Sir John Tenniel's illustrations as used in the first editions of both books. Reverse design by Ffion Gwillim. The common obverse carries the effigy of Her Majesty the Queen by Jody Clark.

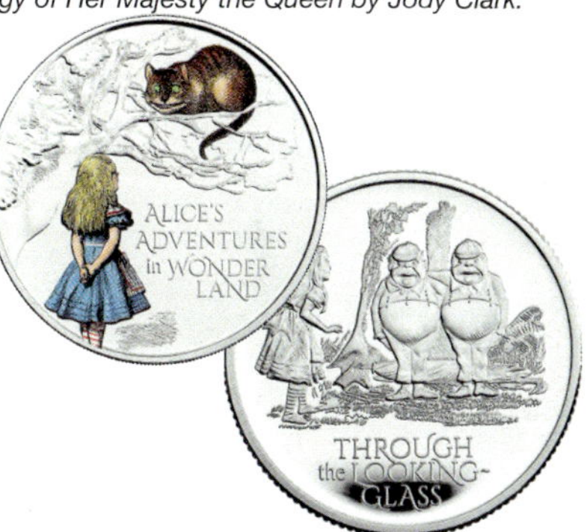

ALICE'S ADVENTURES IN WONDERLAND			
2021 BU	£5	–	£13
2021 — Coloured Coin	£5	1,500	£20
2021 Silver Proof	1/2 ounce /£1	5,510	£65
2021 —— Coloured Coin	1 ounce /£2	3,510	£100
2021 Gold Proof	1/4 ounce/£25	510	£650
2021 ——	1 ounce/£100	160	£2440
THROUGH THE LOOKING GLASS			
2021 BU	£5	–	£13
2021 — Coloured Coin	£5	1,500	£20
2021 Silver Proof	1/2 ounce /£1	5,510	£65
2021 —— Coloured Coin	1 ounce /£2	3,510	£100
2021 Gold Proof	1/4 ounce/£25	510	£650
2021 ——	1 ounce/£100	160	£2440

The latest collections of coins from the Royal Mint are often available in a variety of collector-pack versions.

Myths and Legends Series

Taking inspiration from UK myths and legends, this latest issue from the Royal Mint's bullion series commenced with the story of Robin Hood. Issues thus far are a 999.9 gold one ounce coin and a one ounce silver edition.

ROBIN HOOD			
2021 Silver Proof	1 ounce/£2	–	£25
2021 Gold Proof	1 ounce/£100	–	£1,406
MAID MARIAN			
2021 Silver Proof	1 ounce/£2	–	£25
2021 Gold Proof	1 ounce/£100	–	£1,406
2022 Silver Bullion	1 ounce/£2	–	£25.73
2022 Gold Bullion	1 ounce/£100	–	£1644.51
LITTLE JOHN			
2022 Silver Bullion	1 ounce/£2	–	£25.73
2022 Gold Bullion	1 ounce/£100	–	£1644.51
KING ARTHUR			
2023 BU	£5	–	£14.50
2023 Silver Proof	1 ounce/£2	2,500	£99.50
2023 — —	2 ounce/£5	500	£190
2023 Gold Proof	1/4 ounce/£25	600	£725
2023 — —	1 ounce/£100	200	£2,725

Date	Weight Face value/	Auth. issue qty	Issue price
MORGAN Le FAY			
2023 BU	50p	—	£14.50
2023 Silver Proof	1 ounce/£2	2,500	£102.50
2023 — —	2 ounce/£5	500	£192.50
2023 — —	1/4 ounce/£25	250	£750
2023 — —	1 ounce/£100	200	£2,770

The Music Legends Collection

This series is intended to celebrate famous bands and musicians. The first issue is dedicated to Queen and all four members of the band are named with edge lettering on the silver editions. The subsequent issues carry images synonymous with their subject.

QUEEN

The BU £5 coin comes in a special illustrated pack with one of four designs

Date	Weight Face value/	Auth. issue qty	Issue price
2020 BU (with pack design 1)	£5	—	£13
2020 BU (with pack design 2)	£5	25,000	£15
2020 BU (with pack design 3)	£5	25,000	£15
2020 BU (with pack design 4)	£5	25,000	£15
2020 Silver Proof	half ounce/£1	20,000	£60
2020 — Proof	1 ounce/£2	10,000	£90
2020 Gold Proof	quarter ounce/£25	1,350	£510
2020 — Proof	1 ounce/£100	350	£2020

ELTON JOHN

The BU £5 coin comes in a special illustrated pack with one of four designs

Date	Weight Face value/	Auth. issue qty	Issue price
2020 BU (with pack design 1, 2, 3, 4)	£5	—	£15
2020 Silver Proof	half ounce/£1	15,000	£60
2020 — Proof	1 ounce/£2	10,000	£95
2020 — Proof	2 ounces/£5	500	£95
2020 — Proof	5 ounces/£10	425	£95
2020 Gold Proof	quarter ounce/£25	1,150	£585
2020 — Proof	1 ounce/£100	300	£2320
2020 — Proof	2 ounces/£200	50	£4555
2020 — Proof	5 ounces/£500	50	£2320
2020 — Proof	1 kilo/£100	4	£68,865

DAVID BOWIE

The BU £5 coin comes in a special illustrated pack with one of four designs

Date	Weight Face value/	Auth. issue qty	Issue price
2020 BU (with pack design 1, 2, 3, 4)	£5	—	£15
2020 Silver Proof	half ounce/£1	13,500	£65
2020 — Proof	1 ounce/£2	8,100	£97.50
2020 — Proof	2 ounces/£5	550	£195
2020 — Proof	5 ounces/£10	500	£520
2020 Gold Proof	quarter ounce/£25	1,400	£615
2020 — Proof	1 ounce/£100	400	£2425
2020 — Proof	2 ounces/£200	100	£4760
2020 — Proof	5 ounces/£500	60	£11,815
2020 — Proof	1 kilo/£100	11	£72,195

MUSIC LEGENDS COLLECTION—THE WHO

The BU £5 coin comes in a special illustrated pack with one of four designs

Date	Weight Face value/	Auth. issue qty	Issue price
2021 BU	£5	—	£13
2021 — Coloured coin	£5	10,000	£22.50
2021 Silver Proof	half ounce/£1	10,010	£65
2021 — Proof	1 ounce/£2	8110	£97.50
2021 — Proof	2 ounces/£5	550	£195
2020 — Proof	5 ounces/£10	500	£520
2021 Gold Proof	quarter ounce/£25	1,010	£595
2021 — Proof	1 ounce/£100	360	£2315
2021 — Proof	2 ounces/£200	150	£4530
2021 — Proof	5 ounces/£500	64	£11,225
2021 — Proof	1 kilo/£1000	12	£68,380

Date	Weight Face value/	Auth. issue qty	Issue price
THE ROLLING STONES			
2022 BU	£5	–	£14.50
2022 BU (coloured coin)	£5	10,000	£23.50
2022 Silver Proof	1 ounce/£2	8,000	£105
2022 — —	2 ounce/£5	550	£190
2022 — —	5 ounces/£10	600	£480
2022 Gold Proof	1/4 ounce/£25	1000	£725
2022 — —	1 ounce/£100	350	£2,725
2022 — —	2 ounce/£200	150	£5,215
2022 — —	5 ounces/£500	30	£12,500
2022 — —	1 kilo/£1000	–	£76,135
DAME SHIRLEY BASSEY			
2023 BU	£5	–	£14.50
2023 BU (coloured coin)	£5	5,000	£23.50
2023 Silver Proof	1 ounce/£2	2,500	£105.00
2023 — —	2 ounce/£5	350	£190
2023 Gold Proof	1/4 ounce/£25	350	£750
2023 — —	1 ounce/£100	150	£2,770
2023 — —	2 ounce/£200	70	£5,305
THE POLICE			
2023 BU	50p	–	£14.50
2023 BU (coloured coin)	50p	7,500	£23.50
2023 Silver Proof	1 ounce/£2	6,000	£107.50
2023 — —	2 ounce/£5	700	£192.50
2023 — —	5 ounces/£10	300	£485
2023 Gold Proof	50p	200	£1,220.00
2023 — —	1/4 ounce/£25	500	£750
2023 — —	1 ounce/£100	300	£2,770
2023 — —	2 ounce/£200	150	£5,305
GEORGE MICHAEL			
2024 BU	50p	–	£15.50
2024 BU (coloured coin)	50p	7,510	£24.50
2024 Silver Proof (coloured coin)	1 ounce/£2	3,510	£108.50
2024 — —	2 ounce/£5	360	£195
2024 — —	5 ounces/£10	185	£487.50
2024 Gold Proof	1/40 ounce/50p	2,034	£99.50
2024 — —	1/4 ounce/£25	310	£750
2024 — —	1 ounce/£100	160	£2,770
2024 — —	2 ounce/£200	35	£5,305

In addition to the above, other series, such as the "Tower of London", the "Portrait of Britain", etc. will be found under specific denominations or in the Proof and Specimen sets section.

British Monarchs

The British Monarchs Collection was launched in 2022 to celebrate some of the most iconic Kings and Queens in British history. The series commenced with the House of Tudor and the classic portrait of Henry VII as it would have appeared on the coinage of the time.

Date	Weight Face value/	Auth. issue qty	Issue price
KING HENRY VII			
2022 Silver Proof	1 ounce/£2	1,250	£92.50
2022 — —	2 ounce/£5	700	£180
2022	5 ounces/£10	275	£455
2022 — —	10 ounces/£10	150	£885
2022 Gold Proof	1 ounce/£100	100	£2,370
2022 — —	2 ounce/£200	175	£4,485
2022 — —	5 ounces/£500	75	£10,820

Date	Weight Face value/	Auth. issue qty	Issue price
KING JAMES I			
2022 Silver Proof	1 ounce/£2	1,250	£95
2022 — —	2 ounce/£5	700	£185
2022 — —	5 ounces/£10	275	£465
2022 — —	10 ounces/£10	150	£885
2022 Gold Proof	1 ounce/£100	100	£2,505
2022 — —	2 ounce/£200	150	£4,775
2022 — —	5 ounces/£500	50	£11,430
Two-coin gold set			
2022 Gold Proof Coin 2 ounce/£200/Gold Crown (second coinage)		10	£8,000
KING GEORGE I			
2022 Silver Proof	1 ounce/£2	1,360	£95
2022 — —	2 ounce/£5	756	£185
2022 — —	5 ounces/£10	281	£465
2022 — —	10 ounces/£10	156	£885
2022 Gold Proof	1 ounce/£100	610	£2,625
2022 — —	2 ounce/£200	126	£5,010
2022 — —	5 ounces/£500	56	£12,015
KING EDWARD VII			
2022 Silver Proof	1 ounce/£2	1,360	£99.50
2022 — —	2 ounce/£5	756	£190
2022 — —	5 ounces/£10	281	£480
2022 — —	10 ounces/£10	156	£910
2022 Gold Proof	1ounce/£100	610	£2,725
2022 — —	2 ounce/£200	106	£5,215
2022 — —	5 ounces/£500	56	£12,500
KING HENRY VIII			
2023 Silver Proof	1 ounce/£2	1,350	£99.50
2023 — —	2 ounce/£5	600	£190
2023 — —	5 ounces/£10	250	£480
2023 — —	10 ounces/£10	100	£910
2023 Gold Proof	1ounce/£100	100	£2,725
2023 — —	2 ounce/£200	50	£5,215
2023 — —	5 ounces/£500	20	£12,500
KING CHARLES I			
2023 Silver Proof	1 ounce/£2	1,350	£99.50
2023 — —	2 ounce/£5	600	£190
2023 — —	5 ounces/£10	250	£480
2023 — —	10 ounces/£10	100	£910
2023 Gold Proof	1ounce/£100	100	£2,725
2023 — —	2 ounce/£200	50	£5,215
2023 — —	5 ounces/£500	20	£12,500
KING CHARLES II			
2023 Silver Proof	1 ounce/£2	1,350	£99.50
2023 — —	2 ounce/£5	600	£190
2023 — —	5 ounces/£10	250	£480
2023 — —	10 ounces/£10	100	£910
2023 Gold Proof	1ounce/£100	100	£2,770
2023 — —	2 ounce/£200	50	£5,305
KING GEORGE II			
2023 Silver Proof	1 ounce/£2	1,350	£102.50
2023 — —	2 ounce/£5	600	£192.50
2023 — —	5 ounces/£10	250	£485
2023 — —	10 ounces/£10	100	£950
2023 Gold Proof	1ounce/£100	100	£2,770
2023 — —	2 ounce/£200	50	£5,305

City Views

The City Views Collection celebrates iconic urban landmarks from the world's greatest cities. Starting, of course, with our own capital city, the iconic Tower of London graces the first issue of the series. The series is struck in gold and silver.

LONDON 2022

Date	Weight Face value/	Auth. issue qty	Issue price
2022 Silver Proof	1 ounce/£2	2010	£95
2022 — —	2 ounce/£5	1506	£185
2022 — —	5 ounces/£10	256	£465
2022 — —	1 kilo/£500	52	£2,330
2022 Gold Proof	1 ounce/£100	310	£2,505
2022 — —	2 ounce/£200	256	£4,775
2022 — —	5 ounces/£500	56	£11,430

ROME 2022

Date	Weight Face value/	Auth. issue qty	Issue price
2022 Silver Proof	1 ounce/£2	2010	£99.50
2022 — —	2 ounce/£5	1006	£190
2022 — —	5 ounces/£10	206	£480
2022 Gold Proof	1ounce/£100	210	£2,725
2022 — —	2 ounce/£200	156	£5,215
2022 — —	5 ounces/£500	31	£12,500
2022 — —	1 kilo/£1000	4	£76,135
2022 — —	1 kilo/£1000	56	£69,445

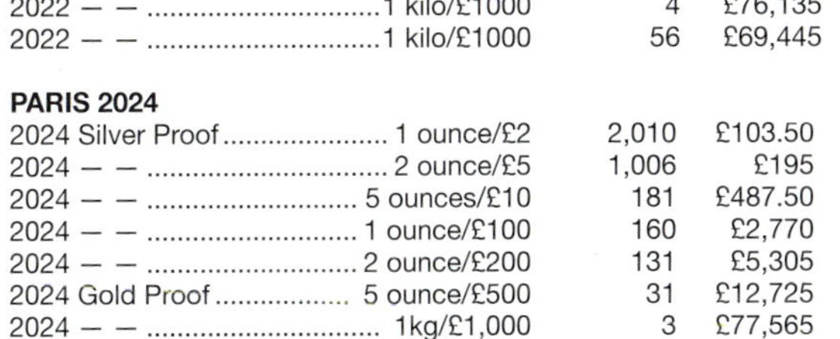

PARIS 2024

Date	Weight Face value/	Auth. issue qty	Issue price
2024 Silver Proof	1 ounce/£2	2,010	£103.50
2024 — —	2 ounce/£5	1,006	£195
2024 — —	5 ounces/£10	181	£487.50
2024 — —	1 ounce/£100	160	£2,770
2024 — —	2 ounce/£200	131	£5,305
2024 Gold Proof	5 ounce/£500	31	£12,725
2024 — —	1kg/£1,000	3	£77,565

The Royal Tudor Beasts

Following the popularity of the Queen's Beast's series, a new collection commenced in 2022 depicting historic and mythical creatures. Based on the ten stone beasts that line the Moat Bridge at Hampton Court Palace—representing the lineage of Henry VIII and his third wife, Jane Seymour—these heraldic symbols make up the Royal Tudor Beasts Collection.

THE SEYMOUR PANTHER

Date	Weight Face value/	Auth. issue qty	Issue price
2022 Cu-Ni BU	£5	—	£13
2022 Silver Proof	1 ounce/£2	7,010	£95
2022 — —	2 ounces/£5	2,006	£185
2022 — —	5 ounces/£10	306	£465
2022 — —	10 ounces/£10	156	£885
2022— —	1 kilo/£500	72	£2,330
2022— —	2 kilos/£1000	56	£4,995
2022 Gold Proof	1/4 ounce/£25	1,010	£650
2022 — —	1 ounce/£100	560	£2,440
2022 — —	2 ounces/£200	356	£4,650
2022 — —	5 ounces/£500	131	£11,125
2022 — —	10 ounces/£500	31	£22,250
2022 — —	1 kilo/£1000	14	£67,500
2022 — —	2 kilos/£2000	5	£147,250

Date	Weight Face value/	Auth. issue qty	Issue price
THE LION OF ENGLAND			
2022 Cu-Ni BU	£5	–	£13
2022 Silver Proof	1 ounce/£2	6,000	£95
2022 — —	2 ounces/£5	2,000	£185
2022 — —	5 ounces/£10	300	£465
2022 — —	10 ounces/£10	150	£885
2022— —	1 kilo/£500	70	£2,330
2022— —	2 kilos/£1000	55	£4,995
2022 Gold Proof	1/4 ounce/£25	1,000	£670
2022 — —	1 ounce/£100	400	£2,505
2022 — —	2 ounces/£200	175	£4,775
2022 — —	5 ounces/£500	70	£11,430
2022 — —	10 ounces/£500	10	£22,855
2022 — —	1 kilo/£1000	3	£69,445
2022 — —	2 kilos/£2000	2	£151,135

Date	Weight Face value/	Auth. issue qty	Issue price
THE YALE OF BEAUFORT			
2023 Cu-Ni BU	£5	–	£13
2023 Silver Proof Two Coin Set	£2	500	£210
2023 — —	1 ounce/£2	5,000	£105
2023 — —	2 ounces/£5	12,500	£185
2023 — —	5 ounces/£10	300	£465
2023 — —	10 ounces/£10	100	£885
2023— —	1 kilo/£500	70	£2,330
2023 Gold Proof	1/4 ounce/£25	750	£700
2023 — —	1 ounce/£100	400	£2,625
2023 — —	2 ounces/£200	100	£5,010
2023 — —	5 ounces/£500	50	£12,015
2023 — —	2 kilos/£2000	1	£158,650

Date	Weight Face value/	Auth. issue qty	Issue price
THE BULL OF CLARENCE			
2023 Cu-Ni BU	£5	–	£14.50
2023 Silver Proof	1 ounce/£2	5,000	£99.50
2023 — —	2 ounce/£5	1,250	£190
2023 — —	5 ounces/£10	250	£480
2023 — —	10 ounces/£10	100	£910
2023— — 2 Coin Set	£2	500	£195
2023 Gold Proof	1/4 ounce/£25	650	£725
2023 — —	1 ounce/£100	300	£2,725
2023 — —	2 ounce/£200	60	£5,215
2023 — —	5 ounces/£500	20	£12,500

Date	Weight Face value/	Auth. issue qty	Issue price
THE SEYMOUR UNICORN			
2024 BU	£5	–	£14.50
2024 Silver Proof	1 ounce/£2	6,260	£102.50
2024 — —	2 ounce/£5	1,256	£192.50
2024 — —	5 ounces/£10	256	£485
2024 — —	10 ounces/£10	106	£950
2024— — 2 Coin Set	£2	750	£210
2024 Gold Proof	1/4 ounce/£25	660	£750
2024 — —	1 ounce/£100	260	£2,770
2024 — —	2 ounce/£200	56	£5,305
2024 — —	5 ounces/£500	26	£12,725

Date	Weight Face value/	Auth. issue qty	Issue price
THE TUDOR DRAGON			
2024 BU	£5	–	£15.50
2024 Silver Proof	1 ounce/£2	5,000	£103.50
2024 — —	2 ounce/£5	1,250	£195
2024 — —	5 ounces/£10	200	£487.50
2024 — —	10 ounces/£10	75	£955
2024— — 2 Coin Set	£2	500	£210
2024 Gold Proof	1/4 ounce/£25	500	£750
2024 — —	1 ounce/£100	250	£2,770
2024 — —	2 ounce/£200	50	£5,305
2024 — —	5 ounces/£500	20	£12,725

Mahatma Gandi

Struck in the 75th year of India's Independence, a series of coins was issued to celebrate the life and legacy of Mahatma Gandhi.The coin depicts an image of a lotus, India's national flower, and a well-known quote from Gandhi—"My life is my message". This is the first time Gandhi has been commemorated on an official UK coin.

Date	Weight Face value/	Auth. issue qty	Issue price
2021 BU	£5	–	£13
2021 Silver Proof	£2	2,500	£95
2021 Gold Proof	£100	185	£2,440

The Platinum Jubilee of Her Majesty the Queen

Her Majesty the Queen became the first British monarch to reach a Platinum Jubilee in 2022 and to mark the occasion one of the Royal Mint's largest coin collections to date was issued—a number of commemorative coins as well as circulating pieces were struck.
John Bergdahl has created a commemorative Platinum Jubilee portrait depicting Her Majesty on horseback and two reverse designs for the occasion. He was also the artist who designed the reverse of the £5 hence his creations were on both sides of the coin.

Date	Weight/Face value	Auth. issue qty	Issue price
2022 Silver Proof	2 ounce/£5	1,006	£185
2022 — —	5 ounces/£10	1,006	£465
2022 — —	10 ounces/£500	156	£885
2022 — —	1 kilo/£500	147	£2,330
2022 Gold Proof	1/4 ounce/£25	1,110	£670
2022 — —	2 ounces/£200	206	£4,775
2022 — —	5 ounces/£500	136	£11,430
2022 — —	10 ounces/£500	56	£22,855
2022— —	1 kilo/£1,000	17	£69,445
2022— —	2 kilos/£2,000	8	£151,135
2022— —	5 kilos/£5,000	2	£385,200

120 Years of Peter Rabbit

To mark 120 years since the first publication of Beatrix Potter's The Tale of Peter Rabbit, *the Royal Mint issued a series of coins (not for general circulaton) as well as a limited edition Peter Rabbit™ 2022 Minty® piggy bank.*

Date	Weight Face value/	Auth. issue qty	Issue price
2022 Cu-Ni BU	£5	–	£13
2022 Cu-Ni BU (coloured coin)	£5	8,600	£17
2022 Silver Proof	1 ounce/£2	3,500	£100
2022 Gold Proof	1 ounce/£100	120	£2505

The Life and Legacy of Dame Vera Lynn

The popular singer, whose career extended well beyond her songs of the war years for which she became famous, the late Dame Vera Lynn was commemorated on a £2 coin as well as a number of bullion issues. Perhaps, her most iconic and for some, most moving recording was that of "We'll Meet Again" which became a war-time anthem for those involved in World War II. The reverse design of the £2 coin depicts a portrait of Dame Vera as she appeared during the height of her fame, accompanied by her name and the dates denoting the years of her life. The coin's edge inscription reads "WE'LL MEET AGAIN". The common obverse bears the effigy of Her Majesty the Queen by Jody Clark.

Date	Weight Face value/	Auth. issue qty	Issue price
2022 BU	£2	–	£10
2022 Silver Proof	£2	3,500	£72.50
2022 — — Piedfort	£2	175	£117.50
2022 — —	5 ounces/£10	240	£465
2022 Gold Proof	£2	350	£1,125
2022 — —	5 ounces/£500	35	£11,430

The Harry Potter Collection

The Harry Potter collection celebrates the 25th publishing anniversary of Harry Potter and the Philosopher's Stone *in the UK. Struck in both precious and base metal and in a variety of denominations, including the 50p, the new collection will comprises four designs in total. The first coins feature Harry himself with subsequent coins showing The Hogwarts Express, Albus Dumbledore and Hogwarts School of Witchcraft and Wizardry.*

HARRY POTTER

Date	Weight/Face value	Auth. issue qty	Issue price
2022 Silver Proof	1 ounce/£2	15,000	£99.50
2022 — —	2 ounce/£5	750	£190
2022 — —	5 ounces/£10	300	£480
2022 Gold Proof	1/4 ounce/£25	650	£725
2022 — —	2 ounce/£200	100	£ 5,215

HOGWARTS EXPRESS

Date	Weight/Face value	Auth. issue qty	Issue price
2022 Silver Proof	1 ounce/£2	15,000	£99.50
2022 — —	2 ounce/£5	750	£190
2022 — —	5 ounces/£10	300	£480
2022 Gold Proof	1/4 ounce/£25	650	£725
2022 — —	2 ounce/£200	100	£5,215

PROFFESSOR ALBUS DUMBLEDORE

Date	Weight/Face value	Auth. issue qty	Issue price
2023 Silver Proof	1 ounce/£2	5,000	£99.50
2023 — —	2 ounce/£5	500	£190
2023 — —	5 ounces/£10	300	£480
2023 Gold Proof	1/4 ounce/£25	500	£725
2023 — —	2 ounce/£200	50	£5,215

HOGWARTS SCHOOL OF WITCHCRAFT AND WIZARDRY

Date	Weight/Face value	Auth. issue qty	Issue price
2023 Silver Proof	1 ounce/£2	5,000	£99.50
2023 — —	2 ounce/£5	500	£190
2023 — —	5 ounces/£10	300	£480
2023 Gold Proof	1/4 ounce/£25	500	£725
2023 — —	2 ounce/£200	50	£5,215

The Coronation of His Majesty King Charles III

Date	Weight Face value/	Auth. issue qty	Issue price
2023 Silver Proof	1 ounce/£2	17,500	£99.50
2023 — —	2 ounce/£5	1,000	£190
2023 — —	5 ounces/£10	1,500	£480
2023 — —	1 kilo/£500	200	£2,390
2023 Gold Proof	1/40 ounce/50p	2,023	£85
2023 — —	1/4 ounce/£25	1,250	£750
2023 — —	1 ounce/£100	500	£2,770
2023 — —	2 ounce/£200	300	£5,305
2023 — —	5 ounces/£500	100	£12,725
2023 — —	1 kilo/£1000	15	£77,565

Star Wars

Working in collaboration with the Walt Disney Company, the four-coin collection depicts the characters from the block-buster, 1970s sci-fi movie. Characters include R2–D2, C-3PO, Darth Vader, Luke Skywalker and Princess Leia, Hans Solo and Chewbacca. The reverse designs are by Royal Mint designer Fion Gwillim.

R2-D2 AND C-3PO			
2023 BU	50p	–	£11.00
2023 BU (coloured coin)	50p	20,000	£20.00
2023 Silver Proof (coloured coin)	50p	12,500	£70.00
2023 — —	1 ounce/£2	3,000	£102.50
2023 — —	2 ounce/£5	750	£192.50
2023 — —	5 ounces/£10	350	£485
2023 Gold Proof	50p	200	£1,220.00
2023 — —	1/4 ounce/£25	500	£750
2023 — —	1 ounce/£100	250	£2,770
DARTH VADER AND EMPEROR PALPATINE			
2023 BU	50p	–	£11.00
2023 BU (coloured coin)	50p	20,010	£20.00
2023 Silver Proof (coloured coin)	50p	12,510	£70.00
2023 — —	1 ounce/£2	3,010	£102.50
2023 — —	2 ounce/£5	760	£192.50
2023 — —	5 ounces/£10	360	£485
2023 Gold Proof	50p	210	£1,220
2023 — —	1/4 ounce/£25	510	£750
2023 — —	1 ounce/£100	260	£2,770
LUKE SKYWALKER AND PRINCESS LEIA			
2023 BU	50p	–	£11.00
2023 BU (coloured coin)	50p	20,010	£20.00
2023 Silver Proof (coloured coin)	50p	12,510	£70.00
2023 — —	1 ounce/£2	3,010	£102.50
2023 — —	2 ounce/£5	760	£192.50
2023 — —	5 ounces/£10	310	£485
2023 Gold Proof	50p	210	£1,220
2023 — —	1/4 ounce/£25	510	£750
2023 — —	1 ounce/£100	260	£2,770
MILLENIUM FALCON			
2024 BU	50p	–	£12.00
2024 BU (coloured coin)	50p	20,010	£21.00
2024 Silver Proof (coloured coin)	50p	7,150	£71.00
2024 — —	1 ounce/£2	3,010	£103.50
2024 — —	2 ounce/£5	506	£195
2024 — —	5 ounces/£10	206	£487.50

Date	Weight Face value/	Auth. issue qty	Issue price
2024 Gold Proof	50p	110	£1,220
2024 — —	1/4 ounce/£25	260	£750
2024 — —	1 ounce/£100	110	£2,770
TIE FIGHTER			
2024 BU	50p	–	£12.00
2024 BU (coloured coin)	50p	20,010	£21.00
2024 Silver Proof (coloured coin)	50p	7,150	£71.00
2024 — —	1 ounce/£2	3,010	£103.50
2024 — —	2 ounce/£5	506	£195
2024 — —	5 ounces/£10	206	£487.50
2024 Gold Proof	50p	110	£1,220
2024 — —	1/4 ounce/£25	260	£750
2024 — —	1 ounce/£100	110	£2,770

The Lion and the Eagle

Obverse Design Martin Jennings, Reverse Design John Mercanti.

Date	Weight Face value/	Auth. issue qty	Issue price
2023 Silver Proof	1 ounce/£2	4,510	£102.50
2023 — —	2 ounce/£5	2,006	£192.50
2023 — —	5 ounce/£10	806	£485
2023 — —	1kg/£500	77	£2,422.50
2023 Gold Proof	1 ounce/£100	385	£2,770
2023 — —	2 ounce/£200	46	£5,305
2023 — —	5 ounce/£500	31	£12,725
2023 — —	1kg/£1,000	7	£77,565

75th Birthday of King Charles III

Date	Weight Face value/	Auth. issue qty	Issue price
2023 BU	50p	–	£14.50
2023 Silver Proof	1/2 ounce/£1	5,000	£72.50
2023 — —	£5	3,000	£97.50
2023 — — Piedfort	£5	1,000	£182.50
2023 Gold Proof	1/40 ounce/50p	2,023	£99.50
2023 — —	1/4 ounce/£25	500	£750
2023 — —	2 ounce/£200	75	£5,305
2023 — —	£5	200	£2,995

Iconic Dinosaurs

Date	Weight Face value/	Auth. issue qty	Issue price
TYRANNOSAURUS			
2024 BU	50p	–	£11
2024 — (coloured coin)	50p	15,000	£20
2024 Silver Proof	50p	500	£60
2024 — — (coloured coin)	50p	5,000	£70
2024 Gold Proof	50p	100	£1,220
2024 Silver Proof		1ounce/£2	£102.50
2024 Gold Proof		1/4 ounce/£25	£750
STEGOSAURUS			
2024 BU	50p	–	£12
2024 — (coloured coin)	50p	15,000	£21
2024 Silver Proof	50p	500	£61
2024 — — (coloured coin)	50p	5,000	£71
2024 Gold Proof	50p	100	£1,220
DIPLODOCUS			
2024 BU	50p	–	£12
2024 — (coloured coin)	50p	15,000	£21
2024 Silver Proof	50p	500	£61
2024 — — (coloured coin)	50p	5,000	£71
2024 Gold Proof	50p	100	£1,220
2024 Silver Proof		1ounce/£2	£103.50
2024 Gold Proof		1/4 ounce/£25	£750

200 Years of the RNLI

2024 BU	50p	–	£12
2024 BU (coloured coin)	50p	–	£21
2024 Silver Proof	50p	4,510	£71
2024 — — Piedfort (coloured coin)	50p	2,084	£123.50
2024 Gold Proof	1/40 ounce/50p	2,034	£99.50
2024 — —	1/4 ounce/£25	510	£750
2024 — —	50p	185	£1,220
2024 — —	2 ounce/£200	81	£5,305

Buckingham Palace

2024 Silver Proof	£5	3,760	£98.50
2024 — — Piedfort	£5	1,060	£185
2024 Gold Proof	1/40 ounce/50p	2,034	£99.50
2024 — —	£5	210	£2,995

The National Gallery

2024 BU	£2	–	£13.00
2024 Silver Proof	£2	2,760	£78.50
2024 — — Piedfort	£2	1,210	£128.50
2024 Gold Proof	1/40 ounce/50p	2,034	£99.50
2024 — —	£2	185	£1,250

80th Anniversary of the D-Day Landings

2024 Cupro Nickel	50p	–	£12.00
2024 Silver Proof	50p	5,000	£61.00
2024 — —Piedfort	50p	1,954	£113.50
2024 Gold Proof	2 ounce/£200	86	£5,305
2024 — —	27.30mm 50p	470	£1,220
2024 — —	1/4 ounce/£25	510	£750
2024 — —	1/40 ounce/50p	2,034	£99.50

The Gruffalo's Child

2024 BU	50p	–	£12.00
2024 BU (coloured coin)	50p	25,000	£21.00
2024 Silver Proof (coloured coin)	50P	7,510	£75
2024 Gold Proof	1/40 ounce/50p	2,034	£99.50

Great Seals of the Realm

2024 Cupro Nickel	50p	–	£15.50
2024 Silver Proof	1ounce/£2	4,007	£103.50
2024 — —	2 ounce/£5	750	£195
2024 — —	5 ounce/£10	356	£487.50
2024 Gold Proof	1/4 ounce/£25	660	£750
2024 — —	1 ounce/£100	260	£2,770
2024 — —	2 ounce/£200	81	£5,305

With an interesting programme of issues intended to promote coin collecting, the Royal Mint produced a series of coins which were offered to the public at face value. The first issue was made in 2013 and was a £20 coin. The series was extended in 2015 to include a £100. In the same year the £50 silver coin in the Britannia series was offered as part of this programme. The issues are listed below.

HUNDRED POUNDS

Following on from the late 2013 introduction of the Twenty Pounds (see below) a "Hundred Pounds for £100" appeared, again a 0.999 Fine Silver coin, of two ounces weight, in early 2015.

DATE	Auth. issue qty	No. Issued	Issue price
2015 Big Ben, BU	50,000	49,147	£100
2015 Buckingham Palace, BU	50,000	47,851	£100
2016 Trafalgar Square	—	14,878	£100

FIFTY POUNDS

A new denomination introduced in 2015, with the slogan "Fifty Pounds for £50". A double first for Jody Clark, minted in 99.99 silver, diameter 34mm.

DATE	Auth. issue qty	No. Issued	Issue price
2015 Britannia BU	100,000	78,644	£50
2016 Shakespeare BU	—	14,948	£60

TWENTY POUNDS

Another new denomination was added in late 2013. Marketed by the Royal Mint under the slogan "Twenty Pounds for £20", it is a 27mm diameter 0.999 Fine silver coin.

DATE	Auth. issue qty	No. Issued	Issue price
2013 Pistrucci St George & Dragon BU	250,000		£24
2014 Centenary of the outbreak of the WWI	—	141,751	£24
2015 Sir Winston Churchill	—	132,142	£20
2015 The Longest Reigning Monarch, New Portrait	—	149,408	£20
2016 The 90th Birthday of Her Majesty the Queen	—	116,354	£20
2016 The Welsh Dragon	—	—	£25
2016 Christmas Nativity	—	29,929	£30
2017 Platinum Wedding Anniversary	70,000	24,223	£25

Up until 2022, the Royal Mint releases for the above issues depicted the relevant coinage profile of Her Majesty the Queen. Post the sad passing of the Queen in September 2022, there was a brief period when these coins were issued posthumously, therefore, you may find 2023-dated coins bearing her obverse portrait. These were a limited issue that had already been minted prior to her death hence the majority of coins of 2023 onwards will feature the new effigy of HIs Majesty King Charles III by Martin Jennings.

DECIMAL PROOF AND SPECIMEN SETS

The following listings are an attempt to include all officially marketed products from the Royal Mint of two coins or more, but excluding those which included non-UK coins. It is appreciated that not all have been advertised as new to the public, but it is assumed that at some time they have been, or will be, available. In a few cases, therefore, the prices may be conjectural but are, nevertheless, attempts at listing realistic values, in some instances based on an original retail price. In the case of Elizabeth II sets, if no metal is stated in the listing, the coins in the sets are of the same metal as the circulation coin equivalent. In addition to the above we have excluded historical gold coin sets, such as sets of sovereigns from different mints, where the dates of the coins vary from one set to another.

DATE	FDC
ELIZABETH II	
1968 Specimen decimal set 10p, 5p and 1971-dated bronze in blue wallet (5 coins)	£5
1971 Proof (issued 1973) 50p–half penny (6 coins)	£20
1972 Proof (issued 1976) 50p–half penny (7 coins including Silver Wedding crown)	£25
1973 Proof (issued 1976) 50p–half penny (6 coins)	£16
1974 Proof (issued 1976) 50p–half penny (6 coins)	£20
1975 Proof (issued 1976) 50p–half penny (6 coins)	£20
1976 Proof 50p–half penny (6 coins)	£18
1977 Proof 50p–half penny (7 coins including Silver Jubilee crown)	£22
1978 Proof 50p–half penny (6 coins)	£16
1979 Proof 50p–half penny (6 coins)	£18
1980 Proof gold sovereign series (4 coins)	£4700
1980 — 50p–half penny (6 coins)	£16
1981 Proof £5, sovereign, Royal Wedding Silver crown, 50p–half penny (9 coins)	£2500
1981 — 50p–half penny (6 coins)	£18
1982 Proof gold sovereign series (4 coins)	£6200
1982 — 50p–half penny (7 coins)	£20
1982 Uncirculated 50p–half penny (7 coins)	£15
1983 Proof gold double-sovereign to half sovereign (3 coins)	£1900
1983 — £1–half penny (8 coins) (includes H. J. Heinz sets)	£25
1983 Uncirculated £1–half penny (8 coins) (includes Benson & Hedges and Martini sets)	£30
1983 — — (8 coins) (only Benson & Hedges and Martini sets) with "2 NEW PENCE" legend	£1350
1983 — 50p–half penny (7 coins) (H. J. Heinz sets)	£16
1983 — — (7 coins) (H. J. Heinz set) with "2 NEW PENCE" legend	£1250
1984 Proof gold five pounds, sovereign and half-sovereigns (3 coins)	£4500
1984 — £1 (Scottish rev.)–half penny (8 coins)	£20
1984 BU £1 (Scottish rev.)–half penny (8 coins)	£16
1985 New portrait proof gold sovereign series (4 coins)	£4800
1985 Proof £1–1p in de luxe case (7 coins)	£25
1985 — In standard case	£20
1985 BU £1–1p (7 coins) in folder	£15
1986 Proof gold Commonwealth Games £2, sovereign and half sovereign (3 coins)	£2000
1986 — Commonwealth Games £2–1p, de luxe case (8 coins)	£30
1986 — — in standard case (8 coins)	£25
1986 BU £2–1p in folder (8 coins)	£20
1987 Proof gold double- to half sovereign (3 coins)	£2000
1987 — £1–1p in de luxe case (7 coins)	£35
1987 — £1–1p in standard case (7 coins)	£25
1987 BU £1–1p in folder (7 coins)	£20
1988 Proof gold double- to half sovereign (3 coins)	£2000
1988 — £1–1p in de luxe case (7 coins)	£35
1988 — £1–1p in standard case (7 coins)	£30

DATE	FDC
1988 BU £1–1p in folder (7 coins) (includes Bradford & Bingley sets)	£18
1989 Proof gold 500th anniversary of the sovereign series set (4 coins)	£8500
1989 — — — double- to half sovereign (3 coins)	£4250
1989 — Silver Bill of Rights £2, Claim of Right £2 (2 coins)	£65
1989 — — Piedfort as above (2 coins)	£125
1989 BU £2 in folder (2 coins)	£25
1989 Proof £2 (both)–1p in de luxe case (9 coins)	£35
1989 — in standard case (9 coins)	£30
1989 BU £1–1p in folder (7 coins)	£25
1990 Proof gold sovereign series set (4 coins)	£4500
1990— — double- to half sovereign (3 coins)	£2000
1990 — silver 5p, 2 sizes (2 coins)	£28
1990 — £1–1p in de luxe case (8 coins)	£35
1990 — £1–1p standard case (8 coins)	£30
1990 BU £1–1p in folder (8 coins)	£20
1991 Proof gold sovereign series set (4 coins)	£4500
1991 — — double- to half sovereign (3 coins)	£2000
1991 — £1–1p in de luxe case (7 coins)	£35
1991 — £1–1p in standard case (7 coins)	£28
1991 BU £1–1p in folder (7 coins)	£18
1992 Proof gold Britannia set (4 coins)	£4800
1992 — — sovereign series set (4 coins)	£5400
1992 — — double- to half sovereign (3 coins)	£2500
1992 — £1–1p including two each 50p and 10p in de luxe case (9 coins)	£75
1992 — £1–1p as above in standard case (9 coins)	£65
1992 BU £1–1p as above in folder (9 coins)	£60
1992 — with Enhanced Effigy on obverse of 20p	£60
1992 Proof silver 10p, two sizes (2 coins)	£25
1993 Proof gold sovereign series set (4 coins plus silver Pistrucci medal)	£4800
1993 — — double- to half sovereign (3 coins)	£2200
1993 — Coronation anniversary £5–1p in de luxe case (8 coins)	£38
1993 — — in standard case (8 coins)	£35
1993 BU £1–1p including 1992 EU 50p (8 coins)	£65
1994 Proof gold sovereign series set (4 coins)	£5200
1994 — — £2 to half sovereign (3 coins)	£2100
1994 — Bank of England Tercentenary £2–1p in de luxe case (8 coins)	£38
1994 — — in standard case (8 coins)	£35
1994 BU £2–1p in folder (9 coins)	£18
1994 Proof gold 1992 and 1994 50p (2 coins)	£450
1994 — "Family silver" set £2–50p (3 coins)	£65
1995 Proof gold sovereign series (4 coins)	£4100
1995 — — £2 to half sovereign (3 coins)	£2000
1995 — 50th Anniversary of WWII £2–1p in de luxe case (8 coins)	£40
1995 — — as above in standard case (8 coins)	£35
1995 BU as above in folder (8 coins)	£16
1995 Proof "Family Silver" set £2 (two) and £1 (3 coins)	£90
1996 Proof gold sovereign series set (4 coins)	£5200
1996 — — double- to half sovereign (3 coins)	£2000
1996 — Royal 70th Birthday £5–1p in de luxe case (9 coins)	£50
1996 — — as above in standard case (9 coins)	£45
1996 BU Football £2–1p in folder (8 coins)	£20
1996 Proof gold Britannia £10 and half-sovereign (2 coins)	£850
1996 — — sovereign and silver £1 (2 coins)	£500
1996 — — "Family silver" set £5–£1 (3 coins)	£125
1996 — silver 25th Anniversary of Decimal currency £1–1p (7 coins)	£175
1996 Circulation and BU 25th Anniversary of Decimalisation 2s 6d–halfpenny (misc.) and £1–1p in folder (14 coins)	£25
1997 Proof gold sovereign series set (4 coins)	£4700
1997 — — — £2 to half sovereign (3 coins)	£2100
1997 — Golden Wedding £5–1p in red leather case	£45
1997 — — as above in standard case (10 coins)	£35
1997 BU £2 to 1p in folder (9 coins)	£25
1997 Proof silver 50p set, two sizes (2 coins)	£55
1997/1998 Proof silver £2 set, both dates (2 coins)	£85

DATE	FDC
1998 Proof gold sovereign series set (4 coins)	£4500
1998 — — double- to half sovereign (3 coins)	£2200
1998 Prince of Wales £5–1p (10 coins) in red leather case	£45
1998 — as above in standard case (10 coins)	£38
1998 BU £2–1p in folder (9 coins)	£16
1998 Proof silver European/NHS 50p set (2 coins)	£60
1998 BU Britannia/EU 50p set (2 coins)	£8
1999 Proof gold Sovereign series set (4 coins)	£4500
1999 — — £2 to half sovereign (3 coins)	£2100
1999 Princess Diana £5–1p in red leather case (9 coins)	£65
1999 — as above in standard case (9 coins)	£45
1999 BU £2–1p (8 coins) in folder	£20
1999 Proof "Family Silver" set. Both £5, £2 and £1 (4 coins)	£150
1999/2000 Reverse frosted proof set, two x £1 (2 coins)	£80
2000 Proof gold Sovereign series set (4 coins)	£4500
2000 — — — double- to half sovereign (3 coins)	£2500
2000 Millennium £5–1p in de luxe case (10 coins)	£50
2000 — — as above in standard case (10 coins)	£45
2000 — Silver set Millennium £5 to 1p plus Maundy (13 coins)	£285
2000 BU £2–1p set in folder (9 coins)	£20
2000 Millennium "Time Capsule" BU £5 to 1p (9 coins)	£30
2001 Proof gold Sovereign series set (4 coins)	£4500
2001 — — — £2–half sovereign (3 coins)	£2100
2001 — Victoria £5–1p in Executive case (10 coins)	£100
2001 — — as above in red leather case (10 coins)	£75
2001 — — as above in "Gift" case (10 coins)	£48
2001 — — as above in standard case (10 coins)	£40
2001 BU £2–1p in folder (9 coins)	£20
2002 Proof gold Sovereign series set, all Shield rev. (4 coins)	£4700
2002 — — — double- to half sovereign (3 coins)	£2400
2002 — — Golden Jubilee set £5–1p plus Maundy (13 coins)	£13500
2002 — Golden Jubilee £5–1p in Executive case (9 coins)	£75
2002 — — as above in red leather de luxe case (9 coins)	£50
2002 — — as above in "Gift" case (9 coins)	£42
2002 — — as above in standard case (9 coins)	£40
2002 BU £2–1p (8 coins) in folder	£16
2002 Proof Gold Commonwealth Games £2 set (4 coins)	£4500
2002 — Silver Piedfort Commonwealth Games £2 set (4 coins)	£500
2002 — — Commonwealth Games £2 set (4 coins)	£125
2002 — Commonwealth Games £2 set (4 coins)	£30
2002 BU Commonwealth Games £2 set (4 coins) in folder	£25
2003 Proof gold Sovereign series set (4 coins)	£4600
2003 — — — series £2–half sovereign (3 coins)	£2000
2003 — type set (one of each £2 reverse) (4 coins)	£100
2003 — £5 to 1p, two of each £2 and 50p in Executive case (11 coins)	£80
2003 — — as above in red leather case (11 coins)	£55
2003 — — as above in standard case (11 coins)	£48
2003 BU £2 (two)–1p in folder (10 coins)	£22
2003 Proof silver Piedfort set. DNA £2, £1 and Suffragette 50p (3 coins)	£180
2003 Proof "Family Silver" set £5, Britannia and DNA £2, £1 and Suffragette 50p (5 coins)	£195
2003 Circ & BU "God Save the Queen" Coronation anniversary set 5s/0d to farthing (1953) and £5 to 1p (2003) in folder (19 coins)	£55
2003 Circulation or bullion "Royal Sovereign" collection, example of each Elizabeth II date (21 coins)	£12000
2004 Proof gold Sovereign series set (4 coins)	£4500
2004 — — — Series £2-half sovereign (3 coins)	£2100
2004 (Issue date) Royal Portrait gold sovereign set, all proof except the first: Gillick, Machin, Maklouf and Rank-Broadley sovereigns, and the 2nd, 3rd and 4th of above half-sovereigns, various dates (7 coins)	£3750
2004 Proof "Family Silver" set £5, Britannia and Trevithick £2, £1 and Bannister 50p (5 coins)	£225
2004 — Silver Piedfort set, Trevithick £2, £1 and Bannister 50p (3 coins)	£225
2004 — £2 to 1p, two each of £2 and 50p in Executive case (10 coins)	£125
2004 — — as above in red leather case (10 coins)	£45

DATE	FDC
2004 — — as above in standard case (10 coins)	£40
2004 BU £2 to 1p in folder (10 coins)	£22
2004 — "New Coinage" set, Trevithick £2, £1 and Bannister 50p (3 coins)	£10
2004 BU "Season's Greetings" £2 to 1p and Royal Mint Christmas medal in folder (8 coins)	£18
2005 Proof Gold Sovereign series set (4 coins)	£4500
2005 — — — series, double to half sovereign (3 coins)	£2100
2005 — Gold Trafalgar and Nelson £5 crowns (2 coins)	£5800
2005 — Silver, as above (2 coins)	£100
2005 — — Piedfort, as above (2 coins)	£200
2005 — Silver Piedfort set, Gunpowder Plot and World War II £2, £1 and Johnson 50p (4 coins)	£250
2005 — £5 to 1p, two of each of £5, £2 and 50p in Executive case (12 coins)	£80
2005 — — as above in red leather case (12 coins)	£60
2005 — — as above in standard case (12 coins)	£45
2005 BU Trafalgar and Nelson £5 crowns in pack (2 coins)	£35
2005 — £2 (two) to 1p in folder (10 coins)	£25
2005 — "New Coinage" set, Gunpowder Plot £2, £1 and Johnson 50p (3 coins)	£10
2005 — "Merry Xmas" £2 to 1p and Royal Mint Christmas medal in folder (8 coins)	£20
2006 Proof Gold Sovereign Series set (4 coins)	£4500
2006 — — — series, double to half sovereign (3 coins)	£2100
2006 — Silver Brunel £2 coin set (2 coins)	£75
2006 — — Piedfort Brunel £2 coin set (2 coins)	£140
2006 — Gold Brunel £2 coin set (2 coins)	£2000
2006 — Silver VC 50p coin set (2 coins)	£80
2006 — Silver Piedfort VC 50p coin set (2 coins)	£130
2006 — Gold VC 50p coin set (2 coins)	£2400
2006 — Silver proof set, £5 to 1p plus Maundy coins (13 coins)	£375
2006 — — — Piedfort collection £5, with trumpets enhanced with 23 carat gold, both Brunel £2, £1, both VC 50p (6 coins)	£200
2006 — £5 to 1p, three of each £2 and 50p in Executive case (13 coins)	£80
2006 — as above in red leather case (13 coins)	£55
2006 — as above in standard case (13 coins)	£45
2006 BU £2 (two), £1, 50p (two) and to 1p in folder (10 coins)	£18
2006 Proof Brunel £2 in folder (2 coins)	£15
2006 — VC 50p in folder (2 coins)	£15
2006 — Gold Half-Sovereign set dated 2005 Noad and 2006 Pistrucci St George and the Dragon (2 coins)	£750
2007 — — Sovereign Series set (4 coins)	£4500
2007 — — — series, double to half sovereign (3 coins)	£2100
2007 — — Sovereign and half-sovereign (2 coins)	£850
2007 — "Family Silver" set, Britannia, £5 crown, Union and Slavery £2, Gateshead £1 and Scouting 50p (6 coins)	£250
2007 Proof Silver Piedfort Collection, as "Family Silver" above but excluding a Britannia (5 coins)	£325
2007 — Silver £1 Bridge series coins, dated 2004 to 2007 (4 coins)	£150
2007 — Silver Proof Piedfort £1 Bridge Series, dated 2004 to 2007 (4 coins)	£290
2007 — Gold £1 Bridge series coins, dated as above (4 coins)	£5000
2007 — £5 to 1p, three £2 and two 50p in Executive case (12 coins)	£85
2007 — as above, Deluxe in red leather case (12 coins)	£65
2007 — as above, in standard case (12 coins)	£50
2007 BU £2 (two) to 1p (9 coins)	£18
2007 50th Anniversary Sovereign set, 1957 circulation standard and 2007 Proof (2 coins)	£1200
2008 Proof Gold Sovereign series set (4 coins)	£4500
2008 — — — double to half-sovereign (3 coins)	£2100
2008 — — Sovereign and half-sovereign (2 coins)	£850
2008 — "Family silver" set, 2x £5, Britannia £2, Olympiad £2 and Royal Arms £1 (5 coins)	£250
2008 — Silver Piedfort Collection, 2x £5, Olympiad £2 and Shield of Royal Arms £1 (4 coins)	£325
2008 — 2 x £5, 2 x £2, £1 to 1p in Executive case (11 coins)	£85
2008 — as above, Deluxe in black leather case (11 coins)	£55
2008 — as above, in standard back case (11 coins)	£60
2008 BU 2 x £2, Royal Arms £1 to 1p (9 coins)	£20
2008 — "Emblems of Britain" ("old" Revs) Royal Arms £1 to 1p (7 coins)	£15
2008 — "Royal Shield of Arms" ("new" Revs) Shield of Royal Arms £1 to 1p (7 coins)	£15
2008 — Above two sets housed in one sleeve	£28
2008 Proof Base Metal "Royal Shield of Arms" set, £1 to 1p (7 coins)	£40
2008 — Silver "Emblems of Britain" set, £1 to 1p (7 coins)	£90
2008 — — "Royal Shield of Arms" set, £1 to 1p (7 coins)	£90
2008 — — Above two sets in one black case	£325
2008 — Gold "Emblems of Britain" set, £1 to 1p (7 coins)	£6000
2008 — — "Royal Shield of Arms" set, £1 to 1p (7 coins)	£6000

DATE	FDC
2008 — — Above two sets in one oak-veneer case	£13,400
2008 — Platinum "Emblems of Britain" set, £1 to 1p (7 coins)	£6500
2008 — — "Royal Shield of Arms" set, £1 to 1p (7 coins)	£6500
2008 — — Above two sets in one walnut veneer case	£12,000
2008 — Silver Piedfort "Royal Shield of Arms" set, £1 to 1p (7 coins)	£180
2008 — Gold set of 14 £1 coins, one of each Rev used since 1983, all dated 2008 (25th anniversary) (14 coins)	£17,000
2008 — Silver with gold Rev highlighting as above (14 coins)	£400
2008 — 2 x £2, Royal Arms £1 to 1p (9 coins) Christmas Coin Sets, two different outer sleeves, Father Christmas or Three Wise men	£20
2009 Proof Gold Sovereign series set (5 coins)	£4700
2009 — — — double to half-sovereign (3 coins)	£2100
2009 — — sovereign and half-sovereign (2 coins)	£800
2009 — "Family Silver" set, Henry VIII £5, Britannia £2, Darwin and Burns £2, £1 and Kew 50p (6 coins)	£250
2009 — Silver Piedfort collection, Henry VIII £5, Darwin and Burns £2 and Kew Gardens 50p (4 coins)	£375
2009 — Silver Set, £5 to 1p (12 coins)	£275
2009 — Base metal Executive set, £5 to 1p (12 coins)	£80
2009 — — — Deluxe set, £5 to 1p (12 coins)	£55
2009 — — — Standard set, £5 to 1p (12 coins)	£45
2009 BU Base metal set, £2 to 1p (11 coins)	£22
2009 — — —, £1 to 1p "Royal Shield of Arms" set (7 coins)	£12
2009 — — —, £2 to 1p (8 coins)	£15
2009 Proof set of 50p coins as detailed in FIFTY PENCE section, CuNi (16 coins)	£350
2009 — Silver (16 coins)	£950
2009 — Gold (16 coins)	£21,000
2009 — Gold Piedfort (16 coins)	£37,000
2009 "Mind" set of £5 coins, silver (6 coins)	£350
2010 Proof Gold Olympic Series "Faster", £100 and £25 (2), (3 coins)	£4500
2010 Proof Gold Olympic Series "Faster", £25 (2), (2 coins)	£1300
2010 — — Sovereign series set (5 coins)	£4700
2010 — — — double to half (3 coins)	£2600
2010 — — — sovereign to quarter (3 coins)	£1300
2010 — "Silver Celebration" set, Restoration £5, Nightingale £2, London and Belfast £1 and Girlguiding 50p (5 coins)	£200
2010 Silver Piedfort set, coins as in "Silver Celebration" set (5 coins)	£375
2010 — Silver Collection, £5 to 1p (13 coins)	£300
2010 — Base Metal Executive Set, £5 to 1p (13 coins)	£80
2010 — — Deluxe set	£50
2010 — — Standard set	£40
2010 BU — Capital Cities £1 (2 coins)	£15
2010 — — Set, £2 to 1p (12 coins)	£35
2010 — — Definitive pack, £2 to 1p (8 coins)	£20
2010 Proof "Body" Collection of £5 coins, silver (6 coins)	£350
2010 Proof "Spirit" Collection of £5 coins, silver (6 coins)	£350
2011 Proof Gold Sovereign set (5 coins)	£4700
2011 — — double to half (3 coins)	£2600
2011 — — sovereign to quarter (3 coins)	£1300
2011 — Olympic gold "Higher" set (3 coins)	£4500
2011 — — — "Faster" (2010) and "Higher" set (6 coins) in 9-coin case	£9500
2011 — Silver Collection, £5 to 1p (14 coins)	£400
2011 — — Celebration set, Duke of Edinburgh £5, Mary Rose and King James bible Cardiff and Edinburgh £1 and WWF 50p (6 coins)	£250
2011 — — — Piedfort, as above (6 coins)	£395
2011 Executive Proof Base metal set (14 coins)	£85
2011 De-luxe Proof Base metal set (14 coins)	£50
2011 Standard Proof Base metal set (14 coins)	£40
2011 BU set including £2, £1 and 50p commemoratives (13 coins)	£26
2011 BU set of Definitives (8 coins)	£25
2012 Proof Gold Sovereign set (5 coins)	£4700
2012 — — Double to Half (3 coins)	£2600
2012 — — Sovereign to Quarter (3 coins)	£1300
2012 BU Sovereign set Double to Half (3 coins)	£2000
2012 Proof Olympic gold Stronger set (3 coins)	£4500
2012 — — — 2x £25 (2 coins)	£1350

DATE	FDC
2010, 2011, 2012 Proof Olympic gold complete set (9 coins)	£14,500
2009, 2010, 2011, 2012 Complete Countdown sets:	
Gold Proof (4 coins)	£12,000
Silver Proof Piedfort (4 coins)	£400
Silver Proof (4 coins)	£325
CuNi BU (4 coins)	£45
2012 Proof Gold set, Diamond Jubilee £5, Dickens & Technology £2, £1 to 1p (10 coins)	£15,000
2012 — Silver set, as above with Selective Gold plating on £1 to 1p coins (10 coins)	£300
2012 — set (Premium) (10 coins)	£100
2012 — set (Collector) (10 coins)	£55
2012 BU set, include Diamond Jubilee £5 (10 coins)	£40
2012 — set, Technology £2 to 1p (8 coins)	£21
2012 Proof Gold, Diamond Jubilee £5 and Double Sovereign (2 coins)	£6000
2012 — Olympic and Paralympic £5 (2 coins)	£8500
2012 — Gold Piedfort 50p set, one each of the coins of Olympic sports in which Team GB gained gold medals (11 coins)	£30,000
2012 Proof Gold Sovereign set (5 coins)	£5000
2012 — — Double to Half (3 coins)	£2500
2013 Proof Gold Sovereign set (5 coins)	£5000
2013 — — Double to Half (3 coins)	£3000
2013 — — One to Quarter (3 coins)	£1750
2013 — Gold £5 Portraits set (4 coins)	£13000
2013 — Silver Portraits set (4 coins) (1,465)	£400
2013 — Silver Piedfort Portraits set (4 coins) (697)	£800
2013 — Gold set, £5 Coronation anniversary to 1p (15 coins)	£16,000
2013 — Gold set of both London Underground £2 (2 coins)	£4500
2013 — Silver Piedfort set, as above (2 coins)	£200
2013 — Silver set, as above (2 coins)	£100
2013 BU set, as above (2 coins)	£20
2013 — Gold set, 30th anniversary of the One Pound coin, reverses from 1983 (Sewell), 1988 (Gorringe) and 2013 (Dent). (3 coins)	£4500
2013 — Silver, as above (3 coins)	£150
2013 BU Sovereign set, Double to Half (3 coins), struck June 2, 2013	£2500
2013 Proof Silver annual set, £5 Coronation anniv to 1p (15 coins)	£600
2013 — — Piedfort commemorative set (7 coins)	£650
2013 — "Premium" set (15 coins plus a "Latent Image" item)	£150
2013 — "Collector" set (15 coins)	£110
2013 — Commemorative set (7 coins)	£65
2013 BU annual set (15 coins)	£50
2013 — Definitive Set (8 coins)	£25
2014 Proof Gold Britannia (Clark) set £100 to 50p (6 coins)	£5000
2014 — — — £50 to £10 (3 coins)	£2500
2014 — — — £25 to £1 (3 coins)	£1500
2014 — Silver Britannia (Clark) set £2 to 5p (6 coins)	£200
2014 — — — 20p to 5p (3 coins)	£45
2014 — Sovereign set (5 coins)	£4000
2014 — — Double to half (3 coins)	£2000
2014 — — One to quarter (3 coins)	£1000
2014 — Gold Commemorative set, £5 Queen Anne, 2 x £2, 2 x £1, 50p (6 coins)	£7500
2014 — Silver Piedfort set, as above (6 coins)	£570
2014 — — set as above (6 coins)	£295
2014 — — all major coins of 2014 (14 coins)	£560
2014 — Premium set (14 coins and a premium medal)	£155
2014 — Collector set (14 coins)	£110
2014 — Commemorative set (6 coins)	£65
2014 BU Annual set (14 coins)	£50
2014 — Definitive set (8 coins)	£25
2014 — Floral £1 set, Scotland and Northern Ireland (2 coins)	£18
2014 Proof Silver Outbreak of First World War set of £5 (6 coins)	£450
2014 — Gold set as above (6 coins)	—
2014 — Silver Portrait of Britain £5 Silver collection (4 coins)	£36
2015 Proof Gold Sovereign set, Rank-Broadley portrait (5 coins)	£4000

DATE	FDC
2015 — — Double to half, Rank-Broadley portrait (3 coins)	£2000
2015 — — One to quarter, Rank-Broadley portrait (3 coins)	£1000
2015 — Gold Commemorative set, 2 x £5, 2 x £2, 2 x £1, 50p, Rank-Broadley portrait (5 coins)	£7500
2015 — Silver Piedfort set, as above (5 coins)	£570
2015 — — set as above (5 coins)	£295
2015 — Base metal set as above (5 coins)	£65
2015 — Platinum definitive set £2 to 1p, Rank-Broadley portrait plus £2 to 1p Clark portrait (16 coins)	£8,000
2015 — Gold ditto	£10,000
2015 — Silver ditto	£480
2015 — Base metal ditto	£120
2015 BU definitive set as per Platinum set above (16 coins)	£50
The above four entries are also available as 8-coin sets with either the Rank-Broadley ("Final Edition") or the Clark ("First Edition" portrait. These are issued at half the prices quoted above.	
2015 Proof Silver set of definitive and commemorative coins, Rank-Broadley portrait (13 coins)	£560
2015 — Premium set as above (13 coins and a Premium medal)	£155
2015 Collector set as above (13 coins and medal)	£110
2015 Proof Double to half sovereign, Clark portrait (3 coins)	£2000
2015 — Silver commemorative set, Anniversary of First World War (6 coins)	£450
2015 Portrait of Britain Silver Proof Collection (4x£5 with colour)	£310
2016 Proof Gold Sovereign set, Butler Portrait (5 coins)	£5000
2016 — — Double to half, Butler Portrait (3 coins)	£2000
2016— — One to quarter, Butler Portrait (3 coins)	£1000
2016 — Gold Commemorative set, £5, 5x £2, £1, 50p (8 coins)	£7500
2016 — Silver Piedfort set, as above (8 coins)	£595
2016 — — set as above (8 coins)	£395
2016 — Base metal set as above (8 coins)	£95
2016 — silver set, commemoratives and definitives (16 coins)	£595
2016 — Base metal set as above, Premium plus Medal (16 coins)	£195
2016 — — Collector set (16 coins)	£145
2016 Portrait of Britain Silver Proof Collection (4x£5 with colour)	£310
2016 BU Annual set including commemoratives (16 coins)	£55
2016 — Definitive set (8 coins)	£30
2016 Proof Silver set of £5 coins, Anniversary of First World War (6 coins)	£450
2016 Beatrix Potter 150th Anniversary 50p coin set (5 coins)	£75
2017 BU Annual "Premium" set (13 coins & premium medal)	£195
2017 BU Annual set (13 coins as above)	£55
2017 — Definitive set (8 coins)	£30
2017 Proof Annual "Collector" set (13 coins & medal)	£145
2017 — Commemorative set (5 coins), 2x£5, 2x£2, 50p	£95
2017 — Silver Piedfort Commemorative set (coins as above)	£595
2017 — Silver Commemorative set (coins as above)	£350
2017 — Silver set (13 coins £5–1p)	£625
2017 — Silver Portrait of Britain Collection (4x£5 with colour)	£310
2017 — Silver Outbreak of First World War set of £5 (6 coins)	£450
2018 BU Annual set (13 coins)	£55
2018 — Definitive set (8 coins)	£30
2018 Proof Annual set (13 coins)	£155
2018 — "Premium" set (13 coins & premium medal)	£210
2018 — Portrait of Britain Silver Proof Collection (4x£5 with colour)	£310
2018 — Centenary of World War I Silver Proof set of £5 (6 coins)	£465
2018 — — Gold (6 coins)	£15,000
2018 — — Silver Piedfort set (5 coins)	£555
2018 Silver set (5 commemorative and 8 circulating coins)	£610
2018 Commemorative coin set (5 coins)	£95
2019 BU Annual set (13 coins)	£55
2019 — Annual definitive set (8 coins)	£30
2019 Proof Annual coin set with Medal (13 coins £5–1p)	£210
2019 — Silver set (13 coins £5–1p)	£610
2019 — Gold Proof commemorative set (5 coins £5–50p)	£5500
2019 — Silver Proof Piedfort commemorative set (5 coins)	£550
2019 — Sovereign Proof set (5 coins)	£8500
2019 — "Premium" Sovereign Proof set (3 coins)	£2000

DATE	FDC
2019 — Sovereign Proof set (3 coins)	£1100
2019 — Paddington Bear Silver Proof set (2 coins)	£65
2019 BU Paddington Bear BU set (2 coins)	£10
2019 Proof set Celebrating 50 Years of the 50 pence (3 types):	
i. *British Military and Culture Set* (10 coins): New 50 Pence, Girl Guides, Kew Gardens, Roger Bannister, Scouting, Battle of Hastings, Battle of Britain, D-Day, Victoria Cross 150th Anniversary, Victoria Cross Heroic Acts, BU	£76.50
ii. *British Military Set* (5 coins): Battle of Hastings, Battle of Britain, D-Day, Victoria Cross 150th Anniversary, Victoria Cross Heroic Acts, BU	£45
iii. *British Culture Set* (5 coins): New 50 Pence, Girl Guides, Kew Gardens, Roger Bannister, Scouting, BU	£70
2019 — — Proof (3,500)	£90
2019 — — Silver Proof (1,969)	£225
2019 — — Gold Proof (75)	£5500
2020 Monumental Coin Designs (5 coins) including Team GB 50p, 75th Anniversary of VE Day £2, 400th Anniversary of the Mayflower £2, Centenary of Agatha Christie £2, 200th Anniversary since the reign of George III £5	—
2020 BU Annual coin set, 1p–£2 plus the 5 above (13 coins)	£55
2020 — Definitive coin set, 1p–£2 (8 current circulating coinage designs only)	£30
2020 Proof Annual coin set (13 coins) (7000)	£155
2020 — Premium set (13 coins) (2500)	£210
2020 — Silver set (13 coins) (500)	£610
2020 — Silver Piedfort set (5 coins, 50p–£5) (300)	£550
2020 — Gold Proof Sovereign series (5 coins) (75)	£6150
2020 — Gold Proof Sovereign series (3 coins) (750)	£1000
2021 BU Annual coin set £2–1p (8 coins)	£30
2021 — including coins from the 5-piece coin set below (13 coins)	£55
2021 Proof Annual coin set (13 coins) (7000)	£155
2021 — Premium Proof set (13 coins) (2500)	£210
2021 — Silver Proof set (13 coins) (550)	£640
2021 — Gold Proof Sovereign series set (5 coins, £5–quarter sovereign)	£4900
2021 — — (4 coins, £2–quarter sovereign)	£2100
2021 — — (3 coins, Sovereign–quarter sovereign)	£1000
2021 — — Special commemorative Sovereign set comprising George V 1926, EII 1957 and a "Struck on the Day" 2021 (3 coins) (100)	£2500
2021 5 piece coin set comprising: 50th Anniversary of Decimal Day 2021 UK 50p, Celebrating the life and work of John Logie Baird 2021 UK 50p, Celebrating the life and work of H. G. Wells 2021UK £2, 250th Anniversary of the birth of Sir Walter Scott 2021 UK £2. The 95th Birthday of Her Majesty the Queen 2021 UK £5. Silver Proof Piedfort (5 coins) (300)	£600
2021 — — Gold Proof (95)	£7100
2021 10 piece coin set comprising: The Lion of England, The Unicorn of Scotland, The Red Dragon of Wales, The Black Bull of Clarence, The Falcon of Plantagenets, The Yale of Beaufort, The White Lion of Mortimer, The White Horse of Hanover, The Greyhound of Richmond, The Griffin of Edward III. Silver Proof 1/4 ounce/50p (1250)	£400
2021 — — Silver Proof 2 ounce/£5 (300)	£2000
2021 — — Gold Proof 1/4 ounce/£25 (250)	£7000
2022 BU Definitive Annual coin set (8 coins) (Unlimited)	£30
2022 13 piece coin set comprising: Platinum Jubilee of Her Majesty the Queen 2022 UK 50p, Birmingham 2022 Commonwealth Games UK 50p, Life and Legacy of Dame Vera Lyynn 2022 UK £2, Life and Legacy of Alexander Graham Bell 2022 UK £2, Platinum Jubilee of Her Majesty the Queen 2022 UK £5 and the following denominations: £2, £1, 50p, 20p, 10p, 5p, 2p, 1p. BU (13 coins. Unlimited)	£60
2022 — Proof set (7000)	£155
2022 — Premium Proof set (2500)	£210
2022 — Silver Proof set (550)	£650
2022 HRH Duke of Cambridge 40th Birthday. 2 piece Gold Coin set comprising 1982 Uncirculated Sovereign & 2022 Quarter ounce/£25 Gold Proof coin (100)	£1400
2022 5 piece coin set comprising: Platinum Jubilee of Her Majesty the Queen 2022 UK 50p, Birmingham 2022 Commonwealth Games UK 50p, Life and Legacy of Dame Vera Lynn 2022 UK £2, Life and Legacy of Alexander Graham Bell 2022 UK £2, Platinum Jubilee of Her Majesty the Queen 2022 UK £5. Silver Proof Piedfort (5 coins) (370)	£600
2022 — Gold Proof set (100)	£7500
2022 — Platinum Proof set (30)	£9000
2022 Dame Vera Lynn two-coin set comprising 1917 Sovereign & 2022 1/4 ounce Gold Proof coin (400)	£1500

DATE FDC

2022 — — comprising 1917 Half Crown & 2022 £2 Silver Proof coin (373) £150
2022 Platinum Jubilee Gold Sovereign Proof set (5 coins, £5–1/4 Sovereign) (700) £7500
2022 Gold Sovereign Proof set (4 coins, Double Sovereign–1/4 Sovereign) (500) £2700
2022 Gold Sovereign Proof set (3 coins, Sovereign–1/4 Sovereign) (1000) £1200
2022 Memorial Gold Sovereign Proof set (5 coins, 5 Sovereign–1/4 Sovereign) (1,200) £5600
2022 Memorial Gold Sovereign Proof set (4 coins, Double Sovereign–1/4 Sovereign) (750) £2600
2022 Memorial Gold Sovereign Proof set (3 coins, Sovereign–1/4 Sovereign) (1,500) £1125
2022 Her Late Majesty the Queen Memorial 10-coin set, with privy mark 26/22 comprising the memorial UK 50p and £5 Coins struck to commemorate Her Majesty's life and legacy as well as the following denominations, £2, £1, 50p, 20p, 10p, 5p, 2p, 1p. BU £75
2022 — Silver Proof (1,500) £465
2022 — Gold Proof (200) £10,750
2022 — Platinum Proof (96) £12,000
2023 Five Piece Coin Sets comprising: 75 Years of Windrush Generations UK 50p, NHS 75th Anniversary UK 50p, The Centenary of the Flying Scotsman UK £2, Celebrating the life and works of J. R. R. Tolkien UK £2, 75th Birthday of His Majesty King Charles III UK £5, BU £50
2023 — Proof (7,500) £105
2023 — Premium Proof (2,750) £145
2023 — Silver Proof (650) £315
2023 — Silver Proof Piedfort (400) £615
2023 — Gold Proof (150) £12,500
2023 — Platinum Proof (30) £10,000
2023 The Coronation of His Majesty King Charles III Gold Sovereign Proof set (5 coins, 5 Sovereign–1/4 Sovereign) . (1,050) £6000
2023 The Coronation of His Majesty King Charles III Gold Sovereign Proof set (4 coins, Double Sovereign–1/4 Sovereign) (575) £2750
2023 The Coronation of His Majesty King Charles III Gold Sovereign Proof set (3 coins, Sovereign–1/4 Sovereign (1,250) £1200
2023 Milestones of His Majesty King Charles III Life—Historic Sovereign Set (3 coins, 1958 Sovereign, Memorial Sovereign, His Majesty King Charles III Coronation 2023 Sovereign) (1,000) £2000

2023 KING CHARLES III Definitives Eight Piece Coin Sets, with Coronation Tudor Crown privy mark, comprising the following denominations:
£2, £1, 50p, 20p, 10p, 5p, 2p, 1p.
2023 — BU (Unlimited) £33.00
2023 — Base Proof (12,023) £99.50
2023 — Silver Proof (3,000) £370
2023 — Gold Proof (125) £7,725

13 Piece Coin Sets comprising: Buckingham Palace £5, Sir Winston Churchill £2, The National Gallery £2, RNLI 50p, Team GB and Paralympics 50p, £2, £1, 50p, 20p, 10p, 5p, 2p, 1p
2024 — BU (Unlimited) £69
2024 — Proof (7,500) £179.50
2024 — Premium Proof (2,024) £240
2024 — Silver Proof (500) £672.50
2024 — Gold Proof (25) £15,495

Five Piece Coin Sets comprising: Buckingham Palace £5, Sir Winston Churchill £2, The National Gallery £2, RNLI 50p, Team GB and Paralympics 50p
2024 — Silver Proof Piedfort (250) £627.50

2024 Brilliant Uncirculated Definitive Coin Set
Eight Piece Coin Sets comprising of:
£2, £1, 50p, 20p, 10p, 5p, 2p, 1p
2024 — BU (Unlimited) £34.50

2024 Gold Proof Sovereign series set (5 coins) quarter sovereign, half sovereign, sovereign, double sovereign, five piece sovereign (450) £5,725
2024 — — (4 coins) quarter sovereign, half sovereign, sovereign, double sovereign (350) £2,435
2024 — — (3 coins) quarter sovereign, half sovereign, sovereign (650) £1,140

In addition to the information on the previous pages, the Royal Mint produce the BU sets detailed above in Wedding and in Baby gift packs each year. Also various patterns and sets have been made available from time to time. These include the following:

1999 (dated 1994) Bi-metal £2, plus three unprocessed or part-processed elements .... —
2003 Set of patterns of £1 coins with "Bridges" designs, in gold, hall-marked on edges (4 coins) .... —
2003 — Silver £1 as above (4 coins) £150
2004 — Gold £1 featuring heraldic animal heads, hall-marked on edge (4 coins) £1500
2004 — Silver £1 featuring heraldic animal heads, hall-marked on edge (4 coins) £150
The Centenary of the Burial of the Unknown Warrior Historic coin set comprising: Remembrance Day 2020 UK Silver Proof £5 Coin, George VI Half Penny, George V Farthing, Sixpence, Shilling, Florin, Half Crown, Penny, Threepence (100) £280

New Coins for a new King

The new coin designs for the new monarch, King Charles III, are called "Definitives". The designs of the new coins depict animals and plants, many of them under threat, from the four nations that make up the United Kingdom. As we move away from the more traditional, heraldic designs, the inclusion of animals on our circulating coinage is sure to engage the young and may perhaps trigger another bout of "change checking". From the £2 down to the lowly 1p, collector versions in Proof, silver and gold ensure the new releases meet the needs of collectors of modern issues. The King's portrait by Martin Jennings graces the obverse while the reverse designs have been created in-house at the Royal Mint. The obverse of each 2023-dated commemorative, as opposed to circulating, coin carries a privy mark that takes the form of the Tudor Crown which is an exclusive addition to this new set of coins.

(Reproduced from the December 2023 edition of COIN NEWS.*)*

THE STANDARD CATALOGUE TO THE

Gold Sovereign Series

The first revised edition of the Token Publishing Ltd imprint of Michael Marsh's The Gold Sovereign was published in 2017 to coincide with the 200th anniversary year of the famous coin. Since then this book, fully revised and updated by Steve Hill of Sovereign Rarities (formerly of Spink and Baldwins) has become the reference work on the sovereign, half sovereign and quarter sovereign.

The second edition, now entitled The Gold Sovereign Series was published in 2021, and was once again updated by Steve with all new sovereigns and fractionals added, Also, for the very first time, the five sovereign and two sovereign coins were included too, Both the first and second editions completely sold out.

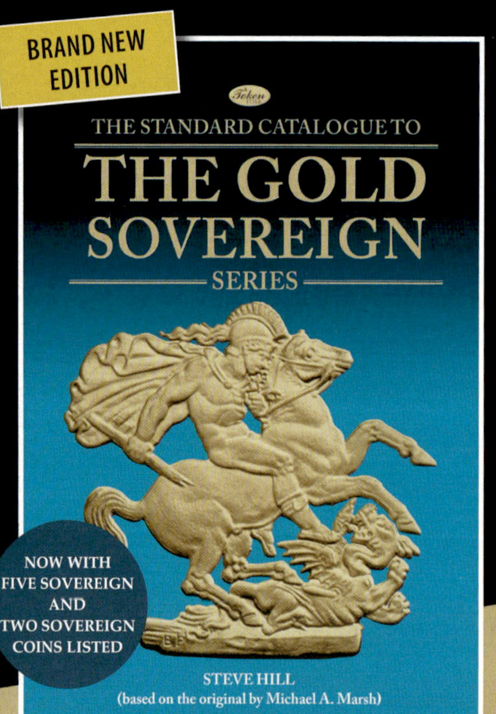

Now the third edition is ready and, for the first time, we have gone all the way back to where it began and include the sovereigns of Henry VII, the half sovereigns of Henry VIII, and on up to the reign of James I. So now not only are all the post-1816 sovereigns, half sovereigns, quarter sovereigns, fives and double sovereigns all included in the book but so too are the hammered coins, making this the absolute go-to reference work, the standard catalogue for this most fascinating of coin series.

ISBN 978-1-908828-69-9

£45.00 *plus p&p*

Visit www.tokenpublishing.com or telephone 01404 46972

SCOTLAND

The coins illustrated are pennies representative of the reign, unless otherwise stated.

DAVID I (1124–53)

Berwick, Carlisle, Edinburgh and Roxburgh Mints

		F	VF
Penny in the name of David		£3000	£10500
Cut Halfpenny		Extremely rare	
Penny in name of Stephen		£1000	£4000

David I

HENRY (1136–52)

Bamborough, Carlisle and Corbridge Mints for the Earl of Huntingdon and Northumberland

		F	VF
Penny		£1500	£6250
Cut Halfpenny		Extremely rare	

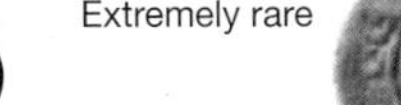

Henry

MALCOLM IV (1153–65)

Berwick and Roxburgh Mints

		F	VF
Penny (5 different types)		Extremely rare	

WILLIAM THE LION (1165–1214)

Berwick, Edinburgh, Dun (Dunbar?), Perth and Roxburgh Mints

		F	VF
Penny - cross pattee early issue	from	£2500	£7000
Penny – pellet & crescent	from	£250	£750
Penny – short cross & stars – mint & moneyer	from	£175	£500
Penny – short cross & stars HVE WALTER & var	from	£150	£375

William the Lion

ALEXANDER II (1214–49)

Berwick and Roxburgh Mints

		F	VF
Penny – in the name of William the Lion	from	£400	£1200
Penny – in own name	from	£650	£1900

Alexander II

ALEXANDER III (1249–86)

FIRST COINAGE (1250–80)

Pennies struck at the Mints at

		F	VF
Aberdeen	from	£160	£425
Ayr	from	£220	£725
Berwick	from	£95	£250
Dun (Dumfries / Dunfermline? / Dundee?)	from	£185	£525
Edinburgh	from	£155	£400
Forfar	from	£320	£950
Fres (Dumfries)	from	£295	£850
Glasgow	from	£295	£850
Inverness	from	£290	£775
Kinghorn	from	£750	£2000
Lanark	from	£270	£825
Montrose	from	£585	£1500
Perth	from	£115	£325
Roxburgh	from	£125	£375
St Andrews	from	£300	£875
Stirling	from	£250	£750

Alexander III First Coinage

SECOND COINAGE (1280–86)

		F	VF
Penny		£85	£225
Halfpenny		£100	£325
Farthing		£275	£825

Alexander III Second Coinage

JOHN BALIOL (1292–1306)

		F	VF
FIRST COINAGE *(Rough Surface issue)*			
Penny	from	£165	£475
Halfpenny	from	£450	Ex. rare
Penny – St. Andrews	from	£250	£750
Halfpenny – St. Andrews	from	£850	Ex. rare
SECOND COINAGE *(Smooth Surface issue)*			
Penny	from	£200	£525
Halfpenny	from	£175	£550
Farthing		Extremely rare	
Penny – St. Andrews	from	£350	£950
Halfpenny – St. Andrews		Extremely rare	

John Baliol

ROBERT BRUCE (1306–29)

Berwick Mint

		F	VF
Penny	from	£700	£1950
Halfpenny	from	£750	£2250
Farthing	from	£850	£2250

Robert Bruce

DAVID II (1329–71)

Aberdeen and Edinburgh Mints

		F	VF
Noble		Extremely Rare	
Groat (Edinburgh)	from	£150	£350
Groat (Aberdeen)	from	£750	£2250
Halfgroat (Edinburgh)	from	£150	£450
Halfgroat (Aberdeen)	from	£600	£1700
Penny 1st Coinage 2nd Issue	from	£85	£250
Penny 2nd Coinage (Edinburgh)	from	£150	£375
Penny 2nd Coinage (Aberdeen)	from	£495	£1350
Halfpenny	from	£250	£775
Farthing	from	£350	£950

David II

ROBERT II (1371–90)

Dundee, Edinburgh and Perth Mints

		F	VF
Groat	from	£125	£325
Halfgroat	from	£150	£495
Penny	from	£95	£250
Halfpenny	from	£125	£350

Robert II

ROBERT III (1390–1406)

Aberdeen, Dumbarton, Edinburgh, Perth Mints

		F	VF
Lion or crown	from	£2500	£6500
Demy lion or halfcrown	from	£2000	£5750
Groat	from	£150	£375
Halfgroat	from	£175	£425
Penny	from	£250	£725
Halfpenny	from	£275	£850

JAMES I (1406–37)

Aberdeen, Edinburgh, Inverness, Linlithgow, Perth, Stirling Mints

		F	VF
Demy	from	£1750	£4500
Half demy	from	£1250	£3950
Groat Edinburgh	from	£225	£625
Groat Other Mints	from	£475	£1500
Penny	from	£250	£650
Halfpenny		Extremely rare	

Robert III Lion

JAMES II (1437–60)

Aberdeen, Edinburgh, Linlithgow, Perth, Roxburgh, Stirling Mints

		F	VF
Demy	from	£1500	£4500
Lion	from	£1750	£5500
Half lion		Extremely rare	
Early groats (fleur-de-lis) Edinburgh	from	£250	£750
Early groats (fleur-de-lis) Other Mints		Extremely rare	
Later groats (crown) Edinburgh	from	£375	£1100
Later groats (crown) Other Mints	from	£675	£2250
Later Halfgroats (crown) Edinburgh	from	£750	£2125
Later Halfgroats (crown) Other Mints		Extremely rare	
Penny (billon)	from	£250	£650

James III Groat, Berwick Mint

JAMES III (1460–88)

Aberdeen, Berwick and Edinburgh Mints

		F	VF
Rider		£2500	£8500
Half rider		£2250	£7000
Quarter rider		£3250	£9500
Unicorn		£3250	£9500
Groat (facing bust) Edinburgh	from	£325	£900
Groat (facing bust) Berwick	from	£750	£2250
Groat (thistle & mullet) Edinburgh		£750	£2250
Groat (threequarter bust) Edinburgh	from	£625	£1750
Groat (threequarter bust) Aberdeen	from	£825	£2500
Halfgroat	from	£550	£1750
Penny (silver)	from	£325	£950
Plack (billon)	from	£175	£450
Half plack)	from	£195	£525
Penny (billon)	from	£150	£425
Farthing (copper)		£200	£650
Penny – ecclesiastical issue	from	£90	£225
Farthing – ecclesiastical issue	from	£125	£350

James IV Unicorn

JAMES IV (1488–1513)

Edinburgh Mint

		F	VF
Unicorn		£2000	£6750
Half unicorn		£2000	£6750
Lion or crown		Extremely rare	
Half lion		Extremely rare	
Groat	from	£950	£2950
Halfgroat	from	£1250	£4950
Penny (silver)	from	£150	£400
Plack	from	£45	£125
Half plack		Extremely rare	
Penny (billon)	from	£50	£145

JAMES V (1513–42)

Edinburgh Mint

		F	VF
Unicorn		£2050	£7500
Half Unicorn		Extremely rare	
Crown		£1350	£4750
Ducat or Bonnet piece	from	£2000	£8500
Two-thirds ducat		£2500	£6500
One-third ducat		£3500	£9500
Groat	from	£375	£1100
One-third groat	from	£325	£975
Plack	from	£50	£125
Bawbee	from	£75	£185
Half bawbee	from	£140	£325
Quarter bawbee		Extremely rare	

James V Ducat or Bonnet Piece

MARY (1542–67)

Edinburgh and Stirling Mints

FIRST PERIOD (1542–58)

		F	VF
Crown		£1750	£6500
Twenty shillings		Extremely rare	
Lion (Forty-four shillings)		£2000	£8500
Half lion (Twenty-two shillings)		£1750	£6500
Ryals (Three pounds)		£5000	£17500
Half ryal		£4500	£12500
Portrait testoon		£8000	£30000
Non-portrait testoon	from	£395	£995
Half testoon	from	£395	£995
Bawbee	from	£125	£375
Half bawbee	from	£150	£425
Bawbee - Stirling		£195	£525
Penny (facing bust)	from	£395	£1250
Penny (no bust)	from	£225	£650
Lion	from	£50	£145
Plack	from	£95	£275

Mary Lion or Forty-Four Shillings

SECOND PERIOD (Francis and Mary, 1558–60)

		F	VF
Ducat (Sixty shillings)		Extremely rare	
Non-portrait testoon	from	£375	£1000
Half testoon	from	£375	£1000
12 penny groat	from	£115	£350
Lion	from	£55	£135

THIRD PERIOD (Widowhood, 1560–65)

		F	VF
Portrait testoon		£5500	£18500
Half testoon.		£4500	£15000

FOURTH PERIOD (Henry and Mary, 1565–67)

		F	VF
Portrait ryal.		£45000	£125000
Non-portrait ryal	from	£875	£2250
Two-third ryal	from	£725	£1850
One-third ryal	from	£925	£2750

FIFTH PERIOD (Second widowhood, 1567)

		F	VF
Non-portrait ryal	from	£850	£1950
Two thirds ryal	from	£550	£1450
One-third ryal	from	£725	£1700

JAMES VI (1567–1603)

(Before accession to the English throne)

FIRST COINAGE (1567–71)

		F	VF
Ryal	from	£550	£1500
Two-thirds ryal	from	£350	£1100
One-third ryal	from	£400	£1200

SECOND COINAGE (1571–80)

		F	VF
Twenty pounds		£25,000	£75,000
Noble (or half merk)	from	£125	£300
Half noble (or quarter merk)	from	£125	£300
Two merks or Thistle dollar	from	£2250	£6750
Merk	from	£3000	£8500

THIRD COINAGE (1580–81)

		F	VF
Ducat		£6500	£17500
Sixteen shillings		£3000	£8500

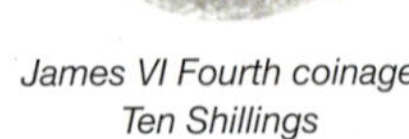

James VI Fourth coinage Ten Shillings

		F	VF
Eight shillings		£2500	£7500
Four shillings		£4500	£12500
Two shillings		Extremely rare	

FOURTH COINAGE (1582–88)

		F	VF
Lion noble		£10000	£30000
Two-third lion noble		£8000	£25000
One-third lion noble		Extremely rare	
Forty shillings		£5750	£18500
Thirty shillings		£800	£2500
Twenty shillings		£500	£1250
Ten shillings		£500	£1250

FIFTH COINAGE (1588)

		F	VF
Thistle noble		£3000	£9000

SIXTH COINAGE (1591–93)

		F	VF
"Hat" piece		£6000	£18000
"Balance" half merk	from	£350	£1150
"Balance" quarter merk		£800	£2200

SEVENTH COINAGE (1594–1601)

		F	VF
Rider		£1500	£4000
Half rider		£1500	£4000
Ten shillings	from	£175	£595
Five shillings	from	£125	£400
Thirty pence	from	£225	£625
Twelve pence	from	£130	£375

EIGHTH COINAGE (1601–04)

		F	VF
Sword and sceptre piece	from	£850	£2350
Half sword and sceptre piece	from	£675	£2100
Thistle-merk	from	£110	£350
Half thistle-merk	from	£65	£175
Quarter thistle-merk	from	£55	£135
Eighth thistle-merk	from	£50	£110

BILLON AND COPPER ISSUES

		F	VF
Eightpenny groat	from	£45	£125
Fourpenny groat	from	£350	£1000
Twopenny plack	from	£130	£375
Hardhead	from	£30	£85
Twopence	from	£80	£230
Penny plack	from	£160	£750
Penny	from	£500	£1250

JAMES VI (1603–25)

(After accession to the English throne)

		F	VF
Unit	from	£1100	£2750
Double crown	from	£1500	£4000
British crown	from	£575	£1750
Halfcrown	from	£750	£2150
Thistle crown	from	£650	£2050
Sixty shillings	from	£750	£2500
Thirty shillings	from	£225	£625
Twelve shillings	from	£175	£575
Six shillings	from	£600	£3750
Two shillings	from	£75	£225
One shilling	from	£125	£350
Copper twopence	from	£25	£70
Copper penny	from	£85	£250

James VI Seventh Coinage Rider

James VI Seventh Coinage 10 Shillings

James VI after accession thirty shillings

CHARLES I (1625–49)

	F	VF
FIRST COINAGE (1625–36)		
Unit	£1500	£4500
Double crown	£2000	£6000
British crown	Extremely rare	
Sixty shillings	£995	£2750
Thirty shillings	£175	£575
Twelve shillings	£175	£575
Six shillings from	£650	£2000
Two shillings	£45	£110
One shilling	£150	£495
SECOND COINAGE (1636)		
Half merk	£120	£300
Forty penny piece	£75	£210
Twenty penny piece	£70	£200
THIRD COINAGE (1637–42)		
Unit from	£1750	£6750
Half unit from	£1225	£3750
British crown from	£675	£2000
British half crown from	£575	£1750
Sixty shillings	£875	£3250
Thirty shillings from	£150	£475
Twelve shillings from	£150	£550
Six shillings from	£125	£325
Half merk from	£120	£395
Forty pence from	£75	£195
Twenty pence from	£35	£95
FOURTH COINAGE (1642)		
Three shillings thistle	£75	£250
Two shillings large II	£50	£145
Two shillings small II	£60	£155
Two shillings no value	£100	£300
COPPER ISSUES		
(1629 Issue)		
Twopence (triple thistle	£25	£70
Penny	£175	£500
(1632-39 Issue)		
Twopence (Stirling turner from	£25	£70
(1642-50 ISSUE)		
Twopence (CR crowned	£20	£55

Charles I Third Coinage Sixty Shillings

Charles I Fourth Coinage Two Shillings

CHARLES II (1660–85)

	F	VF
FIRST COINAGE		
Four merks		
1664 Thistle above bust	£1250	£4000
1664 Thistle below bust	£2500	£7250
1665	Extremely rare	
1670 varieties from	£1550	£6950
1673	£1550	£6950
1674 F below bust varieties from	£1250	£4000
1675	£950	£2750
Two merks		
1664 Thistle above bust	£1000	£2500

Charles II two merks

	F	VF
1664 Thistle below bust	£2500	£7250
1670	£1200	£3000
1673	£750	£1950
1673 F below bust	£1350	£3250
1674	£1200	£3000
1674 F below bust	£1200	£3000
1675	£750	£1950

Merk

	F	VF
1664 varieties from	£250	£715
1665	£275	£780
1666	£325	£950
1668	£325	Ex. rare
1669 varieties from	£100	£275
1670	£145	£375
1671	£110	£300
1672 varieties from	£100	£275
1673 varieties from	£110	£300
1674	£250	£715
1674 F below bust	£225	£650
1675 F below bust	£200	£550
1675	£210	£585

Charles II Dollar

Half merk

	F	VF
1664	£275	£725
1665 varieties from	£325	£600
1666 varieties from	£300	£750
1667	£325	£600
1668	£150	£400
1669 varieties from	£105	£325
1670 varieties from	£150	£400
1671 varieties from	£105	£285
1672	£150	£400
1673	£175	£475
1675 F below bust	£175	£575
1675	£195	£550

Charles II Sixteenth Dollar

SECOND COINAGE

Dollar

	F	VF
1676	£750	£2000
1679	£650	£1650
1680	£750	£1650
1681	£550	£1325
1682	£475	£1250

Half Dollar

	F	VF
1675	£650	£1500
1676	£750	£1950
1681	£400	£1100

Quarter Dollar

	F	VF
1675	£195	£550
1676 varieties from	£100	£295
1677 varieties from	£145	£400
1678	£165	£450
1679	£185	£500
1680	£135	£325
1681	£105	£275
1682 varieties from	£145	£400

Eighth Dollar

	F	VF
1676 varieties from	£85	£210

Charles II Bawbee

		F	VF
1677		£125	£300
1678/7		£195	£495
1679		£300	Ext. rare
1680	varieties from	£150	£345
1682	varieties from	£225	£495

Sixteenth Dollar

		F	VF
1677		£100	£275
1678/7	varieties from	£120	£320
1679/7		£135	£360
1680	varieties from	£135	£360
1681		£75	£175

Copper Issues

		F	VF
Twopence CR crowned	varieties from	£25	£70
Bawbees 1677-79	varieties from	£65	£195
Turners 1677-79	varieties from	£45	£125

James VII ten shillings

JAMES VII (1685–89)

Sixty shillings

		F	VF
1688 proof only	varieties from	–	£5500

Forty shillings

		F	VF
1687	varieties from	£450	£1100
1688	varieties from	£450	£1100

Ten shillings

		F	VF
1687		£165	£525
1688	varieties from	£250	£700

WILLIAM & MARY (1689–94)

William & Mary ten shillings

Sixty shillings

		F	VF
1691		£525	£1950
1692		£850	£2350

Forty shillings

		F	VF
1689	varieties from	£295	£850
1690	varieties from	£185	£525
1691	varieties from	£195	£550
1692	varieties from	£225	£600
1693	varieties from	£195	£550
1694	varieties from	£225	£775

Twenty shillings

		F	VF
1693		£500	£1650
1694		Extremely rare	

Ten shillings

		F	VF
1689		Extremely rare	
1690	varieties from	£295	£750
1691	varieties from	£195	£600
1692	varieties from	£195	£600
1694	varieties from	£250	£700

Five shillings

		F	VF
1691		£200	£575
1694	varieties from	£120	£350

Copper Issues

		F	VF
Bawbees 1691–94	varieties from	£100	£275
Bodle (Turners) 1691–94	varieties from	£55	£180

WILLIAM II (1694–1702)

		F	VF
Pistole		£5000	£15000
Half pistole		£4000	£12000
Forty shillings			
1695	varieties from	£225	£650
1696		£250	£625
1697		£300	£650
1698		£250	£595
1699		£375	£750
1700		Extremely rare	
Twenty shillings			
1695		£200	£625
1696		£200	£625
1697	varieties from	£250	£700
1698	varieties from	£175	£650
1699		£225	£625
Ten shillings			
1695		£150	£375
1696		£150	£375
1697	varieties from	£150	£375
1698	varieties from	£150	£375
1699		£295	£750
Five shillings			
1695		£70	£195
1696		£65	£180
1697	varieties from	£75	£225
1699		£95	£275
1700		£85	£230
1701		£125	£350
1702		£125	£350
Copper Issues			
Bawbee 1695–97	varieties from	£85	£325
Bodle (Turners) 1695–97	varieties from	£50	£150

William II ten shillings

Anne five shillings

ANNE (1702–14)

Pre -Union 1702–7 (For POST-UNION 1707–1 See listing in the English section)

		F	VF
Ten shillings			
1705		£175	£450
1706	varieties from	£225	£650
Five shillings			
1705	varieties from	£85	£225
1706		£85	£225

JAMES VIII (The Old Pretender) (1688–1766)

A number of Guineas and Crowns in various metals were struck in 1828 using original dies prepared by Norbert Roettiers, all bearing the date 1716. These coins are extremely rare and are keenly sought after.

Guinea		
1716 Gold Old Bust Right Type 1	Generally EF+	£12000
1716 Silver Old Bust Right Type 1	Generally EF+	£1500
1716 Silver Young Bust Left Type	Generally EF+	£1750
Crown		
1716	Generally EF+	£2500

Our grateful thanks go to David Stuart of ABC Coins & Tokens for updating this Scottish section of the Yearbook

ISLE OF MAN

Hiberno-Manx silver penny, c.1025

HIBERNO-MANX PENNY

Recent research has established that a Mint did exist in the Isle of Man and evidence suggests that silver pennies were minted on the Island from c.1025. Resulting from finds in various locations on the Island, it had been suggested that Hiberno-Manx pennies were coined at a mint located in the northern area, perhaps Maughold. However, the mint was more likely to have been in the fortress on St. Patrick's Isle at Peel in the west of the Island. They have been found in hoards from Park Llewellyn (Maughold), West Nappin (Jurby), Kirk Andreas and at Kirk Michael. The dies for these Hiberno-Manx silver pennies may have originally come from a moneyer called Færemin in Dublin.

JOHN MURREY'S PENNIES OF 1668

The two known types of John Murrey's penny of 1668

The first Manx tokens to become 'official' legal tender in the Isle of Man are attributed to John Murrey's Pennies of 1668. British coins circulated alongside these tokens, together with much extraneous coinage. At this time there was a severe shortage of pennies and halfpennies. An Act of Tynwald dated 24th June 1679 proclaimed that "...no copper or brass money called Butchers' halfpence, Patrick's halfpence and copper farthings, or any of that nature, shall pass in the Island from the first day of January next." The Act also stated that only the King's (Charles II) farthings and halfpence, and the brass money called Ino Murrey's pence was to pass as currency. Consequently, the Act had the effect of making John Murrey's brass tokens legal tender pennies. The Isle of Man thus had its own distinctive legal currency for the first time. John Murrey was a merchant of Douglas and lived at Ronaldsway near Castletown. Two distinct types of his penny have been recorded and both are rare.

Murrey's coins remained in circulation as legal tender until the 1710 Coinage Act of Tynwald. This Act authorised the new coinage of James Stanley, Earl of Derby, and declared all coins previously circulating to be illegal. When this Act was promulgated, it is believed that a descendant of John Murrey redeemed nearly all the "murreys" then in circulation and destroyed them.

The new Stanley coinage was cast at Castle Rushen in Castletown and dated 1709. The penny and halfpenny were proclaimed legal currency on 24th June 1710.

DATE	F	VF	EF	UNC
PENNY (Copper except where stated)				
"Derby" coinage				
1709 Cast	£55	£185	£350	—
1709 Silver cast Proof	—	—	—	£2000
1709 Brass	£50	£175	£350	—
1733 "Quocunque"	£40	£75	£275	£450
1733 "Ouocunoue"	£45	£85	£300	£750
1733 Bath metal "Quocunque"	£30	£75	£300	—
1733 Silver Proof	—	—	—	£850
1733 Bronze Proof	—	—	—	£500
1733 Proof	—	—	—	£675

Cast penny.

DATE	F	VF	EF	UNC
1733 Cap frosted	£35	£75	£300	£500
1733 Brass, cap frosted	£40	£75	£325	£650
1733 Silver Proof cap frosted	—	—	—	£650
1733 Bronze annulets instead of pellets	£50	£100	£400	£500
"Atholl" coinage				
1758	£30	£50	£250	£450
1758 — Proof	—	—	—	£650
1758 — Silver Proof	—	—	—	£1000
Regal coinage				
1786 Engrailed edge	£35	£65	£275	£450
1786 Engrailed edge Proof	—	—	—	£600
1786 Plain edge Proof	—	—	—	£1000
1786 Pellet below bust	£35	£65	£275	£550
1798	£35	£65	£250	£500
1798 Proof	—	—	—	£450
1798 Bronze Proof	—	—	—	£450
1798 Copper-gilt Proof	—	—	—	£2000
1798 Silver Proof	—	—	—	£2500
1813	£40	£75	£300	£500
1813 Proof	—	—	—	£650
1813 Bronze Proof	—	—	—	£650
1813 Copper-gilt Proof	—	—	—	£2500
1839	£35	£75	£200	£450
1839 Proof	—	—	—	£500

"Derby" coinage.

HALF PENCE (Copper except where stated)

DATE	F	VF	EF	UNC
"Derby" coinage				
1709 Cast	£50	£125	£250	—
1709 Brass	£55	£185	£500	—
1723 Silver	£725	£1250	£3500	—
1723 Copper	£300	£600	£1750	£2500
1733 Copper	£35	£55	£225	£450
1733 Bronze	£35	£55	£225	£450
1733 Silver Proof plain cap	—	—	—	£700
1733 Silver Proof frosted cap	—	—	—	—
1733 Bronze Proof	—	—	—	£500
1733 Bath metal plain cap	£40	£50	£215	—
1733 Bath metal frosted cap	£40	£50	£215	—
"Atholl" coinage				
1758	£40	£50	£215	£450
1758 — Proof	—	—	—	£800
Regal coinage				
1786 Engrailed edge	£30	£45	£120	£350
1786 Proof engrailed edge	—	—	—	£450
1786 Plain edge	£40	£65	£250	£350
1786 Proof plain edge	—	—	—	£650
1786 Bronze Proof	—	—	—	£450
1798	£35	£45	£150	£350
1798 Proof	—	—	—	£450
1798 Bronze Proof	—	—	—	£400
1798 Copper-gilt Proof	—	—	—	£1500
1798 Silver Proof	—	—	—	£1500
1813	£30	£45	£150	£300
1813 Proof	—	—	—	£375
1813 Bronze Proof	—	—	—	£350
1813 Copper-gilt Proof	—	—	—	£1250
1839	£30	£45	£150	£300
1839 Bronze Proof	—	—	—	£450

Regal coinage.

FARTHING

DATE	F	VF	EF	UNC
Regal coinage				
1839 Copper	£30	£45	£150	£300
1839 Bronze Proof	—	—	—	£450
1839 Copper-gilt Proof	—	—	—	£2500

"Atholl" coinage.

MANX DECIMAL COINS FROM 1971

This section lists the circulating coins issued by the Isle of Man Government Treasury. The Royal Mint produced the initial issue in 1971 which satisfied the needs of the Island until 1975. In 1972, 73 and 74 the Pobjoy Mint sent to the Government 1,000 samples of each denomination of the current series in anticipation of securing future contracts for the minting of Manx coins. Pobjoy won the contract in 1975 and minted all Isle of Man coins up to and including 2016. One exception was the 1972 Royal Silver Wedding crown which was minted by the Royal Canadian Mint in Ottawa. In 1975 the Manx Government released the Pobjoy samples into circulation with the 1975 coins. In 2016 the Tower Mint in London won the contract for minting Manx coins from 2017. There are no mint marks on Tower Mint coins.

From 1979 Pobjoy introduced die marks on their coins in the form of small Celtic letters in the form AA, AB, AC, etc. Alternative letter(s) were used for diamond finish and precious metal coins. 'PM' mint marks also appear on most Pobjoy minted coins. The positions of die marks and mint marks can randomly appear on both obverse and reverse. There are many variations on practically all denominations and are outside the scope of this yearbook.

Where known, minting figures are shown in the lists but from about 1986 Pobjoy did not release minting quantities. On the Christmas 50p coins where the 'Minting Limit' is quoted the actual quantities produced were far less, usually up to 5,000 coins for circulation in the Isle of Man.

In some years when no coins were required for circulation, the only source for certain denominations of that year was from uncirculated sets. Unsold sets were often broken up by the Treasury and the coins put into circulation. Coins bearing those dates are, therefore, scarce.

Sculptors of Queen's Profile used on Manx Coins

1971-1984	Arnold Machin
1985-1997	Raphael Maklouf (full bust on Crowns)
1998-2016	Ian Rank-Broadley (full bust on Crowns)
2017-	Jody Clark (full bust version)

Privy and Provenance Marks

Privy marks can be found on a number of Manx circulating coins. A stylised Triskeles was used on coins dated 1979 to commemorate the Millennium of Tynwald - The Manx Parliament. Some coins dated 1982 bore a baby crib to commemorate the birth of Prince William. In 1985 the Manx Year of Sport logo was incorporated into the designs of circulating coins.

Provenance marks may be found on some £1 coins dated 1980 and 1981 minted at the Daily Mail Ideal Home Exhibition in London (D.M.I.H.E.) and minted at the Daily Mail Ideal Home Exhibition in Birmingham (D.M.I.H.E./N.). Also Belfast Ideal Home Exhibition (I.I.H.E.) on the 1981 £1 and £5 coins minted at this location. In 1980 a number of £1 coins bore the T.T. (Tourist Trophy motorcycle races) provenance mark.

A few two pounds (£2) and five pounds (£5) coins dated 1991 bore the privy mark 'RAOB'. Both are scarce

Precious Metals Coins

Many coins have been produced in various precious metals such as silver, gold, platinum and palladium.

Coins not intended for Circulation

Fractional coins, odd denominations and unusual shapes have all featured and a few examples are listed at the end of this section, however, details of these coins are outside the scope of this yearbook.

DATE		Mintage	UNC

HALF PENNY

Metal: Bronze
Size: 17mm diameter

DATE		Mintage	UNC
1971	Cushag (Ragwort)	495,000	£2
1972		1,000	£30
1973		1,000	£30
1974		1,000	£30
1975		705,610	£1
1976	Herring on Map of Island	335,554	£1
1977		887,803	£1
1978		120,225	£2
1979		251,152	£2
1980	Stylised Norse Herring	117,665	£2
1981		169,772	£2
1981	Herring on Map - World Food Day	10,000	£4
1982	Stylised Norse Herring	17,385	£3
1983		24,576	£3
1984	Fuchsia	39,009	£3
1985		25,000	£4

Half pennies are no longer legal tender in the Isle of Man

Cushag

Herring on Map of Island

Stylised Norse Herring

Fuchsia

PENNY

Metal: Bronze up to 1995 then Bronze Plated Steel
Size: 20mm diameter

DATE		Mintage	UNC
1971	Ring Chain Pattern	100,000	£3
1972		1,000	£30
1973		1,000	£30
1974		1,000	£30
1975		826,032	£1
1976	Loughtan Sheep on Map of Island	823,572	£1
1977		479,751	£2
1978		850,415	£1
1979		1,096,285	£1
1980	Tailless Manx Cat	593,401	£2
1981		224,126	£3
1982		324,440	£3
1983		447,820	£3
1984	Cormorant on Shield	406,858	£1
1985		25,000	£2
1986			£3
1987			£2
1988	Metalwork Lathe & Cog		£1
1989			£1
1990			£1
1991			£1
1992			£4
1993			£1
1994			£1
1995			£1
1996	Rugby Ball & Goal Posts		£1
1997			£1
1998			£1
1999			£1
2000	St. Michael's Chapel, Langness		£1
2001			£1
2002			£1
2003			£1
2004	Santon War Memorial		£1
2005			£1
2006			£1
2007			£1

Ring Chain Pattern

Loughtan Sheep on map

Tailless Manx Cat

Cormororant on Shield

Metalwork Lathe & Cog

Rugby Ball & Goal Posts

St. Michael's Chapel

Santon War Memorial

DATE		Mintage	UNC
2008			£1
2009			£1
2010			£1
2011			£1
2012			£1
2013			£1
2014			£1
2015			£1
2016			£1

Pennies are no longer minted for circulation in the Isle of Man.

Cast of Falcons

TWO PENCE

Metal: Bronze up to 1995 then Bronze Plated Steel
Size: 26mm diameter

DATE		Mintage	UNC
1971	Cast of Falcons	100,000	£3
1972		1,000	£30
1973		1,000	£30
1974		1,000	£30
1975		683,549	£1
1976	Manx Shearwater	875,146	£1
1977		458,089	£1
1978		620,695	£1
1979		602,593	£1
1980	Chough & Hiberno-Norse Bronze	569,993	£1
1981		172,170	£2
1982		236,376	£1
1983		371,735	£1
1984	Peregrine Falcon on Shield	178,296	£2
1985		25,000	£3
1986			£2
1987			£2
1988	Ancient Manx Crafts		£1
1989			£1
1990			£1
1991			£1
1992			£1
1993			£1
1994			£1
1995			£1
1996	Racing Pedal Cyclists		£1
1997			£1
1998			£1
1999			£1
2000	Manx Fishermens Evening Hymn		£1
2001			£1
2002			£1
2003			£1
2004	Albert Tower, Ramsey		£1
2005			£1
2006			£1
2007			£1
2008			£1
2009			£1
2010			£1
2011			£1
2012			£1
2013			£1
2014			£1
2015			£1
2016			£1

Two Pence coins are no longer minted for circulation in the Isle of Man.

Peregrine Falcon on Shield

Ancient Manx Crafts

Manx Fishermens Evening Hymn

Albert Tower, Ramsey

FIVE PENCE

Metal: Cupro Nickel to 2016 then Nickel Plated Steel
Size: 23,5mm diameter up to 1989 then 18mm diameter from 1990

DATE		Mintage	UNC
1971	Tower of Refuge	100,000	£3
1972		1,000	£30
1973		1,000	£30
1974		1,000	£30
1975		1,017,103	£1
1976	Laxey Wheel on Map of Island	677,404	£1
1977		201,306	£2
1978		677,031	£1
1979		271,526	£2
1980	Loughtan Ram on Norse Brooch	403,296	£1
1981		67,289	£3
1982		405,381	£1
1983		137,365	£2
1984	Cushag & a la Bouche Shield	313,994	£1
1985		25,000	£3
1986			£2
1987			£3
1988	Windsurfer		£3
1989			£3
1990	Windsurfer (small diameter)		£1
1991			£1
1992			£1
1993			£1
1994	Golf Ball & Crossed Clubs		£3
1995			£3
1996	Golfer in Action		£2
1997			£2
1998			£2
1999			£2
2000	Gaut's Cross		£1
2001			£1
2002			£1
2003			£1
2004	Tower of Refuge, Douglas		£1
2005			£1
2006			£1
2007			£1
2008			£1
2009			£1
2010			£1
2011			£1
2012			£10
2013			£1
2014			£1
2015			£1
2016			£1
2017	Manx Shearwater in Flight	460,000	£1
2018		20,000	£2
2019		2,000	£5
2020		2,000	£5
2021			£5
2023	Manx Shearwater (obv. KCIII)		£1

Tower of Refuge

Laxey Wheel

Loughtan Ram

Golf Ball & Clubs

Gaut's Cross

Tower of Refuge

TEN PENCE

Metal: Cupro Nickel to 2016 then Nickel Plated Steel
Size: 28mm diameter up to 1992 then 24,5mm diameter from 1992

DATE		Mintage	UNC
1971	Triskeles (Three Legs oF Mann)	100,000	£3
1972		1,000	£30
1973		1,000	£30
1974		1,000	£30
1975		1,454,265	£1
1976	Triskeles on Map of Island	1,412,309	£1
1977		483,550	£2
1978		103,383	£3
1979		276,554	£2
1980	Peregrine Falcon	90,657	£3
1981		760,086	£1
1982		378,912	£2
1983		98,797	£3
1984	Loughtan Ram on Shield	289,789	£2
1985		25,000	£3
1986			£2
1987			£2
1988	Portcullis on Map of World		£3
1989			£3
1990			£3
1991			£20
1992			£5
1992	Triskeles (small diameter)		£1
1993			£10
1994			£10
1995			£10
1996	Sailing Boat		£5
1997			£5
1998			£3
1999			£5
2000	St. German's Cathedral, Peel		£2
2001			£2
2002			£2
2003			£2
2004	Chicken Rock Lighthouse		£2
2005			£2
2006			£2
2007			£2
2008			£2
2009			£2
2010			£2
2011			£2
2012			£15
2013			£2
2014			£2
2015			£2
2016			£2
2017	Manx Tailless Cat	220,000	£1
2018		20,000	£3
2019		720,000	£1
2020		500,000	£2
2021			£1
2023	Lesser Mottled Grasshopper (obv. KCIII)		£1

Triskeles

Peregrine Falcon

Portcullis on Map

Triskeles

Chicken Rock Lighthouse

A comprehensive listing of all the coins and tokens produced for the Isle of Man, together with a detailed history and all recorded variations including die marks, can be found in the book *Coins of the Isle of Man* by Mike J. Southall. ISBN 9 780995 738720 third edition.

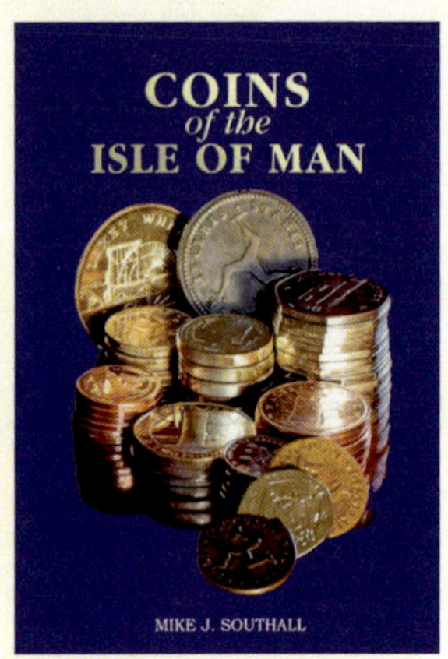

COINS
of the
ISLE OF MAN
MIKE J. SOUTHALL

COINS *of the* ISLE OF MAN

by Mike J. Southall, MBE

This book contains a comprehensive history of coins used in the Isle of Man and a definitive study of Manx decimal coins that have been in circulation since 1971. Adding further interest, the die marks, mint marks, provenance marks, etc. found on the 1979–2016 Manx decimal coins are also included. A section listing the non-circulating, precious metal and bullion coins follows that of the circulating coins.

After John Murrey's first legal penny token of 1668, the first official Manx coins, halfpennies and pennies, were issued by the Lord of Mann, James Stanley 10th Earl of Derby. They were made legal tender by an Act of Tynwald on 24th June 1710. Manx coins, and a variety of tokens, were circulating on the Island until 1839. Thereafter British coins became the only legal currency until decimalisation in 1971.

This updated third edition book makes compelling reading and is a most useful and comprehensive reference work for anyone with the slightest interest in the coins of the Isle of Man.

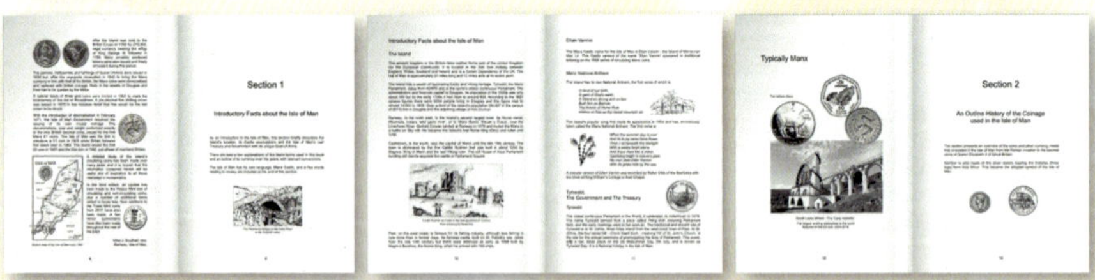

ISBN 9 780995 738720 from Lily Publications Limited, PO Box 33, Ramsey, Isle of Man. IM99 4LP £29.95 plus postage.

TWENTY PENCE

Metal: Cupro Nickel
Wider border with incuse lettering from 1993

DATE		Mintage	UNC
1982	Viking Arms & Armour	824,892	£2
1983		115,610	£2
1984	Three Herrings on Shield	141,393	£2
1985		25,000	£3
1986			£3
1987			£3
1988	Combine Harvester		£3
1989			£2
1990			£2
1991			£2
1992			£2
1993			£3
1994			£3
1995			£3
1996	Rally Racing Car		£2
1997			£2
1998			£2
1999			£2
2000	Manx Bible at Rushen Abbey		£2
2001			£3
2002			£2
2003			£3
2004	Castle Rushen 1597 Clock		£2
2005			£2
2006			£2
2007			£2
2008			£2
2009			£2
2010			£2
2011			£2
2012			£15
2013			£2
2014			£2
2015			£2
2016			£2
2017	Sailing Viking Longship	281,250	£1
2018		262,500	£2
2019		937,500	£2
2020		625,000	£2
2021			£1

Viking Arms

Three Herrings

Combine Harvester

Castle Rushen 1597 Clock

TOURIST TROPHY (TT) FIFTY PENCE

Metal: Cupro Nickel
Size: 30mm diameter up to 1997 then 27,3mm diameter from 1997

DATE		Mintage	UNC
1981	Joey Dunlop	30,000	£20
1982	Mick Grant	30,000	£25
1983	Ron Haslam	30,000	£25
1984	Mick Boddice	30,000	£20
1999	Leslie Graham	4,500	£50
2004	Tourist Trophy (TT)	3,000	£50
2007	Dave Molyneux and Sidecar	3,500	£30
2007	Tourist Trophy (TT)	3,500	£75
2009	John McGuinness	3,500	£40
2010	Suzuki Team Rider		£30
2011	Yamaha Motorcycle		£30
2012	Mark Cavendish Cyclist		£60
2012	Dave Knight Enduro Motorcyclist		£60
2014	John McGuinness Twenty TT Wins		£25
2015	TT Legends, TT Winners, Duke etc		£20
2016	TT Legends, TT Winners, Dunlop etc		£20

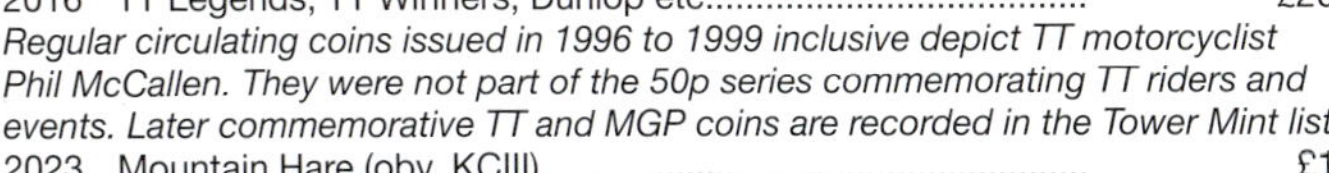

Regular circulating coins issued in 1996 to 1999 inclusive depict TT motorcyclist Phil McCallen. They were not part of the 50p series commemorating TT riders and events. Later commemorative TT and MGP coins are recorded in the Tower Mint list.

DATE		Mintage	UNC
2023	Mountain Hare (obv. KCIII)		£1

Joey Dunlop, TT Champion

Geoff Duke, etc. TT Legends

FIFTY PENCE

Metal: Cupro Nickel
Size: 30mm diameter up to 1997 then 27,3mm diameter from 1997

DATE		Mintage	UNC
1971	Viking Longship	100,000	£3
1972		1,000	£100
1973		1,000	£100
1974		1,000	£100
1975		121,817	£2
1976	Viking Longship on Map	116,242	£3
1977		131,784	£2
1978		76,203	£5
1979		164,316	£2
1979	Odin's Raven Longship	100,000	£5
1979	Odin's Raven, Royal Visit (edge)	50,000	£10
1980	Odin's Raven, New York (edge)	20,000	£20
1980	Stylised Viking Longship	203,138	£3
1981		332,940	£2
1982		118,166	£4
1983		162,524	£3
1984	Viking Longship on Shield	282,567	£2
1985		25,000	£5
1986			£8
1987			£5
1988	Triskelion on Computer Screen		£10
1989			£15
1990			£20
1991			£40
1992			£40
1993			£40
1994			£50
1994	Tynwald Legislative Centenary	2,500	£80
1995	Triskelion on Computer Screen		£60
1996	TT Motorcycle Racing, Phil McCallen	6,000	£200
1997			£250
1997	As above but small 27,3mm diameter		£3
1998			£10
1999			£25
2000	Calf of Man Crucifixion Stone		£5
2001			£5
2002			£5
2003			£5
2004	Milner's Tower, Bradda Head		£5
2005			£15
2006			£5
2007			£5
2008			£5
2009			£5
2010			£3
2011			£3
2012			£25
2012	Queen's Diamond Jubilee		£10
2013	Milner's Tower, Bradda Head		£3
2014			£3
2015			£3
2016			£3
2017	Manx Loughton Sheep	325,000	£2
2018		200,000	£3
2019		937,500	£2
2020		375,000	£2
2021			£2
2023	Peregrine Falcon (obv. KCIII)		£2

Viking Longship

Viking Longship on Shield

TT Motorcycle Racing Phil McCallen

Calf of Man Crucifixion Stone

Milner's Tower Bradda Head

1980 Mona's Isle Paddle Steamer

CHRISTMAS FIFTY PENCE

Metal: Cupro Nickel
Size: 30mm diameter up to 1997 then 27,3mm diameter from 1997

DATE		Mintage	UNC
1980	Steam Packet's Mona's Isle	30,000	£20
1981	Manx Nikki Fishing Boat	30,000	£15
1982	Carol Singers at Castletown	30,000	£20
1983	Model T Ford Car	30,000	£25
1984	Steam Engine No.1 Sutherland	50,000	£25
1985	De Haviland Rapide Aircraft	30,000	£20
1986	Douglas Corporation Horse Tram	30,000	£20
1987	Douglas Vosper Thorneycroft Bus	30,000	£20
1988	Motorcycle & Sidecar at Cregneash	30,000	£20
1989	Laxey Tram Station	50,000	£20
1990	Steam Packet's Lady of Mann	30,000	£25
1991	Nativity Scene	30,000	£40
1992	Manks Mercury Newspaper	30,000	£60
1993	St. Georges Stained Glass Window	30,000	£50
1994	Hunting the Wren	30,000	£125
1995	Snowball scene on S.M.R.	30,000	£115
1996	Choir Boys at Lonan Old Church	30,000	£80
1997	Thomas Edward Brown, Manx Poet	30,000	£50
1998	Victorian Manx Family Scene	30,000	£50
1999	Decorating Christmas Tree	30,000	£50
2000	Manx Bible at Rushen Abbey	30,000	£50
2001	Victorian Fluted Pillar Box	30,000	£50
2002	Charles Dickens Christmas Carol	30,000	£60
2003	The Snowman and James	10,000	£260
2004	The Great Laxey Wheel	30,000	£40
2005	12 Days of Christmas, Pear Tree	30,000	£100
2006	12 Days of Christmas, Turtle Doves	30,000	£100
2007	12 Days of Christmas, French Hens	30,000	£70
2008	12 Days of Christmas, Calling Birds	30,000	£60
2008	The Snowman and James	30,000	£310
2009	12 Days of Christmas, Gold Rings	30,000	£60
2010	12 Days of Christmas, Geese	30,000	£50
2011	Santa with Sack and Parcel	30,000	£50
2012	Christmas Angel	30,000	£35
2013	Christmas Stocking	30,000	£35
2014	Snowman and Snowdog	30,000	£50
2015	No issue	—	—
2016	Christmas Pudding	30,000	£15

1984 Steam Engine No.1 Sutherland

1997 T. E. Brown Manx Poet

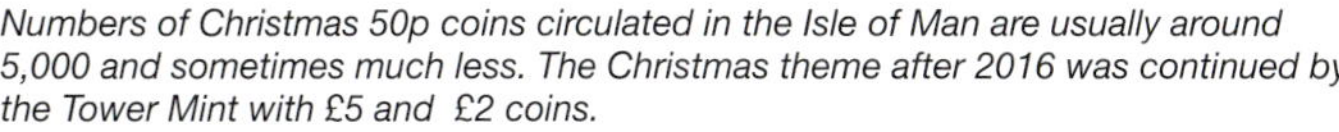

Numbers of Christmas 50p coins circulated in the Isle of Man are usually around 5,000 and sometimes much less. The Christmas theme after 2016 was continued by the Tower Mint with £5 and £2 coins.

2003 The Snowman and James

ONE POUND

Metal: Virenium to 1995. Nickel-Brass from 1996
Size: 22mm diameter x 1,5mm thick to 1982. 3mm thick from 1983 -

DATE		Mintage	UNC
1978	Triskeles on Map of Isle of Man	323,071	£3
1979		67,687	£5
1979	As above, X-oars Prov. Mark	1,000	£75
1980		78,288	£8
1980	As above, D.M.I.H.E. Prov. Mark	100,000	£15
1980	As above, D.M.I.H.E./N Prov. Mk.		£20
1980	As above, T.T. Prov. Mark		£10
1981		12,590	£12
1981	As above, I.I.H.E. Prov. Mark		£75
1982			£50
1982	As above, Baby Crib Prov. Mark		£25

Triskeles on Map

DATE		Mintage	UNC
1983	Town Arms—Peel	19,619	£8
1984	Town Arms—Castletown	25,000	£20
1985	Town Arms—Ramsey	25,000	£40
1986	Town Arms—Douglas		£75
1987	Viking on Horseback		£15
1988	Cellnet Telephone		£6
1989			£5
1990			£5
1991			£5
1992			£5
1993			£5
1994			£5
1995			£5
1996	Douglas Corporation Centenary		£10
1996	Cricket Stumps, Bat and Ball		£5
1997			£6
1998			£6
1999			£6
2000	Triskeles with Millennium Bells		£4
2001			£4
2002			£4
2003			£3
2004	Tynwald Hill and St.Johns Church		£3
2005			£3
2006			£3
2007			£3
2008			£4
2009			£6
2010			£4
2011			£4
2012			£3
2013			£3
2014			£3
2015			£3
2016			£4
2017	Peregrine Falcon & Raven	460,000	£2
2018		20,000	£3
2019		2,000	£10
2020		2,000	£10
2021			£5
2023	Grey Seal (obv. KCIII)		£3

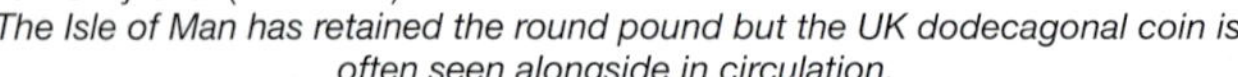

The Isle of Man has retained the round pound but the UK dodecagonal coin is often seen alongside in circulation.

Town Arms Ramsey

Cellnet Telephone

Triskeles with Milennium Bells

Tynwald Hill and St. John's Church

TWO POUNDS

Metal:Virenium up to 1997. Bi-metal Nickel-Brass / Cupro-Nickel 1997

Size: 28,4mm diameter

DATE		UNC
1986	Tower of Refuge (Metal: Virenium)	£15
1987		£15
1988	Manx Airlines BAe 146-100 Jet	£25
1989	Manx Airship Dirigible	£1000
1990	Manx Airlines BAe 146-100 Jet	£25
1991		£25
1992		£30
1993		£30
1993	Nigel Mansell Formula 1	£30
1994	Nigel Mansell PPG Indi Car	£40
1995	Royal British Legion VE / VJ Day	£20
1996	E-Type Jaguar Racing (Virenium)	£25
1997		£25
1997	E-Type Jaguar Racing (Bi-Metal)	£20
1998		£10
1999		£25

Manx Airlines BAe 145-100 Jet

DATE		Mintage	UNC
2000	Thorwald's Cross, Andreas Church		£10
2001			£15
2002			£15
2003			£15
2004	Round Tower Peel Castle		£10
2005			£10
2006			£10
2007			£10
2008			£10
2009			£10
2010			£10
2011			£10
2011	Commonwealth Games, Tosha the Cat		£250
2012	Round Tower Peel Castle		£30
2013			£10
2014			£10
2015			£10
2016			£20
2017	Tower of Refuge	300,000	£4
2018		20,000	£8
2019		176,000	£5
2020		156,000	£5
2021			£5
2023	Basking Shark (obv. KCIII)		£5

E-Type Jaguar Racing
Virenium version

E-Type Jaguar Racing
Bi-metal version

FIVE POUNDS

Metal: Virenium up to 2016. Alpaca (nickel silver) from 2017
Size: 36mm diameter up to 2016. 32mm diameter from 2017

DATE		Mintage	UNC
1981	Triskeles on Map of Isle of Man	22,414	£15
1982		1,075	£35
1983		1,473	£30
1984			–
1984	Knight on Horseback	2,068	£40
1985		25,000	£30
1986			£35
1987			£35
1988	Peel Inshore Fishing Boat		£25
1989			£25
1990			£25
1991			£25
1992			£25
1993			£25
1993	Nigel Mansell, Formula 1		£25
1994	Nigel Mansell, PPG Indi Car		£40
1995	50 Years, End of World War II		£15
1996	Footballers Euro96		£25
1997	Footballers		£30
1997	Royal Golden Wedding Anniv.		£20
1998	Prince Charles 50th Birthday		£30
1998	Footballers		£25
1999			£25
1999	175th Anniversary of RLNI		£30
2000	St. Patrick's Hymn		£25
2001			£30
2002			£30
2003			£30
2004	The Great Laxey Wheel		£30
2005			£30
2006			£50
2007			£30
2008			£30
2009			£50
2010			£50

Knight on Horseback

Peel Inshore Fishing Boat

St. Patrick's Hymn

DATE		Mintage	UNC
2011			£50
2012			£70
2013			£50
2014			£35
2015			£30
2016			£40
2017	Manx Triskele Symbol	20,000	£15
2018		20,000	£25
2019		1,000	£35
2020		1,000	£35
2021			£35
2023	Queen Scallop (obv. KCIII)		£25

The Great Laxey Wheel

ISLE OF MAN CROWNS

Isle of Man crowns minted from 1970 to 2016 have a face value of twenty five pence (25p) or five shillings (5/- 1970 pre-decimal issue). Manx Crowns were revalued at five pounds (£5) by the Isle of Man Government from 2017.

Crowns listed in this section are standard size coins 38.61mm diameter made of cupro-nickel (CuNi) and have a nominal value of 25p. Howsever, the supply and demand for these coins is very erratic according to the retail source, therefore it has been decided not to price them.

Many of these Crowns were also struck from precious metals such as Silver (Ag), Gold (Au), Platinum (Pt) and Palladium (Pd). There are also many odd-shaped Crowns and part Crowns issued in CuNi and various precious metals. Multiple Crown values also exist. These coins to detail individually are outside the scope of this Year Book but a selection is illustrated after this list.

A comprehensive listing of all the coins and tokens produced for the Isle of Man, together with a detailed history and all recorded variations including die marks, can be found in the book *Coins of the Isle of Man* by Mike J. Southall. ISBN 9 780995 738720 third edition.

DATE

1970 Manx Cat
1972 Royal Silver Wedding
1974 Centenary of Churchill's birth
1975 Manx Cat
1976 Bi-Centenary of American Independence
1976 Centenary of the Horse Drawn Tram
1977 Silver Jubilee
1977 Silver Jubilee Appeal
1978 25th Anniversary of the Coronation
1979 300th Anniversary of Manx Coinage
1979 Millennium of Tynwald (5 coins)
1980 22nd Olympics (3 coins)
1980 80th Birthday of Queen Mother
1980 Derby Bicentennial
1980 Winter Olympics—Lake Placid
1981 Duke of Edinburgh Award Scheme (4 coins)
1981 Prince of Wales' Wedding (2 coins)
1981 Year of Disabled (4 coins)
1982 12th World Cup—Spain (4 coins)
1982 Maritime Heritage (4 coins)
1983 Manned Flight (4 coins)
1984 23rd Olympics (4 coins)
1984 Commonwealth Parliamentary Conference (4 coins)
1984 Quincentenary of College of Arms (4 coins)
1985 Queen Mother (6 coins)
1986 13th World Cup—Mexico (6 coins)
1986 Prince Andrew Wedding (2 coins)
1987 200th Anniversary of the United States Constitution
1987 America's Cup Races (5 coins)
1988 Australia Bicentennial (6 coins)

DATE

1988 Bicentenary of Steam Navigation (6 coins)
1988 Manx Cat
1989 Queen Elizabeth II & Prince Philip Royal Visit
1989 Bicentenary of the Mutiny on the Bounty (4 coins)
1989 Bicentenary of Washington's Inauguration (4 coins)
1989 Persian Cat
1989 Royal Visit
1989 13th World Cup Mexico (2 coins)
1990 150th Anniversary of the Penny Black
1990 25th Anniversary of Churchill's Death (2 coins)
1990 Alley Cat
1990 Queen Mother's 90th Birthday
1990 World Cup—Italy (4 coins)
1991 1992 America's Cup
1991 Centenary of the American Numismatic Association
1991 Norwegian Forest Cat
1991 10th Anniversary of Prince of Wales' Wedding (2 coins)
1992 1992 America's Cup
1992 Discovery of America (4 coins)
1992 Siamese Cat
1993 Maine Coon Cat
1993 Preserve Planet Earth—Dinosaurs (2 coins)
1994 Japanese Bobtail Cat
1994 Normandy Landings (8 coins)
1994 Preserve Planet Earth—Endangered Animals (3 coins)
1994 Preserve Planet Earth—Mammoth
1994 World Football Cup (6 coins)
1994 Year of the Dog
1994 D-Day Normandy Landings (8 coins)
1994 Man in Flight—Series i (8 coins)
1995 Aircraft of World War II (19 coins)
1995 America's Cup
1995 Famous World Inventions—Series i (12 coins)
1995 Man in Flight—Series ii (8 coins)
1995 Preserve Planet Earth—Egret and Otter
1995 Queen Mother's 95th Birthday
1995 Turkish Cat
1995 Year of the Pig
1996 70th Birthday of HM the Queen
1996 Burmese Cat
1996 European Football Championships (8 coins)
1996 Explorers (2 coins)
1996 Famous World Inventions—Series ii (6 coins)
1996 Football Championships Winner
1996 King Arthur & the Knights of the Round Table (5 coins)
1996 Olympic Games (6 coins)
1996 Preserve Planet Earth—Killer Whale and Razorbill (2 coins)
1996 Robert Burns (4 coins)
1996 The Flower Fairies—Series i (4 coins)
1996 Year of the Rat
1997 10th Anniversary of the "Cats on Coins" series (silver only)
1997 Royal Golden Wedding
1997 90th Anniversary of the TT Races (4 coins)
1997 Explorers—Eriksson and Nansen (2 coins)
1997 Long-haired Smoke Cat
1997 Royal Golden Wedding (2 coins)
1997 The Flower Fairies—Series ii (4 coins)
1997 Year of the Ox
1998 The Millennium (4 coins)
1998 125th Anniversary of Steam Railway (8 coins)
1998 18th Winter Olympics, Nagano (4 coins)
1998 Birman Cat
1998 Explorers—Vasco da Gama and Marco Polo (2 coins)
1998 FIFA World Cup (4 coins)
1998 International Year of the Oceans (4 coins)
1998 The Flower Fairies—Series iii (4 coins)
1998 The Millennium (16 coins issued over 3 years)
1998 Year of the Tiger
1999 The Millennium (4 coins)

DATE

1999 27th Olympics in Sydney (5 coins)
1999 Rugby World Cup (6 coins)
1999 The Millennium (4 coins)
1999 Titanium Millennium crown
1999 Wedding of HRH Prince Edward and Sophie Rhys-Jones
1999 Year of the Rabbit
2000 The Millennium (4 coins)
2000 Millennium Intertwined MM (Issued to every Manx school child)
2000 18th Birthday of HRH Prince William
2000 60th Anniversary of the Battle of Britain
2000 BT Global Challenge
2000 Explorers, Francisco Piarro and Wilem Brents (2 coins)
2000 Life and times of the Queen Mother (4 coins)
2000 Millennium—own a piece of time
2000 Queen Mother's 100th Birthday
2000 Scottish Fold cat
2000 Year of the Dragon
2001 75th Birthday of HM the Queen
2001 Explorers, Martin Frobisher and Roald Amundsen (2 coins)
2001 Harry Potter (6 coins)
2001 Joey Dunlop
2001 Life and times of the Queen Mother (2 coins)
2001 The Somali cat
2001 Year of the Snake
2002 A Tribute to Diana Princess of Wales—5 years on
2002 Introduction of the Euro
2002 The Bengal Cat
2002 The Queen's Golden Jubilee—i (1 coin)
2002 The Queen's Golden Jubilee—ii (4 coins)
2002 The XIX Winter Olympiad, Salt Lake City (2 coins)
2002 World Cup 2002 in Japan/Korea (4 coins)
2002 Year of the Horse
2003 Golden Coronation Jubilee
2003 XII Olympic Games 2004 (4 coins)
2003 Anniversary of the "Star of India"
2003 Lord of the Rings (5 coins)
2003 Prince William's 21st Birthday
2003 The Balinese Cat
2003 Year of the Goat
2004 Year of the Monkey
2004 100 Years of Powered Flight (2 coins)
2004 Olympics (4 coins)
2004 Ten New EU Entries
2004 Harry Potter—Prisoner of Azkaban
2004 Queen Mary 2—World's Largest Passenger Liner
2004 D-Day Re-enactment—Parachute Jump
2004 Football, Euro 2004 (2 coins)
2004 Lord of the Rings—Return of the King
2004 Tonkinese Cats
2004 Battle of Trafalgar
2004 60th Anniversary of D-Day (6 coins)
2005 60th Anniversary of Peace (coins as 2004 D-Day) (6 coins)
2005 60th Anniversary of Victory in Europe
2005 Bicentenary of the Battle of Trafalgar (6 coins)
2005 175th Anniversary of Isle of Man Steam Packet (2 coins)
2005 400th Anniversary of the Gunpowder Plot (2 coins)
2005 Bicentenary of Hans Christian Andersen
2005 Harry Potter and the Goblet of Fire (4 coins)
2005 Italy and the Isle of Man TT races (2 coins)
2005 Manx Hero Lt. John Quilliam (2 coins)
2005 The Himalayan Cat with kittens
2005 Bicentenary of the Battle of Trafalgar (6 coins)
2006 150th Anniversary of the Victoria Cross (2 coins)
2006 30th Anniversary of the first Translantic Flight
2006 80th Birthday of Her Majesty the Queen (4 coins)
2006 The Battles that Changed the World—Part II (6 coins)
2006 Transatlantic Flight (2 coins)
2006 Exotic Short Hair Cat
2006 World Cup FIFA 2006

DATE

2006 Queen's Beasts
2006 Fairy Tales (2 coins)
2006 Aircraft of World War II—Spitfire
2006 The Battles that Changed the World—Part I (6 coins)
2007 The Tales of Peter Rabbit
2007 Fairy Tales (3 coins)
2007 The Centenary of the Scouting
2007 The Centenary of the TT races (5 coins)
2007 The Graceful Swan
2007 The Ragdoll Cat
2007 The Royal Diamond Wedding Anniversary (4 coins)
2008 50th Anniversary of Paddington Bear
2008 Burmilla Cat
2008 Prince Charles 60th Birthday
2008 The Adorable Snowman
2008 The Return of Tutankhamun (2 coins)
2008 UEFA European Football Championships
2008 Year of Planet Earth
2008 Olympics China (6 coins)
2009 40th Anniversary of the 1st Concorde Test Flight
2009 Fifa World Cup South Africa 2010
2009 The Chinchilla Cat
2009 Winter Olympics (2 coins)
2009 500th Anniversary of Henry VIII (2 coins)
2009 BeeGees—Freedom of Douglas
2009 Fall of the Berlin Wall
2009 40th Anniversary of the First Man on the Moon
2009 Olympics 2012 (6 coins)
2010 Olympics 2012 (6 coins)
2010 Vancouver Olympics 2010 (2 coins)
2010 Buckingham Palace
2010 Abyssinian Cat and her Kitten
2011 A Lifetime of Service—Queen Elizabeth II and Prince Philip
2011 Buckingham Palace
2011 Royal Wedding of HRH Prince William and Catherine Middleton
2011 The Turkish Angora Cat
2011 TT Mountain Course 100 years
2011 Year of the Rabbit
2012 Life of Queen Elizabeth II (2 coins)
2012 Centenary of RMS *Titanic* (2 coins)
2012 European Football Championships (4 coins)
2012 Juno Moneta Coin
2012 Manx Cat Coin
2012 Olympics (6 coins).
2012 River Thames Diamond Jubilee Pageant
2013 Anniversary of Queen Victoria and Queen Elizabeth II Coronations
2013 Kermode Bear
2013 60th Anniversary of Coronation
2013 Siberian Cat
2013 St. Patrick Commemorative
2013 Winter Olympic (4 coins)
2014 Centenary of WWI (2 coins). Coloured Silver Proof.
2014 200th Anniversary of Matthew Flinders
2014 70th Anniversary of D-Day (3 coins)
2014 Snowman and Snow Dog Crown (£5)
2014 Snowshoe Cat
201 Snow Dog
2014 Winter Olympic Games (4 Coin Collection)
2015 175th Anniversary of the Penny Black Stamp (issued in a pack)
2015 200th Anniversary of the Battle of Waterloo—Napoleon
2015 200th Anniversary of the Battle of Waterloo—Wellington
2015 75th Anniversary of the Battle of Britain (search lights in yellow)
2015 Her Majesty the Queen Elizabeth II Longest reigning Monarch
2015 Paddington Bear
2015 Selkirk Rex Cat
2015 Sir Winston Churchill
2016 90th Birthday Queen Elizabeth II
2016 Tobacco Brown Cat

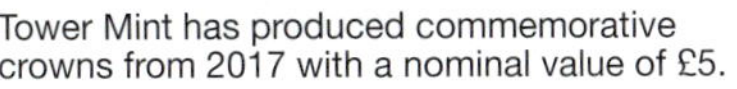
Tower Mint has produced commemorative
crowns from 2017 with a nominal value of £5.

CROWNS FROM THE TOWER MINT

Crowns listed in this section are standard size coins 38.61mm diameter made of cupro-nickel (CuNi) and have a nominal value of £5.Some of these Crowns were also struck from precious metals such as Silver (Ag) and/or Gold (Au) and a few issues were minted piedfort.

2017 Duke of Edinburgh 70 Years of Service
2017 Platinum Wedding Anniversary
2017 Viking Scenes (*CuNi Antique silver plate finish*) (5 coins)
2017 Centenary of the House of Windsor (*CuNi gold plated*)
2017 Sapphire Wedding of Her Majesty and Prince Philip
2018 60th Anniversary of Queen Elizabeth II Coronation
2019 Centenary of the First Man on the Moon
2019 200th Anniversary of the Birth of Queen Victoria (3 coins)
2022 Isle of Man TT Races

Other Crowns Minted only in Precious Metals:
2018 World War I Armistice Centenary (poppies in red and black) *Ag*
2018 Birth of Prince Louis Arthur Charles. *Ag*
2020 Manx Wildlife Series Part I. *Ag, Au*

Coins with High Denominations have also been minted:
2017 £10 King Canute (*Ag with antique finish*)
2018 £10 WWI Armistice Centenary (poppies in red and black) *Ag*
2019 £10 50th Anniversary of the Moon Landing *Ag*
2018 £50 World War I Armistice Centenary (poppies in red) *Ag*
2019 £100 Age of the Vikings (*Ag with antique finish*)

60th Anniversary of Queen Elizabeth II Coronation

Viking Scenes (CuNi Antique silver plate finish) (5 coins)

TT Races

Centenary of the House of Windsor (CuNi gold plated)

Centenary of the First Man on the Moon

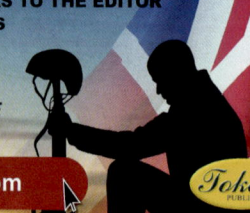

ODD SIZE AND IRREGULAR SHAPED CROWNS

Many odd shaped Crowns have been produced by the Pobjoy Mint and a representative selection is illustrated here. A variety of metals, from cupro-nickel, silver, gold, platinum and palladium have been used in the minting of these coins. Parts and multiples of a Crown struck in precious metals also exist. Denominations that exist for some Crown issues are 1/64 Crown, 1/32 Crown, 1/25 Crown, 1/20 Crown, 1/10 Crown, 1/5 Crown, 1/4 Crown, 1/2 Crown, 2 Crowns, 5 Crowns, 10 Crowns, 13 Crowns, 32 Crowns, 64 Crowns, 100 Crowns and 130 Crowns. Coins illustrated here are not to scale.

Golden Jubilee of Queen Elizabeth II 2002
3kg .9999 fine silver

2010 750th Anniv. of Mongol ruler Kublai Khan

2012 Queen's Diamond Jubilee. ½ Crown silver

2009 Terracotta Army - 1/5 Crown

2008 Tutankhamun's Death Mask ½ Crown. Fine 999.9 gold.

1 crown

Commemorating the 2008 - 09 Tutankhamun Exhibition in London

Tower Mint Crown (£5)

2019 Manannan - First King of Mann. 99.9% Silver Crown.

NOTABLE MANX FIRSTS

1978 World's First £1 Coin

1990 First Black Coin Penny Black Anniversary

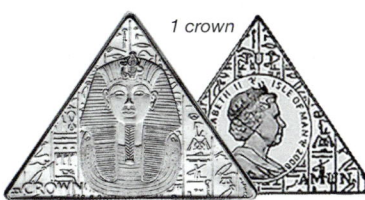

1999 First White Gold Coins 1/25, 1/10, 1/5 and 1/2 Platina

2002 First Spinning Coin Currency Converter

COINS OF OTHER DENOMINATIONS

SOVEREIGNS, PARTS & MULTIPLES

Isle of Man sovereigns, multiples and parts were minted in gold in certain years between the years 1965 and 1993. Sovereigns were of standard imperial size, contained between 91.6% and 99.9% gold and depicted a Viking in armour on horseback.

The 1965 gold coins (Five, One and Half Sovereign) to mark the bicentenary of the Act of Revestment are 98% (23.5ct). They were also minted in 91.7% (22ct) gold.

Sovereigns in 99.99 gold were again minted from 2019 by the Tower Mint in London. A proof silver sovereign was issued in 2022.

The "face value"of a sovereign is one pound sterling (£1) but its intrinsic or bullion value is much greater owing to the value of its metal content.

ANGELS, PARTS & MULTIPLES

In addition to the Sovereign, bullion coinage has been issued in several different denominations, viz. Angels and Nobles. Bullion coins are legal tender and their face value is equal to the current market or bullion value of the metal content in the coins.

The Angel was launched in the Isle of Man for legal tender status purposes on 13th March 1985. However, a token issue of the 1oz gold Angels dated 1984 were struck by the Pobjoy Mint and sent to the United States for 'test marketing' ahead of the official release by the Isle of Man Treasury.

Pobjoy Mint produced Angels until 2016 when Tower Mint continued the series in 2017.

The reverse of the Angel coin depicts the Archangel Michael slaying the Dragon. The series of Christmas 1/20 Angels have been struck in fine gold and others in 22ct. gold and many also exist as proof coins.

NOBLES, PARTS & MULTIPLES

The first Manx 1 Noble coin was issued in 1983 followed by the 1/10 Noble in 1984. The latter was known then as a 'Noblette'. Pobjoy Mint produced Nobles periodically until 2016 when the Tower Mint continued the series in 2017.

The reverse of the Noble coin depicts the Viking Ship 'Thusly' in full sail. Nobles have been struck in fine gold and others in gold and platinum. Proof coins exist for some issues.

A full listing of crowns, with their multiples and parts and a full listing of Angel and Noble coins, with their multiples and parts, can be found in the book *Coins of the Isle of Man* by Mike J. Southall. ISBN 9 780995 738720 third edition.

TOWER MINT CIRCULATING COIN DESIGNS

No Isle of Man **One Penny** or **Two Pence** coins have been produced by the Tower Mint. All 1p and 2p coins from 1971 to 2016 inclusive remain legal tender on the island and circulate with their UK equivalents.

Jody Clark's portrait of Her Majesty the Queen was adopted for use on coins of the Commonwealth countries, including the Isle of Man, and this effigy was first used by the Tower Mint from 2017 for Manx coins. These coins from the Tower MInt are included in the general list of Manx Decimal Coins from 1971.

The **five pence** (5p) design depicts the Manx Shearwater, a medium-sized sea bird of the family *Procellaridae*. It is an amber-listed species of particular conservation concern in the Isle of Man. It is found around the cliffs on the east coast and on the Calf of Man.

The **ten pence** (10p) design depicts the famous Manx tailless cat with its most distinguishing characteristics of its elongated hind legs and rounded head. Manx cats are best known as being entirely tailless and are affectionately called a "rumpy", but some have a small stub of a tail and they are known as a "stumpy".

The **twenty pence** (20p) design depicts a typical sailing Viking longship. The Isle of Man has a significant Viking heritage, particularly with the Viking longship *Odin's Raven*, a replica of which is in the House of Mannan at Peel.

The **fifty pence** (50p) design shows the famous breed of Manx Loaghtan sheep native to the Isle of Man. The sheep, which has dark brown wool, is depicted full-face with its characteristic four horns.

The **one pound** (£1) design depicts a Pergrine Falcon and a Raven. The Isle of Man was granted a coat-of-arms by Queen Elizabeth II in 1966 in which the two birds are shown. They are both symbolically associated with the island.

The **two pounds** (£2) design depicts the Tower of Refuge, an important landmark built on Conister Rock in Douglas Bay. It was built in 1832 by Sir William Hilary, founder of the Royal National Lifeboat Institution, who lived at Fort Anne overlooking Douglas Bay.

The **five pounds** (£5) design depicts the famous Triskelion or Triskele, symbol of the Isle of Man. It is based on the Manx coat-of-arms, dating back to the 13th century. The three legs are known in Manx as "ny tree cassyn".

The Tower Mint produces commemorative coins for general circulation at appropriate intervals. In addition, coins are also minted in various precious metals and in colour for some issues. Bullion coins in precious metals have also been minted.

NEW DESIGNS FROM THE TOWER MINT

New designs bearing the head of King Charles III on Isle of Man circulating coins were introduced in 2023. They were issued to commemorate the 50th Anniversary of the Manx Wildlife Trust.

These coins from the Tower Mint are included in the general list of Manx Decimal Coins.

The **five pence** (5p) depicts the Manx Shearwater, Pibbin Vanninagh, a black and white seabird known for its hunting call and is part of a group of birds called 'tubenoses'.

The **ten pence** (1 Op) depicts the Lesser Mottled Grasshopper, Lheimmeyder-faiyr, a small grasshopper unique to the Area of Special Scientific Interest at Langness peninsular in the south east corner of the Isle of Man.

The **twenty pence** (20p) shows the Mountain Hare, Mwaagh ny Sleityn, that can be found on the hills and mountain in the northern part of the Island. On the Island they are also called Blue Hares and are renowned for turning white in the winter months.

The **fifty pence** (50p) design depicts the Peregrine Falcon, Shirragh y Ree, and are among the fastest animals on the planet. Peregines are making a welcome comeback on the Isle of Man.

The **one pound** (£1) design shows the Grey Seal, Raun Glass, and is the larger of the two Manx seal species. They can be spotted resting on the rocks and beaches around the Island.

The **two pounds** (£2) depicts the Basking Shark, Sharkagh Greiney; the largest shark seen in Manx waters during the summer months. They survive on a diet of plankton and can reach up to 12 metres in length.

The **five pounds** (£5) shows the famous Queen Scallop, Roagan Veg, known on the Island as the Manx Queenie. Local regulations aim to ensure that the Queen Scallop stocks are preserved and sustainable.

COMMEMORATIVE CIRCULATING COINS FROM THE TOWER MINT

*Quantities shown as "No. Minted" are for coins circulated in the Isle of Man, where known. Coins shown thus * were not intended for general circulation.*

DATE		No. Minted	UNC
FIFTY PENCE			
2017	150th Anniversary of House of Keys	33,000	£3
2018	Platinum Wedding Queen & Prince Philip (8 coins)	each design 2,500	£30
2018	Sapphire Coronation of Her Majesty QEII (5 coins)	each design 2,500	£25
2018	Centenary of World War I Armistice, Plain	25,000	£3
2018	Centenary of World War I Armistice, Coloured	15,000	£12
	Coloured coins were given to all school pupils.		
2019	ICC Cricket World Cup (5 coins)	each design 12,000	£20
2019	Peter Pan, Part I (6 coins)	each design 25,000	£20
2020	75th Anniversary of VE Day—Individual letters spelling "VICTORY" on 7 coin designs.	25,000	£25
2020	Rupert Bear (5 coins)	each design 25,000	£30
2020	Peter Pan, Part 2 (6 coins)	each design 25,000	£30
2021	Alice in Wonderland (5 Coins)	each design 10,000	£30
2021	HM Queen 95th Birthday (6 coins)	each design 10,000	£30
2021	Alice through the Looking Glass (5 coins)		£30
2021	Prince Philip in Memoriam		£10
2021	Prince Philip in Memoriam (6 coins)		£120
2022	HM Queen's Platinum Jubilee (5 coins)		£30
2022	HM Queen's Platinum Jubilee—part gold/silver plated (5 coins)	—	£150
2023	Tutankhamun (5 coins)	—	£30
2023	King Charles III National Anthem (5 coins)	—	£30
2023	King Charles III National Anthem—part gold/silver plated (5 coins)	—	£150
2023	Jurassic Britain (5 coins)		£30
2024	King Charles III Inaugural Year (5 coins)		£40
2024	King Charles III Inaugural Year, part gold plated * (5 coins)		£150
2024	History of Manx Motor Racing (5 coins)		£40
2024	D-Day 80th Anniversary (5 coins)		£40
2024	D-Day 80th Anniversary, part gold plated * (5 coins)		£150
TWO POUNDS			
2018	Prince Harry & Meghan Markle Wedding	2,500	£10
2018	Mike Hailwood, TT 40 Years	15,000	£5
2018	Mike Hailwood, TT 60 Years	15,000	£5
2018	Christmas, Hunt the Wren	10,000	£6
2019	D-Day, King George VI	2,500	£10
2019	D-Day, Winston Spencer Churchill	2,500	£10
2019	D-Day, Field Marshall Montgomery	2,500	£10
2019	Steve Hislop's 120mph TT Lap	15,000	£5
2019	Steve Hislop's 11 TT Wins	12,500	£5
2019	Father Christmas	12,500	£6
2020	Operation Dynamo. 80th Anniversary (2 coins)	each design 3,000	£15
2020	Dickens Christmas (3 coins)	each design 3,500	£15
2020	Mayflower 400th Anniversary	3,500	£10
2021	HRH Prince Philip Memoriam	—	£12
2021	Pioneering Women's Suffrage (4 coins)	—	£30
2021	Remembrance Day (2 coins)	—	£15
2021	Christmas "Nollick Ghennal"	–	£10
2022	Isle of Man TT Races (2 coins)	—	£20
2023	Isle of Man TT Races "Parliament Square"		£12
2023	Isle of Man Manx Grand Prix Centenary		£12

DATE	No. Minted	UNC
2023 History of British Railways (5 coins)		£70
2023 Isle of Man Year of the Railways (2 coins)		£30
2023 Christmas "Nollick Ghennal"		£12
2024 TT "Greg-ny-Baa"		£12

FIVE POUNDS

DATE	No. Minted	UNC
2017 110 Years of the Tourist Trophy	20,000	£20
2017 Christmas—Dove of Peace	10,000	£25
2022 HM Queen's Platinum Jubilee	—	£25

IRELAND

As in the English hammered section (q.v.) the prices given here are for the most common coins in the series. For a more specialised listing the reader is referred to Coincraft's *Standard Catalogue of Scotland, Ireland, Channel Islands & Isle of Man*, or other specialised publications. Collectors should be aware that with most of the coins of the Irish series there are many varieties struck at different mints. The coins listed are all silver unless mentioned otherwise. Another important factor to consider when collecting early Irish coins is that few examples exist in high grades.

HIBERNO-NORSE ISSUES (995–1155)

	F	VF
Penny, imitating English silver pennies, many various types	£300	£650

Hiberno-Norse phase II example.

JOHN, Lord of Ireland (1185–99)

	F	VF
Halfpenny, profile		Extremely rare
Halfpenny, facing	£200	£575
Farthing	£500	£1850

JOHN de COURCY, Lord of Ulster (1177–1205)

	F	VF
Halfpenny		Extremely rare
Farthing	£750	£3750

John Lord of Ireland penny.

JOHN as King of England and Lord of Ireland (c. 1199–1216)

	F	VF
Penny	£80	£500
Halfpenny	£185	£5000
Farthing	£650	£2500

HENRY III (1216–72)

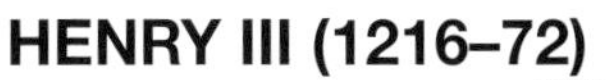

	F	VF
Penny	£150	£585

EDWARD I (1272–1307)

	F	VF
Penny	£75	£250
Halfpenny	£75	£185
Farthing	£150	£450

Henry III penny.

No Irish coins were struck for Edward II (1307–27).

EDWARD III (1327–77)

	F	VF
Halfpenny		Extremely rare

No Irish coins were struck for Richard II (1377–99), Henry IV (1399–1413) or Henry V (1413–22).

HENRY VI (1422–61)

	F	VF
Penny		Extremely rare

Edward I penny.

EDWARD IV (1461–83)

	F	VF
"Anonymous crown" groat	£700	£14500
— penny	£1200	–
"Titled crown" groat	£1600	–
— halfgroat		Extremely rare
— penny		Extremely rare
Cross on rose/Sun groat	£1850	–
Bust/Rose on sun double groat	£2250	£7500
— groat	£2250	–
— halfgroat		Extremely rare
— penny		Extremely rare
Bust/Cross & pellets groat—First issue	£150	£585
— halfgroat	£650	£1700
— penny	£100	£375
— halfpenny		Extremely rare
— Second (light) issue	£150	£550
— halfgroat	£650	£1700
— penny	£100	£250
— halfpenny		Extremely rare
Bust/Rose on cross groat	£570	£1500
— penny	£80	£275
Billon/Copper issues		
Small crown/Cross farthing (1460–61)	£1700	–
— half farthing ("Patrick")	£1100	–
Large crown/Cross farthing (1462)		Extremely rare
Patricius/Salvator farthing (1463–65)	£350	£2000
— half farthing		Extremely rare
Shield/Rose on sun farthing	£250	£1000

Edward IV groat. "Anonymous crown" issue.

Edward IV penny struck in Dublin.

RICHARD III (1483–85)

	F	VF
Bust/Rose on cross groat	£1100	£4000
— halfgroat		Unique
— penny		Unique
Bust/Cross and pellets penny	£100	£3500
Shield/Three-crowns groat	£650	£3000

Richard III bust/rose on cross groat.

HENRY VII (1485–1509)

	F	VF
Early issues (1483–90)		
Shield/Three crowns groat	£170	£575
— halfgroat	£250	£575
— penny	£650	£2600
— halfpenny		Extremely rare
Later issues (1488–90)		
Shield/Three crowns groat	£150	£475
— halfgroat	£200	£650
— penny	£500	£1400
Facing bust groat (1496–1505)	£200	£525
— halfgroat	£1100	–
— penny	£1000	–

LAMBERT SIMNEL (as EDWARD VI, Pretender, 1487)

	F	VF
Shield/Three crowns groat	£1300	£5200

Henry VII groat.

HENRY VIII (1509–47)

	F	VF
"Harp" groat	£150	£4000
— halfgroat	£525	£2750

The "Harp" coins have crowned initials either side of the reverse harp, e.g. HR (Henricus Rex), HA (Henry and Anne Boleyn), HI (Henry and Jane Seymour), HK (Henry and Katherine Howard).

Posthumous (Portrait) issues	F	VF
Sixpence	£185	£575
Threepence	£165	£575
Threehalfpence	£500	£1800
Threefarthings	£650	£2500

Henry VIII Posthumous portrait issues threepence.

EDWARD VI (1547–53)

	F	VF
Shilling (base silver) 1552 (MDLII)	£1100	£3750
Brass contemporary copy	£110	£420

MARY (1553–54)

	F	VF
Shilling 1553 (MDLIII)	£1000	£3500
Shilling 1554 (MDLIIII)		Extremely rare
Groat		Extremely rare
Halfgroat		Extremely rare
Penny		Extremely rare

PHILIP & MARY (1554–58)

	F	VF
Shilling	£350	£1500
Groat	£150	£475
Penny		Extremely rare

Philip & Mary shilling

ELIZABETH I (1558–1603)

	F	VF
Base silver portrait coinage		
Shilling	£500	£1750
Groat	£250	£825
Fine silver, portrait coinage (1561)		
Shilling	£300	£1200
Groat	£350	£1200
Third (base silver) shield coinage		
Shilling	£250	£820
Sixpence	£200	£575
Copper		
Threepence	£275	£725
Penny	£75	£285
Halfpenny	£150	£350

JAMES I (1603–25)

	F	VF
Shilling	£125	£500
Sixpence	£125	£475

Coins struck under Royal Licence from 1613

	F	VF
"Harrington" farthing (small size)	£75	£295
"Harrington" farthing (large size)	£75	£250
"Lennox" farthing	£75	£285

Elizabeth I "fine" shilling of 1561.

CHARLES I (1625–49)

During the reign of Charles I and the Great Rebellion many coins were struck under unusual circumstances, making the series a difficult but fascinating area for study. Many of the "coins" were simply made from odd-shaped pieces of plate struck with the weight or value.

Charles I "Ormonde" crown.

	F	VF
Coins struck under Royal Licence from 1625		
"Richmond" farthing	£65	£250
"Maltravers" farthing	£50	£250
"Rose" farthing	£50	£275
Siege money of the Irish Rebellion, 1642–49		
"Inchiquin" Money (1642)		
Crown	£2500	£6500
Halfcrown	£2000	£5750
Shilling		Extremely rare
Ninepence		Extremely rare
Sixpence		Extremely rare
Groat		Extremely rare
"Dublin" Money (1643)		
Crown	£1000	£3750
Halfcrown	£600	£2750
"Ormonde" Money (1643–44)		
Crown	£575	£1600
Halfcrown	£375	£1275
Shilling	£150	£475
Sixpence	£150	£475
Groat	£120	£435
Threepence	£120	£350
Twopence	£500	£1700
"Ormonde" gold coinage (1646)		
Double pistole. 2 known (both in museums)		Extremely rare
Pistole. 10 known (only 1 in private ownership		Extremely rare
"Ormonde" Money (1649)		
Crown		Extremely rare
Halfcrown	£1300	£4000
Dublin Money 1649		
Crown	£3000	£8000
Halfcrown	£2200	£5500
Issues of the Confederated Catholics		
Kilkenny issues (1642–43)		
Halfpenny	£350	£1000
Farthing	£450	£1200
Rebel Money (1643–44)		
Crown	£2650	£5750
Halfcrown	£2000	£5850
"Blacksmith's" Money (16??)		

A rare Charles I "Rebel" halfcrown.

	F	VF
Imitation of English Tower halfcrown.....	£750	£3500

Halfpenny of Charles I.

Local Town issues of "Cities of Refuge"

	F	VF
Bandon		
Farthing (copper)..................................	Extremely rare	
Cork		
Shilling..	Extremely rare	
Sixpence...	£775	£1500
Halfpenny (copper)................................	Extremely rare	
Farthing (copper)..................................	£635	–
Kinsale		
Farthing (copper)..................................	£425	–
Youghal		
Farthing (copper)..................................	£500	£2500

CHARLES II (1660–85)

	Fair	F	VF	EF
"Armstrong" coinage				
Farthing (1660–61)................................	£75	£250	–	–
"St Patrick's" coinage				
Halfpenny	£235	£475	–	–
Farthing	£85	£200	£600	£1895
Legg's Regal coinage				
Halfpennies				
1680 large lettering...............................	£35	£100	£325	–
1681 large lettering...............................	–	£200	£695	–
1681 small lettering			Extremely rare	
1682 small lettering	–	£200	£675	–
1683 small lettering	£35	£45	£465	
1684 small lettering	£50	£125	£675	–

"St Patrick" farthing of Charles II.

JAMES II (1685–88)

REGAL COINAGE

Halfpennies	Fair	F	VF	EF
1685..	£35	£85	£320	£750
1686..	£35	£65	£200	£635
1687..			Extremely rare	
1688..	£45	£125	£300	£1400

"Gun Money" crown.

EMERGENCY COINAGE

	Fair	F	VF	EF
GUN MONEY				
Most of these coins were struck in gun metal but a few rare specimens are also known struck in gold and in silver				
Crowns				
1690 (many varieties)......................from	£45	£65	£650	–
Large halfcrowns				
Dated July 1689–May 1690 ....from	£35	£65	£250	–
Small halfcrowns				
Dated April–October1690 ....from	£35	£65	£250	–
Large shillings				
Dated from July 1689–April 1690 ....from	£35	£75	£125	£925
Small shillings				
Dated from April–September 1690 ....from	£30	£35	£125	£850
Sixpences				
Dated from June 1689–October 1690 ....from	£35	£60	£300	–
***PEWTER MONEY* (1689–90)**				
Crown	£700	£1200	£3500	–
Groat..			Extremely rare	
Penny large bust..................................	£230	£675	–	–
– small bust	£165	£485	£1500	–
Halfpenny large bust	£130	£345	£950	–
– small bust	£110	£245	£700	–
***LIMERICK MONEY* (1690–91)**				
Halfpenny, reversed N in HIBERNIA......	£35	£75	£275	–
Farthing, reversed N in HIBERNIA.........	£35	£75	£275	–
– normal N	£45	£135	£345	–

William & Mary half-penny of 1693.

WILLIAM & MARY (1689–94)

	Fair	F	VF	EF
Halfpennies				
1692..	£15	£50	£100	£725
1693..	£15	£50	£85	£725
1694..	£25	£75	£135	£895

WILLIAM III (1694–1702)

	Fair	F	VF	EF
1696 Halfpenny draped bust................	£35	£85	£275	–
1696 – crude undraped bust	£45	£275	£950	–

DATE	F	VF	EF	UNC

No Irish coins were struck during the reign of Queen Anne (1706–11).

GEORGE I (1714–27)

Farthings

DATE	F	VF	EF	UNC
1722 D.G. REX Harp to left (Pattern)	£650	£1600	£2500	–
1723 D.G. REX Harp to right	£120	£225	£525	–
1723 DEI GRATIA REX Harp to right	£35	£65	£275	£650
1723 — Silver Proof	–	–	–	£2500
1724 DEI GRATIA REX Harp to right	£60	£150	£365	£885

Halfpennies

DATE	F	VF	EF	UNC
1722 Holding Harp left	£55	£130	£395	£1200
1722 Holding Harp right	£45	£120	£350	£825
1723/2 Harp right	£50	£150	£350	£825
1723 Harp right	£30	£65	£200	£565
1723 Silver Proof	–	–	–	£3700
1723 Obv. Rs altered from Bs	£35	£100	£295	–
1723 No stop after date	£25	£80	£295	£575
1724 Rev. legend divided	£40	£100	£300	–
1724 Rev. legend continuous	£40	£110	£395	–

Halfpenny of George II

GEORGE II (1727–60)

Farthings

DATE	F	VF	EF	UNC
1737	£35	£60	£185	£500
1737 Proof	–	–	–	£525
1737 Silver Proof	–	–	–	£1300
1738	£35	£65	£165	£495
1744	£35	£65	£165	£495
1760	£30	£50	£100	£385

Halfpennies

DATE	F	VF	EF	UNC
1736	£25	£65	£225	£685
1736 Proof	–	–	–	£695
1736 Silver Proof	–	–	–	£1400
1737	£25	£50	£225	–
1738	£30	£60	£225	–
1741	£30	£60	£225	–
1742	£30	£60	£225	–
1743	£30	£60	£200	–
1744/3	£30	£60	£200	–
1744	£30	£60	£375	–
1746	£30	£60	£250	–
1747	£30	£60	£225	–
1748	£30	£60	£225	–
1749	£30	£60	£225	–
1750	£35	£60	£225	–
1751	£30	£60	£225	–
1752	£30	£60	£225	–
1753	£30	£60	£250	–
1755	£30	£110	£350	–
*1760	£35	£75	£250	–

George III proof penny 1805

GEORGE III (1760–1820)

All copper unless otherwise stated

Pennies

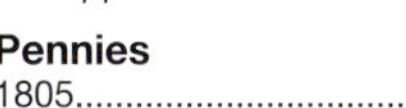

DATE	F	VF	EF	UNC
1805	£20	£40	£185	£525
1805 Proof	–	–	–	£625
1805 in Bronze Proof	–	–	–	£600
1805 in Copper Gilt Proof	–	–	–	£600
1805 in Silver Proof (restrike)	–	–	–	£3500

DATE	F	VF	EF	UNC
Halfpennies				
1766	£30	£55	£165	—
1769	£30	£55	£165	—
1769 Longer bust	£40	£75	£250	£775
1774 Pattern only Proof	—	—	—	£3500
1775	£30	£55	£200	£475
1775 Proof	—	—	—	£675
1776	£55	£140	£400	—
1781	£45	£60	£175	£465
1782	£45	£60	£175	£465
1805	£18	£45	£120	£465
1805 Copper Proof	—	—	—	£465
1805 in Bronze	—	—	—	£325
1805 in Gilt Copper	—	—	—	£475
1805 in Silver (restrike)	—	—	—	£2000
Farthings				
1806	£20	£35	£100	£200
1806 Copper Proof	—	—	—	£375
1806 Bronzed Copper Proof	—	—	—	£275
1806 Copper Gilt Proof	—	—	—	£350
1806 Silver Proof (restrike)	—	—	—	£1600

One of the scarcer dates, a 1776 George III halfpenny.

GEORGE IV (1820–30)

DATE	F	VF	EF	UNC
Pennies				
1822	£20	£40	£195	£525
1822 Proof	—	—	—	£625
1823	£12	£25	£150	£475
1823 Proof	—	—	—	£625
Halfpennies				
1822	£20	£40	£125	£400
1822 Proof	—	—	—	£650
1823	£20	£40	£125	£425
1823 Proof	—	—	—	£695

NB Prooflike Uncirculated Pennies and Halfpennies of 1822/23 are often misdescribed as Proofs. The true Proofs are rare. Some are on heavier, thicker flans.

DATE	F	VF	EF	UNC
Farthings				
1822 (Pattern) Proof	—	—	—	£1875

TOKEN ISSUES BY THE BANK OF IRELAND

DATE	F	VF	EF	UNC
Five Pence in Silver				
1805	£30	£45	£75	£375
1806	£30	£65	£150	£410
1806/5	£60	£145	£450	£1475
Ten Pence in Silver				
1805	£20	£35	£95	£275
1806	£20	£65	£150	£295
1813	£20	£35	£95	£335
1813 Proof	—	—	—	£475
Thirty Pence in Silver				
1808	£45	£100	£250	£685
Six Shillings				
1804 in Silver	£100	£250	£465	£1875
1804 Proof	—	—	—	£1800
1804 in Copper (restrike)	—	—	—	£825
1804 Copper Gilt	—	—	—	£1850
1804 in Gilt Silver	—	—	—	£3100

1804 six shillings.

In this series fully struck specimens, with sharp hair curls, etc., are worth appreciably more than the prices quoted.

IRISH FREE STATE/EIRE

DATE	F	VF	EF	UNC
TEN SHILLINGS				
1966 Easter Rising	—	£12	£18	£45
1966 Cased Proof	—	—	—	£45
1966 Special double case	—	—	—	£110
HALF CROWNS				
Silver				
1928	£7	£12	£45	£100
1928 Proof	—	—	—	£125
1930	£15	£75	£250	£600
1931	£15	£75	£250	£545
1933	£15	£75	£275	£600
1934	£20	£45	£150	£300
1937	£70	£295	£750	£2250
Modified obverse: Eire				
1938				Unique
1939	£7	£17	£30	£85
1939 Proof	—	—	—	£650
1940	£8	£18	£35	£95
1941	£7	£17	£35	£95
1942	£7	£20	£35	£110
1943	£85	£300	£995	£3450
Cupro-nickel				
1951	£2	£3	£20	£75
1951 Proof	—	—	—	£750
1954	£2	£3	£15	£95
1954 Proof	—	—	—	£725
1955	£2	£3	£15	£45
1955	—	—	—	£850
1959	£2	£3	£12	£50
1959 Proof	—	—	—	£850
1961	£2	£3	£25	£60
1961 Obv as 1928, rev. as 1951	£30	£75	£325	£1000
1962	£2	£3	£6	£35
1963	£2	£3	£6	£35
1964	£2	£3	£6	£35
1966	£2	£3	£6	£35
1967	£2	£3	£6	£45
FLORINS				
Silver				
1928	£5	£8	£25	£75
1928 Proof	—	—	—	£85
1930	£5	£25	£150	£500
1930 Proof				Unique
1931	£5	£25	£200	£550
1933	£5	£20	£195	£525
1934	£15	£125	£375	£950
1934 Proof	—	—	—	£3250
1935	£5	£20	£85	£250
1937	£6	£25	£165	£450
Modified obverse: Eire				
1939	£3	£6	£35	£85
1939 Proof	—	—	—	£685
1940	£5	£6	£30	£85
1941	£5	£6	£35	£85
1941 Proof	—	—	—	£875
1942	£7	£15	£30	£100
*1943	£5000	£10000	£20000	£30000

Beware of fake 1943 florins.

DATE	F	VF	EF	UNC
Cupro-nickel				
1951	60p	£2	£15	£50
1951 Proof	—	—	—	£650
1954	60p	£2	£10	£50
1954 Proof	—	—	—	£650
1955	—	£2	£6	£50
1955 Proof	—	—	—	£750
1959	40p	£2	£6	£45
1961	60p	£3	£15	£65
1962	40p	£2	£6	£30
1963	30p	£2	£6	£30
1964	30p	£2	£6	£30
1965	30p	£2	£6	£30
1966	30p	£2	£6	£30
1968	30p	£2	£6	£30

SHILLINGS

DATE	F	VF	EF	UNC
Silver				
1928	£5	£10	£25	£60
1928 Proof	—	—	—	£75
1930	£8	£35	£200	£495
1930 Proof	—	—	—	£950
1931	£3	£17	£95	£485
1933	£3	£17	£95	£470
1935	£3	£15	£60	£170
1937	£20	£95	£350	£1500
1939	£3	£6	£25	£80
1939 Proof	—	—	—	£795
1940	£3	£6	£17	£60
1941	£3	£5	£17	£75
1942	£3	£10	£15	£55
Cupro-nickel				
1951	£1	£2	£6	£25
1951 Proof	—	—	—	£650
1954	£1	£2	£6	£25
1954 Proof	—	—	—	£650
1955	£1	£2	£6	£25
1959	£1	£2	£6	£35
1962	50p	£2	£5	£22
1963	50p	£2	£5	£15
1964	50p	£2	£5	£15
1966	50p	£2	£5	£15
1968	50p	£2	£5	£15

SIXPENCES

DATE	F	VF	EF	UNC
Nickel				
1928	£1	£6	£25	£65
1928 Proof	—	—	—	£65
1934	£1	£3	£18	£100
1935	£1	£5	£35	£170
Modified obverse: Eire				
1939	£1	£2	£10	£65
1939 Proof	—	—	—	£675
1940	£1	£2	£6	£65
Cupro-nickel				
1942	£1	£2	£9	£65
1945	£3	£12	£35	£100
1946	£5	£20	£120	£525
1947	£2	£5	£35	£125
1948	£1	£3	£15	£75
1949	£1	£2	£10	£50
1950	£5	£12	£45	£135
1952	£1	£2	£7	£30

DATE	F	VF	EF	UNC
1953	£1	£2	£5	£45
1953 Proof	—	—	—	£500
1955	£1	£12	£20	£35
1956	£1	£10	£15	£35
1956 Proof	—	—	—	£500
1958	£4	£15	£42	£85
1958 Proof	—	—	—	£600
1959	50p	60p	£3	£25
1960	50p	60p	£2	£25
1961	—	£2	£3	£25
1962	£2	£6	£35	£80
1963	£2	£3	£6	£20
1964	£2	£3	£6	£15
1966	£2	£3	£6	£15
1967	£2	£3	£6	£12
1968	£2	£3	£6	£12
1969	£5	£8	£10	£20

THREEPENCES

DATE	F	VF	EF	UNC
Nickel				
1928	£2	£3	£10	£45
1928 Proof	—	—	—	£45
1933	£3	£13	£75	£400
1934	£1	£3	£15	£85
Modified obverse: Eire				
1935	£2	£4	£30	£235
1939	£3	£7	£60	£400
1939 Proof	—	—	—	£1300
1940	£2	£3	£13	£75
Cupro-nickel				
1942	—	£2	£6	£65
1942 Proof	—	—	—	£850
1943	£2	£15	£45	£90
1946	£2	£10	£15	£65
1946 Proof	—	—	—	£850
1948	£2	£15	£65	£100
1949	—	£8	£10	£50
1950	—	£2	£6	£35
1950 Proof	—	—	—	£700
1953	—	£2	£4	£20
1956	—	£2	£3	£15
1961	—	60p	£2	£5
1962	—	60p	£2	£12
1963	—	60p	£2	£12
1964	—	60p	£2	£5
1965	—	60p	£2	£5
1966	—	60p	£2	£5
1967	—	60p	£2	£5
1968	—	—	£2	£5

PENNIES

DATE	F	VF	EF	UNC
1928	£2	£3	£12	£55
1928 Proof	—	—	—	£75
1931	£2	£4	£35	£125
1931 Proof	—	—	—	£1300
1933	£2	£5	£50	£275
1935	£1	£2	£25	£85
1937	£1	£2	£35	£135
1937 Proof	—	—	—	£1200
Modified obverse: Eire				
1938			Only two known	
1940	£10	£50	£175	£800
1941	£1	£10	£20	£45
1942	—	£2	£5	£25

DATE	F	VF	EF	UNC
1943	—	£2	£6	£50
1946	—	£2	£5	£25
1948	—	£2	£4	£20
1949	—	£2	£5	£25
1949 Proof	—	—	—	£600
1950	—	£2	£6	£40
1952	—	£2	£4	£15
1962	—	£2	£4	£15
1962 Proof	—	—	—	£225
1963	—	—	£2	£20
1963 Proof	—	—	—	£200
1964	—	—	£2	£10
1964 Proof	—	—	—	£550
1965	—	—	£1	£5
1966	—	—	£1	£5
1967	—	—	£1	£5
1968	—	—	£1	£5
1968 Proof	—	—	—	£300

HALFPENNIES

DATE	F	VF	EF	UNC
1928	£2	£3	£15	£45
1928 Proof	—	—	—	£50
1933	£6	£20	£100	£520
1935	£5	£10	£50	£235
1937	£5	£10	£25	£75
Modified obverse: Eire				
1939	£5	£20	£75	£220
1939 Proof	—	—	—	£900
1940	£2	£4	£50	£350
1940 Proof	—	—	—	Ex. rare
1941	£1	£5	£10	£45
1942	£1	£2	£6	£25
1943	£1	£5	£10	£45
1946	£2	£15	£70	£120
1949	£1	£2	£10	£30
1953	—	£2	£3	£12
1953 Proof	—	—	—	£700
1964	—	—	£1	£5
1965	—	—	£1	£6
1966	—	—	£1	£4
1967	—	—	£1	£4

FARTHINGS

DATE	F	VF	EF	UNC
1928	£3	£4	£15	£32
1928 Proof	—	—	—	£45
1930	£3	£4	£12	£35
1931	£4	£8	£20	£40
1931 Proof	—	—	—	£955
1932	£4	£8	£20	£50
1933	£3	£4	£12	£32
1935	£4	£10	£20	£45
1936	£5	£20	£30	£65
1937	£4	£6	£18	£35
Modified obverse: Eire				
1939	£3	£4	£10	£20
1939 Proof	—	—	—	£695
1940	£4	£5	£10	£35
1941	£3	£4	£6	£12
1943	£3	£4	£6	£12
1944	£3	£5	£8	£15
1946	£3	£8	£12	£20
1949	£4	£6	£8	£25
1949 Proof	—	—	—	£475
1953	£3	£4	£5	£12
1953 Proof	—	—	—	£400
1959	£3	£4	£5	£12
1966	£3	£4	£5	£12

For the 1928–50 copper issues it is worth noting that UNC means UNC with some lustre. BU examples with full lustre are extremely elusive and are worth much more than the quoted prices.

IRISH DECIMAL COINAGE

HALF PENCE

DATE	MINTAGE	BU
1971	100,500,000	£5
1975	10,500,000	£6
1976	5,500,000	£6
1978	20,300,000	£5
1980	20,600,000	£4
1982	9,700,000	£4
1985	2,800,000	Rare
1986. Only issued in the 1986 set	19,750,000	£145

ONE PENNY

DATE	MINTAGE	BU
1971	100,500,000	£6
1974	10,000,000	£16
1975	10,000,000	£18
1976	38,200,000	£5
1978	25,700,000	£8
1979	21,800,000	£12
1980	86,700,000	£3
1982	54,200,000	£5
1985	19,200,000	£8
1986	36,600,000	£5
1988	56,800,000	£5
1990	65,100,000	£5
1992	25,600,000	£6
1993	10,000,000	£10
1994	45,800,000	£5
1995	70,800,000	£3
1996	190,100,000	£1
1998	40,700,000	£1
2000	Unknown	£1

TWO PENCE

DATE	MINTAGE	BU
1971	75,500,000	£5
1975	20,000,000	£12
1976	5400,000	£18
1978	12,000,000	£12
1979	32,400,000	£8
1980	59,800,000	£6
1982	30,400,000	£5
1985	14,500,000	£6
1986	23,900,000	£6
1988	35,900,000	£5
1990	34,300,000	£5
1992	10,200,000	£12
1995	55,500,000	£5
1996	69,300,000	£2
1998	33,700,000	£2
2000	Unknown	£2

FIVE PENCE

DATE	MINTAGE	BU
1969 Toned	5,000,000	£12
1970	10,000,000	£5
1971	8,000,000	£8
1974	7,000,000	£11
1975	10,000,000	£11
1976	20,600,000	£5
1978	28,500,000	£5
1980	22,200,000	£5
1982	24,400,000	£4
1985	4,200,000	£10
1986	15,300,000	£5
1990	7,500,000	£8
Size reduced to 18.4mm		
1992	74,500,000	£5
1993	89,100,000	£5
1994	31,100,000	£5
1995	12,000,000	£5
1996	14,700,000	£2
1998	158,500,000	£2
2000	Unknown	£2

TEN PENCE

DATE	MINTAGE	BU
1969	27,000,000	£12
1971	4,000,000	£15
1973	2,500,000	£16
1974	7,500,000	£12
1975	15,000,000	£12
1976	9,400,000	£12
1978	30,900,000	£10
1980	44,600,000	£8
1982	7,400,000	£10
1985	4,100,000	£12
1986. Only issued in the 1986 set	11,280	£320
Size reduced to 22mm		
1992	2 known	—
1993	80,100,000	£5
1994	58,500,000	£5

DATE	MINTAGE	BU
1995	16,100,000	£5
1996	18,400,000	£3
1997	10,000,000	£4
1998	10,000,000	£4
1999	24,500,000	£3
2000	Unknown	£3

TWENTY PENCE

DATE	MINTAGE	BU
1985. Only 600 minted and 556 melted down, only 3 known	Extremely rare	
1986	50,400,000	£9
1988	20,700,000	£6
1992	14,800,000	£5
1994	11,100,000	£5
1995	18,200,000	£5
1996	29,300,000	£5
1998	25,000,000	£3
1999	11,000,000	£3
2000	Unknown	£2

FIFTY PENCE

DATE	MINTAGE	BU
1970	9,000,000	£10
1971	650,000	£8
1974	1,000,000	£55
1975	2,000,000	£55
1976	3,000,000	£45
1977	4,800,000	£55
1978	4,500,000	£45
1979	4,000,000	£45
1981	6,000,000	£25
1982	2,000,000	£25
1983	7,000,000	£25
1986 Only issued in the 1986 set	10,000	£325
1988	7,000,000	£5
1988 Dublin Millennium	5,000,000	£6
1988 — Proof	50,000	£35
1996	6,000,000	£7
1997	6,000,000	£7
1998	13,800,000	£5
1999	7,000,000	£4
2000	Unknown	£4

ONE POUND

DATE	MINTAGE	BU
1990	42,300,000	£5
1990 Proof	50,000	£28
1994	14,900,000	£5
1995	9,200,000	£5
1995 UN silver proof in case of issue	2,850	£200
1996	9,200,000	£5
1998	22,960,000	£4
1999	10,000,000	£5
2000	4,000,000	£5

DATE	MINTAGE	BU
2000 Millennium	5,000,000	£8
2000 – Silver Proof Piedfort	90,000	£50

OFFICIAL COIN SETS ISSUED BY THE CENTRAL BANK

1971 Specimen set in green wallet. 6 coins.............£35
1975 6 coin set.............£65
1978 6 coin set.............£65
1978 6 coin set. Black cover, scarce.............£85
1982 6 coin set. Black cover.............£75
1986 Specimen set in card folder 1/2p to 50p, 7 coins. Very scarce. Most sets have glue problems.............£650
1996 7 coin set.............£70
1998 7 coin set.............£50
2000 Millennium set. Last decimal set.............£150
2000 — With 1999 instead of the 2000 £1 coin £300

Dublin Millennium 50p

OFFICIAL AND SEMI-OFFICIAL COMMEMORATIVE MEDALS

It is probably a strong love of history, rather than the strict disciplines of coin collecting that make collectors turn to commemorative medals. The link between the two is intertwined, and it is to be hoped that collectors will be encouraged to venture into the wider world of medallions, encouraged by this brief guide, originally supplied by Daniel Fearon (author of the *Catalogue of British Commemorative Medals)* and kindly updated again this year by Charles Riley.

DATE	VF	EF
JAMES I		
1603 Coronation (possibly by C. Anthony), 29mm, Silver	£1500	£2500
QUEEN ANNE		
1603 Coronation, 29mm, AR	£1100	£2000
CHARLES I		
1626 Coronation (by N. Briot), 30mm, Silver	£1200	£1800
1633 Scottish Coronation (by N. Briot), 28mm, Silver	£750	£1500
1649 Memorial (by J. Roettier). Struck after the Restoration, 50mm, Bronze	£95	£175
CROMWELL		
1653 Lord Protector (by T. Simon), 38mm, Silver	£700	£1700
— Cast examples	£350	£600
CHARLES II		
1651 Scottish Coronation, in exile (from design by Sir J. Balfour), 32mm, Silver	£3000	£4000
CHARLES II		
1661 Coronation (by T. Simon), 29mm		
— Gold	£4500	£9000
— Silver	£400	£700
1685 Death (by N. Roettier), 39mm, Bronze	£150	£325

James I Coronation, 1603

Charles II Coronation, 1661

DATE	VF	EF
JAMES II		
1685 Coronation (by J. Roettier), 34mm		
— Gold	£4500	£9000
— Silver	£600	£950
MARY		
1685 Coronation (by J. Roettier), 34mm		
— Gold	£4500	£9000
— Silver	£450	£750
WILLIAM & MARY		
1689 Coronation (by J. Roettier), 32mm		
— Gold	£4000	£7000
— Silver	£400	£650
1689 Coronation,"Perseus" (by G. Bower), 38mm, Gold	£4000	£7000
MARY		
1694 Death (by N. Roettier), 39mm, Bronze	£110	£245
WILLIAM III		
1697 "The State of Britain" (by J. Croker), 69mm, Silver	£1250	£2500
ANNE		
1702 Accession, "Entirely English" (by J. Croker), 34mm		
— Gold	£4000	£7000
— Silver	£175	£350
1702 Coronation (by J. Croker), 36mm		
— Gold	£4500	£9000
— Silver	£300	£500
1707 Union with Scotland (by J. Croker, rev. by S. Bull), 34mm		
— Gold	£4000	£8000
— Silver	£250	£350
1713 Peace of Utrecht (by J. Croker—issued in gold to Members of Parliament), 34mm		
— Gold	£4500	£9000
— Silver	£150	£250
GEORGE I		
1714 Coronation (by J. Croker), 34mm		
— Gold	£4000	£7000
— Silver	£250	£450
1727 Death (by J. Dassier), 31mm, Silver	£150	£275
GEORGE II		
1727Coronation (by J. Croker), 34mm		
— Gold	£4000	£7000
— Silver	£250	£350
QUEEN CAROLINE		
1727 Coronation (by J. Croker), 34mm		
— Gold	£4000	£7500
— Silver	£250	£450
1732 The Royal Family (by J. Croker), 70mm		
— Silver	£1500	£3000
— Bronze	£550	£950

Queen Anne, 1702–1713.

George I Coronation, 1714.

DATE	VF	EF
GEORGE III		
1761 Coronation (by L. Natter), 34mm		
— Gold	£4000	£8000
— Silver	£500	£700
— Bronze	£150	£250
QUEEN CHARLOTTE		
1761 Coronation (by L. Natter), 34mm		
— Gold	£3500	£7000
— Silver	£375	£600
— Bronze	£150	£295
1810 Golden Jubilee, "Frogmore", 48mm, Silver	£130	£275
— Bronze	£95	£175
GEORGE IV		
1821 Coronation (by B. Pistrucci), 35mm		
— Gold	£2500	£4500
— Silver	£350	£450
— Bronze	£95	£150
WILLIAM IV		
1831 Coronation (by W. Wyon; rev. shows Queen Adelaide), 33mm		
— Gold	£2500	£4500
— Silver	£200	£450
— Bronze	£95	£150
QUEEN VICTORIA		
1838 Coronation (by B. Pistrucci), 37mm		
— Gold	£3000	£5000
— Silver	£300	£450
— Bronze	£95	£175

George III, Coronation, 1761

Queen Victoria Coronation, 1838

Queen Victoria Diamond Jubilee 1897

DATE	VF	EF
1887 Golden Jubilee (by J. E. Boehm, rev. by Lord Leighton)		
— Gold, 58mm	£6500	£8500
— Silver, 78mm	£250	£500
— Bronze, 78mm	£95	£180
1897 Diamond Jubilee (by G. de Saulles),		
— Gold, 56mm	£6500	£8500
— Silver, 56mm	£95	£125
— Bronze, 56mm	£45	£65
— Gold, 25mm	£850	£1200
— Silver, 25mm	£20	£35

EDWARD VII

1902 Coronation (August 9) (by G. W. de Saulles)		
— Gold, 56mm	£6500	£8500
— Silver, 56mm	£95	£175
— Bronze, 56mm	£45	£65
— Gold, 31mm	£1250	£1500
— Silver, 31mm	£25	£35

**Some rare examples of the official medal show the date as June 26, the original date set for the Coronation which was postponed because the King developed appendicitis.*

GEORGE V

1911 Coronation (by B. Mackennal)		
— Gold, 51mm	£6500	£8500
— Silver, 51mm	£110	£250
— Bronze, 51mm	£35	£65
— Gold, 31mm	£1250	£1500
— Silver, 31mm	£25	£35
1935 Silver Jubilee (by P. Metcalfe)		
— Gold, 58mm	£6500	£8500
— Silver, 58mm	£100	£150
— Gold, 32mm	£1250	£1500
— Silver, 32mm	£25	£35

PRINCE EDWARD

1911 Investiture as Prince of Wales (by W. Goscombe John)		
— Gold, 31mm	£3500	£5000
— Silver, 31mm	£65	£125

EDWARD VIII

1936 Abdication (by L. E. Pinches), 35mm		
— Gold	£1750	£2500
— Silver	£45	£65
— Bronzo	£20	£35

GEORGE VI

1937 Coronation (by P. Metcalfe)		
— Gold, 58mm	£6500	£8500
— Silver, 58mm	£65	£95
— Gold, 32mm	£1250	£1500
— Silver, 32mm	£25	£35
— Bronze, 32mm	£12	£15

George V Silver Jubilee, 1935

Edward, Prince of Wales, 1911

Edward VIII, Abdication, 1936.

DATE	VF	EF
ELIZABETH II		
1953 Coronation (by Spink & Son)—illustrated		
— Gold, 57mm	£5500	£6500
— Silver, 57mm	£65	£125
— Bronze, 57mm	£35	£65
— Gold, 32mm	£750	£950
— Silver, 32mm	£25	£35
— Bronze, 32mm	£12	£15
1977 Silver Jubilee (by A. Machin)		
— Silver, 57mm	—	£70
— Silver, 44mm	—	£40

**The gold medals are priced for 18ct—they can also be found as 22ct and 9ct, and prices should be adjusted accordingly.*

	VF	EF
PRINCE CHARLES		
1969 Investiture as Prince of Wales (by M. Rizello)		
— Silver, 57mm	—	£75
— Bronze gilt, 57mm	—	£40
— Silver, 45mm	—	£50
— Gold, 32mm	—	£1250
— Silver, 32mm	—	£35
— Bronze, 32mm	—	£10
QUEEN ELIZABETH THE QUEEN MOTHER		
1980 80th Birthday (by L. Durbin)		
— Silver, 57mm	—	£65
— Silver, 38mm	—	£38
— Bronze, 38mm	—	£25

N.B.—Official Medals usually command a premium when still in their original case of issue.

Prince Charles, Prince of Wales 1969.

The Royal Mint Museum contains a charming group of medallic portraits of seven of the children of Queen Victoria and Prince Albert. They appear to have been made in 1850 and therefore do not include the two children who were born after that date. The skilfully-executed portraits are the work of Leonard Wyon, a member of the extremely talented family of engravers whose name is so well known to numismatists. The son of William Wyon, he was actually born in the Royal Mint in 1826. These particular portraits were not commissioned by the Mint and little is known about the circumstances in which they were prepared, but for some reason the dies have survived in the Royal Mint Museum, along with single-sided bronze impressions roughly the size of a half-crown.

Images and information courtesy of Dr Kevin Clancy, The Royal Mint.

Directory
section

ON the following pages will be found the most useful names and addresses needed by the coin collector.

At the time of going to press with this edition of the YEARBOOK the information is correct, as far as we have been able to ascertain. However, people move and establishments change, so it is always advisable to make contact with the person or organisation listed before travelling any distance, to ensure that the journey is not wasted.

Should any of the information in this section not be correct we would very much appreciate being advised in good time for the preparation of the next edition of the COIN YEARBOOK.

Club directory

Details given here are the names of Numismatic Clubs and Societies, their date of foundation, and their usual venues, days and times of meetings. Meetings are monthly unless otherwise stated. Finally, the telephone number of the club secretary is given; the names and addresses of club secretaries are withheld for security reasons, but full details may be obtained by writing to the Secretary of the British Association of Numismatic Societies, Bill Pugsley, bill@pugsley.co or visiting the website at www.coinclubs.org.uk.

Banknote Society of Scotland (1994) Meetings are held four times a year in Edinburgh. Email, bnss2019@gmail.com.

Bath & Bristol Numismatic Society (1950). The Globe Inn, Newton St Loe, Bath BA2 9BB 2nd Thu, 19.30. Email: adrian@bathandbristol-ns.org.uk.

Bedfordshire Numismatic Society (1966). 2nd Mon, call for venue details: 07555 048859

Birmingham Numismatic Society (1964). Friend's Meeting House, Bull Street. Email for dates: bhamns@hotmail.co.uk.

Matthew Boulton Lunar Society (1994). The Old School House, Chapel Lane, Birmingham, B47 6JX Tel: 01564 821 582.

British Banking History Society. 22 Delamere Road, Gatley, Cheadle, SK8 4PH.

British Numismatic Society (1903). Call for venue and dates; 02070161802.

Cambridgeshire Numismatic Society (1946). Friends' Meeting House, 12 Jesus Lane Cambridge, CB5 8BA. Call for dates. Tel: 01223 332 918.

Chester & North Wales Coin & Banknote Society (1996). Nags Head, Bunbury, Cheshire, CW6 9PB 4th Tue, 20.00. Tel: 01829 260 897.

Crewe & District Coin and Medal Society. Memorial Hall, Church Lane, Wistaston, Crewe, CW2 8ER. 2nd Tue, (exc Jan & July), 19.30 Tel: 07828 602 611.

Derbyshire Numismatic Society The Friends Meeting House, St Helen's Street, Derby. Tel: 01283 211623.

Devon & Exeter Numismatic Society, Courtenay Room, The St James Centre, Stadium Way, Exeter. 3rd Wed. Tel: 01395 568830.

Essex Numismatic Society (1966). Christchurch URC, 164 New London Road. 4th Fri (exc Dec), 20.00. Tel: 01279 814 216.

Glasgow & West of Scotland Numismatic Society (1947). Ibrox Parish Church Halls, Clifford Street, Glasgow, G51 1QH. 2nd Thu, Oct-April, 19.30. Tel: 07949 194036, Email: glasgowcoinclub@aol.com.

Harrow Coin Club (1968). The Scout Building, off Walton Road, Wealdstone, Harrow, HA1 4UX. 2nd Mon, 19.30. Tel: 0208 8952 8765.

Havering Numismatic Society (1967). Fairkytes Arts Centre, Billet Lane, Hornchurch, Essex, RM11 1AX 1st Tue, 19.30. Tel: 0208 5545 486. Email: mail@havering-ns.org.uk.

Huddersfield Numismatic Society (1947). Lindley Liberal Club, 36 Occupation Road, Huddersfield, HD3 3EQ. 1st Mon (Sept to June) unless Bank Holiday then following Monday. Tel: 01484 866 814.

International Bank Note Society (London Branch) (1961). Spink, 69 Southampton Row, Bloomsbury, London, WC1B 4ET. Last Thu (exc Sept & Dec), 18.30. Tel: 0208 6413 224.

International Bank Note Society (East Mids) , Highfields Community Fire Station, Hassocks Lane, Beeston, Nottingham, NG9 2 GQ. Last Saturday of every odd month. Tel: 0115 928 9720.

Ireland, Numismatic Society of (Northern Branch). Cooke/Instonians RFC, Shaws Bridge Sports Asson, 123 Milltown Road, Belfast. Call for dates; 07843 450597 www.numsocirelandnb.com.

Ireland, Numismatic Society of, Ely House, 8 Ely Place, Dublin 2. For dates and venues visit; 07843 450597, www.numismaticsocietyofireland.com.

Ipswich Coin Club, Archdeacons House, 11 Northgate Street, Ipswich, IP1 3BX. 2nd Tues. Tel; 0789 443 7847, www.ipnumsoc.org.uk.

Lancashire & Cheshire Numismatic Society (1933). Call for venue details. 3rd Sat, 14.00. Tel: 01204 849 469.

Loughborough Coin & Search Society (1964). Rosebery Medical Center, Rosebery Street, Loughborough, Leics, LE11 5DX 1st Thu, 19.30.

Norwich Coin & Medal Society, The White Horse Inn, Trowse, Norwich, NR14 8ST. 3rd Mon. Tel: 07894437847.

Numismatic Society of Nottinghamshire (1948). Highfield Fire Station, Hassocks Lane, Beeston, Nottingahm, NG9 2GQ. 2nd Mon (Sep-Apr). Tel: 0115 928 0347.

Orders & Medals Research Society (1942). Spink, 69 Southampton Row, Bloomsbury, London, WC1B 4ET. Last Monday of the month (except a Bank Holiday) of the odd numbered months plus April and October. 18.00.

Ormskirk & West Lancashire Numismatic Society (1970). The Eagle & Child, Maltkiln Lane, Bispham Green L40 1SN. 1st Thu, 20.15. Tel: 01704 232 494

Peterborough & District Numismatic Society (1967). Belsize Community Centre, Celta Road Peterborough, Cambs. 4th Tue (exc June, July & Aug), 19.30. Tel: 01733 567 763.

Plymouth Numismatic Society. 3rd Tue. Call for venue details. Tel: 07399 276295.

Reading Coin Club (1964). Abbey Baptist Church, Abbey Square, Reading, RG1 3BE 1st Mon, 19.00. Tel: 01344 774 155.

Royal Numismatic Society (1836). Warburg Institute, Woburn Square, London, WC1H 0AB. (some meetings held at Spink, 69 Southampton Row, Bloomsbury Road, London WC1B 4ET). 3rd Tues 18.00. Email: info@numismatics.org.uk. Tel: 0207 323 8541.

Southampton and District Numismatic Society (1953). Email for venue details: sue717@btinternet.com.

South Manchester Numismatic Society. Nursery Inn, 258 Green Lane, Heaton Norris, Stockport, SK4 2NA. 1st and 3rd Tue (Mar–Oct), 1st Tue (Nov–Feb). Tel: 07818 422696.

South Wales & Monmouthshire Numismatic Society (1958). 1st Mon (except Bank Holidays when 2nd Mon), 19.30. For venue call Tel: 02920 561 564.

Tyneside Numismatic Society (1954). The Plough Inn, 369 Old Durham Road, Gateshead, NE9 5LA. 2nd Weds, 19.30. Tel: 07306 896 532.

Wiltshire Numismatic Society (1965). Please ring 07342858799 or email verityjeffery2@gmail.com

Sussex Coin Club (1967). The Durrington Community Centre, Romany Road, Durrington, BN13 3FJ. 2nd Thu, 19.00. For further details, please email sussexcoinclub@gmail.com.

Yorkshire Numismatic Society (1909). Email for venues and dates. Email: yorkshirenumismaticsociety@gmail.com.

Important Notice to Club Secretaries:

If your details listed are incorrect please let us know in time for the next edition of the **COIN YEARBOOK.**

Amendments can be sent via post to:
8 Oaktree Place, Manaton Close, Exeter, Devon EX2 8WA
or via email to:
jayne@tokenpublishing.com

IMPORTANT ORGANISATIONS

ADA
The Antiquities Dealers Association

Secretary: Membership administrator: Beth Hodges, email: bethany@bada.org. Tel: 020 7589 4128.

IBNS
International Bank Note Society

UK Membership Secretary: Claudio Di Sora uk-secretary@theibns.org

ANA
The American Numismatic Association

818 North Cascade Avenue, Colorado Springs, CO 80903, USA

RNS
Royal Numismatic Society

Dept of Coins & Medals, British Museum, London WC1B 3DG.

BNTA
The British Numismatic Trade Association

Secretary: Christel Swan 3 Unwin Mansions, Queens Club Gardens, London, W14 9TH

BAMS
British Art Medal Society

Janet Larkin, Secretary General. email: generalsecretary@bams.org.uk.

IAPN
International Association of Professional Numismatists

Secretary: Frederico Pastrone, IAPN, 57, rue Grimaldi, 98000 MONACO. Tel: +377 93 25 12 96, email: secretary@iapn-coins.org.

BNS
British Numismatic Society

Secretary: Peter Preston-Morley.
Email: secretary@britnumsoc.org

OMSA
Orders & Medals Society of America

Membership Secretary: Clyde L. Tinklepaugh, Jr.
P.O. Box 540, Claymont, DE 19703-0540.

OMRS
The Orders & Medals Research Society

Membership Secretary: Jim Lees, PO Box 248, Snettisham, King's Lynn, Norfolk PE31 7TA

Directory

of auctioneers

Listed here are the major auction houses which handle coins, medals, banknotes and other items of numismatic interest. Many of them hold regular public auctions, whilst others handle numismatic material infrequently. A number of coin companies also hold regular Postal Auctions—these are marked with a Ⓟ

Auction World Company Ltd
1-15-5 Hamamatsucho,Minato-ku,
Tokyo, 105-0013 Japan. www.auction-world.co

Baldwin's Auctions (BNTA)
399 Strand, London WC2R 0LX.
Tel: 020 7930 6879, Email: auctions@baldwin.co.uk,
www.baldwin.co.uk.

Biddle & Webb
Icknield Square, Birmingham B16 0PP.
Tel: 0121 455 8042, www.biddleandwebb.com

Blyth & Co
Arkenstall Center, Haddenham, Cambs CB6
3XD. Tel: 01353 930 094, www.blyths.com

BSA Auctions
Units 1/2, Cantilupe Court, Cantilupe Road, Ross on
Wye, Herefordshire, HR9 7AN . Tel: 01989 769 529,
www.the-saleroom.com

cgb.fr
36, Rue Vivienne, 75002, Paris, France.
Email: contact@cgb.fr, www.cgb.fr.

Chilcotts Auctioneers
The Dolphin Saleroom, High St, Honiton, Devon
EX14 1HT. Tel: 01404 47783,
email: info@chilcottsauctioneers.co.uk

Christies
8 King Street, St James's, London SW1Y 6QT.
Tel: 020 7839 9060.

Classical Numismatic Group Inc (Seaby Coins)
20 Bloomsbury Street, London, WC1B 3QA.
Tel: 020 7495 1888 ,fax 020 7499 5916,
Email: cng@cngcoins.com, www.historicalcoins.com. Ⓟ

The Coinery
Tel 01132 407900, www.auctions.thecoinery.co.uk.

The Coin Cabinet
First Floor, St James's Street, London SW1A 1LE
Tel 020 3808 5855, www.thecoincabinet.co.uk.

Corbitts
5 Moseley Sreet, Newcastle upon Tyne NE1 1YE.
Tel: 0191 232 7268, fax 0191 261 4130.
www.corbitts.com

Croydon Coin Auctions
4 Sussex Street, Rhyl LL18 1SG. Tel: 01492 440763,
www.croydoncoinauctions.com.

Davissons Ltd.
PO Box 323, Cold Spring, MN 56320 USA.
Tel: 001 320 685 3835, info@davcoin.com,
www.davcoin.com.

Duke's
Brewery Square, Dorchester, Dorset DT1 1GA.
Tel: 01305 265 080, enquiries@dukesauctions.com,
www.dukes-auctions.com

David Duggleby Auctioneer
The Vine Street Salerooms, Scarborough,
North Yorkshire YO11 1XN. Tel: 01723 507111

English Coin Auctions
3 Elders Street, Scarborough YO11 1DZ
Tel: 01723 364 760, wwwenglishcoinauctionscom

Jean Elsen & ses Fils s.a.
Avenue de Tervueren 65, B–1040, Brussels.
Tel: 0032 2 734 6356, Email: numismatique@e
lsen.euwww.elsen.eu.

Fellows & Sons
Augusta House, 19 Augusta Street, Hockley,
Birmingham, B18 6JA. Tel: 0121 212 2131,

B. Frank & Son
3 South Avenue, Ryton, Tyne & Wear NE40 3LD.
Tel: 0191 413 8749, Email: bfrankandson@aol.com,
www.bfrankandson.com.

Gadoury
57, rue Grimaldi, 98000 MONACO.
Tel: 0 377 93 25 12 96, Email: contact@gadoury.com,
www.gadoury.com.

Goldberg Coins & Collectibles
11400 W. Olympic Blvd, Suite 800, Los Angeles,
Hills CA 90064. Tel: 001 310.551 2646, info@
goldbergcoins.com, www.goldbergcoins.com,

Gorny & Mosch GmbH
Giessener Münzhandlung, Maximiliansplatz 20,
80333 Munich. Phone: +49-89/24 22 643-0,
info@gmcoinart.de

Halls Auctioneers
Halls Holding House, Bowmen Way, Battlefield
SY4 3DR.
Tel: 01743 450700. www.fineart.hllsgb.com.

Hansons Auctioneers
Heage Lane, Derby DE65 6LS. Tel: 01283 733988,
www.hansonsauctioneers.co.uk

Heritage World Coin Auctions (BNTA)
UK address: 6 Shepherd Street, Mayfair, London W1J 7JE. Tel: 001 214 528 3500, www.ha.com.

HoskerHaynes Auctioneers
Tel: 0330 1336013, email: info@hoskerhaynes.com, www.hoskerhaynes.com

International Coin Exchange
Charter House, 5 Pembroke Row, Dublin 2. Tel: 00353 8684 93355, www.ice-auction.com.

Kleeford Coin Auctions
Tel: 07484 272837, www.kleefordcoins.co.uk email: kleeford@btinternet.com Ⓟ

Fritz Rudolf Künker
Nobbenburger, Strasse 4A, 49076, Osnabrüeck, Germany. Tel: 0049 5419 62020, www.kuenker.de

Lawrence Fine Art Auctioneers
The Linen Yard, South Street, Crewkerne, Somerset TA18 8AB. Tel: 01460 73041, email: enquiries@lawrences.co.uk, www.lawrences.co.uk.

Lockdale Coins (BNTA)
52 Barrack Square, Martlesham Heath, Ipswich, Suffolk IP5 3RF. Tel: 01473 627 110, sales@lockdales.com, www.lockdales.com.

London Coins
Tel: 01474 871464, email: info@londoncoins.co.uk, www.londoncoins.co.uk.

Mavin International
20 Kramat Lane, #01-04/05 United House, Singapore 228773. Tel: +65 6238 7177,

MDC Monaco sarl
Allées Lumières Park Palace, 27 Avenue de la Costa, 98000 Monaco. Tel: +377 93 25 00 42, info@mdc.mc, www.mdc.mc.

Mitchells
47 Station Road, Cockermouth, Cumbria, CA13 9PZ. www.mitchellsantiques.co.uk

Morton & Eden Ltd (BNTA)
Nash House, St Georges Street, London W1S 2FQ. Tel: 020 7493 5344, info@mortonandeden.com, www.mortonandeden.com.

Mowbray Collectables
Private Bag 63000, Wellington 6140, New Zealand
Tel: +64 6 364 8270, email: auctions@mowbrays.nz, www.mowbraycollectables.com

Nesbits Auctioneer & Valuers
7 Clarendon Road, Sooutһsea, Hants, PO5 2ED. Tel: 02392 295568, email: auctions@nesbits.co.uk

Noble Numismatics
169 Macquire Street, Sydney, NSW 2000 Australia. Tel: 0061 2922 34578, Email: info@noble.com.au, www.noble.com.au.

Noonans (IAPN, BNTA)
16 Bolton Street, Mayfair, London W1J 8BQ Tel: 020 7016 1700, www.noonans.co.uk.

Numismatica Ars Classica NAC AG
Suite 1, Claridge House, 32 Davies Street, London W1K 4ND. Tel: 020 7839 7270, email: info@arsclassicacoins.com.

Numis-Or
4, Rue des Barques 1207, Geneva Switzerland email: info@numisor.ch, www.numisor.ch.

Pacific Rim Online Auction
P O Box 847, North Sydney, NSW 2060, Australia. www.pacificrimonlineauctions.com

Penrith, Farmers' & Kidds PLC
Skirsgill Saleroom, Penrith, Cumbria, CA11 0DN. Tel: 01768 890 781,
email: info@pfkauctions.co.uk,www.pfkauctions.co.uk

Royal Wotton Bassett Auctioneers
144 High St, Royal Wootton Bassett, Swindon SN4 7AB
Tel: 01793 840777, www.rwbauctions.com

Chris Rudd Ltd (IAPN, BNTA)
PO Box 1500, Norwich NR10 5WS
Tel: 01263 735 007, email: liz@celticcoins.com, www.celticcoins.com

Simmons Gallery (BNTA)
PO Box 104, Leytonstone, London. Tel: 020 8989 8097. simmonsgallery.co.uk. Ⓟ

Smiths of Newent
The Old Chapel, Culver Street, Newent GL18 1DB. Tel: 01531 821 776, email: enquiries@smithsauction-room.co.uk, www.smithsnewentauctions.co.uk.

Sovereign Rarities Ltd (BNTA)
17–19 Maddox Street, London W1S 2QH Tel: 0203 019 1185, www.sovr.co,uk.

Spink & Son Ltd (BNTA)
69 Southampton Row, Bloomsbury, London WC1B 4ET. Tel: 020 7563 4000, fax 020 7563 4066, email: concierge@spink.com, www.spink.com.

Stacks, Bowers and Ponterio
1231 East Dyer Road, Suite 100, Santa Ana, California, 92705, USA. Tel: 001 800 458 4646, email: info@StacksBowers.com, www.stacksbowers.com

St James's Auctions (BNTA)
10 Charles II Street, London SW1Y 4AA. Tel: 020 7930 7888, fax 0207 930 8214, Email: info@sjauctions.com, www.sjauctions.com.

Tennants Auctioneers
The Auction Centre, Leyburn, North Yorkshire DL8 5SG. Tel: 01969 623 780, email: enquiry@tennants-ltd.co.uk, www.tennants.co.uk.

Teutoberger Auctioneers
Brinkstraße 9, 33829 Borgholzhausen, Germany. E-Mail: info@teutoburger-muenzauktion.de, Tel: 009 5425 930050, www.teutoburger-muenzauktion.de.

The-saleroom.com
The Harlequin Building, 65 Southwark Street, London SE1 0HR. Tel: 0203 725 555, email: sup port@auctiontechnologygroup.com, www.the-saleroom.com.

Thomson Roddick Auctioneers
Auction Centre, Marconi Road, Carlisle CA2 7NA. Tel: 01228 528 939.www.thomsonroddick.com.

Timeline Auctions (BNTA)
The Court House, 363 Main Road, Harwich, Essex CO12 4DN Tel: 01277 815 121, email: enquiries@timelineauctions.com www.timelineauctions.com.

Trevanion and Dean
The Joyce Building, Station Road, Whitchurch, SY13 1RD. Tel: 01948 800 202, email: info@trevanionand dean.co.uk

Warwick & Warwick (BNTA)
Chalon House, Scarbank, Millers Road, Warwick CV34 5DB. Tel: 01926 499 031 fax 01926 491 906, email: richard.beale@warwickandwarwick.com, www.warwickandwarwick.com.

Peter Wilson Fine Art Auctioneers LLP
Victoria Gallery, Market Street, Nantwich, Cheshire, CW5 5DG. www.peterwilson.co.uk.

Woolley & Wallis
51-61 Castle Street, Salisbury, Wiltshire SP1 3SU. Tel: 01722 424500, email: nc@woolleyandwallis.co.uk, www.woolleyandwallis.co.uk

Directory
of fairs

Listed below are the names of the fair organisers, their venue details where known along with contact telephone numbers. Please call the organisers direct for information on dates etc.

Aberdeen
Doubletree by Hilton Hotel Aberdeen TreeTops, Springfield Road, Aderdeen AB15 7AQ.
Alba Fairs Tel: 07767 020343.

ANA National Money Show March 2024
Broadmoor Resort, Colorado Springs, CO.
www.money.org.

Berlin. World Money Fair
Estrel Convention Center, Sonnenalle, 12057 Berlin, Germany. Tel: +41(0)61 3825504.

Berlin
Messegelände am Funkturm, Hall 11/2, Messedamm 22, 14055 Berlin. Numismata International Tel: +49 (0) 89 268 359.

Birmingham
National Motor Cycle Museum, Bickenhill, Birmingham. Midland Stamp & Coin Fair
Tel: 01694 731 781, www.coinfairs.co.uk.

Britannia Medal Fair
Carisbrooke Hall, The Victory Services Club, 63/79 Seymour Street,
London W2 2HF.
Noonans Tel: 020 7016 1700.

Cardiff
City Hall, Cathays Park, Cardiff CF10 3ND.
M. J. Promotions. Tel: 01792 415293.

Cheltenham
The Regency Hotel, Gloucester Road GL51 0SS.
St Andrews United Reform Church, Montpellier, GL50 1SP. Mark Grimsley Tel: 0117 962 3203.

Crewe
Memorial Hall, Church Lane, Wistaston, Crewe. CW2 8ER. Crewe & District Coin & Medal Society.
Tel: 01270 661181.

Dublin Coin Fair
Serpentine Hall, RDS, Ballsbridge, Dublin 4.
Mike Kelly Tel: 00353 86 8714 880.

East Grinstead
Chequer Mead Arts Center, De La Warr Road, East Grinstead, RH19 3BS.
John Perryman Tel: 01903 244875.

Exeter
The America Hall, De La Rue Way, Pinhoe, EX4 8PX. Michael Hale Collectors Fairs Tel: 01749 677669.

Frankfurt 2019
Ludwig-Erhard-Anlage1, 60327 Frankfurt, Hesse.
Numismata International Tel: +49 (0) 89 268 360.

Harrogate
Old Swan Hotel, Swan Road, HG1 2SR.
Bloomsbury Fairs Tel: 01242 898 107.

Inverness
Kingsmills Hotel, Culcabock Road, Inverness, IV2 3LP. Alba Fairs Tel: 07767 020343.

London
Novotel London West, 1 Shortlands W6 8DR.
www.coinfairs.co.uk

COINEX
*Biltmore Hotel, 44 Grosve*nor Square, Mayfair, W1K 2HP.
BNTA. Email: secretary@bnta.net.

London IBNS
Ambassador Bloomsbury Hotel, 12 Upper Woburn Place, Euston, London. WC1H 0HX.
IBNS Web: www.theibns.org.

Maastricht
Maastricht Exhibition & Convention Center, Forum 100, 6229 GV Maastricht, The Netherlands.
mif events Tel: +32 (0) 89 46 09 33.

Munich Numismata March 2024
MOC, Hall 3, Lilienthalallee 40, 80939 Munich.

New York International Numismatic Convention
Grand Hyatt Hotel, 109 East 42nd Street, New York 10022, USA. www.nyinc.info/

Plymouth
The Guildhall, Armada Way, PL1 2ER
Peter Jones Tel: 01489 582673.

Weston-super-Mare
Victoria Methodist Church Hall, Station Road, BS23 1XU.
Michael Hale Tel: 01749 677 669

Worthing
Chatsworth Hotel, The Steyne, Worthing, BN11 3DU. Organised by the Worthing & District Numismatic Society. Tel: 01903 239867

York
The Grandstand, York Race Course, YO23 1EX
York Coin Fair, Tel: 01793 513 431 (Chris Rainey), 020 8946 4489 (Kate Puleston).

Yorkshire
Cedar Court Hotel, Lindley Moor Road, Ainley Top, Huddesfield, HD3 3RH.
Neil Smith Tel: 01522 522 722.

Information correct at the time of going to press.

Dealers directory

The dealers listed below have comprehensive stocks of coins and medals, unless otherwise stated. Specialities, where known, are noted. Many of those listed are postal dealers only, so to avoid disappointment always make contact by telephone or mail in the first instance, particularly before travelling any distance.

Abbreviations:
ADA—— Antiquities Dealers Association
ANA — American Numismatic Association
BADA — British Antique Dealers Association
BNTA — British Numismatic Trade Association
IAPN — International Association of Professional Numismatists
IBNS — International Bank Note Society
Ⓟ —— Postal only
Ⓛ —— Publishes regular lists

ABC Coins & Tokens
PO Box 52, Alnwick, Northumberland, NE66 1YE. Tel: 01665 603 851, www.abccoinsandtokens.com. *British (particularly Scottish) and world coins, tokens.*

Absolutely Banknotes (Chris Burch)
Tel: 07870 504849, www,absolutelybanknotes.co.uk *English and Scottish notes. Treasury to modern.*

A. Ackroyd (IBNS)
62 Albert Road, Parkstone, Poole, Dorset BH12 2DB. Tel/fax: 01202 739 039, www.AAnotes.com. Ⓟ Ⓛ *Banknotes and Cheques*

Allgold Coins
P.O Box 260, Wallington, SM5 4H. Tel: 0844 544 7952, email: sales@allgoldcoins.co.uk, wwwallgoldcoins.co.uk. *Quality Sovereigns.*

A. J. W. Coins
Tel: 08456 807 087, email: andrewwide@ajw-coins.co.uk, www.ajw-coins.com. Ⓟ *Sovereigns and CGS-UK specialist.*

AMR COINS (BNTA)
PO Box 352, Leeds, LS19 9GG. Tel: 07527 569 308, www.amrcoins.com. *Quality English Coins specialising in rare hammered and milled coins of exceptional quality.*

ARL Collectables
P O Box 380, Reigate, Surrey, RH2 2BU. Tel: 01737 242 975, www.litherlandcollectables.com. Coins, Banknotes, Medallions and Paper Emphemera.

Athens Numismatic Gallery
Akadimias 39, Athens 10672, Greece. Tel: 0030 210 364 8386, www.athensnumismaticgallery.com. *Rare & Common Sovereigns. British & World Coins.*

Atlas Numismatics
Tel: 001 718643 4383, email, info@atlasnumismatics.com, www.atlasnumismatics.com New, *Ancient, World and US Coinage*

ATS Bullion (BNTA)
2, Savoy Court, Strand. London, WC2R 0EZ. Tel: 020 7240 4040, email: sales@atsbullion.com, www.atsbullion.com. *Bullion and Modern Coins.*

A. H. Baldwin & Sons Ltd (ANA, BADA, BNTA, IAPN)
399 The Strand, London WC2R 0LX. Tel: 020 7930 6879, fax 020 7930 9450, email: coins@baldwin.co.uk *Coins, Tokens, Numismatic Books.*

Avere Coins (BNTA)
Langstone Park, Langstone Road, Havant, PO9 1SA. *Email: info@averecoins.co.uk, Tel: 01243 915155. www.averecoins.co.uk. British Coins and Banknotes*

B & G Coins
PO Box 1219, Spalding, PE11 9FY. Email: info@bandgcoins.co.uk. *Coins, Banknotes and Medals*

Baird & Co
20 - 21 Gemini Business Park, Hornet Way, London, E6 7FF. Tel: 020 7474 1000, www.goldline.co.uk. *Bullion Merchants*

T. Barna
64 High Street, Lyndhurst, SO43 7BJ. Email: tbarna_and sonuk@hotmail.com. Ancient Greek and Roman Coins.

Bath Stamp and Coin Shop
12 -13 Pulteney Bridge, Bath, Avon BA2 4AY. Tel: 01225 431 918, *Vintage Coins and Banknotes.*

Michael Beaumont
PO Box 8, Carlton, Notts NG4 4QZ. Tel: 0115 9878361. Ⓟ *Gold & Silver bullion, English and Foreign Coins.*

R. P. & P. J. Beckett
Maes y Derw, Capel Dewi, Llandyssul, Dyfed SA44 4PJ. Tel: 01559 395 276, email: beckett@xin.co.uk. Ⓟ *Coin Sets and Banknotes.*

Lloyd Bennett (BNTA)
PO Box 2, Monmouth, Gwent NP25 3YR. Tel: 07714 284 939, email: Lloydbennett@Coinofbritain.biz, www.coinsofbritain.com *English Hammered and Milled Coins.*

Berkshire Coin Centre
35 Castle Street, Reading, RG1 7SB. Tel: 0118 957 5593. *British and World Coins. Militaria.*

Stephen J. Betts
49-63 Spencer Street, Hockley, Birmingham B18 6DE. Tel: 0121 233 2413 Ⓟ Ⓛ, *Medieval and Modern Coins, Counters, Jetons, Tokens and Countermarks.*

Jon Blyth (BNTA)
Office 63, 2 Lansdowne Row, Mayfair, London W1J 6HL. Tel:07919 307 645, jonblyth@hotmail.com, www.jonblyth.com. *Specialists in quality British Coins*

Barry Boswell and Kate Bouvier
24 Townsend Lane, Upper Boddington, Daventry, Northants, NN11 6DR. Tel: 01327 261 877, email: kate@thebanknotestore.com. *British and World Banknotes.*

James & Chester Brett
jc.brett@btinternet.com P L
British and World Coins.

Stephen Betts
4 Victoria Street, Narborough, Leicester, LE19 2DP.
P L *World Coins, Tokens, Countermarks, Jettsons, Medallions etc.*

J. Bridgeman Coins
20 Abbey Street, Accrington, Lancs. Tel: 07816 396276. Telephone for appointment. *Coins, Banknotes & Medals.*

Brittonum (BNTA)
PO Box 3, 41 Oxford Street, Leamington Spa, CV32 4RA Tel: 07768 645 686, email: info@brittonum.com www.brittonum.com. *British Coins and Medals.*

BRM Coins
3 Minshull Street, Knutsford, Cheshire, WA16 6HG. Tel: 01565 651 480. *British Coins.*

Bucks Coins (BNTA)
St Mary's House, Duke Street, Norwich NR3 1QA Callers by appointment only. Tel: 01603 927 020. *English Milled Coins, Celtic and Roman.*

Iain Burn
2 Compton Gardens, 53 Park Road, Camberley, Surrey GU15 2SP. Tel: 01276 23304.
Bank of England & Treasury Notes.

Cambridgeshire Coins (BNTA)
12 Signet Court, Swanns Road Cambridge, CB5 8LA. Tel: 01223 503 073, wwwcambridgeshirecoins.com.
Coins, Banknotes and Accessories.

Castle Galleries
81 Castle Street, Salisbury, Wiltshire SP1 3SP. Tel: 01722 333 734. *British Coins and collectables.*

Cathedral Coins
23 Kirkgate, Rippon, North Yorkshire, HG4 1PB. Tel: 01765 701 400

Cathedral Court Medals
First Floor Office, 30A Market Place, West Ripon, North Yorks HG4 1BN. Tel: 01765 601 400. *Coin and Medal Sales. Medal Mounting and Framing.*

Cathedral Stamps & Coins
Unit B14, KCR Industrial Estate, Ravensdale Park, Kimmage, Co. Dublin, Ireland. Tel: +353 1 490 6392 *Coins, medals, banknotes & accessories.S tockist of Token Publishing titles in Ireland.*

Central Bank of Ireland
PO Box 559, Dublin 1. Tel: +353 (0) 1248 3605, Ireland. *Issuer of new Coin and Banknote*

Lance Chaplin
17 Wanstead Lane, Ilford, Essex IG1 3SB. Tel: 020 8554 7154. www.shaftesburycoins.com.
P L *Ancient, Hammered Coins and Antiquities.*

Chard
32-36 Harrowside, Blackpool, FY4 1RJ. Tel: 01253 343081, www.chards.co.uk, *British and World Coins.*

Charing Cross Collectors' Market
Charing Cross, 1, Villiers Street/Northumberland Ave, London.Tel: 07540 144433, www.charingcrossmarket.com, *Market in Central London with dealers offering coins, stamps, postcards, medals & ephemera.*

Jeremy Cheek Coins Ltd
Tel: 01923 450385/07773 872686, email: jeremycoins@aol.com. *Advice, valuation and representation at auctions.*

Simon Chester Coins
196, High Road, London, Farnham, N22 8HH Tel: 07774 886688, email: simosimonchestercoins. com. *British Milled Coins*

City Coins
www.citycoins.com. Email: admin@citycoins.co.za South African Specialists

Nigel A. Clark
28 Ulundi Road, Blackheath, London SE3 7UG. Tel: 020 8858 4020, email: nigel.a.clark@btinternet. com. P L *17th & 19th century Tokens. Farthings.*

Classical Numismatic Group (IAPN) **(BNTA)**
20 Bloomsbury Street, London, WC1B 3QA. Tel: 020 7495 1888, email cng@cngcoins.com, www.cngcoins.com. P *Ancient and world coins. Publishers of the Classical Numismatic Review. Regular High Quality Auctions of Ancient Coins.*

Paul Clayton (BNTA)
PO Box 21, Wetherby, West Yorkshire LS22 5JY. Tel: 01937 582 693. *Modern Gold Coins.*

André de Clermont (BNTA)
10 Charles II Street, London, SW1Y 4AA. Tel: 020 7584 7200. *World Coins, especially Islamic.*

Philip Cohen Numismatics (ANA, BNTA)
20 Cecil Court, Charing Cross Road, London, WC2N 4HE. Tel: 020 7379 0615, www.coinheritage. co.uk

Coin & Collectors Centre
PO Box 22, Pontefract, West Yorkshire WF8 1YT. Tel: 01977 704 112, email sales@coincentre. co.uk, www.coincentre.co.uk. P *British Coins.*

Coinage of England
P.O. Box 118, 8 Shepherd Market, Mayfair, London, W1J 7JY. Tel: 07557 819 104
Email: info@coinageofengland.co.uk. *Fine and Rare English Coins.*

Coincraft (ANA, IBNS)
45 Great Russell Street, London, WC1B 3JL. Tel: 020 7636 1188 or 020 7637 8785, fax 020 7323 2860, email: info@coincraft.com. L (newspaper format). *Coins and Banknotes.*

The Coinery
Tel 01132 407900, www.thecoinery.co.uk.

Coinote
74 Elwick Road, Hartlepool TS26 9AP. Tel: 01429 890 894. www.coinnote.co.uk. *Coins, Medals, Banknotes and Accessories.*

Coins on a Budget
wwwcoinsonabudget.com. Incorporating budget stamps. World Coins and Banknotes.

Coinswap.co.uk
Swap, Sell or Trade Coins.

Coins of Canterbury
PO Box 47, Faversham, Kent,, ME13 7HX. Tel: 01795 531 980. P *English Coins.*

Coins of the Realm
PO Box 12131, Harlow, Essex, CM20 9LY. www.coinsoftherealm.com. Dealers in Precious and Historical Coinage

Colin Cooke (BNTA)
P.O. Box 602, Altrincham, WA14 5UN. Tel: 0161 927 9524, fax 0161 927 9540, email coins@colin cooke.com, www.colincooke.com. L *British Coins.*

Collectors' World (Mark Ray)
190 Wollaton Road, Wollaton, Nottingham NG8 1HJ. www.collectorsworld-nottingham.com. Tel: 01159 280 347. *Coins, Banknotes, Accessories.*

Colonial Collectables
P.O.Box 35625, Browns Bay, Auckland 0753, New Zealand. Email: richard@colonialcollectables.com British & World Coins.

Colonial Coins & Medals
218 Adelaide Street, Brisbane, QLD 4001. Email: coinshop@bigpond.net.au. *Auctions of World Coins.*

Constania CB
15 Church Road, Northwood, Middlesex, HA6 1AR. P *Roman and Medieval Hammered Coins.*

Coopers Coins
PO Box 12703, Brentwood, Essex, CM14 9RB. Tel: 01277 560348, email: jack@cooperscoins.com. wwwcooperscoins.com. British Coins.

Corbitts (BNTA)
5 Mosley Street, Newcastle Upon Tyne NE1 1YE. Tel: 0191 232 7268, fax: 0191 261 4130. *Dealers and Auctioneers of all Coins and Medals.*

David Craddock (BNTA)
PO Box 3785, Camp Hill, Birmingham, B11 2NF. Tel: 0121 733 2259 L *Crown to Farthings. Copper and Bronze Specialist. Some foreign.*

Roy Cudworth
8 Park Avenue, Clayton West, Huddersfield HD8 9PT. *British and World Coins.*

Curtis Coin Care
www.curtiscoincare.com. *Numismatic accessories and storage solutions.*

Paul Dawson (BNTA)
47 The Shambles, York, YO1 7XL. Tel: 01904 654 769, email: pauldawsonyork@hotmail.com, www.pauldawsonyork.co.uk. *Ancient and British coins, medals.*

Mark Davidson
PO Box 197, South Croydon, Surrey, CR3 0ZD. Tel: 020 8651 3890. *Ancient, Hammered & milled Coinage.*

Paul Davies Ltd (ANA, BNTA, IAPN)
PO Box 17, Ilkley, West Yorkshire LS29 8TZ. Tel: 01943 603 116, fax 01943 816 326, paul@pauldaviesltd.co.uk. P *World Coins. British Gold and silver bullion.*

Paul Davis (BNTA)
PO Box 418, Birmingham, B17 0RZ. Tel: 0121 427 7179. *British and World Coins.*

R. Davis
Tel: 01332 862 755 days / 740828 evenings, email: robdaviscc@gmail.com. *Maker of Traditional Coin Cabinets.*

Ian Davison
PO Box 256, Durham DH1 2GW. Tel 0191 3750 808. L *English Hammered and Milled Coins 1066–1910.*

Davissons
PO Box 323, Cold Spring, MN, 56320, USA. Tel: (001)320 685 3835, Email: infodavcoin.com, www.davcoin.com. North American Specialists. British Coins, Tokens and Medals.

Dei Gratia
PO Box 3568, Buckingham MK18 4ZS Tel: 01280 848 000. P L *Pre–Roman to Modern Coins. Antiquities, Banknotes.*

Den of Antiquity (BNTA)
PO Box 1114, Cambridge, CB25 9WJ. Tel: 01223 863 002, www.denofantiquity.co.uk.) *Ancient and Medieval Coins.*

C. J. Denton (ANA, FRNS)
PO Box 25, Orpington, Kent BR6 8PU. Tel: 01689 873 690. P *Irish Coins.*

Michael Dickinson (ANA)
Ramsay House, 825 High Road Finchley, London N12 8UB. Tel: 0181 441 7175. P *British and World Coins.*

Douglas Saville (BNTA)
Tel: 0118 918 7628, www.douglassaville.com. *Out of Print, Second-Hand, Rare Coin & Medal Books.*

Eagle Coins
Winterhaven, Mourneabbey, Mallow, Co. Cork, Ireland. Tel: 010 35322 29385. P L *Irish Coins.*

East of England Coins
Leprosy Mission Orton Goldhay, Peterborough, Cambridgeshire, PE2 5GZ. Tel: 01733235277 *Coins, Tokens and Banknotes*

John Eccles
www.eccleswellington.co.nz. New Zealand and Pacific Islands Coins and Banknotes

Educational Coin Company
Box 892, Highland, New York 12528, USA. Tel:001 845 691 6100. *World Banknotes.*

Christopher Eimer (ANA, BNTA, IAPN)
PO Box 352 London NW11 7RF. Tel: 020 8458 9933, email: art@christophereimer.co.uk P *Commemorative Medals.*

Malcolm Ellis Coins
Petworth Road, Witley, Surrey, GU8 5LX. Tel: 01428 685 566, www.malcolmelliscoins.co.uk). *Collectors and Dealers of British and Foreign Coins*

Elm Hill Collectables
41-43 Elm Hill, Norwich, Norfolk NR3 1HG. Tel: 01603 627 413. *Coins & Banknotes .*

Europa Numismatics (ANA)
PO Box 119, High Wycombe, Bucks HP11 1QL. Tel: 01494 437 307 P *European Coins.*

Evesham Stamp & Coin Centre
Magpie Antiques, Manchester House,1 High Street, Evesham, Worcs WR11 4DA. Tel: 01386 41631. *British Coins.*

Robin Finnegan Stamp Shop
83 Skinnergate, Darlington, Co Durham DL3 7LX. Tel: 01325 489 820/357 674. *World coins.*

B. Frank & Son
3 South Avenue, Ryton, Tyne & Wear NE40 3LD. Tel: 0191 413 8749, Email: bfrankandson@aol.com, www.bfrankandson.com. *Coins, notes, tokens.*

Galata Coins Ltd (ANA)
The Old White Lion, Market Street, Llanfylin, Powys SY22 5BX. Tel: 01691 648 765. P *British and World Coins.*

A. & S. Gillis
59 Roy Kilner Way, Wombwell, Barnsley, South Yorkshire S73 8DY. Tel: 01226 750 371, www.gilliscoins.com. *Ancient Coins and Antiquities.*

Richard Gladdle—Northamptonshire (BNTA)
Suite 80, 29/30 Horse Fair, Banbury, Oxfordshire, OX16 0BW. Tel: 01327 858 511, email: gladdle@plumpudding.org. *Tokens.* P L

GM Coins
Tel: 01242 627 344, email: info@gmcoinsco.uk, www.gmcoins.co.uk. *Hammered and Milled Coins.*

Adrian Gorka Bond
Tel: 07500 772 080, email: sales@ 1stsovereign.co.uk, www.1stsovereign.co.uk. *World gold coins*

Goulborn
4 Sussex Street, Rhyl LL18 1SG. Tel: 01745 338 112. *English Coins and Medallions.Organiser of Chester Coin Auctions.*

Ian Gradon
PO Box 359, Durham DH7 6WZ. Tel 0191 3719 700, email: rarebanknote@gmail.com, www.worldnotes.co.uk. Ⓛ *World Banknotes.*

Eric Green—Agent in UK for Ronald J. Gillio Inc
1013 State Street, Santa Barbara, California, USA 93101. Tel: 020 8907 0015, Mobile 0468 454948. *Gold Coins, Medals and Paper Money of the World.*

Philip Green (GB Classic Coins)
Suite 207, 792 Wilmslow Road, Didsbury, Manchester M20 6UG. Tel: 0161 440 0685. *Gold Coins.*

Gurnhills of Leicester
8 Nothampton Street, Leicester, LE1 1PA.Tel: 07434 010 925. *British and World Coins and Banknotes.*

Halls Hammered Coins (BNTA)
From early Saxon to late Stuart. Tel: 07830 019 584 www.hallshammeredcoins.com

Anthony Halse (BNTA)
PO Box 1856, Newport, Gwent NP18 2WA. Tel: 01633 413 238.Ⓟ Ⓛ*English/Foreign coins, tokens.*

A. D. Hamilton & Co (ANA)
7 St Vincent Place, Glasgow, G1 2DW. Tel: 0141 221 5423, email: jefffineman@hotmail.com, www.adhamilton.co.uk.*British and World Coins.*

Hammered British Coins (BNTA)
PO Box 2330, Salisbury, SP2 2LN. Tel: 07825 226 435, www.hammeredbritishcoins.com. *British Coins.*

Peter Hancock
40–41 West Street, Chichester, West Sussex, PO19 1RP. Tel: 01243 786 173. *World Coins, Medals and Banknotes.*

Hattons of London
PO Box 3719, Newcastle, ST55 9HH. Tel: 0333 234 3103. Email: enquiries@hattonsoflondon.co.uk Ⓛ *Rare and Exclusive Coins.*

Tom Hart Coins
Based in Devon. Tel: 07745 985 510. Email: woosworlduk@aol.com. Coins, Medals and Antiques.

Munthandel G. Henzen
PO Box 42, NL – 3958ZT, Amerogngen, Netherlands. Tel: 0031 343 430564 fax 0031 343 430542, email: info@henzen.org, www.henzen.org. Ⓛ*Ancients, Dutch and Foreign Coins.*

History In Coins (BNTA)
Tel: 07944 374600, email:historyincoins@gmail.com, www.historyincoins.com. *Hammered to milled, English, Irish and Scottish coins.*

Craig Holmes
6 Marlborough Drive, Bangor, Co Down BT19 1HB. Ⓟ Ⓛ*Low cost Banknotes of the World.*

R. G. Holmes
11 Cross Park, Ilfracombe, Devon EX34 8BJ. Tel: 01271 864 474. Ⓟ Ⓛ *Coins, World Crowns and Banknotes.*

HTSM Coins
26 Dosk Avenue, Glasgow G13 4LQ. Tel: 0141 562 9530, www.thomasgreaves1.comⓅ Ⓛ *British and foreign coins and Banknotes.*

M. J. Hughes Coins (BNTA)
27 Market Street, Alton, Hampshire, GU34 1HA. Tel: 01420 768 161, email: info@mjhughes.co.uk *World Coins and Bullion.*

T. A. Hull
15 Tangmere Crescent, Hornchurch, Essex RM12 5PL.Ⓟ Ⓛ *British Coins, Farthings, Tokens.*

J. Hume
107 Halsbury Road East, Northolt, Middlesex UB5 4PY. Tel: 020 8864 1731.Ⓟ Ⓛ *Chinese Coins.*

D. A. Hunter
Email: coins@dahunter.co.uk, www.dahunter.co.uk/coins. Ⓟ Ⓛ *UK and World Coins.*

D. D. & A. Ingle
380 Carlton Hill, Nottingham, NG4 1JA. Tel: 0115 987 3325. *World Coins.*

R. Ingram Coins
2 Avonbourne Way, Chandlers Ford, Eastleigh, SO53 1TF. Tel: 023 8027 5079, email: info@ringramcoins.com, www.ringramcoins.com.Ⓟ Ⓛ *Dealers in UK Coins.*

F. J. Jeffery & Son Ltd
Haines Croft, Corsham Road, Whitley, Melksham, Wilts, SN12 8QF. Tel: 01225 703 143.Ⓟ Ⓛ, *British, Commonwealth and Foreign Coins.*

Richard W. Jeffery (BNTA)
Tel: 01736 871 263. Ⓟ *British,World Coins, notes.*

JN Coins
PO Box 1030, Ipswich, OP1 9XL. Tel: 07916 145 038, info@jncoins.co.uk, www.jncoins.co.uk). *British Coins from Celtic to Modern.*

KB Coins (BNTA)
PO BOX 499, Stevenage, Herts, SG1 9JT. Tel: 01438 312 661, fax 01438 311 990. www.kbcoins.com Ⓛ *English coins and medals. Specialists in gold sovereigns, rare dates and varieties.*

Kleeford Coins
Tel: 07484 272 837, kleeford@btinternet.com www.kleefordcoins.co.uk, . Ⓟ *Monthly Auctions of Coins, Banknotes, Tokens & Medals.*

K&M Coins
PO Box 3662, Wolverhampton WV10 6ZW. Tel: 0771 238 1880, email: M_Bagguley@hotmail.com. *English Milled Coins.*

Knightsbridge Coins (ANA, BNTA, IAPN, PNG)
43 Duke Street, St James's, London, SW1Y 6DD. Tel: 020 7930 8215/7597, info@knightsbridgecoins.com. *Quality Coins of the World..*

Liberty Coins and Bullion
17g Vyse Street, Birmingham, B18 6LE. Tel: 0121 554 4432, www.libertycoinsbullion.co.uk. *Coins and Precious Metals.*

Lindner Publications Ltd (Prinz)
Unit 20A, Longrock Industrial Estate, Longrock, Cornwall TR20 8HX. Tel: 01736 751 910, email: prinzpublications@gmail.com. Ⓛ *Coin Albums, accessories. Lindner range.*

Jan Lis
Beaver Coin Room, 57 Philbeach Gardens, London SW5 9ED. Tel: 020 7373 4553 fax 020 7373 4555. By appointment only. *European Coins.*

Keith Lloyd
1 Dashwood Close, Pinewood, Ipswich, Suffolk IP8 3SR. Tel: 01473 403 506.Ⓟ Ⓛ *Ancient Coins.*

Lockdale Coins (BNTA)
52 Barrack Square, Martlesham Heath, Ipswich, Suffolk, IP5 3RF. Tel: 01473 627 110, www.lockdales.com.Ⓛ *World Coins, Medals and Banknotes.*

Stephen Lockett (BNTA)
4–6 Upper Street, New Ash Green, Kent, DA3 8JJ. Tel: 01474 871464. *British and World Coins.*

The London Coin Company (BNTA)
PO Box 495, Stanmore, Greater London, HA7 9HS Tel: 0800 085 2933, 020 8343 2231, www.thelondoncoincomany.com. *Modern Gold and Silver Coins.*

The London Mint Office
Tel: 0330 024 1001, londonmintoffice.org Gold, Silver and Commemorative Coins.

MA Shops
www.mashops.com. On-line coin mall. *Coins, Medals, Banknotes and Accessories.*

Manston Coins of Bath
8 Bartletts St. Antique Centre, Bath. Tel: 01225 487 888. *Coins, Tokens and Medals.*

C. J. Martin Coins (BNTA)
The Gallery, Trent Park Equestrian Centre, Bramley Road, London, N14 4UW. Tel: 020 8364 4565, www.ancientart.co.uk. (P) (L) Bi– monthly catalogue. *Greek, Roman & English Hammered Coins.*

Maverick Numismatics—Matt Bonaccorsi
07403 111843, www.mattbonaccorsi.com. *Coin and Currency Design.*

M. G. Coins & Antiquities
12 Mansfield, High Wych, Herts CM21 0JT. Tel 01279 721 719. (L) *Ancient and Hammered Coins, Antiquities.*

M & H Coins
PO Box 10985, Brentwood, CM14 9JB. Tel: 07504 804 019, www.mhcoins.co.uk. (L) *British Hammered and Milled Coins.*

Michael Coins
PO Box 3100 Reading RG1 9ZL. *World Coins and Banknotes.*

Middlesex Coins
www.middlesexcoins.co.uk. Tel: 07753618613, Email: marksaxby25@hotmail.com. Quality rare coins specialists since 1999

Timothy Millett
PO Box 20851, London SE22 0YN. Tel: 0208 693 1111, www.historicmedals.com. (L) *Historical Medals.*

Nigel Mills
PO Box 53126, London, E18 1YR. Email: nigelmills@onetel.com, www.nigelmills.net *Coins and Antiquities.*

Monetary Research Institute
PO Box 3174, Houston, TX 77253-3174, Tel: 001 713 827 1796, email: info@mriguide.com. *Bankers Guide to Foreign Currency*

Moore Antiquities
Unit 12, Ford Lane Industrial Estate, Ford, nr. Arundel, West Sussex BN18 0AA. Tel: 01243 824 232, email moore.antiquities@virgin.net. *Coins and Artefacts up to the 18th Century.*

Mike Morey
19 Elmtrees, Long Crendon, Bucks HP18 9DG. (P) (L) *British Coins, Halfcrowns to Farthings.*

Peter Morris (BNTA, IBNS)
1 Station Concourse, Bromley North Station, Bromley, BR1 1NN or PO Box 223, Bromley, BR1 4EQ. Tel: 020 8313 3410, email: info@petermorris.co.uk, www.petermorris.co.uk *British and World Coins, Proof Sets and Numismatic Books, Medals and Banknotes.*

Colin Narbeth & Son Ltd (ANA, IBNS)
20 Cecil Court, Leicester Square, London,WC2N. 4HE .Tel: 020 7379 6975, www.colin–narbeth.com *World Banknotes.*

Newcastle Coin Dealers
7 Nile Street, North Shields, NE29 0BD. Tel: 07939 999 286, email: newcastlecoin@outlook.com, www.newcastlecoindealers.co.uk. *Modern British and World Coins/Banknotes.*

John Newman Coins (BNTA)
P O Box 4890, Worthing, BN119WS. Tel: 01903 239 867, email: john@newmancoins.co.uk, www.johnnewmancoins.co.uk. *English hammered coins, British Milled Coins and British Tokens.*

Wayne Nicholls
PO Box 44, Bilston, West Midlands. Tel: 01543 45476. (L) *Choice English Coins.*

North Wales Coins Ltd
1b Penrhyn Road, Colwyn Bay, Clwyd. Tel: 01492 533 023. *British Coins.*

NP Collectables
9 Main Street, Gedney Dyke, Spalding, Lincs PE12 0AJ. Tel: 01406 365 211 (P) (L). *English Hammered and Milled Coins.*

NumisCorner
www.NumisCorner.com
Coins, Banknotes, Medals and Tokens

Numitrading.com
Online market place/trading platform. Tel: 01702 667420, email: info@numitrading.com, www.numitrading.com.

Odyssey Antiquities
PO Box 61, Southport PR9 0PZ.Tel: 01704 232 494. *Classical Antiquities, Ancient and Hammered Coinage.*

Glenn S. Ogden (BNTA)
Tel: 01626 859 350 or 07971 709 427, email: glennogdencoins@hotmail.com, www. glennogdencoins.com, (P) (L) *English Milled Coinage.*

John Ogden Coins
Hodge Clough Cottage, Moorside, Oldham OL1 4JW. Tel: 0161 678 0709 (P) (L) *Ancient and Hammered.*

Don Oliver Gold Coins
Stanford House, 23 Market Street, Stourbridge, West Midlands DY8 1AB. Tel: 01384 877 901. *British Gold Coins.*

Del Parker
PO Box 310 Richmond Hill, GA 31324. Tel: + 1 2143521475, Email: irishcoins2000@hotmail.com www.irishcoins.com. *Irish, American Coins.*

Pavlos S. Pavlou
58 Davies Streer, Mayfair, London W1K 5JF. Tel: 020 7629 9449, email: pspavlou@hotmail.com. *Ancient to Modern.*

PCGS
Tel:+33 (0) 949 833 0600, email:info@pcgs.com, www.pcgs.com. *Coin Grading and Authentication Service.*

Penrith Coin & Stamp Centre
37 King Street, Penrith, Cumbria CA11 7AY. Tel: 01768 864 185.*World Coins.*

Pentland Coins (IBNS)
Pentland House, 92 High Street, Wick, Caithness KW14 L5. (P) *British, World Coins & banknotes.*

Philatelic Heritage
35a High Street, Hungerford, RG17 0NF. Email philatelicheritage@gmx.com. Tel: 01488 684008 Coins & Stamps.

B. C. Pickard
1 Treeside, Christchurch, Dorset BH23 4PF. Tel: 01425 275763, email: bcpickard@fsmail.net). (P) *Stone Age, Greek, Roman Items (inc. coins) for sale.*

George Rankin Coin Co Ltd (ANA)
Tel: 020 7739 1840. www.rankinsjewellers.co.uk. *World Coins, banknotes, medals, watches, general bullion bought and sold.*

Mark Rasmussen (BNTA, IAPN)
PO Box 42, Betchworth, Surrey, RH3 7YR. Tel: 01306 884 880, email: mark.rasmussen@rascoins.com, www.rascoins.com. (L) *Quality Hammered, Milled Coins.*

Mark T. Ray (see Collectors World)

Rhyl Coin Shop
12 Sussex Street, Rhyl, Clwyd. Tel: 01745 338 112. *World Coins and Banknotes.*

Chris Rigby
PO Box 181, Worcester WR1 1YE. Tel: 01905 28028. P L *Modern British Coins.*

Roderick Richardson (BNTA)
The Old Granary Antiques Centre, King's Staithe Lane, King's Lynn, PE30 1LZ. Tel: 01553 670 833, www.roderickrichardson.com. L *English, Hammered and Early Milled Coins. High quality lists.*

Charles Riley (BNTA)
PO Box 733, Aylesbury HP22 9AX. Tel: 01296 747 598, charlesrileycoins@gmail.com, www.charlesriley.co.uk. *Coins and Medallions.*

Robin–on–Acle Coins
193 Main Road Essex CO12 3PH. Tel: 01255 554 440, email: enquiries@robin–on–acle–coins.co.uk. *Ancient to Modern Coins and Paper Money.*

Royal Australian Mint
www.ramint.gov.au. *Official new coin issues for Australia.*

Royal Gold
PO Box 123, Saxonwold, 2132, South Africa, Tel: +27 11 483 0161, email: royalg@iafrica.com, www.royalgold.co.za. *Gold Coins bought and sold,*

Colin de Rouffignac (BNTA)
57, Wigan Lane, Wigan, Lancs WN1 2LF. Tel: 01942 237 927. *P. English and Scottish Hammered.*

R. P. Coins
PO Box 367, Prestwich, Manchester, M25 9ZH. Tel: 07802 713 444, www.rpcoins.co.uk. *Coins, Books, Catalogues and Accessories.*

Chris Rudd Ltd (IAPN, BNTA)
PO Box 1500, Norwich, NR10 5WS P L
Tel: 01263 735 007 www.celticcoins.com. *Celtic Coins.*

Colin Rumney (BNTA)
PO Box 34, Denbighshire, North Wales, LL16 4YQ. Tel: 01745 890 621. *All world coins including ancients.*

R & J Coins
21b Alexandra Street, Southend-on-Sea, Essex, SS1 1DA. Tel: 01702 345 995. *World Coins.*

Safe Albums (UK) Ltd
16 Falcon Business Park, 38 Ivanhoe Road, Finchampstead, Berkshire RG40 4QQ. Tel: 0118 932 8976 fax 0118 932 8612. *Accessories.*

Saltford Coins
Harcourt, Bath Road, Saltford, Bristol, Avon BS31 3DQ. Tel: 01225 873 512, email: info@saltfordcoins.com, www.saltfordcoins.com P *British, Commonwealth, World Coins and medallions.*

Satin Coins
PO Box 63, Stockport, Cheshire SK4 5BU. Tel: 07940 393 583 answer machine.

Scotmint Ltd (BNTA)
68 Sandgate, Ayr, Scotland KA7 1BX
Tel: 01292 268 244, email: rob@scotmint.com, www.scotmint.com. *Coins, Medals and Banknotes. Retail shop.*

David Seaman
PO Box 449, Waltham Cross, EN9 3WZ. Tel: 01992 719 723, email: davidseamancoins@outlook.com. P L *Hammered, Milled, Maundy.*

Mark Senior
553 Falmer Road, Woodingdean, Brighton, Sussex Tel: 01273 309 359. By appointment only. P L *Saxon, Norman and English hammered.*

Sharps Pixley
54, St James's Street, London SW1A 1JT Tel: 020 7871 0532, www.sharpspixley.com. *Safe deposit boxes in St James's, buying and selling Gold Bullion.*

Silbury Coins (BNTA)
PO Box 281, Cirencester, Gloucs GL7 9ET. Tel: 01242 898 107, email: info@silburycoins.com, www.silburycoins.com. *Iron Age, Roman, Saxon, Viking, Medieval Coins and later.*

Simmons Gallery (ANA, BNTA, IBNS)
PO Box 104, Leytonstone, London E11 1ND Tel: 020 898 98097, simmonsgallery.co.uk. L *Coins, Tokens and Medals.*

E. Smith (ANA, IBNS)
PO Box 348, Lincoln LN6 0TX Tel: 01522 684 681. P *World Coins and Paper Money.*

Neil Smith
PO Box 774, Lincoln LN4 2WX. Tel: 01522 522 772 fax 01522 689 528. *GB and World Gold Coins 1816 to date, including Modern Proof Issues.Organiser of the Yorkshire Coin Fair.*

Jim Smythe
PO Box 6970, Birmingham B23 7WD. Email: Jimdens@aol.com. P L *19th/20th Century British and World Coins.*

Sovereign Rarities Ltd (BNTA)
17–19 Maddox Street, London W1S 2QH Tel: 0203 019 1185, www.sovr.co,uk. *Quality British & World Coins.*

SP Asimi
Cabinet at The Emporium, 112 High Street, Hungerford, RG17 ONB. Tel: 01488 686959. British Milled Coins 1662-1946

Spink & Son Ltd (ANA, BNTA, IAPN, IBNS)
69 Southampton Row, Bloomsbury, London. WC1B 4ET. Tel: 020 7563 4000, email: info@spinkandson.com, www.spink.com. *Ancient to Modern World Coins. Medals, Banknotes.*

Stamford Coins
65–67 Stamford Street, Bradford, West Yorkshire, BD4 8SD. Tel: 07791 873 595, email: stamfordcoins@hotmail.co.uk.

Stamp & Collectors Centre
404 York Town Road, College Town, Camberley, Surrey GU15 4PR. Tel:01276 32587 *World Coins and Medals.*

St Edmunds Coins & Banknotes
PO Box 118, Bury St Edmunds IP33 2NE. Tel: 01284 761 894.

Drake Sterling Numismatics Pty Ltd
GPO Box 2913, Sydney 2001, Australia. UK callers Tel: 020 7097 1781, www.drakesterling.co.uk. *British and British Colonial Gold Coins.*

Studio Coins (ANA)
Studio 111, 80 High Street, Winchester, Hants SO23 9AT. Tel: 01962 853 156 email: stephenmitchell13@bttconnect.com. P *English Coins.*

The Britannia Coin Company (BNTA)
143 High Street, Royal Wootton Bassett,Wilts, SN4 7AB. Tel: 01793 205007. wwwbritanniacoincompany.com. Ancient, Hammered and Milled, Sovereigns, Investment Gold, Royal Mint New Issues.

The Coin Cabinet (BNTA)
First Floor, 60 St James's Street, London, SW1A 1LE. Tel: 020 3808 5855. Email: contact@thecoincabinet.com. www.thecoincabinet.com. World Coin Dealer and Auctioneer.

The Coin House
Tel: 01935 824 878, email: thecoinhouse@btinternet.com. *Quality Investment Coins and Silver Bars.*

The East India Company
Tel: 0203 205 3394, email, service@theeastindiacompany.com. *Gold and Silver Coins, retail premises.Gifts and collectables of historic interest.*

The Royal Mint
Llantrisant, Pontyclun, CF72 8YT. Tel: 01443 222111. *New coin minter/issuer. Also historic numismatics.*

Time Line Originals (BNTA)
PO Box 193, Upminster, RM14 3WH. Tel: 01708 222 384/07775 651 218, email: sales@time–lines.co.uk.

Stuart J. Timmins
Smallwood Lodge Bookshop, Newport, Salop. Tel: 01952 813 232. *Numismatic Literature.*

R. Tims
39 Villiers Road, Watford, Herts WD1 4AL. Ⓟ Ⓛ *Uncirculated World Banknotes.*

Michael Trenerry
PO Box 55, Truro, TR1 2YQ. Tel: 01872 277 977, email: veryfinecoins@aol.com. By appointment only. Ⓛ *Roman, Celtic and English Hammered Coins and Tokens.*

Robert Tye
7–9 Clifford Street, York, YO1 9RA. Tel: 0845 4 900 724, email: orders@earlyworlscoins.com. *www.uk–coins.com. Rare Historical Medals*

Vale
Tel: 01322 405 911, email: valecoins@ntlworld.com *British Coins and Medals.*

Van der Schueren, John-Luc (IAPN)
14 Rue de la Borse, 1,000 Bussels, Belgium. Email: iapnsecret@compuserve.com, www.coins.be. . *Coins and Tokens of the World and of the Low Countries.*

M. Veissid & Co (The Collectors Centre) (BNTA)
Tel: 01743 600951,www.veissid.com. *Buying and selling coins, medals, notes and emphemera.*

Victory Coins (BNTA)
PO Box 948, Southsea, Hampshire, PO1 9LZ. Tel: 023 92 751908. *British and World Coins.*

Mark J. Vincenzi
Rylands, Earls Colne, Essex CO6 2LE. Tel: 01787 222 555. Ⓟ *Greek, Roman, Hammered.*

Mike Vosper
PO Box 32, Hockwold, Brandon IP26 4HX. Tel: 01842 828 292, email: mikevosper@vosper4coins.co.uk, www.vosper4coins.co.uk. *Roman, Hammered.*

Weighton Coin Wonders
50 Market Place, Market Weighton, York, Y043 3AL, Tel: 01430 879 740, www.weightoncoin.co.uk. *Modern Gold, Silver Proofs and Sets.*

Wessex Coins (BNTA)
PO Box 482, Southampton, SO30 9FB. Tel: 02380 972 059, email: info@wessexcoins.co.uk, www.wessexcoins.co.uk. *Ancient Greek, Roman, English Hammered Coins and Antiquities, also Shipwreck Treasure.*

Pam West (IBNS)
PO Box 257, Sutton, Surrey, SM3 9WW. Tel: 020 8641 3224, email: pam@britishnotes.co.uk, www.britishnotes.co.uk. Ⓟ Ⓛ *English Banknotes and related publications.*

West Essex Coin Investments (BNTA, IBNS)
Croft Cottage, Station Road, Alderholt, Fordingbridge, Hants SP6 3AZ. Tel: 01425 656 459. *British and World Coins and Paper Money.*

Whitmore Coins, Tokens & Medals
Tel: 01568 720536, www.whitmorectm.com *Coins, tokens and medals.*

West Wicklow Coins
Blessington, Co Wicklow, Ireland. Tel: 00353 45 858 767, email: westwicklowcoins@hotmail.com. Irish and *World Coins.*

Simon Willis Coins
43a St Marys Road, Market Harborough, LE16 7DS. Tel:07908 240 978, swcoins@simonwilliscoins.com, www.simonwilliscoins.com. *Quality Hammered and Early Milled British Coins.*

Worldwide Coins (IBNS)
PO Box 11, Wavertree, Liverpool L15 0FG. Tel: 0845 634 1809, email: sales@worldwidecoins.co.uk, www.worldwidecoins.co.uk. *World Coins and Paper Money.*

World Treasure Books
PO Box 5, Newport, Isle of Wight PO30 5QE. Tel: 01983 740 712. Ⓛ *Coins, Books, Metal Detectors.*

There is no better place to learn about coins and coin collecting than one of the many coin fairs organised up and down the country. The annual Harrogate Coin Fair, which took place on April 19–20 at the Old Swan Hotel, Harrogate, perhaps boasts the most elegant surroundings for such an event, hence its popularity amongst dealers and collectors.

Advertisers directory

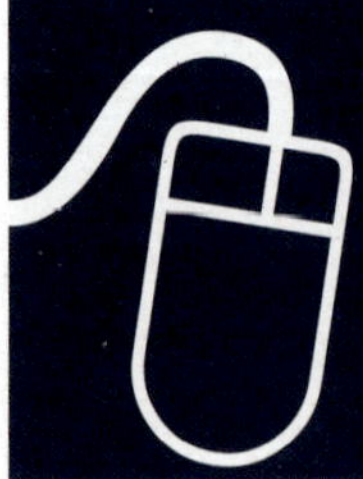

See our website at tokenpublishing.com for up-to-date dealer entries, with hyperlinks taking you directly to their websites.